# AMERICAN
## JEWISH
# HISTORY

EIGHT VOLUME SET ISBN 0-415-91933-9

VOLUME 1: ISBN 0-415-91920-7
    VOLUME 2: ISBN 0-415-91921-5
    VOLUME 3: ISBN 0-415-91943-6 (SET)
        VOL 3, PART 1: ISBN 0-415-91922-3
        VOL 3, PART 2: ISBN 0-415-91923-1
        VOL 3, PART 3: ISBN 0-415-91924-X
    VOLUME 4: ISBN: 0-415-91925-8
    VOLUME 5: ISBN 0-415-91944-4 (SET)
        VOL 5, PART 1: ISBN 0-415-91926-6 (SET)
        VOL 5, PART 2: ISBN 0-415-91927-4
        VOL 5, PART 3: ISBN 0-415- 91928-2
    VOLUME 6: ISBN 0-415-91945-2 (SET)
        VOL 6, PART 1: ISBN 0-415-91929-0
        VOL 6, PART 2: ISBN 0-415-91930-4
    VOLUME 7: ISBN 0-415-91931-2
    VOLUME 8: ISBN 0-415-91932-0

# AMERICAN JEWISH HISTORY

A EIGHT-VOLUME SERIES

Edited by Jeffrey S. Gurock

SPONSORED BY

The American Jewish Historical Society

**R**OUTLEDGE   A Routledge Series

# CONTENTS OF THE SET

AMERICAN JEWISH HISTORY: VOLUME 3

# EAST EUROPEAN JEWS IN AMERICA, 1880-1920: IMMIGRATION AND ADAPTATION

Edited by Jeffrey S. Gurock

**IN THREE PARTS**

PART TWO

Routledge

New York ◆ London

**Library of Congress Cataloging-in-Publication Data**

East European Jews in America, 1880-1920 : immigration and adaptation
   / edited by Jeffrey S. Gurock.
      v. <1  > cm. — (American Jewish history ; 3)
      Includes bibliographical references and index.
      ISBN 0-415-91943-6 (lib. bdg. : alk. paper)
      1. Jews, East European—United States.   2. United States—Ethnic
relations.   I. Gurock, Jeffrey S., 1949–  .  II. Series.
E184.J5E37    1998
973'.04924—dc21                                              97-27128

Published in 1998 by
Routledge
29 West 35th Street
New York, NY 10001

Published in Great Britain by
Routledge
11 New Fetter Lane
London EC4P 4EE

Case design: Helene Benedetti
Printed in the United States of America on acid free paper.

VOLUME 3:     ISBN  0-415-91943-6  (SET)
                 PART ONE        ISBN  0-415-91922-3
                 PART TWO        ISBN  0-415-91923-1
                 PART THREE      ISBN  0-415-91924-X

# Contents

## Volume One

# Volume Two

# Volume Three

# East European Jews in America, 1880–1920

# ABRAHAM CAHAN AND THE NEW YORK
## *COMMERCIAL ADVERTISER:*
## A STUDY IN ACCULTURATION

### By Moses Rischin*

Abraham Cahan (1860–1951), the doughty editor of the *Jewish Daily Forward* for nearly half a century, achieved a fame and eminence that extended far beyond the confines of the Jewish immigrant community with which he was associated. Yet little is known of the diverse influences that entered into his career. It is the contention of this writer that the years 1897 to 1902, when Cahan was employed by the New York *Commercial Advertiser*, comprised a seminal period in his journalistic apprenticeship. An understanding of this interval in Cahan's life provides a vital key to an understanding of his subsequent achievements as editor of America's renowned Yiddish daily newspaper, the *Forward*.[1]

447

It was in August, 1897, that the immigrant journalist, teacher, labor organizer and socialist orator, Abraham Cahan, then a youthful and ebullient thirty-seven, severed his connections with the newly organized *Jewish Daily Forward* due to eloquent and bitter disputations over the policy to be pursued by that as yet unstable journal.[2]

Cahan left the *Forward* in a state of physical exhaustion with no other immediate means of earning a livelihood and with no savings. His highly praised first novel, *Yekl*, brought him no royalties. Inspired reviews, including the laudatory article by William Dean Howells, dean of the new American literature, only aided sales in the first few weeks; the American public, like the American critics, had no interest in the unmoral love story of a Jewish immigrant. Nor was the dearth of appreciation for Cahan's style of writing and his theme due to an anti-Semitic bias, for novels dealing with the Irish were equally unsuccessful. The American reading public, mainly women, desired to read about aristocrats, the rich and the well-born, and looked askance upon stories about immigrants; also

---

* Mr. Rischin has been appointed instructor in American Civilization at Brandeis University.

[1] An indispensable work is Ephim H. Jeshurin's *Abraham Cahan Bibliography* (New York, 1941).

[2] Abraham Cahan, *Bleter fun mein Leben* [*Leaves from My Life*], vol. III (New York, 1926), p. 493.

10

still taboo were literary intimations about the less romantic aspects of the relations between the sexes.[3]

Cahan ceased to entertain dreams of deriving a munificent income from the writing of realistic novels depicting Jewish life. His finances had reached so low an ebb that the thought of writing fiction became prohibitory. The fifty dollar fee he had received for his story, *Circumstances*, had long disappeared and he had failed to write any tales in English for a number of months. Nor had he troubled to nurse the requests of newspapers for sketches and they therefore ceased soliciting his contributions. He might have written short stories and sent them to the magazines but he found it impossible to engage in creative activity when beset by economic insecurity.[4] "When it rains, it pours"; and so it was with Cahan. At a time when his need for a steady source of income was crucial, he lost his job as an adult evening school teacher, a position he had held for eleven years. The Yiddish journalist was informed of the reason for this abrupt dismissal upon accidentally encountering Gustave Straubenmüller, the school's assistant principal, in the Astor Library. It seemed that one of the trustees of the school had noticed the nocturnal pedagogue delivering a socialist speech during the previous year's election campaign, a political heresy which that gentleman believed intolerable.[5] Cahan's only resort was to submit articles to the American press. Although his friend, Erasmus Darwin Beach, was no longer with the *Sun*, one of his feuilletons was accepted on its own merits and Cahan was assured of a weekly article in that paper. Unfortunately, the income from the sale of a single weekly article was insufficient to keep body and soul together and so the former Yiddish journalist sallied forth to the offices of the *Evening Post*, located in an old house on Fulton Street, off Nassau. The *Evening Post* like the *Sun* appealed to a small number of cultivated and intelligent readers and its Saturday supplement contained the same sort of feature material Cahan had sold to the morning paper.[6]

At this time Lincoln Steffens was assistant city editor at the *Evening Post*. It was his task to decide whether Cahan's manuscript was acceptable. After reading the sketch with great enthusiasm and wonderment, Steffens gingerly stepped out of his small office and warmly greeted Cahan, complimenting him on *Yekl* which the editor had read with intense pleasure. Steffens was keenly interested

448

[3] *Ibid.*, vol. IV (1928), p. 70.

[4] *Ibid.*, vol. IV, p. 71; cf. A. Cahan, "Circumstances," *The Cosmopolitan*, vol. XXII (April, 1897), pp. 628–640.

[5] A. Cahan, *Bleter, supra*, vol. IV, pp. 71–72.

[6] *Ibid.*, vol. IV, pp. 72–73.

in literature. He and Cahan spoke of the latter's future literary plans and of the writings of Stephen Crane and William Dean Howells. The two kindred spirits continued to bristle with literary conversation as they strolled over to Steffens' home on Fifty-fourth Street where Cahan was introduced to the editor's wife, the former Josephine Bontecou, and her mother.[7]

Only a few of Cahan's articles were published in the *Evening Post* and it became necessary for him to prospect for additional means to augment his slender earnings. Steffens recommended Cahan to the editor of the New York *Commercial Advertiser*, formerly the *American Minerva*, and one of the oldest papers in New York, having been established by the renowned philologist, Noah Webster, during the French Revolution. Although the paper had a small circulation, among its readers were numbered the oldest and the wealthiest families of New York City and its environs. While the *Commercial* received a respectable sum from its advertisers, it was not self-supporting and depended upon the multi-millionaire railway magnate, Collis P. Huntington, for economic sustenance. The *Advertiser* was rarely seen in Jewish immigrant neighborhoods, nor was it to be found displayed extensively elsewhere. The paper was sustained by the Huntington family for its influence, the resultant prestige accruing to the family name, and as a hobby. Despite its limited number of readers, the *Advertiser* was highly respected.[8]

449

Norman Hapgood, the *Advertiser*'s drama critic whose pungent criticism was beginning to arouse the attention of discriminating intelligent Americans, introduced Cahan to the paper's editor-in-chief, the Scotsman, Harry J. Wright. Wright immediately assigned Cahan to write a description of the Jewish holidays, *Sukkot* and *Simhat Torah*, which began that sundown. The following morning, the erstwhile Yiddish journalist submitted his finished article and it appeared that afternoon.[9]

In the fall of 1897, the newly organized City of Greater New York elected its first mayor. Tammany Hall, the Republican party, the newly formed Citizens' Union, and the remnants of the Henry George following of a decade earlier, nominated their respective

---

[7] *Ibid.*, vol. IV, p. 73. Cf. Joseph Chaiken, *Yidishe Bleter in Amerika* [*Yiddish Press in America*] (New York, 1946), pp. 152 ff.

[8] A. Cahan, *Bleter, supra*, vol. IV, p. 74; cf. Lincoln Steffens, *The Autobiography of Lincoln Steffens* (New York: Harcourt, Brace and Company, 1931), p. 311. In this article we shall quote several passages from Steffens' *Autobiography*. We wish to thank the publishers of this book, Harcourt, Brace and Company, for kindly granting us permission to do so. See also F. L. Mott, *American Journalism* (New York, 1941), p. 483.

[9] A. Cahan, *Bleter, supra*, vol. IV, p. 76; cf. New York *Commercial Advertiser* [=*CA*], Oct. 10, 1897.

candidates.[10] The *Commercial*, a Republican organ, campaigned for Benjamin V. Tracy of Brooklyn, the G. O. P. standard bearer. Wright assigned Cahan to attend a political rally for Tracy so that he might write a character portrait of that gentleman, a most unhappy chore for a pious socialist. Upon informing Wright of his predicament and the problem of political ethics with which he was faced, the worthy editor evinced deep concern. He convinced Cahan that all he desired of him was a description of Tracy's appearance, his manner of speech, the type of impression he made, and a few lines on the meeting itself; otherwise, Cahan might write as his conscience dictated. Cahan's article on Tracy, needless to say, remained unpublished. Wright excused this omission by informing Cahan that he had merely wanted to see a sample of his writing style. "Belles lettres was one thing and writing for a newspaper was another." Wright understood the nature of Cahan's idealistic and political compunctions. In the future the work of the former Yiddish journalist concentrated around the writing of human interest sketches of the various quarters of the city and the portayal of its diverse types. Thus three months after leaving the nascent, strife-torn *Forward*, Cahan was writing for three distinguished American journals, the *Sun*, the *Evening Post*, and the *Commercial Advertiser*.[11]

In November, 1897, Lincoln Steffens left the *Evening Post* to become city editor of the *Commercial Advertiser*. Upon Steffen's request, Cahan was employed as a regular member of the reportorial staff. Provided with the steady position that his temperament required, Cahan now could return to the pursuit of serious literature. The former Yiddish journalist had an intimate knowledge of the Jewish socialist movement, the Jewish labor organizations, and the Jewish world in general. Conscious of the limited orbit of his experience, he passionately desired to familiarize himself with the diverse class, nationality and occupational groupings in the city, and to explore the many facets of the cosmopolitan metropolis, — opportunities afforded him in his new position.[12] Since Cahan insisted upon assignments that would bring him into close touch with the throbbing life of the city, he was given the job of police reporter, thus allowing him free reign for the satisfaction of his curiosity.[13]

450

[10] A. Cahan, *Bleter*, *supra*, vol. IV, p. 76; cf. Cleveland Rodgers and Rebecca B. Rankin, *New York: The World's Capital City* (New York, 1948), p. 82; cf. Lothrop Stoddard, *Master of Manhattan, the Life of Richard Croker* (New York, 1931).

[11] A. Cahan, *Bleter*, *supra*, vol. IV, pp. 77–78.

[12] *Ibid.*, vol. IV, p. 79; L. Steffens, *Autobiography*, *supra*, pp. 311–312.

[13] A. Cahan, *Bleter*, *supra*, vol. IV, p. 79.

While Cahan was only a "cub" reporter, it must be remembered that around the turn of the century, the ordinary reporter's calling was highly respected; a first class journalist was better paid than a drama critic or a subeditor. Jacob Riis, chief reporter for the *Sun*, who had already achieved considerable fame for his crusading activities in the tenement districts had become friendly with Steffens a few months earlier. Steffens gave Cahan a letter introducing him to Riis at police headquarters on Mulberry Street, near Houston. Steffens commended Cahan to Riis as the author of *Yekl*, as a writer, and as a thinker of acute perceptions. Understandably, the bespectacled blond moustachioed Riis neither appreciated Cahan's contempt for American writers nor his militant espousal of a socialist creed; Cahan, for his part, viewed Riis's opinions as anachronistic. Despite these differences, Riis graciously instructed Cahan in all the details of his new assignment, and introduced him to the many reporters and public officials who congregated at police headquarters.[14]

451

Cahan's first task as a police reporter was to familiarize himself with the use of the telephone. As the gadget was still a rarity on the East Side, certainly an unheard of luxury in the offices of the *Forward*, Cahan's experience with this still mystifying invention was limited. The ability to distinguish between the transmitter and the receiver was insufficient to instill him with confidence in its use. The role of tutor in the intricacies of the telephone played by an Italian apothecary for a perspiring immigrant police reporter, marked a hilarious incident in the annals of American journalism.[15]

Cahan prospered. His fifteen dollar weekly salary as a "cub" reporter was increased to twenty-five dollars; he was able to earn additional sums by writing feuilletons for the Saturday supplements and received occasional honoraria for magazine stories. His extraordinary experiences at police headquarters supplied him with copy for newspaper articles as well as raw material for his own literary work. Every newsworthy incident contained fictional potentialities for Cahan. The artistic qualities that distinguished his articles were recognized by newspapers in distant cities which reprinted them. If as gatherer of news the eccentric police reporter fell short of perfection, his talents as an observer and writer were superb. Cahan's sensitivity to color and dramatic content were so sharply electrified that the most prosaic scenes revealed their lyrical qualities to his pen, a talent the city editor did not neglect to employ upon the least provocation.[16]

[14] *Ibid.*, vol. IV, pp. 82–83.　　　[15] *Ibid.*, vol. IV, pp. 85–87.

[16] *Ibid.*, vol. IV, pp. 91–92.

Two articles, the gifted police reporter wrote for the *Commercial Advertiser* very early in his career, poignantly revealed the literary heights a sensitive reporter could attain. Appearing in the Saturday supplement of August 6, 1898, "Imaginary America: How a Young Russian Pictured It" was an autobiographical gem:

> I do not know through what association of ideas the image came into my head, but I remember distinctly that the word American would call to my mind a luxuriant many-colored meadow, with swarms of tall people hurrying hither and thither along narrow footpaths. They were all young and beardless and they were all men. Why the scene contained not a single woman I cannot explain no more than I can account for the color of the spring overcoats the men wore, which were exclusively gray.
>
> When a child I was fond of Cooper's and Mayne Reid's stories, which I read in a Russian translation, and it may be that something in some of these stories it was which painted the meadow and the gray-coated people in my mind. Later I read of Washington and Lincoln and liked them both. When Garfield was assassinated I read the news in a St. Petersburg paper. I can almost see the page and the upper part of the column on which the despatch was printed and the feeling of indignation with which I was discussing it with my classmates. We were all more or less "tainted" with Nihilism and while we applauded those who blew up the palace of our own Czar, the man who would lay his hand on the chosen representative of a free people was in our eyes nothing short of a demon.
>
> ... I knew some people who could speak English, but I do not think I ever heard them speak it: At all events, I never had any personal impressions as to how that language sounded. But then Turgeneff [*sic!*] says somewhere in his writings that English is the language of birds, so, accepting that, I would imagine Englishmen twittering, warbling and chirping in their efforts to produce French words. This had nothing to do with my beardless Americans, however, who I somehow could not get to speak the "language of birds." To be sure, I was aware that my gray-coated young fellows were of the same stock and spoke the same tongue as the inhabitants of Great Britain, but the composite picture of the English nation in my brain was so distinct from my image of an American that I could not get them to speak the same language either, and if the truth must be told my gray-coated Yankee must have been a dumb creature, for I do not seem ever to have thought of him as speaking or singing or doing anything except push his way through that bright-hued meadow of his.
>
> [1882] I set foot on American soil on a scorching day in July, and the first American I saw was an old customs officer, with a white beard and in the blue uniform of his office. The headless men in gray vanished as if at the stroke of a magic wand, but then, gleaming green, fresh and beautiful, not many hundred yards off, was the shore of

452

Staten Island, and, while I was uttering exclamations of enchantment in chorus with my fellow passengers I asked myself whether my dreams of a meadow had not come true.

Still, pretty as America was, it somehow did not seem to be genuine, and much as I admired the shore I had a lurking impression that it was not the same sort of grass, trees, flowers, sod as in Europe, that it was more or less artificial, flimsy, ephemeral, as if a good European rainstorm could wipe it all off as a wet sponge would a colored picture made with colored chalk on blackboard.

I remember joking of the seeming unreality of things in my new home. "The ice here is not cold," I would say, "The sugar is not sweet and the water is not wet." And a homesick German thereupon added in the words of a famous poet of his that America was a country where "the birds had no sing, the flowers no fragrance and the men no hearts." Why I should have doubted the actuality of things in the New World I do not know. Now that I try to account for that vague, hidden suspicion which the sky and clouds of New York arouse in me, it occurs to me that it may have been due to my deep-rooted notion of America as something so far removed from my world that it must look entirely different from it. If Staten Island had the appearance which its reflections had in the water, if the trees, and the cliffs were all upside down, I should have been surprised but satisfied.

... One of the first things I beheld on the pier as we were landed was a big Maltese cat. I can just see her squatting by the side of the gangplank and eyeing me as I came down. Nor shall I ever forget the queer sense of joy which the sight of her gave me. "Why they have cats here!" I exclaimed to myself. "And just like ours, too!" I felt like flinging myself on the little creature, hugging her, shaking her paw and introducing myself to her as a fellow countryman. At the next instant, however, I was surveying that same cat to make sure that she was really a cat like our cats at home, a living creature and not a mechanical imitation of one; the more so since I knew of the prevalence of machinery in the United States, and of the inventive genius of its people. I had read of the artificial hatching of chickens, and by a stretch of imagination I could see artificial dogs and artificial cats. I knew that this cat was a genuine one, and I inwardly made fun of my suspicions as well as of my joy, but the suspicions held their own, and altogether I was two men in one.

"Oh, come, it's a cat; can't you see?" said one.

"Of course it is. Who says it isn't?" the other retorted with cowardly insincerity.

When I found myself on the street and my eye fell on an old rickety building I expressed a feeling akin to surprise. I could only conceive of America as a brand-new country, and everything in it, everything made by man, at least, was to be spick and span, while here was an old house, weatherbeaten and somewhat misshapen with age. How did it get time to get old?

453

The first American who left an impression on me was a tall, gray-haired missionary whom I saw preaching from a bench on Union or Madison Square — I do not remember which. One of his hands was bandaged and as he stood against the blue sky with the disabled member resting against his breast and his flowing beard looming dazzlingly white in a flood of sunshine, the picture at once moved me to pity and thrilled me with reverence. The old man's speech at first impressed me like the monotonous thrumming noise which is produced by playing upon the loose end of a thin, flexible strip of steel whose other end is made fast to some stationary object. As I stood listening to it I had the sense of being in the presence of self-denying piety, and again I was wondering whether it was not a sort of *fata Morgana*. My idea of America had so little to do with what stood before me that I was timidly asking myself whether the man was a genuine man, his beard a genuine beard, the bandages on his hand real bandages. But presently he began to speak faster and the illusion fled. His English now sounded in my ears like the snapping noise made by running a stick across the rods of a metal gate or fence. The sound at once became annoying to me, and the man was suddenly transformed into a heartless, vulgar, supercilious creature. His voice set my teeth on edge, and I remember the malicious feeling with which I set to analyzing it. "How does he get that confounded metallic sound of his?" I asked myself, and after listening a few minutes I made the discovery that he pronounced the "R" utterly unlike any people I had known. "Do they all speak like that?" I said to myself with disgust, trying to imitate him for sheer hatred, and getting all the more disgusted with him because I failed. The preacher's manner, his scant gesticulations, the way he aimed his fist in the air and then brought it down on nothing, his projecting lower lip when he shut his mouth, his grey eyes, everything about him seemed to me intensively repulsive and anything but human. He struck me as a species of frog, and try as I would I could not get myself to imagine that the sounds he uttered were words and that the crowd around him understood their meaning.

Subsequently, when I had mastered English enough to understand the old preacher and to make myself understood, more or less, to him, I made his acquaintance, and my original impressions gave away to others. I found him to be a very pleasant and interesting man. I liked him and my second image of him is one of my dearest portraits in my mental album of American races.[17]

The erstwhile Yiddish journalist was much impressed with the literary talents of his mentor at police headquarters, Jacob Riis. Although highly critical of the able son of Denmark, he no doubt was influenced by him. It was apparent to Cahan, however, that while

---

[17] A. Cahan, "Imaginary America — How a Young Russian Pictures It," *CA*, Aug. 6, 1898; see also A. Cahan, "Back to Dear Old Russia," *CA*, April 5, 1899.

454

Riis was an able writer, he reported through the eyes of another — through the eyes of "a little old round, happy Jewish boy," Max Fischel. Max, the semiliterate son of Hungarian-Jewish immigrants, would be sent to the scene of the disaster. Upon his return, he would describe it to Riis and Riis would thereupon compose an article. Riis made no attempt to conceal the relationship between the two "genuises," as Steffens called them. In Cahan's opinion, Max not only provided Riis with the factual skeleton for the article but with its soul as well. Max was endowed with keen powers of observation, subtle intuition and genuine artistry. His gifts were best illustrated upon the occasion of a fire that Cahan reported for his paper. The *Advertiser*'s police reporter described a particularly resplendent aspect of the conflagration certain to elude the eyes of the other reporters. To Cahan's surprise this feature of the fire was limned in the New York *Sun* by that paper's chief reporter. Since Cahan knew that Riis had not been at the scene of the fire, it was evident that Fischel had instinctively sensed the splendor of the crimson sun shining through the white mask of smoke. At one time Cahan intended to write a story entitled "Jimmy McAllister" depicting the symbiotic relationship between the educated Dane and the untutored Jewish boy.[18]

455

Indeed, the nonconforming police reporter cut rather unconventional capers in journalistic circles. But, then, the New York *Commercial Advertiser* had become a unique venture in journalism with the advent of Lincoln Steffens. Upon becoming city editor in November, 1897, the California-born journalist summarily dismissed two thirds of the reportorial staff. In their places he installed inexperienced young college men with literary ambitions — young men from Harvard, Yale, Princeton, and Columbia — who had no desire to become newspapermen.[19]

Steffens' ideals and procedures were unique in American journalism:

> ... "We" had use for anyone who, openly or secretly, hoped to be a poet, a novelist, or an essayist. I could not pay them much in money, but as an offset I promised to give them opportunities to see life as it happened in all its news varieties. No one would be kept long in any department; as soon as a reporter became expert in one branch of work, he would be turned into another. When a reporter no longer saw red at a fire, when he was so used to police news that a murder was not

[18] A. Cahan, *Bleter, supra,* vol. IV, pp. 93–94; cf. L. Steffens, *Autobiography, supra,* p. 203.

[19] L. Steffens, *Autobiography, supra,* p. 314; A. Cahan, *Bleter, supra,* vol. IV, p. 102.

a tragedy but only a crime, he could not write police news for us. We preferred the fresh staring eyes to the informed mind and the blunted pencil. To express, if not to enforce this, I used to warn my staff that whenever a reporter became a good all-around newspaperman he would be fired, and to encourage each man to form and write in his own style, I declared that if any two reporters came to write alike, one of them would have to go. There was to be no *Commercial Advertiser* style, no *Commercial* men. So also there were no rules about promptitude, sobriety, accuracy; no lists of friends or enemies of the paper; no editorial policy; no "beats"; and best of all, there was no insistence even on these rules, which were broken at anyone's convenience.[20]

456

The exceptional intellectual and working conditions of the *Commercial* gave Cahan extremely favorable opportunities to become acquainted with fellow members of the staff upon terms of mutual consideration, respect, and understanding, fostered by a reciprocal interchange of ideas, opinions, and prejudices. The *Advertiser* police reporter associated with such diverse personalities as Chapman, the English telegraph editor, with Allen, the athletic debonair young society editor, and with Cooper, the literary editor who possessed what Cahan regarded as phenomenal, a capacity to read a book of from three to four hundred pages in an hour. His friends included Hutchins and Norman Hapgood, Carl Hovey, Edwin LeFevre, Pitts Duffield, Norman Duncan, and the vitriolic Irishman, Robert Dunn. An interesting employee of the *Advertiser* was Professor Harry Thurston Peck of Columbia University who found literary criticism for the *Commercial* and other newspapers more remunerative than his academic duties. Cahan viewed Peck's evaluations of contemporary literature as insipid and pedestrian, corresponding closely to the taste of the average reader for sentimental hokum. Peck's axiom that all stories should have a happy ending so that the spirits of the readers would be uplifted was shared by his American colleagues and was antithetical to Cahan's staunch espousal of realism in literature. The efforts of the amiable Wright to persuade his police reporter of the beauties of Tennyson's romantic poetry proved of no avail.[21]

Among so ambitious and learned a body of journalists, literary discussion and disputation was inevitable. Every afternoon after the paper had been "put to bed," the college-bred reporters would gather around a long hard table with Steffens and Cahan at the helm and the daily ritual would begin. Although Cahan was considerably older than his colleagues, this was of slight importance;

[20] L. Steffens, *Autobiography, supra*, pp. 314–315.
[21] A. Cahan, *Bleter, supra*, vol. IV, pp. 107–109.

of real significance was the fact that Cahan was the author of a novel and stories that were published in reputable periodicals with nation-wide circulations; of greatest moment, however, was the fact that Cahan had adamant and irrepressible convictions about literature. These young men acknowledged that American literature was barren of a high order of creativity. In their ingenuous search for a path leading out of the literary wilderness, they never wearied of discussing writers and books. But Cahan felt that they had no standards of their own. The sweet-scented pabulum served up by the literary journals and recognized critics provided no palpable aid. The most popular novels featured the adventures, heroics, and intrigues of the plumed knights of the Middle Ages. These ornately penned romances, printed in fine type, and attractively embossed, were treated by the critics with the utmost seriousness as works of art. Howells' realism, for all its virtues, was too tepid for masculine appetites.[22]

457

In a time of crisis in religious, moral and intellectual values, the erstwhile Yiddish journalist and American novelist became the center of attention. A stormy petrel, Cahan wielded a powerful influence in a circle, still accustomed to the genteel art of literary chit-chat. With his impassioned iconoclasm, he shattered all their literary idols from the meticulous Dickens to the majestic Thackeray to the romantically sentimental Rudyard Kipling. His auditors were deeply unsettled by his philippics and his well-reasoned heresies irritated them to the point where they were gradually won over.[23]

During these heated sessions, the unassuming city editor would stand by leisurely puffing his pipe, every now and then unleashing a pointed remark, while the future editor of the *Metropolitan Magazine*, the lanky blue-eyed Yankee, Carl Hovey, cigar in mouth, would venomously attack the *Commercial's* fiery police reporter. One Saturday afternoon before going home, Hovey stopped in at Brentano's upon Cahan's suggestion and spent a very precious dollar and a half for Turgeniev's *Dmitri Rudin* (1885). Upon completing this Russian novel, all the fictional works which he had read previously seemed cheap and trite to Hovey. Within a few months, he had

---

[22] *Ibid.*, vol. IV, pp. 110–112; cf. A. Cahan, *The Imported Bridegroom and Other Stories of The New York Ghetto* (Cambridge, 1898); cf. *idem*, *Yekl* (New York, 1899); cf. *idem*, "Rabbi Eliezer's Christmas," *Scribner's Magazine*, vol. XXVI (Dec., 1899), pp. 661–668; *idem*, "The Apostate of Chego Chegg," *The Century*, vol. LIX (Nov., 1899), pp. 94–104; *idem*, "The Daughter of Reb Avrom Leib," *The Cosmopolitan*, vol. XXIX (May, 1900), pp. 53–64; *idem*, "A Marriage by Proxy," *Everybody's Magazine*, vol. III (Dec., 1900), pp. 569–574.

[23] A. Cahan, *Bleter*, *supra*, vol. IV, pp. 112–113; L. Steffens, *Autobiography*, *supra*, p. 316.

enthusiastically gobbled up all of Turgeniev and Tolstoy as well, upon Cahan's advice, although he could ill afford the price of these volumes.[24]

Cahan and his journalistic associates extended their social relationships by mutual visits with each other's families. A number of them expressed deep confidence in his literary judgment and discretion, entrusting their stories and sketches to him before sending them to the magazines. This literary group was something of "an aristocracy in the editorial office, a kingdom within a kingdom."[25]

Among Cahan's close associates was the financial reporter, Edwin LeFevre. A laughing young man of mixed Spanish and English parentage, he did not participate in the literary discussions; his reportorial duties restricted him to the unrhymed verse of Wall Street stock manipulation. He surprised the police reporter on one occasion, however, by asking him to read one of his stories. Their unexpected common interest in literature soon made them fast friends.[26]

Pitts Duffield, a scion of one of the wealthiest families in Ohio, was also employed by the *Advertiser*. Once, upon speaking about Jews, he remarked in passing that his great-grandfather was a Jew. From that time on Pitts Duffield received the favor of the *Commercial*'s lone Russian-Jewish employee.[27]

The former Yiddish journalist regarded himself as the only Jew among the forty employees of the paper until one day he espied the political reporter who revealed his antecedents to Cahan by the cast of his smile. Cahan immediately realized that he was an American-born "Yehudi" who strenuously desired to conceal his origins. He was uninterested in literary matters and diligently avoided any contact with the unmistakably Jewish police reporter.[28]

Lincoln Steffens, whose name was of German origin, though partially of Irish stock, lunched with Cahan daily. They would take long walks in each other's company and Cahan often visited the city editor at his home. Whenever Cahan essayed to broach the subject of socialism, Steffens would suggest that he would prefer to discuss literature.[29]

Hutchins Hapgood, of all Cahan's friends, was closest to him in temperament. In the estimation of the former Yiddish journalist,

[24] A. Cahan, *Bleter, supra*, pp. 113–114.

[25] *Ibid.*, vol. IV, p. 115.

[26] *Ibid.*

[27] *Ibid.*, vol. IV, p. 117.

[28] *Ibid.*, vol. IV, p. 116.

[29] *Ibid.*, vol. IV, pp. 117–119.

"Hutch" resembled the Russian intellectual type, although out-
wardly a genuine Yankee Anglo-Saxon. Devoid of cunning, sincere,
somewhat temperamental, and with a genuine and tender love for
good books, "Hutch," like a Russian nihilist or a sincere artist from
the Montmartre quarter of Paris, hated all cant or ceremony.
Although he later became the central figure in one of the most
radical groups in Greenwich Village, in the years that Cahan worked
with him on the *Commercial,* radical ideas interested him as little
as they did Steffens. Hapgood and Cahan along with Carl Hovey
would attend the American theaters in each other's company, often
spending an evening at the Harvard Club where Hapgood and Hovey
were members.[30]

459

"Hutch" was fascinated by the religious life of the Jewish quarter
and the many interesting types it contained. Cahan would act as
his liaison agent and interpreter introducing him to some of his
friends and acquaintances. "Hutch" soon began to write descriptions
of the Lower East Side and its personalities for the *Advertiser.*
Cahan often wrote on these themes but more often than not, he would
leave them to Hapgood. It was rewarding to see how warmly and
beautifully "Hutch" could write on a subject so dear to the heart of
the former Yiddish journalist. One of the legendary characters of the
ghetto to whom "Hutch" was introduced was Eliakim Zunser, the
jester and folk-poet. Hapgood's tender description vividly limns
the subsequent scene.

> So as he chanted his poems he seemed to gather up into himself
> the dignity and pathos of his serious and suffering race, but as one who
> had gone beyond the suffering and lived only with the eternities. His
> wife and children bent over him as he recited, and their bodies kept
> time with his rhythm. One of the two visitors was a Jew, whose child-
> hood had been spent in Russia, and when Zunser read a dirge which
> he had composed in Russia twenty-five years ago at the death by
> cholera of his first wife and children — a dirge which is now chanted
> daily in thousands of Jewish homes in Russia — the visitor joined
> in, although he had not heard it for many years. Tears came to his
> eyes as memories of his childhood were brought up by Zunser's famous
> lines; his body swayed to and fro in sympathy with that of Zunser
> and those of the poet's second wife and her children; and to the Anglo-
> Saxon present this little group of Jewish exiles moved by rhythm,
> pathos, and the memory of a far-away land conveyed a strange
> emotion.[31]

---

[30] *Ibid.,* vol. IV, pp. 119–120.

[31] *Ibid.,* vol. IV, p. 121; H. Hapgood, *The Spirit of the Ghetto,* (second edition, New
York: Funk & Wagnalls Company 1909), p. 94. We wish to thank Funk & Wagnalls

Of course, the Russian with the tear-stained cheeks was Abraham Cahan.[32]

Interestingly enough, the *Commercial Advertiser* published the first poem in an English translation by the sweatshop lyricist of the East Side, Morris Rosenfeld, and again it was "Hutch" Hapgood who introduced this dreamer of the ghetto to an American audience. The pathos of Rosenfeld's earnest, almost childlike simplicity was enshrined in the two stanzas of the poem, "I Know Not Why."

> I lift mine eyes against the sky,
> The clouds are weeping — so am I;
> I lift my eyes again on high,
> The sun is smiling — so am I.
> Why do I smile? Why do I weep?
> I do not know; it lies so deep.
>
> I hear the winds of autumn sigh,
> They break my heart, they make me cry.
> I hear the birds of lovely spring,
> My hopes revive, I help them sing.
> Why do I sing? Why do I cry?
> It lies so deep, I know not why.[33]

460

Hapgood later assembled his articles on the Jewish quarter from the *Atlantic Monthly*, the *Bookman*, the *Critic*, the *World's Work*, the Boston *Transcript*, the *Evening Post*, and the *Commercial Advertiser*, and in 1902, published them in a classic work of compassion and understanding entitled, *The Spirit of the Ghetto*. Upon its publication, Cahan praised Hapgood "as the only gentile who knows and understands the spirit of the ghetto." Writing from Florence, Italy, the celebrated Anglo-Jewish novelist, Israel Zangwill, no stranger to the ghetto, stated:

> It is a criticism of life, and moreover a criticism tending toward sweetness and light. For it is the work of no prejudiced Jew but the work of an outsider of culture, able to interpret what he sees: to understand its ratios: and finally to define the deep springs of idealism that transfuse the ghetto with a poetry that the larger American life often loses . . . .[34]

Company for its kind permission to quote this passage, as well as others from Hapgood's book. Cf. *CA*, Dec. 31, 1898. See also, Sol Liptzin, *Eliakum Zunser: Poet of His People* (New York, 1950), pp. 227, 234 f.

[32] A. Cahan, *Bleter, supra*, vol. IV, p. 121, and see also *ibid.*, vol. I, p. 88.

[33] *CA*, Dec. 17, 1898; cf. H. Hapgood, *Spirit of the Ghetto, supra*, pp. 90–112.

[34] H. Hapgood, *Spirit of the Ghetto, supra*, p. 314.

Mr. Hapgood explained with deep warmth the purpose of his studies in the preface to the first edition of his book:

> The Jewish quarter of New York is generally supposed to be a place of poverty, dirt, ignorance, and immorality — the seat of the sweat-shop, the tenement house, where "red Lights" sparkle at night, where the people are queer and repulsive. Well-to-do persons visit the Ghetto merely from motives of curiosity or philanthropy; writers treat of it "sociologically," as of a place in crying need of improvement.
> That the Ghetto has an unpleasant aspect is as true as it is trite. But the unpleasant aspect is not the subject of the following sketches. I was led to spend much time in certain poor resorts of Yiddish New York not through motives either philanthropic or sociological but simply by virtue of the charm I felt in men and things there. East Canal Street and the Bowery have interested me more than Broadway and Fifth Avenue. Why, the reader may learn from the present volume — which is an attempt made by a "Gentile" to report sympathetically on the character, lives and pursuits of certain east-side Jews with whom he has been in relations of considerable intimacy.[35]

461

The *Commercial Advertiser* devoted many columns to interpreting the East Side Jew to its readers. Almost every Saturday, its supplement contained an article depicting a phase of the life of the immigrant Jew.[36] Cahan's influence was to be seen on every hand. Steffens happily accused the future editor of the *Jewish Daily Forward* of bringing the spirit of the East Side into the editorial offices of his paper. The city editor joyously recorded that the contentious Jews of the Ghetto were split into parties over the question of realism in the arts and that his police reporter, Abraham Cahan, had taken his fellow journalists, one by one as he could get them, or in groups to the cafés where the debate was on at every table and to the theaters where the audiences divided into factions:

> . . . . A remarkable phenomenon it was, a community of thousands of people fighting over an art question as savagely as other people

---

[35] *Ibid.*, p. 5; cf. Mark Wischnitzer, *To Dwell in Safety* (Philadelphia, 1949), p. 49, for a scholarly appreciation of Hapgood's writings.

[36] *CA*: "East Side Journalism," Feb. 12, 1898; "Yiddish Comedy," Feb. 26, 1898; "Schiller Garnished," March 26, 1898; "Literature of the Slums," April 9, 1898; "Ghetto War Spirit," May 14, 1898; "Reb Yehudah Pereles," May 21, 1898; "Ghetto Letter Writing," Aug. 13, 1898; "Zangwill in the Ghetto," Dec. 10, 1898; "Tailor and Poet," Dec. 17, 1898; "The Ghetto Poet's Life," Dec. 31, 1898; "A Prophet not at Home," Jan. 14, 1899; "In An East Side Cafe," April 22, 1899; "Researches of a Rabbi," June 3, 1899; "A Socialistic Poet," April 14, 1900; "Shakespeare in Vogue," June 9, 1900; "Some East Side Rabbis," July 14, 1900; "A Yiddish Sketch," Nov. 10, 1900; "Hamlet in the Bowery," Jan. 26, 1901; "The Real Poit Pinchas," March 16, 1901.

have fought over political or religious questions, dividing families, setting brother against brother, breaking up business firms, and finally forcing the organization of a rival theater with a company pledged to realism against the old theater, which would play any good piece.

I rejoiced when this East Side controversy flowed over into my paper. I had enjoyed and profited by my police reporter's interest in the picturesque ghetto and I knew it was good — good journalism and good business — for my reporters to follow and report the happenings over there. It increased our circulation; the Jews read the *Commercial*, and it broadened the minds of our staff and of our readers. Norman Hapgood reviewed the Yiddish theaters or let Cahan and other reporters write criticisms of their shows; he often put their plays and perform-

462     ances at the head of his column, where they often belonged. The Yiddish stage was about the best in New York at that time, both in staff and in acting . . . .[37]

Steffens had already taken an interest in the East Side Jews while employed as a reporter for the New York *Evening Post*, nearly losing his job for his avid coverage of the Jewish quarter. Edwin L. Godkin, the renowned editor of the *Nation* and the *Evening Post*, once required his reporter to call on a socially prominent "Hebrew" lady who resented the fact that

> so much space was given to the ridiculous performances of the ignorant, foreign East Side Jews and none to the uptown Hebrews.[38]

Steffens thereupon savored the pleasure of informing her of the comparative beauty, significance, and character of the uptown and downtown Jews. The impudent gentile must have excelled in his exposition for she threatened to have him discharged from the *Evening Post*. Fortunately for Steffens however, the editorial writers were also under pressure from prominent Jews to back up their side of a public controversy over the blackballing of a wealthy Jew by an uptown social club.[39]

Cahan's influence must not be overly exaggerated. Although the interest of the *Commercial Advertiser* in East Side life was extraordinary at the turn of the century, it must be remembered that the New York *Daily Tribune*, the *Evening Post*, and the other papers which did not benefit from the vital stimulus of the erstwhile Yiddish journalist, were generous in their reporting of Jewish matters. The *Tribune* religiously covered the Jewish holidays, carefully explaining their significance. Articles were devoted to Jewish marriage customs,

[37] L. Steffens, *Autobiography, supra*, p. 318.
[38] *Ibid.*, p. 243.
[39] *Ibid.*

education, health, vocations, and events on the East Side.[40] But the *Tribune*'s reports did not possess the informed luminous charm which distinguished the writing on the ghetto for the *Advertiser*.

Cahan's assignments were not wholly restricted to police reporting. Norman Hapgood, the drama critic, less intense and more sophisticated than his brother, once assigned him to attend a performance of "Macbeth," starring Helena Modjeska. Cahan's review was uncomplimentary to this most celebrated Shakesperian actress and the mild well-mannered Hapgood, one of her most ardent admirers, recoiled in horror upon reading Cahan's critique. Not wanting to offend Cahan, the future editor of *Collier's Weekly*, simply informed him that a few changes and deletions might have to be made. Upon reading the paper the following day, Cahan noted that his unfavorable criticism had been converted into a column of praise.[41] Needless to say, just as Wright never again asked Cahan to write a political article after reading his piece on Tracy, so Hapgood never again requested him to write a criticism of a play performed in the American theater. It is instructive to sample Cahan's polemical dramatic criticism. His critique of Zangwill's *The Children of the Ghetto*, reveals the area of perception and sensibility he was striving to illuminate:

463

> In the literary anarchy which marks the exit of the nineteenth century aesthetic emotion is often confounded with interest in plot and incident. The same human nature which is thrilled by the clever disentanglement of an ingeniously entangled set of events may also take keen delight in a picture of simple life; but there is no more reason why we should confuse these two sources of enjoyment than there is to put the pleasure of a mathematician unravelling a complex problem side by side with that of a schoolboy watching a fight. These elements of emotional activity may have some points of contact; but they belong to two distinct classes of psychical phenomena and should be treated separately. However difficult the definition of art, one thing is clear: It is a source of aesthetic enjoyment and has as little to do with what may be called a plot interest as it has with sportsmanship. To judge of the art of a novel or a drama by the amount of plot it contained would be like measuring silk by the bushel or time by the yard. Yet this is what is done every day by reviewers of books and plays, and what was done recently by some of the critics of Israel Zangwill's drama, "The Children of the Ghetto."

[40] Cf. New York *Daily Tribune*: Jan. 9, Feb. 20, April 6, Sept. 16, Oct. 1, 1898; Jan. 29, March 26, May 27 and 28, June 4, 8, 24, 29, July 23, Aug. 20, Sept. 5, 9, 13, 14, 15, 24, 27, Nov. 12, 1899.
[41] A. Cahan, *Bleter, supra*, vol. IV, pp. 122–123.

The storm of discussion which the production of this play has raised is one of the literary events of the year. Few works of art have awakened so much acrimony, on the one hand, and so much enthusiastic praise, on the other, as has the Zangwill play. One of the chief faults pointed out by its adverse critics is the meagreness of the story which forms the framework of the drama, and the abundance of character-portraiture the omission of which would increase the rapidity of movement. This reminds one of the little girl who will skip all the descriptive passages in her novel that she may sooner find out whether the hero married the heroine. "The Children of the Ghetto" is not a blood-and-thunder production. It is a piece of art; and the interest it is intended to arouse is one of pure aesthetics.

464

The central motive of the play flows from one of the most unique and interesting situations ever exploited by the stage; and the artistic detail which the critics have found superfluous is made up of pulsating bits of life, each contributing to the reality of vital parts of the play, and all harmoniously blending into an ensemble of singular power and beauty. So far from retarding the progress of the drama these character-studies seem to quicken it by adding to the convincing force of the story. The play consists of a mass of human interest — as varied in its fun and sadness as life itself — out of which the basic event shapes itself in the most natural way. It belongs to the same class as Hauptmann's "Die Weber," where a multitude of types and seemingly detached scenes combine to throw into high relief the central idea of the play.

"The Children of the Ghetto" depicts the world of Talmudic Judaism crumbling under the pressure of modern culture. It shows two civilizations seventeen centuries apart at the point of collision, and the desperate struggle of the past for existence under the crushing weight of the present. It is a breathing throbbing picture of a social phenomenon instinct with historical as well as dramatic interest. The present home of the Talmudic Ghetto is in the smaller towns of Russia, Poland, Galicia, Hungary, and Rumania. In modern London or New York it is an immigrant; and it has in it both the tragedy and the comedy of a foreigner struggling to make himself at home amid uncongenial surroundings. The crowding out of the Talmudic spirit by modern influences is going on in the most out-of-the-way town in Poland as well as in London; but in the former the process is almost imperceptible, while in the Ghetto of the English metropolis it is clearly visible to the naked eye. In Zangwill's play the old world triumphs over the new; yet the inevitable doom of this wonderful old world gives a mournful echo to the most irresistible fun of the work and lends special meaning to every stroke of the artist's brush.

When, for example, you meet a Jew with sidelocks on his way from Broadway to Hester Street, in New York City, you see a man going from the nineteenth century to the second. To boast of a lack of interest in Reb Shemuel or Moses Ansell, therefore, as some of the critics of "The Children of the Ghetto" play have done, is to pride one's self on a lack of interest in the living, but rapidly crumbling, relic of a musty past bubbling over with intellectual and emotional energy. He who does so cannot sincerely admire the dumb statues in the Roman corridor of the British Museum or the excavations of Pompeii. It is only in business that the Jews know how to put their best goods in the window. Outside of it their slight faults are apt to catch the eye more readily than their important virtues. Some of their noblest and most interesting things are hidden from view; and some of these are shown by Zangwill in his "Children of the Ghetto."[42]

Cahan's relations with his gentile associates continued to bear the ripe fruit of mutual esteem and sympathy. Hovey, LeFevre, Duncan, and Parrish, all valued his company and wisdom. In Cahan's judgment, Hovey, a practical Yankee with a fine mind, would have made an excellent literary critic had he been born in Russia. From a contrasting species of mankind stemmed Edwin LeFevre. Devoid of Hovey's New England reserve, he resembled a Frenchman or Italian in the ease with which he could be approached. His first novel, *The Woman and the Bonds*, a product of his Wall Street experiences, was in Cahan's judgment one of the most talented novels of the period and had LeFevre been living in France, Germany, or Russia, he would have become an important writer. He was a procrastinator, however, and easily became intoxicated with the fame he enjoyed as the author of humorous stories on finance, neglecting to make artistic integrity his prime ideal. It was fame rather than money which corrupted LeFevre for he had been able to acquire great sums of money with ease through his connections on the stock exchange.[43]

465

Upon one occasion, Cahan was assigned to do a piece on the Syrian quarter on Washington Street about which Norman Duncan had once written for the *Evening Post*; the kindly Canadian provided Cahan with a list of the acquaintances he had made in that neighborhood. The former Yiddish journalist did not become inspired with this quarter although Duncan whom he encountered there wrote a romantic piece lyrically describing this middle eastern outpost in the

---

[42] A. Cahan, "Zangwill's Play 'The Children of the Ghetto,'" *Forum*, vol. XXVIII (Dec., 1899), pp. 504–505; for other Cahan critiques in the American periodical press see: A. Cahan, "The Younger Russian Writers," *Forum*, vol. XXVIII (Sept., 1899), pp. 119–128; *idem*, "The Mantle of Tolstoy," *Bookman*, vol. XXVI (Dec., 1902), pp. 328–333; *idem*, "Zangwill's 'The Gray Whig,'" *Bookman*, vol. XXVII (May, 1903), pp. 256–257; *idem*, "Maxim Gorky's 'The Spy,'" *Bookman*, vol. XXXIII (March, 1909), pp. 90–92.

[43] A. Cahan, *Bleter*, *supra*, vol. IV, pp. 123–125.

heart of New York City. Unhappily, the literary career of this dreamer was abruptly terminated by a premature death.[44]

A curious figure was the tall, beardless real estate editor, the only member of the *Advertiser* staff who enjoyed talking about socialism with Cahan. He even invited him to his home to discuss this subject with his friends, one of whom was a single-taxer.[45]

The outbreak of the Spanish-American War in April, 1898, gave Cahan a real opportunity to broaden his knowledge of the United States and to measure the pulse of its inhabitants. In order to fully partake of the soldiers' experiences, Cahan visited a training camp on Long Island. He slept with the volunteers on their pallets, ate with them, and listened to their stories and jokes. Those whom he questioned candidly admitted that they had volunteered out of a lust for adventure; the more practical minded felt that should they be shipped to the Philippines, attractive economic opportunities awaited them there. The former Yiddish journalist was very much fascinated by the vivid sense perception of men under fire. Upon visiting a convalescent hospital for soldiers on Staten Island, he spent some time questioning the veterans about their recollections of the experience under fire with very spotty results. Among the wounded, he talked to a Jewish boy named Jacobs from Pitt Street on the Lower East Side.[46]

Cahan was also privileged to interview the renowned American military and naval luminaries. Generals Joseph Wheeler and William Shafter and Admirals Winfield S. Schley and George Dewey. The reporter for the *Commercial Advertiser* spent many hours with "Fighting Joe" Wheeler in his hotel apartment, remaining all night and into the early hours of the morning. As the early evening's shadow blackened into night, Cahan jokingly remarked that it was unnecessary for Wheeler to light the lamp, since his uniform would illuminate the room with a poetic glow. The general insisted that the journalist join him at supper. They continued their conversation afterwards, the articulate Wheeler responding in warm and zealous tones. They discussed a huge variety of topics. Cahan, ever on the alert, ventured to ride one of his favorite hobby horses, the theory and practice of socialism, to whose elucidation Wheeler listened attentively. For obvious reasons, Cahan promised the distinguished officer he would not report the last portion of their conversation in his paper.[47]

[44] *Ibid.*, vol. IV, pp. 125–126; cf. "Swarthy Syrians," *CA*, June 25, 1898.
[45] A. Cahan, *Bleter, supra*, vol. IV, p. 128.
[46] *Ibid.*, vol. IV, pp. 137–139.
[47] *Ibid.*, vol. IV, pp. 141–142.

During the war period, Cahan frequently spent all night on an assignment. When an important military or naval personality was expected or when a shipload of wounded soldiers or sailors was scheduled to reach port, the newspapermen from New York and the other large cities, numbering well over a hundred, would assemble to spend many hours expectantly waiting on the docks. The interval was usually filled with an endless stream of indelicate bits of humor or with a debate over a fact or some practical matter rather than over ideas. Cahan with his delight in abstract thought found these preoccupations not to his taste.[48]

At this time, the former Yiddish journalist lived a major part of his life in the emotional world of American newspaperdom. When Fitzgerald, the gifted son of Erin employed by the dignified *Evening Post*, scooped the journalistic community by gaining an interview with the triumphant Admiral Dewey off the shores of Staten Island, Cahan's heart burst with pride. Although Admiral Dewey was the idol of the broader universe, Fitzgerald was the hero of the world of the fourth estate and of Abraham Cahan.[49]

467

In these years the future editor of the *Jewish Daily Forward* seems to have taken an uncanny interest in the observation and recording of various criminal trials.[50] His devotion of many detailed pages to these matters in his memoirs is only understandable in the light of Steffens' dictum with regard to the reporting of murder trials. Steffens' interesting attitude toward the arraignment of murderers was best expressed in his autobiography:

> The flash of a murder would come in. I did not rush a man to get the news first; Lachaussee would write a short bulletin for the next edition while I would call up, say Cahan; I would ask him to sit down and then, without any urge, tell him quietly what to do.
>
> "Here, Cahan, is a report that a man has murdered his wife, a rather bloody, hacked up crime. We don't care about that. But there's a story in it. That man loved that woman once well enough to marry her, and now he has hated her enough to cut her all to pieces. If you can find out what happened between the wedding and this murder, you will have a novel for yourself and a short story for me. Go on now, take your time, and get this tragedy, as a tragedy."
>
> Our stated ideal for a murder story was that it should be so understood and told that the murderer would not be hanged, not by our readers. We never achieved our ideal but there it was; and it is scientifically and artistically the true ideal for an artist and for a

---

[48] *Ibid.*, vol. IV, pp. 142–144.
[49] *Ibid.*, vol. IV, pp. 174–175.
[50] Cf. *ibid.*, vol. IV, pp. 151–166.

newspaper: to get the news so completely and to report it so humanly that the reader will see himself in the other fellow's place.[51]

Cahan was given broad scope for his unlimited compassion for human misery and full reign for his artistic ability to evoke an equally forbearing emotion in the hearts of his readers.

Cahan's duties also included some special reporting. He was given the opportunity to interview the highly publicized Boss of New York's Tammany machine and the living epitomy of municipal corruption, Richard Croker. The press was unrelenting in its twice-daily denunciations of the Democratic chieftain although he granted no interviews; reporters found it impossible to get a word out of him. There was a perennial and avid speculation as to whom the Tammany chieftain would place in public office or to whom he would give the opportunity to make a few hundred thousand dollars on a city contract. Meanwhile, a caricature of Croker's feline visage superimposed upon the vilified head of Nast's Tammany tiger would be on constant public display in the daily press. Cahan spent the long evening of Election Day, 1898, with Croker in the Democratic Club on Fifth Avenue where the widower maintained his permanent residence. The election results were quite conclusive very early in the evening. It was apparent that Theodore Roosevelt, the Republican candidate, had soundly trounced Tammany's Augustus Van Wyck, a brother of the Tammany mayor, for the governorship. Although little hope was entertained for the Democratic candidate, Croker, like a seasoned gambler, maintained a merry countenance all evening. Among those present was the opulent August Belmont. Belmont, unlike his wealthy cronies who if interested in politics at all supported the Republican party, yielded his allegiance to the Grand Sachem of Tammany Hall. The *Commercial* reporter found it instructive to observe the young banker humbling himself before so poorly varnished a product of New York's gutters and saloons, as Richard Croker. One journalist compared Croker to a laughing tiger. A laughing Croker was far more dangerous, chimed another. Later in the evening after most of the reporters had left leaving only Cahan and four other die-hards, Croker became more amiable and loquacious. Cahan jotted down some notes on the Tammany leader's observations. Croker exploded with rage. Despite reassurances from another reporter that Cahan's word, that he would not report the conversation to his newspaper, was reliable and unequivocal, the politician regarded him suspiciously thereafter.[52] Indeed Cahan's

468

---

[51] L. Steffens, *Autobiography, supra*, p. 317.
[52] A. Cahan, *Bleter, supra*, vol. IV, pp. 167–172; cf. Lothrop Stoddard, *Master of Manhattan, The Life of Richard Croker* (New York, 1931).

earlier impressions of American politicians were now categorically confirmed.

September 9, 1899, saw the end of the second trial of Alfred Dreyfus. The court's decision was momentarily awaited by the New York press. Although Cahan's co-workers on the *Advertiser* had only superficial knowledge of the case, they knew that Jews viewed Dreyfus as a martyr. They sincerely shared in the despair of their fellow journalist when the verdict of "guilty" was received over the wire.[53]

Among Cahan's further experiences were encounters with such notables as President William McKinley, William Cody, popularly known as Buffalo Bill, Russell Sage, Bishop Henry Codman Potter, Peter Kropotkin, Theodore Roosevelt, and Samuel Gompers. From each he gained a deeper insight into the paradoxes constituting the foundation blocks of American life.

469

The former Yiddish journalist's interview with McKinley took place aboard a ferry crossing the Hudson from New Jersey to New York. As yet new to the art of reporting for the American press and crowded in with a host of other reporters, Cahan was barely able to put a few questions to the chief executive in the short time available.[54]

A far more gratifying experience was Cahan's meeting with hospitable Buffalo Bill, at his circus location on Staten Island. Cody had been informed that Cahan was a man of literary interests, not just an ordinary reporter. He graciously demonstrated the intricacies of the art of the rodeo to the reporter and invited him to lunch. Cahan felt as though he were the honored guest of the chief of a wild primitive tribe from the Pacific Islands or darkest Africa.[55]

One morning, Russell Sage, reputedly one of America's most frugal millionaires, found time to converse with Cahan, as they walked down Fifth Avenue from Sage's home on Forty-second Street to his office on Wall Street. Despite Sage's desire to avoid discussing business, he responded to the journalist's query regarding his need for such vast wealth by exclaiming that he simply enjoyed acquiring it. Cahan was sceptical of this reply and in his autobiography, he pointed to an incident which supported his view that Sage gained a great deal of pleasure from hoarding his riches.[56]

One of Cahan's most pleasant recollections was that of Bishop Potter, head of the Protestant Episcopal Church in New York, whom he admired for his masterly pronunciation of the English

[53] A. Cahan, *Bleter, supra*, vol. IV, p. 130.
[54] *Ibid.*, vol. IV, p. 98.
[55] *Ibid.*, vol. IV, pp. 178–179.
[56] *Ibid.*, vol. IV, pp. 181–182.

language and his rich quality of speech. In Cahan's estimation, only the carefully inflected and musical elocution of the veteran English Shakespearian actor, Henry Irving, compared with the prelate's gifts.[57]

The former Yiddish journalist's acquaintance with the grinning ultra-vigorous Theodore Roosevelt of Oyster Bay was limited to a brief appraisal. The then Governor of New York came into the *Advertiser* office to greet Steffens with whom he had become friendly at police headquarters when he had been police commissioner of New York City and the editor, a police reporter for the *Evening Post*. Cahan suspected that "Teddy" called partially to show that he was democratic and partially out of honest good fellowship.[58]

470

The future *Forward* editor was afforded a warm acquaintance with Samuel Gompers in the aristocratic Nineteenth Century Club. There the lonely President of the American Federation of Labor vigorously defended the trade union movement against the verbal sallies of the Harvard professor, Edward Atkinson, whom Cahan characterized as the court-economist of "King Capitalism." To Cahan's surprise, Gompers, despite his non-socialist position, acquitted himself so admirably that the enthusiastic journalist could not restrain himself from rushing forward to shake the hand of the unattended and neglected labor leader. The two immediately became friends and spent the early hours of the morning in each other's company, walking, talking, and sipping coffee.[59]

Another in the heterogeneous company whom Cahan encountered in his journalistic capacity was the gentle Russian anarchist, Prince Peter Kropotkin, with whom Cahan had enjoyed a brief acquaintance in London. Upon his arrival in New York, Kropotkin was interviewed in his hotel apartment by the local reporters. Despite his flawless command of English, he asked Cahan to stay during the interrogation, probably to render him moral support. The Prince was not disappointed in his fearful expectations. One journalist, pen and paper in hand, entreated: "Tell me, Prince, how does one make a bomb?"[60] As was to be expected, an embarrassing silence ensued; the anarchist philosopher could hardly expect aid from his socialist companion in this instance.

Cahan's career with the *Commercial Advertiser* came to an abrupt conclusion shortly after the resignation of Lincoln Steffens from the paper in 1901. The new city editor brought a vastly different

[57] *Ibid.*, vol. IV, pp. 182–183.
[58] *Ibid.*, vol. IV, p. 175.
[59] *Ibid.*, vol. IV, pp. 176–178.
[60] *Ibid.*, vol. IV, pp. 186–187.

character to the *Advertiser*. Although Cahan was not disturbed in his work, the paper lost all interest for him. Wright readily discerned Cahan's reaction and was prepared to accept his resignation. It was arranged that Cahan would continue to contribute articles to the Saturday supplement of the *Commercial* as a free lance writer. Cahan also agreed to write for the Sunday edition of the New York *Sun* and to have his writings syndicated in newspapers of other cities.[61]

A few days before resigning his regular job with the *Advertiser*, Cahan suddenly had his eyes covered from behind as he paced down Chambers Street; of course — it was Lincoln Steffens. The late city editor of the *Advertiser* who had just returned from a tour of some of America's larger cities was violently aroused by the universal prevalence of social injustice and municipal corruption. Cahan now realized that what abstract discussions had failed to accomplish, concrete experience had impressed upon Steffens as a reporter for *McClure's*. While in earlier years, Steffens had viewed the discussion of the problem of the ills of society as a wearisome bore, he now regarded these matters as vital to the health and preservation of a society which boasted of its democratic institutions. Steffens' new outlook was reflected in his articles in *McClure's*, increasing the circulation of that magazine to over one hundred thousand and making him famous as "King of the Muckrakers." *McClure*, however, felt that Lincoln Steffens' and John S. Phillips' articles were too radical. The two "radicals" therefore decided to found the extremely successful *American Magazine*. Upon being informed of this new enterprise, Cahan asked his friend whether the new publication would be more literary than *McClure's*. Steffens hurriedly cited a few details and then insisted that they discuss socialism. Cahan wryly reminded him that in earlier years when he had attempted to broach this subject, the muckraking journalist had insisted on talking about literature. Steffens laughed heartily and they proceeded to discuss the principles of socialism.[62]

So ended the career of Abraham Cahan as a journalist for the American press. Vested with the aplomb and dignity acquired through success in the greater American sphere, he rejoined the immigrant community with a chastened impression of American life. More than four eye-opening years with the *Advertiser* allowed him to divest himself of many prejudices which the East-European

471

---

[61] *Ibid.*, vol. IV, pp. 226–230; cf. Lincoln Steffens, *The Shame of the Cities* (New York, 1904).

[62] A. Cahan, *Bleter, supra*, vol. IV, pp. 226–230.

Jew, often unknowingly, brought with him to the seaports on the Atlantic coastal plain. The Americanization of Abraham Cahan heralded a process that affected all Russian-Jewish immigrants in varying degrees as their roots became more firmly embedded in America's fertile soil.

Cahan returned to the tottering *Jewish Daily Forward* an accomplished literary craftsman and polished journalist. Two decades in the United States had provided him with a varied apprenticeship — factory hand, lecturer, teacher, labor organizer, law student, socialist preacher, and editor and contributor to five Yiddish periodicals, capped by his experiences as a journalist for the *Sun, Evening Post,* and *Commerical Advertiser.* His subsequent career as editor of the *Jewish Daily Forward* was grounded in the experiences of these impressionable years. Above all, his association with the *Commercial Advertiser* left a deep impress. In the eyes of the immigrant Jewish community, Cahan had become a real American whose advice was to be heeded. Not only had he achieved an English literary style of distinction but his colleagues assured him that his Yiddish had been improved in the process.

With his natural talent for journalism, Cahan transformed the *Jewish Daily Forward* single-handedly from an obscure sectarian newspaper into the leader and pacemaker of Yiddish journalism in the United States.[63] A deep and obsessive interest in human problems, a stethoscopically attuned ear to the aches and aspirations in his readers' hearts, and an overweening conviction in the infallibility of his judgments, led Cahan away from the narrow dogmatic paths pursued by the socialists of the book and the formula. The "socialism" of Lincoln Steffens made it clear to Cahan that social and political convictions were defined by actions rather than by an easy flow of words punctuated by labels. Although Cahan remained a pious socialist, his socialism was indistinguishable from social reform. Despite a loyal adherence to Marxian terminology and ritual, however tenuous, his keen intuition guarded him from trampling upon the deepest sensibilities of the *Forward's* hundreds of thousands of readers. In practice, socialism came to mean a fervent almost personal concern with all human problems and a deep sympathy for the miserable and oppressed of all lands, races, and creeds.

Nor was Cahan's love and admiration for the magnificent literary standards erected by the great Russian novelists ever dimmed. His passion for literature was not only reflected in the character and

472

---

[63] Cf. M. Osherowitch, *Di Geshichte fun Forverts, 1897–1947* [*The History of the Forward, 1897–1947*] (typescript in the Jewish Division of The New York Public Library).

warmth of his own articles and editorials and those of his colleagues but in the grand creative literature which Cahan nursed and encouraged. The acknowledged masters of modern Yiddish poetry and prose, Sholem Asch, I. J. Singer, Abraham Reisen, and Abraham Liessin, published their major works in the pages of the *Jewish Daily Forward*. Literature was a guide to life. Whether as a novel or the report of a murder trial, it had much to teach the most ordinary reader about ethical problems and the vagaries of human nature.

Unlike a number of gifted journalists cultivated by the Yiddish press whose powers of observation were blotted out by an inflationary capacity for clever but fruitless polemics hovering about a magically fascinating idea, Cahan doggedly kept his ear to the ground. Just as Cahan brought the excitement of the East Side into the offices of the *Commercial Advertiser* so he carried back with him to the *Forward* the refreshing liberal American spirit that animated that paper. The socialist inspired *Jewish Daily Forward* has become a monument to the unquenchable individualism of Abraham Cahan.

473

# All, All Alone: The Hebrew Press in America from 1914 to 1924*

By MICHAEL GARY BROWN

## I

The First World War proved to be a watershed for American Jewish history. Cut off from their former European sources, American Jews had to create their own institutional and spiritual life. This was particularly true of the new immigration from Eastern Europe, which had in large part continued to look upon itself as a branch of the Old World. But it was not only the war which cut off the Americans from Europe and caused a new flowering. For the first time Jews discovered that creative talent — some of which, to be sure, had arrived only because of the crises in Europe and Palestine — existed in America. Thus, during the war years, Jewish welfare work in America came into its own; the Congress movement developed, groping for some form of quasi-national organization for American Jews; and the Rabbi Isaac Elchanan Theological Seminary was organized for the training of modern American Orthodox rabbis.

Hebrew circles, too, experienced new vitality and activity: "The War brought the fullness of life . . . to . . . [Hebrew] literature. . . ."[1] In 1916 the Histadruth Ivrith was founded to further the dissemination of Hebrew language and culture in the United States. There was agitation for better Hebrew schools and, particularly among the teachers, for better pay and working conditions. Perhaps the sphere of Hebrew activity that most thrived during the War and the immediate post-War years was the Hebrew press.

Hebrew periodicals had appeared in America many years before the first World War. In 1871 a former Russian *maskil* with middling talents, Hirsch Bernstein, began to publish the first Hebrew language periodical in the United States. This first meager publication managed to survive for five years, a respectable length of time,

* The author would like to express his thanks to Dr. Salo Baron who supervised the original research for this paper at Columbia University.

[1] Daniel Persky, "Hebrew Literature in America," *Luaḥ Aḥiever* (1918), p. 63.

as later events were to show.[2] Altogether, in the more than forty years between the publication of Bernstein's *Hatsofe b'erez hachadosho*[3] and the beginning of the First World War, some 49 Hebrew periodicals (including supplements to Yiddish and English publications) appeared in the United States.[4] Only two of these were still publishing in 1914.[5] As one observer put it, "It is a fact ... that ... the Hebrew press in America already has, thank God, its own [well-populated] graveyard. ...."[6] According to most critical observers, the pioneers of the American Hebrew press had well merited their early demise. Second-rate at best, they were out of touch with contemporary affairs and enamoured with aphorisms.

The decade 1914–1924 witnessed a significant growth in the number of Hebrew journalists and in their intellectual maturity and responsibility. During this decade alone almost as many Hebrew periodicals appeared as had in the 43 years since the publication of the first.[7] One of them is still being published. Two appeared for over eleven years, and nine others for more than three years.

The list of journalists who were "temporary residents" of America during the War included many illustrious names, among them David Ben Gurion, Yitzhak Ben Zvi, Eliezer Ben Yehuda, Hemda Ben Yehuda, Nahum Slouschz, Shmarya Levin and I. D. Berkowitz. In 1916, the *American Jewish Chronicle* noted:

> The Jewish press in this country has, strangely enough, been the one institution to profit by the war. With the outbreak of the conflict there began an influx of prominent Jewish writers and journalists who began immediately to take their place in the Jewish press. Bringing with them years of experience, training and a developed literary taste, they [have] imparted to the ... [American Jewish press] a cultural character which ... [has been] readily distinguishable.[8]

To the uninitiated this list of names would seem to indicate unlimited growth potential. But the Hebrew press was unlike any other immigrant press. It was not created to serve the needs of

476

---

[2] For a complete discussion of America's first Hebrew periodical, see Moshe Davis "Hatsofe b'erez hachadosho" in *Alexander Marx Jubilee Volume* (New York: 1950).

[3] The transliteration of Hebrew titles used herein are those used by the periodicals themselves.

[4] Fannie M. Brody, "The Hebrew Periodical Press in America, 1871–1931: A Bibliographic Survey," *PAJHS*, xxxiii (1934), 127–170.

[5] *Bei Doar Ivri* and *Hatoren*.

[6] Reuben Brainin, "The Hebrew Press in America," *Hatoren* (Jan. 7, 1921).

[7] Brody.

[8] *American Jewish Chronicle*, May 12, 1916.

a public that did not yet read English. The Hebrew press came into being here as it had in Europe, because it was felt that people *should* read Hebrew, not because they wanted to or could. In actuality, although the number of journalists increased, the reading public did not.

No one expected Hebrew periodicals to be profit-making ventures. They were primarily a labor of love. Thus, while 88 of 110 men in a 1927 survey of Hebrew journalists were professionals,[9] it is significant that only two of them made their living directly and entirely from the Hebrew press.[10] This was even true of the financiers of the Hebrew press. Israel Matz, active in the publication of *Hatoren*, *Hadoar* and other periodicals, was the founder and head of the Ex-Lax Corporation. Through subsidies and by placing ads for his product in the magazines, Matz helped keep many of the publications running. Of a similar mold was Saul Lamport, a wealthy textile manufacturer. These men came from the same Russian background as the journalists and differed from them only in that they had grown rich.

The group of men involved in the publication of Hebrew periodicals during these years was a tiny, close-knit circle of like-minded individuals with similar backgrounds, almost all of whom had to devote themselves to some other occupation in order to earn a living. Still they seemed to have unlimited human resources available for the cause. It is remarkable how the same names appear simultaneously in several publications. Of the twenty-two men who served as editors during this decade, seventeen were connected on more than a casual basis with at least one other American Hebrew periodical, and all can be found as authors of articles in several. These journalists also found time to publish in the European Hebrew press, in the American Yiddish press and frequently in the non-Jewish press as well. Max Lipson, editor of *Hatoren*, *Haibri* and the *Luah Ahiever*, and editor-in-chief of the daily *Hadoar*, was at one time or another a correspondent for most of the major European Hebrew newspapers and a co-editor of the first Yiddish newspaper in Belgium. Before World War I, he had collaborated on the Hebrew daily, *Ha-Yom* (1909), on a short-lived Hebrew humor magazine, and served also for a considerable time as editor of *Dos Yiddishe Folk*, the official Yiddish organ of the Zionist Federation of America. The scope of Lipson's involvement gives us some idea of how a small group of men can give the impression of so much activity.

477

---

[9] Daniel Persky, "A Chapter of our New Literature," *Hadoar Jubilee Volume* (New York: 1927).

[10] Another eighteen were professional journalists with the Yiddish press.

Equally small but less impressive was the audience for which these men labored. Estimates of the number of Hebrew readers in America were made by several contemporary journalists. Kalman Whiteman, in 1918, estimated that there were about 80,000 Hebrew readers in America, a number, he felt, never even exceeded in Russia.[11] Another estimate put the figure at 100,000 for the United States and Canada.[12] A third writer merely stated that there were tens of thousands of Hebrew readers in North America.[13] It is, of course, impossible to know whether any of these figures were at all realistic, since the Hebraists were continually accused of over-enthusiasm in estimating their potential audience.[14] The few circulation figures available seem to indicate that these estimates were high, although in all likelihood these periodicals were passed around from one devotee to another.[15] A Hebrew reader was not necessarily a subscriber to a Hebrew publication. Many of the readers were undoubtedly too poor to purchase their own copies. *Haibri* was aware of this condition:

> How great are the expenses of a newspaper in these days.... The price of paper and printing materials goes up daily. In order to meet these rising costs, all the papers find it necessary to raise their prices.... But because we recognize that the Hebrew readers are not well-to-do, we have decided to bear more than our share of the burden and not to raise prices presently.... We hope to make up the deficit through additional subscriptions....[16]

Except for their poverty and paucity, it is difficult to obtain a clear picture of the readers. Contemporary analyses of the American Hebrew reading public conflict. One ebullient admirer described them as: "men and women of culture, Hebrew scholars, thinkers,

478

[11] Kalman Whiteman, "The Hebrew Reader in America," *Hatoren* (Nov. 29, 1918).

[12] Kolmos, "Hebrew Work," *Haibri* (Nov. 24, 1916).

[13] Persky, "Hebrew Literature."

[14] Herman Eliassof, "Journals Printed in the Hebrew Language," *The Reform Advocate* (May 27, 1916), pp. 524–534.

[15] *The American Newspaper Annual and Directory* lists some figures. *Der Volksfreund* of Pittsburgh with its Hebrew supplement has a listed circulation of 5,000 for the years 1916–1922, although this does not necessarily reflect its Hebrew readership, since it was primarily a Yiddish journal. *Hatoren* is listed with 13,300 readers for 1921–23 and 10,000 for 1924. Persky in "Hebrew Literature" states that, after its first issue, *Hatoren* had 2,000 subscribers. The only other periodical for which figures exist is *Miklat*, which in the issue of March 25, 1921, states that the number of subscribers never rose to 1,000. Persky however notes that, in its first year, *Miklat* had 1,921 subscribers and that this number gradually dwindled to 749.

[16] *Haibri*, Jan. 2, 1920.

intellectual leaders . . ."[17] But, although the Hebrew reading public may have looked upon itself as a kind of Jewish intelligentsia, many journalists did not find it very intelligent. Max Lipson stated that the American reader was completely different from the Russian.[18] In Russia a Hebrew reader had been either a comfortable bourgeois continuing a tradition or an intellectual, immersed in Hebrew culture. In America, by contrast, he identified readers as *maskilim*, who read the Hebrew press only to carp about its deterioration and who refused to pay for their subscriptions unless the journal published their scribblings; bourgeoisie, many of whom were willing to donate money on the condition that they not receive the journal (which, Lipson felt, was due to a lack of time for anything cultural or from a fear of being mocked for reading Hebrew, but some may simply have not found them interesting); and the rabbi. Although in Russia the rabbi's home had been an intellectual center, American rabbis were either too busy, too uneducated or too afraid of anti-religious writing to concern themselves with modern Hebrew.

479

Lipson also asserted that crude advertising and personal publicity were "American diseases," which could not be found in the Hebrew press, but only in the Yiddish press. Therefore the people were reading Yiddish, and those whose tastes were more refined, particularly among the young, were assimilated.

Estimates of the quality of the Hebrew periodicals also vary. One contemporary critique of the Hebrew press described them as

> a small but virile and well educated group of Hebrew periodicals, poor in circulation and diminutive in form, yet exercising an influence altogether disproportionate to their resources and the number of . . . readers. It has generally been conceded that one good article by a prominent, or even obscure, Hebrew author, in a Hebrew paper will create a much deeper impression than would a similar article in the Yiddish or English press.[19]

Others, however, asserted that the chief characteristic of all the Hebrew periodicals of the time was their universal dryness and dullness.[20]

All of them were modeled after their Russian precursors. Unlike American periodicals, all the Hebrew ones published advertisements

---

[17] Joseph Esterman, "The American Jewish Press," *The American Weekly Jewish News* (June 14, 1918), p. 262.

[18] Max Lipson, "A Year of the Hebrew Press in America," *Haibri* (Jan. 12, 1917).

[19] Esterman.

[20] H. L. Gordon, "The Hard Beginning," *Hadoar Jubilee Volume* (May 11, 1927), pp. 74–77.

only at the front and back, despite the consequent loss of revenue. Articles were always continuous, making for a ponderous, unattractive layout. Even the spelling of foreign words frequently followed the Russian rather than the American method. The journalists just could not forget what they had learned in Europe.[21]

The Hebrew periodicals of this decade fall into two categories, those appealing to special interests and those of a general nature. Of the former, the largest number was written by or for children. These included the publications of the students of several Hebrew "high schools" (almost the only source of publication in Hebrew outside of New York City), e. g., *Ner Maarovi*, issued by the students of the Rabbi Isaac Elchanan Theological Seminary, a supplement to the *Young Judean*, *Eden*, an illustrated periodical published by Berkowitz and Persky, and the relatively long-lived *Shaharut*, published by the Bureau of Jewish Education of New York and edited by Zvi Scharfstein. Most of these efforts were so insignificant that they were ignored by contemporary critics of the Hebrew press.[22] Of the general periodicals, all but two (*Mikeren Zovith* of Detroit and *Bei Doar Ivri* of Pittsburgh) were published in New York City. *Hadoar* still appears and is today one of the oldest continuously published Hebrew periodicals in the world.

One of the longest-lived was *Bei Doar Ivri* (1909–1922), which appeared as a supplement to a Yiddish weekly with about 5,000 readers. Unlike the other publications, it was published by a middle-aged peddler, Joseph Selig Glick. Its Hebrew style was poor, heavily laced with Aramaic archaisms, and it was ignored by its Hebrew contemporaries.

Some of the smaller periodicals are quite interesting. The only literary-scholarly annual to appear, *Luah Ahiever*, was published only twice, in 1918 and 1921, and was a direct imitation of the European annuals. The appearance of the *Luah* marked a milestone, with its careful and deliberate planning, although one critic declared that, "if this be *belles lettres*, then there is nothing ugly in the world."[23]

All the publications of the period were unsuccessful financially and of questionable literary value with the possible exception of *Miklat*, which received excellent critical notices and was one of the few sufficiently capitalized ventures. Abraham Joseph Stybel,[24] the publisher, owned the Stybel Publishing House of Warsaw, probably

[21] Lipson.

[22] Ephraim Deinard, *Kohelet Amerika* (St. Louis: 1926); Josef Lin, *Die Hebräische Presse, Werdegang und Entwicklungstendenzen* (Berlin: 1928).

[23] Deinard.

[24] Zalman Reisen, *Lexicon of the Yiddish Literature, Press and Philology* (Vilna: 1926).

the largest Hebrew publishing house in the world, and was determined that *Miklat* be financially secure. It was the first American
Hebrew periodical to pay contributors, and the printing and paper
were of the highest quality. Each issue sold far fewer than the 5,000
copies printed, and after fifteen monthly issues, *Miklat* suspended
publication in 1921.[25]

Despite the evident lack of reader enthusiasm, almost all contemporaries agreed that *Miklat* was a fine journal, except for Ephraim
Deinard who felt that if its "poems and stories written in the language of Satan would be fed to mice, literature would lose nothing."[26]
Book-size, *Miklat* included fiction, poetry, literary criticism and
scholarly monographs. I. D. Berkowitz was one of the best and
most experienced editors in America. The material was original,
and every effort was made to stay clear of partisanship. The publication was aimed not only at the American public but also at Europe.
It is said to have been well-received abroad. The enthusiastic critical
reception, the good direction and the adequate financing notwithstanding, *Miklat*, like its less impressive contemporaries, died an
early death, leaving little impression on the American Hebrew scene.

481

## II

In fact, of the forty-two Hebrew periodicals which appeared in
the United States during the decade, only three can be classed as
major undertakings. To be sure, even these were insignificant when
compared with English or Yiddish publications. Longevity, literary
and material resources, and comprehensiveness, however, made
*Haibri*, *Hatoren* and *Hadoar* important enterprises. A successful
Hebrew periodical needs "capital," "personality," a "public" and a
"purpose."[1] From 1914–24, only these three publications approached
those criteria. Although they resembled their less successful cousins
and were produced largely by the same men, only they attempted
seriously to cover all of Jewish life for a wide Jewish public. All
three had inadequate financial resources which eventually contributed to their foundering. Still they had better backing than any
previous publication, except *Miklat*. Two of them even benefited
from organizational subsidies.

[25] Persky, "A Chapter"; Brainin, *op. cit.*; *Haibri*, March 25, 1921.
[26] Deinard, p. 89.

[1] Eliassof, *op. cit.*, p. 525.

The first of the three periodicals to appear was *Haibri*. *Haibri* was founded in Berlin late in 1910 as a weekly by Rabbi Meir Berlin (later Bar-Ilan).[2] An early issue carries a description of the purposes of the magazine as well as a list of its sponsors. The notice calls *Haibri* a

> weekly non-party paper dedicated to all the affairs of Israel, faithful in its spirit to our religious tradition and to our national renaissance.[3]

Most of the sponsors were from Berlin, but the distinguished roster included Jews from Russia, America, England, Palestine and Greece. Among them were Baron Ginzberg, the eminent Russian financier, Professors Max Hildesheimer, Israel Friedlander, Samuel Margoliuth, Nahum Slouschz and Abraham Isaac Kook, later chief rabbi of Palestine. Some of the foremost Hebrew writers of both Europe and America promised their participation in this religious Zionist Hebrew publication.

The geographical distribution of the sales agents of *Haibri*, as opposed to that of the sponsors, indicates that the public to whom it appealed was Eastern European. An early list records forty agents, of whom twenty were in Russia and only three in Germany.[4] (Four were listed in America.) The impressive roster of sponsors and correspondents and a long list of agents, however, did not insure prosperity. No circulation figures are available, but the number of agents listed in various issues declined, until in September, 1913, only eight were listed, although it was stated that subscriptions were taken in all Mizrachi offices.[5] Evidently the agents were not reliable. There were continual pleas in the periodical for the agents to send in the money they had collected from subscribers. The general apathy of the Hebrew reading public, however, suggests that they may have been doing just that.

Advertisements apparently were as unsure a source of revenue as subscriptions. They followed about the same pattern of decline until, by the final issues of the European edition, there were few left. The advertisements do, however, give an idea of what sort of people it was thought were reading *Haibri*. There were always ads by publishers in Poland, Germany, Russia and Palestine for Jewish books and periodicals, especially Hebrew ones. There were also a few ads for kosher hotels in Germany and for tombstones.

---

[2] Curiously in his memoirs *From Volozhin to Jerusalem* (New York: 1933) Berlin has almost nothing to say about *Haibri*.

[3] *Haibri*, Jan. 6, 1911.

[4] *Ibid.*, Nov. 4, 1911.

[5] *Ibid.*, Sept. 23, 1913.

These were standard for all Jewish periodicals in any language anywhere in the world. Among the largest advertisers and the most steady, at least at first, was the Hamburg-America Line, appealing not to immigrants but to the tourist trade. In general, the advertisements seemed to cater to middle and upper class Germans. The N. Israel Department Store was one of the most regular large advertisers. There were also ads for bread and tea and for Suchard chocolate. Among the less regular advertisers were a piano dealer, a jeweler and a clothier. All products and goods advertisers were German, in fact, all from Berlin. From the ads, one might assume that the magazine was going to the relatively well-to-do Hebraists who were by no means numerous in Germany. This contrasts with the dealerships which were in Eastern Europe, perhaps indicating one of the publication's problems.

Diminishing numbers of advertisers and agents mirrored the waning fortunes of the magazine. Its message of the "realisation of Zionism through the foundation of the Jewish tradition thus bringing about a positive end to the Jewish question and the question of Judaism"[6] was the official message of the Mizrachi Organization. It appeared with monotonous regularity in increasingly similar articles. Fiction and poetry were almost non-existent. Literarily as well as financially the journal became progressively weaker. The issue of June 14, 1912, appeared a week late "for technical reasons." The next issue did not appear.

Over a year later, on June 20, 1913, *Haibri* reappeared in "a new form." The management was the same, but each issue was now only half the size of former issues. Moreover, this reduced version almost without advertisements appeared bi-weekly rather than weekly. In the beginning of 1914, the editor, Rabbi Berlin, left for New York. Although, according to reports in *Haibri*, he had every intention of returning, he did not. In his absence *Haibri* ceased publication in April, 1914. Although it was later claimed that the coming of the war in 1914 caused the Berlin *Haibri* to cease publication and to emigrate to America with its editor, its pallid, frail form indicates that its own health dictated a change of climate.[7]

An editorial in the new series of *Haibri* summarized the Berlin era of the periodical well, if a bit complimentarily:

> The five years of its existence in Berlin . . . earned for *Haibri* a modest position well overshadowed by literature and scholarship.

[6] Lin, *op. cit.*, p. 42.
[7] *Haibri*, Jan. 2, 1920.

483

> *Haibri* did not appeal to a wide public in those years. . . . It was
> neither literary nor journalistic . . . but . . . it fulfilled its function. . . .
> It was a Hebrew teacher to many . . . penetrating many houses that
> had been closed for generations to the Hebrew language. . . .[8]

The unsteady and "overshadowed" beginning, admittedly "modest," would not seem to have boded well for a prosperous future. Hebrew journalism, however, was rather unlike any normal business operation. Its devotees were seldom long discouraged by a lack of public acceptance. Greener pastures were always only a short distance away in time or space. Moreover, "wherever Meir Berlin went, a Hebrew periodical was sure to follow."[9] Thus on January 7, 1916, a reinvigorated *Haibri* appeared in New York, the first of the weekly issues that were to appear regularly for the next five years.[10]

The New York *Haibri* was published by "The Hebrew Press Association." The president of the association and the editor of the periodical was Rabbi Meir Berlin. The other officers of the company changed over the years but were always rabbis or members of the New York Orthodox community. Foremost among them were the Redelheims, Abraham and Jacob, but there were other names as well. The post of business manager was particularly vulnerable and difficult, changing at least once a year. During much of the period the managing editor and chief collaborator of Berlin was Max Lipson.

In New York *Haibri* became the official spokesman of the American branch of the Mizrachi, making it the only Hebrew periodical acceptable to many of the Orthodox. In 1917 the offices of *Haibri* were located in the Mizrachi Building on the lower East Side of New York City, and the journal was receiving financial support from the organization. Berlin and his co-workers recognized the importance that Mizrachi support had for the periodical:

> Until last year *Haibri* was partially supported by the American-
> Canadian Mizrachi, which took upon itself as a duty, the support
> of the only Hebrew publication faithful to all the traditions of our
> nation. . . .
> In the past months, the Mizrachi has been putting its funds more
> and more into settlement work in Palestine and into the periodical
> *Ha-Tor* edited by Rabbi Y. L. Fishman in Palestine, its official
> organ. . . . Thus the Mizrachi Organization cannot continue to

---

[8] *Ibid.*

[9] Author's interview with Abraham Spicehandler, Dec. 18, 1962.

[10] According to early issues, a quarterly was originally projected but never appeared.

support *Haibri* . . . [and *Haibri* is therefore forced to suspend operations].[11]

*Haibri* did not, however, subsist wholly on donations and subsidies. Its circulation, while not large, was respectable for a Hebrew periodical. It achieved fairly wide distribution in America, although lists of its agents indicate that its former following in Eastern Europe was completely lost. Nevertheless, revenue from circulation at $3.00 a year and seven cents a copy (up to $4.00 a year and ten cents a copy in 1921 with the postwar inflation) could not have been very great.

Advertising does seem to have been considerably more remunerative in America than it had been in Europe. Ads were more numerous and came from much more varied sources. There were, of course, the old standbys: Hebrew books, kosher foods and wines, and hotels. Through 1919, there were also many other types, large and small. There were ads from New York East Side banks as well as from the Schiff and Company Bank in Chicago. There were ads for products which new householders — immigrants — would need: silverware, furniture, instruction in English, and that sine qua non of Lower East Side business, the pushcart. Only occasionally were there political ads, but in 1916 the periodical was successful in securing a considerable amount of legal advertising from the State of New York. Most of the ads were directed to people living in New York City, and one can assume that most of the subscribers were there as well. The many ads for small shops on the Lower East Side seem to indicate where most of the subscribers lived.

To some extent *Haibri* was a "local" newspaper. There was one important exception to this rule. During the first nine months of 1918, *Haibri*, in the style of the *Christian Science Monitor*, carried as many as four pages of inserts from Chicago firms. The short duration of these inserts would seem to indicate that there was no sizable following of the magazine in Chicago, and that there was only a devotee who sought out the ads. While major national advertisers avoided the periodical — as they did all Hebrew periodicals — there were a few exceptions. Ex-Lax, the staple of American Hebrew publications, never advertised, but its competitor, Marmalax, was a regular advertiser. The Borden Milk Company, several typewriter companies and a fly liquid firm were the only other national advertisers to appear frequently. *Haibri* succeeded in attracting more advertising than any American Hebrew periodical had done before. There was, however, a failure to secure a broad

485

---

[11] *Haibri*, Nov. 18, 1921.

base of advertisers. After 1920 a steady decline set in, and ads became ever more parochial. The failure to lift circulation beyond 2,000 must have limited the attractiveness of the periodical to advertisers.

If "capital" was not a strong point of *Haibri*, "purpose" was. As it had in Europe, *Haibri* spoke for the religious Zionist point of view, but it also looked outward.

> In America, where the groundwork for a Hebrew newspaper has never been laid ... *Haibri* has not chosen new paths for itself, but has conducted itself as it had previously ... It has covered in its pages all of Hebrew life, gathering around itself the best Hebrew writers of every party, ... and it has viewed questions from ... a Hebrew vantage point.[12]

486

It was, of course, always "faithful to the religious tradition and to the national renaissance."[13]

While it is true that the contents of the magazine, and especially the editorial column, were entirely Jewish and Zionist, there was a real attempt at variety and at the inclusion of the best talent available. Although poetry gradually disappeared from *Haibri*, there was some fairly good fiction by men such as S. Y. Agnon and Opatoshu. Berlin and Rabbi Y. L. HaCohen Fishman, the secretary of the Mizrachi Organization, were ever present, but there was plenty of room for outsiders. Many writers who were far from the Mizrachi camp, like Reuben Brainin, who leaned to the Communists in his later life, and the secularist Eliezer Ben-Yehuda were regular contributors. The number of authors appearing in *Haibri* compares favorably with that of the other two major American Hebrew publications.[14]

By contemporary critics *Haibri* was praised for its fairness and for its accomplishments. Even the bitter Ephraim Deinard conceded that "in its internal form it is neither better nor worse than the other periodicals ..."[15] A more generous and doubtless more accurate appraisal was given by Daniel Persky.

> Even though *Haibri* was faithful to the religious tradition ... it did not confine itself to the narrow limits of party thinking. ... On the contrary, *Haibri* served an important function in the development of a modern Hebrew press in America, with its living and exact

---

[12] *Ibid.*, Dec. 28, 1917.
[13] *Ibid.*, July 1, 1921.
[14] In 1916, for example, sixty-one individuals contributed to the periodical.
[15] Deinard, *op. cit.*, p. 101.

style. . . . *Haibri* penetrated a number of homes which no other Hebrew paper could have entered.[16]

*Haibri* survived in America for five years. As it had not done in Germany, it put out its weekly issues with scrupulous regularity. If America did not provide sufficient readers, advertisers or subsidizers to keep *Haibri* in business after 1921, it was nevertheless recognized by the management of the periodical that America had been kind. In 1920, well before the end had been foreseen, *Haibri* editorialized about what it had gained from its existence in America:

> New York has given much to *Haibri*. She brought *Haibri* out of the shadows and put it in the midst of public affairs. . . . Here in America *Haibri* became a living journal. . . .[17]

*Haibri* had grown and prospered in America. Josef Lin asserted that "the best direction of the paper was . . . when it was in America, where the Mizrachi possessed a strong party organization."[18] Even in its final message, it spoke of America as an excellent place for a Hebrew periodical, a land "of many possibilities and of great promise."

Chronologically the second of the three major periodicals was *Hatoren*. *Hatoren* was the only publication to span the period under study, appearing in New York from 1913 to 1925. *Hatoren* had four distinct phases. In a sense one can speak of four different periodicals, each of which used the name, *Hatoren*.

One of the longest-lived Hebrew periodicals ever to appear in America, and one of the most substantial, *Hatoren* had probably the greatest influence and importance of any of the periodicals appearing during the decade under study. An overstated contemporary evaluation asserted that its

> articles and editorials are echoed and re-echoed throughout the land, reaching every section and stratum of Jewry. . . . Men reckon with the utterances of *Hatoren*, because they know that back of it is . . . a profound thinker and brilliant statesman . . . who has wrought a revolution in the life of American Jewry, Dr. Shmaryahu Levin. . . .[19]

Although such inflated prose exaggerated the impact of *Hatoren*, it may indicate its relative importance. At times the periodical did indeed justify such high-flown praise, but its composition and

487

---

[16] Persky "A Chapter"; *Hadoar*, Nov. 21, 1921.
[17] *Haibri*, Jan. 2, 1920.
[18] Lin, *op. cit.*, p. 42.
[19] Esterman, *op. cit.*

purposes fluctuated with the changes in management and format, and thus its influence and quality also varied.

In June, 1913, the first *Hatoren*, a monthly, appeared as a publication of the "Histadrut Ahiever." It continued as a monthly until November 1915, although between June, 1914, and January, 1915, there were no issues. Persky stated that the "Histadrut Ahiever" labored for over a year and a half in preparing for the publication of *Hatoren*. The frequent early failure of American Hebrew periodicals had made it imperative that this venture not fail if the name of the Hebrew press were to be saved. The laborious preparations appear to have been worthwhile, for with the first issue subscriptions reached the then substantial figure of 2,000.[20]

Even in this earliest phase, the periodical had agents in twenty-one cities in fourteen states covering the United States, although, naturally, concentrated in the East. Still, at $1.00 a year and ten cents a copy, circulation could not have been a major source of revenue. Advertising could not have provided much income either. Seldom were there more than enough ads to cover the covers, and those that there were were the old standbys: books and newspapers (Yiddish and Hebrew), kosher wine and foods, personals and, of course, Ex-Lax. P. Lorillard and the Bank of the United States were about the only general advertisers attracted to *Hatoren*.

At first *Hatoren* was edited by a group of men, which included some of the most active and prominent American Hebraists: Simeon Ginzburg, Abraham Goldberg, Shalom Baer Maximon, Daniel Persky and Benjamin Silkiner. All of them were involved with other American Hebrew publications, and every one of them had also been a correspondent for one or more European publications. After its six-month lapse in 1914, *Hatoren*'s editorial board consisted of Maximon, Dr. S. M. Malamed and Persky.

The goal that all these men set for themselves in their new venture was set forth in the prospectus for *Hatoren*:

> Our principal goals [are] . . . to unite and to join together the "lone wolves" as an active force, as a channel of influence; to bring into our secular lives here, a new wave, new hope; and, principally, to bring the new generation under the wings of Hebrew literature and to attach it irrevocably to our national heritage.[21]

These aims were to be achieved in a periodical of varied contents. Much of the material consisted of reasonably scholarly articles on Jewish subjects. In addition, there was a considerable amount of poor poetry and fiction, the latter consisting largely of stories of

---

[20] Persky, "Hebrew Literature."

[21] *Prospectus for the Publication of a Hebrew Monthly in America Called Hatoren* . . .

less than *Saturday Evening Post* calibre. As in every other Hebrew periodical, articles were serialized for months on end. Therefore the periodical didn't change much from issue to issue. A page of contents provides a fair sample of what was found in the first *Hatoren*:

1) Poems — Ephraim Lisitsky
2) "The Monotheistic Value of the Nationalist Mythology in the Bible" — Prof. David Neumark
3) "After the Fact," a story — Yakir Warshawsky
4) "To . . .," a poem — Israel Ephros
5) "Why Am I Reformed?" — Dr. Max Raisin
6) Parables — N. Liberman
7) "Sonnet" — Asher Barash
8) "From the Life of a Hebrew School (from the notebook of a principal)" — Y. Kahana
9) "Contemporary Questions (a general view)" — Y. Z. Frishberg
10) "In Honor of the Sixth Issue of *Hatoren*," a feuilleton — Yekutiel Ginzburg[22]

489

The magazine was unquestionably Zionist at this early stage, and although not religious, nonetheless traditional in tone. An overwhelming number of the issues was devoted largely to nationalism and to Palestine. Free speech was not suppressed, however, and a dissenting article like the above-cited one of Max Raisin on Reform was not unusual.

The last issue of the first *Hatoren* appeared in November, 1915. The periodical was resurrected as a sixteen-page weekly on March 3, 1916. This second period marked the apogee of *Hatoren*. While "the Hebrew press was [being] shattered in the old world in the wake of the World War, *Hatoren* became the spiritual refuge and the meeting-place for Hebrew creative energy."[23]

The management and operation of the weekly are somewhat more difficult to follow than were those of the monthly. The publisher of the renewed venture was the Hatoren Publishing Association. The officers of this association were all fairly well-to-do businessmen, with the exception of Shmaryahu Levin, who became the president of the Association in June, 1916. In the spring of 1919, the Zionist Federation of America became the publisher of *Hatoren*, and the offices of the periodical moved to Zionist headquarters at 55 Fifth Avenue.

The assumption of control by the Zionist Federation represented only the formalizing of a situation which had existed *de facto* for some time previous. *Hatoren* itself reported that for the year 1916–17

[22] *Hatoren*, Nov., 1913.
[23] Lin, *op. cit.*, p. 44.

the Zionist Federation had given the periodical a subsidy of $1,000.[24] Deinard claimed that the Federation was spending "eight thousand shekels" a year on *Hatoren* during this period of its existence, but this is nowhere substantiated.[25] A report for the year 1920 stated that *Hatoren* lost $18,000 in that year and that the Zionist Federation could no longer support the journal. Specific figures are nowhere quoted except for 1916–1917. It can be assumed, however, that Zionist expenditures were considerable.[26]

Aside from the Zionist subsidies, *Hatoren's* revenues during this second phase came from greatly increased circulation. In addition to regular methods of solicitation, prizes (*The Works of Reuben Brainin* and *Luah Ahiever*) were offered to new subscribers. Thus *Hatoren* achieved a circulation of about 13,000, probably the greatest ever reached by a Hebrew periodical in America at any time.[27] Subscriptions cost $3.00 a year and single copies seven cents ($4.00 and ten cents in October, 1918).

With increased circulation, advertising also increased. It remained quite similar in character to what it had been in the first phase, but there were some changes. Aside from the regular Jewish advertisers, many of the same general companies that advertised in *Haibri* and some new ones, such as Remington, Community Silver, the Manhattan School and a number of banks appeared. Hebrew and Yiddish books and notices of meetings still formed the bulk of the advertising.

The first editor of the weekly *Hatoren* was Isaac Dov Berkowitz. After a year Shmaryahu Levin became a co-editor with Berkowitz, and in April, 1918, both were replaced by Reuben Brainin, who remained as editor until the final demise of *Hatoren*. All three editors maintained pretty much the same format, although each had a few minor distinguishing characteristics of his own. The stories of Sholom Aleichem, for example, appeared regularly under the reign of Berkowitz, Sholom Aleichem's son-in-law. The unchangeable features of the weekly were the editorial column, "Weekly Portion," and three specialized news columns: "News and Events," "The National Movement" and "Miscellanies." Outside of the news columns, which occupied only a small part of the periodical, *Hatoren* during this period was little more than a mouthpiece for Zionist propaganda. Much less scholarly than it had previously been, *Hatoren* presented Zionist pleas and excoriations ad nauseam,

[24] *Hatoren*, July 6, 1917.
[25] Deinard, *op. cit.*, p. 148.
[26] *Hatoren*, Mar. 18, 1921.
[27] *Ibid.*, Mar. 1, 1918.

interspersed with second-rate fiction and poetry. Again a sample table of contents serves to illustrate the make-up of the journal:

1) "On the Threshhold of a New Era," a plea for money for re-construction work in Palestine
2) "Burgers," a critique of the bourgeoisie — Kalman Whiteman
3) "Decaying Leaves," a poem — A. S. Schwartz
4) "The Pot," a serialized story — Sholom Aleichem
5) "*Knesset*," a review of the anthology by Bialik — Reuben Brainin
6) "From the World of the Spirit," a critique of the internal spirit of American Jewry — Simeon Zack
7) "News and Events"
8) "The National Movement"
9) "Miscellanies"[28]

491

The magazine's expenses began to mount just as its readership began to diminish. This dwindling support is already reflected in the list of agents which *Hatoren* published in the summer of 1917, showing a considerable decline from the previous year.[29] Abraham Spicehandler asserts that "little by little *Hatoren* deteriorated, until Brainin turned it into a monthly." The periodical thus drifted into its third phase in June, 1921, with the first of the new monthly issues. The publisher and the editor of the new monthly *Hatoren* were the same as had produced it in its weekly existence, the Zionist Federation of America and Reuben Brainin. In this transitory phase, *Hatoren* was little more than a monthly reproduction of the weekly.

Radically different was the monthly which began to appear in March, 1922. After a lapse of three months, *Hatoren* reappeared in its fourth and final form and remained on the American scene until 1925. The publisher now was the Safruth Publishing Company, composed, like the Hatoren Publishing Association of well-to-do businessmen. Notable among them was Israel Matz, who, according to Abraham Spicehandler, almost single-handedly bank-rolled the whole enterprise. The Zionist Federation, though not now the publisher, still assisted to some extent. The offices of *Hatoren* continued to be at Zionist Headquarters on Fifth Avenue. Additional revenues were secured by raising the subscription to $5.00, five times the original price. (There had been a significant inflation during the intervening years, so it is doubtful that much of the raise went into real added income.) Advertising in this last

---

[28] *Ibid.*, Oct. 4, 1918.
[29] *Ibid.*, Aug. 3, 1917.

phase was not very important. Almost the only ads were for meetings or books. This was in full keeping with the new character of the magazine.[30]

The fourth *Hatoren* was a scholarly and literary journal. Each issue now had approximately ninety pages, occasionally running to as many as 190. A sample table of contents illustrates its character:

1) "Freedom and Inscription," on the eternality of Judaism — Dr. Jacob Klatzkin
2) "From the Talmud to Spinoza," on the Talmud — Dr. Jacob Frimer
3) "Creative Moments," on the function of literature — M. B. Lazevnik
4) "The Cantor in Israel" — Abraham Zvi Edelson
5) "A Welcome," philology — Dr. Samuel Kraus
6) "The Scroll of Beth-Av" — Dr. M. Hertzberg
7) "Woman," a sketch — Jacob Hurgin
8) "Broken Panes," poems in prose — A. Z. Ben-Fishai
9) "Crusades," a poem — Zalman Shneur
10) "From the Notebook of a Librarian," book reviews — A. Ben-Shefat
11) "From Palestinian Literature" — Dr. Simeon Bernstein
12) "A Heritage for Generations," a critique of Nathaniel Rothschild's interest in entomology — Reuben Brainin
13) "Monthly Review," news commentary
14) "Uri Nissan Gnessen," a biography and a bibliography — Z. Fishman[31]

This specialized *Hatoren* could hardly have had wide appeal. No longer was *Hatoren* a periodical "produced by many . . . for the general public." In many ways the new version represented a decline from the previous forms. Persky asserted that under Brainin there were changes which were "not always for the better." The editing was careless and consequently the style as well. This new version contained little Zionism, little fiction, few poems and many translations. "Therefore its influence among the modern Hebrew readers in America . . . declined so greatly."[32] Spicehandler also speaks of the decline of the periodical's relevance to the American Hebrew scene, and lays the decline at Brainin's feet. "That was Brainin's way," he said. "He had no perseverance to finish what he had begun. He was either too old or too weak."[33] *Hatoren*, in a

---

[30] Author's interview.
[31] *Hatoren*, Oct., 1925.
[32] Persky, "A Chapter."
[33] Interview.

longer time to be sure, went the way of Brainin's previous publishing efforts in America, although not all the blame can be ascribed to him. The fate of America's Hebrew periodicals was too consistent for anyone to bear special responsibility for an individual failure.

The climax of this era of the Hebrew press in America came with the appearance of *Hadoar*. None could know that it was the only publication fated to survive. Although it began to appear in its present form during the decade under consideration, that part of its history belongs to a later era. It is rather the predecessor of the present *Hadoar* which epitomized the decade from 1914 to 1924. The daily *Hadoar* (and the weekly that succeeded it in the same format for almost a year) was the fruit of the greatest optimism of the period and of the greatest concentration of literary and material energies ever mustered by the Hebrew press in America. As Abraham Spicehandler described this brief flowering, "The first days were really holidays. Afterwards we grew accustomed to rising in the morning and finding *Hadoar* on the doorstep."[34]

The first Hebrew daily in the United States had lasted for two days. Another daily was projected, but never appeared. Knowing the troubled history of the Hebrew press, contemporaries must have been skeptical of the rumors heralding the forthcoming birth of a new daily. All the more so since, by November 1, 1921 — the date of the first issue of the daily *Hadoar* — *Miklat*, *Haibri*, and the weekly *Hatoren* had already failed. At the same time Hebrew papers were dead or dying outside the United States as well. The last Hebrew daily in Europe, *Hacefira*, perished the same month that *Hadoar* came to life (although it was revived for a time later). For five months *Hadoar* was the only Hebrew daily in the world outside of Palestine.[35]

The publisher of the daily *Hadoar* was the Hebrew Publishing Company,[36] the name of which was changed to Hadoar Publishing Company a month after the paper first appeared. "At its inception, Hadoar's creators and editors were young dreamers...."[37] The businessmen-dreamers, the managers of the paper, consisted of Wolf Fischer, president, Nathan Hermoni, Nathan Elkan and a fourth man who was ousted when he was found not to possess the investment capital he had originally promised. After a short time,

493

---

[34] Abraham Spicehandler, "Some of My Memories of *Hadoar*," *Hadoar* (Nov. 28, 1924).

[35] Gordon, *op. cit.*

[36] Not to be confused with the book publishing firm of the same name.

[37] Menachem Ribalow, "A Period of Twenty Five Years," *Hadoar 25 Year Jubilee Volume* (New York: 1947), p. 696.

Abraham Spicehandler became the business manager of the paper and remained in that position until the demise of the daily.[38]

As many foreign-language papers in America, and particularly a number of the Yiddish papers (viz., *The Forward*), *Hadoar* was founded on pennies. A number of the Yiddish papers had succeeded in overcoming this original lack of capital and had grown quite prosperous by 1921. The founders of *Hadoar* felt that they might be able to emulate their success.

At the time, Jewish dailies had relatively little difficulty in securing national advertisers if they were able to prove, by staying alive for at least a year, that they were substantial operations. Because it could not do this, the amount of advertising that *Hadoar* could attract was limited. Again the Ex-Lax Company was a principal advertiser, purchasing $1,000 worth in six months. The standard Jewish ads were augmented only by a regular advertisement for the Yiddish Art Theater. In addition there were ads for some New York East Side banks and for Thos. Cook and Sons. There were also ads for neighborhood businesses, particularly on the East Side.

494

The unorthodox methods which were unsuccessfully used to secure ads for the new paper were described in an article in the paper entitled, "What Can We Do to Increase the Number of Ads in *Hadoar?*"[39] The article advised all the readers to emulate the "rich Sephardic Jews." They had demanded that their record dealer, The Oriental Music Shop, advertise in *Hadoar*, which he then did. This pressure, however, could not have been very successful for the Music Shop ads appeared only a few times.

Low advertising income was not greatly augmented by the subscription fees of $9.00 a year and three cents a copy. Spicehandler estimates that circulation was approximately 12,000 copies at first, declining gradually. There is no substantiation of this figure anywhere, and the files of the daily *Hadoar* have disappeared.[40]

An attempt at overcoming low advertising and subscription revenues was made with a sustaining fund. It was planned to raise a "Foundation Fund" of $50,000, and for that purpose the editor, Max Lipson, set out on a cross-country trip. The lists published in *Hadoar* of bond purchasers responding to this campaign were singularly unimpressive. Only 175 different contributors were listed, and most of these had bought only ten dollars' worth of bonds.

---

[38] Interview.
[39] *Hadoar*, Nov. 16, 1921.
[40] Statement of present editor of *Hadoar*.

Later the original goal was lowered to $30,000, but even this proved unattainable.[41]

A final search for funds was made through private and institutional subsidies. The Mizrachi Organization had been assisting by providing space for the editorial offices in an unventilated, dark room in its headquarters building. As the daily reached the end of its resources in June, 1922, an agreement was reached with Israel Matz and the Histadruth Ivrith to contribute $8,000 and $6,000 respectively for the continued operation of the daily, on the condition that the Zionist Federation also contribute $6,000. Just as this arrangement was to go into effect, a member of the Zionist Federation with a grudge against the administration of *Hadoar* torpedoed the Zionist contribution. As a consequence the daily *Hadoar* died.[42]

495

*Hadoar* went the way of other American Hebrew periodicals during this decade. Its demise caused the usual loss to the small investors who had pooled their funds to create it. Its end proved to be a financial disaster for at least one man. The owner of the plant where the paper had been printed was a German immigrant, who had continued to print the paper even when the bills could not be met. The $20,000 owed to him by *Hadoar* bankrupted his business. He died shortly after the failure. Even the workers lost considerable sums. The paper was threatened with a strike each Monday because it had not paid them. The enthusiasm and idealism of the founders had trickled down, however, and the workers continued to work for reduced wages. Most of them had donated the equivalent of a week's salary to the fading paper, and others had agreed to work for half wages until such time as the paper could pay them.[43]

From July, 1922, until October, 1923, hope was maintained that the daily would yet be revived. In the interim *Hadoar* continued to appear in the same format (except that news was replaced by more features) but only once a week. The Histadruth Ivrith now became the publisher, and Menahem Ribalow replaced Max Lipson as editor. Endless pleas and meetings came to nothing. Money to renew the daily was not forthcoming. On December 9, 1923, after a lapse of six weeks, *Hadoar* appeared in substantially its present format, and all expectations of renewing the daily were abandoned. It had fallen prey to the usual ills of American Hebrew periodicals and to the special difficulties which America experienced in 1921–22.

[41] *Hadoar*, June 29, 1922.
[42] Gordon, *op. cit.*; Interview with Spicehandler.
[43] Spicehandler, "Some of My Memories."

> *Hadoar*, like every publication in its first year, has fought hard for its existence, and the present economic crisis in this country has heightened the difficulty. Large advertisers have reduced their advertisements, hitting particularly hard at a new paper.[44]

The daily *Hadoar* was not just another, more frequently issued Hebrew paper. Technically it was primitive, operating without typesetting machines and without an adequate plant. Its regular press run was only four pages. Still, Hadoar attempted to fulfill all the functions of a daily newspaper and of a Jewish periodical. It succeeded remarkably well.[45]

The first of its four pages, quite naturally, was devoted to news items, about half of them of general interest and half of exclusively Jewish interest. Two regular features of the front page were a table of exchange rates and a list of the boats arriving in New York harbor. The second and third pages were devoted to editorials and features. Some of these were translations from *The Freeman*, *The Nation* or *The New Republic*, since Lipson was a political radical. Most, however, were original essays, largely about Jewish topics, particularly Zionism and Palestine. There were also many essays dealing with current affairs as well as some poetry and a considerable amount of serialized fiction. Some of this was by such writers as S. Y. Agnon, Opatoshu, Brandstatter and I. D. Berkowitz, among the best Hebrew fiction writers of the time. Literary and art criticism included translations of the writings of Stefan Zweig and Leonid Pasternak as well as original pieces by Bialik and Joseph Haim Brenner. In addition to these occasional pieces, there were certain regular features: "Literary News," "Items and Remarks" (Jewish news), "Anniversaries of the Week" and "Writers and Books." Every Friday there was a large children's column with stories, poems and games. There was also a regular column about the weekly Bible portion and a health column written by Dr. Leon Golden.[46] The fourth page of the paper was for advertisements and, when there were not enough ads to fill it, for the continuation of articles.

Although it was not able to remain alive long, the daily *Hadoar* had a number of considerable achievements to its credit, and it succeeded in attracting much favorable comment from both American and foreign critics. Josef Lin described it and its successor weeklies as "a free tribunal for the critical evaluation of the social, political

---

[44] *Hadoar*, Feb. 3, 1921.

[45] Gordon, *op. cit.*

[46] Golden was the publisher of two Hebrew periodicals devoted to medicine which appeared during this decade, *Luaḥ Magen David Adom* and *Rephuah*.

and intellectual phenomena in the entire spectrum of Jewish life."[47] Persky asserted that the daily, with its good editing, logical arrangement and careful style made a greater impression among the Hebrew reading public than had any previous publication. In fact, such care was taken over linguistic style that arguments over it among the editors were quite common.[48] A superficial comparison with *Ha-Aretz*, the contemporary Palestinian Hebrew daily, or even with *Hacefira*, the veteran Warsaw daily, will demonstrate the comparative good taste and exact style and language which characterized the American daily. Through Stygian efforts, Lipson and his assistants on the editorial board, Persky, H. L. Gordon and Dr. M. Katz, succeeded in making the daily *Hadoar* both a public and an artistic success. That, however, did not make up for the small number of potential readers, and the marginality of the Hebrew press. If the readers of *Hacefira* had really immigrated to America, as its former editor, the veteran Zionist Nahum Sokolow, claimed,[49] they were no longer searching for a Hebrew daily to read, not even a first-class one.

497

> We know how many of the enemies of Hebrew were expecting our downfall, and how few of our friends believed in our success, and especially, how few stood ready to support us with action and not just with words of encouragement.[50]

## III

The technical and business operations of periodicals, while an interesting and significant aspect of their life, represent their least important side for readers. Ultimately the success or failure of any periodical depends upon the appeal of its policies and features. The editorial columns help explain what type of reader the publication is trying to attract and what the publishers' views are. The Hebrew press in America from 1914 to 1924 was no exception and reflected certain consistent attitudes and views of world affairs, of the United States, of the Jewish community and of itself. Only in *Haibri*, *Hatoren* and *Hadoar* were these positions fully developed, the other publications being either too parochial or too short-lived for such trends to be definitively expressed, and it is these three periodicals on which the present analysis is based.

[47] Lin, *op. cit.*
[48] Persky, "A Chapter"; author's interview with Spicehandler.
[49] Spicehandler, "Some of My Memories."
[50] Gordon, *op. cit.*

Because the three periodicals did not appear concurrently, it is somewhat difficult to speak of their approach to world affairs. Moreover, the small amount of space devoted to "foreign" affairs was not always adequate for the expression of mature views. There were, however, certain basic attitudes common to all three.

To some degree the concerns of the American Hebrew publications were dictated by the nature of world events during the decade: the World War, the Balfour Declaration and the British conquest of Palestine, the Russian Revolution, and the realignment of Europe. Although all of these events were important to American Hebraists, they could at most merely comment on them, since they could not hope to exert any influence upon primarily European affairs.

498

Perhaps the most basic tenet of American Hebraists concerned the relationship of the Jews to the family of nations. All American Hebrew periodicals considered the Jews one of the small nations to whom justice was to be meted out in the peace settlement. In *Haibri* this separatist attitude became evident in some of the articles dealing with Germany and the entry of America into the World War and later in articles dealing with the Balfour Declaration.

> It is natural, after the great upheavals in the life of our nation, that when it comes to making a choice between the "Central Powers" and the "Allies," the Jews tend to choose the latter. This is because of their positive attitude towards the Palestine question.[1]

In the editorial columns of *Hadoar* this attitude was considerably more explicit. The nationalist movements of Ireland, India, the Philippines and even Egypt were supported by *Hadoar* as those of fellow small nations striving to free themselves of alien sovereignty. Ireland especially was seen as akin to Palestine, inasmuch as the Irish were attempting a cultural as well as national revival. No small nation's rights were to be suppressed. "We do not wish the enslavement of any nation, not even the Arabs."[2] *Haibri* also supported the proposal for a Jewish legion to enable Jews to have a hand in conquering their own country.

Palestine was not just a refuge for the oppressed of Eastern Europe, rather it was to be the homeland of all the Jewish people. The Hebraists actually anticipated that many American Jews would settle in Palestine if given the opportunity. All three devoted a great deal of space to Palestine and to Zionism.[3]

Given these basic premises, the views of the periodicals on most

[1] *Haibri*, Apr. 5. 1918.
[2] *Hadoar*, Dec. 2, 1921, Dec. 19, 1921, Dec. 28, 1921, Jan. 26, 1922, Mar. 2, 1922.
[3] E. g., *Haibri*, Sept. 7, 1917, Jan. 9, 1918; *Hatoren*, Nov. 29, 1918.

political issues were readily determined. Pre-revolutionary Russia, post-war Poland, and Roumania were ever condemned for their anti-Jewish policies, and, despite fairly strong pro-German sentiment for a time among many American Jews and the fact that many Hebraists had lived or been educated in Germany, little favorable comment was to be found about Germany.[4]

The gradual disillusionment of American liberal sentiment with the peace settlements was reflected in the Hebrew press as well. *Hadoar* noted:

> The participation of America in the War was very strange from the beginning. America jumped into the sea of fire and blood with closed eyes, out of exaggerated idealism. Wilson ... created for himself a god, ... democracy.... And the god ... became Molech, and upon his altars the citizens of America sacrificed their children.[5]

499

France, in particular, was deplored for renascent militarism and her attempts to wreck the Naval Disarmament Conference, and Japan was similarly condemned. The harsh criticism reserved for Wilson and his naive idealism was a part of general, rather than specifically Jewish, reaction.[6] *Hadoar* spoke out strongly against Wilson:

> The ideals of ... Wilson have already become empty.... He took America into the War for the sake of making a better world ... and the world is not even a little bit better.... The same militarism that ruled before the War, rules now also.... He spoke about principles ... and they answered ... [with] thieving and ... enslavement. Wilson accustomed the European nations to look upon America as an innocent country, easily seduced.... Wilson increased the forces of reaction in the country, [and] made the presidency an autocracy. The American people evaluated him properly during the last elections, [when they elected in his stead] ... a simple man, an ordinary newspaperman, Harding....[7]

The attitude of the American Hebrew periodicals toward Russia on the other hand was determined largely by the nationalism of the publications. Before the Revolution, there was nothing but dislike on the part of almost all Jews for Russia. After 1917, Jewish liberals, like their American counterparts, were enthusiastic about the new social ideals of Russia and the new freedoms officially granted to its Jews, but the Hebrew periodicals were quick to see through the facade and strongly opposed Bolshevism.[8]

[4] *Haibri*, Jan. 28, 1916, May 9, 1919.
[5] *Hadoar*, Mar. 23, 1922.
[6] *Ibid.*, issues for Nov, 1921–Jan. 1922.
[7] *Ibid.*, Jan. 17, 1922.
[8] *Haibri*, Jan. 9, 1920; *Hadoar*, Nov. 9, 1920, Jan. 9, 1922, Feb. 1, 1922.

> The Jewish commissars . . . have set out for themselves one goal, the destruction of Judaism. . . . And this whole Bacchanalia replete with insanity and stubbornness, is very dangerous to the surviving remnant of Russian Jewry.[9]

There were, of course, some aspects of world politics which had no relation to Zionism or Jews. But, since as Jews they saw themselves as underdogs, with regard to non-Jewish problems, too, the American Hebrew press championed the cause of the oppressed, be he a striking coal miner, or a vanquished Germany. In general the periodicals dealt with foreign affairs as spokesmen of the Jewish nation. They felt that they were protecting Jewish interests against a basically hostile world, fighting for justice for a defenseless people vulnerable to oppression throughout the world. These same feelings were evinced toward the American environment in which the periodicals were published, and toward their Jewish milieu as well.

Just as the Hebrew periodicals considered Jews in the world at large to be an entity apart from the nations among whom they dwelt, they considered the situation in America no different. This attitude was in marked contrast to the other immigrant presses in the United States. Analysts of the Polish, the Norwegian and the German language presses in America have stressed the Americanizing function of these publications.[10] The immigrant press was "concerned with preserving the cultural ties of the immigrant with the land of his origin, promoting the activities of the group in its new home, and keeping the mother tongue alive as long as possible."[11] But these were largely secondary tasks, the inevitable product of an instinct for self-preservation.

The Yiddish press in particular seems to have devoted itself to "adjustment" or, perhaps, assimilation. A study of the Yiddish press for the period 1914 to 1924 showed that most of the readers subscribed because of its Jewish content and continued to do so even after they had mastered English only because the English press did not have adequate Jewish coverage. The papers themselves, however, saw their primary task as the assimilation of their readers into the mainstream of American life. An overwhelming amount of space was devoted to "general" rather than Jewish news; editorials were largely concerned with non-Jewish topics and invariably de-

500

---

[9] *Hadoar*, Dec. 12, 1921.

[10] Edmund G. Olszyk, *The Polish Press in America* (Milwaukee: 1940); Arlow William Andersen, *The Immigrant Takes His Stand — The Norwegian American Press and Public Affairs* (Northfield, Minn.: 1953); Carl Wittke, *The German Language Press in America* (New York: 1957).

[11] Wittke, p. 21.

voted to Americanizing their readers.[12] While they may not have aimed consciously for such results, their very success made them superfluous. So, too, the first Hebrew periodical in America featured articles about Jesuits and Mormons, about the strange America to which its readers had come or were to come.

But in general, the Hebrew press, in its conception of itself and in the goals it set out for itself, was much different. It aimed to keep its readers a separate and distinct entity. To a very large degree it was trying to recreate the multi-lingual and multi-national atmosphere of Eastern Europe, where the Jews could easily maintain their own language (although this had been Yiddish and not Hebrew). *Haibri* even noted that New York might be made as Jewish as was Warsaw, Cracow or Frankfurt if the authorities would only regulate *kashrut* and the Sabbath.[13] At the very least the Hebrew press was preparing Jews for the day when they might be able to speak their own language in their own country.

Isolation, not only from their gentile American surroundings but from the Jewish public as well, was one of the most persistent themes of Hebrew journalism in America during the decade. The attitude of a group under siege trying to defend the national heritage against the onslaught of a hostile society was best described by Haim Nahman Bialik, the Hebrew "national poet," in a letter to *Hadoar*.

> Upon you and upon those like you our little world stands. You have revivified the nation of God.... One small modest legion like you is equal in my eyes to ten legions of sword-bearers....
> [You are] fighting mightily for the establishment of our tongue in the land of dollars, working ... to erect for it a frail tent among the walls and pillars of iron in America....[14]

The encomia of Bialik and the accompanying encouragement for the beleaguered were never minimized by the American Hebrew journalists when they spoke of their own work. Thus, in a plea for new subscriptions, *Hatoren* editorialized in its usual tone:

> We have done ... all that was in our limited power to do to put some Hebrew national content into our work.... We have no hope here ... except the unbounded idealism of the few....[15]

The Hebrew journalists even found themselves isolated from those Americans they might legitimately have hoped to find on their side.

501

[12] Mordecai Soltes, *The Yiddish Press: An Americanizing Agency* (New York: 1950).
[13] *Haibri*, Feb. 11, 1916.
[14] *Hadoar*, Mar. 31, 1922.
[15] *Hatoren*, Aug. 24, 1917.

The Zionist Federation did subsidize *Hatoren,* and the Mizrachi Organization supported *Haibri* during its ten years of existence. Yet while the Hebrew journalists and their periodicals were all Zionist, and Hebrew and not Yiddish was obviously to be the language of Palestine, American Zionists were not overly eager to support the Hebrew periodicals. Although the masses can not be reached through a Hebrew medium, still today the Zionist Organization, much concerned with cultural affairs, is an ardent supporter of all Hebrew causes. Nevertheless, in the decade under consideration, when the Zionists were much more of a political group, concerned chiefly with political and not with cultural activities, they chose to express themselves in whatever languages could reach the most readers. The American Zionists' main organ during these years was *Dos Yiddishe Folk.* It also sponsored a number of English periodicals, including *The New Palestine.* The Hebraists felt abandoned.

502

> In Europe . . . all of our cultural work is done with the help and participation of the Zionist Organization. Here there is no tie between the Zionist Federation and the Hebrews who have centered themselves in the Histadrut Ivrith. . . . The stubborn group . . . around the Histadrut Ivrith and *Hadoar* feels . . . isolated among the official Zionist leadership. There is no help, no participation — there isn't even any interest. . . .
>
> The Zionist Federation ought at least to take upon itself some of the worries about the fate of Hebrew work in America. . . .[16]

This chosen or enforced isolation from American and Jewish life occurred side by side with a criticism of almost every facet of both. For the Hebrew press, Jewish life in America was bad because it was becoming "Americanized," that is, vulgarized, and this vulgarization was particularly evident in the Yiddish press, which copied the tone and business methods of the American yellow press.[17] *Hadoar* was particularly vehement in its denunciation of the Yiddish press, particularly *The Forward,* which it found not only vulgar but anti-nationalist.

> . . . The one newspaper which simple . . . Eastern Jews have succeeded in placing on a secure foundation [is *The Forward*]. But when we are reminded of its character . . . and its spiritual qualities, of its literary standards . . . and its educational influence — our soul shrinks back from it and from its anniversary. The twenty-five years of its [vulgar] existence are not cause for celebration but for mourning.[18]

[16] *Hadoar,* June 25, 1922.
[17] *Haibri,* June 30, 1916.
[18] *Hadoar,* Apr. 23, 1922.

This contempt for the deference of the Yiddish press to the popular taste had, of course, another side. The Yiddishists were generally opposed to Hebrew as the national language, and the radicals among them felt that the return to Hebrew as well as the return to Palestine was a reactionary attempt to impede the inevitable flow of progress. The Hebraists resented the success of the Yiddishists in America.

The Hebrew journalists were neither unmindful of nor ungrateful for the freedom which they found in America: "There is no place where we are as free as in this country. . . ."[19] When the war broke out, there was unqualified support for America and its allies and unstinted patriotism. Nevertheless, the attitude towards America, at least towards the America in which they lived as Jews, could hardly be called positive. All Hebrew papers were bitter over the imposition of immigration quotas which discriminated against Jews. They also suffered from the wartime restrictions placed upon foreign-language papers in America,[20] and they were upset over the continued imprisonment of Debs. The post-war period in America, following the heady and hollow moral enthusiasm of the war, was generally one of disillusionment.

Out of this isolation and general disillusionment, developed what might otherwise be considered rather strange attitudes towards specific issues. Thus the Hebrew press often avoided American politics. There was always the question of how a certain election might affect the Jews, but, if it were decided that it did not matter, the Hebrew press remained neutral. This was in marked contrast to the Yiddish press which entered into political campaigns and battles with glee.[21] After the Congressional elections of 1918, *Haibri* said that it was not

> . . . commenting here on the victory of the Republicans, on their revolt against Wilson. That is an internal question of state, which does not affect us as Jews. Our purpose here is to talk about the downfall of the Jewish socialists.[22]

In *Hatoren*, at least at first, a different political position was attempted.

> The Jewish voters . . . [have] a very important political power . . . that, if they knew how to use it, would get them anything in the world. . . . Not as Jews, holders of a particular faith, but as residents

503

---

[19] *Haibri*, Jan. 7, 1916.

[20] This meant primarily that a correct translation of all articles had to be provided, an expensive requirement.

[21] *Haibri*, Nov. 5, 1920; Soltes, *op. cit.*

[22] *Haibri*, Nov. 6, 1918.

of a particular district, as people of a special culture, the Jews have specific interests.[23]

But this policy was out of touch with the reality of American politics and of Jewish demography and psychology in the United States. The Jews were not content to be residents of segregated districts, and the possibility of their taking political action as a group was decreased by their relatively small numbers. Moreover, bloc political action has, until recently, been popularly disapproved of in America and could not be undertaken proudly and openly, as had been done in Eastern Europe. *Hatoren* was unable to maintain such a political stance for long. It did not reject the policy openly, but gradually ceased to relate itself to America.

Dovetailing neatly with demands for Jewish bloc voting was the almost universal enthusiasm engendered in the Hebrew press for the ideas of the "Kehilla" for New York City Jewry and the "Congress" for American Jewry. Had they succeeded in their original aims, both these organizations would have become quasi-national representative bodies for all Jews in their respective areas. Although neither would have had any legal power, by their sheer inclusiveness they might have wielded enormous real power and might have done much to alter the disorganization of American Jewry. The Congress idea occupied much editorial space in 1916, especially in *Haibri*. By 1917, when the Congress came into existence, it was already apparent that it could not achieve its goals. Interest declined, and the American Hebrew press even joined the opposition.

*Hadoar* did not present quite the same simple attitude towards American politics, nor could it have done so as a daily paper. American politics received fairly adequate coverage, and the daily did evince an interest in national affairs. *Hadoar* was partially an American political animal. It was a liberal defender of the rights of the little man. It attacked Andrew Mellon's proposed tax cut because it favored the wealthy. Similarly, it supported the strikes of the clothing workers, coal miners and milkmen as socially and economically justified.[24] *Haibri* had favored such strikes only because they were likely to bring about a five-day week and thereby make it possible for Jews to celebrate their Sabbath in the traditional manner. This was the only real issue for *Haibri*.

Perhaps easiest to understand of the American political attitudes of the Hebrew press in America during these years was the united stand on immigration. Here the Hebrew press was more in accord

[23] *Hatoren*, Sept., 1913.
[24] *Hadoar*, Nov. 10, 1921, Dec. 9, 1921, Feb. 13, 1922

with other immigrant presses, although it stood in opposition to the mainstream of American thought. Articles imploring the Congress not to close the doors to further immigration and attacking the decision once it was made occupied much of the editorial and feature space of all three periodicals after the war, when the question came to a head.

The spiritual and intellectual aloofness from American life which the Hebrew journalists felt and propounded was reinforced by their own way of life in America. Their occupational break-down shows that most of them managed to remain wholly within the Jewish world even for business or culture. By being Hebrew teachers or by writing for the Yiddish press, the Hebraists managed to keep themselves as well as their publications insulated from general American life. It is not to be gainsaid, however, that this view might be inverted. Perhaps because most of them had been almost entirely molded by their European Jewish experience, the Hebrew journalists were incapable of acclimating themselves fully to America. Consequently, they sojourned in an unreal land, more Jewish and more European than American, seeking always the unrealizable goals of recreating a world which had ceased to exist or creating a new and completely different one elsewhere.[25]

Not unexpectedly the American Hebrew publications spoke for the Jews of Eastern European origin, frequently decrying abuses on the part of those who had originally come from Western Europe or who had been in the United States long enough to become "Westernized." *Hatoren's* attack on Western Jews was launched on several fronts. The failure of the "Kehilla" was laid at the doorstep of the Western Jews because of their contempt for public opinion, that is, the opinion of the Easterners.[26] The Educational Alliance, the institution set up on New York's Lower East Side for the new immigrants by the "American" Jews, was lambasted for its assimilationist Americanization program:

> Except for a tiny corner . . . Judaism has no place in the institution. . . . In all of the activities of the institution, one aspiration is recognizable, the Americanization of the immigrants; or better still, the forcing upon them of Americanism.[27]

The Hebrew periodicals were quick to recognize that the integration of Americanized Jews and their success in the non-Jewish world

505

[25] Persky, "A Chapter."
[26] *Haibri*, Jan. 6, 1911, Nov. 17, 1916; *Hadoar*, Nov. 4, 1921, Dec. 13, 1921, Dec. 25, 1921; *Hatoren*, June, 1913.
[27] *Hatoren*, Mar.–Apr., 1915.

of America did not necessarily bode well for Jews *per se*. *Haibri* minimized the Jewish importance of the appointment of Brandeis to the Supreme Court.

> The nationalists, who see things as they are . . . don't place any special importance upon the nomination of one or two Jews . . . [to high office]. The nationalists know that in every place at every time there have been those who were "close to the rulers.". . .[28]

The rich and the successful, the "Americans," were clearly not the people for whom *Haibri* was writing, or whose views it was expressing. Even stronger language was used by the periodical in attacking the leadership of Americanized Jews.

> The Western Jews are accustomed to deceiving the Eastern Jews . . . [by making the Easterners think of themselves as] unruly and un-disciplined. . . . All this guilt is a figment of the imagination. . . . The Eastern Jews have their institutions . . . and all of them operate well. . . . And if anyone be . . . ill-mannered it is the Western Jews themselves. Their relationships with the Eastern Jews prove it.[29]

Intimately connected with this antagonism towards the Western or Americanized Jews was the democratic spirit of the American Hebrew press and its general stand against privilege and wealth. Thus there was criticism of the attempts by American Jews to send immigrants to farms in order not to crowd the cities. The general feeling in the Hebrew press was that Eastern Europeans were being railroaded by undemocratic Westerners.[30]

Another facet of the East-West controversy played out in the pages of the American Hebrew press was the debate over religion. As representatives of the Eastern European community, the Hebrew periodicals were arrayed against Reform, which was almost entirely a movement of Americanized Jews. It was, moreover, most often a movement of the wealthier elements, who were resented and opposed because of their usurpation of communal leadership. In addition to their opposition to Reform, and not infrequently to the Conservative movement as well, the Hebrew periodicals opposed the Yiddish secularism which was indigenously Eastern European. Thus the periodicals were perforce defenders of Orthodoxy, or at least of tradition.

The periodicals discussed Reform and Conservative Jews in tones of scorn. Their religious leaders were always called "rabbis" and

506

---

[28] *Haibri*, Feb. 4, 1916.
[29] *Ibid.*, June 20, 1919.
[30] *Haibri*, Nov. 5, 1919, May 21, 1920; *Hatoren*, Nov., 1913.

never *rabbanim* as correct Hebrew usage demanded. *Haibri* found the graduates of the Conservative Jewish Theological Seminary Jewishly ignorant at best. "The place . . . which promised to be a fitting home for Jewish learning and for the education of faithful and enlightened rabbis . . . has not kept its promise."[31] Although the Yiddish papers generally published on the Sabbath, *Hadoar* did not. None of the weeklies published on Jewish holidays, always having a double issue either before or after the holiday.

The Hebrew periodicals also concerned themselves much with the state of religious education, and particularly the daily *Hadoar* campaigned for higher pay and better conditions for Hebrew teachers. Such interest cannot be attributed solely to the fact that many of the Hebrew journalists were Hebrew teachers. There was a genuine interest in the condition of Judaism. Still, much of the affinity with tradition must have resulted from the fact that Americanized Reform Jews were the most assimilated, the least nationalistic, and the least susceptible to the message which the Hebrew press had to offer. Moreover, they were unlikely to be able to read Hebrew.

This concern with and closeness to traditional Judaism was not an uncritical acceptance, even on the part of *Haibri*, the one officially religious publication. Those Orthodox rabbis and laymen who opposed the Zionist program were always under attack for their "shortsightedness." There were demands for the reform of many facets of Judaism, for the elimination of the vulgarity and the obscurantism that they felt had infected much of Orthodoxy, and for restructuring traditional Jewry on modern lines.[32]

This is not to say that the nationalist, traditionalist mass of Eastern European Jews in America was reading the periodicals which spoke in the name of their interests. Most of them could not or simply did not. The periodicals were, in fact, isolated from almost the whole of the American community. Not only were their sympathizers often unable to read the periodicals, but they were also frequently on a different cultural and intellectual plane from that of the journalists. The "American" Jews could not read the periodicals at all, and most likely they would not have cared to do so had they been able.

This isolation of the Hebrew journalists did much to color their periodicals, giving them a singular tone and an unusual attitude towards their readers. All too frequently their articles were eulogistic, and the reader could only feel that he was participating in a funeral.

507

---

[31] *Haibri*, June 16, 1916, June 11, 1920, July 9, 1920; *Hatoren*, Nov., 1913.
[32] *Haibri*, Apr. 27, 1917, June 1, 1917; *Hatoren*, May 25, 1917; *Hadoar*, Nov. 20, 1921.

There was unanimous consent that America was not a hospitable home for the Hebrew muse, that its environment might well provide cause for lament. However, with the dedication of true believers, the Hebrew journalists took to their task.[33]

To this hallowed cause, the Hebrew journalists brought unbounded love and enthusiasm. Abraham Spicehandler typified this zeal. He has described his feelings about the Hebrew press and what it represented to him as a young immigrant boy in America.

> At every opportunity I used to try to publicize its existence. Every day when I would travel on the subway, I used . . . to read [Ha-Leum] . . . in order to arouse the attention of [the other] travelers.
> And how great was my joy when a Jew would approach me and talk. . . . And I, on my side, would seize the opportunity to test my inclination for "missionary work" and try to win him over . . . to the readers of our language and its literature.[34]

Yet laments over the fate of the periodicals, their almost inevitable decline and failure, were always externalized by the journalists. In a way which would be unthinkable to someone who found himself publishing a fading periodical in English, the Hebrew journalists in America placed the blame for their failure upon their American surroundings. Caught up in their sacred task, convinced of the right as they saw it, the Hebrew journalists could not be convinced that the causes of their failures were in themselves and not in their readers.

This displeasure with their audience was most often expressed in pleas, or more rightly demands, for the support which the Hebrew journalists felt was the due of the Hebrew press. These pleas were neither subtle nor gentle. The monotonous appeals to duty, no matter how justified they may have been, must have annoyed the readers of the periodicals. Moreover, they could easily have undesirable effects. Considering subscription to Hebrew periodicals a duty and not a pleasure, Hebraists were all too often apathetic about reading and paying for them. There was seldom fear in anyone's heart that his subscription might stop coming if he failed to pay the bill. Most were willing to take the chance.[35]

In all fairness, however, it must be noted that the self-righteous attitude of the Hebrew journalists predated their arrival in America. It had been the old and honored stance of Hebrew journalists in Europe, and it continued there after the war. In Europe, however,

[33] Haibri, Dec. 2, 1910, Feb. 7, 1919; Hatoren, June, 1913.
[34] Abraham Spicehandler, "A Remembrance of Pioneers," Hadoar (May 23, 1947).
[35] Hadoar, Feb. 5, 1922; Hatoren, Aug. 24, 1917; Haibri, Mar. 25, 1921.

the duty had seemed somewhat more natural, for Jewish national life was less escapable than it was in the America of 1914.[36]

Although the years from 1914 to 1924 were years of change and activity for the Jewish community of the United States and for world Jewry, the apparently encouraging American environment failed to fulfill its promise to the Hebrew press. By the end of 1921 it was evident that the flurry of publication would not result in permanent achievement. Developments after that year seemed to indicate that the Hebrew press in America was destined to become a specialized press, for scholars and children.

Much of the difficulty which faced the Hebrew periodicals and their promoters was a lack of sufficient capital to establish them on a secure footing. But this was a problem faced by most of the young foreign-language periodicals in the United States, and it was one which many of them succeeded in overcoming. Yiddish papers had done so remarkably well. *The Forward*, begun with small contributions from workingmen at a ball, grew into the largest and most prosperous foreign-language daily in the United States.

Perhaps more damaging was the adherence to European technical methods, the failure to develop an indigenous American style and the universal drabness of the periodicals. Here, too, the Hebrew periodicals were not unique. Other immigrant periodicals were European in style, and an all-pervading "gloom . . . [hung] over the spirit of every newspaperman who . . . [was then writing] in a foreign tongue to the immigrants of America," and who realized that his professional career was sure to be a short one.[37]

But in one respect at least, the Hebrew press in America between 1914 and 1924 was unlike other immigrant presses. It refused to pander to the tastes of its potential public. Little rapport with the audience was established or even sought unless it could be on the terms of the intellectuals themselves. Thus there were attempts at producing specialty journals (medical, literary, etc.) which could not possibly have attracted sufficient followers to have kept them alive. Frequently the general journals produced were derivative products, of which people capable of reading another language surely had no need.

The Hebrew periodicals often expressed contempt and dislike for America. Their formal attitude was one of "neutrality" and disengagement from their new home. This was in contrast to the attitude and aims of most of the immigrant presses in the United

509

---

[36] *Hacefira*, Jan. 2, 1921.

[37] Oscar Ban, "Death Comes to the Foreign Press," *The New Outlook* (July, 1933).

States. As has been noted, "the immigrant press ... [generally] worked at two contradictory tasks: to promote the Americanization of its readers, and to preserve their feeling of being different from the Americans."[38] While it is true that the other immigrant presses eventually put themselves out of business with their Americanization programs, as their readers were integrated into the general American scene, the Hebrew press was never really in business. The mass of Jews in America was not ready to respond to its "non-American" message. Most of them had come to stay and were sufficiently caught up in the new American experience not to have the desire or the leisure for such attitudes as those propounded by the Hebrew press.

510

The result was that the Hebrew periodicals really had no public. The only people who seemed actually to need the Hebrew press were the unemployed Hebrew journalists in America. Everyone who could read Hebrew periodicals could also read periodicals in other languages. Those who purchased a Hebrew publication did so out of devotion.

Devotion on the part of its small public and the journalists did much to keep the Hebrew press together and in operation in what was obviously a most hostile atmosphere. The isolation which characterized the Hebrew press helped to create an élan, the sort of group pride that can hold a beleaguered group together in the face of potentially overwhelming divisive forces. This intellectual isolation was reinforced by the similar backgrounds and upbringing of the journalists, by their occupational distribution and by their geographic concentration in New York City.

The periodicals were nonetheless the work of amateurs, of devotees, who, taking their own convictions and feelings of obligation to the Hebrew cause as a touchstone, demanded the same devotion on the part of their readers. By the end of the decade, many of the most able and prominent of the American Hebrew journalists had either left America or now devoted their time and capabilities to other occupations. The experience of this decade, which had appeared to be so propitious at its opening, seemed to indicate incontrovertibly that America was not to be more than a *Nachtasyl* for the Hebrew muse.

The demise of the Hebrew press in Europe at the same time, however, argues that the causes for the failure of the American Hebrew press were not entirely local. Perhaps the maladies which

---

[38] Albert Parry, "Good-bye to the Immigrant Press," *The American Mercury* (Jan., 1933).

afflicted the Hebrew press in America were also to be found in Europe, even in a period of heightened Jewish consciousness and Zionist success which promised to make the Hebrew language a practical tool at least for those who chose to go to the emerging homeland. Quite apart from the specific career of the American Hebrew press, it remains questionable whether any foreign-language periodical can survive in an environment where that language is not spoken. The question is particularly cogent for such a place as America where all residents are increasingly integrated into a similar life-pattern, where there are fewer and fewer pockets of differing cultural or religious activities or language peculiarities. It may be that, in such an environment, foreign-language periodicals are doomed to be the playground of scholars.                    511

## APPENDIX

### List of American Hebrew Periodicals, 1914–1924

אביב. New York, June–November 1915. Illustrated juvenile weekly, published by the Hebrew Teachers' Federation of the United States and Canada. Edited by Wolf Frishberg, and then a board of editors.

אוצר הדרוש וההטפה. Brooklyn, 1918–1919. Published by the Pardes Publishing House and edited by Rabbi Shalom Rabinowitz.

האמה. New York, 1915. Weekly, published by S. Zeligson and edited by Aaron Frankel.

512a

אפריון. Yonkers, 1923–1928. Monthly, edited and published by Samuel Miller.

בי דואר עברי [The Jewish Post]. Pittsburgh, 1909–1922. Weekly supplement to דער פאלקס-פריינד. Edited and published by Joseph Selig Glick.

בית ספרנו. New York, 1919–1920. Monthly of the pupils of the National Hebrew School.

הדאר [The Post]. New York, 1921–date. Daily to June 1922, weekly thereafter. Publishers: The Hebrew Publishing Company, Hadoar Publishing Company, and lastly, the Histadruth Ivrith, Editors: Max Lipson (daily), Menahem Ribalow (weekly, through 1924).

הד המורה [The Echo of the Teacher]. New York, 1915. Monthly, published by the Hebrew Teachers' Federation of the United States and Canada. Edited by Akiba Fleischman.

ינדיל תורה. Brooklyn, 1915–1920. Monthly, later bi-monthly. Published and edited by Rabbi Moses B. Tonashoff.

יהודה הצעיר [The Young Judean]. New York, 1914. Monthly supplement to the Young Judean. Published by the Young Judea Organization.

יזרעל. New York, 1917. Illustrated juvenile monthly. Published by the Young Judea Organization. Edited by M. Neiman. Appeared three times.

הירדן. New York, 1919–1924. Monthly, published and edited by Rabbi Moses Leiter.

הכרם. Roxbury, Massachusetts, 1915. Bi-monthly, published by the "Ivrith" School. Appeared three times.

לנלו. New York, 1924–1925. Annual, published by "the jokesters" of "Herzliah" High School. Appeared twice.

לוח אחיעבר. New York, 1918, 1921. Annual, published by the Histadruth Achiever. Edited by Simeon Ginzburg, Dr. S. M. Melamed and Zvi Scharfstein (1918) and by Max Lipson (1921).

לוח מגן דוד אדום". New York, 1919. Annual, edited and published by Dr. Leon Golden.

המאחד. New York, 1923. Irregularly published by the Meahad Organization. Edited by M. Trotzky. Appeared once.

המורה. New York, 1924. Monthly, published by the Teachers' Organization of Greater New York. Edited by J. N. Adler, M. Glick, A.
Levine and Y. Z. Frishberg. Appeared once.

מחג לחג. New York and Baltimore, 1915–1917. Three-times-yearly, published by the Okeanus Company and edited by Israel Ephros. Appeared twice.

המנהל. New York, 1920. Monthly, published by the Hebrew Office of the
Education Department of the Zionist Federation. Edited by Kalman
Whiteman.

מקלט. New York, 1919–1920. Monthly, published by Stybel Publishing
Company and edited by I. D. Berkowitz.                                512b

מקרן זוית. Detroit, 1921. Published by Neriyah Publications and edited
by Bernard Isaacs and Aaron David Markson. Appeared once.

הנוער. New York, 1922. Published by the pupils of the National Hebrew
School. Appeared once.

נימים. New York, 1923. Published by Chawerim Publications and edited
by Hillel Bavli. Appeared once.

נעורים. Albany, New York, 1922. Monthly, published by the Hebrew
Club, "Lovers of the Nation," of the Albany Hebrew School. Appeared once.

נר מערבי. New York, 1923–1925. Published by the students of the Isaac
Elchanan Theological Seminary.

סמדר. Philadelphia, 1923–1924. Monthly, published by the pupils of the
High School of the Philadelphia Hebrew Schools.

סנסן. Minneapolis, 1923–1926. Annual, published by the students of the
Hebrew School of Minneapolis.

העברי. Berlin and New York, 1910–1921. Weekly (bi-weekly for a time
in Germany), published in America by the Hebrew Press Association.
Edited by Rabbi Meir Berlin, with the collaboration of Rabbi Y. L.
Ha-Cohen Fishman and (during the American period) Max Lipson.

העברי הצעיר. Bronx, 1923. Published by the students of the "Torah of
Moshe" School. Appeared once.

עדן. New York, 1924–1925. Illustrated juvenile weekly. Published by
Bathsheba Grabelski. Edited by Daniel Persky, and then by I. D.
Berkowitz.

על המפתן. Baltimore, 1918. Published by the graduating pupils of the
Hebrew School (Talmud Torah). Appeared once.

העם. New York, 1916. Weekly, published and edited by S. Zeligson.

פרח לבנון. New York, 1918. Quarterly, published and edited by Rabbi
Eliezer Lippa Weissblum. Appeared four times.

הצעיר. Newburgh, New York, 1919. Published twice by the "Young
of Zion."

קדימה. New York, 1923–1931. Annual, published by the pupils of the East Side Hebrew Schools.

קונטרס מודיעין. New York, 1917. Published by the Information Office of the Education Department of the New York Kehilla. Edited by Israel Kanowitz. Appeared three times.

רפואה. New York, 1923, 1927. Annual, published by Rephuah Publications and edited by Dr. Leon Golden.

שחרות [*The Youth*]. New York, 1916–1921. Monthly for children, published by the Bureau of Jewish Education of New York City and edited by Zvi Scharfstein.

תרבות. New York, 1919–1920. Monthly, published by the Histadruth Ivrith and edited by Zvi Scharfstein.

התרן [*The Mast*]. New York, 1913–1925. Monthly, then weekly, then monthly again. Published by the Histadruth Achiever, then the Hatoren Publishing Association, then the Zionist Federation of America, and lastly the Safruth Publishing Company. Edited by Simeon Ginzburg, Abraham Goldberg, Shalom Baer Maximon, Daniel Persky and Benjamin Silkiner; and then by Max Lipson, Dr. S. M. Melamed and Daniel Persky; then by I. D. Berkowitz; then by Berkowitz and Shmarya Levin; and lastly by Reuben Brainin.

512c

# WORLD OF OUR MOTHERS: THE WOMEN'S PAGE OF THE JEWISH DAILY FORWARD

by Maxine S. Seller

With a daily circulation approaching 200,000, the Jewish Daily Forward in 1919 was one of the most important foreign language papers in the United States, the leading Yiddish newspaper in the world, and the voice of a vibrant left wing workingclass Yiddish culture.[1] Although Karl Marx's call for the workers of the world to unite adorned the masthead and news was covered from a labor perspective, the Forward attracted the apolitical as well as the political. The paper was lively, easy to read, secular (though respectful of traditional religion) and committed to the Americanization as well as the politicization of the immigrant. Its influence was immense. "In our house the 'Bible' was Der Forverts, the literary work that determined our outlook and decided our patterns of conduct....In my parents' time everyone they knew read and followed the Forward," wrote a nostalgic admirer, with perhaps only slight exaggeration.[2]

While much has been written about the role of the Forward in the education and Americanization of immigrants, the special pages addressed to women have not been specifically examined. Women did not confine their reading of the Forward to the women's pages, nor can it be assumed that these pages were read exclusively by women. Nevertheless, many women did read the women's pages and were, presumably, influenced by them.[3]

Like the Forward of which it was a part, the women's page changed with the times and with the increasing Americanization of its intended audience. In 1919, however, it spoke to women who were still rooted in working class, radical Yiddish culture. Moreover, it spoke to them in the Indian summer of that culture, in the glowing aftermath of Bolshevik and feminist victory, before it was widely recognized that the Soviet Union suppressed civil liberties and that the Nineteenth Amendment did little to improve women's lives. Yet even in 1919 and even in the works of a socialist and feminist such as Esther Luria, Americanization emerged as

513

MAXINE SELLER is in the Department of Educational Organization, Administration and Policy at the University of Buffalo (SUNY), Buffalo NY 14210.

The Journal of Ethnic Studies 16:2

the first priority. Despite their radical background, Luria and other columnists who wrote for the women's page in 1919 were helping their readers move toward mainstream, middle class American life. The women's page at this fascinating point in history provides insight into the multiple and sometimes conflicting agendas of the "progressive" Yiddish speaking community's most influential newspaper and, indirectly, into the rapidly changing lives of the readers it described and influenced.

Although in 1919 the workers' movement was more important than the women's movement to most of the columnists who wrote for the women's page and the needs of Americanization shaped their approach to both, conflicts among these three agendas produced conflicting advice for readers. Women were told to be loyal participants in the workers' movement but were assured that it was all right to move into the middle class as long as they were ethical and compassionate. They were told to be active in public life but, at the same time, to fulfill the traditional (and time-consuming) roles of homemaker, wife, and mother. They were encouraged to enter American life with enthusiasm and grace, but Americanization was defined in terms of the familiar Jewish values, albeit in altered form, of the male-headed nuclear family and of educational achievement.

It would be simplistic to attribute these contradictions solely to the multiple priorities of the staff of the Forward. They also reflected the contradictions in the lives of readers, women beginning the transition from "Yiddishkeit" to middle class American life. If the women's page underscored the contradictions inherent in this transition, it also suggested ways in which those contradictions could be resolved. Idealistic working class women could move into the middle class without guilt when socialism was defined, as it was in the women's page, less as a specific economic program than as an ethic, a democratic and compassionate outlook on public and private life. With socialism thus redefined, politically "progressive" women could move from admiration for Lenin in 1919 to support for President Franklin Roosevelt's New Deal in the 1930s.[4] The women's page suggested that women could take part in public and private life without challenging traditional sex roles if they did so sequentially. This suggestion was made indirectly, through columns such as Botvinnik's which tacitly assumed that women participated in the paid labor market, the unions, and the socialist movement while single and devoted themselves entirely to domestic concerns after marriage. This assumption both reflected and helped shape reality for the majority of

514

readers, although some continued work or political activity after marriage, and others, such as Rose Schneiderman and Pauline Newman, never married at all.

By defining Americanization in terms of the familiar Jewish values of the stable nuclear family and educational achievement (now defined as secular rather than religious study and expanded to include women as well as men) the women's page once again both reflected and helped shape women's choices. Finally, by giving Americanization priority over socialism and feminism, the women's page foreshadowed the fate of the radical working class culture for which it and the Forward spoke, a culture that would ultimately be transformed, if not defeated, by time, social mobility, Stalinism, and McCarthyism.

Like the Forward of which it was a part, the women's page walked a fine line between leading and following public opinion. Even in 1919, a peak time for socialist and feminist activism, it did not urge readers to make radical changes in their values or lifestyles, nor did it emphasize conflict either between the classes or the sexes. Rather, it reinforced the democratic, progressive approach to public affairs already head by many of its readers, educated others toward that approach, and offered its readers sympathetic if limited help in adapting their private lives as wives and mothers to the American environment.

Most single women at that time were in the paid workforce, usually the garment industry, and married women, who usually left the garment shops to become "housewives," often continued to earn by keeping boarders or "minding" a small individual or family business. This high level of participation in economic activity continued an East European pattern in which women were accustomed to earning some, and occasionally all, of the family income and to moving freely and independently outside the home in order to do so.[5] Extensive participation in political life also continued a pattern begun in Europe, where a conspicuous minority had been active in anti-Czarist revolutionary parties, trade unions, Zionism, and the socialist Bund. In the United States many more participated in massive strikes in the garment industry, in tenant and consumer actions, in school protests, and in the suffrage and socialist movements.[6]

While about half of the columns on the women's page in 1919 dealt with public life, the remaining half dealt with private or domestic matters. These columns discussed polite behavior, social life, love, marriage, child psychology, and the education of children. The prevalence

515

of such topics reflects the fact that most of the readers were young women who, regardless of their other interests, considered marriage and motherhood central to their lives either as present realities or as future goals.

Despite the traditional pictures on the masthead and the readers' interest in family life, much of the domestic material commonly found in publications read by middle class American born women was not found in the women's pages of the Forward in 1919. There were no consumer reports, no food lore nor recipes, no instructions on housecleaning, laundering, or sewing, and the few articles on fashion or beauty were either satirical or disparaging. The absence of homemaking instruction may indicate that the staff and readers thought such things were best learned at home, or perhaps Jewish women, immersed in housekeeping chores, preferred in their rare moments of leisure to read about something else. Articles of sewing instruction would certainly have been superfluous to veterans of the sweatshops, while consumer news, beauty, and fashion were dismissed by the staff (though probably not by most readers) as inappropriate for the serious socialist woman.[7]

Cutting across the categories of women's public and private lives and permeating the entire women's page in 1919 were three major themes: socialism, feminism, and Americanization. The Forward had been founded to bring the working class Jewish immigrant to socialism, a goal which had been reinforced by the recent victory of socialism in the Soviet Union. It is not surprising, therefore, that the paper's commitment to socialism was clearly visible in the women's page. While the Forward had no formal commitment to feminism, socialists gave at least verbal support to the women's movement, and editor Cahan was sympathetic to the problems of his female constituency. It was also not surprising that feminism was a major theme in the women's page in the year of the passage of the Nineteenth Amendment. Most salient of all was the third theme, Americanization, a long standing interest of the paper and, especially during and immediately after World War I, a major concern of the American population as a whole.

Despite its editorial support of the Bolshevik Revolution in the Soviet Union (which would later be withdrawn), the Forward favored a democratic, gradualist approach to socialism in what editor Cahan considered the more open and less class-conscious society of the United States.[8] This was also the position taken by the women's page in 1919. Columnists who wrote for the women's page assumed that their reader

516

understood the general socialist outlook (if not the intricacies of dialectical materialism) and was in sympathy with it. Their columns frequently referred to capitalism negatively and to the proletariet positively, but specific allusions to class struggle were rare and were often muted by gender solidarity. Their goals were the cultural and personal growth of the individual worker as well as the economic advancement of the working class, and their perspective was international. Most important, they used socialism not only as a political program for the reconstruction of society but also as a source of insight into the daily problems of the reader and as a to moral behavior in both public and private life.

517

A feature article on kitchen work, "Her Realm—Slavery" illustrates many of these generalizations. The author deplored the plight of the "proletariet wife" enslaved by kitchen work in the "contemporary capitalist order," but defined the problem in humanistic as well as political terms. Kitchen "slavery" was condemned because it deprived women of the opportunity to contribute to the worker's movement--a recognition of the potential conflict for women between the demands of public, or political, and private, or domestic, life. Kitchen "slavery" was also condemned on apolitical grounds because it was hard, unappreciated and stifling; it "takes all her skill, devours all her thoughts, and leaves her no time for any other human interests." Class conflict was muted by gender solidarity. Although the article was addressed to the working woman, it expressed sympathy rather than hostility toward the rich homemaker with servants because "the work of management is not light, if she has a taste for beauty and cleanliness as well as order." Thus gender solidarity overruled class antagonism.[9]

The solution to kitchen slavery was kitchen socialism, the replacement of private kitchens with cooperatives, although no details were provided as to how the cooperatives would work. The article concluded with an international perspective; cooperatives, the reader was informed, were familiar to progressive minded Europeans and had freed women in Austria, Germany, and Russia for participation in the Revolution. The columnist did not inform readers that cooperatives for housework and childcare had for years been proposed by American feminists such as Charlotte Perkins Gilman, a symptom of the social distance between most immigrants and middle class American feminists.[10]

The women's page provided socialist insights into the problems of women working outside as well as inside the home, focussing in the spring of 1919 on the issue of women's wages. Low wages were a major concern to the many Jewish women supporting themselves and who were often dependent on half the meager sums paid to their male counterparts. Columnists acknowledged the value of revolution in achieving justice for workers, including women, in other countries, but recommended that American women attack the problem of their low wages through unionization and legislative action.

In a feature article on women's wages, Dr. Esther Luria defended the revolutionary solution in the Soviet Union. Somewhat unconvincingly, she denied reports that women physicians there were paid less than men: "the Russian woman [physician] is often idealistic and wants to help the peasants. If there is no vacancy, she will work as a nurse at lower wages." Showing the impact of America on her own ideology, the former revolutionary recommended trade unionism, not Bolshevism, as appropriate for the United States. She urged her readers to join unions, holding up as a model the cultural and intellectual life made possible by the higher wages paid to the members of the Ladies Waist and Dressmakers Union. Despite her own commitment to a broader socialist ideology, Luria's column focused the reader's attention on personal improvement rather than on social change.[11]

Unlike Samuel Gompers, leader of the American Federation of Labor, columnists who wrote for the women's page did not consider socialism to be in opposition to trade unionism; rather, the two were considered complementary means to the same end, the advancement of both the individual worker and the working class. A third, equally legitimate means to the same end was the legislative process in which women, who had won the right to vote in New York state in 1917, could now participate. The weekly news column "Notes from the Women's World" urged readers to campaign for a state minimum wage applicable to both men and women and high enough to insure all workers a comfortable standard of living. "Then employers will not be able to exploit women, lower the wages of men, and make trouble in general for the trade unions."[12] "Notes from the Women's World" reported with evident approval lobbying and political demonstrations in the interests of the woman worker by gender based coalitions across class and ethnic lines, including the Women's Suffrage Party, the Women's Trade Union League, the National Council of Jewish Women, and the Women's Christian Temperance Union.[13] Thus, in the women's page socialism was in effect redefined as any economic or political action undertaken alone or with

518

middle class allies, to better the immediate condition of the working woman.

In 1919 concerned groups were debating whether women needed special protection in the workforce because of their maternal functions and supposed moral and physical vulnerability. Opponents of protective laws argued that these laws put women at a disadvantage in the job market and proposed protection for both sexes. Most middle class American reformers favored special protective legislation, but the women's page of the Forward disagreed. Coming from a culture that viewed the working woman as strong rather than weak, its columnists favored equal protection for workers of both sexes, including an effective system of inspection in which both women and men would participate. Given a high enough minimum wage, women could protect their own health and morals.[14]

519

Although socialists usually viewed the struggle for women's wages as part of the greater struggle for justice for the working class, Luria understood that women's economic problems were the result of sex as well as class. Luria offered the traditional explanations for women's low wages—that parents invested in the training of sons but not daughters, that women worked in unskilled and unorganized trades, and that, considering their jobs temporary, women would not acquire skills or pay union dues. However, she also pointed out the role of sex discrimination. She noted that skilled women who did exactly the same work as men— replacing them in heavy industry during World War I, for example, or practicing "male" professions—still earned less than their male counterparts. She attributed this to prejudice against women workers and to the unfounded belief that women were always supported by men and therefore had little need for money.[15]

Recognizing that male workers sometimes resented the presence of women in the workplace, columnists defended the interests of working women. They insisted that men must accept the fact that women were entitled to pursue their own economic interests and to get "equal pay for work of equal worth."[16] The women's page did not share the view, widespread even among socialists, that women should be at home rather than in the paid labor force. To the contrary, Luria applauded the entry of women into a broad range of formerly male occupations during the recent war and predicted, optimistically but inaccurately, that the gains would be permanent, a position not shared by most male workers or their unions.[17]

While columnists acknowledged tensions between men and women in the workplace, they rarely saw, or would not acknowledge, tensions between men and women within the workers' movement. Trade unionists who opposed the appointment of Francis Perkins to the New York State Industrial Commission, "to our shame," were scolded for breaking what the columnist apparently considered a long standing and universally accepted alliance between labor and women; "the great struggle for women and the worker formerly went hand in hand."[18] The columnists were silent, however, on the problematic status of women in the Socialist Party and on the discrimination women faced within the trade unions, even in unions representing predominantly female trades, although Jewish women had complained of this discrimination as early as the shirtwaistmakers strike of 1909.[19]

The use of socialism as a class conscious guide to public morality appeared in articles demanding justice for American Blacks. While much of the nation was indifferent to the worsening plight of Blacks, columnist Michael Zametkin informed Jewish women about the loss of Black voting rights in the South; "we have democracy in one part of the land but not in the other."[20] "Notes from the Women's World" cited shocking statistics on Black maternal deaths and infant mortality. Justice for Blacks was to be achieved through socialism; the government must provide free doctors and nurses. To make this happen, women and workers must have political power. Here the women's page linked socialism and feminism; realization of a socialist goal, state medical care, depended upon the realization of a feminist goal, women's suffrage.[21]

The women's page used socialism or, perhaps more accurately, the class consciousness derived from socialism, to provide perspectives on private a well as public morality. In columns containing wonderful descriptions of the newly prosperous and ostentatious "allrightniks," with their expensive clothes and jewelry and country vacations, columnists warned their still predominantly working class audience against selfishness, pretentiousness, and other moral pitfalls which they identified with movement into the middle class. Regina Freshwater criticized "allrightniks" for making a public show of large charitable contributions, while ignoring the needs of their own poor relatives. She contrasted their hypocritical behavior with the true generosity of the Workman's Circle, the socialist lodge that could be relied upon to care for sick workers and their families. An ambivalent rather than condemnatory attitude among socialist Jews toward mobility into the middle class is indicated by the

520

fact that the Workman's Circle lent money to impoverished members so that they might become capitalists, albeit humbly, in businesses of their own—a practice which socialist columnist Freshwater praised.[22]

Her socialism apparently tempered by the realities of American life, Freshwater did not condemn "allrightniks" for getting rich, but for behaving badly once they did so. She criticized women "allrightniks" for exaggerating their husbands' financial success and wearing expensive jewelry bought on credit. Her columns portrayed rich women who vacationed in the country as playing cards all day while their neglected children drowned or were killed in traffic. Freshwater urged the working class woman to forego cardplaying, "a product of our present materialistic life style...the passion to grasp an 'easy' dollar." Instead, she should join educational and cultural clubs that provided uplifting activity without taking too much time or money from the family.[23] Thus the women's page gave readers advice not only about improving their situations as workers, but also about the behavior and lifestyle appropriate to the socialist woman and her husband.

521

As already noted, Luria demonstrated a feminist as well as a socialist perspective in recognizing the impact of sex discrimination on women's wages, and socialist goals such as state financed medical care were linked to the feminist goal of women's suffrage. A feminist perspective permeated many other areas of the women's page as well, appearing in columns about both public and private life. Feminism was explicit in columnists' commitment to women's political and economic equality and implicit in their concern for women's problems and the value placed upon their activities.

Political feminism in 1919 focussed, as might be expected, on the campaign to pass the Nineteenth Amendment in Congress. When that was successfully accomplished, the task was to win its ratification in the state legislatures. Regular "Notes from the Women's World" columns and feature articles provided sophisticated political analysis of the progress of the Amendment in the United States and, by placing political feminism in an international perspective, applauded advances toward political equality in England, France, Italy and India. Nowhere did a columnist on the women's page argue, as many of their American born counterparts did, that women needed the ballot in order to protect the sanctity and sobriety of the home. Columnists apparently recognized that for the immigrant generation of Jewish women, whose culture had never confined them to the household, interest in public affairs was normal rather than exceptional and was important to young, single women for whom issues of protecting the family were not yet relevant.

Significantly, the women's page did not feel it necessary to argue the cause of political equality for women at all; its correctness was considered self-evident and the support of readers, many of whom had been active in recent state suffrage campaigns, justifiably assumed.[24] Columnists who had only recently witnessed the defeat of Tsarism and Kaiserism considered the victory of women's suffrage an inevitable sign of the enlightenment and progress of the age.[25] Nevertheless, they gave full credit to Susan B. Anthony, Dr. Marie Shaw and other suffragists. Veterans of the long battle for socialism, columnists understood and noted that the vote was not being "given" to women; women had won it through more than fifty years of struggle.[26]

While middle class, American born feminists focussed their attention almost exclusively on suffrage in 1919, columnists of the women's page of the Forward defined feminism in broader terms. They reminded readers that many state laws discriminated against women in marriage, divorce, property and inheritance rights, and family life and warned that "these remainders from barbarism must be erased from all the law books."[27] They called attention to the importance of psychological as well as legal barriers to women's equality; "it will take time to uproot...[men's] prejudices about the 'weaker sex' and before women themselves will look upon themselves as completely equal in ability with the 'stronger sex.'"[28] Finally, unlike most middle class American feminists, they were careful always to link political equality to economic equality. "There should be for equal work, equal pay. This is naturally of the greatest importance to working women."[29]

Like other women's publications, the women's pages included many feature columns about notable women, past and present, but in 1919 these often had a feminist and sometimes also a socialist perspective. While stories about the wives of public figures also appeared, much more space was devoted to accounts of women who were important for their own achievements. Columnist Jacob Padalier wrote about powerful women of the past, including the medieval Johanna who supposedly served as Pope John VIII until pregnancy revealed her identity.[30]

Moving from myth to history, Padalier wrote a lengthy series on women heroes of the French Revolution. Although these articles told of the personal lives and love affairs as well as the political activities of Madame Roland, Chalotte Cordee, and others, their content was

522

implicitly feminist. Padalier showed that women could aspire to public power and change the course of events. He also showed the problems women faced in doing so; women's attempt to participate fully in the French Revolution were resisted not only by aristocratic reactionaries, but also by fellow revolutionists opposed to equality for women.[31]

Obituaries of contemporary women in public life, usually Jewish labor activists, provided "role models" for political activism closer to home. Readers of the women's page learned, for example, about Julia Pollock, self-educated intellectual, member of the Social Revolutionary Party, operator of a cooperative dressmaking shop and a revolutionary press in Russia, and tireless supporter of the workers' movement in the United States. They also learned about Amelia Barr, an immigrant from England, "a mother of thirteen children and a writer of seventy novels.... One often found her, with a child in hand, sitting and reading a book." Here intellectual achievement, traditionally valued only for Jewish men, was endorsed by the women's page as praiseworthy for women as well, whether combined with politics or motherhood.[32]

The women's page honored women's contributions in private as well as public life. A column entitled "There Are Also Good 'Busybodies'" praised the homemaker whose lively interest in her neighbors enabled her to help them in emergencies (such as the influenza epidemic) with money or needed services.[33] By expressing appreciation for the homemaker, the traditional caretaker, as well as for the working woman and the political activist, the women's page fostered the self-respect of all types of readers.

A feminist perspective was implicit, though not explicit, in columnists' perceptive descriptions of the problems their women readers faced in every day life. The best example was a poignant series, "The Seven Stages in the Life of a Woman," by Beryl Botvinnik (written under the pen name "Lead Pencil").[34] Taking his cue from Shakespeare—"the world's a stage" the author followed a "typical" woman through seven successive phases of life in which, like a skilled actress, she played one role after another—school girl, "princess," shop girl, young wife, mother, middle aged woman, and old woman. Botvinnik noted that women's roles were determined by the men (suitors, then husbands) who constituted their audience and paid for their performance and that therefore women moved through life with few real choices. Seeing no prospect for change, he recommended silence, a silence which, ironically, his column had already broken. "Only a brute, a murderer" would tell the hopeful young girl what a "drab path" awaited her.[35]

523

Botvinnik left a vivid picture of the immigrant woman's life in the early twentieth century industrial city. Every stage of life had both positive and negative features. Botvinnik described the positive—the pleasures of courtship, the pride of the first job, the elation of new motherhood, the satisfaction of companionship with grown children, and the renewed zest for life that came in the later years.

More memorable, however, were his descriptions of darker times—the woman's panic at approaching thirty still unmarried, "she trembles at every compliment, hoping it is not just 'small talk'...she smiles, but it is a lie. Life has taken her in its claws"; the loss of personal autonomy that came with the long desired marriage "she has left the authority of the foreman...only to be under the authority of her husband...she is not saying or thinking her own language and thoughts, only his....She has stopped belonging to herself...she lives because of him"; motherhood in the tenements, "the glow that came...with the first child has disappeared. She has another and another and another, and she has only anguish and fear. The beautiful name of mother is no more than a cover for the work of the woman who is in truth a maid, a baby nurse, and an incubator...for children against whom she has turned with a knife so that they shouldn't come..."; the frustrations and longings of every day life, "every time she takes a child's jacket in her hand she feels a burst of happiness....But how tightly she is imprisoned by those jackets...the woman, the human being restrained, awakens in her....She has lived so little...."[36]

Some of the problems described by Botvinnik were related more closely to readers' social class than to their gender. The difficulty of rearing a large family was clearly felt by fathers as well as mothers and was related primarily to poverty; nevertheless, the problem was experienced differently by the woman who was, after all, the one who bore the children (or, as in Botvinnik's column, tried to avoid bearing them) and who provided daily care. Other problems, such as the tremendous pressure to marry and the loss of personal autonomy and decline of contact with the wider world after marriage, were specific to women, although the form they took might vary with social class. In identifying these problems, and in recognizing that financial dependence on men made it difficult for women to control their own lives, Botvinnik wrote from an implicitly feminist.

While middle class American publications for women portrayed homemaking as feminine fulfillment or, alternatively, an opportunity for the display of scientific management, the women's page of the Forward

524

acknowledged that housework was repetitive and unpleasant and that marriage and motherhood were restrictive as well as fulfilling.[37] The woman who read Botvinnik's columns may have been reassured simply to learn that her frustrations were not unique, but the women's page offered her no practical help other than the vague proposal for kitchen cooperatives. Nowhere in the women's pages in 1919 appeared the suggestion that men should participate in housework or childcare. Although paid work was viewed as appropriate for women and men, homemaking was seen as appropriate only for women, individually or, in the case of the kitchen cooperatives, collectively. Progressive in their advocacy of equality in the workplace and the voting booth, columnists supported traditional sex roles within the home.

Despite the excitement engendered by the recent Bolshevik Revolution and the ongoing campaign for the Nineteenth Amendment, Americanization was more prominent in the women's page in 1919 than either socialism or feminism and, in case of conflict, appeared to take priority over both. The predominance of Americanization reflected not only the Forward's longstanding editorial policy on this matter, but also the views of most of its readers. Like other immigrants, Jews were sometimes homesick for the scenes of their birthplace, but even in the optimistic aftermath of the Russian Revolution relatively few (compared to other immigrant groups) returned to Europe. The women's page implicitly endorsed their decision to remain in the United States. The "old country" was rarely mentioned in its columns and nostalgia was nonexistent. Women were told, in effect, to look ahead, not back. Nor was the emphasis on Americanization modified in 1919 by concerns about the preservation of Jewish tradition. Although many readers were observant Jews from conviction or habit, religious holidays such as Passover and Shavuot went unmentioned. Jewish women were not urged, as women were in other immigrant publications, to be the guardians of religion or ethnicity.[38]

Columnists were eager to help women adjust their public lives to American values and conditions. They encouraged women to express political and social activism in ways that were acceptable and appropriate to the United States; for example, by participation in labor unions, lobbying, and political parties. Columnists were equally eager to help readers Americanize their private lives, to behave as individuals and as members of families in ways that were acceptable and appropriate to the United States. Help in Americanizing private life was offered in the form

525

of advice on social behavior, courtship, marriage, "progressive" childrearing, and education. If followed, much of this advice could facilitate not only Americanization, but also--ironically, considering its socialist sponsorship—entry into the middle class.

An example of this kind of advice is a column entitled "What Does 'Interesting Company' Mean?" in which Regina Freshwater encouraged readers to move from the aggressive, outspoken female culture of the East European "shtetl" (and American tenement) to the more subdued behavior of an idealized middle class American "lady."[39] According to Freshwater, readers who wanted to be considered "interesting company," must learn to be good listeners. They must also learn not to complain. Freshwater expressed sympathy for the woman who had lost a child, or who was sick, or whose aging sister could not find a husband, leaving for today's reader a description of the familiar tragedies of immigrant life. Her main interest was not description, however, but prescription; "of these things [tragedies] it is not good to talk when people come together because everyone has his own pack of troubles which he would like to forget for a little while." To be "interesting company" one must be not only willing to listen and always cheerful, one must also be agreeable. Freshwater admonished her apparently argumentative readers not to dispute every point with their companions because "no one wants to be shown in front of others that he is wrong."[40]

Verbal assertiveness was important, indeed, indispensable, in America as well as Europe for ordinary women who survived by buying and selling in the streets and marketplaces and for intellectuals and political activists who argued in the union halls and coffee shops. In advising women to subdue this assertiveness Freshwater was advising them to give up behavior associated with economic and political activism in the interest of Americanization and, more specifically, entry into the middle class. Women who followed her advice would have found it more difficult to achieve their goals in public life but easier to achieve what some defined as success in private life—marriage to an upwardly mobile, Americanized man.

The many columns dealing with courtship, love, and marriage offered help with familiar problems in an unfamiliar environment. These columns met a need for women whose mothers, aunts and other trusted advisors were often far away and whose advice, had they been here, may have seemed inappropriate in urban America. In Europe, marriages had traditionally been arranged and contact between the sexes closely

526

supervised (although by the late nineteenth century this had begun to change). In America, however, most young women sought romance on their own in the factory, the dancehall, or the streets, sometimes with unfortunate results. Married women, too, faced new problems, as immigration, poverty, and adjustment to a different lifestyle aggravated the normal tensions of family life. The women's page offered these women sympathy and understanding while guiding them toward goals endorsed by Jewish tradition, American social workers, and the staff of the Forward, the establishment and maintenance of stable nuclear families.

Sometimes this guidance was addressed to parents. Columnist Yetta Gold warned parents, for example, to protect patriotic and emotional young daughters from being seduced by homecoming soldiers during the abnormal postwar period.[41] Freshwater warned parents of the dire consequences of insisting, in traditional European fashion, that daughters marry in birth order.[42]

Usually advice was addressed to the young women themselves, often in the form of morals drawn from sensational court cases or melodramatic stories about love, jealousy, adultery, and divorce. Typical of such advice stories was that of Lili, a Jewish working girl who flirted with the Black elevator operator at the "shop." The young man fell hopelessly in love with her and wanted to marry her. Consumed with guilt, Lilli quit her job, leaving the young man broken hearted. The columnist excused Lilli's "love play" at the factory as an attempt to add interest to a hard and barren life but used her story to warn readers of the dangers of flirting. "Sometimes the boy is the victim and sometimes the girl. It starts with a joke and ends with a broken heart."[43] Similar stories warned against hasty marriages and against choosing partners columnists considered too old, too rich, too poor, or otherwise inappropriate.[44]

Reflecting the age of most of its readers, the women's page was usually sympathetic to young wives as opposed to mothers-in-law, although young women who complained of the latter were reminded that they too would someday be mothers-in-law.[45] Although a small percentage of Jewish immigrants, including the famous anarchist Emma Goldman, believed in free love and rejected conventional marriage, the women's page endorsed traditional sexual morality for both men and women. A column about socialite Austin Flint Gibson, who sued for divorce because his wife had lovers before marriage, condemned the sexual double standard. "We think the men should be as pure as they want

527

the women to be...when there is no double morality...truth and purity will reign in family life."[46]

Reflecting the viewpoint of its intended audience, the women's page was usually more sympathetic to the viewpoint of women than of men. Freshwater, for example, criticized husbands for refusing to pay their wives' bills or, worse still, for being unfaithful. She warned, however, that women often shared the blame for such problems. "There are women that have the nature to make themselves loathsome to their husbands and then are amazed that the husbands do something bad to them...." Freshwater's desire to champion the cause of women proved secondary to her interest in preserving the nuclear family; the wife was given the traditional advice that, to avoid marital problems, she must meet her husband more than half way. "If a woman wants understanding from her husband, she should first show understanding."[47]

While the women's page supported the traditional family even on occasion, as Freshwater's advice suggests, at the expense of the wife, it also supported limiting the size of that family, a position both advantageous to the wife and consistent with the example set by the middle class American family. Interestingly, family limitation was not suggested as a means of increasing the social mobility of children but of improving the life of the mother. Botvinnik wrote sympathetically of the harassed young mother who attempted self-afflicted abortion. Luria warned that the physical and economic hardships of too many children could drive a woman to suicide.[48] Freshwater warned that women with many children must expect to worry about their future, bear the blame if they turned out badly, and risk being neglected by them in old age.[49]

Explicit references to birth control in 1919 would have resulted in the Forward's losing its mailing privileges, but the topic was not new to its readers. The Socialist Party had expressed a tentative interest. More important, Emma Goldman, Rose Pastor Stokes, and other radical Jewish women had been active in the early birth control movement before World War I, and Margaret Sanger's first birth control clinic had been opened—and welcomed—in the heavily Jewish Lower East Side of New York City in 1916. Hints about the desirability of smaller families in the women's pages are therefore not surprising and are compatible with Jewish women's interest in Americanization and social mobility as well as their interest in socialism and feminism.[50]

Whether the family was large or small, most married women considered childrearing their central task, a focus reflected in regular

528

articles on the subject in the women's pages. Childrearing may have been even more important to Jewish women in the United States than it had been in Europe, since many consoled themselves for the hardships of their own lives with high hopes for the future of their children; in America anything was possible. American children brought problems as well as possibilities, however. Women found the tasks of childrearing complicated by the absence of their own mothers and other helpers, the dangers of urban street life, and the demands of a new environment in which their own upbringing seemed an unreliable guide.[51]

To women eager to be successful in the parenting of a new American generation, the women's page offered what was in its time sophisticated and timely guidance. Although American-born social workers in the postwar years gave foreign-born women instruction in feeding, bathing, and dressing their children, the women's page ignored these mundane matters. It offered instead a steady stream of articles, usually by Dr. Esther Luria, on child psychology and on public education, subjects of widespread interest in both radical and conservative circles in the early twentieth century. In articles such as "The Child and the Community," "The Child and Its Interests," "The Child and Its Memories," and "Sympathies Felt by Children," Luria introduced the work of educational experts such as John Dewey, and G. Stanley Hall (though she did not mention them by name) to her immigrant readers.

Reflecting the enlightened American opinion of the day, columnists deplored corporal punishment and recommended protecting children from premature exposure to harsh realities. They also admonished mothers to recognize the importance of fantasy and play as well as study in the development of the child's personality.[52] Adopting the techniques of the union to the needs of the family, Luria urged mothers to organize for the purpose of bringing children's theatre and wholesome movies to their neighborhoods.[53]

Recognizing the eagerness with which many Jewish mothers exposed their offspring to cultural and educational activities, the women's page warned against pushing children into experiences they had neither the interest nor maturity to appreciate; an active five-year-old, for example, should not be taken to a museum.[54] While American born social workers often accused immigrant mothers of neglecting their children, the women's pages cautioned against too much interference. "One cannot make from a child what one wants. You must look at their inclinations.... Parents and teachers can't play with a child's soul, even when they do their best."[55]

529

Offering comfort to immigrant mothers whose children did not live up to their expectations, Luria acknowledged that bringing up children was hard and that despite one's best efforts the results were unpredictable; "some will break up their own lives and others." She did not favor the permissiveness and emphasis of self expression advocated by the more radical progressive educators, however, seeing them incompatible with the development of social responsibility, a value central to socialism and Judaism. Children should be made to help at home according to age and ability. "The child must learn to consider the parents, brothers, and sisters and then after that the community. Then he will be able to leave the house in the future."[56] The goal of childrearing was to produce an adult who would be both socially responsible and autonomous.

530

Unlike many Roman Catholic immigrants who built parochial schools, the vast majority of Jewish immigrant parents in the early twentieth century sent their children to the expanding public schools. Luria gave readers sensible advice on how to help their children do well in these schools. Since the schools considered the acculturation of immigrant children, and through them of their parents, to be one of their most essential tasks, advice that helped children succeed in school could facilitate the Americanization of the entire family.[57]

The women's page was supportive but not uncritical of public education. Like many American born educators of her day, Luria attacked the schools for being "mechanical" and cold. As a socialist, she also criticized them for failing to develop "comradely feelings" among the children and for contradicting the values socialist parents inculcated at home. Recognizing that the values of socialism often differed from those of the competitive public school, Luria resolved these contradictions in favor of the schools. Despite her misgivings, she urged parents to reinforce what their children learned in school. Mothers should provide plants in the home, for example, to support the nature programs in the schools and see that children studied every day instead of just before examinations.[58]

Luria informed parents about the different curricula offered in the new comprehensive high schools, warned them that the academic track did not prepare for jobs, and urged them to seek the advice of the principal in making career and education decisions for their children.[49] Her socialist convictions led her to express strong reservations about the eagerness of working class parents to launch their children through education into the middle class. She reminded readers that entering a profession was not the equivalent of entering the garden of Eden, and that the intelligent working person was deserving of respect. At the same time, her interest in Americanization and, even more important, her respect for education led her to encourage adults as well as children to get as much schooling as possible.

The women's page of the Forward remains a valuable historical source because it is both descriptive and prescriptive. Astute observers of the immigrant Jewish community of which they were a part, journalists who wrote for the women's page in 1919 left vivid and authentic pictures of the activities and problems of Jewish women moving from the old world into the new. They also left a record of the guidance a popular and trusted paper offered to the women making this transition.

531

The content of the woman's page was shaped by the events of the day, the policies of the paper (dominated over the years by editor Abraham Cahan) and the needs and interests of the readers. In 1919 at least half of the page was devoted to political and economic issues, including a regular column of national and international news called "Notes from the Woman's World" and featured articles on suffrage, wages, and notable women, usually political or social activists. This heavy emphasis on public affairs, unusual for a women's page, reflected the political ferment of the post-war period and the labor activist orientation of the paper. Equally important, it reflected the interests of its Jewish immigrant readers, many of whom in 1919 were deeply involved in the economic and political life of their new country.

NOTES

[1]For background on the Jewish Daily Forward, see Barbara Ann Portnoy Berman, Environmental Impact on the Ideology of a Social Movement Organization: The Jewish Daily Forward 1887-1966. PhD Diss. Univ. of Michigan, 1972; Melech Epstein, Jewish Labor in the U.S.A.: An Industrial, Political, and Cultural History of the Jewish Labor Movement 1882-1914, Vol. I, Chapter 18, Ktav Publishing House, 1950, 1969; Irving Howe, World of Our Fathers. Harcourt, Brace, and Jovanovich, 1976; Ronald Sanders, The Downtown Jews: Portraits of an Immigrant Generation. New American Library, 1969, 1976; and the autobiography of editor Abraham Cahan, Bleter fun Mayn Lebn. 5 volumes, The Forward Association, 1926-1931. (1969). See also Mordecai Soltes, The Yiddish

Press, An Americanizing Agency. Teachers College Columbia University, 1925 and Robert E. Park, The Immigrant Press and Its Control. Harper and Brothers, 1922. For further bibliography on the Forward and other Yiddish newspapers, see Robert Singerman, "The American Jewish Press 1823-1983: A Bibliographic Survey of Research and Studies," American Jewish History LXXIII, no. 4 (June 1984), 422-444. Circulation figures are from Berman, 35-36. Soltes (38-39) suggests that circulation figures should be augmented by 75% to approximate the actual number of readers.

[2]Jack Sheinkman, "A Concern for How Jewish People Lived," Forward, May 23, 1982. Sheinkman's article is one of many nostalgic and laudatory testimonials in a special celebratory issue of the Forward.

[3]Audiences of Jewish women in several cities have told the author that their mothers, aunts, or grandmothers were regular readers of the Forward in the post World War I period and that they frequently repeated anecdotes and discussed materials from it. Although most informants did not distinguish between the women's page and other parts of the paper, one noted that her aunt specifically saved the women's page. Soltes states that a third of the readers of the Yiddish press were women and that feature sections (including, presumably, the women's page) were especially popular with women readers. Soltes, 37, 45.

[4]For material on the political behavior of Jewish women, especially in recent years, see Susan Welch and Fred Ulrich, The Political Life of American Jewish Women. Biblio Press, 1984.

[5]For background on East European Jewish women in Europe and America see Mark Zborowski and Elizabeth Herzog, Life Is with People: The Culture of the Shtetl, Schocken, 1960, 131; Baum, Hyman, and Michel, op. cit.; Jacob Rader Marcus, The American Jewish Woman 1645-1980 and The American Jewish Woman: A Documentary History. Ktav Publishing House, 1981; Rudolph Glanz, The Eastern European Jewish Woman, Vol. I, The East European Jewish Woman. Ktav Publishing House, 1976; and Maxine S. Seller, ed. Immigrant Women. Temple University Press, 1981.

[6]On Jewish women as socialists and trade unionists, see Mari Jo Buhle, Women and American Socialism 1870-1920. University of Illinois Press, 1981; Meredith Tax, The Rising of the Women: Feminist Solidarity and Class Conflict 1880-1917. Monthly Review Press, 1980; Alice Kessler-Harris, op. cit. and Maxine S. Seller, "The Rising of the Twenty Thousand: Sex, Class, and Ethnicity in the Shirtwaist Makers Strike of

532

1909" in Dirk Hoerder, ed. Struggle a Hard Battle: Essays on Working Class Immigrants. Northern Illinois University Press, 1986, 254-279. On other areas of activism, see Elinor Lerner, "Jewish Involvement in the Woman Suffrage Movement," American Jewish History LXX, no. 4 (June 1981), 442-461; Paula Hyman, "Immigrant Women and Consumer Protest: The New York City Kosher Meat Boycott of 1902," American Jewish History LXX, no. 1 (September 1980), 91-105; and Diane Ravitch, The Great School Wars, New York City 1805-1973: A History of the Public Schools as Battlefield of Social Change. Basic Books, 1974, 224-225.

[7]See "New Styles for Women," (no author), Forward, "Women's Interests," March 22, 1919 and article by Sadie Vinacker, June 7, 1919. See also Seller, 256.

[8]For Cahan's views on the relative lack of class consciousness among Jewish workers in the United States, see Cahan, vol. IV, 553-555. Berman provides a survey over time of Cahan's editorial positions and political ideology. For background on the relationship between socialism and Judaism in the immigrant Jewish community of the late nineteenth and early twentieth centuries, see Moses Rischin, The Promised City: New York's Jews 1870-1914. Harvard University Press, 1962, 1977, 148-168.

[9]A. Litvak (pseud.) "Her Realm as Slavery," Forward "Women's Interests," April 11, 1919. This and all subsequent translations from the Yiddish are my own. Citations from the Forward for March through June 1919 are from the Chicago edition of the Forward. Citations beginning in July 1919 are from the New York City edition.

[10]On women's domestic cooperatives, see Dolores Hayden, The Grand Domestic Revolution: A History of Feminist Designs for American Homes, Neighborhoods, and Cities. The MIT Press, 1982. On the distance between Jewish immigrant and American, middle class feminists, see Tax, op. cit., 170-179. See also Aileen Kraditor, The Ideals of the Woman's Suffrage Movement 1880-1920. Norton, 1981.

[11]Dr. Esther Luria, "Why Do Women Receive Lower Wages Than Men?" Forward, "Women's Interests," March 8, 1919.

[12]"Notes from the Women's World," Forward, "Women's Interests," May 17, 1919.

[13]"Notes from the Women's World," Forward, "Women's Interests," April 11, 1919.

[14]"Notes from the Women's World," Forward, "Women's Interests," May 17, 1919.

533

[15] Luria, op. cit.

[16] "Notes from the Women's World," Forward, "Women's Interests," May 17, 1919.

[17] Luria.

[18] "Notes from the Women's World," Forward, "Women's Interests," March 1, 1919.

[19] See Buhle, passim, and Alice Kessler-Harris, "Where Are the Organized Women Workers?" Feminist Studies 3:1 and 2 (Fall 1975) 92-110. See also Seller, "The Uprising of the Twenty Thousand."

[20] M. Zametkin, "Women's Rights in the Coming Election," Forward, "Women's Interests," June 21, 1919.

[21] "Notes from the Women's World," Forward, "Women's Interests," March 8, 1919.

[22] Regina Freshwater, "Help for the Sake of Advertisement and True Human Help," Forward, "Women's Interests," March 15, 1919.

[23] Regina Freshwater, "Feminine Complaints Against the Country," Forward, "Women's Interests," May 31, 1919; Regina Freshwater, "Why People Avoid Sunday by Playing Cards," Forward, "Women's Interests," March 29, 1919.

[24] Lerner, 443, documents the important role played by the Jewish women of the Lower East Side in support of women's suffrage both through the Socialist Party and through suffrage associations in the state referendums of 1914 and 1917.

[25] Zametkin.

[26] Ibid.

[27] "Notes from the Women's World," Forward, "Women's Interest," April 5, 1919.

[28] Ibid.

[29] Ibid.

[30] Jacob Padalier, "A Woman Once Was Pope of Rome," Forward, "Women's Interests," April 5, 1919.

[31] Jacob Padalier, "Women Heroes in the Great French Revolution," Forward, "Women's Interests," April 26; May 17, 24, and 21; June 7, 19, and 29; July 12, 20, and 27, 1919.

[32] Philip Kranen, "To the Memory of Julia Pollock," Forward, "Women's Interests," May 10, 1919; "Amelia Barr," Forward, "Women's Interests," March 22, 1919.

[33] "There Are Also Good Busybodies," Forward, "Women's Interests," April 16, 1919.

534

[34]Lead Pencil, Forward, "Women's Interests," "The Schoolgirl," March 29, 1919; "The Marriageable Young Woman," April 11, 1919; "The Young Wife," May 2, 1919; "A Mother," June 11, 1919; "Her Duties to Her Home, Her Children, Herself," June 29, 1919; "A Woman in the Middle Years," July 20, 1919; "Second Youth," August 3, 1919. The author was identified as Beryl Botvinnik by Simon Weber, current editor of the Forward, in a telephone interview, October 26, 1984. For biographical information on Botvinnik, see Leksikon, Vol. I, 212-213.

[35]Ibid. March 29, 1919.

[36]Ibid. April 11, May 2, June 29, 1919.

[37]On middle class American views of housework, see Barbara Ehrenreich and Deirdre English, For Her Own Good: 150 Years of the Experts' Advice to Women. Anchor Books, 1979, 141-182.

535

[38]Glos Polek, organ of the Polish Women's Alliance, for example, was comparable to the woman's page of the Forward in its feminist and labor orientation, but not in its commitment to preservation of the Polish language and cultural heritage. See Thaddeus Radziolowski, "Let Us Join Hands: The Polish Women's Alliance," in Maxine Seller, ed., Immigrant Women, 174-179.

[39]For an insightful description of cultural change and its impact on East European Jewish immigrant women, see Baum, Hyman and Michel, 187-233.

[40]Regina Freshwater, "What Does 'Interesting Company' Mean?" Forward, "Women's Interests," August 31, 1919.

[41]Yetta Gold, "Thousands of Young Women Seduced Because of the War," Forward, "Women's Interests," May 10, 1919.

[42]Regina Freshwater, "Family Tragedies Because of Older Sisters," Forward, "Women's Interests," April 5, 1919.

[43]"A Jewish Girl Who Broke the Heart of a Negro," Forward, "Women's Interests," March 22, 1919.

[44]For example: "Old Men are More Independent than Young Ones," Forward, "Women's Interests," May 14, 1919; "Can a Rich Girl Be Married to a Poor Boy?" Forward, "Women's Interests," June 21, 19 9.

[45]Regina Freshwater, "The Lament with the Mothers-In-Law That Remains Always New," Forward, "Women's Interests," June 21, 1919.

[46]Yetta Gold, "A Divorcee Because She Has Not Revealed Her Past," Forward, "Women's Interests," May 21, 1919.

[47]Regina Freshwater, "When Women Will Be Protected," Forward, "Women's Interests," May 10, 1919. See also Freshwater, "Breaking

Hearts in the Country," Forward, "Women's Interests," June 29, 1919 and S. Zeligson, "Are Men Always Wrong?" Forward, "Women's Interests," May 17, 1919.

[48] Dr. Esther Luria, "The Child as a Person for Itself," Forward, "Women's Interests," April 28, 1919.

[49] Regina Freshwater, "Better to Be Childless Than to Have Bad Children," Forward, "Women's Interests," June 11, 1919.

[50] On Jewish women in the birth control movement, see Buhle, 276 and Emma Goldman, Living My Life. Vol. 2, Knopf, 269-272.

[51] For a famous social worker's view of the adjustment problems of the immigrant housewife and mother, see Sophonisba Breckinridge, New Homes for Old. Harper and Brothers, 1921.

[52] Dr. Esther Luria, "Should One Whip Bad Children?" Forward, "Women's Interests," July 27, 1919; S. Ravitch, "Should One Tell Children About Death?" Forward, "Women's Interests," March 15, 1919; Dr. Esther Luria, "Games Introduce a Child to Fantasy," Forward, "Women's Interests," March 22, 1919.

[53] Dr. Esther Luria, "The Child and the Theatre," Foward, "Women's Interests," September 21, 1919.

[54] Dr. Esther Luria, "The Child and Its Interests," Forward, "Women's Interests," April 11, 1919. See also Luria, "The Child and Its Memories," May 10, 1919.

[55] Luria, "The Child as a Person for Itself."

[56] Ibid.

[57] On Americanization in the schools, see David B. Tyack, The One Best System: A History of American Urban Education. Harvard University Press, 1974, 229-255; Selma Cantor Berrol, Immigrants at School: New York City 1898-1914, Ph.D. Diss. New York University, 1968; and Bernard J. Weiss, ed., American Education and the European Immigrant. University of Illinois Press, 1982.

[58] Luria, "The Child and Its Memories."

[59] Dr. Esther Luria, "Further Education for Children Ending Public School," Forward, "Women's Interests," June 21, 1919.

536

*Eli Lederhendler*

⊛

# GUIDES FOR THE PERPLEXED:
# SEX, MANNERS, AND MORES
# FOR THE YIDDISH READER IN AMERICA*

"What is culture?", asked Dr. Ben-Zion Liber, an early advocate of progressive health education and preventive medicine, introducing a short article on "Physical Culture."[1] Culture, he argued, is everything that enhances the quality of life. Taking a holistic view of human existence, Liber insisted—Jewish proclivities to the contrary notwithstanding—that culture is not confined to music, literature, art, and the sciences—aspects of culture that engage the mind. Rather, he argued, the concept of "culture" ought to include the "cultivation" and care of the body. Culture began with self-knowledge and involved, ideally, all of one's faculties.[2]

This is an essay on Jewish immigrant culture in America, or one phase of it, at least. But it is also about Liber's question and its significance for the writing of social history. What historians generally speak of as "Jewish culture" is fairly narrowly and rigidly defined, and therefore there are some aspects of Jewish culture that are often overlooked. I am referring not only to the problem of "popular culture"; I have in mind the fact that even popular or "low-brow" culture tends to be conceptualized as mass-consumption analogues of "high culture" equivalents. Folklore and folk customs, folk music, the melodramas of the Yiddish stage, and pulp novels are patently alternate, "poor man's" versions of the literature, religion, poetry, music, and art of the elite. Culture in a broader, anthropological or social historical sense—the sum total of a group's social behaviors and responses to its environment—is relatively under-appreciated.

Such pedestrian matters as food, dress, sexual mores, family relations, and social etiquette go a long way toward defining a society. They might not appear quite as crucial as ideologies and social movements, masterworks of scholarship, great literature, and other creations of the spirit, but they are matters of prime concern to most people.

The following literary example, that exposes some of the fault

Originally published in *Modern Judaism*, 11 (October 1991). Reprinted by permission of The Johns Hopkins University Press.

lines of cultural and social dynamics in modern East European Jewry, shows what I mean about the importance of these aspects of culture:

> Fradl . . . was a student in Zvihil. She liked to dress up and speak Russian. . . . This Fradl was considered the black sheep of the family. The *khasidim*, who were my grandfather's enemies, claimed that because of his contempt for their *rebeim* he had been cursed with a heretic granddaughter . . . who spoke gentile languages and wore patent-leather shoes. . . . I gaped when she took a cigarette from Uncle Joseph's box and let the smoke drift from her mouth and nose at the same time, all the while bickering furiously with her father. . . . Uncle Joseph did not punish his daughter for her un-Jewish ways. But he did say that she was wasting her time going to school instead of staying home in Bilgoray and accepting a match with some eligible young man. Fradl shrieked in a way no decent Jewish woman would dare in Bilgoray. "Marry some Itche Mayer and rot in this dump? Not me." . . . "Then what are you looking for?" her father asked, blowing smoke in her face. "To study and become a dentist," she shot back, blowing smoke in his face. . . . I could only keep staring at this fantastic creature . . . and wonder how she could be my blood relative.[3]

538

The combined abominations of a woman smoking, wearing alien clothes and shoes, blatantly and loudly challenging patriarchal authority and rejecting social norms marked this young woman as an outsider—practically a non-Jew—because they went against the grain of basic elements in Jewish society and culture.

The importance of these elements for an understanding of Jewish social and cultural history ought to be apparent to anyone approaching the topic of immigrant history, generally, and the subject of Americanization in particular.[4] They do not readily fit into conventional definitions of religious life, but properly belong to the study of secular or ethnic culture.

The broader ramifications of this essay, then, relate to our perceptions of a certain Jewish ambience: the secular culture of first-generation immigrants between roughly 1910 and 1930. I use the term "secular" in two senses: first, to denote cultural phenomena that do not necessarily derive from or directly relate to sacred institutions and traditions; and second, in speaking about consciously anti-traditional values and attitudes. To address these issues, I will look at them through the lens of "how-to" books and pamphlets that instructed small but substantial Jewish audiences in the ways of the world.

What this involves is not a study of culture in a static sense, but the dynamics of cultural change. We are dealing with a population that was undergoing culture shock. In its encounter with an alien environment, foreign values, and strange habits, that population came to internalize much of what it found in America and (to one degree or another) reshaped its life accordingly. But the conduits of cultural osmosis—apart from such obvious ones as schools and the press—are not easily identified. The examples to be cited in this essay may, therefore, shed some light on an ill-defined area of social history.

Finally, a few words need to be said about secular Jewish culture as a concept and as a historical phenomenon. In the period under study, secular Jewish culture was still in its heyday, buoyed up by the cultural optimism that characterized the pre-"death of ideology" era. The hallmarks of secularism were a critical stance vis-à-vis traditional norms (social and religious), and a pervasive individualism that sanctioned the idea of personal growth. Secular Jewish culture, in that period, was expressed in Hebrew and Yiddish, in America, in Europe, and in Palestine. The parameters of that culture were much wider than many today might credit, and ranged from the agrarian-utopian experiments of young workers in Palestine, to secular schools and youth clubs in Eastern Europe, to such artifacts as I shall be examining here.

539

What made all of this "Jewish" was clearly not what is conventionally understood as "Jewish content." The Jewishness, very often, was in the medium and the social context. Ben-Zion Liber noted, for example, that although he could easily have translated into Yiddish one of several books on the subject of sexuality, he felt that there simply was no book that precisely fit his purpose: "to address the viewpoint of the Yiddish reader, whose needs I understand so well." His work (*Dos geshlekhts lebn* [*Sex Life*]), therefore, was "especially written for the kind of Jew who would read such a book in Yiddish," and he dedicated it as "A gift to the Jewish people." Interestingly, Liber reports (in his foreward to the third edition) that it was only when he settled in America that the Jewish community became his chief arena of public activity, and it was only there, in the new Jewish metropolis of New York, that he learned Yiddish. He did so in order to be able to speak directly to this mass audience.[5]

As for translated materials (some of which will figure in this essay), these made aspects of Euro-American culture accessible to Jewish immigrant audiences. Though they may not rank with Yiddish classics in terms of cultural creativity, they nevertheless helped to determine patterns of Jewish cultural consumption and social behavior, and served to integrate Jewish with international cultural trends.

Forging such cosmopolitan links was, indeed, a prime function of secular Jewish culture. Typical of the readers' letters published in Liber's health journal, *Unzer gezund* (*Our Health*: monthly, 1910–1917), was one that criticized the local Jewish intelligentsia for or-

ganizing fine discussions on Ibsen and Nietzsche, but failing to organize "to clean the filth from the streets where they live."[6] Although
neither Ibsen nor Nietzsche qualify for the adjective "Jewish," the
immigrants' encounters with their ideas were undoubtedly Jewish encounters, filtered through the particular experience of uprootedness
and of life in the slums, and, indeed, undertaken in an effort to
transcend the squalor of tenement life. Secular culture, then, was an
agent of cultural change because it mediated between the particular
and the general.

Given how new, exciting, and different America was, it is no
wonder that immigrant Jews needed a "user's guide" in the form of
secular Jewish culture. But Ibsen and Nietzsche were hardly the most
challenging or even the most novel paths to be negotiated: such intellectual stimulation came right out of the Russian tradition. Far more
perplexing were the truly new, day-to-day challenges of private life.
Guidebooks were written on parenting, sex education and sexual hygiene, love, marriage, and polite behavior. In such matters many
immigrants were at a loss, in a double sense. Not only did they have
to find their way in new surroundings and cope with children raised
in an alien environment, but in many cases they had to do all of this
alone, without the cultural, social, and family support mechanisms
that had been available back home. This much is suggested by the
figures on Jewish immigration in this period, which show a pre-
ponderance of young adults and children.[7] Consider, especially,
the predicament of single immigrant girls, young women, and new
mothers, who had few people they could rely on for back-up and
guidance.[8]

It is true that neighborhood networks and the friendship-kinship
ties of the *landsmanshaftn*—fraternal hometown associations—could
function as surrogate families. But guidebooks such as Margaret Sanger's "What Every Girl Should Know" (in Yiddish translation) still
fulfilled a basic need and, therefore, found a ready market.[9] It was
published twice (1916 and 1921), and sold for thirty cents. Ben-Zion
Liber's *Unzer gezund* (superseded by *Rational Living*) reached some
four thousand subscribers in its first year, and could not keep up with
demand for reprints.[10] His book, *Dos geshlekhts lebn*, went through four
editions (1914, 1918, 1919, and 1927). On the topic of progressive
child-rearing and behavior modification, one could consult a Yiddish
translation of Herbert Spencer's *Education* (*Di ertsiung: gaystig, moralish,
un fizish*), that also went through two editions.[11] The nouveau-bour-
geois could turn to the popular writer Tashrak's *Etikette* (1912).[12] And
those who needed to conduct their private and social lives by mail, or
who wanted to impress someone with their mastery of formal English,

could use the model letters published in Alexander Harkavy's *Amerikanisher briefen-shteller* (*American Letter-Writer*: New York, 1902).

Lucy Dawidowicz once wrote about the wild sense of freedom that young immigrant Jews experienced in urban America: freedom from the limits and constraints of parental supervision, rabbinical chastisement, and social pressure.[13.] This heady freedom was surely as disorienting as it was intoxicating. Redefining codes of behavior and absorbing new social models and ground rules became part of a larger cultural reorientation, a process that was probably aided by guides and handbooks like the ones I shall discuss.

541

### SEX EDUCATION

The issue of sex education touched on a number of sensitive areas simultaneously. In the first instance, it was related to the desire to combat prostitution and reduce the spread of venereal diseases. The proliferation of the one, and the transmission of the other to unsuspecting wives, were held to be the products of an abysmal ignorance: "One reason why girls are driven to promiscuity is their utter lack of knowledge on sex and sexual relations."[14] Such ignorance was compounded by parents of adolescent boys and young men who encouraged their sons to seek "professional" sexual outlets, lest they fall victim to masturbation, nocturnal "pollutions," acne, and other alleged perils of unfulfilled manhood.[15]

But although these issues loomed large on the agenda of those who wrote and published sex education tracts, other matters were at stake, as well. To Ben-Zion Liber, sex education was but one point and a natural consequence of his overall program, which he announced in the form of a credo (published in the second edition):

> Greater freedom for the individual to develop his personality.
> Greater freedom for the child, at home and in school; an open and free education for children.
> If one wants to accomplish something in life, one must first of all live rationally and do all one can to prevent disease.
> Enlightenment and science should be disseminated as widely as possible.
> Thinking people should regulate the number of children they have.
> Never be enslaved by one's habits, theories, or principles; they can change if one's convictions change.[16]

Margaret Sanger, too, adhered to a broad social vision which, she felt, was pertinent to her discussion of sexual development and to the education of girls generally:

Women must finally understand that they are not just mothers—
they are people [in their own right], too. They are more than baby
machines. Women have been taught to believe that their only mission
in life is motherhood. . . . Today's woman is more fortunate. She is
gradually liberating herself from such outmoded concepts. . . .

Another word about sexuality and the economic problems of
our day: It is impossible to speak of prostitution, syphilis, etc. without
mentioning [that] . . . the world is going through a great crisis. The
entire edifice of our society is rotten. Capitalism is rotten. In today's
society young girls do not stand a chance of leading a pure life; youth
is unable to develop its physical capabilities [properly]. . . .

Women will take their fate into their own hands. Women are
the natural enemies of our rotten social order. All women must rise
up as one against the prevailing system that enslaves women sex-
ually. . . . We will declare war on the slavery that binds both men
and women—a war of life and death.[17]

542

In short, these authors looked at the matter of sex education as one
facet of a wide-ranging campaign to educate a new, liberated generation and to enlighten society at large. Sanger's pamphlet, therefore,
was a treatise on how to raise a modern, forward-looking American
girl—and herein lies its chief interest for us.

For instance, Sanger advocated a more open, equal, and friendly,
rather than authoritarian, parenting style. An unembarrassed and
educationally sound approach to children's questions on childbirth
and sexuality was predicated on establishing trust and mutual understanding between the generations.[18] This counsel, though obviously meant originally for English readers, bore added significance
(far beyond the specific point being made about sex education) for
immigrant mothers facing a very real generation gap with their children.

A somewhat similar (if more conservative) message comes across
to the Yiddish reader of Spencer's *Education*, in the sections dealing
with discipline, values, behavior, and parental authority.[19] The translator (a Dr. Morrison) noted that the entire subject of proper childrearing was often discussed in what he called "intelligent circles,"
radical circles in particular, in terms of the need for "free" (i.e., liberal)
education; but that precious little had been published in Yiddish on
the subject until then. Hence, he believed, many people would find
this book useful.[20]

Beyond building trust and friendship, it was the responsibility of
parents to be sensitive to the physical needs of growing youngsters.
Liber was fanatic on the subject of the benefits of fresh air and proper
ventilation. Alongside such aphorisms as, "The best cure for all disease
is social revolution," he warned readers of *Unzer gezund* to keep their

windows open, so as to ventilate their dank tenement apartments.[21] Sanger, too, urged parents of working girls to see to it that, after factory or shop hours, their daughters have the opportunity to run, play, dance, and exercise in the open air in order to counter the deleterious effects of the work environment on bone structure, circulation, and posture.[22] On a related subject, she strictly warned against wearing corsets, at least until age 21, because they could be harmful to the lungs, bone growth, and reproductive organs. "Every girl should consider the corset question very carefully, if she values her health."[23]

But above all, her pamphlet communicated to her readers an image of the robust, active American girl, raised to believe in and assert her independence and her own worth:

543

> Long ago girls were supposed to be delicate, fragile, with under-developed breasts and small appetites. Those days are past. Nowadays we understand that a girl must be physically strong, healthy, and energetic. Today's girl does not wish . . . to sit home all day, sewing and playing with dolls. Mothers no longer require this of them. . . . We no longer worry if a girl learns to swim, ride, play ball and shoot[!]. . . . She *should* not be inferior to boys, and she *is* not inferior. Happy is the girl born in this day and age, who can calmly contemplate her physical development.[24]

At the same time, Sanger reacted very strongly against any impulse to stifle or inhibit young women's desires for self-adornment and self-expression of any kind (music, poetry, flights of fancy, dreams of fame and romance, etc.). This was something she warned parents against, stressing the great value of the feminine aesthetics of the young. She also held it against social reformers that they, out of patrician and disparaging attitudes toward the working class, denounced as "frivolous" and wasteful the money spent by working women on clothes. "It is high time that the social reformers stop trying to correct all the ills of our world and instead pay closer attention to the injustices they themselves perpetrate."[25] That must have rung a bell or two in the immigrant quarter!

Sanger dwelled on the question of love (and its distinctness from mere physical attraction) and on the sound bases for enduring relationships between husbands and wives.[26] But she also had encouraging things to say to single women regarding their potential role in social movements and about the new professional opportunities opening up for them. These, she maintained, were creating chances for fulfillment outside the conventional wife-and-mother framework.[27]

As a pamphlet addressed primarily to mothers of adolescent girls and for the edification of single young women, "What Every Girl

Should Know" did not take up subjects that would be encountered only in literature addressed to married couples (and which, in any case, were liable to violate obscenity laws controlling distribution of such materials through the mail). Sanger did not, for example, discuss sexual intercourse per se, or touch on birth control—a subject that concerned her deeply. In 1916, the year her pamphlet was translated and published in Yiddish, she opened the first birth control clinic on the Lower East Side of Manhattan.[28]

544

The topic of birth control *was* addressed by Liber; indeed, planned parenthood and the promotion of smaller families was one of his chief interests.[29] Moreover, his book (in comparison with Sanger's pamphlet) was far more clinical and comprehensive, with 300 pages of text and illustrations. It addressed the anatomy of male and female reproductive organs, pregnancy and childbirth, "normal" sexual relations, masturbation, eugenics, love, sex education for children, various sex-related problems ("anomalies") and diseases, and medical charlatanism in the sex field.

It is, of course, difficult to know how such publications (and public lectures)[30] actually impinged on immigrant culture and society. Perhaps their influence was restricted to a specialized class of reader, defined by their "progressive" and secular outlook. Still, in view of the fact that a market did exist for such materials (and we can assume that the number of readers exceeded somewhat the number of copies sold), it is safe to say that here we can pinpoint one conduit along which cultural information, American social values, and "radical chic" passed into the immigrant community.[31]

While gauging how well such ideas were received and implemented may be difficult, reader response is one indicator. Some people were sufficiently bothered by questions related to pregnancy, childbirth, and sexuality to direct queries to the relevant authors and health authorities. Liber's *Unzer gezund* published readers' letters and also a column of Liber's answers to medical questions. These ranged over various health-related concerns, but a significant proportion dealt with sex education, sexual development, and sexual performance. Naturally, as Liber explained, only a small portion of readers' queries could be answered in print; he was inundated by mail, and selected only those letters he felt were representative or likely to interest others.[32] It is worth noting that, at least geographically, *Unzer gezund* seems to have reached a diverse readership. Letters came from, among other places, Montreal, Boston, Paterson (New Jersey), Philadelphia, Providence, Milwaukee, Chicago, Detroit, Lynn (Massachusetts), and Liberty (New York), as well as from New York City, from the national Jewish sanitarium in Denver, and even from Paris and from Russia.[33]

Health officials in New York, too, were in a position to assess the relative impact of such literature on the consciousness of the immigrant quarter. The medical adviser to the venereal clinic run by the city's Health Department reported (in 1914):

> For the past few months we have been somewhat mystified . . . by a certain class of cases which have come to us for advice. These cases all had a number of peculiarities: they were Hebrews, spoke English very indefinitely, had very up-to-date views on eugenics [and] . . . asked many other questions which I could not hope to answer. Upon inquiring further, I found that they had been reading a journal called *Unzer gezund*.[34]

545

An interesting light is cast on our American evidence by comparing it with Yiddish tracts on sex, marriage, and related subjects that were published in Poland. For one thing, literature that was available to Jews in New York in the 1914–1920 period appears to have become available to Jews in Warsaw only during the 1930s. For another, the European materials seem less concerned with prostitution, although promiscuity and venereal diseases are prominently dealt with. On the other hand, there seems to have been great concern with problems of male impotence and sexual performance generally.[35] Also of note is the fact that, in Poland as in New York, there was a certain amount of reliance on translated materials. Finally, the publications from Poland do not seem to derive from politically radical sources, in contrast to the American cases we have looked at.

These distinctions and comparisons aside, there is internal evidence in some of the publications from Poland that suggests the appearance of such literature in Yiddish was linked to a process of sociocultural change, comparable to the situation facing East European Jews who went to America. To take one example, which seems to be representative, Dr. G. Weber's book, *Dos geshlekhts lebn fun mener un froyen* (*The Sex Life of Men and Women*): The author contrasts the "clean-living" generations of the past with the "dissipated youth of today," asserting that modern youth began sexual activity much too early in life, with the consequence of impaired virility in middle age, unlike their grandfathers' generation.[36] Similarly, he notes that modern couples seemed far too preoccupied with the material aspects of marriage, to the neglect of the "spiritual side."[37] In addition, there are comments on the status of women in society, on women's employment, and on the respective roles of husbands and wives in household decisionmaking that clearly indicate a perception of change with regard to gender and social roles.[38] As for birth control, Weber called this "the most burning issue on the agenda today," given the concern of middle-class families for planning, forethought, and material status. Modern couples, he asserted, were reversing the time-honored priorities, placing sexual pleasure above procreation. Nonetheless, he refused to recommend, or even condone, any method of contraception, with the sole exception of the douche.[39]

Finally, it bears noting that what characterizes all the materials reviewed here—from Poland as well as from America—is their deadly earnestness. Throughout, there is barely a suggestion that sex is to be enjoyed. Whether discussing "normal sex," masturbation, or venereal disease, they tend to preach at and intimidate the reader, rather than simply inform. They are unrelievedly prescriptive and, overall, make for fairly dull reading.

546

## "THE ORDEAL OF CIVILITY" OR "*DOS PAST NISHT*"

Guides to social etiquette remind us that culture is not only related to ethnicity, but also to social class. Concern over propriety and conformity is conventionally associated with the middle-class ethic, although rather rigid codes of conduct are hardly the exclusive burden of those in the middle reaches of the social pecking order. The desire to know what is "the right way to behave" in any given social encounter is a function of unfamiliarity with certain situations and the fear of not being regarded as acceptable in particular social sets. That is, a need to learn a code of etiquette reflects social mobility or aspirations to rise on the social ladder.

That such guides should have been published by and for Jewish immigrants in this period is consistent with what we know about their social and economic mobility. They were already heading toward middle-class status, and they were unfamiliar with the ways "real" Americans behaved in society.[40] They were people in transition between the vaguely disreputable status of newcomers and the elusive goal of social acceptance.

Entrée into a new class and a new culture was not easily earned. Only mastery of the right gestures, passwords, choice of clothing, and eating habits could qualify one for membership. To "pass" as a native one had to know how to make the right signals.

The author of one Yiddish handbook on the subject, *Etikette*, was a popular author and well-known columnist in the Orthodox press, Israel Zevin, who went under the *nom de plume* of Tashrak.[41] He was well attuned to the nature of his audience:

> We often encounter people whose material standing . . . may not allow them to stick to all the niceties of fashion and worldly manners;

but their clean and tidy appearance, their innate respect for others, their care and attention to others' comfort, [their consideration] for women and older people, make so fine an impression that we recognize them as true gentlemen and ladies, even if they are hampered by the lack of a certain polish. With the proper knowledge they would surely be able to improve. That is the class of people who will find this book helpful.[42]

Tashrak points out that ideally, ethics and etiquette ought to go hand in hand; in modern society, however, it was necessary to be educated in the outward forms of civility, even if one happened to be naturally good-hearted and moral, so as to "avoid embarrassment."[43]

This field guide to good taste and good manners is incredibly detailed: from the proper form of a handshake to the art of conversation; from drinking and smoking etiquette to rules for train rides and ocean voyages; from the advisability of having clean fingernails to ballroom courtesies; from table manners to card playing; from the theater to the telephone. All possibilities are foreseen and accounted for. In addition, a full third of this 300-page tome is devoted to matters of love, marriage, and family life.

547

What ties Tashrak's book to the problem of acculturation and to the question of culture itself raised earlier is the fact that it is as much about the acquisition of culture as it is about social refinement. Civility is the master key not only to being a fine human being, but to being a fine American and "a credit to one's race." The desire to Americanize, "civilize," and otherwise make the immigrants appear "less Polish and more polished," is something that historians have most often associated with the German-American uptown Jewish establishment. This is patently an oversimplification. *Etikette* is a good example of Americanization at work at the grass roots level, within the immigrant community.

It is significant, for instance, that Tashrak began with two introductory sections: one, a collection of proverbs and parables on ethics and etiquette culled from the Talmud and ancient rabbinic lore; the other, "George Washington's Rules of Polite Conduct—Wise and Useful Rules Written by the Father of his Country, that Still Apply."[44]

Or, again, we can take his treatment of decorum in the synagogue—the concern for which is often attributed to the more Americanized Jews of the German immigration stream, but to which East European Orthodox middle-class immigrants (and especially the younger generation) were sensitive, as well.[45] Giving full credit where it was due, Tashrak commended the Reform temples for two things: first, for the dignity and decorousness of their services, which contrasted sharply with the unfortunate picture he drew of the typical downtown prayer hall; and second, for the creditable way Reform

Jews presented Judaism to their gentile neighbors and guests.[46] The good opinion of non-Jews, Tashrak argued, was not to be dismissed lightly; and it was something that Judaism deserved because it was a dignifying, sacred, and uplifting faith—though, to judge by the way some Jews took God's house for granted, this was sometimes difficult to discern.[47] The advice Tashrak gave was both Jewishly respectable and explicitly *American*:

> In America we enjoy all civil rights and freedoms. What does freedom mean? It means self-control, [it means] following the rules of common decency. The Talmud teaches us: "Who is truly respected? He who respects his fellow creatures," that is, all people. Whoever understands the concept of respect for others will understand how to behave correctly . . . in any social setting, but especially in . . . the house that is dedicated to the honor of God and the brotherhood of men.[48]

548

Self-control, tolerance, and following the rules—these were key elements of the civility that Tashrak found in America and hoped to promote in his own community. Thus, in his section on behavior at meetings and public gatherings we find counsel on "the obligation to listen to others," on the wisdom of keeping one's speeches short, on the duties of a president, and so on[49]—a subject of direct relevance to immigrant life, with its plethora of lodges, fraternal societies, and political groups.

Indeed, alongside its emphasis on socialization into American ways, familiarity with the special circumstances and sometimes unique features of Jewish immigrant life is one of the strong points of this book. Returning to the section on the synagogue, the reader finds rules for non-believers who might have occasion to visit a house of prayer—a not unusual occurrence in the complex world of the Jewish immigrant. The "freethinker" was urged to behave like a "gentleman" and a guest, to refrain from open mockery or inappropriate clowning. "Even if he does not keep God's commandments, he can still show that he is a decent human being."[50]

It has been suggested that Anglo-Saxon civility, which was basic to the fabric of American culture, was especially foreign to the Jew newly arrived from Eastern Europe, precisely because of its differentiation between inner feelings and outward expression—with a premium placed on the latter.[51] Tashrak pointed out this distinction to his readers, but in mediating between rabbinic ethics and American etiquette he attempted something of a synthesis. Etiquette, he claimed, was the natural "daughter" of ethics, being based on the morality of "Do not do unto others what you would not have done unto you."

The greatest gentleman he ever met, he said, had been an impoverished, small-town schoolteacher (*melamed*). His point throughout is that the exterior forms of refinement should reflect sincere inner sensitivity—not mask a coarse interior. As far as he was concerned, people who certainly looked *salonfähig* could be "utter boors" in private, and thus miss the essential point. The title of "lady" or "gentleman" had to be earned through nobility of character.[52]

Of course, the standards of behavior that applied were taken directly from the values of the American milieu. The "real American" was a master or mistress of moderation and restraint, understated rather than ostentatious, never flashy, intense, or loud. Elegant eveningwear might convey a superficial impression of sophistication; but a woman with a shrieking laugh, no matter how well dressed, immediately gave away the fact that she was "no lady" ("*a proste yente*").[53]

Although appearances could, thus, deceive, correct dress was still an important component of good taste. The stress here is on three elements of self-presentation: neatness, color coordination, and sensible—rather than faddish—style. Everyone, even those who could not afford new clothes, could take the time to use a clothes brush before going out, our author admonished his reader. There was no excuse for slovenliness.[54] As for color and style, Tashrak tried to impress his female audience, especially, with the distinction between plebeian taste and crass parrotting of the latest fashion craze, on the one hand, and "real American" sophistication, on the other. "Good taste is an art, and it takes talent to dress well."

> It is actually among the poorer classes that women blindly follow the dictates of fashion. . . . It is well known that affluent American women prefer very simple clothing—of the finest fabrics, to be sure—and they are never the first to jump at a new style. . . . It is awful what poor taste most Jewish girls have. Consider the garish colors you can see on a Saturday or a holiday on Jewish streets. Any man with an ounce of taste can only shudder at the way girls and young women—who may be otherwise quite attractive—ape the latest fashions. . . . If fashion decrees that women should wear red [this season], does it follow that a woman with red hair and freckles must dress in a color that makes her look like a scarecrow?[55]

It should be noted that what we are dealing with, here, is obviously a stage at which European garb had already been exchanged (in the younger set) for American clothing; Tashrak was hoping to take this one step further.

Given the heavy involvement of immigrant Jews (both men and women) in the needle trades, it is hardly surprising that they, of all

549

people, were keenly aware of the latest trendy styles. The point Tashrak was making is that a little knowledge could be a dangerous thing.
To aid those without a trained eye, he included a guide to "harmonious color combinations." He also advised on the proper clothes for
young girls, for elderly matrons, for the businesswoman, and for
maternity wear. Similarly, he addressed the questions of jewelry, per-
fume, and makeup, and the issue of how to spend money on clothes.[56]
Finally, on the ubiquitous "corset question," he gave his qualified
approval:

> A corset, if it is the right kind, made out of good material and well
> constructed, and if it is not too tight-fitting, is healthy to wear, quite
> apart from the fact that it smooths the figure, makes a woman look
> slimmer . . . and improves her looks. Nowadays there are scientifi-
> cally designed corsets, known as "common sense corsets." There are
> even special corsets that may be worn quite safely by pregnant
> women.[57]

As already noted, a significant part of Tashrak's book is devoted to
love, marriage, and family relations. It is worth pointing out that
romantic love, as a social norm, was relatively new for East European
Jews, and any advice on the subject was bound to reflect the adoption
of standards and points of view from non-Jewish cultures.

The uninitiated were thought to be easily tripped up by the attendant dangers and pitfalls of romance, and therefore needed to be
cautioned.[58] As for gender roles and ideals, Tashrak tended toward
the Victorian: the gentle but manly and assertive male, and the educated, refined, practical and reliable, but modest, female.[59] He also
gave pointers on the etiquette of betrothals, receptions, and weddings,
and on relating to in-laws. In this connection, he also returned to the
question of "freethinkers," and dealt with the issue of marriages that
joined religious and non-religious people[60]—something that was not
a rarity in immigrant Jewish society. Secularization was a major component of the immigrant experience and deeply affected patterns of
acculturation.

Turning to parenting, our author-advisor took his point of departure from the child-centeredness of the Jewish family, on the one
hand, and the crucial early childhood experiences that would determine socialization, on the other. He emphasized the importance of
play and of imagination, the child's need for playthings and art sup-
plies, and the short attention span of young children.[61] At the same
time he advocated orderliness, firm guidance to discourage negative
behaviors, strict attention to cleanliness, and punishment for lying.[62]

In light of the problems facing immigrant families in the area of parental authority, it is worth noting how Tashrak tried to deal with this issue, which he thought was a matter of projecting confidence, stability, and character:

> Parents' chief responsibility is to demonstrate their worthiness to exercise authority. They should never reveal to the child the unhappy side of life. They must not let on to their children if there is anything amiss between them. They must never utter words that children should not hear. They should set an example.[63]

As in the case of sex manuals, it should be pointed out here, too, that there were also East European etiquette guides, and even something of a tradition behind them. A very early example was a Hebrew work by Fayvl Shiffer, called *Mehalkhim 'im anashim* (*How to Conduct Oneself with People*: Warsaw, 1866). It covered, in brief, some of the same aspects of social relations that we find in Tashrak's book, including relations between men and women, husbands and wives, parents and children—though Shiffer's perspective and cultural ambience were, of course, quite different. There is even a satirical work that parodied the posturing Jewish social climbers of the day: *Der mode ustav* (*A Course in Fashionableness*: Warsaw, 1894), by Be"Z. These works, in turn, were modern, secularized reincarnations of even older forms of ethical conduct literature and social criticism, known as *musar* books.

551

Finally, a contemporary work fully parallel to Tashrak's guide was *Gutte ziten un shehne manieren* (*Proper Conduct and Fine Manners*: Warsaw, 1930), by G. Whiteman. Like its American counterpart, this book was clearly intended for the novice. In the present context it is impossible to go into a textual comparison between the two books, although a close examination would doubtless reveal interesting contrasts, as well as similarities in bourgeois etiquette in the Old World and the New.

It is a fallacy to regard East European Jewish society as socially naive and homogenized: as one big *shtetl*, without a code of its own to define proprieties and outward formalities, class-based rituals and transactions, and subtle distinctions of status conveyed by details of attire and grooming.[64] The immigrants to America did not suddenly discover the importance of civility or style; rather, as they thought about moving into a different social class and began to make themselves over in a more "American" image, they needed to decipher and learn an intricate new choreography.

CONCLUSION

The importance of "culture" with a small "c" for social history is no longer a novel idea. In offering this small contribution to American Jewish social history, the main point I wish to make is that we ought not to overlook potentially rich sources of information.[65]

The problem, of course, is that we risk overlooking them only because we would never think of searching for them, if our own view of Jewish culture is blinkered or truncated. Yiddish sex manuals and guides to etiquette hardly fit the categories conventionally used to define Jewish culture; but once encountered, their existence makes eminent sense. To think of Jewishness as something limited by institutional, ethno-political, or religious definitions, is to rule out automatically a rich vein of cultural media and experience whose Jewishness derives more from context than from content.

Along with the reservoir of knowledge we already have, such media can aid us in coming to grips with the main issues we face when we ask ourselves about processes of social transformation.

HEBREW UNIVERSITY OF JERUSALEM

NOTES

*Research for this essay was generously supported by a grant from the Institute of Contemporary Jewry of the Hebrew University of Jerusalem.

1. Ben-Zion Liber, "Fizishe kultur," *Yidishe kultur*, March 1955, pp. 37–39. Liber, who immigrated to the United States from Romania in 1904, was a medical doctor with political ties to socialist, Zionist-socialist (Poale Zion), and anarchist groups. He wrote prolifically and lectured widely on public hygiene, vegetarianism, art, and education until his death in 1958 in New York City, where he was associated with the New York Psychiatric Institute and was professor emeritus of psychiatry at the New York Polyclinic Medical School. At his death he was eulogized by *Yidishe kultur*, in the inimitable style once perfected by *Pravda*, as "[a man] who was well-known and much beloved among the broad working masses" (*Yidishe kultur*, June–July 1958, p. 58). See: Ephraim Auerbach, *et al* (eds.), *Leksikon fun der nayer yidisher literatur* (New York, 1963), Vol. 5, cols. 53–54; Zalman Raizin, *Leksikon fun der yidisher literatur* (Vilna, 1927), Vol. 2, cols. 117–119.

2. Liber, "Fizishe kultur," p. 37.

3. I. J. Singer, *Of a World that is No More* (New York, 1971), pp. 124–125, as quoted in Roskies and Roskies, *The Shtetl Book* (New York, 1975), pp. 298–299.

4. I understand that a major project on the cultural impact of Ameri-

canization on immigrant women is currently being undertaken by Hannah Kliger and Barbara Schreier, both of the University of Massachusetts. Dr. Kliger presented a paper on Yiddish etiquette manuals at the Tenth World Congress of Jewish Studies (Jerusalem, August 1989).

5. Liber, *Dos geshlekhts lebn* (New York, 1918), p. 13, and "Foreword" to the 1919 edition.

6. *Unzer gezund*, No. 3, 1910, pp. 213–214.

7. Simon Kuznets, "Immigration of Russian Jews to the United States: Background and Structure," *Perspectives in American History*, Vol. 9 (1975), pp. 94–100. Among Jews immigrating between 1899 and 1914, 24.4 percent were under 14 years old, 69.8 percent were between age 14 and 44, and only 5.8 percent were age 45 and over. In 1913, 28.8 percent of all Jewish arrivals were single adults (HIAS, *Annual Report 1913*, p. 56 [Table 3]).

8. Figures on the arrival of unaccompanied women were compiled by representatives of the Hebrew Sheltering and Immigrant Aid Society (HIAS). Figures for the year 1913 showed that a total of 16,093 "unaccompanied Jewish girls" had arrived in the United States (at five major ports—most of them in New York: 13,588)—constituting a quarter of all female Jewish immigrants. Of these, nine thousand (56 percent) were met by family members; 6,533 (40.6 percent) were met by other relatives; and 555 were met by friends or intended husbands (3.4 percent). HIAS, *Annual Report 1913*, pp. 56 (Table 3), 60 (Table 16).

553

For the first five months of 1914, a total of 4,813 (28.7 percent of all arriving Jewish females) were in the "unaccompanied" category. Of these, 55.9 percent were met by family members, 41.2 percent by other relatives, and 2.9 percent by friends or intended husbands. *Jewish Immigration Bulletin* Vol. 4, No. 7 (July 1914), p. 9 (Table 11).

These women were carefully classified and tabulated according to countries of origin, ports of departure, ports of entry, month of entry, state and city of destination, and amount of money shown on arrival.

The isolation of the immigrant woman from home and family, and the attendant need for other sources of advice and guidance in such matters as love, marriage, and parenting contributed to the usefulness of advice columns in the Yiddish press. This point is stressed by Maxine S. Seller, "Defining Socialist Womanhood: The Women's Page of the *Jewish Daily Forward* in 1919," *American Jewish History*, Vol. 76, No. 4 (1987), pp. 429–431.

9. "Vos yedde meydl darf visn," 71 pp., translated from the English by K. Tepper, published by the Max N. Maisel Press for Literature and Knowledge, at 424 Grand Street on Manhattan's Lower East Side.

10. *Unzer gezund* No. 4, 1911. *Unzer gezund* was sold to subscribers at the rate of ten cents per monthly issue, or one dollar a year. The printing cost per copy came to twenty-five cents each for a press run of one thousand copies; twenty cents each for a press run of two thousand. Liber sold out his entire press run of the first issue which (if the ten-cent charge is a proportional reflection of printing costs) can be estimated at four thousand copies, and he received many requests for reprints (No. 4, 1911, p. 286). Liber's first edition of *Dos geshlekhts lebn* (1914) was also sold out within the first few months. See "Foreword to the second edition," p. 12.

11. Also the work of the Maisel Press, the book appeared in 1910 and 1911.

12. Hebrew Publishing Co., also a Lower East Side enterprise.

13. Lucy Dawidowicz, "From Past to Past," *Conservative Judaism*, Vol. 22, No. 2 (1968), pp. 24, 26.

14. Sanger, "Vos yedde meydl darf visn," p. 5. See also Liber, *Dos geshlekhts lebn*, p. 33. On the salience of the prostitution problem in urban America and in the Jewish community in particular, see: Edward Jay Bristow, *Prostitution and Prejudice: The Jewish Fight Against White Slavery, 1880–1939* (Oxford, 1982), pp. 146–180, 220–225, 233–235; Jenna Weissman Joselit, *Our Gang: Jewish Crime and the New York Jewish Community, 1900–1940* (Bloomington, 1983), pp. 45–53; Arthur Goren, *New York Jews and the Quest for Community* (New York, 1970), pp. 139ff.; Judith L. V. Joseph, "The Nafkeh and the Lady: Jews, Prostitutes and Progressives in New York City, 1900–1930," Ph.D. dissertation, State University of New York at Stony Brook, 1986.

15. Liber, *Dos geshlekhts lebn* (1918), pp. 29–33. The physiological necessity for young men to have sexual relations was "one of the first things a young man learns" (*ibid.*, p. 32). This passage was deleted from the 1927 edition, at the behest of the U.S. Post Office.

16. *Ibid.*, pp. 19–20. See also the foreword to the 1919 edition. Other points in Liber's credo included: "The Jewish people will be free only when it lives in Eretz Israel on such a basis that no capitalist institutions will exist there. . . . More art for everyone, and greater artistic freedom. . . . All religions are dangerous and are an obstacle to progress and freedom. . . . People with any sense of justice should not eat meat. . . . With enough determination, it is always possible to avoid bloodshed."

17. Sanger, "Vos yedde meydl darf visn," pp. 70–71.

18. *Ibid.*, pp. 6, 9. See also Liber, *Dos geshlekhts lebn*, p. 32, 135ff., 146–147.

19. Spencer, *Di ertsiung*, pp. 182–188.

20. *Ibid.*, translator's introduction. Yiddish works on the subject appeared somewhat later: e.g., H. G. Salutsky's *Gaystige ertsiung fun kind* (New York, 1920).

21. "One of the first principles of a modern education ought to be: the child must be taught the benefits of following the rules of proper health habits, so that the need for fresh air becomes ingrained in him. . . . Radical parents—remember this!" *Unzer gezund* No. 3, 1910, p. 167; cf. *ibid.*, pp. 170, 117–179, 187ff.

22. Sanger, "Vos yedde meydl darf visn," p. 12. Exercise and lots of outdoor physical activity was also recommended as a way to tire girls out before bedtime, which would minimize the risk of masturbation (*ibid.*, pp. 31–34).

23. *Ibid.*, pp. 10–11. See also the cartoon about corsets in *Unzer gezund* No. 3, 1910, p. 171.

24. Sanger, "Vos yedde meydl darf visn," p. 10.

25. *Ibid.*, pp. 15–17.

26. *Ibid.*, p. 36.

27. *Ibid.*, p. 36–37.

28. Seller, "Defining Socialist Womanhood," pp. 433–434. Cf. Mari Jo Buhl, *Women and American Socialism 1870–1920* (Urbana, 1981), p. 276.

29. Liber, *Dos geshlekhts lebn*, pp. 14, 159ff., 180ff. Sections on birth control were banned by the Post Office and deleted from the 1927 edition.

30. E.g., Liber's lectures on childbirth and on "parents, children, and physical hygiene," in New York in January 1911, and on "normal sex life" and "sexual diseases" in Boston, later the same month: *Unzer gezund* No. 4, 1911, p. 287.

31. There is some anecdotal evidence available on the popularity of Margaret Sanger among young Jewish women in New York: see Neil M. Cowan and Ruth Schwartz Cowan, *Our Parents' Lives: The Americanization of Eastern European Jews* (New York, 1989), pp. 170, 172, 183.

32. *Unzer gezund* No. 4, 1911, p. 278.

33. One of Liber's correspondents was Emma Goldman, who supported his efforts (see No. 4, 1911, p. 282).

34. Printed in the front matter of the second to fourth editions of *Dos geshlekhts lebn*.

35. E.g., Ivan Bloch, *Dos geshlekhts lebn fun unzer tsayt* (Warsaw, 1934–1936); G. Weber, *Dos geshlekhts lebn fun mener un froyen* (Warsaw, 1936); *idem.*, "Kreftungs-mitlen in geshlekhts lebn" (pamphlet: Warsaw, n.d.); Reinhold Gerling, "Der mansparshoyn mit velkher [*sic*] men tor nisht khassene hobn," and "Dos meydl mit velkher men tor nisht khassene hobn" (Warsaw, 1928); H. Grinboym, *Di bavustzinike shvangershaft* (Warsaw, 1937); G. Vandeli, *Vi azoy dergreykht men erfolg in der libe?* (Warsaw, 193?); T. Veld, *Libe un hayrat* (Warsaw, 1930); Emil Jason, *Dos seksuele lebn bay mener un froyen* (Warsaw, 1934); B. Mannheim, "Vi azoy farhit men zikh fun onanizm" (Warsaw, 1934); Alexander Parczewski, *Moreh nevukhim: menlikhe geshlekhts-shvekhe iz a kultur-krankhayt fun unzer tsayt* (Warsaw, 1937); Lev. S. Friedland, *Vegn vos me redt nisht: notitsn fun a doktor vegn geshlekhts laydn* (trans. from Russian: Warsaw, 1931).

36. Weber, *Dos geshlekhts lebn fun mener un froyen*, pp. 9–10; "Sadly, these days only a small proportion of young men are chaste until their wedding night" (p. 52).

37. *Ibid.*, pp. 29–30. One consequence of the preoccupation with material concerns was the postponement of marriage, especially among men. Weber recommended that women marry between age 21 and 26, and that men marry between ages 27 and 31. He noted that the actual average age at marriage among middle class couples was 26 for women and 30 for men. Among working class couples, the respective ages were lower.

38. *Ibid.*, pp. 30–32, 44–45, 92–96.

39. *Ibid.*, pp. 71–76. A more helpful attitude may be found in a TOZ (Jewish Health Organization) pamphlet, "Yidishe froy, dervakh! vi azoy zikh tsu farhitn fun umgevunshener shvangershaft" ("Jewish Women, Awake! How to Prevent Unwanted Pregnancies": Lemberg, 1934).

40. Thomas Kessner, "The Selective Filter of Ethnicity: A Half Century of Immigrant Mobility," in David Berger (ed.), *The Legacy of Jewish Migration: 1881 and its Impact* (New York, 1983), pp. 172, 178. Between 1880 and 1905, the share among Russian Jewish heads of households of those who were employed in upper white collar jobs rose from 5.2 to 15.1 percent, and those

555

in lower white collar jobs rose from 15.8 to 25.1 percent. Among their off
spring, 58.1 percent filled white collar jobs in 1925.

41. Israel Joseph Zevin (Tashrak) immigrated to the United States from
Russia in 1889, at the age of 17. He edited and wrote for two Orthodox
Yiddish newspapers in New York, the *Tageblatt* and the *Morgen Journal*; many
of his popular articles appeared in the latter paper's "Home and Family"
column. In addition, he wrote numerous short stories and feuilletons, mostly
humorous vignettes about immigrant life in America, and also wrote com-
pilations of *midrash*. He continued his association with the Orthodox community, serving as a warden (*gabbai*) in an Orthodox synagogue. See Raizin,
*Leksikon*, Vol. 4, cols. 902–912.

42. Tashrak, *Etikette*, pp. 36; cf. *ibid.*, pp. 14–15.

43. *Ibid.*, p. 36.

44. *Ibid.*, pp. 26–30.

45. Jeffrey Gurock points out the importance of this issue to the young,
American-raised Orthodox Jews of Harlem when they set out to found their
own synagogues in the early years of the twentieth century. "The organizers
of [Congregation Shomre Emunah] promised services conducted according
to 'Orthodox ritual in an impressive, decorous manner.' They pledged to
their prospective American constituency that the unsightly noise, commotion
and blatant commercialism that attended the immigrant landsmanshaft congregation would find no place in the up-to-date Orthodox synagogue." See
his book, *When Harlem Was Jewish* (New York, 1979), p. 117.

46. Tashrak, *Etikette*, pp. 114–118.

47. *Ibid.*, p. 114. Among his criticisms of the Orthodox immigrant *shul* or
*beis medresh* (*beit midrash*) were the following: gossip, business discussions and
joking during services, disorder (people sitting down and standing up to their
own rhythm), the lack of English-speaking ushers, and the frequently dirty
appearance of prayer shawls. "Cleanliness is godliness ("*getlikhkayt*") and courtesy is human decency ("*menshlikhkayt*")," he summed up (p. 118.)

48. *Ibid.*, p. 117.

49. *Ibid.*, pp. 107–113.

50. *Ibid.*, p. 117.

51. John Murray Cuddihy, *The Ordeal of Civility* (New York, 1974), pp.
12–14: "The differentiations most foreign to the *shtetl* subculture . . . were
those of public from private behavior and manners from morals. . . . Civility
requires . . . the bifurcation of private affect from public demeanor. . . .
'Niceness' is as good a name as any for the informally yet pervasively institutionalized civility expected—indeed, required—of members (and of aspir-
ant members) of that societal community called the civic culture. Intensity,
fanaticism, inwardness—too much of *anything*, in fact—is unseemly and bids
fair to destroy the fragile solidarity of the surface we call civility. . . . [Civility]
is not merely regulative of social behavior; it is an order of 'appearance'
constitutive of that behavior."

52. Tashrak, *Etikette*, pp. 15, 31.

53. I.e., coarse: *ibid.*, p. 33. Interestingly, the internalization of this middle
class American view of loudness has been noted in the Yiddish socialist press,
as well. See Seller, "Defining Socialist Womanhood," p. 436.

54. Tashrak, *Etikette*, p. 35.

55. *Ibid.*, pp. 42–43. American women, he asserted, were known the world over as the best dressed. Here, again, it is noteworthy that Tashrak's objections to loud dress and to excessive attention to fashion were also echoed in the *Forward*: see Seller, "Defining Socialist Womanhood," p. 434.

56. Tashrak, *Etikette*, pp. 44–63, 248–249, 303–307.

57. *Ibid.*, p. 305.

58. *Ibid.*, pp. 145–155, 170–171, 176–181, 238–245, 307–310. On divorce, see 263–271. On the perils of love, see also Seller, "Defining Socialist Womanhood," pp. 429–430.

59. Tashrak, *Etikette*, pp. 155–168, 228–238.

60. *Ibid.*, pp. 196–228.

61. *Ibid.*, p. 249.

62. *Ibid.*, pp. 252–256.

63. *Ibid.*, p. 254.

64. Cuddihy (*The Ordeal of Civility*, p. 14) makes this error, and approvingly quotes Irving Howe's poetic assessment of *shtetl* life: "Having love, they had no need of politeness" (Howe, "Sholem Aleichem: A Voice of Our Past," *A World More Attractive: A View of Modern Literature and Politics* [New York, 1963], p. 215).

65. I myself stumbled over this material by chance, spotting Liber's book at a used book sale.

# Jewish Mothers and Immigrant Daughters:
# Positive and Negative Role Models

SYDNEY STAHL WEINBERG

MALE REMINISCENCES and novels have created familiar stereotypes of the domineering "Jewish mother" and the struggle of sons for independence. This study suggests that such descriptions do not as readily apply to relationships between immigrant mothers and daughters.[1] The view presented here has grown out of an intensive oral history project, supplemented by traditional research in memoirs and autobiographies. The oral histories explore the lives of forty-six women who left Eastern Europe for the United States by 1925 and were old enough when they emigrated to have some memory of their early home.[2] These women differed in their area of birth, social class and circumstances of departure.[3] Yet they had much in common. Despite the dislocations involved in entering a highly industrialized society, most of them emphasized the importance of their mothers as role models of some kind. The majority also felt that their order of birth and age at time of immigration determined relationships within their families.[4] Almost all the women interviewed shared the belief that one or both of these factors exerted a significant effect upon their lives.

Dora W., for example, believed that she had come to America at just the right age. As the third child and second of three daughters who had emigrated with her parents when she was eight years old, Dora felt that her relationship with her parents was better than that of her sisters because of her particular situation. "We were once in my house, my sisters and I," she recalled, "having discussions of older times. We spoke about our parents, and it was fascinating. You would think that the three of us had different sets of parents. And maybe we did. You wouldn't recognize *my* parents from what my older sister said or what my younger sister said." Dora went on to explain why she and her sisters held such diverse impressions. Her older sister hated her father for taking her away from Russia at fifteen, leaving behind school, a boyfriend, and a familiar life. A sensitive and educated girl, she was too old for school in America and had to work in a garment shop where she was miserable. As the oldest daughter, she also bore heavy responsibilities for helping her mother at home.

559

Originally published in *Journal of American Ethnic History* (Spring 1987). Reprinted by permission of Transaction Publishers.

When she wanted to go out with friends or keep some of her salary for herself, her father refused to permit such liberties. She never managed to "Americanize," or to do the next best thing—marry an American man—and she blamed her father for her unfulfilled life. Dora's younger sister resented her parents for a different reason. She was born in America and shared the unfortunate trait of some American-born children—shame at being part of a foreign-born family. As the youngest, she was a favorite of her father and mother, but she wanted them to be like the parents of her American friends and felt embarrassed by their poor home on Manhattan's Lower East Side.

560

Dora, however, believed that she had "the best of both worlds." She remembered enough of her life in Russia to appreciate the difficulties her parents faced in leaving and creating a new life in America. Dora understood that they had done this for the sake of their children, and she felt that she had benefited from their decision more than her sisters. She had attended school here, as her older brother and sister could not, but she still had to make the effort to learn a new language and way of life, which her American-born sister took for granted. Thus, as poor as her family was, Dora knew that life was going to be better in America than it would have been in Russia; she always felt that she was "upward bound."

The sisters' differences in age shaped attitudes towards their parents and led to very different life experiences. Dora's eldest sister remained within the immigrant culture, while the youngest blamed her mother and father's foreign ways for preventing her from being accepted as "a real American." Dora believed that she alone had successfully bridged the gap between cultures and felt comfortable with both her European origins and her life in America.

Birth order was also crucial in determining a daughter's responsibilities in the home. Generally, older daughters were expected to act as their mothers' chief assistants in caring for the home and younger children. Particularly when families were poor, the daily struggle to put food on the table placed heavy burdens on these girls. Many older daughters felt overworked by their duties, cooking and cleaning and watching over their siblings. Some even took charge completely while their mother was out earning a living. "I had no freedom," asserted Rose G., echoing the statements of others, "no childhood at all." These women believed that their brothers had easier lives. Although boys, too, might leave school at a young age to work, their childhood years were relatively free of family obligations. Few attended day-long Hebrew schools, as they would have in Eastern Europe,[5] nor were they expected to help with the household chores and younger children. "My brother really enjoyed his life," recalled Fannie C. "I had all the responsibilities."

These attitudes are reflected in the different perceptions of their mothers' kitchens recorded by the sons and daughters of this generation. For boys, it was a refuge where they were coddled guests. In the memories of sons, the mother's performance of her chores assumes an almost mystical quality, as in Sholem Asch's *The Mother*, where in an impoverished family, "Sarah Rifke turns to her magical cooking pots to provide for her family. She could milk her pots as though they were cows. They never denied her anything. She gave them cold water and the pots yielded yesterday's carrot soup anew. . . . When the pots heard mother sigh it was as though she had repeated a secret incantation over them with which she adjured them to supply the pitifully meager bit of nourishment which was all she demanded for her large brood."[6] Alfred Kazin described his mother's sabbath preparations in a similar manner. "By sundown," he wrote, "the curtains had been drawn, the world put to rights. Even the kitchen walls had been scrubbed and now gleamed in the Sabbath candles. On the long white tables were the company dishes." Kazin's mother accomplished her tasks without effort, almost magically. "When my father came home from work," he recalled, "she had somehow mysteriously interrupted herself to make supper for us, and the dishes cleared and washed, was back at her machine."[7] This was a woman's world, viewed through a romantic haze created by a complete lack of experience with the efforts it took.

561

Girls knew that it was hard work rather than magic that put food on the table. Because of the different roles mothers played in the lives of their male and female children, girls' perceptions of their mothers' chores were more precise than the descriptions recorded by sons. For older daughters, the family kitchen was a school and workshop where labor seldom ceased. Fannie C. remembered that her mother "was busy the whole day long. She was an immaculate housekeeper—she used to sew too. She made all my clothes. She always had people in, and she did everything herself. For Friday, she got up early to bake the challah [sabbath bread] and the little cakes. Then she would make the gefilte fish and roll out dough to make the noodles." Before she was old enough to go to school, Fannie learned to help with these tasks. Anzia Yezierska, a well-known writer in the 1920s, provides a less rosy but equally graphic description of her mother, who "dried out her days fighting at the push-carts for another potato, another onion into the bag, wearing out her heart and soul and brain with the one unceasing worry—how to get food for the children a penny cheaper."[8] In their mother's lives, daughters saw with fear or anticipation what they themselves might become.

If sons generally held a favored position in the family, youngest children, even if they were girls, also had an easier time than their older siblings. They often escaped most household chores and there were no younger children for them to care for. As the baby, they were frequently spoiled by parents or older sisters. As Dora W. explained the relationship within her own family, her father had mellowed and was less restrictive when she was growing up than he had been with his older children. Her brother and sister had to fight for their privileges, while she was permitted more freedom without a struggle. Part of this change she credited to age, but part was also due to the respect her father had for his more Americanized child. Gussie M. similarly attributed her mother's closeness to her youngest child to a change in attitude after emigrating. In her village of birth, children had been expected from their earliest years to labor for the family, with few rewards or thanks—a system similar to that of working-class families throughout the western world in the nineteenth century, where parents considered children as "their own flesh, blood and labor supply."[9] When they came to the United States, however, Gussie's mother saw how people treated children—"with respect, with ice cream cones, and she learned." Her youngest daughter reaped the benefit.

Middle-class families in Europe and America, particularly in urban areas, were already treating young children *as* children rather than as an economic investment.[10] This did not mean that daughters no longer had obligations to the family, but rather that their efforts were often appreciated rather than taken for granted. If a daughter's work in the home or a factory was appreciated by her parents, it could provide a source of fulfillment and was not considered a chore. "I felt a great deal of responsibility towards my parents," observed Fannie C., "and I felt that they loved and appreciated me." Pauline H., who at fourteen had to keep house for her father and brothers, recalled with pride the words of praise she earned. "They used to say, '*A junge kindt un an alte kopf*,' [a young child with an old, or wise head]. Anna S., who ruined her health working to bring her parents to America remembers her mother thankfully saying "This is my daughter's miracle." Only when they were taken for granted did such women later resent their sacrifices.[11] In general, the closer the relationship, the more willingly did daughters assist their mothers, although all girls were expected to work in the home.

This relationship also helped determine a daughter's attitude towards contributing her wages to the family. In most western nations, this was

562

expected of working daughters,[12] and statistics indicated that girls contributed to a greater extent than their brothers.[13] A common refrain was "people were depending on me." Many women used the example of their mothers' selflessness to explain why they had been willing to work to help the family. Furthermore, despite the American emphasis on individualism, responsibility to one's family became a more generally accepted value after the onset of the Great Depression.[14]

Often older daughters helped support their families while brothers attended school,[15] but age just as frequently as sex determined whether a child attended school or went to work. In a Census Bureau survey of Jewish immigrants who were forty-five years and older in 1950, the men averaged 8.1 years of schooling and the women 5.8. But the years of education either sex achieved was low compared to their younger siblings. Among younger foreign-born Jews, twice as many boys as in the older group, but three times as many girls graduated from high school. Children who came to this country younger thus had a greater chance of receiving a high school education, and the difference in years of education between girls and boys is narrow. Among the American born men and women, many of whom were the youngest children of immigrant parents, the difference is insignificant.[16] Thus, although sons were initially favored slightly if a family could afford to permit only one of its children to remain in school rather than work, once financial security was established, younger children of both sexes had greater access to education than either their older sisters *or* brothers.

563

For older girls in particular, if the family needed their income, there were few options besides the factory. "We were the lost generation," observed Fannie K., who came to America at the age of twenty. "If we were born here, who knows what we could have been?" "I saved the family," recalled Anna S., who had worked steadily since she was fourteen, "but it almost killed me." These young women who had come too late to get an education themselves could sometimes cope with disappointment by transferring their desire for learning to the youngest child or children. Several women I interviewed went to high school and one even finished law school because older siblings had worked and insisted that they complete their education. They were aware of the sacrifices of these older sisters, and of their limited horizons regardless of talent or intelligence. "She was the oldest and I'm the youngest," mused Marie F., who became an opera singer. "It made all the difference in the world."

Apart from the order of their birth, an important influence on women's lives was the role their mothers had played in the family. Although many daughters became Americanized and most worked steadily before marrying they did not assume that a homebound mother was less important than a wage-earning father. In fact, the most common observation about a mother was that she was "a great manager," when managing meant everything from looking after their husband and children's needs to taking in boarders and doing piecework to controlling the family's expenditures—the key to most women's importance throughout urban society at that time.[17] The smooth functioning of the household thus depended on a wife's ability to "manage." Her sense of competence as well as her daughter's appreciation came from the ability—as one woman succinctly put it—"to make two pennies out of one." Rose G. remembered her mother "saving up the pennies she and her brother had earned—and every one counted. She used to say, 'My little bags will outlive other people's big sacks of money.' And they did, because she was very good at it." Women remembered such qualities and prided themselves on following their mothers' example. Rose L. recalled that "any money my husband had, he gave it to me. Thank God, like my mother, I was always a good manager."

These women learned from their mothers to place the well-being of their families before the demands of pride or status. Sometimes fathers became demoralized at having to accept a low-paying, low-status job in this country and never succeeded in earning enough to care for their families adequately. The wives of such men usually managed to keep food on the table by taking a temporary job or earning money in the home when times were hard. Status did not matter as much to these women. As Riva P. observed, for her mother, "the important thing was that the family be taken care of." Ethel B.'s mother worked in her husband's business and secretly put away a small amount of money each week. When the business failed during the Great Depression, she had saved $1,000 to start over. Rose G., who still works at eighty-six, remembered that her mother loved going out to work with her husband. "She was happy when she was needed and busy," Rose observed, "like I am too."

Some young unmarried daughters, athough very few in this survey,[18] had an ambivalent relationship with their mothers. One source of this ambivalence was based upon a subtle kind of rivalry. Although parents generally had emigrated so their children might lead an easier life, some mothers could not help but envy the opportunities which contrasted so vividly with their own limited lives. As a woman saw her daughter exceeding her in education, in adjusting to America, in possibilities for a satisfying life, the only advantage the mother held was in the performance of her housewifely duties. Thus, while she usually took pride in her daughter's

564

accomplishments, a mother might at the same time withhold the finer points of cooking or baking and would give her instead the less skilled tasks to perform in the home.[19]

Parents could also be ambivalent about their children's "American" ways. Some mothers and fathers made great efforts to learn the language—more Jewish adults than those of any other immigrant group attended night school.[20] A few refused to permit books written in any language but English into their homes. Even if they sought to retain old customs, most parents nevertheless seemed proud of their Americanized children. Several women, who were the youngest children in the family and therefore the most Americanized, commented upon this pride and observed that in their parents' eyes they could do no wrong. Yet sometimes the apparent requirements of "Americanization" created tensions within families. Conflict could erupt over a daughter's decision to work on the Sabbath, spend money on clothing, attend dances or union meetings in the evenings, go to movies, and in general, seek more freedom. Tanya N. had to leave home for a few days to avoid her father's wrath after she "bobbed" her long hair. Fannie C. resented her father's refusal to permit her to attend a high school prom with schoolmates. In many families, a daughter's desire to express her individualism, a trait fostered by American society, clashed with a parent's insistence on the primary importance of family needs or the assertion of patriarchal authority.[21] Urbanization and industrialization had altered life irrevocably, and a mother's homebound existence offered few clues to behavior in this new world. Girls would insist that parents did not understand them, and mothers could no more provide role models for these teenage daughters on the Lower East Side of New York than they could in the working-class areas of Bialystok or Odessa.[22] Some young women working in factories found an alternative focus to family life in union activities or in socializing with their peers. Those who did not work lacked this option and their lives were more restricted. Some even chose to work because of the greater freedom this would gain for them; one fourteen year old girl decided to take a job when her mother told her that only those who worked needed new clothes and shoes.

Despite such conflicts, mothers seemed less likely than fathers to impose their values upon daughters. The term "fanatical," frequently applied to a dictatorial father, was never used to describe a mother, no matter how religious she was. Furthermore, mothers often served the function of mediator—a bridge between the old ways and the new—or simply between a rigid father and a daughter (or son) desiring more free-

565

dom.[23] For example, when Dora W. got a good job requiring her to work on Saturday, her father refused to speak to her for a year, but her equally pious mother accepted Dora's wages and eventually secured a reconciliation. When the mother of Mildred L., a simple, devout woman, learned that her troubled daughter was attending a Christian Science church, she kept it from her husband and told the girl "if it's doing you good, it has to be good, and I want you to have it." Fannie K.'s mother, more religious than her father, accepted her daughter's lesser piety and helped hide from her husband the dresses Fannie bought lest he object to the unnecessary expense. Although mothers usually maintained their old country traditions, they generally accepted their children's signs of entry into the modern world more readily than fathers. These women perhaps could vicariously achieve through their daughters a freedom they were seldom permitted in Eastern Europe. Possibly they believed that their own traditions might prevent their children from assimilating and thus reaping the benefits of becoming Americans.[24] Perhaps they simply wanted to keep peace within the family. Regardless of the reason, mothers seemed to accept the Americanization of their daughters with relative equanimity.[25]

Although ambition to be anything but a wife and mother was not considered appropriate for young women of any ethnic background,[26] Jewish immigrant mothers, while accepting traditional roles for themselves, sometimes encouraged their daughters' ambitions, or at least passed on a mixed message. The mother of Marie F., for example, opposed her going on the stage, preferring that she be "safely married," but when her daughter proved adamant, they both moved to Chicago to help with Marie's career. When Sophie Abrams Flint, as a child, read until late at night, her mother would wake up and say, "The light is still on? What do you expect to be, a doctor or a lawyer? What's the use of all this reading and writing? Don't be foolish, a woman never needs to know anything!" But under her breath, Sophie would hear her mutter, "A talented child has hands of gold."[27] Despite the desire that their daughters marry, such mothers encouraged in them a sense of independence, sometimes without themselves being aware of it.[28]

Many mothers seem to have encouraged their daughters' desire for education in part because of their own thwarted ambitions or limited lives, and in part because they followed a time-worn tradition of wanting them to be self-supporting if necessary. Mollie Linker remembered her mother wanting something better for all her children, but especially for the girls,[29] and the mother of Hattie L., who made a career out of helping other immigrants get settled, was proud when her daughter became a nurse. In Abraham Cahan's *The Rise of David Levinsky*, Dora, an illiterate immigrant woman, lives her life through her daughter, whom she views with a combination of pride and envy. "My own life is lost," she thought, "but she shall be educated."[30] This was a common attitude. Riva P.'s mother, like Dora, used to berate her daughter when she did poorly in school and told her how lucky she was to be able to get an education. "If I were raised in this country," she told her repeatedly, "do you imagine what I would have become?" Very few mothers, though, would go as far as Kate Simon's did. "Study, learn. Go to college," she urged her daughter. "Don't get married, at least not until you can support yourself and make a careful choice. Or don't get married at all, better still."[31]

567

Even if a relationship between mother and daughter faced strains when a daughter was in her teen years, the tie usually became closer once the younger woman married.[32] Possible tensions arising from a girl wanting to date, buy clothing, or lead a relatively independent life were replaced by concerns similar to those of the mother: how to manage a home, deal with a husband, and raise children. Mothers and daughters now would share more interests. They could help each other with shopping, household activities and baby-sitting,[33] a connection common to women of other ethnic groups as well after a daughter's marriage.[34] At this point, young women could accept their mother as role models. Women who wanted their lives to follow a different path were still aware of the effect their mother exerted in forming their attitudes. "My life," asserted Rose Chernin, "you can only understand if you know my mother."[35]

Apart from learning housekeeping skills, many women had learned from observing their mothers how to make important decisions in their own homes while maintaining, for the sake of their husbands' egos, that these decisions were made by the men. Rose G., for example, insisted that she, like her mother, had continually deferred to her husband. "Louis," she remembered telling him, "please don't come down from your pedestal." In most cases, however, the creation of this male dominant role was a convenient fiction. Like Rose, Fannie C. asserted that her father made the decisions, but went on to explain that her mother had ways of getting what she wanted. "Many of the decisions my father made," Fannie concluded, "were really hers to start with. But as children we were under the impression that it was my father's decision." It was important that men *appear* to be the heads of the family, making all important decisions. The reality was somewhat different, as it was among other immigrant groups where it was important to maintain the public posture of male leadership.[36] In such families, the men were "ceremonial leaders," assuming credit for decisions the women convinced them they had made on their own.[37] One woman described how she had learned this strategy from her mother: "She lets him think he is boss but when anything really important comes up she usually handles it without letting him know she is doing it. When it is disposed of, he pats himself on the back and claims all the credit. And she lets him get away with it, never contradicts him. She tipped me off to that system when I got married and I guess that is why my husband and I get along so well."[38] These women were, as Frances F. put it, "the power behind the throne." Many women acted in this circumspect way to help maintain the egos of husbands who had difficulty adjusting to a low status and poorly-paid jobs. In their households, as in those of their daughters, solutions to most problems were based on the input of both parents rather than imposed by the father alone, regardless of outward appearances.[39]

568

The way women ran a home and raised their children were also affected by what they had learned from their mothers. More than half the women in this survey asserted that they had consciously followed their mothers' example in their own marriages. Like many others, Jennie H. and Mollie Linker kept Kosher homes more because their mothers did than because of religious conviction. "It's the heritage; it's embedded in me," Mollie explained. "I want my grandchildren to remember . . . just like my children remember what my mother did." Her mother, the backbone of the family, also taught her how to raise children—"Not to curse or raise the voice," and, Mollie insisted, she was "the best teacher."[40] Many other women also emphasized that they had learned how to bring up their children from their mothers. Sometimes the similarities between their attitudes or mannerisms and those of their mothers took them by surprise: Rose G. remembered as a child making fun of her mother praying for her children. "Now," she observed with amusement, "I'm doing the same thing."

Many women internalized their mothers' caring attitudes towards people. They insisted that they had learned to derive great satisfaction from helping others. Anna R. asserted that in this characteristic, she resembled her mother—a "people's person,"—the kind of woman who, as Irving Howe described his own mother, "blooms through sustaining others."[41] Anna and Janet A. learned from their mothers to keep an open house and an open heart to anyone in need, not because it was an obligation, but because "it was the way to be." Hattie L. remembered her mother, not yet able to speak much English, travelling to Ellis Island to meet other immigrants and help them get settled. "She had nothing," Hattie recalled, "but she had her work. She had gratification. She became a real social worker, and that's what she left with me—it must have rubbed off." Hattie herself became a psychiatric nurse. Quite possibly, these daughters also learned that such activities which made the home the focus of social life also enhanced their mothers' status in the family.[42]

A few women attributed a stoical acceptance of life's tribulations to their mothers' example. The mother of Fannie C. found life here more difficult than she had anticipated but ultimately accepted its limitations. She learned to seek satisfaction in her children, as did the mothers of Fannie G. and Riva P. who endured philandering husbands. Several women learned to face adversity with the saving grace of humor, as their mothers had done. Whenever she mispronounced an English word, Janet A.'s mother would laugh at herself instead of reacting with embarrassment, and went on with the arduous task of learning a strange language. The mother of Tanya N. also used humor to provide color to a drab existence. For example, a friend once asked her where she got all the sunflower seeds she liked so much. "I'll tell you," she replied. "When I scrub the floor, I also plant seeds between the boards. And in the summertime, I have sunflowers." "She was always imaginative," Tanya recalled. "Even when things were bitter, she never gave up. She understood her hardships and faced them with humor."

569

Among the majority of women who held such positive views of mothers, or felt that they had sacrificed for their children's welfare, relationships tended to be strong, with mothers often living near or with daughters after marriage. For example, Sara B., speaking of the nine years her mother had spent under her roof, observed that "I always felt that my mother was a *tsirung* in the house—something very beautiful and decorative." One woman, Minna S., instead of marrying, lived at home and cared for her mother devotedly until her death. Another, Rose S., married not as much to gain a husband, but in the futile hope of finding in her new mother-in-law a replacement for her dead mother—her "best friend." Sometimes the connection persisted despite the effects of distance. Louise C., who fled a life of poverty in Russia, remained close to her mother through their correspondence. On the very day Louise left for the hospital to give birth to her first child, a letter arrived from her mother to urge her "to have the courage to give birth." "In spite of the fact that you were an ocean apart," observed Louise, "the umbilical cord was never really cut. The tie was there."

In a few families, however, relationships between mothers and daughters were distant. This situation generally occurred when a daughter re-

jected her mother as part of the East European background she wanted to
shed, particularly when the parent was unwilling or unable to take any
steps towards Americanization, or at least towards understanding the
needs of a daughter who wanted to be "all-American." Shame at having an
obviously foreign parent, unfortunately, was not unusual,[43] although it
was seldom encountered in this survey. Some children were mildly embarrassed when parents came to school to speak to their teachers in inadequate English. Riva P. always felt that teachers looked down on her
parents because of their accent. And although she loved them, she remembered thinking often, "I wish they were American!" Children might feel
570     that they were judged by their parents. For this reason, in one of Anzia
Yezierska's short stories a young girl works to no effect to modernize her
dowdy, old-country mother. "I dressed her in the most stylish Paris models," she tells her brothers, "but Delancey Street sticks out from every inch
of her. Whenever she opens her mouth, I'm done for."[44] This more intense
kind of rejection was shared by a few women like Mildred L., who was
ashamed of her poor, illiterate mother and sought singlemindedly to dissociate herself from her and to become a "real American." She spent her
money on scented soaps and fashionable clothing and chose only American-born friends whom she refused to bring home to meet her parents.
"My growing up didn't do me any good," she stated, still passionate with
feelings of deprivation after more than fifty years, "because I had nobody
to learn from." Mildred had what sounds like a nervous breakdown at
sixteen, which she attributed to the strain of trying to escape from her
hated immigrant environment. Such daughters, as Sonya Michel has observed, may have suffered from a kind of identity crisis, because although
they rejected the behavior and personality traits of their mothers, they had
also internalized them and were therefore fearful of seeing these traits
emerge in themselves.[45]

Thus, in the few instances where a daughter rejected a mother, she
would still consider her as a role model, but a negative rather than a
positive example. "Everything that my mother did," asserted Gussie M.,
"I decided to do the opposite." One woman, an oldest daughter who had
to forego an education and stay home to help with the younger children
without any appreciation, branded her mother's methods and attitudes
"primitive" and swore to raise her own children in a more enlightened
way.[46] Another, who saw her mother broken by the constant battle for
survival was obsessed by the desire to lead a different and better life.
"Always I struggled," she recalled with passion, "never to be like mama."[47]

Despite such exceptions, most women felt close to their mothers and seem to have derived particular satisfaction from caring for them late in life. Jewish girls, and indeed girls of many ethnic groups, were socialized to assume such obligations, and there is little question that many achieved gratification from fulfilling what they perceived to be a filial responsibility.[48] After being widowed, the mother of Rose S. lived in turn with each of her three daughters, all of whom urged her to remain, but she refused to stay with her son and his wife. Hannah F. and her three sisters also fought over what they considered the privilege of caring for their mother, but again the brothers were not involved. Sons were expected to contribute financially to the care of an elderly parent, but this was the extent of their obligation. Their responsibility for a sister was even more limited. One dying mother told her devoted daughter that after her death the girl would be alone—a prophecy that became true—because her brother "is a man and will go his own way."[49] Women, not men, were expected to be the caretakers. When the mother of Rose G. was terminally ill with cancer, Rose left a good job to nurse her continuously for a year, with her brothers paying the bills and visiting every month or two. She remembered, as a child, her mother closing the eyes of her dead grandmother, and she felt privileged to do the same for her own mother. "It was no sacrifice," Rose insisted, for she had given this care not out of obligation, but because of the example her mother had set before her. "It was a natural thing to do," she explained, "because she was always so sweet and self-effacing." Occasionally, the mother-daughter relationship was cemented late in life by this apparent role-reversal—a daughter caring for her mother. Frieda M. observed that her mother "was never important to me until I had to take care of her. And then," she explained simply, "she was."

Although most daughters felt close to their mothers, even those who had been alienated gained insight into the older women's lives in their own mature years. The few women who believed their mothers had not loved them or treated them properly—all from very poor families—explained that they understood that their lives had been too bitter or harried to enable them the luxury of love. "My mother happened to be a selfish woman," observed Rose G. in discussing her own impoverished youth. But she went on to explain that her mother "had no real childhood" of her own and had suffered great deprivation that affected her attitudes. Jennie Herbst recalled her own mother's "caustic and sarcastic retorts" that often made her young daughter cry. "Love was never talked about," she remembered, "nor was there ever a gesture or intimation that such a thing existed between mother and child." Yet after Jenny married, she thought about her mother's sorry life "with pity and commiseration."[50] Even for these women, age brought reconciliation.

Thus, most women eventually seemed able to accept differences in values or behavior between themselves and their mothers[51] without simultaneously rejecting the parent. Perhaps one reason for this tolerance is that the majority of mothers had also accepted the values or behavior of their children although they may not have shared them. Relatively few relationships seemed to founder on the shoals of intergenerational strife.

Few immigrant mothers could offer their daughters advice on how to be Americans—how to speak properly, dress or behave—for in this country 572  as in the cities of Russia or Poland, the culture of young people was diverging from that of their parents. What young immigrant women *could* learn from their mothers, though, were the basic values and attitudes that would affect their lives as mature women, once the initial desire to "fit in" with American society was satisfied. Girls of every ethnic group learned from their mothers what it took to run a home properly. They saw their mothers shopping, baking, cooking, cleaning, sewing, managing the family's money and sometimes earning it themselves. They learned how to do the emotional housework of dealing with the psychological needs of husbands and children. These mothers set important examples for their daughters in understanding how to approach life and relate to their families and others. Although girls could learn individual values from fathers, from mothers they absorbed a whole system of values that would affect them profoundly as adults—in a positive way if the relationship was sound, and negatively in the few cases where it was not.

As members of a generation which emphasizes self-fulfillment, we might not easily understand the satisfactions of those who lived their lives for and through others. Like their mothers, the women of the immigrant generation, whatever their ethnic origin, were socialized to consider others before themselves. Older daughters in particular seemed to bear more responsibility than either brothers or younger children, and the order of a girl's birth and her age at time of emigration greatly affected her later life. It seems clear, though, that these Jewish immigrant daughters were profoundly influenced by their mothers' example of service and self-sacrifice. Yet they demanded something in return. These young women's attitudes toward their own sacrifices depended on the response of parents and siblings, and if their efforts were rewarded by an appreciative family, they, like their mothers, learned to achieve gratification from such a life. How these values are affecting the more varied lives of the next generation is an intriguing topic for further study.

## NOTES

1. Among recent writers to be concerned with such issues are Sonya Michel, "Mothers and Daughters in American Jewish Literature: The Rotted Cord," in *The Jewish Woman*, ed. Elizabeth Koltun (New York, 1976), pp. 272–82; Kim Chernin, *In My Mother's House* (New Haven, 1983); Eleanor Mallach Bromberg, "Mother-Daughter Relationships in Later Life," (Ph.D. diss., Columbia University School of Social Work, 1982).

2. Women I have interviewed are identified only by their first name and last initial to preserve confidentiality, and quotations from their testimony are not footnoted. The author's complete name is given for published or other open sources which are cited in footnotes.

3. The first fifteen women interviewed were selected based upon the availability of informants. The second group of thirty-one were chosen in an attempt to achieve more balance in the following areas: area of birth, social class, circumstances of emigration (for example, did they emigrate alone or with parents), age at time of emigration, number of children in the family, and birth order of the informant.

4. These interviews were loosely-structured, so although I had many specific questions, the women were free to emphasize what they believed were important factors in determining their lives. Initially, I had been seeking other information, but these two major points—the importance of mothers as role models and the significance of the child's birth order and age at time of emigration—emerged from the narratives of so many women that I realized that they formed an important pattern and altered some of my subsequent questions accordingly. However, because of the advanced age of some of my informants, the fact that a few resisted talking about their parents, and because material from other sources is interspersed with evidence from the interviews, I make no claims for scientific methodology and avoid using percentages of the women interviewed to support a particular attitude. I do attempt to indicate whether an attitude or pattern of behavior was one shared by many women or a small minority—whether it seemed dominant or deviant.

5. In 1916, there were only two Yeshivoth (Jewish high schools) in the United States, and only 24 percent of Jewish elementary school children received a Jewish education. See Charles S. Liebman, "Religion, Class and Culture in American Jewish History," *The Jewish Journal of Sociology*, 1 (December 1967): 227–42, esp. p. 231.

6. Sholem Asch, *The Mother*, (New York, 1937), p. 10.

7. Alfred Kazin, *A Walker in the City* (New York, 1931), pp. 52, 53, 66–67.

8. Anzia Yezierska, "The Fat of the Land," in *Hungry Hearts* (Boston, 1920), pp. 208–09.

9. Mary Ryan, *The Cradle of the Middle Class: The Family in Oneida County, New York, 1790–1865* (New York, 1981), p. 26.

10. Joan Scott and Louise A. Tilly, *Women, Work and Family* (New York, 1978), p. 107.

11. Some examples of this resentment can be seen in Elizabeth W. Ewen, "Immigrant Women in the Land of Dollars, 1890–1920," (Ph.D. diss., SUNY, Stony Brook, 1979), pp. 126–27; Laura Schwartz, "Immigrant Voices from Home, Work and Community: Women and Family in the Migration Process, 1890–1938" (Ph.D. diss., SUNY, Stony Brook, 1983), p. 615; and Elizabeth Hasanovitz, *One of Them* (New York, 1918), p. 42.

12. Scott and Tilly, *Women, Work and Family*, pp. 108, 111, 115.

13. A Department of Labor Survey indicated that sons gave an average of 83 percent of their wages to parents, while daughters gave 95 percent. See Schwartz, "Immigrant Voices," pp. 610–12.

573

14. Winifred Wandersee, *Women's Work and Family Values, 1920–1940* (Cambridge, Mass., 1981), p. 116.

15. This was a fairly typical pattern. See Schwartz, "Immigrant Voices," pp. 613–15.

16. Among twenty-five to forty-four year old foreign-born males, 44 percent of males graduated from high school, while 36 percent of women in this age group did so. The median years of schooling for this male group was 10.9, for the women, 9.7. This is a narrower gap than for the older group, where the males had a median of 8.1 years of schooling, and the women 5.8. Among native-born children, in contrast, the gap between male and female education is narrower still. Males in the younger age group averaged 12.7 years of schooling, and 72 percent had at least completed high school, while women averaged 12.4 years of school, and 69 percent of them had graduated from high school. See Census Survey in Miriam Cohen, "From Workshop to Office: Italian Women and Family Strategies in New York City, 1900–1950." Ph.D. diss., University of Michigan, 1978), p. 251.

17. See Scott and Tilly, *Women, Work and Family*, pp. 142–44, 205, esp. p. 106.

18. Almost all the women whose mothers came to this country had a good relationship with them in their later years, and this might have modified memories of earlier strife. The few women who seem not to have been close with their mothers were reluctant to speak about them at all except to say that they were difficult people.

19. On this point, see Ruth Landes and Mark Zborowski, "Hyypotheses Concerning the Eastern European Family," in *The Psychodynamics of American Jewish Life*, ed. Norman Kiell (New York, 1967), pp. 33–66, esp. pp. 36–37.

20. In Pittsburgh, one study indicates that Jews also had the lowest rate among immigrant families of the European language being spoken in the home. See Corinne Azen Krause, *Grandmothers, Mothers and Daughters: An Oral History Study of Ethnicity, Mental Health and Continuity of Three Generations of Jewish, Italian and Slavic American Women* (New York, 1978), p. 29.

21. On this important issue, see Elizabeth W. Ewen, "City Lights: Immigrant Women and the Rise of Movies," *Signs*, supplement to vol. 5, #3 (Spring 1980): 545–65, esp. pp. 549–50; Ewen, "Immigrant Women in the Land of Dollars." pp. 196–97; Schwartz, "Immigrant Voices from Home, Work and Community," p. 696.

22. In "Mothers and Daughters," p. 275, Michel pointed out that immigrant mothers were unable to provide their daughters with role models in the United States, but she seems to have assumed that what was true in youth remained constant throughout these women's lives.

23. See, for example, Beverly G. Bienstock, "The Changing Image of the American Jewish Mother," in *Changing Images of the Family*, eds. Virginia Tufte and Barbara Myerhoff (New Haven, 1979), pp. 173–91, esp. pp. 173–74, 177.

24. Michael R. Weisser, *A Brotherhood of Memory: Jewish Landsmanshaftn in the New World* (New York, 1985), p. 274.

25. Rudolph Glanz, *The Jewish Woman in America: Two Female Immigrant Generations 1820–1929.* vol. 1: *The Eastern European Jewish Woman* (New York, 1976), p. 58.

26. Alice Kessler-Harris, *Out to Work: A History of Wage-Earning Women in the United States* (New York, 1982), p. 126.

27. Unpublished Manuscript Autobiography No. 92, YIVO Archives, New York.

28. On this point, see Alice Kessler-Harris, "Organizing the Unorganizable: Three Jewish Women and their Union," in *Class, Sex and the Woman Worker*, eds. Milton Cantor and Bruce Laurie (Westport, Conn., 1977), p. 147.

29. Sydelle Kramer and Jenny Mazur, eds., *Jewish Grandmothers* (Boston, 1976), p. 98.

574

30. Abraham Cahan, *The Rise of David Levinsky* (1917; reprint ed., New York, 1960), pp. 242–43, 254–55.

31. Kate Simon, *Bronx Primitive: Portraits in a Childhood* (New York, 1982), p. 48.

32. This is generally true in mother-daughter relationships. See Edith Neisser, *Mothers and Daughters: A Lifelong Relationship* (New York, 1967), p. 170.

33. Bromberg, "Mother-Daughter Relationships," pp. 32, 210.

34. For example, among Italian women, see Janet Theophano, "'It's Really Tomato Sauce But We Call It Gravy': A Study of Food and Woman's Work Among Italian-American Families" (Ph.D. diss., University of Pennsylvania, 1982), p. 135.

35. Chernin, *In My Mother's House*, p. 29.

36. On this point for Italian immigrant families, see Cohen, "From Workshop to Office," p. 52; and Leonard Covello, *The Heart is the Teacher*, Reissued as *The Teacher in the Urban Community* (Totowa, N.J., 1970), p. 210.

37. For this ceremonial role, see Barbara Myerhoff, *Number Our Days* (New York, 1979), p. 247.

38. WPA interview, transcribed in the 1930s of Marie Esposito, a Jewish woman married to an Italian man. Cited in Schwartz, "Immigrant Voices from Home, Work and Community," pp. 586–87.

39. For a model of such family decision-making, see Marilyn Manser and Murray Brown, "Bargaining Analyses of Household Decisions," in *Women in the Labor Market*, eds. Cynthia B. Lloyd, E.S. Andrews, and C.L. Gilroy (New York, 1979), p. 5.

40. Kramer and Mazur, *Jewish Grandmothers*, pp. 98–99.

41. Irving Howe, *A Margin of Hope: An Intellectual Autobiography* (New York, 1982), p. 7.

42. See, for example, Michelle Z. Rosaldo, "Women, Culture and Society: A Theoretical Overview," in *Women, Culture and Society*, eds. Rosaldo and Louise Lamphere (Stanford, Calif., 1974), p. 46.

43. For some examples, see C. Baum, P. Hyman and S. Michel, *The Jewish Woman in America* (New York, 1976), pp. 205–06.

44. Yezierska, "The Fat of the Land," pp. 208–09.

45. Michel, "Mothers and Daughters," p. 278.

46. Kramer and Mazur, *Jewish Grandmothers*, p. 14.

47. Chernin, *In My Mother's House*, pp. 15, 39.

48. Bromberg, "Mother-Daughter Relationships," p. 239.

49. Esther Bender, "Looking Back," *National Jewish Monthly*, November 1977, pp. 28–34, esp. p. 34.

50. Jenny Herbst to Beatrice Weinreich, 18 September 1984, reprinted with permission of the author, YIVO Archives.

51. Bromberg, "Mother-Daughter Relationships," p. 35.

# "Send Me My Husband Who Is In New York City":* Husband Desertion in the American Jewish Immigrant Community 1900-1926

by Reena Sigman Friedman

In 1908, a despondent young woman wrote the following letter to the "Bintel Brief" section of the *New York Daily Forwards*:

> Max: The children and I now say farewell to you. You left us in such a terrible state. You had no compassion for us. . . . Have you ever asked yourself why you left us? Max, where is your conscience; you used to have sympathy for the forsaken women and used to say their terrible plight was due to the men who left them in dire need. And how did you act? I was a young, educated decent girl when you took me. You lived with me for six years, during which time I bore you four children. And then you left me. Of the four children, only two remain, but you have made them living orphans. Who will bring them up? Who will support us? Have you no pity for your own flesh and blood. Consider what you are doing. My tears choke me and I cannot write any more. . . .[1]

Such letters appeared quite frequently in *The Forwards* and other Yiddish newspapers in the early years of the twentieth century. The desertion of the breadwinner had become a fact of life for numerous immigrant Jewish families during this period. In 1905, 14.6 per cent of the cash relief funds administered by the United Hebrew Charities were granted to deserted women, second only to that provided to widows and their children.[2] The records of the United Hebrew Charities for 1909 indicate that, for every three applications for relief submitted by widows, two were received from deserted women.[3] Jewish charitable organizations in a number of American cities expended considerable sums in their efforts to deal effectively with the desertion problem. In 1909, the budgets of Jewish charities in Chicago, Baltimore and and New York City indicated desertion expenditures of $11,600, $3,000, and $37,000, respectively.[4] Finally, by 1911, the Jewish community acknowledged the seriousness of the problem by establishing a National Desertion Bureau, of nationwide and even international scope, with headquarters in New York City.

Nevertheless, most American Jewish historians have chosen to ignore the evidence. They have consistently maintained that the American Jewish family emerged virtually unscathed from the twin traumas of migration and Americanization. As Ronald Sanders has argued, "Foremost among the public virtues was— despite the element of gangsterism and prostitution that had arisen in the initial shock of transplantation from Eastern Europe to America—a steady revival of the family as an institution in the life of the New York Jewish quarter. . . ."[5] The tendency of these writers has been to gloss over the sordid aspects of East European Jewish life on New York City's Lower East Side and elsewhere in the late nineteenth

1

Originally published in *Jewish Social Studies* (Winter 1982). Reprinted by permission of Indiana University Press.

and early twentieth centuries. Those who have addressed themselves to the question of family conflict have generally focused on the tensions between parents and children rather than the gulf separating husbands and wives.

This article examines the phenomenon of husband desertion within the East European Jewish community in the United States during the period from 1900 to 1926. The areas to be discussed include the causes of desertion, its impact upon the individuals involved, and a comparison of the general and Jewish populations with respect to desertion. It should be noted at the outset that much of this material is based on data collected by various Jewish communal and philanthropic agencies. The questions posed, and therefore the conclusions reached, reflect the personal biases of the survey-takers regarding deserters and their motivations, and must be evaluated in light of that fact.

The following analysis focuses on the work of the National Desertion Bureau, a nationwide organization established in 1911 and charged with coordinating the work of the many organizations concerned with desertion. A survey of the objectives and *modus operandi* of the Bureau is followed by an evaluation of its achievements. Finally, the Bureau's program is viewed within the context of both the efforts of "uptown" Jews to rapidly integrate the immigrants into American society and the dominant trends in American social work at the beginning of the twentieth century.

To a large extent, the Jewish family exhibited remarkable strength and resilience throughout the transitional period. Desertion was largely confined to the lower socioeconomic classes and the available figures do not indicate that the problem was overwhelming in scope. Moreover, the extended family, at least, remained quite cohesive, as evidenced by frequent examples of women being supported by relatives following the desertions of their husbands. Yet the fact that, during this period, very serious threats were posed to the "traditional" solidarity of the Jewish family cannot be dismissed lightly. The dangers were real and they certainly were not limited to an isolated few. As one author of a study on Jewish desertion observed:

> The popular conception, borne out by the Jewish historical background, is that family ties are exceptionally strong in the Jewish people. . . . But, family disorganization does exist among the Jews . . . particularly as changes in the social and economic phases of modern society affect all members of that society. In view of the changing system of values, one would expect an increased amount of family disorganization among the Jews, just as is true of all other groups.[6]

*Migration, Americanization, and the Jewish Family*

The Jewish family has traditionally been credited with helping to preserve Jewish religion and group life. East European Jewish immigrants, however, entered the United States *en masse* just as it was undergoing transformations of seismic proportions, many of which threatened the survival of the family unit. Most social scientists agree that the industrialization process, which fostered economic individualism, was incompatible with the strong family ties associated with home production. Urbanization, too, tended to weaken the control of primary groups over the individual. Thus, American divorce rates rose drastically after the Civil War, a time of rapid industrialization and technological development. Between 1909 and 1912, public ferment over family breakdown reached new heights.[7] Americans were clearly concerned about the future of the traditional extended family during the modern age.

The masses of immigrants inundating American cities in the late nineteenth and early twentieth centuries experienced considerable family disorganization, largely in response to the pressures of migration and acculturation. Each immigrant group reacted somewhat differently, depending upon the nature of its cultural and religious values regarding the family.[8] Symptoms of familial discord were present in Jewish homes as they were in those of all other immigrant groups. As Irving Howe has asserted:

> Every recollection of Jewish immigrant life that is concerned with more than the trivia of "local color" notices that as soon as the Jews moved from Eastern Europe to America there followed a serious dislocation of the family. Patterns of the family had been firmly set, indeed, had been allowed to become rigid in the old country. The moral authority of the father, the formal submission of the wife, together with her frequent dominance in practical affairs, the obedience of children softened by parental indulgences. In the turmoil of the American city, traditional family patterns could not long survive.[9]

579

The roles traditionally played by Jewish parents and children were reversed in the context of the immigrant family. That this situation was painfully familiar to the immigrants is demonstrated by the preoccupation of American Jewish authors with generational conflict. Mary Antin, who arrived in the United States as a young child, somberly recalled the tensions within her own family:

> My parents [felt] . . . that the American way was the best way . . . they must step down from their throne of parental authority and take the law from their children's mouths; for they had no other means of finding out what was good American form. The result was that laxity of domestic organization, that inversion of normal relationships which makes for friction, and which sometimes ends in breaking up a family that was formerly united and happy.[10]

Somewhat less perceptible, yet probably more significant, was the transformation that took place in the positions of husband and wife within the family. While the men became more aggressive under the influence of American capitalism, the women generally assumed more submissive roles than they had filled in Eastern Europe. As they entered the middle class, Jewish men and women increasingly conformed to the sex role models current in Victorian America.[11] Even in the early phases of the immigrant experience, husbands and wives accommodated to American norms at different rates, resulting in a great deal of friction within the home. This dissonance was reflected by Jewish literature of the period. In some cases, such as that of Mary Antin's father, the husband was more eager to become Americanized than was his wife, and repeatedly urged her to discard her outmoded religious practices.[12] In others, an aggressive husband went so far as to divorce the wife who represented all that was repugnant to him in the Old World culture, and to marry a woman whose demeanor better suited his newly acquired "American" tastes.[13]

The aspect of the immigrant experience which proved most disruptive to Jewish family life, however, was the long separation endured by families whose breadwinners journeyed to America some time before their dependents. Abraham Cahan portrayed this state of affairs in his characteristically vivid manner. The hero of his novel, *Yekl*, enters the United States, leaving his family behind in Russia. In typical fashion, he is terribly disappointed in his "Old World" wife when she arrives, and eventually divorces her to marry an Americanized Jewish woman.[14] Such sketches were clearly drawn from the real-life situations of immigrant Jews. One letter received by the Socialist newspaper, *Warheit*, in 1903, expressed its writer's concern that he would no longer be able to love the wife who was about to join him in America after all the emotional changes he had undergone since his arrival. In other instances, such separations resulted in dramatic transformations of the wife's condition. Another letter received that year by the *Warheit* described the despair of a man who had secured his wife's passage to the United States, only to discover that she was pregnant with her brother-in-law's child.[15]

Another major cause of Jewish family dislocation in America was the presence of boarders in most immigrant households. Abraham Cahan's classic novel, *The Rise of David Levinsky*, illustrates the detrimental effect the husband-wife-boarder triangle had upon family relationships.[16] The Yiddish play, *Minna*, recounts the story of a Jewish woman who is attracted to her boarder for his "advanced ideas," which contrast sharply with the crude behavior of her husband, an ignorant laborer. Minna finally commits suicide when societal censure becomes overwhelming.[17]

A fourth highly disruptive feature of Jewish family life in late nineteenth and early twentieth century America was the frequent incapacitation or death of the breadwinner caused by occupational accidents or illness. Widows who could not obtain adequate relief were compelled to relinquish their young children to the care of orphan asylums. The economic and emotional stress of caring for an invalid husband and father, or of his removal to a sanatorium, was very great. In addition to strained relationships within the unified family, various forms of family disorganization were quite prevalent in the Jewish community. Family disorganization is defined as the partial or total dissolution of the family unit owing to separation, divorce or desertion.[18]

Divorce, in the ascendancy in the general American population, was, at the turn of the century, generally restricted to upper-income groups. Desertion, on the other hand, was most common among the poorer classes, although it often resulted in divorce. From 1887 to 1906, for instance, of the total number of divorces granted in the United States, 38.9 per cent were demanded on grounds of desertion.[19] In fact, desertion has been termed the "poor man's divorce" because it involves no financial expense or costly legal proceedings. For the poverty stricken, desertion constitutes a temporary "escape from responsibility" rather than a commitment to permanent separation.[20]

*Desertion: Dimensions of the Problem*

"Desertion" has been defined by the Jewish Social Service Association of New York City as "the act by which either or both parents abandon their children, the husband leaves the wife or the wife leaves the husband, whereby the one leaving avoids, neglects or refuses to support or maintain the other."[21] Desertion is probably as ancient as Jewish history itself. During the Middle Ages, public demands for restrictions on the absences of husbands seeking work resulted in a twelfth-century decree limiting the length of time away from home to 18 months. A treatise published in Salonica in 1651, *Kontres Ha'agunah*, deals exclusively with the problem of desertion. Section 17 of the *Shulhan Arukh* is concerned with the dilemma of the *agunah*, the abandoned wife.[22]

The problem of Jewish desertion, however, reached particularly alarming proportions in the early years of the twentieth century. Throughout the period from 1900 to 1911, the proportion of relief funds administered by Jewish charitable agencies to deserted women remained at approximately 15 per cent of their total annual disbursements.[23] After 1911, this percentage gradually declined because of the success of the National Desertion Bureau in apprehending and prosecuting deserters. The incidence of desertion was largely confined to the lower-class immigrant community and the rate of recidivism was high. Although deserters were almost always male, there are several recorded instances of women deserting their husbands, usually as a result of extramarital relationships.

According to a study of 423 desertion cases undertaken in 1926 by Charles Zunser (then director of the National Desertion Bureau, and a prominent figure in the desertion field), the typical Jewish deserter was between the ages of 27 and 36, and was employed in a seasonal occupation. Most men had been married between one and six years prior to the first desertion and had fewer than three children, aged five to eleven. Infidelity on the part of either spouse was given as the cause of desertion in a large majority of the cases.[24] This profile of the Jewish deserter does not differ markedly from that of his non-Jewish counterpart. Both Jewish and gentile deserters tended to be poor, to be married for a short time, to have small families, and to have personality traits regarded as leading to domestic discord. Jewish deserters were distinguished only by their earlier ages upon marriage, higher intermarriage rates, and somewhat smaller families.[25] The reasons given for desertion are also different for Jews and non-Jews, according to some surveys. Morris Waldman, in his study of 260 desertion cases in 1902–1903, discovered that, while 33 per cent of the desertions in his non-Jewish sample were attributable to the alcoholism of the husband, only 3 per cent of the Jewish men were accused of intemperance. On the other hand, 30 per cent of the Jewish husbands were charged with adultery, as compared with 11 per cent of the non-Jewish deserters.[26]

581

Desertion was clearly as prevalent in the general American population, particularly among immigrant groups, as it was in urban Jewish quarters throughout the country. The United Hebrew Charities recorded that 11.6 per cent of the cases that it handled in 1906–1908 concerned desertion. A report of the New York City Charity Organization Society (a major non-Jewish charitable organization) for the same period indicated that 12.12 per cent of its cases were desertion-related.[27] Charles Zunser noted that, in 1922, 10 to 15 per cent of all people receiving aid from Jewish charities were deserted families. On the other hand, deserted wives and children accounted for 15 to 20 per cent of non-Jewish social service cases.[28]

1. Causes of Desertion

A survey of husband desertion in the Jewish population for the period from 1910 to 1923 conducted by the United Hebrew Charities revealed that the major causes of desertion were: "immorality of husband, or wife, or both; incompatibility of temper; shiftlessness; intemperance; economic conditions including industrial disturbances; financial depression; insufficient wages; illness; discrepancy in ages; interference of relatives; differences in nativity; forced marriages; and immigration of the husband ahead of his family."[29] Opinions vary about which of these factors most commonly led to desertion, depending upon the survey.

Most often cited as the principal cause of desertion was "immorality," that is, marital infidelity. Morris Waldman, in his aforementioned study, attributed more desertions to immorality than to economic hardship.[30] To a large extent, the long period of separation between men and their families remaining in Europe was responsible for the extramarital relationships in which many husbands became involved. In some instances, a well-intentioned husband remarried in the United States on the basis of alleged reports that his wife had been killed in a pogrom or during wartime hostilities. Other men, who lost contact with their families owing to wartime conditions, remarried in the United States, later to be confronted by their former families on their arrival in the United States.[31]

The most common reason for a wife's desertion of her husband was her involvement with another man, usually a boarder. One forsaken husband wrote a letter to the *Forwards* in 1906, in which he described his wife's affair with the boarder and her elopement. He concluded:

> I know, dear Editor, that you cannot advise me now, but for me it's enough that I can pour out my suffering on paper. I can't find a place for myself. I miss the children. Life is dark and bitter without them. I hope that my wife will read this letter in the *Forwards* and that she will blush with shame.[32]

Competing with "immoral behavior" as a major impetus for desertion was economic hardship, encompassing both low wages and seasonal or chronic unemployment. As Charles Zunser affirmed in 1906, "Lack of work . . . has driven more men away from their families than any other single factor."[33] Maurice B. Hexter, too, in an article entitled, "The Business Cycle, Relief Work and Desertion," written in 1924–25, concluded that there was a clear correlation between the index of desertion and seasonal unemployment in the textile and clothing trades. Based on a sample of 5,002 desertion cases filed with the National Desertion Bureau from the New York City area (excluding Brooklyn) between 1912 and 1921, Hexter discovered that there was a pronounced seasonal variation in rates of desertion, with the largest number of abandonments occurring in January and June, and the smallest number in April and early fall.[34]

According to some commentators, the impoverished, unsanitary, and often cheerless home lives of the urban immigrant masses were sufficiently demoralizing to impel men to desert their families. A report of the National Desertion Bureau for 1919 regarded this factor as one of supreme significance: "A man without resources for his leisure hours, a woman whose life is narrowed to hard work, children fretful and clamorous, all confined within a few small, dreary rooms — that is the condition in a thousand tenements throughout the city . . . it is nearly always out of such dull domesticity that the desertion of wives and families ensues."[35] Many writers concluded that manual laborers had to be provided with sufficient opportunities for recreation and relaxation,[36] and that young women should receive instruction in domestic science in the public schools. Thus, the burden of creating a more attractive home environment for her husband was shifted to the woman.[37]

In the opinion of M. Baranov, among others, the lower-class origins of potential deserters, combined with their attraction to American cultural values, evoked a type of *wanderlust* in many young Jewish men. He depicted the experience of these immigrant Jews in the following manner:

In Europe . . . their road to life was narrow, but they could not get lost. . . . In America young Jews are hurled into a world of freedom — no fences, no police, no community judgment. It's every man for himself. . . . Conscience and honor fall by the waywide. . . . Such a young man gets married. . . . He fights with his wife, who doesn't let him out of the house. There are gay young girls out there, and carefree bachelors. The anarchists preach free love; the freethinkers guarantee there is no God, no punishment in the after life. The young man thinks, "I'm a free person, who cares what they say," and one fine day he leaves home and forgets to come back. He becomes a missing husband.[38]

Poor health was a perennial concern of all immigrants, and was cited as a significant factor in many cases of Jewish desertion. Although Jews were not as affected by tuberculosis, cholera or typhus as were large sectors of the immigrant population, neurasthenia, hysteria, and diabetes were consistently identified as "Jewish ailments." Moreover, venereal disease became progressively more common among young Jewish men in the early years of the twentieth century.[39] "Health defects" of either husband or wife were frequently cited as reasons for desertion. In Jeanne Levine's sample of 115 desertion cases, for example, approximately half of the 222 individuals studied suffered from some illness which they felt had contributed to marital friction.[40]

583

Of some significance in inducing desertions was "incompatibility" between husband and wife caused by the excessive interference of relatives or the repugnant personality traits or behavior of either spouse.[41]

## 2. Impact of Desertion

Abandoned wives suffered both psychological trauma and severe financial deprivation as a result of their husbands' conduct. Often, a husband who had deserted his family long before continued to torment his wife. One such man threatened his wife with physical violence if she persisted in having him traced by the National Desertion Bureau. He wrote: ". . . I will not send you any money, if you should stand on your head, or if I should see you sick, but there is one thing that I will do for you. I would break your head if you will trouble me again. So you see I don't care for you any more. Do as you please about it and go to H_____ or get run over. . . ."[42] The emotional trauma resulting from desertion occasionally reached terrifying proportions. Although the incidence of suicide among Jews in Eastern Europe had been negligible, suicides in the United States were reported quite frequently in the American Yiddish press around the turn of the century.[43] Abandoned wives were among those most likely to take their own lives.[44]

Although financial support for deserted women and their children was available from a number of Jewish charitable institutions, the amount granted was often minimal and always difficult for proud women to accept. In many cases, women were so completely dependent on their husbands for support that they refused to testify against them once the men were apprehended and presented for prosecution.[45] Many took back their chronically deserting husbands time and again, and even sought monetary support from husbands living with other women and their illegitimate children.[46]

A striking number of abandoned women turned to prostitution as a means of earning a living. In the Bedford Reformatory, which housed numerous Jewish inmates, 14.5 per cent of the 671 prostitutes interviewed claimed that their prostitution had resulted from their husbands' desertion. The Chicago Vice Commission, which studied the problem in 1911, concurred that a clear connection existed between desertion and prostitution.[47] For the fortunate few, various Jewish charities throughout the country sponsored "workrooms" for unskilled widowed or deserted mothers of young children. Entrusting their children to the care of local day nurseries, women could earn a portion of their total relief package by working several hours a day in the production of baby outfits, linens, and other garments. Most of these workrooms, however, were short-lived enterprises and, while they were in operation, could only afford to employ a limited number of women.[48]

In contrast, mothers who were refused relief, or who received insufficient aid, were often compelled to place their children in orphan asylums or in the foster care of private individuals. One woman poured out her bitterness in a letter to the "Bintel Brief" (1910):

> The local Jewish Welfare Agencies are allowing me and my children to die of hunger and this is because my "faithful" husband brought me over from Canada just four months ago and therefore I do not yet deserve to eat their bread. I, the unhappy young mother, am willing to sign a contract, with my heart's blood, stating that the children belong to the good people who will treat them tenderly. Those who are willing and able to give my children a good home can apply to me.[49]

In fact, in 1913, a committee appointed to study the desertion problem in New York City disclosed that as many as 20 per cent of the children housed by municipal institutions were from deserted families. One of every two inmates of juvenile reformatories or industrial schools was a child from a broken home.[50] In 1915, it was estimated that New York City municipal authorities and private orphanages expended $700,000 and $300,000 per year, respectively, for the care of abandoned children.[51] Jewish orphanages proliferated in the United States during the first decade of the twentieth century, in an effort to accommodate the large numbers of children requiring shelter owing to the death or desertion of their parents.[52] Even those children who remained with their families suffered from both parental neglect and their need to work to supplement the family income. The full impact of desertion upon children often did not surface until later in their lives when it emerged in the form of emotional instability or delinquency. A letter received by the National Desertion Bureau from a 12-year old boy in 1912 reveals the extent to which the children of abandoned families were compelled to assume adult responsibilities overnight:

> I cannot read Jewish but my mother read to me your advertisement that there is (sic) some kind people who formed a society and are willing to help find husbands who have went (sic) away from their wives and families. Well, my father went away from my mother and family about four years ago. . . . He left us just as somebody was throwed (sic) into the water and left to struggle for himself. . . . I will let you know that . . . William Siff is my uncle, but not Jacob Schiff. I wish he would be my uncle, I would not have to know about father.[53]

In addition to the trauma suffered by women and children, husband desertion created severe financial problems for national, state, and municipal authorities. In 1919, for instance, it was estimated that New York City public and private charities expended a million dollars annually for the maintenance of deserted families. One family in ten seeking relief from a charitable agency was said to be abandoned.

Finally, one of every four children admitted to public and private orphanges in the city had been deserted by one or both parents.[54]

### *Early Jewish Communal Efforts to Deal with Desertion*

Leaders of the Jewish community were sensitive to the fact that Jewish immigrants, particularly large numbers of abandoned Jewish families, were heavily dependent on state funds for their support. In keeping with their desire to prevent them from becoming financial burdens, the leaders strove to provide Jewish charitable relief for these immigrants and to encourage the majority to become self-supporting.[55]

The leaders of the "uptown" Jewish community (mostly German Jews who were generally well established in America by 1880, when the great influx of Jewish immigrants from Eastern Europe began) hoped to rehabilitate the deserting husbands who were "a blot on the fair name of Israel."[56] The "uptown" leadership assumed the responsibility of "(elevating) the general tone of our poorer coreligionists and (impressing) upon them the honorable duty of providing for their families under all circumstances.[57] In eliminating the desertion evil, among others, from their midst, the American Jewish benefactors sought to preserve the security that they had, at long last, achieved in America.

As early as December 1900, Max Senior, president of the National Conference of Jewish Charities, included husband desertion in a discussion of the major concerns confronting American Jewry.[58] It was Morris Waldman's study of 260 desertion cases for the United Hebrew Charities in 1902–1903, however, which finally succeeded in focusing public attention on the problem. Nearly all subsequent treatments of the desertion issue addressed themselves to the questions raised by Waldman's analysis.[59]

By 1905, the public debate sparked by this study set the machinery of systematization in motion. The focus of anti-desertion work between 1905 and 1911 was almost entirely legalistic. Two years of agitation by pioneers in the desertion field culminated in the passage, in 1905, of a New York State law which classified the abandonment of minor children in destitute circumstances as a felony. This was regarded as a milestone by prominent figures in desertion work since, as long as the crime had been labeled a misdemeanor, it had been extremely difficult to secure extradition of the deserter to his home state.[60]

Once the new law was passed, the apprehension and prosecution of deserters by Jewish social service agencies began in earnest. With financial support from the United Hebrew Charities, the National Conference of Jewish Charities established a "Committee for the Protection of Deserted Wives and Children" in 1905, under the direction of Charles Zunser. The Committee immediately embarked on a massive publicity campaign aimed at apprehending deserters and deterring future abandonment. Notices were placed in all major Yiddish newspapers, urging deserted wives to appear before the Committee with as much information as possible regarding their missing husbands. Deserters were informed, through the press, that they might avert punishment only if they returned home at once. The Committee handled a total of 591 cases between October 1905 and May 1906.[61] In a paper presented before the National Council of Jewish Charities in 1906, Lee Frankel described the work of the

585

Committee to date and proposed a detailed program for dealing with desertion in the future. He stressed the need for cooperation among Jewish social service organizations in various states, in order to confront the desertion problem in a more comprehensive manner.[62] A new entity, designed to coordinate the efforts of the numerous Jewish agencies concerned with the problem, was soon to emerge.

### The Work of the National Desertion Bureau, 1911-1926

The National Desertion Bureau (NDB) was created by the National Council of Jewish Charities in 1911, along the lines proposed by Lee Frankel in his 1906 address to the Conference. The New York Foundation contributed a sum of $5,000, which enabled the Bureau to function for 14 months under its first director, Monroe Goldstein. By 1914, the Bureau was incorporated as an independent entity, with headquarters in New York City. Until the formation of the Federation of Jewish Philanthropies in 1917, the Bureau was funded entirely by private donations and sums from charitable organizations. From 1917 on, however, the Bureau derived most of its moral and financial support from the Federation.[63]

The NDB's approach to the desertion problem was strongly influenced by the concept of "scientific philanthropy," which was gaining currency within American social work circles at the time. This movement stressed the importance of: systematic inquiry into the causes of dependency in order to eliminate them; orderly procedures in social service organization; and sensitive responses to the needs of individual clients.[64] The Bureau's early program clearly reflected the legalistic thinking common to all social work agencies during the first two decades of the twentieth century. It gradually adopted a social case work approach, however, which addressed the underlying roots of dependency.[65]

At the time of the Bureau's incorporation, its president was Walter H. Liebman and its directors included many outstanding attorneys and professionals in the Jewish social work field. Among the Bureau's first executives were Fred Butzel, Felix Frankfurter, Minnie Low, Julius Mayer, Joseph Proskauer and Morris Waldman. Charles Zunser was appointed president in 1920, on Liebman's resignation.[66] By 1923, Abraham Cahan was also listed among the NDB's directors.[67] The Bureau's objectives were stated in its Articles of Incorporation:

> To ascertain the whereabouts of men who desert their wives and children and to induce them to reunite with and support their families . . . and in proper cases to aid in bringing about the conviction and imprisonment of such deserters. Its endeavor primarily is to unite and reconcile contending spouses and to keep the family and the home intact. . . . The Bureau's beneficiaries are women who are referred to it by various Jewish charitable organizations in the United States who are poor and unable to otherwise engage legal assistance.[68]

According to an NDB report published in 1929, the Bureau handled approximately 2,500 cases annually. Cases were referred by affiliated Jewish social service agencies in the United States, Canada, and many other nations.[69]

The NDB's program encompassed four major areas: 1). efforts to trace deserting husbands and fathers; 2). attempts to effect a reconciliation between deserters and their families; 3). arrangements for the husband's financial support of his family if a reconciliation could not be achieved; and 4). prosecution of those men who refused or failed to provide for their families. The Bureau accepted cases involving both abandonment and "non-support." "Non-support" refers to situations in which the husband lived at home but made no attempt to secure steady employment.[70]

The Bureau's principal task was the discovery and apprehension of deserters. On receiving a report on a missing husband, the NDB required wives to furnish information regarding their husbands' name, physical condition, occupation, wages, date of disappearance, cause of desertion, complete physical description, and photograph, in addition to clues about his possible whereabouts. The wife was also asked to sign an affidavit certifying that she had been abandoned and authorizing the Bureau to act on her behalf. Descriptions of the missing man were subsequently forwarded to labor organizations, friends, relatives, and employers in the hope that these individuals might have some pertinent information. Blurbs and photographs were also placed in major Yiddish newspapers published in New York, Chicago, Cleveland, Montreal and Toronto, in a section of each paper entitled the "Gallery of Missing Husbands." The total circulation of these newspapers was estimated at 250,000.[71]

Once the man was apprehended, the NDB attempted to reconcile him with his family. If this endeavor proved successful, the Bureau's referral agency maintained contact with the family for at least one year, to monitor its adjustment. Often, however, reconciliation was impossible. In such instances, if the husband could not be persuaded to support his family through extralegal means, he was placed under court probation and compelled to do so. The NDB occasionally served as an "alimony" collection agency, mediating the financial transactions between the estranged husband and wife.[72]

Although the Bureau generally recommended prosecution of offenders only as a last resort, a significant number of deserting husbands were subject to extradition and prosecution for repeated abandonments or continued failure to support their families. If moral suasion proved insufficient to reclaim the husband, he was arrested, extradited and brought to trial. In most states, he could be sentenced to up to two years imprisonment or fined as much as $1,000. In its capacity as a pioneer "legal aid" agency,[73] the Bureau provided all legal services *gratis* to deserted women and often supplied their transportation to the trial sites.[74] In fact, the NDB soon established its reputation as a legal authority on all aspects of domestic relations. It offered advice to social agencies in the United States and abroad regarding divorce, desertion, annulment, separation, and adoption of children.[75]

In the course of their legal work, NDB personnel frequently became embroiled in controversies with state law enforcement officials. District attorneys repeatedly refused to extradite offenders in desertion cases, arguing that the cost was prohibitive. NDB leaders claimed, on the other hand, that the cost of maintaining deserted families or youngsters in orphanages was far greater. The Bureau also opposed the antiquated state court systems that refused to confine desertion and non-support cases to family courts. In the Bureau's view, only these courts were adequately equipped to handle domestic relations cases.[76]

Foreign cases, in which the husband abandoned his family in Europe, and then journeyed to America, were most often referred to the NDB by the Hebrew Immigrant Aid Society (HIAS) or the Immigrant Aid Department of the National Council of Jewish Women. The Bureau assumed the task of locating the man and compelling him to furnish transportation for his dependents or to meet his family at the point of disembarkation if they had already arrived.[77] The situation was rendered more complex when it was the deserter who fled to another country. The policies of foreign governments often impeded the Bureau's search for missing husbands. For example, the Russian authorities refused to assist in the apprehension of American deserters, ostensibly because they regarded marriage as a "private affair."[78] Many men chose Canada as their refuge, since the extradition treaty between Canada and the United States did not allow for the legal removal of those charged with child-abandonment.[79] Within the United States, the NDB in 1923 was instrumental in passing a law regarding the procedures followed by Domestic Relations Courts. Under previous regulations, deserted women were compelled to declare themselves "likely to become public charges" in order to testify against their husbands in court. Such a declaration would, however, place them in danger of deportation. The new provisions removed the "declaration" requirement, thereby encouraging more women to participate in the prosecution process.[80]

A number of organizations, Jewish and non-Jewish, cooperated with the NDB in resolving desertion cases that were international in scope. Among the most active, particularly after World war I, were the HIAS, National Council of Jewish Women, American Jewish Joint Distribution Committee, International Migration Service and Society for the Protection of Girls and Women of London.[81]

In the first year of its existence (1 February 1911–31 March 1912), the Bureau handled 852 cases. By the end of the year, 561, or 66 per cent, of the deserters were located and, of these, 326 were either reconciled with their families or compelled to support them.[82] Those who refused a reconciliation but were willing to comply with separate support agreements, had generally deserted for reasons of incompatibility or "immorality," rather than financial hardship.[83] Only twenty of the men were subject to arrest and prosecution; two of these were charged with bigamy, because they had remarried since their desertion.[84] In 21 of these cases, the applications were dismissed owing to fraudulent charges. On investigation, the Bureau discovered that the husband and wife had collaborated in filing the desertion complaint in an effort to subsidize their income with charitable donations. In a few instances, the woman had forcibly evicted her husband from their home and then feigned desertion to qualify for relief funds. Finally, many women refused to prosecute once their husbands had been apprehended, usually because they feared the loss of his income.[85]

Between 1912 and 1915, the NDB's scope of activity expanded to include 3,286 cases, referred by 93 constituent agencies in 67 cities. The Bureau located 73 per cent of the men (2,405), who were traced to 239 cities in the United States, Canada, England and Russia. Of the 2,405 men, 372 were prosecuted in New York City and were sentenced to imprisonment of six months to two years or fines from $500 to $1,000. In the majority of cases (1,389), however, the Bureau succeeded in effecting reconciliations or negotiating support arrangements.[86]

By 1919, the NDB processed 1,242 cases of desertion. In 70 per cent of the cases (831), the recalcitrant husbands were apprehended.[87] In 1922, 2,108 deserters were pursued by the Bureau, 1,596 of whom were located.[88] In sum, the NDB handled 12,413 cases between 1911 and 1922. Of these, 6,085 originated in New York City (as the largest Jewish center in the United States and a city whose anonymity made it a convenient haven for fugitive husbands), 4,221 were referred by interior communities and the balance were derived from foreign sources.[89]

In addition to the NDB's considerable success in bringing deserters to justice, its achievements are noteworthy in at least two other respects. The Bureau's work realized the goals set by its founders in that it cut by half the sum of relief funds administered to deserted families by the United Hebrew Charities. The total relief disbursements were reduced from $31,251 in 1910 to $15,659 in 1918.[90] In part, this precipitous decline must be attributed to the deterrent effect that the Bureau's widely publicized program had on potential deserters, since the number of families granted relief during that period also was reduced from 521 to 185. The reconciliation and support agreements mediated by Bureau personnel thus must be credited with removing large numbers of families from the relief rolls.

Finally, by World War I, the NDB's reputation as an anti-desertion agency had become so firmly established that it served as a model for the creation of parallel non-Jewish organizations. The desertion departments established in 1914 by the major New York City relief organizations—the New York City Association for Improving the Condition of the Poor, and the New York City Charity Organization Society—patterned themselves after the NDB and were founded in cooperation with the Bureau.[91]

The NDB's record of achievement in the desertion field is quite impressive. The Bureau succeeded in establishing itself as the clearing house for desertion cases within the American Jewish community. A broadly based organizational network had been created and the entire operation appears to have functioned in a reasonably efficient manner. In view of the many legal obstacles confronting the Bureau, it fared remarkably well in reaching a definitive resolution of most cases.

589

### Conclusion

To a large extent, the leadership of the NDB shared the concerns of the entire "uptown" Jewish community, of which it was a part. Confronted with the rapid influx of impoverished "hordes" of their East European coreligionists, more established Jews feared they would be associated with the immigrants in the minds of native Americans. By the 1870s, there were already clear indications of nascent, domestic antisemitism, primarily taking the form of social exclusion. Thus, in an effort to "clear the name of Israel," leaders of the "uptown" community sought to eradicate the evils associated with immigrant Jewish quarters and reduce the number of Jewish recipients of public relief funds. Precursors of the NDB regarded husband desertion as one of many objectionable features of "downtown" Jewish life, along with crime, prostitution, and juvenile delinquency. They resolved that "all our charitable institutions should endeavor, through the means of friendly visiting, the pulpit, the press, and at public meetings, to elevate the general tone of our poorer coreligionists. . . ."[92]

The Bureau's work also reflected its leaders' sincere sympathy for the women and children who were most often the victims of desertion. Although Bureau staff members acknowledged the existence of collusive desertions or those in which the wife was undoubtedly at fault, their efforts reflected a distinct bias in favor of wives and children in the immigrant community. In the words of Charles Zunser, "Let us so shape our methods and procedure that the welfare of the abandoned mother and children be conserved at all costs short of justice and truth."[93] The NDB must also be credited with establishing desertion as a major public concern, and with rallying support for its campaign in both the Jewish and non-Jewish communities. It succeeded in removing many abandoned families from public and private relief rolls. The Bureau's legal work was particularly exemplary, and it became the prototype for subsequent desertion bureaus established with its cooperation.

Yet, precisely because the Bureau was founded in a period dominated by a legalistic approach to social service questions, it placed relatively little emphasis on counseling. From the available records, it appears that the Bureau engaged in little or no "follow-up work" with deserted families, although it is unlikely that the superficial reconciliations mediated by the Bureau could be maintained without at least temporary external support. Given the fact that social case work was coming into widespread use by the 1920s with the increasing professionalization of social work, it is surprising that the Bureau's work does not reflect this shift in emphasis.

The NDB's apparent lack of concern with long-term solutions to the desertion problem is also manifested by its failure to seek employment for abandoned women that would have enabled more of them to provide for their young children instead of placing them in orphanages. Organizations other than the NDB made feeble attempts in this area by establishing "workrooms" for unskilled women. As previously mentioned, however, the workrooms assisted only a tiny proportion of the total number of deserted wives. Evidently, the creation of such programs for working mothers of preschool children was an idea whose time had not yet come.

It is readily apparent that the statistics on husband desertion presented in this article are far from overwhelming. Although higher than might be expected, given the myth of Jewish family solidarity, they might be dismissed as mere "exceptions to the rule." Yet the extant evidence by no means conveys the total picture. The fact that a separate, nation-wide Bureau, with international jurisdiction, was established to devise mechanisms for dealing with desertion attests to the salience of the problem in the minds of both "uptown" and "downtown" Jews. The Bureau was founded in response to the urgent need of Jews to grapple with this most serious matter. Moreover, the data presented in the NDB's records excludes the many instances of desertion which probably went unreported owing to fear or shame on the part of the wives. That this was a frequent response in Jewish families is amply demonstrated by the many women, cited by the NDB, who waited an inordinate length of time before reporting their husbands' disappearance. One typical case history, reported by the Bureau in 1912, indicated that, because the family had waited four years to inform the Bureau of the desertion, it was unable to prosecute since the two-year period specified in the statute of limitations had elapsed.[94] Charles Zunser, in his 1926 desertion study, noted that some of the women in his sample delayed as long as 9 to 13 years before reporting the desertion.[95]

The extent of the problem would probably be more accurately represented in statistics on the number of female-headed households in the Jewish population, the proportion of "one-parent" Jewish children enrolled in public schools, and the precise number of Jewish children admitted to state and private orphan asylums as a result of desertion. The number of households headed by foreign-born, white women fifteen years or older in New York State was approximately 166,776 out of a total of 1,201,766 such females in 1910. Those households headed by foreign-born, white women in the entire country numbered 954,733 out of a total of 6,184,432 in 1920.[96] An investigation into additional sources of data must be reserved for a future study.[97]

Jewish immigrant families experienced severe internal stress during the period of their accommodation to American life and values, whether or not these tensions were manifested in an overt manner. Such inner conflict clearly emerges in the voluminous immigrant memoir literature and fictional accounts produced in these tumultuous years. Jewish family ties did remain strong in America owing to the traditional centrality of the family in Jewish life and observance. It is time to recognize, however, that whether family disorganization emerged in the form of internal friction, desertion, separation or divorce, the traumas of migration and acculturation have taken their toll upon Jewish family life in America.

## NOTES 591

* This request appeared on a postcard sent by a deserted woman from San Francisco to the National Desertion Bureau in 1911.

1. Charlotte Baum, Sonya Michel, and Paula Hyman, *The Jewish Woman in America* (New York, 1976), p. 117.

2. Harry Lurie, *A Heritage Reaffirmed, The Jewish Federation Movement in America* (Philadelphia, Pa., 1961), p. 66.

3. Morris Waldman, "Report of the Committee on Desertion," *Proceedings,* 7th Biennial Conference, National Conference of Jewish Charities (1912), p. 56. See Note 23 below for a listing and dates of other Biennial Conferences held by the National Conference of Jewish Charities, hereafter called NCJC.

4. Waldman, "Report," p. 56.

5. Ronald Sanders, *The Downtown Jews* (New York, 1969), p. 351.

6. Jeanne Levine, "Jewish Family Desertion in Cases Carried Cooperatively by the National Desertion Bureau and Other Social Agencies in New York City, 1934" (Unpublished M.A. Thesis, Graduate School for Jewish Social Work, New York, 1939), p. 3.

7. *Ibid.,* p. 230.

8. For example, Virginia Yans McLoughlin has demonstrated that the Italians living in Buffalo, New York succeeded in avoiding those occupations which would interfere with their cultural norms concerning strong family ties. As a result, they experienced markedly low levels of family disorganization. See her *Family and Community: Italian Immigrants in Buffalo, 1880–1930* (Ithaca, N.Y., 1977), *passim.*

9. Irving Howe, *World of our Fathers* (New York and London, 1976), pp. 172–73.

10. Mary Antin, *The Promised Land* (Boston and New York, 1962), pp. 270–71.

11. Baum, et al., *Jewish Woman,* Ch. 4.

12. Mary's father wrote to her mother still in Eastern Europe, on the eve of her departure, that progressive Jews in America didn't spend their days in prayer and that she should leave her wig in Pobrzk as a first step toward progress, in Antin, *Promised Land,* pp. 244–48.

13. Hutchins Hapgood, *The Spirit of the Ghetto, Studies of the Jewish Quarter of New York* (New York, 1902), p. 85. Many other novels by Yiddish authors deal with strained relationships between husbands and wives in the immigrant Jewish family. See Bernard Cohen, *Sociocultural Changes in American Jewish Life as Reflected in Selected Jewish Literature* (Rutherford, Madison, and Teaneck, N.J., 1972), pp. 117–18.

14. Hapgood, *Spirit of Ghetto,* p. 89.

15. Sanders, *Downtown Jews,* pp. 356–59.

16. Abraham Cahan, *The Rise of David Levinsky* (New York, 1917; 1951).

17. Hapgood, *Spirit of Ghetto,* p. 90.

18. Levine, "Jewish Family Desertion," i–xxiii.

19. *Ibid.,* p. 44.

20. *Ibid.,* p. 230.

21. *Ibid.*, p. 19.

22. Morris Waldman, "Family Desertion," *Proceedings,* 6th Biennial Conference, NCJC (1910), p. 55.

23. *Proceedings,* Biennial Conferences, NCJC (1900–1911) [1st Conference = 1900; 2nd = 1902; 3rd = 1904; 4th = 1906; 5th = 1908; 6th = 1910, and 7th = 1912].

24. Charles Zunser, "Family Desertion — Report on a Study of 423 Cases," *The Annals of the American Academy of Political and Social Science,* 145 (September 1929), 98–104.

25. Levine, "Jewish Family Desertion," p. 250.

26. Morris Waldman, "Family Desertion, A Historical View of the Problem," *Jewish Charity,* 5, nos. 3–4 (December 1905-January 1906), 52. Other issues of *Jewish Charity* concerned with desertion are: 3, no. 5 (Feb. 1904); 4, no. 5 (Feb. 1905); 5, no. 2 (Nov. 1905); and 5, no. 5 (Feb. 1906).

27. *Proceedings,* 6th Conference, NCJC (1910), pp. 54–55.

28. Herman N. Stein, "Jewish Social Work in the United States, 1654–1954," *American Jewish Year Book* (1956), 29.

29. Baum, et al., *Jewish Women,* p. 116.

30. Charles Zunser, "The National Desertion Bureau — Its Functions, New Problems and Relationships With Local Agencies," Paper read at the annual session of the National Desertion Bureau [hereafter called NDB] in Washington, May 1923, p. 4.

31. One such husband, who was informed by reliable sources that his wife had been among the missing after his village had been completely destroyed in a pogrom, remarried a few months later and had a child. When, four years later, the NDB discovered that his family was alive, the husband promptly sent for them and sued for an annulment of his second marriage, despite his second wife's protestations. Ultimately, he returned to live with his original family while continuing to support the child of the second marriage. *Ibid.*, p. 5.

32. Isaac Metzker, ed., *A Bintel Brief* (Garden City, N.Y., 1971), p. 107.

33. Charles Zunser, "Impressions of a Worker in a New Field," *Jewish Charity,* 5, nos. 3–4 (1905/06), 59. In some instances, a man who had preceded his family to the United States sincerely wished to be reunited with them, but was humiliated by his inability to find respectable, lucrative work. One such husband, discovered by the NDB, was working as a farmhand and earning $10 a month. He tearfully recounted his story: "I was a failure and never earned enough to help myself. How could I help my family? I was ashamed to write home. One day, I determined to hide and have kept in hiding ever since. . . . What I wouldn't give to get out of the rut, to have my family join me!" The Bureau representatives granted the man a loan of $125 with which he was able to provide transportation to the United States for his family. In addition, the NDB found him a job in New York City. See also the *Annual Report,* NDB, 1912-15, pp. 10–11. Other *Annual Reports* were issued by the NDB in 1916, 1919, and 1922.

34. In addition, Hexter noted that there was a marked relationship between the incidence of desertion and the birthrate in the population under study. Thus, he assigned greater significance to "pregnancy desertions" than did other writers on the subject. See Maurice Hexter, "The Business Cycle, Relief Work and Desertion," *The Jewish Social Service Quarterly,* 1 (February 1924-February 1925), 3–33.

35. *Annual Report,* NDB, 1919, p. 10.

36. *Ibid.*

37. C. C. Carstens, "How to Aid Deserted Wives," *Jewish Charity,* 4 (February 1905), 140.

38. Howe, p. 180, *World of Our Fathers,* quotes M. Baranov, "Missing Husbands," published in the *Forwards* (25 February 1910).

39. Moses Rischin, *The Promised City: New York Jews, 1870-1914* (Cambridge, Mass., 1962), p. 88.

40. Levine, "Jewish Family Desertion," pp. 197–98.

41. Levine's study demonstrated that Jewish deserters were less likely to be alcoholics than were men in the general population; however, they were more inclined to engage in gambling and extramarital sexual activity than their non-Jewish counterparts, *ibid.*, p. xxi.

42. Report of the Committee on Desertion, *Proceedings,* 7th Biennial Conference, NCJC (1912), p. 14.

43. Rischin, *Promised City,* p. 88.

44. *Annual Report,* NDB, 1912-15, pp. 10–15.

45. Lee Frankel, Report of the Committee on Desertion, *Proceedings,* 7th Biennial Conference NCJC (1912), pp. 58–63.

46. Waldman, "Family Desertion, Historical View," pp. 53–54.

47. Levine, "Jewish Family Desertion," p. 53.

48. Among the organizations which sponsored such workrooms were the United Hebrew Charities, the Chicago Women's Aid Organization and the New York City Charity Organization Society. See Charles Bernheimer, *The Russian Jew in the United States* (Philadelphia, Pa., 1905), pp. 69 and 90–91.

49. Metzker, *Bintel Brief,* p. 108.

50. Levine, "Jewish Family Desertion," p. 52.

51. *Annual Report,* NDB, 1912–15, p. 3.

52. Baum, et al., *Jewish Woman,* pp. 117–18.

53. Report of the Committee on Desertion, *Proceedings,* 7th Biennial Conference NCJC (1912), pp. 29–30.

54. *Annual Report,* NDB, 1919, p. 11.

55. Jewish social service workers consistently stressed the Jewish inclination toward self-support in their addresses before non-Jewish audiences. As Lee Frankel put it, "Among [the traits of Jewish immigrants in America] . . . are the love of home, the inherent desire to preserve the purity of the family and the remarkable eagerness which they show for education and self-improvement. . . . The history of Jewish charities in the United States demonstrates . . . that the Jewish immigrant . . . readily adapts himself to his American environment . . . and even though he may temporarily require assistance, rapidly becomes independent of charitable interference." Bernheimer, *Russian Jew in United States,* p. 67.

56. *Annual Report,* NDB, 1955, p. 4.

57. Lee Frankel, Report of the Committee on Desertion, *Proceedings,* 4th Biennial Conference, NCJC (1906), 47.

58. *American Jewish Year Book* (1900–01), VIII, 138–39. An examination of the United Hebrew Charities' relief records reveals that 1,052, or 10 per cent, of the applications for aid received in New York City came from deserted women. In Chicago, for instance, the figure was 15 per cent. (See Solomon Lowenstein, "Jewish Desertions," *Jewish Charity,* 4 [Feb. 1905], 143). In 1905, the proportion of applicants who were abandoned women was 11 per cent, and in 1910, it was 10.5 per cent, according to Levine, "Jewish Family Desertion," pp. 49–50.

59. Zunser, "National Desertion Bureau," p. 2.

60. Frankel, Report, *Proceedings* (see Note 57 above), p. 50.

61. *Ibid.,* pp. 52–55.

62. Levine, "Jewish Family Desertion," p. 107.

63. *Ibid.,* pp. 107–10.

64. Stein, "Jewish Social Work," p. 22.

65. Levine, "Jewish Family Desertion," pp. 76–77.

66. *Ibid.,* p. 112.

67. Zunser, "National Desertion Bureau," p. 1.

68. Levine, "Jewish Family Desertion," p. 111.

69. Zunser, "Family Desertion—Report," p. 98.

70. *Annual Report,* NDB, 1912–15, p. 6.

71. Report of the Committee on Desertion, *Proceedings,* 7th Biennial Conference, NCJC (1912), pp. 12–13. A typical entry in the "Gallery" of the *Forwards* in 1910 read: "I am looking for my husband, Nathan Cohen, known as . . . Moshe Mendele Shenker's from Nashelsk, Russia-Poland, umbrella peddler, twenty-two years old, the little finger of his right hand is bent. He abandoned me and a five-month old baby in great need. Whoever knows of him should have mercy on a young woman and infant and get in touch with Bessie Cohen, 1415 Snagman Street, Chicago," as quoted by Howe, *World of Our Fathers,* p. 179.

72. Levine, "Jewish Family Desertion," pp. 120–26.

73. *Annual Report,* NDB, 1919, p. 6.

74. *Annual Report,* NDB, 1912–15.

75. Levine, "Jewish Family Desertion," p. 113.

76. *Annual Report,* NDB, 1919, pp. 5–15.

77. Levine, "Jewish Family Desertion," pp. 130–31.

78. *Ibid.*

79. Charles Zunser, "Family Desertion," in Kehillah of New York City, *The Jewish Communal Register of New York City, 1917–18,* (New York, 1918), pp. 1,323–24.

80. Levine, "Jewish Family Desertion," pp. 131–32.

593

81. Zunser, "National Desertion Bureau," p. 82.

82. Report of the Committee on Desertion, *Proceedings,* 7th Biennial Conference, NCJC (1912), pp. 2-3.

83. *Ibid.*, p. 20.

84. *Ibid.*, p. 25. In serveral of the cases, no action was taken by the Bureau because of legal obstacles that proved insurmountable. For example, those men who had been traced to foreign countries were often beyond the scope of American legal action and therefore, if moral suasion failed to induce them to return, nothing more could be done. In other instances, legal minutia undermined the judicial process. In one case, the failure of a family to report the desertion immediately resulted in its inability to prosecute because the time period outlined in the statute of limitations had expired. *Ibid.*, pp. 29-30.

85. *Ibid.*, pp. 32-33.

86. *Annual Report,* NDB, 1912-15, p. 3.

87. *Annual Report,* NDB, 1919.

88. Zunser, "National Desertion Bureau," p. 2.

89. *Ibid.*, p. 3. Hexter, in his "Business Cycle, Relief Work and Desertion" (see Note 34 above), parallels these figures in his study of Cases from New York City (excluding Brooklyn) Handled by the National Desertion Bureau from 1912 until 1921. There he cites the following: 1912 — 610 cases; 1913 — 468; 1914 — 456; 1915 — 593; 1916 — 493; 1917 — 560; 1918 — 423; 1919 — 371; 1920 — 558; and 1921 — 470, for a total of 5,002 cases.

90. *Annual Report,* NDB, 1919, p. 7.

91. Zunser, "Family Desertion," p. 1,326.

92. Hexter, "Business Cycle, Relief Work and Desertion," pp. 27-28.

93. Zunser, "National Desertion Bureau," p. 19. That a special relationship existed between immigrant women and the Jewish social service agencies was reflected in a letter written by 37 husbands who had been imprisoned for non-support on Blackwell's Island. They bitterly complained that their wives had abused the compassion of the Jewish charity workers. Although obviously biased, this letter shows the Bureau's prejudices in this area: ". . . The worst offense is committed by the Jewish charity organizations. They sympathize with the wife when her husband is in jail. They forget, however, that they 'manufacture' the grass widows and living orphans when they help the women. As soon as the wife tastes an easy and a free dollar, as soon as she discovers that the 'charities' won't let her starve, she doesn't care that her husband is condemned. She lives a gay life, enjoys herself and doesn't think of her husband. . . ." See Metzker, *Bintel Brief,* pp. 110-13.

94. Report of the Committee on Desertion, *Proceedings,* 7th Biennial Conference, NCJC (1912), pp. 29-30.

95. Zunser, "Family Desertion," p. 100. See also Howe, *World of Our Fathers,* p. 179.

96. These approximate figures were obtained by adding the numbers of foreign-born, white women, fifteen years and older, classified as widowed, divorced and "condition not reported" (since no category "female, head-of-house" exists) in the U.S. Federal Census Reports of 1910 (13th Census, I, 563), and 1920 (14th Census, II, 388–89). Presumably, many women who identified themselves as "single" may also have been heads of households. It is impossible to obtain the number of Jewish female-headed households from federal government records, since there are no classifications based on religion.

97. Useful to the student of the subject, but not cited above, are the following sources: (primary), Family Location Service, Report, 1905-55 (New York, 1955); (secondary — books), Boris D. Bogen, *Jewish Philanthropy — An Exposition of Principles and Methods of Jewish Social Service in the United States* (New York, 1917); Stanley Brav, *Jewish Family Solidarity, Fact or Myth?* (Vicksburg, Miss., 1940); Abbott Ferriss, *Indicators of Change in the American Family* (New York, 1970); *Fifty Years of Social Service: The History of the United Hebrew Charities of New York* (New York, 1926); William J. Goode, *The Family* (Englewood Cliffs, N. J., 1964); Harry S. Linfield, *The Community Organization of Jews in the United States, 1917* (New York, 1930); Richard Morris and Michael Freund, *Trends and Issues in Jewish Social Welfare in the United States, 1899-1952* (Philadelphia, Pa., 1966); William O'Neill, *Divorce in the Progressive Era* (New Haven, Conn., 1967); and (secondary — articles), Lloyd Gartner, "The Jews of New York's East Side, 1890-93," *American Jewish Historical Quarterly,* 53 (1964); Walter H. Liebman, "Some General Aspects of Family Desertion," *Social Hygiene,* 6 (April 1920); Samson Oppenheim, "The Jewish Population in the United States," *American Jewish Year Book,* (1918-19), XVI, 2-74; Manheim Shapiro, "Changing Life Styles, the Jewish Family and the Jewish Community," *Congress Monthly,* 42 (1975), 14-21; and P. V. Young, "The Reorganization of Jewish Family Life in America," *Social Forces* (December 1928).

# Saints and Sinners: The Underside of American Jewish History

595

*by Arthur A. Goren*

*The American Jewish Archives, Cincinnati, 1988*

Originally published in *American Jewish Archives* (1988). Reprinted by permission of the American Jewish Archives.

*For Avner and Yedida and for Amos and Hagar*

596

And on the first of the intermediate days of Passover in the year 5662 the hevra kadisha of Adath Israel was established; and today, in the year 5671, it numbers 114 members. These saintly men, learned in the law who are also enlightened scholars, perform acts of true kindness conscientiously and uprightly for the glory of the Holy One. And when, heaven forbid, a man or woman of Adath Israel dies, the sexton calls them to carry out the ritual preparation of the body for burial which they do without remuneration to please the Creator. Praised and honored, this hevra kadisha is the finest to be found among the holy congregations of New York.

–from the Book of Chronicles of the
Adath Israel Society of New York,
translated from the Hebrew[1]

597

ספר

דברי הימים

לחברה עדת ישראל

אף נויארק

אשר נתיסדה

ע׳ המיסד רב העלילית

ר׳ אלטער בן ציון שפירא

ביום יד מרחשון תרסב

The title page of the Adath Israel pinkas (official history).

*Sheenie Mike sleeps in a bronze casket.*
*A kingdom of twelve blocks weeps for him*
*And so do his mother's wig and his father's old beard.*
*His orphaned cronies stand on the street corners*
*Rolling cigarettes with nervous thin fingers*

. . . . . . . . . . .

*Terror and guardian, king and commander*
*from around and around twelve whole blocks,*
*he lies there, all dandied up, asleep.*
*His mother's wig bewails yet another virtue:*
*that he never let his old parents*
*become a burden to others.*
*But his father's beard is ashamed in his old age*

. . . . . . . . . . .

*that Sheenie Mike, fallen, now sleeps*
*in a bronze casket.*

*—Yaacov Glatstein, "Sheenie Mike"*
*translated from the Yiddish* [2]

**Y**aacov Glatstein drew his portrait of the death of a Jewish gangster with irony and poignancy: irony, because Sheenie Mike's "orphaned" hoodlum underlings no less than his parents grieved for him; and poignancy, because of the virtue, "that he never let his old parents / become a burden to others." Ambivalence, however, dominated the poet's probe into this dark corner of Jewish immigrant life. The gangster son's filial devotion enabled the pious "half-blind father" to sit "over a tattered book / teaching the children the meaning / of shulkhn, a table, and kise, a chair," while a knowing mother haplessly watched "her child . . . quickly scrambling up the ladder / from pickpocket to the very peak / of empire . . . " Bewildered, they mourned the death of their wayward son, a victim of the golden land of opportunity, now laid out in a "bronze casket all dandied up," a desecration of the sacred rite. Glatstein also strikes a note of ambiguity. The "terror" of the neighborhood was also, enigmatically, its "guardian." And finally Sheenie Mike evo-

kes awe: Did they (the parents) know that under the same roof / lived a king /
who ruled mightily / till he fell by an enemy's hand?"³

Published in 1928, "Sheenie Mike" reflects Glatstein's first-hand knowledge of the Jewish underworld of those years. As rewriteman, columnist
and then city editor of the Yiddish daily, the *Morgen Zhurnal*, he understood
the appeal Jewish crime held for his readers. Indeed in the crime-reporting
of the Yiddish dailies, like that of the general press, one finds a fascination
with the gangster – with his character, motivations, family life, drive for
success, and with the sheer drama of combat, of gang against gang and the
police against the gangs – a theme we will return to. Thus for contemporary
readers, "Sheenie Mike" summoned up the alluring, tragic, and familiar
nether world of Jewish crime.

599

Brief accounts of the demise of two Jewish underworld chiefs, the killing
of Kid Dropper [Nathan Kaplan] in August 1923 and the killing of Arnold
Rothstein in November 1928, will fill out Glatstein's sparse lines for us.

Kaplan's kingdom was never much larger than "twelve square blocks," his
royal court a poolroom on Madison Street on the lower East Side. From there,
he directed his followers in the gangwars endemic to the New York garment
and service industries until he himself was shot dead by a certain Louis
Cohen, a member of Little Augie's (Jacob Orgen's) mob, Kaplan's principal
rival. Newspaper accounts quoted Kaplan's brother in the defense of the Kid:
"I'm telling you the East Side is mourning because he is dead. He was an
honorable son and he gave every cent he made to his family and friends. He's
been supporting his sick father for years." A Dropper mobster added, "Out in
Sullivan Country his father, Morris Kaplan, lies a hopeless paraplytic. Kid
Dropper kept him there. They call the Kid a murderer and a thief, but I know
what he did for the old man. It's lucky the old man can't read English, ain't
it?" His wife, Irene, contributed this character reference: "Why, I could have
asked Nathan to scrub the floor or wash dishes for me and he'd have done it.
I could have slapped him in the face and he'd never have said a word. He was
a real guy and I love him."⁴

With a relish for detail the press reported the funeral. The estimate of the
number present varied from 5,000 to 2,000, as did the estimate of the number of attending policemen (from seventy-five to fifty). Because of the considerable police presence, a rival gang abandoned its plan to send a jazz band
into the house adjacent to the funeral parlor in order to disrupt the funeral
ceremonies with blasts of jazz music. Nor did the Dropper's henchmen hold

the "parade" they had planned as a show of strength. But someone did call in a false-alarm, and the fire department arrived just as the body was being moved from the funeral home to the hearse. The *Morgen Zhurnal* noted with approval that Kaplan was laid out in the traditional shroud, prayer shawl, and skull-cap, and *The World* reporter observed that detectives frisked the gangsters who attended, but "none brought guns to so solemn an occasion." Motorcycle patrolmen led the funeral procession to Mt. Hebron Cemetery in Flushing where either Reverend Doctor Housman *(Morgen Zhurnal)* or Rabbi Rudolf Grossman *(New York World)* officiated.[5]

Understandably, Arnold Rothstein's murder received even greater coverage than Kid Dropper's. King of New York gamblers and banker for commercial crime, Rothstein moved comfortably in the entertainment, sports and political worlds of the city, far removed from the milieu of the Jewish immigrant neighborhoods. Conservative in his tastes and life style ("he never smoked, drank or fell for women," the *Morgen Zhurnal* wrote), Rothstein lived in an upper Fifth Avenue apartment with offices on West 57th Street in mid-town Manhattan. In the annals of American crime, Rothstein is considered a key figure in transforming crime from petty larceny into big business. Like Sheenie Mike, he was also the son of observant parents and, like Glatstein's creation and Kid Dropper, a devoted son. His father, Abraham, a successful businessman, was a pillar of the New York Orthodox community and gave generously to charity, as did Arnold.[6] Out of respect for the elder Rothstein, the son received – as reported in the Yiddish press – a "strictly Orthodox funeral" marked by decorum and suppressed grief and limited to two hundred mourners. *Der Tog* matter-of-factly reported one conspicuous infraction of Orthodox tradition: Rothstein's body wrapped in a *talith* was laid in a bronze casket – worth $5,000 the paper noted – rather than in the simple and inexpensive wooden coffin called for by religious law.[7] Worthy of note is the fact that not even the freethinking *Forverts* commented on what it might have described as the hypocrisy of the affluent Orthodox. Nor did any of the Yiddish dailies point out the impropriety of a renowned Orthodox rabbi, Leo Jung, delivering the eulogy. The rabbi praised the gambler as a great *ba'al tzedakah* – a philanthropist – who had aided many charitable institutions, and who also gave charity anonymously, the highest form of giving. The *Forverts* stressed Rothstein's involvement in the bitter garment industry strikes of the mid-1920s when gangs of hoodlums under his control hired themselves out to both sides, until he "mediated" a settlement in favor

600

of the Communist faction of the union.[8] However the dominant tone of the Yiddish dailies was one of awe if not admiration for Rothstein's business successes, his rise to power, the fame he had won, and his generosity. *Der Tog*, for example, in describing the hospital scene as Rothstein lingered between life and death – the stream of visitors, the high-placed and the low, coming to give blood or express their concern – concluded its report with this thought: "And so it seems that there he lies, not like one who belongs to an inferior class, but a sort of saint." Saints were, of course, good family men. When the *Morgen Zhurnal*, his greatest admirer, reviewed the dead man's life it cavalierly slurred over the existence of a mistress to whom Rothstein willed most of his money, and portrayed him as "a devoted husband."[9]

601

These episodes of violent death and Jewish funerals return us to the opening epigraph: the founding of the *hevra kadisha*, the holy burial society, established by Adath Israel, the United Hebrew Community of New York, in 1902.

The information on the founding of the *hevra kadisha* is drawn from a remarkable document: the *pinkas*, or official history of Adath Israel, written in the ornate style of classical Hebrew scholarship and in the practiced hand of a *sofer*, a copyist of Scriptures. Written by Yehuda L. Kaletsky, scion of a line of Orthodox Jewish literati and a leading member of the organization, the "Book of Chronicles" breaks off in 1912 with the death of Kaletsky "when no one could be found to fill his place."[10]

The saintly virtues the author ascribed to the members of the *hevra kadisha* were in keeping with European tradition. Since attending the dying and burying the dead without personal gain, as Jewish law required, was considered the most exhalted of *mitsvas*, only devout and established members of the community were eligible for membership. And because the *hevra kadisha* exemplified the highest form of public service, it also occupied an esteemed place in the structure of Jewish associational life. With this tradition in mind, the founders of Adath Israel were determined to reestablish the communal character of the management of death as a first step towards reviving the Jewish communal order as they had known it.

For the immigrant, ensuring a proper Jewish burial for oneself and one's family acted as a powerful incentive for joining a congregation or benevolent society. Organized for the most part on a *landsmanshaft* basis by Jews originating from the same town or region in Eastern Europe, these associations often provided other forms of assistance as well, such as sick benefits and interest free loans, which were part of the communal tradition the immigrants brought with them. However, even a cursory look at the immigrant societies reveals the considerable attention they gave to death benefits. These included: an assured grave in a section of a cemetery owned by the organization, the services of the society's *hevra kadisha*, coverage of the minimal funeral expenses, and the presence of members at the home of the deceased, at the funeral, and during the mourning period. Probably, the item that appeared most frequently on the agenda of the *landsmanshaft* societies was the purchase and maintenance of cemetery land.[11]

This anxiety is understandable when one considers the decommunalization and commercialization of death in America. A family not covered by death benefits faced exorbitant costs in buying a cemetery plot privately and paying a funeral director for his services, or they suffered the humiliation of turning to charity. Sholom Aleichem, the Yiddish author and humorist, writing in New York, lampooned the Jewish funeral. He described a well-off Jewish immigrant taking his wife on a tour of cemeteries to pick out desirable plots for themselves and their children, bargaining over the price, and finally arranging at the "funeral office" the type and cost of the funerals.[12]

In the "old home," the Jewish community handled death as one of its public responsibilities. It recognized a single *hevra kadisha* that had exclusive control of the communal cemetery and met all the needs of the bereaved family. For the destitute, the society provided its services gratis and supported the family during the period of mourning. For others, it used a sliding scale of fees, charging according to the financial status of the deceased, and using the income to support charitable institutions, a practice that gave the *hevra kadisha* considerable communal power. The burial society also applied sanctions against those who had violated communal norms: it assigned the offender a less desirable plot, charged his heirs excessive fees, or in extreme cases punished the culprit with a "donkey's funeral" which entailed burial outside sanctified cemetery land.[13]

Schooled in this tradition, the founders of Adath Israel approached their task. The most formidable obstacle they confronted was the reality of a fragmentized immigrant population holding on to narrow parochial loyalties. In a tour de force, Adath Israel's Hebrew chronicler placed this state of affairs in historical context. He recounted the sacred saga of Jewish survival together with the Jewish propensity for schism, from the days of the divided kingdom to modern times. "And when many tens of thousands," the chronicle reads, "fled the darkness and barbarity of Russia and Romania for the asylum which the Guardian of Israel prepared for them in the land of freedom, particularly in its capital, New York, they brought their different factions, customs, and rituals with them. The city became a veritable ingathering of the exiles. Societies, synagogues, and houses of study sprang up in the city like grass in the land. All were distinguished by piety, filled with the glory of Torah, and attaining the splendor of Israel's faith."[14]

Yet these achievements, the chronicler declared in the name of Adath Israel, also carried the seeds of chaos:

"Most of the societies in New York," he wrote, "are named after the city in the homeland from which their founders came. Only those from that particular city or at least those who come from the same region have rights of membership. If one comes from another area, or another state – a Lithuanian to a German or Hungarian society – he will not be accepted, how much more so a person from the sect of Polish hasidim mixing with hasidim from Volyn, and certainly a hasid will be refused by a society of mitnagdim. So, one sect has been estranged from another throughout our history."[15]

603

What agitated the founders most was the callousness one frequently encountered among the members of these benevolent societies. It was in response to one such case that Alter Ben Zion Shapiro, a leading figure in the Orthodox community at the turn of the century, took the first steps in establishing Adath Israel. Shapiro was present at the meeting of a "certain society" while it was considering the admission of an applicant. The majority were opposed because of the applicant's age – unless he paid the high initiation fee of seventy-five dollars. The account, which appears in a jubilee book, continues:

"The proposed member was a respectable and learned Jew, formerly quite well to do in Vilna. He was somewhat over sixty years old, and in the best of health. . . . During the discussion one heard such remarks as: he is too old; he would be a financial loss; he already stood with both feet in the grave. One member expressed the idea that they already need to warm water (to cleanse the corpse). Meanwhile the unhappy subject sat on the other side of a partition and listened to all this."[16]

Shapiro, who had founded the Hebrew Free Loan Society in 1891, now moved to combat both evils: the iniquity of sectarianism represented by the myriad of *landsmanshaft* benevolent societies and the absence of true charity that one encountered in these societies. Shapiro proposed establishing an association that would offer Jews irrespective of their origin, or age (no medical examination to be required) or financial means, the essential communal supports, first and foremost death benefits. For a standard fee of three dollars a year members and their families would be assured a burial plot and insured against funeral expenses. Shapiro's strategy, which became Adath Israel's distinguishing feature, was predicated upon the same free enterprise principle that had exacerbated the splintering effect of the transfer to America of Old World loyalties. By undercutting the costs of existing communal services, Adath Israel would create a united community. Large numbers, moreover, would enable the organization to maintain these low costs.

604

Within a decade of its founding Adath Israel had six thousand members (i. e. heads of families), and had established branches in Harlem and Brownsville. It had also organized its own sick fund, free-loan society, and synagogue. The annual report listed thirty seven institutions and charities as receiving help from the society. A further indication of Adath Israel's communal aspirations was the appointment of the eminent rabbi, scholar and preacher, Gabriel Ze'ev Margolis, as its spiritual leader. Margolis, supported handsomely by the society, established a *bet din*, a rabbinical court, and offered his services without compensation for supervising the kosher meat industry. Although Adath Israel continued to grow and became the largest organization of its kind – eleven thousand families by 1940 – it failed to live up to the ambition incorporated in its legal English name, the "United Hebrew Community of New York." Nevertheless Adath Israel does illustrate the communal energies that were latent in the venerable "holy society."[17]

The transition from life to death is a time of public judgment, of determining who the saints are and who the sinners are. In the European traditional society, or in a society where traditional institutions still possessed some influence, the *hevra kadisha*, acting for the community, played a critical role in making this judgment. In a sense, with each burial the community reaffirmed its common values. Through the details of the final rites of passage, the person was placed somewhere on a well-calibrated scale which ran from saint to sinner. The funeral procession of a saintly scholar, rabbi, great benefactor, or important functionary would pause at the synagogue and other institutions with which the deceased was associated. At each station, and at the cemetery, the deceased would be eulogized by distinguished members of the community, and then interred among the esteemed who had gone to their reward. All who possibly could would accompany a person of such standing from home to cemetery. When common people died, relatives and friends assembled at the dead person's home to accompany the body to the cemetery where a prominent person, not necessarily the rabbi, delivered the eulogy. At the other extreme of the scale, as in the case of an informer's corpse in a small eastern European community, the dead received the most ignoble treatment. He was placed on a garbage wagon, and dragged by a lame horse to the cemetery accompanied by gangs of shouting boys and barking dogs.[18]

605

In the New World, as we have intimated, there was confusion as to who the saints and sinners were. The pious ideals announced by Adath Israel's chronicler did not go much beyond the privatism of immigrant associational life. Outsiders perceived the virtuous founders of the society to be no more than ordinary functionaries, although in Europe they would have been recognized as saintly figures. In the case of Arnold Rothstein, the Yiddish press, an arbiter of sorts of Jewish public opinion, portrayed him in laudatory terms, closer to the saint's end of the scale than the sinner's end, as did an important Orthodox rabbi. Indeed, it is precisely this confusion in categorization that requires further elaboration.

Big Jack Zelig (William Alberts) was Rothstein's contemporary. In the years prior to Zelig's murder in October 1912, both were active figures in New York's underworld, a criminal collusion that linked politicians, police, thieves, racketeers, and purveyors of commercial crime. Rothstein owned and managed gambling casinos. Zelig headed one of the most notorious gangs in the city. In keeping with the times, he protected illicit businesses against their competitors' thugs or the threat of using his own, supplied toughs at election time to intimidate the rival party's followers, and hired out his "gorillas" to commit murder or mayhem as enforcers and labor racketeers. Where Rothstein served a general clientele – his elegant gambling halls in mid-town Manhattan catered to New York's wealthy – Zelig's power base was the Jewish lower East Side.[19]

Like Sheenie Mike, Zelig began his criminal career picking pockets and quickly won the reputation of being "one of the best." He was also known as "a very good stone getter (jewelry thief), perhaps one of the best in the world."[20] Both specialties – together with shoplifting, burglary, and extortion – led to forming gangs able to impose order and efficiency among the many hundreds of competing thieves, and capable of obtaining immunity from police harassment. The gang had its fence, lawyer, police and political connections, and its hangouts, where members met to exchange information and to socialize. The arena of this criminal activity – the gang's "territory" – coincided with an ethnic neighborhood. At a critical moment when murders and arrests disrupted the existing hierarchy of gang rule on the lower East Side, Zelig moved in to fill the vacuum and become the "terror" and "commander" of downtown's Jewish underworld, and for some, the quarter's "guardian"as well.[21]

606

Commercial crime – the systematic provision of illegal goods and services, like gambling, prostitution, and narcotics – was a central part of Zelig's domain. A 1913 report on crime conditions on the lower East Side- – prepared for the New York Kehillah, a federation of Jewish organizations – reflects in part the potential wealth and power of that domain. The report listed 914 hangouts, mostly saloons where various forms of gambling took place, 423 disorderly houses, and 374 pool parlors which were fronts for horse betting. Many of the owners, managers, employees, collectors, and protectors of these enterprises were dependent upon Zelig. Fear of Zelig also gripped the small businessmen. In a cynical borrowing of popular ways of raising funds for philanthropic purposes, Zelig and his gang periodically sponsored "benefit"balls. (The name of the sponsoring organization, as it appeared in the press, was, "the Boys of the Avenue Pleasure Association.") His henchmen would force storeowners and peddlers to buy tickets and advertising space in the journals printed for the occasion. At one such affair campaign type pins featuring a photograph of Zelig were distributed or sold. The income, it was announced, was to be allocated to needy members of the association who required bail or legal assistance.[22]

While Zelig's murder by a minor hoodlum was portrayed in the press as just retribution, a surprisingly different image of the gangleader emerges from another source, the confidential reports prepared by a private investigator for the New York Kehillah. In August 1912, Rabbi Judah L. Magnes, the Kehillah's chairman, hired Abraham Shoenfeld to serve as chief crime investigator of the organization's "vigilance committee" (the name was later changed to Bureau of Social Morals). The immediate stimulus for the unprecedented undertaking was the gangland killing of Herman Rosenthal, a Jewish gambler. For months, while the perpetrators of the crime were pursued, apprehended, tried, sentenced to death and executed, public attention was riveted on the prominence of Jews among those connected with the murder and those involved in the wider world of gambling, police and political corruption, and violence.[23]

The Kehillah's effort to uproot crime in the Jewish quarter depended on gathering precise and trustworthy intelligence that could be used to pressure the politicians and the police department to act expeditiously and forcefully. Shoenfeld's veracity and experience were crucial to the success of the operation. Although only twenty-one at the time, he came with respectable credentials having served under George J. Kneeland in the Rockefeller-financed study of commercialized vice in New York City. Magnes regularly scrutinized Shoenfeld's reports, as did Harry Newburger, a reputable lawyer who handled the legal work of the Kehillah, and both vouched for his credibility and expertise. Finally, a board of distinguished citizens, among them bankers Jacob Schiff, Felix Warburg, William Salomon, Adolph Lewisohn, lawyer Louis Marshall, and Judge Samuel Greenbaum, monitored the activities of the vigilance committee and its chief investigator to assure the reliability of the undertaking.[24]

For Shoenfeld this was not only the moment to "clean up" the East Side, but also the opportunity to educate uptown Jewry's most influential notables about the social world of Jewish criminality. Shoenfeld laced his facts on crime with personal observations, analysis and exhortations. In flamboyant prose, he warned of the decadence, corruption and iniquity infesting the Jewish quarter, and in brief profiles he depicted the brutality and depravity of the more infamous hoodlums, pimps, madams and thieves. Incredibly, the crusading investigator found much to admire in Zelig, the Zelig whom *The World* described as "the most notorious gunman, gang leader and pickpocket in the city." For Shoenfeld he was also defender of the Jewish quarter and a model of manhood.[25]

Both themes appear in the opening page of a long account of Zelig's criminal career, most likely written in August 1912, three months before his murder. Shoenfeld announces the manhood motif in these words:

> "He [Zelig] is about twenty-six years old; five foot eleven inches; somewhat bandy legged; raw boned; broken nose; clean shaven; healthful dark fearless eyes; splendid disposition and a very good conversationalist. ... At

607

all times he has had the reputation amongst his friends and associates as being a good scrapper and above all a man of principle which readily understood is a quality seldom found amongst thieves. You may find honor but never principle."[26]

Shoenfeld then states the defender motif:

"The city has been stirred by the means of copies of newspapers containing his name and pictures and his awful record, but I wish to state that if ever a man has done real good work for the East Side unknowingly it was he. Outlaw he may be classed but he has done one thing and that is, he has rid the East Side of Italian pimps and thieves."

608

From their base in downtown's Little Italy, gang-leaders like Paul Kelly (Paulo Vaccarelli) and Jack Sirrocco ordered their hoodlums and procurers into the neighboring Jewish quarter to hold up gambling houses and to lure young Jewish women from the dancing halls and balls into prostitution. The raids on the gambling houses located in his territory, according to Shoenfeld, challenged Zelig's reign and threatened a lucrative income, while the presence of Italian procurers offended his moral and Jewish sensibilities. To reassert his power – whenever that was necessary – Zelig retaliated. He struck at the saloon headquarters of the rival chiefs, terrorized their "dives" and "hangouts" and barred Italians – by murder on at least one occasion – from attending social affairs held in his domain. His goal remained the brutal exploitation of the small gamblers, madams, and merchants in his district. Nevertheless those who paid tribute to him in exchange for a measure of peace and stability also saw him as defender of the quarter from outside gangs.[27] Shoenfeld describes a ball Zelig ran at the height of his career:

"Not alone did crooks, gamblers and others attend this ball but Eastside businessmen, young and old, came to pay willing tribute to Jack Zelig. There was a large crowd of legitimate businessmen.... Jack was very popular. Half of these people he had never seen nor spoken to in all his life."

Towards the end of his report, written after the gangster's death, Shoenfeld summed up Zelig's contribution:

"He cleared the East Side of Italians who were wont to holdup stuss houses and legitimate business places. He cleared the East Side of Ital-

*ians who could be seen walking through the streets with Jewish girls whom they were working into the business of prostitution. He prevented more hold-ups and other things of a similar nature during his career than one thousand policemen."*

Such successes depended on personal prowess and acquiring a reputation as a dauntless and invincible battler, a reputation that would intimidate friend and foe. Zelig, Shoenfeld reported, was only a fair shot with the gun, "but he is a fighting terrier. The man is a demon when his blood is boiling. He can fight fifty men at once if he has them in front of him and is not taken unawares, and when he hits with his fist it descends like a lion's paw." On one occasion Zelig and two of his henchmen walked into a saloon in the Italian quarter, unarmed, looking for and then finding Jack Sirrocco. Other Italian gang-leaders entered the saloon. "At once his [Zelig's] suspicions were aroused and his thoughts were augmented by the fact that twenty Italians had hastily gathered in the saloon which is in front of the dive . . . and were holding whispered conversations in the Italian language." As Zelig tried to leave he was insulted and ridiculed by Sirrocco. "Jack did not dally but suddenly struck Sirrocco an awful punch on the jaw with his fist which knocked him down and out. Zelig and his two friends took the mob of Italians by surprise. . . . The Italians fought wildly but the twenty or more of them were routed and whipped by the three Jew boys, as they were known to the Italians, and to prove this, it is only necessary to state that when the police arrived on the scene, there were only two Italians left in the place, but every Jew was there."

609

In addition to Zelig's fearlessness, he enjoyed other attributes that swelled Shoenfeld's ethnic pride. Although by nature one who always looked after his own affairs, Zelig "is built so that he cannot bear to see an innocent bystander or unsuspecting person being taken advantage of or wrongfully abused." Fearlessness and fairness led to civic virtue. In the fight for the Democratic Party leadership of the 10th Assembly District in 1911, a Dr. Morris Klein challenged the Tammany incumbent, Larry Mulligan, the step-brother of Big Tim Sullivan. The issue was Tammany's use of gorillas and repeaters at the polls. Klein hired "Jack Zelig and his friends to protect the voters." Zelig went from booth to booth "driving away Italian gorillas one after the other. He was not doing any gorilla work, nor were his men. They were endeavoring to keep things straight." Shoenfeld claims that Zelig's defiance of Sullivan and his hired thugs marked the turning point in the fall of the Sullivan clan and in Tammany's hold on the lower East Side.

*The New York American* elaborated upon Shoenfeld's portrait of Zelig as the embodiment of manhood. "Best Husband That Ever Lived, Says Gunman's Wife" – ran the headline of a long interview with Zelig. The heart of the interview was the gangleader's moving account of his nine-year old son and his plans for the boy's future. When asked what he was doing to train his son "so that he may not also go wrong," Zelig laid down some rules for the upbringing of boys "that might well be pasted up on the wall of every father's room. Make an athlete of your boy; keep him off the streets; never let him play marbles for keeps; keep him away from small dice and poolrooms; make a companion and chum of him." Playing marbles for keeps was morally the most dangerous for "it gives a boy his first taste of gambling." The interview also touched on Zelig's hobbies (swimming and reading). His favorite authors were Shakespeare, Victor Hugo and Eugene Sue. "I like *Les Miserable* best of all. Isn't that part fine where he goes up that wall?"[28]

There is the stuff of instant legend in Shoenfeld's depiction of Zelig, even though it was intended for the eyes of the sober-minded men of affairs who supervised the undertaking. Indeed, herein lies the distinctive value of Shoenfeld's testimony: that his portrait of the gang chief echoed the sentiments held by many at a time when crime was public and fixed, a fact of life, in the immigrant quarters and when ethnic self-esteem was low. What Shoenfeld said in private, the popular press on occasion stated openly. It humanized Zelig, ascribed American virtues to him, and identified him as a proud Jew. Fifty years after the death of Zelig this writer asked Judge Jonah Goldstein who had been a young lawyer at the time and involved in local politics why so many attended his funeral. Did the East Side look upon him as a hero? The judge replied:

> "Going to Coney Island, you take the street car at the Brooklyn Bridge. Jack Zelig and a couple of his thugs would hire some Jews with berd [beards] to ride on the open trolley cars. Then some good for nothing loafers would come along and pull the Jews' beards. They'd give it to those who pulled the beards. They didn't want a Jew's beard pulled. They had never been educated in Hebrew, didn't go to shul, but they weren't going to have a Jew tossed around because he was a Jew. ... These fellows made it possible for the Jews not to get tossed around."[29]

The murdered Zelig received one of the most stately and memorable funerals the Jewish quarter had seen. His confederates hired a fleet of cars to carry the mourners to Washington Cemetery in Brooklyn where they buried him in a choice plot between the graves of Jacob Gordin, the well-known Yiddish playwright, and a "famous rabbi."[30] When the coffin was taken out of Zelig's Broome Street headquarters, a group of Talmud Torah children walked behind it reciting psalms as the funeral procession made its way to Delancey Street and then to the Manhattan Bridge. According to the *Varheyt*, ten thousand gathered to watch the procession, and three thousand followed the coffin on foot across the East River. At the cemetery Cantor Goldberg of the Shaare Shamayim synagogue and his choir sang the traditional *El maleh rahamim* prayer, and Rabbi Adolf Spiegel of the Shaare Zedek synagogue delivered the eulogy. The ever-observant Shoenfeld noted in his report that "only the funeral of Rabbi Jacob Joseph surpassed this, the funeral of Jack Zelig."[31]

611

What did this mean? For four days following Zelig's murder the Yiddish dailies were preoccupied with the question. As to Zelig, he was "the chief of a gang that for money cracked heads, broke bones and routinely committed murder." Absent was any mention of the mitigating deeds Shoenfeld and others described. The Yiddish press detailed the protection rackets, the "taxing" of gambling houses, and the strong-arm jobs carried out for the politicians during election time and for the unions and the employers during the strikes as a calamity for Jews and for the Jewish East Side. The papers also asked why so notorious a gangster as Zelig had walked the streets of New York with impunity and carried on his criminal activities openly. And, simultaneously, they continued the searing self-analysis of the causes of Jewish crime begun only months before with the murder of Herman Rosenthal.

But the magnificent funeral, how was one to understand that? "Imagine," the *Forverts* asked, "if a greenhorn fresh from Ellis Island came upon this impressive funeral. He would have surely assumed that it was for a man of great distinction in Israel, perhaps a luminary in the Torah, and if not a respected figure in the community then at least a great philanthropist. So it would be in the old home. How astonished the greenhorn would be to hear that the parade to the cemetery was for a leader of robbers, murderers and cadets whose greatest virtue was his iniquity." The *Forverts* reproached the respectable Jews whose passivity had enabled hoodlums like Zelig to attain

612

A photograph of Big Jack Zelig's gravestone in Washington Cemetery, Brooklyn, New York.
(Courtesy Dr. Tessa Lebinger and Dr. Martin Lebinger)

power. But there was a further shame. *Kley kodesh* – religious functionaries – were hired for pay to glorify the dead gangster. True, in Europe wealth bought honors in life and in death, "but thoroughly vile criminals, murderers and cadets received a donkey's burial, a grave beyond the cemetery fence." The *Varheyt* echoed the *Forverts'* anguish. "Imagine if all this had happened in a Jewish ghetto in the old home, with the values of the old home, with its moral consciousness and sense of duty, imagine the sort of funeral such as Zelig would have had and where he would have been buried."[32]

Corrupting or discarding altogether the old world practice of judging the departed symbolized communal disorder and the collapse of the once powerful way that a community reasserted its collective values. "Weep not for the dead," the *Tageblat* intoned, "best weep for those who followed behind the coffin. . . . And weep, too, for those who sent Talmud Torah pupils to recite Psalms, mocking the Jewish religion and Jewish honor. We should weep that there are such Talmud Torahs that sent children to say 'and righteousness shall go before him' for Big Jack Zelig. Cry out, too, for the chaos and the licentiousness that reigns among us that such an episode could happen."[33]

613

Thus in America while the rites of death remained important and a spur to communal organization, the powerful *hevra kadisha* became an adjunct to the synagogue or benevolent society, or it functioned as a group of religious specialists hired by a funeral director. No longer did it discriminate between saints and sinners. Other devices in some small measure filled the vacuum, the press for one. The Yiddish press declared Zelig a public enemy and a menace to the Jewish community. And yet an element of ambiguity remains. The ten thousand who turned out for his funeral surely included hundreds from the underworld and perhaps hundreds more of the curious, as the Yiddish newspapers claimed. But many may have come to pay their last respects to Zelig, a defender of his people, the cocky American-made Jew who had made it in the no-holds-barred contest for riches and power. In fact, a decade and a half later, the Yiddish press that had condemned Zelig praised Rothstein.

It is worth noting that the Catholic Church faced a parallel situation. The funerals of gangsters of the Catholic faith presented a dilemma for the church. Many of them were lavish affairs carried out with pomp and dignity. In Chicago, thousands attended the funerals of Jim Colosimo and Dion

O'Banion including judges, congressmen, state senators and aldermem. However, the Archbishop of Chicago issued an order refusing a Christian burial to gangsters. "Any gangster who, because of his conduct, is looked upon as a public sinner or who by his refusal to comply with the laws of his church regarding attendance at church services and Easter duty, such a man is to be refused a Christian burial."[34] In the case of O'Banion, "it was admitted by friends that every effort had been made to have his funeral services conducted in some church." Occasionally hard bargaining won a measure of leniency: no ceremonies at the church, but a priest was allowed to officiate at the cemetery, or, the priest was allowed to say a prayer in the street outside the church.[35] But in New York, when Frank Aiello (Yale) – Brooklyn gunman, bootlegger, neighborhood philanthropist and supporter of his parish church – was buried, a mass was celebrated for "the Robin Hood of Brooklyn," as some called him. Two hundred cars were in the funeral procession, stores and businesses of the neighborhood closed in respect for the "good Samaritan," and houses were draped in black cloth. *Progresso Italo-Americano* reminded its readers of his donation which made possible the construction of the Italian parochial school next to the Church of Santa Rosalia. "Although mixed in shady dealings, Aiello had a generous heart and liked to protect the weak."[36] Despite its hierarchic and disciplined organization, the Catholic Church was hard put to enforce its control over the burial of the dead.

For a moment, one memorable occasion appeared to promise a restoration and American adaptation of the venerated tradition of a community paying homage to its saintly figures. When Sholom Aleichem, the beloved Yiddish author, died in New York in 1916, the Yiddish press declared a day of collective mourning. It called upon Jews to stay away from work and attend the funeral. The Kehillah took charge of the funeral arrangements. For two days and nights the body lay in state in Sholom Aleichem's apartment with a changing guard of Jewish writers keeping vigil. The procession stopped at the Ohel Yitzhak Congregation where a memorial service was held, and then it paused at the *Forward* Building, the Kehillah offices in the United Hebrew Charities Building, HIAS headquarters where Sholom Aleichem's son recited the *kaddish*, and Kessler's Theater. At all of these places spokesmen for the institutions eulogized the famous author. A second memorial service took place in the Educational Alliance where Judah Magnes, the poet Yehoash (Solomon Bloomgarden), Israel Friedlaender of the Jewish

614

Theological Seminary, the dramatist David Pinski, and the popular Yiddish preacher, Hirsch Masliansky, spoke, and Yossele Rosenblat, the famous cantor of the day, sang the *El male rahamim*. The eminent guests sitting on the platform included Jacob Schiff. Abraham Cahan, the *Forverts's* editor, was one of the honorary pallbears, an American invention that Sholom Aleichem would have surely satirized to the entertainment of his readers. The *hevra kadisha* of Congregation Ohavei Zedek handled the ritual internment of the body which took place at the Workmen Circle's Mount Carmel Cemetery in Brooklyn. There were more eulogies at the graveside where the Yiddish writers Sholem Asch and Abraham Raisin spoke, as well as the Yiddish socialist poet, Morris Winchevsky, the renowned European Zionist, Shmaryahu Levin, and the socialist Zionist leader, Nahman Syrkin.[37]

615

The celebration was an extraordinary ecumenical event, uniting the most disparate elements in a demonstration of affection for their cultural hero. The Yiddish press stirred the Jewish public, and the most representative agency in the community succeeded in enlisting the secularists and the religious, the Zionists and the socialists in a common expression of grief and tribute. But it was a one-time event. Neither before nor after did New York Jewry so honor one of its own. The public's response to Zelig's funeral, the spectacle of Sholom Aleichem's funeral, the Yiddish press' respectful leave-taking of Rothstein and the virtuous intentions of the Adath Israel founders, represented old values and traditions floundering about in the cross-currents of a new day and a new land.

In Sheenie Mike, the mother laments over the aloneness of a family branch cut off from its source and over the chasm between the father's submission to adversity and the son's dream of a kingdom.

> "The grandfathers, the pious watercarriers and greasy
> godfearing butchers,
> stayed in their cemeteries across the ocean.
> They didn't intercede
> when the red-eyed father expansively
> took poverty into his house, chanting:
> Now, shulkhn, a table, and kise, a chair.

# Notes

Part of the research for this paper was conducted at the American Jewish Archives of the Hebrew Union College – Jewish Institute of Religion in Cincinnati while I held a Senior Lowenstein-Wiener Fellowship. I also made use of the American Jewish Archives' collection in Jerusalem. I wish to express my thanks to Dr. Abraham Peck, the administrative director of the American Jewish Archives, for making it possible to spend time in Cincinnati and for making the visit all that a researcher could wish. I am also thankful to the Central Archives of the History of the Jewish People where I once more made use of the Judah L. Magnes Papers and for permission to quote extensively from the collection. A grant by the Israel Academy of Sciences and Humanities provided some of the funding for sustained research.

I am grateful to Professors Ezra Mendelsohn, Deborah Dash Moore, and Khone Shmeruk for their perceptive reading of this paper. Their comments and suggestions were invaluable. I benefitted from discussions with Professor Shlomo Slonim on Jewish funeral customs and law. My thanks also go to Mr. David Jacobson, executive vice president of the United Hebrew Community of New York (Adath Israel) who gave me valuable information about the organization in two interviews in August 1983 and granted me access to the early records of Adath Israel. Finally, I wish to acknowledge as well the help of Scott Miller who has been an efficient and resourceful research assistant.

616

1. The original is in the possession of the United Hebrew Community of New York (Adath Israel), the translation is by the author.

2. *The Selected Poems of Jacob Glatstein*, translated from the Yiddish with an Introduction by Ruth Whitman (New York: October House, 1972), p. 35.

3. *Ibid.*, p. 36. An analysis of the poem may be found in Janet R. Hadda, *Yankev Glatshteyn* (Boston: Twayne Publishers, 1980), pp. 42-45. Hadda agrees with Ruth Whitman that Sheenie Mike is "an imaginary composite of several real gangsters who grew up in the lower East Side of New York in the nineteen twenties. Professor Shmeruk called my attention to the fact that the poem first appeared in *Inzich*, March 28, 1928 and was included in the selection of Glatstein's entitled *Kreydos* which appeared in 1929.

4. *Morgen Zhurnal*, August 29, 1923, p. 1, August 30, pp 1, 6, August 31, pp. 1, 4; *Forverts*, August 29, 1923, p. 1, August 30, pp. 1, 3, August 31, p. 1; *Der Tog*, August 29, 1923, p. 1, August 30, p. 1; *New York World*, August 30, 1923, p. 15. For a brief summary of Kid Dropper's career, see Albert Fried, *The Rise and the Fall of the Jewish Gangster in America*, (New York: Holt, Rinehart and Winston, 1980), pp. 133-36.

5. *Morgen Zhurnal*, August 31,1923, p. 1; *Forverts*, August 31, 1923, p. 1; *Der Tog*, August 31, 1923, p. 1; *The World*, August 31, 1923, p.13.

6. Jenna Weissman Joselit, *Our Gang: Jewish Crime and the New York Jewish Community: 1900-1940* (Bloomington, Ind.: Indiana University Press, 1983), pp. 140-44; *Der Tog*, November 5, 1928, p. 1, November 6, p. 1, November 7, pp. 1, 8, November 8, p.1; *Morgen Zhurnal*, November 7, 1928, p. 1, November 9, p. 1, November 12, p. 9; *New York Times*, November 7, 1928, p. 28.

7. *Der Tog, November 8, 1928, p. 1.*

8. *Morgen Zhurnal*, November 8, 1923, p. 1; *Forverts*, November, 6, 1928, p.1.

9. *Der Tog*, November 7, 1928, p.8; *Morgen Zhurnal*, November 12, 1928, p. 9; *New York Times*, November 12, 1928, pp. 1,16, December 18, p.2, February 8, 1929, p. 25, April 16, p. 60; Leo Katcher, *The Big Bankroll* (New York: Harper, 1958), pp. 330-35.

10. *Jubilee Journal on the twenty-fifth anniversary of the Adath Israel of New York, United Hebrew Community, 1901-1926* (Yiddish Section), pp. 15-16. Kaletsky was the grandson of Rabbi Judah Bachrach who wrote novellae and glosses to the Talmud and to the works of Alfasi and Maimonides. In 1899, Kaletsky published in New York a history of Jewish persecution during the Crusader period in Hebrew titled, *She'erit Yisrael*.

11. Isaac E. Rontch, ed., *Di yidishe landsmanshaftn fun new york* (New York, I L Peretz Yiddish Writer's Union, 1938), pp. 14, 45-51, 77, 174; Hannah Kliger, "Traditions of Grass-Roots Organization and Leader-

ship: The Continuity of Landsmanshaftn in New York, "*American Jewish History*, 76 (September, 1986), 29-31; Michael R. Weisser, *A Brotherhood of Memory: Jewish Landsmanshaftn in the New* World (New York, Basic Books, 1985), pp. 92-99, 163-74.

12. Scholem Aleichem, *Kleyne mentschelekh mit kleyne hasoges, Berl Ayzik, Ale verk fun Scholem Aleichem*, vol. 6, pp. 251-54, Vilna-Warsaw, 1925.

13. Arthur A. Goren, "Traditional Institutions Transplanted: the *Hevra Kadisha* in Europe and the United States, "*The Jews of North America: Immigration, Settlement, and Ethnic Identity*, edited by Moses Rischin, (Detroit, Wayne State University Press, 1987), pp. 66-68.

14. "Chronicles of the Adath Israel Society of New York," pp. 973-71. The chronicle is hand-printed in a numbered ledger book beginning on page 998; because of the Hebrew the pagination is in reverse order.

15. *Ibid.* p. 968.

16. *Jubilee Journal of Adath Israel of New York*. (Published on the twenty-fifth anniversary, 1926), p. 28.

17. *Forty Years, 1901-1941, United Hebrew Community of New York* (unpaginated English section).

18. Goren, *The Jews of North America*, p. 77, note 11.

19. For a general account of Jewish criminality on the lower East Side of New York, see Fried, *The Rise and Fall*, pp. 7-36, and for a portrait of Zelig's career, see Herbert Asbury, *The Gangs of New York: An Informal History of the Underworld* (New York: Knopf, 1928), pp. 328-343.

20. "Reports of the Vigilantes Committee," Bureau of Social Morals of the New York Kehillah, file 1780, Judah L. Magnes Papers, Central Archives for the History of the Jewish People, Jerusalem.

21. *Ibid.*; *New York World*, October 6, 1912, p. 2; *New York American*, October 6, 1912, p. 1; Joselit, *Our Gang*, p. 41-44.

22. Arthur A. Goren, *New York Jews and the Quest for Community* (New York, Columbia University Press, 1970), p. 171; Asbury, *Gangs of New York*, p. 333; Story 14, File 1780, Story 747, File 1788, Magnes Papers; interview with Abraham Shoenfeld, February 6, 1965. For a dramatic account of such benefit balls, see *New York Times*, January 11, 1914, pp. 1-2.

23. Goren, *New York Jews*, pp. 148-151, 154-57.

24. *Ibid.* pp. 158-64, 169-75.

25. Interview with Abe Shoenfeld.

26. Story 14, File 1780, Magnes Papers. Subsequent quotations by Shoenfeld about Zelig are from this source and will not be cited.

27. Asbury, *Gangs of New York*, pp. 329-36; *New York American*, December 3, 1911, p. 9; Fried, *The Jewish Gangster*, pp. 31-33.

28. *New York American*. August 21, 1912, p. 2. The newspaper reprinted the interview on October 6, 1912, p. 3.

29. Interview with Judge Jonah J. Goldstein, October 24, 1964.

30. I wish to acknowledge the help of Dr. Tessa Lebinger and Dr. Martin Lebinger who visited Washington Cemetery to confirm the location of Zelig's grave and who supplied me with the following information. The inscription on the tombstone reads: "In memory of my beloved husband / Selig Harry Lefkowitz / Born May 13, 1888 / Died October 5, 1912 / May his soul / rest in peace." However, the death card in the cemetery office reads: "Albert, Zelig / Society, Jehuda Wisternitza / Row 3, Grave 4, Cemetery 4 / N. W. Siegel Plot #2 / Died - October 5, 1912 / Buried - October 7, 1912 / Cause of death - Pistol shot wound / Age - 24 years / Place of death - in transit to Bellevue Hospital / Next of kind - (left blank). The Lebingers found the grave of Jacob Gordin about fifty feet to the left of Zelig's grave. The "famous rabbi" mentioned in the newspaper accounts and in Shoenfeld's report may have been buried in a plot marked by one of turned-over tombstones or one of the tombstones whose inscription was rubbed off to be found to the right of Zelig's grave. The cemetery office was unable to provide any further information on this point.

31. Shoenfeld, Story 14, Magnes Papers; *Varheyt*, October 8, 1912, p. 4; *Forverts*, October 8, 1912, p. 4; *The World*, October 8, 1912, p. 2.

617

32. *Forverts*, October 8, 1912, p. 4; *Varheyt*, October 8, 1912, p. 4.

33. *Tageblat*, October 9, 1912, p. 4.

34. John Landesco, *The Illinois Crime Survey: Part III – Organized Crime in Chicago*, pp. 1026.

35. *Ibid.*, pp. 1028-1030, 1032-1036, 1039.

36. *Progresso Italo-Americano*, July 3, 1928, p. 3; July 4, p. 3. I appreciate the help of Dominick Romeo who examined the Italian press for me.

37. *Forverts*, May 14, 1916, p. 1, May 16, p. 1; *New York Times*, May 16, 1916, p. 13; *American Hebrew*, May 19, 1916, p. 45; Marie Waife-Goldberg, *My Father Sholom Aleichem* (London: Victor Gollancz), pp. 315-16.

618

# An Answer to Commissioner Bingham: A Case Study of New York Jews and Crime, 1907

By Jenna Weissman Joselit

(YIVO Institute for Jewish Research)

In September 1908, New York City's Police Commissioner, Theodore A. Bingham, a former general in the United States army, published an article in the prestigious *North American Review* which contained several astounding statistics. First he asserted that the overwhelming majority of New York City criminals were foreigners. "Eighty five out of every one hundred of our criminals," he wrote, ". . . is of exotic origin." Peppering his article with a variety of statistics, Bingham went on to say that half the city's underworld was composed of "Russian Hebrews." Furthermore, this group had a distinctive criminal profile: as burglars, firebugs, pickpockets and highway robbers.[1]

The police commissioner also contended that Italians, a "rifraff of desperate scoundrels," were responsible for twenty percent of Gotham's crime and that they committed such crimes as bomb throwing, kidnapping and murder. Finally, Bingham divided the remaining thirty percent of New York criminals "among representatives of other alien races" and native born Americans.[2]

Shortly after the article appeared, New York's Yiddish press printed long excerpts from it. At the same time, they protested

121

Originally published in *YIVO Annual of Jewish Social Science* (1983). Reprinted by permission of YIVO Institute for Jewish Research.

against the commissioner's "groundless and irresponsible remarks"
and called for an apology. When none was forthcoming, New York
Jewry, especially its Yiddish speaking population, "rose in wrath"
demanding Bingham's resignation.

To date, scholars have paid a good deal of attention to the
so-called "Bingham affair." Arthur Goren, for example, has demonstrated how New York Jewry's concern over Bingham's allegations
gave rise to the New York Kehillah; others have viewed the Bingham
affair as an example of the antisemitic episodes which dot American
Jewish history.[4] Why, then, another study?

For one thing, none of the extant works deal with the episode
on its own terms, as a chapter in the history of Jewish criminality.
During the early years of this century, and for several decades thereafter, Jews were thought to be disproportionately represented
among New York's criminal population. Writing at the turn of the
century, one observer found the lower East Side to be a "nursery
of crime" and its inhabitants the "worst element in the entire make-
up of New York City life" while as late as 1930, a Washington, D.C.
magistrate charged the Jews with creating a "Jewish crime wave."[5]
Nor was New York Jewry blind to the problem: the community's
establishment of a network of probation societies and reformatories
demonstrated that its concern with Jewish criminality was real.
Nevertheless, American Jewish historians have ignored the subject
of Jews and crime, relegating it, at best, to a minor footnote in the
history of American Jewry.[6] This essay, however, by placing the
Bingham affair in the larger context of Jewish criminality, attempts
to correct that omission.

Another reason for reexamining the Bingham affair are the
recent methodological advances, particularly in the field of quantitative history, which allow the historian to deal with issues which,
for technical reasons, have long escaped his grasp; criminal history
is one area which has enormously benefited from this development.
Investigating the history of crime is by its very nature difficult; it is,
after all, for good reason that the life of the criminal is popularly
referred to as the "underworld," for much of it lies hidden from
view. Police and court records, however, can serve as clues to the
nature of criminal activity and are for that reason quite valuable. At
the same time, the volume of information contained in these records
is so vast that without the aid of a computer, the historian can barely
begin to interpret them. Through a statistical examination of the

unpublished records of New York County's criminal justice system to ascertain the nature and extent of Jewish criminality in 1907, this essay can also be seen as a case study in the methodology of criminal history.[7]

## I. The Charge

Characterizing the Police Commissioner's remarks as "antisemitic poison", an "ugly libel" and as a modern kind of "blood accusation,"[8] all of the Jewish communal newspapers and some of the metropolitan press were quick to denounce what they perceived to be the unfair imputation of wrongdoing to a lawful and quiet people. "He speaks of the Jews with venom and prejudice," noted the usually restrained *American Hebrew,* the voice of middle class Jewry, while the *Yudishes tageblat,* a religious daily, forecast that the term "Jewish criminal" would soon become a household word. People will point their fingers at us, explained the paper, and our "green" immigrants will be automatically looked upon as candidates for prison. The *New York American,* for its part, labeled the police official's remarks "as idiotic as they were atrocious" and called for his resignation while the New York *World* termed Bingham's remarks "grossly unjust." Not one to mince words, Judge Otto Rosalsky, magistrate of the Court of General Sessions, suggested the high ranking city officer "ought to go back to building breakwaters in Buffalo where he was before he came here," a proposal which many Jews undoubtedly seconded.[9]

621

Even as Jewish communal figures and newspapers were giving vent to their anger and embarrassment over Bingham's remarks, they were busily engaged in demonstrating its statistical flabbiness. "He exaggerates facts, and he exaggerates figures . . ." noted the *Forverts;* its competitor, *Varhayt,* found that with the exception of two minor points, what Bingham printed in his article was a "hodgepodge(kasha) of unsubstantiated quotes, clippings and interviews." One New York magistrate thought the piece "ill digested, ill considered and malapropos." Noting that in the course of his long tenure on the bench he had not encountered anything remotely resembling that which the Police Commissioner described, the judge concluded that "even if the statistics showed any such state of things, I would not trust them."[10]

Still, denouncing Bingham's statistics was not quite the same thing as disproving them. Thus, various elements of the Jewish community tried to account for the figures in their own fashion. Some argued that Bingham erroneously labeled as criminal those persons arrested for committing what was, by most accounts, a trivial offense. Does Bingham think "pushcart peddlars commit felonies when they violate a city ordinance," asked Judge Rosalsky. Expanding on this point, the *American Hebrew* contended that Jewish criminals were guilty of such heinous crimes as putting newspapers in ash cans and of leaving banana peelings on the sidewalk; one wit suggested that Jews could be arrested for their inability to speak English properly.[11]

Perhaps the most engaging attempt to account for Bingham's statistics was suggested by one who called himself a "Thief *(ganef)* from the Tombs." In a letter to the *Forverts,* the correspondent wrote that based on his ten year experience as a professional thief, he knew for certain that Bingham was wrong. How the police officer came to place the number of Jewish criminals at fifty percent of the total could be explained by two factors, suggested this veteran of the underworld. First, the Jew tends to be arrested more frequently than his Gentile counterpart; unable or unwilling to shoot a policeman, the Jewish criminal prefers to be incarcerated rather than harm another human being. Second, once in jail, the Jew leaves more easily than other prisoners and is thus back on the streets and susceptible to arrest more often than his non-Jewish confreres. In the long run, observed the Ganef from the Tombs, it was not that the Jew was inherently more criminal than the Gentile; rather, the nature of the Jewish criminal experience was such that a very high number of Jews landed in jail.[12]

Others sought the provenance of Bingham's figures in the internal workings of the New York Police Department. The *Forverts* argued that frequently those Jews arrested were part of an indiscriminate police round-up. Ostensibly a periodic clean-up of local thieves, it was also used as a device, explained the paper, to shore up the number of arrests made by local cops.[13] Since the more names one had on a roster, the more industrious one seemed to be, Jewish names were frequently repeated. The *Morgn zhurnal* had another twist: too many Jews when arrested, it noted, give non-Jewish names for fear of disgracing their families; by doing so, they arouse police suspicions: "When those with black eyes, long noses and Yiddish accents have Irish or English names" is it any wonder that the police, as a matter of course, place the number of Jewish arrests at a high level?[14] Still others wanted to know on what basis racial and religious affiliation was decided. Thus, members of the Jewish community demanded from the Police Commissioner a "bill of particulars."[15]

New York Jewry did not, however, wait for either Bingham or members of his department to provide them with one for they were busy compiling their own set of statistics. On the evening of September 5, one hundred New York Jews, representing a broad spectrum of the community's ethnic and political divisions, met to discuss the implications of Bingham's article. After deliberating until two o'clock in the morning, those assembled decided to establish several committees: one immediately to examine available court and police records so as to "offset" the commissioner's remarks; the other to engage in a long-term study of Jewish criminality. Similarly, editorials, day after day, harped on the importance of having a sober statistical analysis of Jewish crime; several newspapers even published their own statistics.[16]

623

This stress on the importance of presenting a statistically oriented reply to Bingham was in part a response to the terms of the debate set forth by the police official in his article. To mount an effective rebuttal, defenders of the Jews would have to meet the Commissioner on his own terms: with numbers. In this respect, Jewish communal figures were also responding to the tenor of the times. As part of what one historian has called the "factual generation", these leaders, like their gentile counterparts, tried to address difficult social problems—housing, poverty or crime—objectively and empirically. This was a period, writes a student of social reform, "when the solution to every problem seemed to lie in submitting it to a group of good citizens and disinterested experts . . . the path to reform lay through research."[17] As the first step towards solving the problem of Jewish criminality, community leaders submitted the issue to a panel of statisticians who would initially determine the extent of the problem and then (and only then) suggest remedial measures. In the final analysis, though, one wonders whether the casting of what was inherently a highly charged issue in the form of a statistical inquiry was an attempt by Jewish leaders to assume a pose of objectivity in order to mask their true feelings.

Interestingly enough, much of what passed for authoritative statistical analysis barely qualified. *Varhayt's* publication of the daily court calendar of the Court of General Sessions (the felony court) in order that "the reader will be able to determine for himself how many Jewish names there really are" illustrates the community's tendency to seek the authority of numbers regardless of whether or not it truly understood them. On one day, out of 39 criminal cases on the court's agenda, there were eight with Jewish names. Proudly pointing to this one statistic, *Varhayt* affirmed that Jewish criminals accounted for no more than twenty percent of New York's criminal population.[18]

624

A notable exception to the community's flimsy efforts at quantitative analysis was a study of Jewish criminality prepared under the aegis of the Federation of Jewish Organizations, a group which (theoretically, at least) represented five hundred Jewish societies throughout New York State. The Federation's decision to sponsor such a project was fueled by several factors, among them the unavailability of detailed statistics on ethnic criminality. As early as 1907, Edward Lauterbach, the organization's president, had asked the New York Police Department to furnish him with a breakdown of arrests by nationality: a comment made by journalist Frank Marshall White that two-thirds of recent additions to the infamous Rogues Gallery were Russian Jews caught the community leader's attention and he wanted the Police Department to verify it for him.[19] A year passed and Lauterbach's request went unanswered. In the interim, members of the Federation's Executive Committee became alarmed by what they saw as the growing incidence of Jewish criminality and suggested the Federation "shed light upon this important problem." Accordingly, in February 1908, Lauterbach assigned his private secretary, Mark J. Katz, the task of combing through the records of the Court of General Sessions for the year 1907 to ascertain the number of Jews charged with felonies.[20]

Five months later, Katz published his findings in the June issue of the *Federation Review,* the house organ of the Federation of Jewish Organizations. His figures showed that in relation to population, Jews were half as likely to be convicted of a felony than Gentiles. Katz also found that Jewish convicts accounted for 16.4% of the total convicted population of New York County in 1907. Finally, his data indicated that 88% of Jews convicted of felony charges were guilty of property crimes.[21]

The Federation's timing could not have been better: two months after Katz published his research, Bingham sent shock waves throughout the Jewish community by alleging that Jews comprised fully half of Gotham's underworld. Armed with Katz's authoritative examination of Jewish criminality, New York Jewry was able nevertheless to deliver a "crushing and convincing reply."[22]

## II. A Bill of Particulars:

In reexamining the available criminological literature, one finds that Bingham was indeed guilty of overestimating the extent of both foreign born criminality in general and Jewish criminality in particular. The following section, an examination of the published reports of the New York City Police Department and criminal courts and the unpublished files of the New York County District Attorney's office, shows how Bingham erred in his estimation of New York City criminality.

625

The published annual reports of the Police Department contain information on the number of persons arrested in any given year and the nature of their offenses. Supplementing the police records are the published annual reports of the Magistrates Court which list the number and nativity of defendants brought before it. The Magistrates Court functioned as the court of first instance. A person arrested for committing an offense would be taken first to the local police station where his name and the charge would be recorded; after this initial booking, he would be taken to the local magistrate court. There, the presiding judge would determine the category into which the alleged offense fell—whether felony, misdemeanor or a minor offense—and once that was ascertained, decide upon an appropriate judicial course of action. Thus, the magistrate would send a person charged with committing a felony to the District Attorney who, in turn, would prepare a case against the defendant to be heard by the Grand Jury. The latter would decide whether to prosecute the offender or to dismiss him. If indicted by the Grand Jury, the defendant would stand trial in the Court of General Sessions. The Magistrates Court had jurisdiction over such offenses as vagrancy, disorderly conduct, violation of sanitary and corporation ordinances.[23] The third and fullest source of information used in this study are records known as "pedigree sheets." Compiled by the District Attorney, they contain the name, age, sex, place of birth, occupation and other social characteristics of those convicted of a felony.[24]

Material drawn from the published annual reports of the New York City police department indicates that the majority of those arrested during the early years of the century committed a minor offense. Between 1900 and 1905, major felonies such as burglary, felonious assault, grand larceny, homicide and robbery accounted for approximately 5% of all arrests; in 1906 and in 1907, *total* felony arrests accounted for 11.1% and 9.9% respectively of all arrests made by the police in those years.[25] This suggests that an overwhelming proportion of those arrested—even if eighty five percent of them were foreigners, as Bingham would have it—were hardly what one would call criminals in the strict sense of the word.

626

Unfortunately, the information contained in the police records is sketchy; nativity of those arrested is usually not given.[26] The published reports of the Magistrates Court, however, supplement the police records in precisely this area. As Table 1 shows, the majority of those "held for trial or summarily tried and convicted"

## Table 1

### Origins of Those "Held for Trial or Summarily Tried and Convicted" in the Magistrates Court of New York County, 1907

| Country | Number | Percent | |
|---|---|---|---|
| United States | 30,261 | 42.5 | |
| Russia | 9,254 | 12.9 | |
| Italy | 8,243 | 11.6 | |
| Ireland | 8,061 | 11.3 | |
| Germany | 4,219 | 5.9 | |
| Greece | 3,039 | 4.3 | Foreign born=57.3% |
| England | 1,044 | 1.5 | |
| France | 869 | 1.2 | |
| Scotland | 473 | 0.6 | |
| Other | 5,790 | 8.1 | |
| | 71,253 | 100.0 | |

Source: Thirty-fourth Annual Report, Board of City Magistrates, First Division, 1907, p. 83.

in the Magistrates Court in 1907 were foreigners. Moreover, those from Russia and Italy accounted for the two largest foreign born ethnic groups.

When the percentage of foreign born "held for trial or summarily tried and convicted" in the Magistrates Court is compared with available population figures, the foreign born were disproportionately represented. According to the 1910 federal census, those born abroad constituted 45.4% of New York County's population; yet this group accounted for close to sixty percent of those whose cases were tried by the Magistrates Court.[27] Similarly, both Russians and Italians were slightly over-represented among those charged with committing minor crimes: with 11.3% of New York County's population in 1910, Russians comprised 12.9% of those tried before the Magistrates Court while Italians, with 8.1% of New York County's population, comprised 11.6% of those charged with minor crimes.[28]

That a significant proportion of the Magistrates Court's cases was composed of the foreign born certainly suggests that a correlation between immigrants and crime did exist, as Bingham would have it. But a closer look at the material published in the annual report of the court qualifies that contention. It would show that the crimes committed by the immigrant population were largely minor. As Table 2 demonstrates, the profile of the offenses committed by

627

## Table 2

### Type of Offenses for which Russian Born were Held for Trial or Committed to a Reformatory and Other Institutions, 1907 (in percent)

| | |
|---|---|
| Disorderly conduct | 27.0 |
| Violation Corporation Ordinance | 34.0 |
| Violation Sanitary Ordinance | 14.8 |
| Miscellaneous | 24.2 |

Source:   Computed from Table "F": "Showing Nativity of all Persons Held for Trial or Committed to a Reformatory and Other Institutions," Thirty-fourth Annual Report, Board of City Magistrates, First Division, 1907.

Russians "tried or convicted" by the magistrates is rather topheavy with what are in reality civic, as opposed to criminal, cases.

In this regard, the Russian offender differed little from the Italian or, for that matter, from any other member of the "new immigration," for all had high rates of committing relatively "benign crimes." The New York State Immigration Commission in 1908 found, for example, that "a large percentage of the offenses committed by immigrants in New York City . . . are such non-criminal offenses as the violation of corporation ordinances and the sanitary code." These violations, concluded members of the commission, "do not imply actual criminality or criminal motivations on the part of violators."[29]

628

What did imply "actual criminality," though, was the conduct of a person who committed a felony—murder, grand larceny, rob-

## Table 3

## Place of Birth of Those Convicted of Committing a Felony in New York County, 1907

| Country | Number | Percent | |
|---|---|---|---|
| America | 302 | 64.3 | |
| Italy | 44 | 9.4 | |
| Russia | 28 | 6.0 | |
| Germany | 22 | 4.7 | |
| Austria | 19 | 4.0 | |
| Ireland | 19 | 4.0 | |
| Hungary | 7 | 1.5 | |
| Scandinavia | 5 | 1.1 | |
| England | 5 | 1.1 | Foreign born=35.7% |
| Rumania | 4 | 0.9 | |
| Scotland | 3 | 0.6 | |
| Canada | 2 | 0.4 | |
| France | 2 | 0.4 | |
| Bohemia | 1 | 0.2 | |
| Holland | 1 | 0.2 | |
| China | 1 | 0.2 | |
| Poland | 1 | 0.2 | |
| Other | 4 | 0.9 | |
| | 470 | 100.0 | |

bery—and who was convicted of that offense. For that reason, I drew a sample of the convicted population of New York County for 1907; my sample numbered 470 persons.[30]

Contrary to Bingham's allegation that the majority of criminals in New York were foreigners, Table 3 makes it clear that most were in fact native Americans.

Furthermore, when the percentage of foreign born convicted of a felony is compared with the proportion of foreign born in New York County's population, the former was under-represented. According to the 1910 federal census, the foreign born of Manhattan and the Bronx accounted for 45.4% of the population—as contrasted with 35.7% of New York County's convict population.

Of this group of convicted felons, fewer than twenty percent were Jewish (Table 4). Here, too, when the percentage of Jews convicted of committing felonies is compared with the percentage of Jews in the population, the Jews are under-represented. With an estimated 29.2% of New York County's population in 1910,[32] Jews accounted for slightly less than twenty percent of those convicted of major crimes. There is no question, then, that Bingham greatly overestimated the extent of Jewish criminality in New York. Still, Jews accounted for what was indeed a substantial proportion of New York's criminal population in 1907!

Bingham's remarks on the extent of Italian criminality also

629

### Table 4

### Number of Jews* Convicted of Committing a Felony, by Place of Birth, 1907[31]

| | |
|---|---|
| America | 28 |
| Russia | 26 |
| Austria | 16 |
| Germany | 5 |
| Rumania | 4 |
| Hungary | 3 |
| England | 1 |
| Poland | 1 |
| | 84 |

*Name, place of birth and residence were the criteria used to define a defendant as Jewish.

## Table 5

### Criminal Profile of Foreign Born and Native Born Convicts

|              | Property | Person | Both* | Other** |          |
|--------------|----------|--------|-------|---------|----------|
| Foreign born | 104      | 51     | 3     | 10      | (N=168)  |
| Native born  | 241      | 44     | 4     | 13      | (N=302)  |
|              | 345      | 95     | 7     | 23      |          |

*Robbery is an example of a crime classified as "both" insofar as it is an offense against the person and his/her property.
**Gambling, book-making, policy, and the violation of liquor tax regulation are classified as "Other."

appear to be incorrect. Though he charged Italians with committing twenty percent of Gotham's crime, available evidence shows they were responsible for half that (see Table 3). Yet relative to their proportion of the population, Italians, unlike the Jews, were over-represented: with 8.1% of New York County's population, they accounted for 9.4% of its criminal class.

Interestingly enough, Bingham's assessment of the respective criminal proclivities of the Jews and Italians holds up. As Table 5 indicates, the foreign born, with more than one-third of the con-

## Table 6

### Criminal Profile of Foreign Born Italians, Jews and Other Foreign Offenders
### (N=168)

|          | Property | Person | Both | Other |          |
|----------|----------|--------|------|-------|----------|
| Italians | 15       | 24     | 1    | 1     | (N=44)*  |
| Jews     | 41       | 12     | 1    | 1     | (N=56)   |
| Others   | 48       | 15     | 1    | 4     | (N=68)   |
|          | *In Row Percentages* |  |  |  |   |
| Italians | 34.1     | 54.5   | 2.3  | 2.3   |          |
| Jews     | 73.2     | 21.4   | 1.8  | 3.6   |          |
| Others   | 70.6     | 22.0   | 1.5  | 5.9   |          |

*The nature of the criminal offense of three Italians is, for some unexplained reason, not given.

victed population, committed more than one-half of those crimes classified as violent.

The criminal behavior of the Italian offender accounted for the excessive amount of violence found among foreign born convicts: the Italian felon committed 47.1% of all violent crimes perpetrated by the foreign born criminal population and 25.3% of the total number of violent crimes. With only 9.6% of the total population of convicts, the Italian offender had a higher proportion of violent crimes than his percentage of the criminal population warranted.

There are obvious significant differences between the type of offenses for which foreign born Jews were convicted and those for which foreign born Italians were convicted: the former had an extremely high number of property offenses and relatively few violent ones. The tendency for the Jewish offender to commit property crimes is strengthened further when foreign born Jews and native born Jews are classed together (Table 7).

631

Nevertheless, Jews committed such offenses more or less in accord with their proportion of the population: with 17.8% of the total convicted population, they perpetrated 19.7% of all property crimes (see Table 5).

A thorough analysis of the available criminal records for 1907 shows that Police Commissioner Bingham had, as one of his critics put it, "absurdly exaggerated" the extent of foreign crime in general and Jewish crime in particular. At the very most, the foreign born were responsible for committing a third of all felony offenses in New York County; in fact, figures published by the New York County District Attorney record that this percentage had remained constant since 1904 (Table 8).

## Table 7

A Comparison of the Criminal Profile of the Foreign Born Jewish Offender with that of the Native Born Jewish Offender (N=84)

|  | Property | Person | Both | Other |  |
|---|---|---|---|---|---|
| Foreign born | 41 | 12 | 1 | 2 | (N=56) |
| Native born | 27 | 1 | - | - | (N=28) |
|  | 68 (81.0) | 13 (15.5) | 1 (1.2) | 2 (2.4) |  |

## Table 8

A Comparison of the Percentage of Foreign Born Offenders with
Native Born Offenders, 1904–1907

|              | 1904 | 1905 | 1906 | 1907 |
|--------------|------|------|------|------|
| Foreign born | 35.0 | 34.3 | 35.5 | 35.7 |
| Native born  | 65.0 | 65.7 | 64.5 | 64.3 |

Source: Annual report of the District Attorney for New York County, 1907, Table
XVIII, p. 48.

Similarly, the police official overestimated, by a wide margin, the
total number of Jews and Italians involved in the criminal enterprise. Yet his belief in the excessive criminality of the foreign born
was shared by many Americans, who regarded the immigrant as an
unfailing source of criminal behavior.[35] "The dishonest among
them [the Jews] are all out of proportion to their numbers" asserted
one New Yorker in the aftermath of the Bingham affair while another noted that "Bingham had the right idea about the large proportion of Jewish criminals."[36] Some Americans, advocates of a
fierce policy of immigration restriction, believed the immigrant to
be inherently criminal; others probably took a quick look at the
large number of immigrants crowding the Magistrates Court and
concluded immediately that there was an unmistakeable connection
between them and crime.

To what camp did Bingham belong? Was the police commissioner an unabashed xenophobe sharing his thoughts (fears?) with
kindred spirits through the high-toned *North American Review?* Or
was he such a statistical innocent that he was simply unaware of the
implications of his remarks? Perhaps the city official was so immature a politician that he felt his remarks would go unnoticed by the
city's immigrant groups. In a word, one wonders just how culpable
Bingham was. No doubt, Bingham was probably a combination of
xenophobe, statistical innocent and immature politician. By all accounts a man of little tact and discretion, Bingham had become a
thorn in the side of Mayor McClellan who had first appointed him
as police commissioner in January 1906. "He was always getting
himself and incidentally me into hot water", the mayor later recalled. Similarly, *The New York Times* found Bingham to be brusque,

direct and totally "unaware that discretion is sometimes the better part of valor." Thus, writing the *North American Review* article may very well have been just another one of the many blunders committed by this "bluff soldier" of a city official.[37]

Yet, it would also seem that Bingham shared no fondness for the city's immigrants. In charge of an armed police force in daily contact with the city's millions, surely he calmed no fears when he used words that suggested that he was three-quarters prejudiced, one-quarter fair. Bingham was referring to a city that teemed with the foreign born; in expressing his ethnic biases, he was arraying himself not against the law breakers but against the citizenry.

Whatever his biases, Bingham publicly issued a retraction two weeks after his remarks had first appeared. In his lengthy and often unclear statement, the police official contended that he had no animus against the foreign population of New York, nor for that matter had he intended to damage its reputation. Rather, the purpose of the *North American Review* article, he explained, was to press for the creation of a new police unit capable of dealing with the city's ethnic groups where the regular police force was not. "It was only incidentally," Bingham added, "that the remarks were made which have been challenged."[38]

633

## III. Image and Reality

Glad for the opportunity to prove publicly that Jews did not constitute fifty percent of New York City's criminal population, members of the Jewish community hailed Bingham's retraction as a "manly admission of error" and saw it as the conclusion to a painful episode in New York Jewish history. Privately, though, the issues raised by the police official still rankled. If to some, the Bingham affair demonstrated that the "Jews are entitled to more criminals but thank God don't have them", to others, that New York Jewry harbored a criminal population, no matter how statistically small (or legitimate) was cause for great alarm. That Jews comprise even a small proportion of New York's convicted population is far too many for the people who gave the world the *Torah*, editorialized the *Yudishes tageblat*, a sentiment echoed in turn by the *American Hebrew*. "It doesn't matter if the Commissioner's figures were absurdly exaggerated," noted the weekly. "It doesn't matter if the proportion of Jewish criminals was only as low as ten percent. There ought to be no Jewish criminals at all."[39]

In order to understand fully why New York Jewry took Bingham's remarks so to heart, one must realize that the community had a set of perceptions or "working myths" about itself: that of the earnest, hard-working and law-abiding community was one much cherished notion. In addition to defining itself in such terms, the community tried eagerly to project this image, and others like it, publicly. By portraying the Jews as a collection of deviants, Bingham robbed those images of much of their reality. In order, then, to reinstate both for itself and for the general public the image of the Jew as honest and upstanding (and, of course, deserving of American citizenship), New York Jewry labored so diligently, indeed passionately, to prove the police official incorrect. This was not simply an idle gesture, an effort to save face, for Bingham's allegations appeared at a time when anti-immigrant sentiment or what is known as nativism was at its height. His allegedly sophisticated and scientific description of foreign born criminality in New York threatened to lend support to the claims of immigration restrictionists that the presence of foreigners was potentially dangerous to American society. The political implications of Bingham's article were not lost on the community; from the very outset, the *Yudishes tageblat,* for example, noted that the police commissioner's observations would provide antisemites and nativists with the best weapons with which to fight the Jews.[40] Realpolitik as well as a concern for image dictated the shape of New York Jewry's response to Bingham.

From an historical perspective, the Bingham affair is significant for several reasons. First, the Kehillah, New York Jewry's famed attempt to unify the disparate elements of the community into an organized whole, was one of its legacies. Second, and perhaps most importantly, Bingham's article provoked the *entire* New York Jewish community into realizing certain unpleasant facts about itself, facts which earlier many had refused to acknowledge. Though Bingham's figures were heavily inflated, there was no denying that crime among New York Jews was a very real social problem. As Louis Marshall put it: "Let us not deceive ourselves that we are entirely *kosher* . . . for the fact remains that a cancer is gnawing at our vitals."[41] From this point on, the elimination of Jewish criminality would be one of the community's chief priorities.

# NOTES

It is my pleasure to thank Professor Walter Metzger of Columbia University and Professor Arthur Goren of Hebrew University for their assistance.

1   Theodore A. Bingham, "Foreign Criminals in New York," *North American Review* (hereafter *NAR*), 187 (September 1908), 383.
2   *Ibid.*, pp. 385–7.
3   *New York Evening Journal*, September 2, 1908.
4   Arthur Goren, *New York Jews and the Quest for Community* (New York, 1970), Chapter Two; see also, Henry Feingold, *Zion in America* (New York, 1974), p. 139.
5   Frank Moss, *The American Metropolis* (New York, 1897), I, 161; *Jewish Daily Bulletin* January 2, 1930.
6   There are a few works on the topic of Jews and crime but their collective leitmotif is that Jews have less of a problem in this area than other ethnics. See for example, Saul Alinsky and A.J. Jaffe, "A Comparison of Jewish and Non-Jewish Convicts," *Jewish Social Studies*, 1:3 (1939), 359–366; Lee Levinger, "A Note on Jewish Prisoners in Ohio," *Jewish Social Studies*, 2:2 (1940), 309–313; Nathan Goldberg, "Jews in the Police Records of Los Angeles," *YIVO Annual of Jewish Social Science*, 5 (1950), 266–91. For an exception, see Alan Bloch, "Lepke, Kid Twist and the Combination," (unpublished PhD thesis, UCLA, 1975). For a critical bibliography of works on Jewish criminality, see Robert A. Silverman, "Criminality among the Jews: An Overview," *Issues in Criminology*, 6:2 (1971), 1–38.
7   Although Bingham referred to the five boroughs of New York City in his article on foreign crime, I limited my study to an examination of the criminal court records of New York County: Manhattan and the Bronx. I did so because of the unavailability of criminal court records for the remaining boroughs.
        At the time of the Bingham affair, several New Yorkers roundly criticized Edward Lauterbach, the sponsor of a study of Jewish criminality in New York County, for only examining the documents of that borough. In response to this criticism, Lauterbach wrote that the choice of restricting the inquiry to Manhattan and the Bronx "shows the worst possible situation . . . we have selected the place where the argument can be made the most strongly against us, no one can accuse us . . . that the statistics are inconclusive and of little value." Edward Lauterbach to Paul Abelson, September 12, 1908, Abelson papers, American Jewish Archives.
        One last note: the findings of this paper should be regarded as suggestive inasmuch as it is limited to an examination of court records for only one year. For a fuller inquiry into Jewish criminality, see the author's Columbia University PhD thesis, "Dark Shadows: N.Y. Jews and Crime, 1900–1940".
8   *Forverts* (hereafter *F*), September 1, 1908; *Yudishes tageblat* (*YT*), September 1, 1908.
9   *American Hebrew* (*AH*), September 4; *YT*, September 1; *New York American*, September 18; *New York World*, September 17; Judge Rosalsky quoted in the *New York American*, September 2.

¹⁰   *F,* September 1; *Varhayt (V),* September 1; Magistrate John Walsh quoted in *AH,* September 11.

¹¹   Rosalsky quoted in *New York American,* September 4; *AH,* September 11, *F,* September 4; *New York Evening Journal,* September 2.

¹²   *F,* September 14.

¹³   *F,* September 1.

¹⁴   *Morgn zhurnal (MZ),* September 2.

¹⁵   Isaac Hourwich, *Federation Review (FR),* 2; 10 (September 1908), 2.

¹⁶   *AH,* September 11; *New York American,* September 5; September 6; September 7; *New York Times,* September 7; *YT,* September 6; September 7; *V,* September 3; September 7; *F,* September 6; *MZ,* September 3; September 8.

   The decision to establish a permanent organization able to speak authoritatively in the name of New York Jewry was also made at this meeting. See Goren, pp. 30–33.

¹⁷   Robert H. Bremner, *From the Depths: The Discovery of Poverty in the United States* (New York, 1956), p. 157; See also, Robert Wiebe, *The Search for Order* (New York, 1967), Chapter 6.

¹⁸   *V,* September 3; September 15.

¹⁹   Frank Marshall White, "New York's Ten Thousand Thieves," *Harper's Weekly,* 50: 2610 (December 29, 1906), 1892. Surprised by this statistic, Lauterbach wrote to Police Commissioner Bingham on January 9, 1907 asking whether it was "accurate." Bingham replied that it was "substantially correct." Repeatedly throughout the course of the year, Lauterbach asked the police department to furnish him with "figures on criminality with reference to various classes and denominations." It was never done. On this exchange, see "The Police Department's Correspondence with the League," *FR,* 2: 2 (October 1907), 7.

²⁰   "To Investigate Criminality Among the Jews," *FR,* 2: 5 (April 1908), 14.

²¹   "Jewish Criminality in New York in 1907," *FR,* 2:7 (June 1908), 1. The article, replete with tables, was continued in Volume 2, No. 8 (July 1908).

²²   "Jewish Sensitiveness," *AH,* September 11, 1908.

²³   On the Magistrates Court, see Mary Roberts Smith, "Social Aspects of New York Police Courts," *American Journal of Sociology,* 5:2 (1899), 145–54; Raymond Moley, *Tribunes of the People* (New Haven, 1932).

²⁴   The "pedigree sheets" are housed in the New York City Department of Records and Information Services. The files of the New York County District Attorney also contain the docket books and case files of all defendants who appeared before the New York County Grand Jury. They, too, are housed in the New York City Department of Records and Information Services.

²⁵   Computed from the *Report of the Police Department of the City of New York,* 1900, p. 42; *Report of the Police . . .,* 1901, p. 43; *Report of the Police . . .,* 1902, p. 47; *Report of . . .,* 1903, p. 46; *Report of . . .,* 1904, p. 58; *Report of . . .,* 1905, p. 48, *Report of . . .,* 1906, p. 152; *Report of . . .,* 1907, p. 170.

²⁶   Information on the ethnicity of those arrested *city-wide* for the years 1900–1905 is available. It shows that by 1905, the majority of those arrested were foreign born.

|              | 1900 | 1901 | 1902 | 1903 | 1904 | 1905 |
|--------------|------|------|------|------|------|------|
| Native born  | 55.5 | 54.8 | 54.9 | 52.2 | 50.2 | 43.0 |
| Foreign born | 44.5 | 45.2 | 45.1 | 47.8 | 49.8 | 57.0 |

Source: Computed from "Nativity of Persons Arrested," the *Report of the Police Department of the City of New York*, 1900–1905.

There is, however, no way of ascertaining the ethnic composition of those arrested on the borough level; what percentage of New York County's arrested population was foreign born remains unknown.

27    Computed from the Thirteenth United States Census, New York State, Population, 1910, Table 13.

28    Smith, p. 154. Contemporaries named the Magistrates Court the "poor man's court" for those who appeared before it were largely from the poor and immigrant classes of the city. "Magistrates Court in New York," *Charities and Commons*, 20 (April 18, 1908), 96; Moley, p. 21.

29    New York State *Report of the Commission on Immigration*. (Albany, 1909), p. 63. See also, United States Senate Documents, *Reports of the Immigration Commission*, "Immigrants and Crime," 26 (Washington, 1911), 96–7.

30    I took a systematic sample—one out of every tenth name—from the 1907 pedigree sheets; this resulted in a sample population of 470 persons. The data was placed in machine readable form and using SPSS, I performed various calculations. I would like to thank the staff of the Columbia University Center for the Social Sciences for its assistance.

For examples of the methodology used in studying the history of crime, see Eric Monkonnen, *The Dangerous Class* (Cambridge, 1975); V.A.C. Catrell and T.B. Hadden, "Criminal Statistics and their Interpretation" in H.A. Wrigley, ed., *Nineteenth Century Society: Essays in the Use of Quantitative Methods for the Study of Social Data* (Cambridge, 1972), pp. 336–396.

31    It is quite likely that among the persons classified as "foreign born" were Jews who came to America either as infants or as young children; from a sociological perspective, this group ought to be considered as native born Americans rather than as foreign born. Unfortunately, since the pedigree sheets do not list length of residence in America or age at time of entry, how many Jews fall into this category cannot be discerned. What is known, though, is the age of the foreign born Jewish convict population; as the following table shows, the majority was quite young.

Age of Foreign Born Jewish Convict Population, 1907
(N-56)

| 15–19 | 20–24 | 25–29 | 30–34 | 35–39 | 40 and Over |
|-------|-------|-------|-------|-------|-------------|
| 21(37.5) | 15(26.8) | 10(17.9) | 3(5.4) | 6(10.7) | 1(1.8) |

32    Cities Census Committee, "Religious Composition of the Population, 1855–1930," in Walter Laidlaw, ed., *Population of the City of New York, 1890–1930* (New York, 1932), Table 63.

[33]  Computed from the Thirteenth United States Census, New York State Population, 1910, Table 13.

[34]  The United States Immigration Commission's study of the immigrant and crime found that in most cases the criminality of the second generation differed from that of its parents insofar as "the movement of second generation crime is away from the crimes peculiar to immigrants and toward those of the American of native parentage." "Immigrants and Crime," p. 14.

Jews, however, were an exception to this rule. ". . . the percentage of the Hebrew second generation differs from that of the first generation," wrote the Commission, "away from the percentage of the native white of native father instead of towards it.", "Immigrants and Crime," p. 69.

My data support this finding. Instead of decreasing his percentage of property crimes, as one might expect, the native born Jewish felon had a higher incidence of property crimes than the foreign born Jewish convict.

638

A Comparison of the Criminal Profiles of the Native Born Jewish Convict, the Foreign Born Jewish Convict and the Native American Convict   (In Percent)

|             | Property | Person | Both | Other |
|-------------|----------|--------|------|-------|
| American    | 78.8     | 15.4   | 1.5  | 4.8   |
| Native Jew  | 96.4     | 3.6    | -    | -     |
| Foreign Jew | 73.2     | 21.4   | 1.8  | 3.6   |

[35]  "Immigrants and Crime," p. 1.

[36]  "Because You Are A Jew," *The Independent,* 65 (November 26, 1908), 1214–5.

[37]  For biographical information on Bingham, see *New York Times,* December 30, 1905; July 2, 1909; September 7, 1934; *New York Herald,* December 30, 1905, George B. McClellan, *The Gentleman and the Tiger,* ed., Harold Syrett (New York, 1956), p. 295.

[38]  *New York Times,* September 17, 1908.

Bingham's claim was not without merit. In April 1908 the commissioner wrote a lengthy memorandum to Mayor McClellan in which he contended that since the city held great "attraction" for criminals of all sorts, an increase in the number of police officers was imperative. See Theodore Bingham, "Notes on the Necessity for an Increase in the Police Force," April 30, 1908, Police-McClellan files, McClellan papers, Location 25, New York City Department of Records and Information Services.

[39]  *AH,* September 18; *YT,* September 8; *AH,* September 25.

[50]  *YT,* September 1.

[51]  Louis Marshall is quoted in the *AH,* September 25.

*Medical History*, 1981, **25**: 1–40.

# HEALTH CONDITIONS OF IMMIGRANT JEWS ON THE LOWER EAST SIDE OF NEW YORK: 1880–1914

*by*

DEBORAH DWORK*

'Golden thread, you are part of the weaving now.'

639

## I

HEALTH CONDITIONS of immigrant Jews on New York City's Lower East Side are discussed in light of the circumstances of their lives before and during migration. In addition to morbidity and mortality data, the interrelated effects of poor sanitation, occupational hazards, and poverty are shown on the physical, emotional, and family health of these turn-of-the-century immigrants. Also examined is the surprising finding that despite conditions which normally engender disease, the physical health of Jews was remarkably good in comparison to that of both non-Jewish immigrants and native-born Yankees.

This was true not only of immigrant Jews in America; surprisingly, Jews in Europe were, on the whole, also healthier than their Christian countrymen. Although the great majority of Jews in Europe as well as America lived in the most overcrowded and unsanitary quarters of the cities, and under difficult social conditions, available statistics (some fragmentary, others extensive) and contemporary reports of practising physicians show that they had lower morbidity and mortality rates than their non-Jewish neighbours.

Contemporary medical and social investigators believed three major factors to be responsible for the Jews' generally low disease rates: rare alcoholism, religious law, and social customs, particularly family structure, traditions and behaviour patterns. Infant and child mortality rates were lower among Jews than their neighbours, and this was thought to be the result of Jewish concern for child welfare. These possible explanations will be discussed more fully later. Interestingly, these factors which fostered health among Jews were most severely strained by the Americanization process.

## II

The mass immigration of Eastern European Jews to the United States occurred between 1880 and 1914.** From 1881 to 1900, 675,000 Jews entered the United

* Deborah Dwork, B.A., M.P.H., Wellcome Institute for the History of Medicine, 183 Euston Road, London NW1 2BP.
** Between 1820 and 1870, Jews comprised 0.4 per cent of the total number of immigrants to the United

1

States; from 1901 to 1914 the number doubled to approximately 1,346,000.[3] The dates 1880–1914 are related to specific historical events: the assassination of Tsar Alexander II with its subsequent pogroms, and the beginning of World War I. In the thirty-three years between these two events, over two million Jews, or one-third of the Jewish population of Eastern Europe, came to the United States. Prior to 1881, Jews emigrated in search of a less oppressive society. Then, as a result of three events, the character of Jewish emigration changed. First, the assassination of Tsar Alexander II unleashed a fury of pogroms, which continued intermittently at least until World War I. A mass exodus of Russian Jews occurred following the 1881 pogroms, the 1903 Kishinev massacre, and pogroms following the unsuccessful revolution of 1905. Second, the increased legal restrictions on Jews, such as the so-called May Laws of the 1880s, forced Jews to abandon their previous employments and way of life and to migrate to urban centres. Prohibited from owning or renting land outside towns and cities, industrialization encroaching rapidly on their occupations as artisans and craftsmen, Jews turned to the industrial labour force. The population of Jews in Lodz soared from eleven in 1793 to 98,677 in 1897 and 166,628 in 1910. Similarly, Warsaw had 3,532 Jewish inhabitants in 1781 and 219,141 in 1891.[4] These migrations within Russia and Poland were often only temporary solutions to the problem of survival, especially for young skilled Jews who saw no future in the cities. Finally, the decline of Central European emigration to America encouraged the German transatlantic passage companies to seek out Eastern Europeans as new passengers.[5]

There were also more private reasons for leaving: to escape military service; lack of a dowry; hunger. They left because the others were dead, or had left already. They left because "the struggle for living was too great and hard.... The persecution of the Jews became unbearable."[6] "People who got it good in the old country don't hunger for the new."[7]

The Jewish immigration was a movement of families. Between 1886 and 1896, an average of 41.6 per cent of Jewish immigrants entering the port of New York were women, and 33.8 per cent were children under sixteen years of age. This continued after the turn of the century. From 1899 to 1910, women accounted for 43.4 per cent

640

---

States. Between 1871 and 1880, this rose to 2.5 per cent, and from 1881 to 1890, it again rose to 3.8 per cent. From 1891 to 1900 the Jewish ranks swelled to 10.8 per cent. This translates into 850,000 to 900,000 Jews entering the United States during the nineteenth century. Of these 700,000–750,000 were Eastern European and approximately 150,000 were Germans.[1] It is important to note that exact statistics are not available because the term "Hebrew" was not adopted in the United States until 1899; prior to that immigrants were classified by country of origin. Numerical estimates were made using the combined records of philanthropic organizations and the government.[2]

[1] Jacob Lestschinsky, 'Jewish migrations, 1840–1956', in Louis Finkelstein (editor), *The Jews*, vol. II, New York, Harper, 1960, p. 1561.
[2] Ibid., p. 1553.
[3] Ibid., p. 1554.
[4] Moses Rischin, *The promised city*, Cambridge, Mass., Harvard University Press, 1962, p. 24.
[5] Ibid., pp. 19–20.
[6] Michael Charnofsky, *Jewish life in the Ukraine*, New York, Exposition Press, 1965, p. 223.
[7] Anzia Yezierska, *Hungry hearts*, Boston, Houghton, Mifflin, 1920, p. 56.

of the Jewish immigrant population, and children under fourteen years of age for 24.9 per cent. Nearly 70 per cent of Jewish immigrants were between the ages of fourteen and forty-four.[8]

For most, it was a permanent move. A smaller percentage of Jews returned to the Old World than of any other immigrant group. Between 1908 and 1924, 94.8 per cent of the Jewish immigrants, as contrasted with two-thirds of the total immigrant population, remained in the United States.[9]

The occupational training of Jewish immigrants changed considerably before and after 1900. Prior to 1900, there were fewer industrial workers and more artisans and people engaged in middle-man occupations. The years between 1880 and 1900, however, saw great industrial and urban development both in Eastern Europe and the United States. Thus, later immigrants had the opportunity to learn industrial skills in Europe. Immigrants wrote to their family and friends still in Europe, extolling the virtues and necessity of industrial skills. For example, due to the geometric growth of the U.S. garment industry, young people began to take sewing lessons in preparation for emigration. "By 1900 even the daughters of respectable householders had turned their energies and talents to it."[10] The hero of Abraham Cahan's novel, *The rise of David Levinsky*, recounts his arrival in New York:

641

> "You're a tailor, aren't you?" [the contractor] questioned him.
> My steerage companion nodded. "I'm a ladies' tailor, but I have worked on men's clothing, too," he said.
> "A ladies' tailor?" the well-dressed stranger echoed, with ill-concealed delight. "Very well; come along I have work for you."
> ..."And what was your occupation? You have no trade have you?"
> "I read Talmud," I said confusedly.
> "I see, but that's no business in America."...[11]

The immigration statistics verify this emphasis on skilled labour. Although Jews constituted only 10.3 per cent of the total immigrant population between 1900 and 1925, they accounted for one-quarter of the skilled industrial workers entering the United States – nearly one-half of the clothing workers, jewellers, and watchmakers; one-third of the printers; 41.4 per cent of the leather workers; and one-fifth of the shopkeepers and merchants.[12] From 1899 to 1914, "Jews ranked first in 26 out of 47 trades tabulated by the Immigration Commission, comprising an absolute majority in eight."[13]

Immigrants often encountered great difficulties arranging passage to America. Often the male members of the family would leave first, sometimes one at a time, and live depriving themselves of all but bare necessities until they had enough money to "bring over" their wives, mothers, sisters, and children. In Anzia Yezierska's short story, *Brothers*, the hero Moisheh tries to save money for ship tickets for his mother and two brothers:

[8] Samuel Joseph, *Jewish immigration to the United States*, Ph.D. thesis, Columbia University, New York, 1914, pp. 176–177.
[9] Irving Howe, *World of our fathers*, New York, Harcourt, Brace, Jovanovich, 1976, p. 58.
[10] Rischin, op. cit., note 4 above, p. 27.
[11] Abraham Cahan, *The rise of David Levinsky*, New York, Harper, 1917, pp. 90–91.
[12] Lestschinsky, op. cit., note 1 above, p. 1569.
[13] Rischin, op. cit., note 4 above, p. 59.

... Moisheh the Schnorrer they call him. He washes himself his own shirts and sews together the holes from his socks to save a penny. Think only! He cooks himself his own meat once a week for Sabbath and the rest of the time it's cabbage and potatoes or bread and herring. And the herring what he buys are the squashed and smashed ones from the bottom of the barrel. And the bread he gets is so old and hard he's got to break it with a hammer.[14]

Even if a ticket were sent, money was needed for travel from the village or town to a port of embarkation. People simply sold all their possessions and left for America by cart, train, or on foot, with packs on their backs held in feather bedding – if that hadn't already been sold as well. If the immigrant was male and of conscription age, he had to be smuggled out of the country, and often left with no passport or identifying papers.[15] Steerage from Hamburg, Bremen, or Antwerp cost $34; from Liverpool $25. Bribing various officials was another major expense.[16]

642

At the port the immigrants were examined by a physician. This was not done for their health, but rather with an eye to the ship company's profit: upon arrival at Castle Garden, and after 1892 Ellis Island, immigrants with incurable or contagious diseases or conditions had to return to Europe at the ship company's expense. The medical examination is the subject of the short story *Off for the Golden Land* by the great Yiddish author Sholem Aleichem:

The time comes to go on board the ship. People tell them that they should take a walk to the doctor. So they go to the doctor. The doctor examines them and finds they are all hearty and can go to America, but she, that is Goldele, cannot go, because she has trachomas on her eyes. At first her family did not understand. Only later did they realize it. That meant that they could all go to America but she, Goldele, would have to remain here in Antwerp. So there began a wailing, a weeping, a moaning. Three times her mamma fainted. Her papa wanted to stay here, but he couldn't. All the ship tickets would be lost. So they had to go off to America and leave her, Goldele, here until the trachomas would go away from her eyes. . . .[17]

The vast majority of immigrants travelled steerage class (Fig. 2). They were crammed into the bowels of the ship; some companies even locked them in to prevent them from going on the upper decks and mingling with the second-class passengers. For many the food was inedible since it was not kosher. The non-observant found it equally inedible because it was so disgusting and decayed. Many people subsisted on a diet of black bread, herring, and tea. Some were fortunate enough to have cheese and butter. Sanitation was terrible, with a few salt water basins used as dishpans, laundry tubs, and for personal hygiene. The condition of the toilets was worse – open troughs that were rarely flushed and even more rarely cleaned. Throughout their memoirs and oral histories, people recounted tales of terrible seasickness, explaining that the filth and foul smell of their surroundings alone caused nausea.

The voyage lasted anywhere from ten days to three weeks, usually it was a two-week trip. They arrived, dazed, confused, weak from hunger and seasickness, at "The Island of Tears", Ellis Island. From all reports – those of the immigrants, officials, and the Hebrew Immigrant Aid Society – Ellis Island was a bewildering experience, full of the pain of displacement. During the late nineteenth century, a few thousand immigrants had arrived at Castle Garden each week; throughout the early years of the twentieth century, tens of thousands arrived at Ellis Island each week.

[14] Anzia Yezierska, *Children of Loneliness*, New York, Funk & Wagnalls, 1923, p. 127.
[15] Benjamin Lee Gordon, *The memoirs of a physician*, New York, Bookman Associates, 1962, p. 130.
[16] Howe, op.cit., note 9 above, p. 39.
[17] Sholem Aleichem, 'Off for the Golden Land', *Jewish Immigration Bull.*, February 1917, p. 10.

643

Figure 2. Immigrants on Atlantic liner, c. 1906. (Edwin Levick, Library of Congress.)

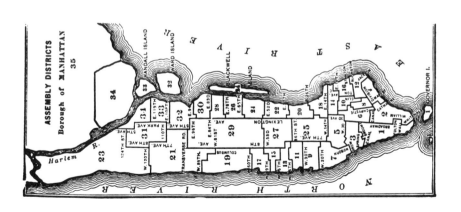

Figure 1. Assembly districts, Borough of Manhattan.

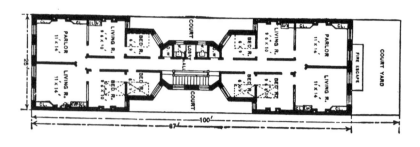

Figure 3. The dumb-bell plan, 1879.

Figure 4. Ludlow Street sweatshop. (Museum of the City of New York.)

Figure 6.    Hester Street, 1899. (Museum of the City of New York.)

Figure 5.    Yard between two rear shop buildings. Shop in Ridge Street which was condemned and vacated. (From *First annual report* of the Joint Board of Sanitary Control in the Cloak, Suit, and Skirt Industry, 1911.)

Figure 7. A cobbler in a Ludlow Street coal cellar, Sabbath Eve. (Museum of the City of New York.)

## III

Each immigrant was given a medical and cursory mental examination. People with suspected problems were marked with symbols drawn in chalk on their outer garments. One immigrant recalled that day with horror:

> It was so crowded and noisy. I was a small child then and held fast to my mother's hand. A man in uniform leaned down and drew a letter on my coat. I was frightened. My mother made as if it was hot and opened her cloak wide, doubling it back over her shoulders. Then, after we passed that man, she did the same to me. There were so many people, no one noticed. That's how I got into America.[18]

Trachoma was the cause of more than half the medical detentions, and according to a contemporary article in Scribner's magazine, "most of those detained by the physicians for trachoma are Jews."[19]

Some immigrants were met by relatives, others, sometimes unexpectedly, by landsmen, or fellow-villagers. One immigrant writes that his rabbi in Russia had written to the *landsmanshaften* (a fraternal organization or lodge composed of fellow-townspeople) in New York on his behalf. Thus, to his surprise, he was met at the pier by an old neighbour.[20] Still others were met by contractors on the watch for "greenhorns" (newcomers) experienced at their trade but not in American ways. And finally there were those, like David Levinsky, Abraham Cahan's fictional protagonist, who were simply pointed in the direction of the Lower East Side, and walked until they were greeted with recognizable signs and understandable speech.

Between 70 per cent[21] and 90 per cent[22] of the Jewish immigrants remained in New York, for a number of reasons. Social ties were very important. Family, friends, or neighbours might have already established themselves there. The desire to settle in a Jewish community was also of great importance. Despite a decrease in strict religious observance, certain essentials were necessary: kosher meat, a rabbi, a minyan (the mandatory minimum of ten men necessary to hold religious services). Many immigrants recalled the great uprooting and intense loneliness mitigated by homely companionship and customs. And, finally, New York was attractive because industrial work was more readily available there than in other parts of the country.

The Jewish immigrant population concentrated in the seventh, tenth, eleventh, and thirteenth wards of lower Manhattan. By 1900, Jews comprised an average of 79 per cent of the population of these wards, or an estimated 252,821 individuals. Thus, these can be considered "Jewish" wards.

The living conditions in these wards must not be romanticized. There is a common notion that poor today is not like poor then; old-time poverty was clean, honest, and upright. This is utter nonsense. Poverty, as it existed on the Lower East Side of New York, was noisy, foul smelling, diseased, hungry:

> The squalid humans that swarmed about . . . the raucous orchestra of voices, the metallic bedlam of elevated trains, the pounding of horses . . . the teeming ghetto . . . haggling pushcart peddlars . . . the dirt and din of screaming hucksters. . . . The slattern yentehs lounging on the stoops, their dirty babies at

---

[18] Oral history, Mrs. B., now living in New Haven, Conn.
[19] Arthur Henry, 'Among the immigrants', *Schribner's Mag.*, 1901, **29**: 302.
[20] Charnofsky, op. cit., note 6 above, p. 224.
[21] Richard Wheatley, 'The Jews in New York', *Century Mag.*, 1892, **43**: 323.
[22] George Price, 'Russian Jews in America', *Amer. Jew. Hist. Soc.*, 1958, **48**: 42.

their breasts. . . . . Wedged in, jumbled shops and dwellings, pawn shops and herring-stalls, strained together. . . . . Broken stoves, beds, three-legged chairs sprawled upon the sidewalk.[23]

The congestion was overwhelming. The *New York Times* reported on 18 January 1895 that sections of the Lower East Side were more densely populated than the most crowded areas of Bombay or Prague, and immigration had not yet reached its peak. The tenth ward was more densely populated than any European city, with 626.25 persons per acre as compared with 485.4 in Prague and 125.2 in Paris.[24] Tables I–IV illustrate the rise in population throughout Jewish wards.

TABLE I. TOTAL POPULATION OF JEWISH WARDS IN 1890, 1900 AND 1910 AND
% JEWISH IN 1900

| Ward | Approx. Assembly District | 1890[a] | 1900[b] | 1910[c] | % Jewish in 1900[d] |
|------|---------------------------|---------|---------|---------|---------------------|
| 7 | 4 | 57,366 | | 99,721 | 60% |
| 10 | 8 | 57,596 | 71,879 | 109,107 | nearly 100% |
| 11 | 16 | 75,426 | | 61,415 | 80%+ |
| 13 | 12 | 45,884 | 64,117 | 78,010 | 75%+ |

TABLE II. RUSSIAN POPULATION[e] IN JEWISH WARDS

| Ward | 1890[b] | 1910[c] |
|------|---------|---------|
| 7 | 16,295 | 46,036 |
| 10 | 30,476 | 70,341 |
| 11 | 3,149 | 2,921 |
| 13 | 13,190 | 14,549 |

TABLE III. POPULATION PER ACRE AND NUMBER OF ACRES IN JEWISH WARDS

| Ward | No. of Acres | 1880[a] | 1890[c] | 1900[c] | 1910[a] |
|------|--------------|---------|---------|---------|---------|
| 7 | 166 | 252.9 | 289.7 | 478.1 | 495.6 |
| 10 | 98 | 432.3 | 523.6 | 653.5 | 609.5 |
| 11 | 165 | 350.9 | 384.8 | 515.3 | 641.0 |
| 13 | 160 | 352.2 | 428.8 | 599.2 | 593.1 |

TABLE IV. RANK ACCORDING TO DENSITY OF JEWISH WARDS AMONG THE 22 WARDS
OF MANHATTAN

| Ward | 1880[a] | 1890[c] | 1900[c] | 1910[a] |
|------|---------|---------|---------|---------|
| 7 | 6 | 6 | 4 | 5 |
| 10 | 1 | 1 | 1 | 3 |
| 11 | 3 | 3 | 3 | 2 |
| 13 | 2 | 2 | 2 | 4 |

[a]John Shaw Billings, *Vital statistics of New York and Brooklyn*, 1890, pp. 230, 235.
[b]Charity Organization Society, *A handbook on the prevention of tuberculosis* (Lilian Brandt), 1903, p. 85.
[c]1910 statistics for corresponding assembly districts, 13th census, vol. 3, pp. 523–524.
[d]Maurice Fishberg, *American medicine*, 2 November 1901, p. 697.
[e]"Russian population" was considered to be Jewish according to the census authorities.

[23] Anzia Yezierska, *Salome of the tenements*, New York, Boni & Liverwright, 1923, pp. 9–14.
[24] *New York Times*, 18 January 1895, reprinted in Allan Schoener, *Portal to America*, New York, Holt Rhinehart & Winston, 1967, p. 212.

6

In 1905, there were 115 blocks on the Lower East Side with an average density of 750 or more persons per acre, and 39 with a density of 1,000 or more per acre.[25] In Manhattan in the early years of this century, 70 per cent of all workers engaged in manufacturing, 67 per cent of the factories, and 28 per cent of the city's inhabitants were located below 14th Street on 1/100 of the city's land area.[26] Furthermore, the Lower East Side had only 29.8 acres of park space, or 2 per cent of the city's total park area.[27]

There was an astounding variety of activity in the Lower East Side. The University Settlement Report of 1896 included a social census of the tenth ward. There were 989 tenement houses; eight public schools; three theatres, with a total seating capacity of 9,500; sixteen stables, with a capacity of 210; thirteen pawn shops; seventy-two restaurants; forty-one churches, of which thirty-one were synagogues; sixty-five factories; 172 garment makers' shops; 236 saloons, of which 108 were Raines Law Hotels, a combination saloon and brothel of the seediest type; and eighteen "Disorderly Places". There were thirty-four bathtubs; four in private houses, twelve in barber shops, and eighteen in lodging houses.[28] In 1904 David Blaustein, Superintendent of the Educational Alliance, took a private census of approximately thirty-two streets south of Houston Street and east of the Bowery. He found 5,007 tenements housing 64,268 families engaged in eighty-four different occupations. There were 306 synagogues, and so few public schools in comparison to need that the children could only attend half-day sessions.[29]

649

The Lower East Side also had a burgeoning red light district centred on Allen Street. As the neighbourhood became increasingly Jewish in character, the saloons moved out; Jews were temperate, and business became slack. The red light district, by contrast, became more prominent. Allen Street was not simply a spectacle in the ghetto. It was part of the way of life of the poor. Michael Gold, an active Communist, remembers the neighbourhood in which he grew up:

> The East Side of New York was then the city's red light district, a vast 606 playground under the business management of Tammany Hall.... There were hundreds of prostitutes on my street. They occupied vacant stores, they crowded into flats and apartments in all the tenements.... On sun-shiny days the whores sat on chairs along the sidewalks. They sprawled indolently, their legs taking up half the pavements. People stumbled over a gauntlet of whores' meaty legs.... Earth's trees, grass, flowers could not grow on my street; but the rose of syphilis bloomed by night and by day.[30]

## IV

Living conditions for the families of the Lower East Side were dictated largely by the conditions of their homes. The tenements, in turn, were fundamental to the health conditions of Lower East Side inhabitants. Legally, "tenement house" was defined in

[25] Harold Finley, 'The congestion of Manhattan', *Federation*, 1908, **5**: 17–18.
[26](a) Manufacturing and land area: Edward E. Pratt, *Industrial causes of congestion of population in New York City*, New York, Columbia University, 1911, p. 42. (b) Population figure: Finley, op. cit., note 25 above, p. 16.
[27] Ibid.
[28] *Annual report of the University Settlement Society*, 1896, p. 10.
[29] Miriam Blaustein, *Memoirs of David Blaustein*, New York, McBride, Nast, 1913, pp. 138–139.
[30] Michael Gold, *Jews without money*, New York, Horace Liverwright, 1930, pp. 14–15.

1867 as, "any house, building ... occupied as the home or residence of more than three families living independently of one another, and doing their own cooking on the premises, or by more than two families upon a floor, so living and cooking and having a common right in the halls, stairways, yards, water-closets, or privies, or some of them. . . ."[31] This definition could also suit flats and apartment houses, which were not then or now known as tenements. Jacob Riis, an ardent reformer and pioneer photographer-journalist, described the tenement:

> It is generally a brick building from four to six storeys high on the street, frequently with a store on the first floor which, when used for the sale of liquor, has a side opening for the benefit of the inmates and to evade the Sunday law; four families occupy each floor, and a set of rooms consists of one or two dark closets, used as bedrooms, with a living room twelve feet by ten. The staircase is too often a dark well in the centre of the house, and no direct ventilation is possible. . . .[32]

The immigrants' descriptions were more pithy, if less precise. "Our tenement was nothing but a junk-heap of rotten lumber and brick. . . . The plaster was always falling down, the stairs broken and dirty. . . . There was no drinking water in the tenement for days."[33] "The bedbugs lived and bred in the rotten walls of the tenement, with the rats, fleas, roaches. . . ."[34] "In America were rooms without sunlight."[35]

650

The number of houses without light, ventilation, hot running water, baths, or water closets was overwhelming. In 1900, the Tenement House Committee of the Charity Organization Society illustrated this problem by exhibiting a cardboard model of an entire block. The chosen block, bounded by Chrystie, Forsyth, Canal, and Bayard Streets, was in the tenth ward. The 80,000 square foot area boasted thirty-nine tenement houses (nearly all six storeys high) with 605 apartments. These buildings housed 2,781 people, 2,315 over five years of age and 466 under five. There were 264 water closets; only forty apartments had hot water. The one bathtub on the block, wedged in an air shaft, was obviously unusable. Of the total 1,588 rooms, 441 or 27.7 per cent were completely dark, with no access to outer air; 635 rooms or 40 per cent were ventilated only by dark, narrow air shafts. The rent roll was high, at $113,964 a year. The disease toll was also high. During the preceding year (1899), thirteen cases of diphtheria had been reported to the Health Department; during the past five years (1895–1900), thirty-two cases of tuberculosis had been reported.[36] It was estimated that "not over two-thirds of the cases are actually reported to the department."[37] Startling as they may seem, these conditions were by no means unique. Table V illustrates that the block was typical.

The tenement house was not a new invention at the turn of the century, manufactured to accommodate the late mass immigrations. Tenement houses had been a social, political, and health problem in New York City since the early 1800s.

[31] L. Veiller and R. De Forest (editors), *The tenement house problem*, vol. 1, New York, Macmillan, 1903, p. 94.
[32] Jacob Riis, *How the other half lives*, New York, Hill & Wong, 1957, pp. 13–14.
[33] Gold, op. cit., note 30 above, p. 248.
[34] Ibid., p. 72.
[35] Yezierska, op. cit., note 7 above, p. 264.
[36](a) Veiller and De Forest, op. cit., note 31 above, p. 113. (b) Jacob Riis, *The peril and preservation of the home*, Philadelphia, George W. Jacobs, 1903, pp. 126–127.
[37] Veiller and De Forest, op. cit., note 31 above, p. 449.

TABLE V.   HOUSING STATISTICS OF THE JEWISH WARDS OF NEW YORK CITY, 1900[a]

| Description | Ward 7 | Ward 10 | Ward 11 | Ward 13 |
|---|---|---|---|---|
| Acres | 206 | 109 | 213 | 109 |
| Tenement houses | 1,500 | 1,179 | 2,031 | 1,123 |
| Rear buildings | 0 | 142 | 182 | 114 |
| Apartments | 17,597 | 15,313 | 21,771 | 13,195 |
| Vacant apartments | 852 | 181 | 1,468 | 755 |
| % Vacant apartments | 4.8 | 1.1 | 6.7 | 5.7 |
| Families | 16,745 | 15,132 | 20,303 | 12,440 |
| Population in tenement houses | 72,446 | 76,073 | 89,361 | 55,564 |
| Children < 5 years | 11,473 | 10,633 | 14,058 | 9,414 |
| Tenement houses 7 storeys | 0 | 3 | 28 | 0 |
| Tenement houses 6 storeys | 13 | 198 | 251 | 105 |
| Tenement houses 5 storeys | 1,049 | 678 | 694 | 501 |
| Tenement houses 4 storeys | 245 | 179 | 801 | 218 |
| Tenement houses 3 storeys | 173 | 110 | 237 | 266 |
| Tenement houses 2 storeys | 1 | 0 | 5 | 4 |

[a]Lawrence Veiller, 'A statistical study of New York's tenement houses', *The tenement house problem*, Vol. I, (Veiller and De Forest, eds.), New York, Macmillan, 1903, pp. 199–204.

651

Public action, however, was not taken until the middle of the century. In 1842, Dr. John H. Griscom, a city inspector of the State Board of Health, drew attention to tenement house conditions and urged that legislative action be taken to ameliorate the situation. Although this was not done, in 1846 The New York Association for Improving the Condition of the Poor (AICP) began investigating slum conditions. An 1854 report disclosed the startling extent of poverty and disease which the AICP had found, and prodded the public conscience by stressing the great need for reform. As a result of this report, the State Legislature appointed a Commission to study the tenement situation and to propose ameliorative legislation. However, in 1857, the Legislature turned down the Commission's reform bill.

Public interest waned until the draft riots of 1863 and high death rates stimulated a group of prominent New Yorkers to form a Citizens' Association. A sub-committee on sanitary conditions, the Council of Hygiene and Public Health, included eminent physicians. Despite the Council's reports on the loathsome sanitary conditions of New York City, the State Legislature still did not act. Finally, in 1865, after cholera appeared in Europe, fear of an epidemic in New York convinced the Legislature to establish a Metropolitan Board of Health for New York City (1866), and a Tenement House Law (1867).[*][38]

The fact that these measures were passed at all was highly significant. It demonstrated the development of a legal consciousness of the importance of the public health. With the Tenement House Law, society recognized the right to limit the entrepreneurial freedom of builders in the interest of public health. However, the law itself was vague, and standards were low. Most requirements could be altered at the discretion of the Board of Health; and the requirements themselves were not sufficient

[*] At this time there were approximately 15,000 tenements in the city.

[38] Information on the history of tenement house reform, 1834–1867: (a) Veiller and De Forest, op. cit., note 31 above, pp. 71–97; (b), Roy Lubove, *The progressives and the slums*, Pittsburgh, University of Pittsburgh Press, 1962, pp. 1–28; (c) Roy Lubove, 'The New York Association for Improving the Conditions of the Poor: the formative years', *N.Y. hist. Quart.* 1959, pp. 307–327.

to protect the inhabitants. Among the major provisions: tenements had to have fire escapes or some other means of egress; a water tap had to be furnished either indoors or outside. Only one water closet or privy had to be provided for each twenty inhabitants, and it could be located outdoors (usually in the rear yard). Water closets and privies had to connect with sewers, but only if such existed. Cesspools were forbidden, except where necessary. There was no limit on the percentage of the lot which the building might cover.[39]

In 1879, the history of the tenements took a sharp turn. During December of the previous year, editor Charles F. Wingate held a $500 competition in Henry C. Mayer's new trade journal, the *Plumber and Sanitary Engineer*. The competition, entitled "Improved Homes for Workingmen" or "The Model Home Competition", called for erection on a standard city lot (25 × 100 feet) of a brick building which provided "security against conflagration (including fireproof staircases open to the air), distribution of light, ventilation, drainage and other sanitary appointments ... inexpensiveness."[40]

652

James E. Ware won first prize; his construction, commonly known as the "dumb-bell" or "double-decker" tenement (Fig. 3), was published in March 1879. Despite the magazine's exhortations that "it is irrational to suppose that a commodious and healthful house for a large number of families can be built upon an ordinary lot 25 × 100"[41] and that "the present competition has demonstrated that stringent restrictions should be made upon the erection of houses of this class,"[42] the dumb-bell tenement was mass-produced for the working class in New York between 1879 and 1901.*[43]

The competition stimulated public interest in tenement house reform. On Tenement House Sunday (23 February 1879), concerned New York clergy preached on the subject. On 28 February, at Cooper's Union, Mayor Cooper presided over a large public meeting, again dealing with tenement house reform. Within days, the Mayor's Committee of Nine was formed with a mandate to devise reform measures.

[39] Veiller and De Forest, op. cit., note 31 above, pp. 71–92. Lubove, op. cit., note 38b above, pp. 1–28.
[40] 'Improved homes for working men', *Plumber and Sanitary Engineer*, December 1878, pp. 1, 32.
[41] Ibid., 1879, **2**: 89.
[42] Ibid.
* The dumb-bell tenement was a brick structure five to seven storeys high, 25 feet wide, and 75 to 90 feet deep. It merely modified the old system of dividing the lot into front and rear buildings by connecting the front to the rear with a narrow hall. The two front ground-floor apartments were generally stores in front with living rooms behind. Between them ran the entrance hallway, less than three feet wide, more than 60 feet deep, and almost totally dark. The staircase was located approximately 50 feet back. Opposite the stairway were two water closets, each ventilated by the air shaft and each shared by two families. Sometimes a dumb waiter was provided between them. Each floor contained four apartments or fourteen rooms. seven on each side of the hallway, running straight back along the hallway. The front apartment consisted of four rooms, the rear apartments of three. The largest room was the front parlour, which measured 10½ by 11 feet; bedrooms measured 7 by 8½ feet. Only four of the fourteen rooms received direct light. The rest were supposed to be illuminated by the air shaft, an enclosed indentation in the side of the building which measured 28 inches by 50 to 60 feet and as tall as the building itself.[44] At the turn of the century, the rent for a front apartment was about $15 a month, that of a rear apartment $11–12.[45]
[43] Lubove, op. cit., note 38b above, p. 31.
[44] Information on the dumb-bell: (a) Veiller and De Forest, op. cit., note 31 above, pp. xiv, 8–9; (b) Lubove, op. cit., note 38b above, pp. 31–32; (c) *Plumber and Sanitary Engineer*, op. cit., note 41 above, pp. 90–91.
[45] *Annual report for the University Settlement Society*, 1899, p. 20.

Approximately one month later, it introduced a successful bill amending the Tenement House Law of 1867. While the bill modified various regulations of the preceding law and provided for thirty sanitary police to enforce the housing code, it still subjected all requirements to the discretionary power of the Board of Health. It did, however, limit the percentage of space a new building could occupy to 65 per cent of the lot, and required a window measuring a minimum of twelve square feet in rooms used for sleeping.

There was no new legislation or important public agitation until 1884, when Professor Felix Adler, founder of the Society for Ethical Culture, again roused public interest and energy with a series of lectures decrying the tenement blight. This renewed public concern forced the Legislature to appoint a second legislative Commission, whose recommendations stimulated the passage of further amendments to the Tenement House Law in 1887. The number of sanitary police was increased to forty-five. Running water on every floor and one water closet per fifteen inhabitants were now required. The Board also took responsibility for inspecting every tenement semi-annually.

653

The mayoral Tenement House Commissions of 1894 and 1900 produced further landmarks of tenement house reform. The 1894 Commission was created due to public anger caused by series of exposés published by a newspaper, the *Press*. The resulting Tenement House Law of 1895 provided for two small parks on the Lower East Side and five recreation piers to be built along the river.

The Commission of 1900 grew out of interest stimulated by the Charity Organization Society's (COS) Tenement House Committee exhibit. Lawrence Veiller, who directed this Committee, was appointed secretary of the Commission. Its recommendations, adopted in their entirety in 1901, prohibited the future erection of dumbbell type tenements. In new construction, the space between buildings was to be enlarged from an air shaft to a court. A separate water closet had to be installed in each apartment.[46] Although baths were not required, an inspection of 311 new tenement houses revealed that 125 of them, or 40 per cent, had a private bath for each apartment. Veiller also reported that many landlords voluntarily improved the plumbing on their property. Clearly, the tenement population desired toilets, sinks with running water, and baths, and were willing to repay the landlord for his investment through increased rent.[47]

Unfortunately, at least initially, the majority of Jewish immigrants were not in a position to take advantage of the major innovations of the 1901 law. For example, the tenth ward had been built up during the last decades of the nineteenth century, and by 1901 little land was left for new construction. The few new apartments built after 1901 were in great demand, especially by those immigrants who had been in New York for a number of years and could afford the luxury. Often, the apartments were rented even before they were completed.[48]

---

[46] Information on the history of tenement house reform, 1868–1901: (a) Veiller and De Forest, op. cit., note 31 above, pp. 98–115; (b) Lubove, op. cit., note 38b above, pp. 28–33, 81–149.

[47] Veiller and De Forest, op. cit., note 31 above, p. 47.

[48] Cahan, op. cit., note 11 above, p. 250.

11

In existing tenements, landlords were required by the 1901 law to install a window in any room which had none. School sinks (sewer-connected privies) and privy vaults had to be replaced with individual water closets. The Commission also detailed specifications for fire-proofing, fire-escapes, and the lighting of public hallways of existing and future tenements. These measures to safeguard the public health were influenced by contemporary medical knowledge. The bacteriological origins of disease set forth by Koch and Pasteur in the 1870s were by this time becoming popularly understood and accepted. The importance of sunlight and ventilation in destroying the tubercle bacillus was stressed in the Commission's report.[49]

As Table V shows, within the Jewish wards the dumb-bell tenement was the predominant housing structure, and there were a significant number of rear buildings as well.[50] The latter were built prior to 1879 and, without direct access to the street, were less well ventilated and sunlit, and more of a fire hazard than the dumb-bell tenement. The dumb-bell structure, built between 1879 and 1901, was characterized by an air shaft which was supposed to provide light and air to the rear rooms. In fact, the air shaft was as much a hazard as a convenience. It conveyed noise and odours, and acted like a huge flue in a fire. According to Jacob Riis, "more than half of all fires in New York occur in tenement houses," and the air shaft, functioning like a chimney, "added enormously to the fireman's work and risk."[51] The air shaft also served as a garbage dump, and, consequently, was even more infested with rats and vermin than the other parts of the tenement structure. Statistics prove that landlords were slow to comply with the 1901 window requirements, designed to succeed where the air shaft had failed in providing light and air. There were 350,000 dark interior rooms in Manhattan in 1902.[52] In 1908, there were still 300,000 south of Houston Street alone.[53]

Tenement houses were not just inadequate, unsanitary homes – they were also inadequate, unsanitary work sites. It was not possible to separate "workshop" from "living quarters" among immigrant Jews.

> Let us follow one [immigrant man] to his home and see how Sunday passes in a Ludlow Street tenement.
>
> Up two flights of stairs, three, four, with new smells of cabbage, of onions, of frying fish, on every landing, whirring sewing machines behind closed doors betraying what goes on within, to the door that opens to admit the bundle [of unfinished garments] and the man. A sweater, this, in a small way. Five men and a woman, two young girls, not fifteen, and a boy who says unasked that he is fifteen and lies in saying it, are at the machines sewing knickerbockers, "knee-pants" in the Ludlow Street dialect. The floor is littered ankle-deep with half-sewn garments. In the alcove, on a couch of many dozens of "pants" ready for the finisher, a bare legged baby with pinched face is asleep. A fence of piled-up clothing keeps him from rolling off on the floor. The faces, hands, and arms to the elbows of everyone in the room are black with the colour of the cloth on which they are working. . . .
>
> They are "learners," all of them, says the woman . . . and have "come over" only a few weeks ago.[54]

[49] Hermann M. Biggs, 'Tuberculosis and the tenement house problem', and Arthur R. Guerard, 'The relation of tuberculosis to the tenement house problem', in Veiller and De Forest (editors), op. cit., note 31 above.

[50] Ibid., vol. 2, p. 87.

[51] Jacob Riis, *Children of the tenement*, New York, Macmillan, 1903, pp. 252–253.

[52] Veiller and De Forest, op. cit., note 31 above, p. xvii.

[53] Claude H. Miller, 'The menace of crowded cities', *World's Work*, 1908, 16: 10269.

[54] Riis, op. cit., note 32 above, pp. 92–93.

654

V

The immigrants arriving in New York found employment wherever they could. "Everyone grabbed the type of job he could get, and changed it very often. . . . Today, one can be a shoemaker; tomorrow, a tailor, and the day after tomorrow he is forced to become a farmer; later a bookkeeper and so on ad infinitum," wrote George Price.[55] Price himself worked in six different types of factories, taught, did manual labour, worked in ditches and on trains, and finally became a prominent physician in the trade union movement.

The majority of immigrant Jews found work in the needle trades shortly after arrival. Tailoring was easy to learn and was not physically demanding – an excellent combination for the immigrants. Some were snatched up by a contractor at Castle Garden or Ellis Island. Many others entered the needle trades following the example of family or friends who had preceded them. By and large they sought employment among other Jews. This enabled them to observe religious law and eliminated a formidable language barrier. An 1890 survey by the Baron de Hirsch Fund found that 14,316 or 55 per cent of the employed permanent residents of wards 7, 10, and 13, worked as tailors, cloakmakers, and labourers in white goods and other branches of the needle trades. There were also 452 furriers and 309 dealers in clothing. Peddling, the second most common occupation, employed another 9.3 per cent or 2,440 people. The survey found 1,382 clerks, 976 cigar-makers, 633 shoemakers, and 500 who owned tailor stores.[56] By 1897, according to the 12th Annual Report of the Factory Inspector of New York, 75 per cent of the 66,500 workers in the clothing industry in Manhattan[57] and 80 per cent of the 15,000 cloakmakers were Jewish.[58] Manhattan was rapidly becoming the hub of the industry; by 1905, half of the clothing manufactured in the United States was produced in New York. [59] The predominance of Jews in the needle trades continued well into the closing years of our study. The fur trade in 1910 was 75 per cent Jewish.[60] In 1911, the Joint Board of Sanitary Control in the Cloak, Suit and Skirt Industry reported that 85–90 per cent of its workers were Jewish.[61] The dress and waist industry reported in 1913 that 77.7 per cent of its workers were female, and that 56.16 per cent of these women were Jewish.[62]

By the late nineteenth century, the needle industry in New York was also overwhelmingly owned and operated by Jews. Historically, Jews had always been involved in the clothing industry. Christians in the United States had allowed Jews to deal in second-hand clothing because this was considered a despicable occupation.[63] This

655

[55] Price, op. cit., note 22 above, p. 47.

[56] Lloyd P. Gartner, 'The Jews of New York's east side, 1890–1893', *Amer. Jew. hist. Quart.*, March 1964, pp. 268–272.

[57] *Twelfth annual report of the Factory Inspector of the State of New York* (1897), published 1898, p. 45.

[58] Judith Greenfield, 'The role of the Jews in the development of the clothing industry in the United States', *YIVO Ann. of Jew. Soc. Sci.*, 1947, **2**: 187–188.

[59] Pratt, op. cit., note 26a above, p. 80.

[60] Rischin, op. cit., note 4 above, p. 66.

[61] *First annual report of the Joint Board of Sanitary Control in the Cloak, Suit, and Skirt Industry of Greater New York*, New York, October 1911, p. 39.

[62] Joint Board of Sanitary Control in the Dress and Waist Industry, *Special report on sanitary conditions in the shops of the dress and waist industry*, May 1913, p. 7.

[63] Jesse E. Pope, *The clothing industry in New York*, University of Missouri, 1905, p. 1.

traditional foothold in the clothing industry enabled Jews to take advantage of its fantastic growth during the second half of the nineteenth century.

Three factors greatly stimulated this growth: the Civil War created an unprecedented demand for mass-produced uniforms, the invention of the sewing machine in 1846 provided a means of manufacture, and the large influx of Irish and, later, German immigrants during the mid-century provided the labour force. After the Civil War, the demand for uniforms decreased, but the industry created a consumer market by providing fashionable clothing at much lower cost than custom tailoring. Until the early 1880s skilled German tailors and Irish cutters controlled production.[64] Then competition arrived in the form of Eastern European Jews who had spent time in London learning not only the tailor's craft but also English language and customs. These tailors broke into the production business and paved the way for future immigrants. The clothing industry thus became one of the few in which Jews were employers.[65]

656

Within the American needle industry, there were three systems and three sites of production. Most antiquated was the so-called "family system", which had become the dominant system of production under German immigrant influence in the mid-nineteenth century. Irish tailors worked in shops, but the Germans worked at home, dividing the labour among family members. Usually the husband was the most skilled worker, the master tailor. He operated the sewing machine while his wife and children did the basting, buttonholes, and finishing touches. This "homework" was done in the family's tenement apartment.

The contracting or "sweat-shop" system grew out of the family system. As competition and the volume of work increased, much time had to be spent obtaining work to do; picking up the cloth or, more commonly, pre-cut, unsewn garments; and then delivering the completed product to the warehouse. Enter the contractor. He knew English and had lived in America at least longer than the greenhorns. He contracted with the manufacturer to do X work for Y price by Z date, and was then free to conduct his business as he chose. This seemed ideal to newly arrived immigrants; they could communicate in their own language, observe the Sabbath on Saturday, and maintain other religious laws.

There were a few variants to the contracting system. The contractor could act as a middleman between the working family and the manufacturer, or hire labourers of his own (who would also work in the tenement, either in the contractor's own apartment, or one rented for work purposes), or he could sell the job to a sub-contractor who performed the same function as the contractor himself. Until the last decade of the nineteenth century, the cloak, suit, and skirt trade was primarily controlled by these petty manufacturers. One estimate ascribed 90 per cent of all ladies' coats and suits produced in New York City in 1890 to the contractor.[66] Dr. George Price, by then chairman of the investigative committee of the Joint Board of Sanitary Control in the Cloak, Suit, and Skirt Industry, explained the proliferation of contractors. "Very

---

[64] Ibid., p. 27.
[65] Ibid., p. 49.
[66] Greenfield, op. cit., note 58 above, p. 191.

little capital was needed for the establishment of a shop, as the workers were compelled to furnish their own machines, which were run with foot power. The workers were also often compelled to pay deposits for the privilege of work. All the enterprising manufacturer had to invest was his ability to get work, and perhaps capital enough to pay for the rent of his 'factory'."[67] These factories were located in lofts, tenement house apartments "converted" for industrial use, or in the tenement home itself. A "cockroach sweater" was the lowest man on the contractor totem pole; his was a small business with few employees, usually run in his own tenement apartment.

The third production site was the inside shop, in which the manufacturer dealt directly with the store buyer, hired his own workers, and ran his own factory. The manufacturer usually worked with a designer, who created fashions or imitated famous designs. The manufacturer displayed these models to the store buyer, who ordered them for the season.

As was generally the case in industry, the physical conditions in which garment workers laboured ranged from poor to foul. The lack of light, space, ventilation, plumbing, and sanitation in tenements has been described already. This situation was exacerbated by the use of the tenements for manufacture. Jacob Riis described the filth and penury over and over again in prose and with photographs. The third annual report (1888) of the New York factory inspectors also discussed the problem of Jewish homework. "They usually eat and sleep in the same room where the work is carried on, and the dinginess, squalor and filth surrounding them is abominable."[68] (Fig. 4). Annie S. Daniel (1858–1944), an eloquent physician interested in the welfare of the poor and particularly concerned about public health, perceived the problem in 1904–5 from another standpoint:

657

> These "homes" of working men and women consist of from two to four rooms. In one room, that which opens on the street or yard, is carried on all the domestic life. This room serves for parlor, dining-room, and kitchen; and in this room in addition is carried on the manufacturing. It is quite obvious that the word home was never intended to apply to such an apartment.... Every garment worn by a woman is found being manufactured in tenement rooms.... [Some] I have seen being made in the presence of small-pox, on the lounge with the patient.... Among the 150 families [I attended who did] manufacturing in the living rooms, 66 continued to work during the entire course of the contagious disease.[69]

Conditions in the sweatshops and most factories were equally abominable. In his memoirs, Gregory Weinstein describes a printshop of the 1880s: "Dark shops in rickety buildings; climbing up four, five and six flights of wooden stairs; cases full of dust and rat dirt; working under gas-light from seven o'clock in the morning till six in the evening."[70] Nearly twenty years later, in 1903, conditions in the needle trades were just as bad. Yetta, the heroine of Arthur Bullard's *roman-à-clef, Comrade Yetta*, views her surroundings: "She saw the broken door to the shamefully filthy toilet, saw the closed, unwashed windows, which meant vitiated, tuberculosis-laden air, saw the backs of the women bent into unhealthy attitudes, saw the strained look in their eyes."[71]

[67] *First annual report of the Joint Board*, op. cit., note 61 above, p. 35.
[68] *Third annual report of the Factory Inspector of the State of New York*, 1888, published 1889, p. 27.
[69] Annie Daniel, 'The wreck of the home', *Charities*, 1905, **14**: 624–629.
[70] Gregory Weinstein, *The ardent eighties*, New York, International Press, 1928, p. 46.
[71] Arthur Bullard, *Comrade Yetta*, New York, Macmillan, 1913, p. 108.

By 1910, homework was in Italian immigrant hands; Jewish labour had moved into inside shops.[72] Unfortunately, most workshops were not a great improvement. In 1910, inspection of 228 waist shops employing 11,000 workers showed that 62 per cent used inadequate artificial light, and 60 per cent provided no protection against the glare. Thirty per cent had filthy water closets with no light or ventilation, and in 28 per cent of the shops the general conditions were labelled "extremely dirty".[73] Loft buildings housed 91 per cent of the inspected establishments, and over one-half of the employees worked above the sixth floor.[74] This was basically the case in all branches of the needle trades. Loft buildings had improved sanitary conditions in the industry; they were new edifices with large windows providing natural illumination and ventilation, and had up-to-date plumbing facilities. But they posed a much greater fire hazard than previous work sites. Building materials were flammable, fire-escapes were either not provided or inadequate, and the loft buildings were simply too high – the Fire Department could not handle fires above the seventh floor.[75] This dilemma was horribly illustrated by the famous fire at the Triangle Waist Company on 25 March 1911, which killed 146 employees.

658

A 1913 inspection of 700 dress and waist shops revealed that 97.3 per cent were located in loft buildings, 2.7 per cent in converted buildings, and none in tenements or cellars. The sanitary conditions of the loft buildings were considered very good, with only 5 per cent using artificial light and 3 per cent having no protection from glare. Only 4.5 per cent had dirty water closets. However, if anything, the danger from fire had increased, as there were now more people working at greater heights. A little over 50 per cent of those in the industry, or 18,417 persons worked on or above the sixth floor, and nearly 10 per cent, or 3,530 persons worked on or above the twelfth floor. The Fire Department was still incapable of handling fires at these heights, and only 7 per cent of the shops practised fire drills. Fifteen shops had no fire escapes; forty-seven had obstructed access to the fire-escape; and forty-six had no safe means to escape from the fire-escape, which meant that workers could be trapped in an enclosed courtyard or alley – a tunnel of fire (Fig. 5). A full 30 per cent of the shops had doors which opened inwards, making escape difficult and dangerous. Finally, as in the Triangle fire, a few employers still illegally locked their employees in the work room, making escape impossible.[76]

Similar conditions prevailed in the predominantly male cloak, suit, and skirt industry.*[77] After the great cloakmakers' strike in 1910, a Joint Board of Sanitary Control was established to study and ameliorate shop conditions. In 1911, the com-

---

[72] (a) State of New York, *Preliminary report of the Factory Investigating Commission*, 1912, vol. III, Albany, Argus, p. 1766. (b) State of New York, *Second report of the Factory Investigating Commission*, 1913, vol. II, Albany, J. B. Lyon, p. 684.

[73] State of New York, op. cit., note 72a above, vol. I, p. 277.

[74] Ibid.

[75] *First annual report of the Joint Board*, op. cit., note 61 above, p. 49.

[76] Joint Board of Sanitary Control, op. cit., note 62 above, pp. 10–13.

*In the five inspections prior to and including 1913, 77 per cent of the workers were male (while 77.7 per cent of the workers in the dress and waist industry were female). At this time the industry employed more than 60,000 people in 2,000 establishments, 90 per cent of which were located below 34th Street.

[77] Ibid., p. 7.

mittee of investigation published its report on 1,738 shops.[78] Two-thirds were found deficient in fire protection and/or sanitary conditions.[79] At a time when chewing tobacco was common and spitting was not considered impolite, over 99 per cent of the shops had no cuspidors (in direct opposition to the law), thus increasing the risk of tubercular infection. The legal limit of one water closet for every twenty-five persons was also largely ignored – some shops had only one water closet for eighty-five workers. Hot water, towels, and rubbish bins were nearly unheard of, and 6.8 per cent of the shops were poorly ventilated. Lunch was eaten in the shop room itself. As in the dress and waist industry, however, fire was by far a greater danger to the workers than were the poor sanitary conditions. Loft buildings housed 90 per cent of workers, 50 per cent between the sixth and twelfth floors. The interiors of the buildings were hazardous, and rapid escape difficult. The halls were narrow; there were only 1,951 stairways in 1,738 buildings. Thus, most shops had only one means of egress, built either of stone, which heated quickly and then crumbled when wetted, or of wood, which burned easily. The vast majority of shops (84 per cent) had only one fire-escape, often narrow, leading into an enclosed courtyard or alley.[80]

659

In 1911, the Joint Board of Sanitary Control adopted sanitary standards which included fire precaution and prevention regulations. Certificates were given to worthy shops. In February 1912, shops employing 40 per cent of the workers were so certified, and in September 1912, shops employing 61 per cent of the workers were found sanitary. By September 1913, 79 per cent of the workers were employed in certified shops. In May of the same year the Joint Board published an alphabetical list of approved establishments.[81]

Thus far, we have primarily examined the physical and sanitary conditions of two branches of the ladies' garment industry. While the great majority of Jewish immigrants were industrial workers, not all were employed in the clothing industry. Industrial conditions in general were on a par with those of the needle trades prior to the 1910 cloakmakers' strike and subsequent formation of the Joint Board of Sanitary Control. George Price, reporting in 1912 for the Factory Investigating Commission (which had been established in response to the public's outcry after the Triangle fire), noted that 54 per cent of the shops had no, or insufficient, washing facilities, and an even larger percentage had no hot water. Few had lunch rooms; the great majority of workers ate in the work room. Poor toilet accommodations were the rule. Very few shops had emergency rooms or first aid facilities in case of illness or accident. The worst offender was the food industry, with baking, nutpicking, and ice cream manufacture commonly done in the tenement.[82]

[78] *First annual report of the Joint Board*, op. cit., note 61 above, p. 35.

[79] Lillian Wald, 'Sanitary control of an industry by the industry itself', *Transactions of the fifteenth International Congress on Hygiene and Demography*, vol. III, part II, Washington, D.C., Government Printing Office, 1913, p. 883.

[80] *First annual report of the Joint Board*, op. cit., note 61 above, pp. 64–68, 46–53.

[81] (a) George Price, 'Ten years of industrial sanitary self control', *Tenth annual report of the Joint Board of Sanitary Control in the Cloak, Suit, and Skirt, and Dress and Waist Industries*, New York, 1921, pp. 23, 27, 29. (b) Joint Board of Sanitary Control in the Cloak, Suit and Skirt Industry, *Directory of certified shops*, New York, May 1913.

[82] State of New York, op. cit., note 72a above, vol. I, pp. 135–138, vol. II, pp. 87, 210.

Not only were the physical conditions of the workplace disgusting, degrading, and unhealthy, but the long hours and low wages increased the strain on the worker's constitution. Lillian Wald, founder of the Henry Street Settlement, wrote:

> ... from the windows of our tenement home we could look upon figures bent over the whirring foot-power machines. One room in particular almost unnerved us. Never did we go to bed so late or rise so early that we saw the machines at rest, and the unpleasant conditions where manufacturing was carried on in the overcrowded rooms of the families we nursed disquieted us more than the disease we were trying to combat.[83]

It is impossible to discern exactly how many hours per day or week people worked. Hours differed from industry to industry, from "outside" shop to "inside" factory, and from rush to slack seasons. In 1891, New York factory inspectors reported a sixty-six- to seventy-two-hour minimum work week during the slack season in the clothing industry (if the worker were lucky enough to maintain his position), and sixteen to nineteen hours a day, seven days a week during the busy season.[84] Dr. Annie Daniel reported women working at home nineteen hours a day, seven days a week during the busy season in 1904–5.[85] Workers were hard put to decide which was worse: the anxiety and poverty of the slack season with little or no employment, or the hours and tension of the rush season with greater and greater work demands. Hours in the factories were slightly better. In 1894 the cloakmakers' union went on strike for – and won – a ten-hour day, reduced from the standard twelve to fifteen hours. In 1901, nearly all clothing union workers sought a fifty-nine-hour week.[86]

Wages depended upon position, piece-work, sex, and whether the worker was employed by a contractor or in a factory. In all cases, wages were low, the difference being between poverty and penury. In 1888, male cloakmakers in inside shops earned an average weekly wage of $12.[87] Annie Daniel reported that female homeworker wages averaged $1.04 a week in 1904–5, and the average weekly income from the man's work was $3.81.[88] Jacob Riis gives various piece-work prices: there were knee-pants "for which the manufacturer pays seventy cents a dozen," or another grade of knee-pants at 42c. a dozen. The finisher of the garment "gets ten and the ironer eight cents a dozen; button-holes are extra, at eight to ten cents a hundred."[89] According to the United States Industrial Reports, between 1880 and 1901 the weekly wage of New York coat-makers in task shops fell nearly 17 per cent. The work day increased by 20 per cent and productivity increased by 66 per cent.[90] There were no significant technical advances during this period, nor any improvement in the division of labour. The workers simply worked harder and longer.

## VI

Clearly, these abominable conditions – poorly lighted, filthy surroundings,

[83] Lillian Wald, *The house on Henry Street*, New York, Henry Holt, 1915, p. 281.
[84] Pope, op. cit., note 63 above, p. 139.
[85] Daniel, op. cit., note 69 above, p. 625.
[86] Pope, op. cit., note 63 above, p. 140.
[87] Ibid., p. 89.
[88] Daniel, op. cit., note 69 above, pp. 625, 627.
[89] Riis, op. cit., note 32 above, pp. 93, 95.
[90] Greenfield, op. cit., note 58 above, p. 202.

incredibly low pay, and exceedingly long hours of repetitive work alternating with equally long seasons of unemployment – had a significant impact on the mental and physical health of the immigrant proletariat. However, before discussing the predicted and real effects of housing, work, and a new way of life on the immigrants, we must know their physical condition upon arrival. The immigrants who made their way to the Lower East Side of New York had already been medically examined two or three times. If they left Russia legally, they were examined at the border. They were further examined by the shipping companies prior to embarkation, and finally, by the medical authorities at Castle Garden or Ellis Island. On the average European Jews were 162.1 cm. tall, with an arm span of 169.1 cm. and a chest girth of 81 cm. This made them the shortest and narrowest of all European peoples.[91] In addition, Eastern European Jews had a poorly developed muscular system and were frequently anaemic.[92] Thus, it is clear that they were not physically equipped for heavy manual labour; as we have seen, the majority of immigrants joined the industrial work force.

Good health was of the utmost importance for survival, and immigrants soon learned (if they did not already know) to dread the workshops as a cause and site of disease. Emma Goldman, who later became a political radical, worked in a corset factory in New York. After a few weeks, she found the strain unbearable, and wrote, "I suffered most from violent headaches."[93] Contemporary novels recognized curvature of the spine as an occupational hazard of needle workers. [94] And tuberculosis was called "the tailors' disease".[95]

For many years it had been understood in a general way that industry was carried on under conditions harmful to health.[96] It was known, for example, that factory workers were more susceptible to disease than other workers; the death rate for males was 20.2 per 1,000 among the labouring and servant class in 1910, while it was 12.1 among the mercantile and trading class.[97] It was also known that factory workers and the workers in tenements were more likely to contract tuberculosis than were persons otherwise employed. This was ascribed to malnutrition, lack of air and light, and congestion in the factory and at home. Ignorance about causes of and precautions against disease in general, and tuberculosis in particular, was also thought to be a primary factor in the high incidence rates.[98]

The fear of tuberculosis – "the shop sickness, the plague of Dollar Land"[99] – figures large in the immigrant literature. However, it was some time before this fear was transformed into exploratory studies or ameliorative action. Until 1910 there were few or no formal demands by workers for improved sanitary conditions in the shop, although there was always a general complaint against them. The strike of 1910

661

---

[91] Maurice Fishberg, 'Tuberculosis among the Jews', *Amer. Med.*, 2 November 1901, p. 697.
[92] Charles Bernheimer, *Half a century of community service*, New York, Association Press, 1948, p. 283.
[93] Emma Goldman, *Living my life*, Garden City, N.Y., Garden City Publishing Co., 1931, p. 37.
[94] Bullard, op. cit., note 71 above, p. 12.
[95] Wald, op. cit., note 83 above, p. 54.
[96] State of New York, op. cit., note 72a above, vol. I, p. 141.
[97] Ibid., p. 18.
[98] Ibid., vol. II, p. 637.
[99] S. B. Ornitz, *Haunch, paunch and jowl*, New York, Boni & Liverwright, 1923, p. 43.

19

focused attention on the related problems of industrial sanitation, occupational hazards, and worker health. In the few years following the strike several studies were undertaken to assess these problems. "The best standard of the healthfulness or dangers of an industry would be a direct study of the physical conditions of its employees. ... Medical examinations of workers ... have been almost entirely neglected."[100]

In 1911 the United Hebrew Trades, a conglomerate of eighty-six local Yiddish-speaking unions, requested that the Factory Investigating Commission medically examine the employees of the Furriers' Union, who worked under unusually poor conditions. Three-quarters of the fur shops were located in old tenement houses with wooden stairs, no ventilation, and no separate drying rooms – causing the work area to stink. Seventy per cent of the fur was dyed with what proved to be harmful chemicals, and the fur itself constituted a dust hazard. Conditions were so poor that many insurance companies would not sell policies to furriers.[101]

Eighty-three furriers were examined, 94 per cent of them male. Only 10.8 per cent were completely healthy; 89.2 per cent had one or more illnesses or unhealthy conditions. Catarrh (chronic rhinitis), and inflammation of the nasal mucous membrane caused by inhalation of dust and fur particles, afflicted 50.6 per cent of the furriers. Similarly, 30.1 per cent suffered from bronchitis, inflammation of the mucous membrane of the bronchial tubes. Another 25.3 per cent had some type of skin disease caused by dyes; 13.3 per cent had asthma, "a condition that is almost purely due to fur,"[102] and which came to be known as "furrier's asthma". Six per cent had phthisis (pulmonary tuberculosis).[103] In the medical examiner's opinion, "The sphere they labour in and the fact that their lungs are always irritated, both by the furs and the dust would tend to make them more susceptible to [phthisis] than if they were otherwise employed."[104]

In 1912 the Joint Board of Sanitary Control examined 800 cloakmakers in a similar study. While the percentage may have been considerably higher, at least 47.4 per cent of the examined workers can be safely classified as Jews. Only 37.3 per cent of the workers were healthy; 62.7 per cent suffered from one or more diseases. The examiners found that 21.7 per cent were anaemic, 6.4 per cent had eye problems, 7 per cent suffered from acute bronchitis, 21 per cent had a "digestive disorder" (disease of the pharynx, 13.2 per cent; stomach disease, 5.7 per cent; hernia, 2.1 per cent), and 1.6 per cent suffered from tailors' disease (phthisis). Syphilis and gonorrhoea were rare, with only one worker suffering from each.[105]

In 1911 George Price examined the health and working conditions of 800 New York City bakers, at least one-third of whom were Jewish. Only 33 per cent of the Jewish workers were free of disease; the remaining 67 per cent suffered from one or

662

---

[100] George Price, 'Occupational diseases and the physical examination of workers', *Transactions of the fifteenth International Congress on Hygiene and Demography*, op. cit., note 79 above, p. 845.
[101] State of New York, op. cit., note 72a above, vol. III, p. 1625.
[102] Ibid., p. 1632.
[103] State of New York, op. cit., note 72b above, vol. II, p. 422.
[104] Ibid., vol. III, p. 1632.
[105] Wald, op. cit., note 79 above, pp. 887–888.

more illnesses. Among the Jewish workers, 28.5 per cent were anaemic; 23 per cent suffered from bronchitis, perhaps due to, and probably exacerbated by, the high temperature and humidity and the generally poor ventilation of the workshop. Eye infections, which afflicted 16.5 per cent of the workers, were ascribed to working in an artificially lighted, dusty cellar, in front of an oven. "Baker's itch", a distinctly occupational disease, and other skin ailments affected 7.6 per cent. Another 6.8 per cent had cardiac problems, 10 per cent had flat feet, there were two cases of venereal disease, and 2.8 per cent had tuberculosis. Price concluded that morbidity and mortality were "affected by the general conditions under which the work of a baker is carried on, including excessive hours, unsanitary conditions of bake shops, night work, etc."[106]

The most comprehensive occupational health study was conducted in 1913 by J. W. Schereschewsky of the United States Public Health Service. Approximately 3,000 workers of the cloak, suit, and skirt, and dress and waist industries were examined. About two-thirds of the subjects were male and 96.7 per cent of the males were Jewish. They averaged 64.5 inches in height and 140 pounds in weight; 90 per cent were between twenty and forty years old. Only 15.5 per cent showed signs of poor nutrition, but only 29.5 per cent were physically well developed. Of the female workers, 88.8 per cent were Jewish. Because it was common for Jewish women to work only prior to marriage, their average age was considerably younger than the men's, with 92 per cent under thirty years old. In general they were better physically developed than the men, and appeared to be well nourished; 83 per cent were between 57 and 63 inches tall, and the average weight was 120 pounds.[107]

Only about 2 per cent of the examined workers were free of defects or disease.[108] Anaemia was found in 4.6 per cent of the males and 11.9 per cent of the females; 13.4 per cent of the males and 6.5 per cent of the females had defective hearing. About 7 per cent of the total population suffered from chronic catarrhal or suppurative middle-ear disease. These percentages were considered higher than those occurring in the general population; they were attributed to exposure to continuous noise* and to the catarrhal conditions of the nose and throat commonly seen in garment workers. Rhinitis was found in 29.3 per cent of the males and 19.8 per cent of the females, and chronic bronchitis in 3.9 per cent of the males and 1.1 per cent of the females. One-quarter of the sample suffered from chronic constipation, one-quarter from defective teeth, and nearly three-quarters from defective vision (only 11.7 per cent of these wore glasses, and only 20 per cent of the bespectacled had their vision corrected). Half the men and one-fifth of the women had some degree of spinal curvature ("it was a rather rare circumstance to encounter a spine completely

663

---

[106] State of New York, op. cit., note 72a above, vol. I, pp. 228, 232.
[107] J. W. Schereschewsky, 'The health of garment workers', *Publ. Hlth Bull.*, May 1915, **71**: 28–30, 46–48.
[108] Ibid., p. 94.
*Immigrant memoirs, oral histories, and novels evoke the same image of the work place: "It was gehenna [hell], so noisy, all the clakety-clack of the machines. You couldn't hear yourself think, and you had to shout to the people next to you."[109]
[109] Oral History, Mrs. D., now living in the Bronx, New York.

straight") and/or faulty posture.[110] The most important and serious disease from which garment workers suffered was tuberculosis, with 3.1 per cent of the men and 0.9 per cent of the women actively tubercular. An additional twenty-nine persons were suspected of having tuberculosis, and many more had had it previously. The men's rate was ten times that of the United States Army, and the women's was nearly three times as great. It must be remembered that, on average the men were ten years older than the women, and had worked in the industry twice as long.[111]

The examiner reported that "no class of disorders peculiar to the garment trades was found, or which would not probably be found with like frequency in similar groups of workers engaged in sedentary, indoor occupations."[112] Yet, "while the garment trades in themselves did not necessarily induce faulty postures, provided the postural habits of the worker were originally correct, occupation in the garment trades had a strong tendency to intensify incorrect postural habits."[113] The report acknowledged that garment workers' constant inhalation of the airborne particles or "fly" from cloth predisposed them to developing tuberculosis.[114] In addition to physical ills, 10 per cent of the male workers and 3.2 per cent of the females suffered from neurasthenia or other psychological disorders. A considerably larger number "gave a strong impression of being predisposed to neuropathic affections."[115]

The peculiar nature of the clothing industry affected mental health. One person, known as the "speeder", set the work pace. The heroine of *Comrade Yetta* described another woman, who had been the speeder for her task force but could no longer keep up:

> She had entered the trade strong and healthy and had been well-paid at first, when she had the great desideratum – Speed. It had seemed like good pay then. But now she knew better. They had been buying not only her day-by-day ability, they had bought up her future. For the wages of less than ten years they had bought all her life.[116]

The seasonal nature of the work also endangered mental health. Less than 18 per cent of the workers studied by Schereschewsky were employed year round.[117] "When there is work in the clothing factory, the short seasonal, body-destroying rush, he sits at his sewing machine . . . twelve hours, fourteen hours, and thinks nothing of a twenty hour stint."[118] "There are two factors . . . which tend to cause over-strain . . . the temptation to overspeed for the purpose of earning high wages when work is brisk, followed by a period of inactivity in the slack season, during which time is afforded for introspection, consideration of the future, worry as to whether work will be forthcoming during the next season, depression over the present bad season. . . ."[119]

Work was not the only predisposing factor to disease. The deplorable conditions of

[110] Schereschewsky, op. cit.,, note 107 above, p. 61.
[111] Ibid., p. 84–85.
[112] Ibid., p. 60.
[113] Ibid., p. 73.
[114] Ibid., p. 95.
[115] Ibid., p. 79.
[116] Bullard, op. cit., note 71 above, p. 26.
[117] J. W. Schereschewsky, B. S. Warren, and Edgar Sydenstricker, 'Health of garment workers', *Publ. Hlth Rep.*, 26 May 1916, **31**: 1304.
[118] Ornitz, op. cit., note 99 above, p. 28.
[119] Schereschewsky, op. cit., note 107 above, pp. 79–80.

the tenements in which immigrant Jews lived determined their health as well. There are no statistics on accidents due to unlit or dimly lit tenement halls, rotten stairs, and lack of gratings on low windows. The immigrant literature, and case studies by settlement workers[120] and reporters like Jacob Riis[121] who were interested in social reform, lead to the inevitable conclusion that such accidents did occur.

There is better information about the relationship between housing and infectious diseases, especially tuberculosis and diphtheria. The discovery of the cause of tuberculosis led the New York City Department of Health to investigate the effect of living conditions on the incidence of the disease. Beginning in 1894 Dr. Hermann N. Biggs of the Department of Health mapped all reported tuberculosis deaths in Manhattan and Brooklyn, by date and house.[122] The patterns of cases showed that the houses themselves became infected. Consumptive tenants expectorated sputum which contained virulent bacilli. When the sputum was not properly disposed of, it dried into dust, was blown into cracks and crevices, and could be inhaled by future tenants. "Tuberculous dust has been found by experiment to remain virulent and infectious for months and even years after it was deposited."[123] Had the expectorate or dust been exposed to either direct or diffused sunlight, the bacillus would have died in a matter of minutes to days. Had the tenement apartment been properly ventilated, the dust would not have been allowed to settle, and might perhaps have been carried outdoors. "But in too many houses in New York City there is never sufficient thorough cleaning to remove the infection, and sunlight, daylight, and fresh air sufficient to destroy the tubercle bacilli cannot enter."[124]

665

Like their working and housing conditions, the living habits of immigrant Jews affected their health. Wages were low and rents high, so families took in boarders who paid 10c. a night to sleep; meals cost extra. At one time or another, most people either had or were boarders. Boarders constituted 7 per cent of the population in the Baron de Hirsch census.[125] The emotional stress of this situation and the strains it put on family life will be discussed later. The important point here is that boarding increased congestion, lowered the standard of living, and increased the risk of contagious infection.

An exhibit concerning the evils of housing congestion was held in 1908 at New York's American Museum of Natural History. One display of a census of 250 "typical" Lower East Side families showed that 50 per cent slept three or four per room, 25 per cent slept two per room, and the rest slept five or more per room.[126] This was, if anything, an improvement on former sleeping arrangements. George Price recalled that during his tenure working for the Sanitary Society in the 1880s, "in one home, consisting of three rooms (each eight by ten or nine feet), you could find a family made up of the husband, the wife, a sick father, and six children, ranging from

[120] *Annual report of the University Settlement Society*, 1897, p. 29.
[121] Jacob Riis, *Children of the poor*, London, Sampson, Low, Marston, 1892, p. 37.
[122] Veiller and De Forest, op. cit., note 31 above, vol. I, p. 448.
[123] Ibid., p. 464.
[124] Ibid., p. 447.
[125] Gartner, op. cit., note 56 above, p. 270.
[126] Miller, op. cit., note 53 above, p. 10270.

one month to thirteen years, and thirteen roomers who came to sleep in these rooms"[127] – a total of twenty-two people. According to Dr. Biggs of the Health Department, "The density of population always bears a more or less constant ratio to the prevalence of tuberculosis, the mortality increasing with an increasing density."[128]

We have already discussed the common misconception that past poverty was "clean". The equally common idealization that immigrant Jewish housewives were particularly fastidious housekeepers is contradicted by the immigrant literature and the reports and memoirs of settlement workers. Immigrants from the ghettos of Eastern European cities had no training in hygiene or housekeeping. And the habits of immigrants from the villages and shtetls – sweeping dirt floors and airing the bedding – were not adaptable to the congested, airless quarters of New York. None of the immigrants was prepared for the degree of urbanization found in New York, and cleanliness in the home suffered accordingly. In a discussion about hygiene education for Jewish immigrants, Jacob Riis wrote, "The homes are too hopeless, the grind too unceasing. The [teachers] know it, and have little hope of the older immigrants."[129] Even those immigrants who either came with or learned clean habits found that maintaining sanitary conditions was next to impossible. There was rarely hot water in the apartment, and often no running water at all. There were few bathrooms and wash basins. Closet space was minimal. To thwart further efforts at sanitation, garbage collection and street cleaning were erratic before 1894. As if the lack of space and paucity of facilities were not bad enough, immigrant women were stymied by their ignorance of ways to deal with them. Jewish immigrant females were far less educated than their male counterparts, and the untrained, untutored mind often cannot devise ingenious methods to cope with a new environment.

Social habits were frequently not conducive to good health. There was "not even enough crockery or eating things. Two soup plates must do for the four of us. Mother has it that respectability requires that the family must eat together. So mother and father eat out of one plate and Philip and I share the other."[130] Often, people simply ate with their fingers.[131] Expectorating was a common habit. "Everybody is busy spitting," one immigrant wrote.[132]

Finally, some habits which evolved in an effort to cope with living conditions were potentially harmful. To escape the hot, airless rooms in summer, people slept on the roofs and fire-escapes, frequently without precautions against falling. Because there was no refrigeration and few people had ice boxes, food was kept on the fire-escape or window-sill on the airshaft, exposed to insects and vermin.

Food shopping was primarily done within the Jewish district. The central shopping area was the Hester Street Market (Fig. 6), where housewives believed great bargains could be obtained from pushcart peddlars. Small quantities were bought at a time; a few cents' worth of milk was purchased in the shopper's own vessel, and butter was

[127] Price, op. cit., note 22 above, p. 54.
[128] Veiller and De Forest, op. cit., note 31 above, vol. I, p. 447.
[129] Riis, op. cit., note 121 above, pp. 56–57.
[130] Ornitz, op. cit., note 99 above, p. 29.
[131] Yezierska, op. cit., note 14 above, p. 101.
[132] Ornitz, op. cit., note 99 above, p. 138.

sold in pats. The most commonly purchased items were flour, sugar, coffee (one pound sufficed a family of six for three weeks), eggs, beans, rice, rye bread, rolls for breakfast, milk, butter, and dried fruit.[133] Fish, either fresh or tinned, was a staple in the diet of the immigrant Jew. Fresh kosher meat and poultry were less common and sold in small quantities. A common diet included rolls and coffee or tea for breakfast; a hunk of bread and a few cents' worth of herring for lunch; and, for dinner, soup, bread, potatoes, and a bit of baked fish or roasted or boiled (in the soup) meat or poultry.[134] Herring was probably the single most common food eaten by immigrant Jews, and in 1898 cost between two and four cents a pound.[135]

Very poor Jewish families "live[d] for days on bread, herring and tea alone."[136] People were forced by poverty to go to great lengths to obtain cheaper food. They bought stale bread, bruised or near rotten produce (pickles, onions, potatoes, and cabbage were the most popular vegetables), and the dregs of the fish stall or butcher's shop.

667

## VII

The tenth ward of New York was the dirtiest and most crowded district in the city. Jews lived there amid incredible congestion and squalid working, housing, and living conditions. Yet, surprisingly, a review of the incidence of the disease* among Jews in the Lower East Side shows that the tenth ward was the healthiest in New York.[137] In 1890, 22,000 Jews reported themselves as being in good health, while 657 rated their health as not good.[138] The Charity Organization Society (COS) in 1902 appointed a Committee on the Prevention of Tuberculosis, consisting of sixteen physicians and sixteen interested lay persons to study the social aspects of the disease and to educate the medical, political, and general community about the proper prevention of and care for tuberculosis. The Committee's report revealed many interesting facts about Jewish disease rates. The death rate from consumption per 100,000 people between fifteen and forty-four years of age in 1900 was listed according to birthplace of mothers. The death rates for Russians, Hungarians, and Poles, "nearly all Jews", were 131.1, 113.5 and 67.4 respectively.[139] These were the lowest mortality rates from consumption for all nationalities. When these figures were further scrutinized, they indicated a difference between male and female susceptibility to the disease. In 1902, 29 per cent of all deaths among Russian and Polish men in Manhattan and the Bronx were due to consumption. The percentage of deaths among females was much lower: 16.6 per cent. The figure for males was the third lowest and for females the lowest among all

---

[133] *Annual report of the University Settlement Society*, 1898, pp. 15–19.
[134] Oral history, Mrs. R., now living in New Haven, Conn.
[135] *Annual report of the University Settlement Society*, 1898, p. 19.
[136] Maurice Fishberg, 'Health and sanitation of the immigrant Jewish population of New York', *Menorah Monthly*, August 1902, 33: 77.
*Due to statistical limitations, I deal largely with mortality and not morbidity rates.
[137] Riis, op. cit., note 121 above, p. 40.
[138] Gartner, op. cit., note 56 above, p. 271.
[139] COS, *Handbook on the prevention of tuberculosis*, New York, 1903, pp. 53, 55.

nationalities in New York.[140] This was among the largest differences in disease susceptibility found between the sexes. It was believed to be "due to the Jewish ideals which keep the woman in the home, and protect her as far as possible from the struggle for existence, as well as to the almost incredible efforts which the husband and father makes in the struggle, and the character of his usual occupations."[141]

Similarly, death rates according to occupation proved lower in Jewish industries than would have been expected considering the working conditions. Tailoring combined many of the characteristics of employment which were thought to make consumption especially prevalent: low wages which caused privation at home, unsanitary conditions in the shop, exposure to "fly" from cloth, continued strained work position, close confinement within doors, and long and irregular hours. Yet the death rate from consumption among tailors was 218.2 per 100,000, well below the average of 240.[142]

Consumption statistics were also studied in relation to density of population (Table VI) and quality of housing. Despite dense population, the Jewish quarter as a whole had the lowest mortality rates from consumption in the city. "It is the large Hebrew element in the tenth ward ... which gives this notoriously congested spot a comparatively low rate of tuberculosis. For the same reason the seventh, eleventh and thirteenth, which rank next the tenth in density, have the very least consumption."[143]

668

TABLE VI.   RELATIONSHIP BETWEEN DENSITY AND TB DEATH RATE IN THE JEWISH WARDS OF NEW YORK, 1890 AND 1900[a]

|  | Ward 7 | | Ward 10 | | Ward 11 | | Ward 13 | |
|---|---|---|---|---|---|---|---|---|
|  | 1890 | 1900 | 1890 | 1900 | 1890 | 1900 | 1890 | 1900 |
| Population | 57,366 | 89,237 | 57,596 | 71,879 | 75,426 | 99,144 | 45,884 | 64,117 |
| Persons per acre | 290 | 478 | 524 | 653 | 385 | 513 | 429 | 599 |
| Rank according to density* | 6 | 4 | 1 | 1 | 3 | 3 | 2 | 2 |
| Death rate/100,000 from TB† | 373 | 156 | 307 | 201 | 328 | 136 | 284 | 102 |
| Rank according to death rate** | 7 | 3 | 4 | 5 | 6 | 2 | 2 | 1 |

[a]Charity Organization Society, *A handbook on the prevention of tuberculosis*, (Lilian Brandt), 1903, p. 85.
*Rank figures indicate relationship to the other wards, "1" being the most densely populated.
**Rank figures indicate relationship to the other wards, "1" having the lowest death rate.
†Death rate and rank are for the years 1890 and 1901.

The death rate, however, may not have been an accurate index to morbidity from tuberculosis. By 1906, 1,200 out of every 100,000 Jews living on the Lower East Side

[140] Ibid., p. 58.
[141] Ibid., p. 61.
[142] Ibid., p. 68.
[143] Ibid., pp. 87–88.

suffered from consumption.[144] Statistics were also distorted because Jews were thought to have pthisis for an average of eight to ten years, compared with other peoples who died quickly from "fulminant" or "galloping" tuberculosis. By the time death occurred for a Jewish patient, it could have been recorded as due to another cause.[145] By 1900, one-quarter to one-third of all deaths in New York among persons between the ages of fifteen and sixty-five were due to this most dreaded of diseases.[146]

Tuberculosis was not the only disease studied. According to the 1890 U.S. census report for New York City and Brooklyn, the mortality rates of those whose mothers were born in Russia and Poland were the lowest of all recorded nationalities (1,485 per 100,000). Child mortality was also lowest among Eastern European Jews (2,867 per 100,000). More specifically, death rates due to scarlet fever, consumption, measles, and diseases of the nervous system were lower in Jewish wards than in the city as a whole. The Jews were not so fortunate with regard to diphtheria and croup, diarrhoeal diseases, and pneumonia (Table VII).

669

TABLE VII. AVERAGE ANNUAL DEATH RATE PER 100,000 FROM VARIOUS DISEASES IN THE JEWISH WARDS AND NEW YORK CITY, 1890[a]

|  | Scarlet fever | Diphtheria and croup | Diarrhoeal diseases | Consump-tion | Pneumonia | Measles | Diseases of the nervous system |
|---|---|---|---|---|---|---|---|
| New York City | 52.19 | 181.63 | 316.85 | 391.75 | 287.89 | 45.67 | 241.96 |
| Wards 7, 10, 11, 13 | 51.38 | 184.78 | 318.24 | 322.91 | 304.90 | 39.79 | 217.68 |
| Ward 7 | 52.96 | 174.62 | 326.55 | 373.15 | 365.89 | 36.63 | 239.39 |
| Ward 10 | 59.77 | 187.57 | 305.57 | 306.80 | 276.76 | 38.00 | 191.86 |
| Ward 11 | 48.16 | 181.73 | 315.54 | 327.58 | 281.69 | 44.53 | 219.67 |
| Ward 13 | 44.66 | 195.19 | 325.32 | 284.12 | 295.29 | 40.04 | 219.83 |

[a] J S. Billings, *Vital statistics of New York and Brooklyn*, 1890, p. 250.

"In spite of narrow chests and slight stature, in spite of extreme poverty and still greater frugality, in spite of mental overexertion, lack of exercise, employment in the sweated industries, and the probability of contact with infection in second-hand clothing",[147] and from living in such congested quarters without air or sunlight, Jews were not only healthier than their gentile immigrant neighbours, they were healthier than the Yankees. This situation was not unique to New York. According to John Shaw Billings's special census report, the average annual mortality among Jews living in the U.S. was 711 per 100,000 population, or a little more than half that found among other people of the same social class. The statistics for deaths due to consumption in the country in general mirror the pattern found in New York City: the rate per 1,000 deaths was, among Jews (1890), 36.67 for males and 34.02 for females, while in the total population (1880) it was 108.79 and 146.12 respectively.[148] As noted above,

[144] Howe, op. cit., note 9 above, p. 149.
[145] COS, op. cit., note 139 above, p. 56.
[146] Veiller and De Forest, op. cit., note 31 above, vol. I, p. 448.
[147] COS, op. cit., note 139 above, p. 56.
[148] John Shaw Billings, *Vital statistics of the Jews in the United States*, Special report for the Eleventh Census of the United States (Census Bulletin No. 19), Washington, D.C., G.P.O., 1894, p. 10.

the mortality rate of children under fifteen years old was lowest (of a total of nine nationalities) among those whose mothers were born in Russia and Poland (2,867 per 100,000). The mortality rate of those whose mothers were born in the United States was 5,401 per 100,000.

This general pattern of a lower mortality rate among Jews, and specifically lower mortality rates from consumption and among children, is found in Europe as well. In Budapest during the years 1885–1893 the general death rate for Jews was approximately half that of Christians.[149] Similarly, in Prussia during the years 1888–1892, the mortality rate among Jews was 1,571 per 100,000 population as compared with 2,326 among Christians, and from 1893 to 1897, 1,473 as compared with 2,184.[150] There are numerous and extensive studies on comparative mortality rates from tuberculosis which indicate a consistently lower rate among Jews. The mortality rate from consumption per 100,000 population in Tunis (1894–1900) was 75 among Jews and 513 among non-Jews; in Berlin (1905) 98 per 100,000 among Jews and 216 among non-Jews; in Vienna (1901–1903), 179 and 496; in London (1901–1906) 133 and 179; in Cracow (1896–1900) 205 and 664; and in Budapest 219 and 460 respectively.[151]

The lower mortality among Jewish children was also noted with interest by several investigators, as infant mortality rates are a crucial index of the general state of health of a population. At a meeting of the British Medical Association in 1892, J. M. Rhodes presented figures showing that whereas there were 198 deaths per 1,000 children under one year old in the City of Manchester (1892), there were only 124 deaths per 1,000 in Cheetham, a densely populated and impoverished quarter of the city inhabited by Jews. This pattern continued; during the ten years 1894–1903 the average infant mortality in Cheetham was 115 as compared with 184 for the whole city.[152] In Baden in 1882 the mortality rate of children under one year old was 220 per 1,000 live births among Jews, 280 among Protestants and 310 among Catholics.[153] The Russian census of 1897 reported the low mortality of Jewish infants (up to one year) in the (agrarian) Pale of Settlement, with a rate of 132.1 deaths per 1,000 births as compared with 259.2 deaths among non-Jewish infants.[154] Similarly, in Budapest between 1886 and 1890 the mortality rate of children under five years old was 76 per 1,000 among Jews and 160 among Catholics.[155] The mortality statistics of Jewish children under fifteen years old in Prussia are remarkable. They were the lowest in Western Europe at the time. Between 1888 and 1892, 5.06 Jewish children less than fifteen years old died per 1,000 population, as compared with 12.17 Christian children, and

---

[149] Josef von Körösi, *Die Sterblichkeit der Haupt- und Residenzstadt Budapest von 1882–95 und deren Ursachen*, Berlin, 1898.
[150] Arthur Ruppin, "Die Sozialen Verhältnisse der Juden in Preussen", *Jahrb. Nationalökonomie und Statistik*, 1902, p. 380.
[151] Max Grunwald (editor), *Die Hygiene der Juden*, Dresden, Verlag der Historischen Abteilung der Internationalen Hygiene-Austellung, 1911, p. 294.
[152] Ministry of Health (Gt. Britain), *42nd annual report on infant and child mortality*, London, H.M.S.O., 1913, pp. 76, 79.
[153] Maurice Fishberg, 'Mortality', *Jewish Encyclopedia*, p. 31.
[154] *Voskhod*, March, 1904, pp. 116–117, quoted in ibid., p. 33.
[155] Körösi, op. cit., note 149 above.

between 1893 and 1897 the figures were 3.96 and 11.47 respectively.[156] Of every 100 Jewish deaths in Prussia in 1907, 16.73 were children under fifteen years old, whereas among Christians there were 45.14.[157]

## VIII

The reasons for this phenomenon were, and remain, unknown, but there was much speculation. At first, Jews were thought to be relatively immune to contagious disease, especially tuberculosis.[158] When it became evident that this was not true, Jews were popularly endowed with a peculiar sort of resistance, "the special heritage of their race, a physical and nervous endurance."[159] This was most often ascribed to "agelong observance of the strict dietary regulations of Moses."[160]

Contemporary medical and social investigators believed three major factors responsible for the Jews' generally low disease rates: rare alcoholism, religious law, and social customs. Alcoholism was known to increase susceptibility to tuberculosis, and Jews were correctly reputed to be not only infrequent alcoholics ("a rare vice among Jews"),[161] but infrequent drinkers of alcohol at all.[162]

671

Jewish law was thought to be helpful in preventing contagion. Men were required to cut their finger- and toenails at least once a week, wash their hands before and after each meal, rinse out the mouth after each meal, and not walk four steps from bed without washing the face and hands. Jewish women were required to bathe at least once a month, and finger- and toenails were to be cut off frequently. Diet, too, was strictly regulated. There were rules for the slaughter of animals, and meat was thoroughly inspected by religious authorities before it was allowed to go on sale. The inspector examined the viscera, particularly expanding the lungs by blowing air into them. Sometimes this was done under water so that any perforation would be indicated by air bubbles rising to the surface. Any abnormality in any organ (e.g. adhesions, perforations, nodules) caused the entire animal to be discarded as unfit for human consumption. This rule was rather stringently enforced both in Russia and the United States: in Russia, 50 per cent of the slaughtered animals were rejected, and in the United States, 30 per cent.[163] Moreover, meat and fowl were considered "kosher" or clean for only three days after slaughter. Thus, ingestion of infected meat was kept to a minimum.

By 1908, many of the theories relating observance of Mosaic law to low disease rates had been put into perspective by one of their formerly most ardent supporters. In an address before the Sixth International Congress on Tuberculosis, Dr. Maurice Fishberg, author of a comprehensive text on tuberculosis, gave a relatively new explanation for Jewish resistance to tuberculosis and to contagious disease in general.

[156] Ruppin, op. cit., note 150 above, p. 380.
[157] Grunwald, op. cit., note 151 above, pp. 292–293.
[158] Wald, op. cit., note 83 above, p. 53.
[159] Bullard, op. cit., note 71 above, p. 133.
[160] Ibid., p. 133.
[161] Ibid., p. 7.
[162] Fishberg, op. cit., note 91 above, p. 698.
[163] Ibid.

> The incidence of tuberculosis among Jews depends more on their economic and social environment than on racial or ritual affinities. . . . The Jews have only the advantage of having passed through a process of infection during past centuries. Hence, their lower mortality today from tuberculosis . . . the Jew does not make any material change in his milieu by changing his abode from eastern Europe to America. He lived there in a city, and here again settles in a city; he worked there at some indoor occupation, and does the same here; he lived there in an overcrowded dwelling, and moves here into a "double-decker" tenement. He has paid the price for urbanization already for several hundred years.[164]

Social customs of Jews were considered to be conducive to health. Although bathing was prescribed at set intervals by religious law, it was also simply customary. When Eastern European Jews came to New York, they built and operated sweat baths for profit. "The Russian baths are very numerous in the Jewish quarter, and very much frequented. 'I cannot get along without a "sweat" (Russian bath) at least once a week,' many a Jew will tell you."[165] In 1880, possibly two of the twenty-four bathhouses in New York were owned by Jews; by 1897, over half of the city's sixty-two bathhouses were Jewish-owned.[166] Philanthropic and municipal organizations also accommodated the Jewish demand for baths by building bathhouses throughout the Lower East Side. At one bath opened in 1900 by the University Settlement, Jews willingly paid the 5c. charge for soap and towel, though the same nickel could have paid for a meal.[167]*

Despite the grim conditions, Jewish housewives often succeeded in maintaining cleanliness in the home – a nearly impossible task. According to Lilian Brandt of the COS, Jewish homes were more hygienic than those of their Italian counterparts.[168] Dr. Fishberg concurred, pointing out that contrary to the immediate impression of disorder in the kitchen upon entering a tenement home, close inspection revealed that the cooking range was kept sparkling clean. However, even Dr. Fishberg admitted that a rear bedroom was kept only as well as "the readiness of the housekeeper to work and clear it of vermin."[169] The home was cleaned at least once a week in preparation for the Sabbath, and was treated to a real "spring cleaning" prior to Passover.[170]

The kitchen was the focal point of the family, and preparation and consumption of food were of major importance. Contemporaries reported that "the Jew is well nourished . . . as a whole his food is well chosen and better prepared . . . than is that of the mass of industrial workers."[171] If food was always a pre-occupation, it was imperative for the Sabbath and Passover. No matter how harried the week, how poor business, or how infrequently the entire family was assembled in one place, every Friday evening, the household sat down together for a full meal. Jacob Riis described such a scene:

[164] Maurice Fishberg, 'Tuberculosis among the Jews', *Sixth International Congress on Tuberculosis*, vol. III: *Hygiene, social, industrial and economic aspects of tuberculosis*, Philadelphia, William F. Fell, 1908, pp. 423–425.

[165] Fishberg, op. cit., note 136 above, p. 74.

[166] Rischin, op. cit., note 4 above, p. 87.

[167] Veiller and De Forest, op. cit., note 31 above, vol. II, pp. 35, 46–53.

*The University Settlement (on the corner of Rivington and Eldridge Streets) provided ten showers and three tubs. During the month of August, 4,919 baths were taken.

[168] COS, op. cit., note 139 above, p. 61.

[169] Fishberg, op. cit., note 136 above, p. 74.

[170] Wheatley, op. cit., note 21 above, p. 327.

[171] Pope, op. cit., note 63 above, pp. 176, 178.

It happened once that I came in on a Friday evening at the breaking of bread, just as the four candles upon the table had been lit with the Sabbath blessing upon the home and all it sheltered. Their light fell on little else than empty plates and anxious faces; but in the patriarchal host who arose and bade the guest welcome with a dignity a king might have envied I recognized with difficulty the humble peddlar I had known only from the street. . . . [172]

By and large, the Sabbath meal consisted of three courses: soup, the main dish (most popularly fish), potatoes, vegetables, braided bread, fruit and nuts, or cake (Fig. 7).

There was one class of illness which was more prevalent among Jews than other people, and for which urbanization in Eastern Europe was as inefficacious a preparation as cleaning, good housekeeping, and full meals were preventive. Jews suffered from mental and emotional disorders. As we have noted, these were sometimes due to the stress of work, with its busy and slack seasons. But the pain and rupture of dislocation caused other health problems with both physical and psychological manifestations. Neurasthenia and hysteria were more common among Jews than among other immigrants. Mental alienation was two to five times more frequent among Jews than non-Jews. Suicide, which was rare in Europe, was an ever more frequent occurrence in New York,[173] and immigrants remember the headline "Genumen di gez" (took gas) appearing often in the Jewish newspapers.

673

The social manifestations of dislocation included a rise in venereal disease among Jews, although the numbers were still low compared to other groups.[174] Prostitution, which is closely connected to venereal disease, was rampant on the Lower East Side for several reasons. The East Side housed many single men, men who had come alone either to earn money and return to their homelands, or, as with the Jews, to send for their families. Second, among religious Jews the woman is not a suitable sexual partner for approximately one third of every month. Third, the crowded living conditions may have inhibited sexual activity between husband and wife, thus creating a market for prostitution. And finally, there were few outlets for entertainment. Physical development and athletic activity were much deprecated by Jews, and many other sources of amusement were beyond their means.

Contemporary novels and reports on the "social evil" claimed that economic conditions and the lure of an apparently easy and luxurious life encouraged women to become prostitutes. Such was the finding of the Committee of Fifteen, a group of concerned New Yorkers who organized in 1900 to investigate and combat prostitution. Their report, published in 1902, stressed the economics of vice. "A season of nonemployment presents [industrial women] with the alternatives of starvation or prostitution." Alternatively, "they may be employed at living wages, but the prospect of continuing from year to year with no change from tedious and irksome labor creates discontent and eventually rebellion."[175]

Important as was prostitution, the breakdown of the family was the most dramatic evidence of the stress of immigration. Husbands deserted wives, and children

[172] Riis, op. cit., note 121 above, p. 44.
[173] Fishberg, op. cit., note 136 above, pp. 169, 172.
[174] Ibid., p. 174.
[175] The Committee of Fifteen, *The social evil*, New York, C.P. Putnam's Sons, 1902, p. 11.

abandoned their parents. Boarders and crowded conditions eroded family structure. "Seduction was commonplace, and many a man considered a trip across the ocean tantamount to a divorce."[176] Wife desertion became so common that the popular newspaper the *Jewish Daily Forward*, with the help of the National Desertion Bureau, ran a regular feature entitled "The Gallery of Missing Husbands". This published a picture and a short biography of the man, and requested him, or anyone who knew or saw him, to make his whereabouts known. The Jewish Information Agency also had a bureau seeking such husbands. In a column called the "bintel brief", which was Abraham Cahan's version of the modern "Dear Abby", the *Forward* printed letters asking for the return of errant husbands:

> Max, where is your conscience: you used to have sympathy for the forsaken women and used to say their terrible plight was due to the man who left them in dire need. And how did you act? . . . Be advised that in several days I am leaving with my two orphans for Russia. We say farewell to you and beg you to take pity on us and send us enough to live on.[177]

674 Women on both sides of the ocean would frequently not admit that they were an "agunah", or deserted wife. The common explanation that the absent husband was away seeking work was used both legitimately and illegitimately.[178] Women in Russia sometimes had to raise the money for passage themselves and then, alone or with children, emigrate to the United States in search of their husbands.

The system of boarding also created strains between husband and wife. Although some boarders fitted in like members of the family, relations were not always so cordial, and occasionally they were too cordial. Reformers blamed overcrowding and the system of lodgers for the immorality they found among the tenement population. Abraham Cahan's protagonist, David Levinsky, had amorous adventures with his landladies, and tried to convince one to leave her husband for him. David was not a "home wrecker"; he could not have disturbed a happy marriage. But his presence in the house exacerbated the problem of an unfulfilled husband-wife relationship.

Schism between parents and children was also a frequent outgrowth of the Americanization process. The children were educated in public schools; they spoke English and learned American habits. They were upwardly mobile. Through the parents' efforts, the children were educated beyond the parents' level and were able to achieve a higher social position. In a sense, then, the parents created monsters: they worked to have their children rise in society, learned to admire their children's achievements, and finally lost control of them. The exaggerated admiration for all that was "American" and upwardly mobile, and the concomitant scorn for all that was immigrant European, standards held by parent and child alike, created great familial stress. A popular saying at the time was, "In America, the children bring up the parents."[179] One settlement worker observed the process of separation between parent and child:

> At first the new ideas of the child are transmitted to its parents; but soon we find the [child] rapidly assimilating himself with our institutions and customs. . . . The home then becomes to the child a place to

---

[176] Ornitz, op. cit., note 99 above, p. 53.
[177] Isaac Metzker, *A bintel brief*, Garden City, N.Y., Doubleday, 1971, p. 84.
[178] Wald, op. cit., note 83 above, pp. 74–75.
[179] Metzker, op. cit., note 177 above, p. 24.

sleep and eat.... It is no longer a home.... The Jewish mother ... loves the child very much, so that after a time the child begins to control the parent instead of being controlled by her.[180]

Story after story by immigrant authors express the pain of this separation between parents and children – the bewilderment and anger of the older generation and the disgust and guilt of the younger. To Anzia Yezierska they were all "the children of loneliness".

## SUMMARY

We have seen that despite the foul housing and work conditions, Jews on the whole were physically healthier than their neighbours, both immigrant and Yankee. The tenth ward was the healthiest in Manhattan; Jewish mortality rates for tuberculosis, measles, scarlet fever, and diseases of the nervous system were the lowest in the City. While Jews were physically healthy, however, they were not spared the emotional illnesses and conditions which stemmed from the rupture with tradition and the pain of dislocation. Depression, suicide, gonorrhoea, and nervous disorders were more common among European Jews in America than in the old country. Neurasthenia, hysteria, and mental alienation were more common among Jews than among their non-Jewish neighbours.

675

By and large the Jewish immigration was successful. Many people prospered and very few returned to Europe. They were, in addition, inordinately healthy. Yet scars were left as the immigrants passed through the crucible of Americanization.

## ACKNOWLEDGEMENTS

I am very grateful to the men and women who spent many hours with me, remembering the days of their youth. From each I have the gift of a little bit of history. They gave not only their time, but also of themselves.

## BIBLIOGRAPHY

I PRIMARY SOURCES

A. *Official and annual reports of municipal, civic, and charity organizations*

1. *Annual report of the Department of Street Cleaning, City of New York*, 1914.

2. *Annual reports of the University Settlement Society*, 1894–1904, 1914, 1915–16. Also, *University Settlement Studies Quarterly.*

   These reports are essential to any study of immigrant Jews on the Lower East Side of New York during those years.

3. *Jewish Charity*, New York, vols. 2, 3, 4, and 5 (1903–1906).

4. The Committee of Fifteen, *The social evil*, New York, G. P. Putnam's Sons, 1902.

5. The Mayor's Committee on Public Baths and Public Comfort Stations, *Report*, New York, January 1897.

6. Society for the Alumni of City (Charity) Hospital, *Report for 1904*, New York City, 1904.

B. *Vital statistics and analyses*

1. Hermann M. Biggs, 'Preventive medicine in the City of New York', *Br. med. J.*, 11 September 1897.

[180] *Annual report of the University Settlement Society*, 1892, p. 27.

2. John Shaw Billings, *Vital statistics of the Jews in the United States*, and *Vital statistics of New York City and Brooklyn*, 31 May 1890, Special Reports for the Eleventh Census of the United States (1890), Washington, D.C., Government Printing Office, 1894.

3. Emil Bogen, 'Diseases among the Jews', *Medical Leaves*, 1943, **5**: 151–159.

4. I. Davidsohn, 'Cancer among the Jews', ibid., 1939, 19–27.

5. Martin Engländer, *Die Auffallend Häufige Krankheitserscheinungen der Jüdischen Rasse*, Vienna, 1902.

6. Maurice Fishberg, 'The comparative pathology of the Jews', *N.Y. med. J.*, 30 March 1901, pp. 537–543: 6 April 1901, pp. 576–581.

7. Maurice Fishberg, 'Health and sanitation of the immigrant Jewish population of New York', *Menorah Mthly*, August 1902, **33**, no. 2: 73–82; September 1902, **33**, no. 3: 168–180.

8. Maurice Fishberg, *The Jews: a study of race and environment*, London, Walter Scott, 1911.

9. Maurice Fishberg, 'Consumption', 'Idiocy', 'Insanity', 'Morbidity', 'Mortality', in *Jewish encyclopedia*, 1901–1906 ed.

10. Max Grunwald (editor), *Die Hygiene der Juden*, Dresden, Verlag der Historischen Abteilung der Internationalen Hygiene-Ausstellung, 1911.

11. Hugo Hoppe, *Krankheiten und Sterblichkeit bei Juden und Nichtjuden*, Berlin, S. Calvary, 1903.

12. Joseph Jacobs, *Statistics of the Jewish population in London, 1873–1893*, London, E. W. Rabbinowicz, 1894.

13. Joseph Jacobs, *Studies in Jewish statistics*, London, D. Nutt, 1891.

14. Josef von Körösi, 'Einfluss der Confession des Wohlstandes und der Beschäftigung auf die Todesursachen', *Publicationen des Statistischen Bureaus d. Hauptstadt Budapest*, Berlin, 1898.

15. Joseph von Körösi, *Die Sterblichkeit der Haupt- und Residenzstadt Budapest von 1882–95 und deren Ursachen*, Berlin, 1898.

16. Lagneau, 'Discussion sur la pathologie de la race juive'. *Bull. Acad. Méd. Paris*, 8 September 1891.

17. Cesare Lombroso, *L'antisemitismo e le scienze moderne*, Turin, 1894.

18. Ministry of Health (Great Britain), *42nd annual report on infant and child mortality*, London, H.M.S.O., 1913, pp. 19, 76, 79.

19. Alfred Nossig, *Jüdische Statistik*, Berlin, 1903, esp: H. Rimalovsky, 'Zur Statistik der Bulgarischen Juden', pp. 316–321; L. Wengierow, 'Die Juden in Königreich Polen', pp. 293–310.

20. Sir Humphry Rolleston, 'Some diseases in the Jewish race', *Bull. Johns Hopk. Hosp.*, 1928, **43**: 117–139.

21. Arthur Ruppin, *The Jews of today*, London, G. Bell, 1913.

22. Arthur Ruppin, 'Die Sozialen Verhältnisse der Juden in Preussen', *Jahrb. Nationalökonomie und Statistik*, 1902.

23. Heinrich Singer, *Allgemeine und Spezielle Krankheitslehre der Juden*, Leipzig, B. Konegen, 1904.

676

23 *Thirteenth Census of the United States* (1910), vol. III, 'Population', Washington, D.C., Government Printing Office.

24 Hugo Ullmann, 'Zur Frage der Vitalität und Morbidität der Jüdischen Bevölkerung', *Arch. Rassen- und Gesellschafts-Biologie*, vol. 18, Munich, 1926, pp. 1–54

25 Also, various reports in: *Bulletin of the International Statistical Institute; Statisches Jahrbuch der Stadt* (Berlin); *Veröffentlichungen des Bureaus für Statistik der Juden.*

(c) *Industry, industrial conditions, industrial health*

1 Joint Board of Sanitary Control in the Cloak, Suit, and Skirt Industry, *Directory of certificated shops in the cloak, suit, and skirt industry*, New York, Allied Printers, May 1913.

2 Joint Board of Sanitary Control in the Cloak, Suit, and Skirt Industry, *First annual report*, New York, October 1911.

3 Joint Board of Sanitary Control in the Cloak, Suit, and Skirt Industry, *Six years' work and progress of the Joint Board of Sanitary Control in the Cloak, Suit, and Skirt, and Dress and Waist Industries*, New York, October 1916.

4 Joint Board of Sanitary Control in the Dress and Waist Industry, *Special report on sanitary conditions in the shops of the dress and waist industry*, New York, Allied Printers, May 1913.

5 Jesse Eliphalet Pope, *The clothing industry in New York*, University of Missouri, 1905.

6 Edward E. Pratt, *Industrial causes of congestion of population in New York City*, Columbia University Ph.D. thesis, New York, 1911.

7 *Preliminary report of the Factory Investigating Commission of the State of New York*, 1912, vols. I, II, and III, Albany N.Y., Argus, 1912.

8 George Price, *Handbook on sanitation*, New York, John Wiley, 1911.

9 George Price, *Report for the year 1926 of the Union Health Center*, New York, Allied Printers, 1926.

10 George Price and Theresa Wolfson, *Seating and posture*, New York, Allied Printers, 1923.

11 George Price, *Ten years of industrial sanitary self control*; the Tenth Annual Report of the Joint Board of Sanitary Control in the Cloak, Suit, and Skirt, and Dress and Waist Industries, New York, 1921.

12 George Price, *The Joint Board of Sanitary Control in the Cloak, Suit, and Skirt, and Dress and Waist Industries*, New York, October 1924.

13 George Price, *The modern factory*, New York, John Wiley, 1914.

14 George Price and Rudolph Miller, *Fire hazard in factory buildings*, New York, December 1922.

15 *Report* for 1924 of the Union Health Center of the I.L.G.W.U. New York Locals, New York, Allied Printers, 1924.

16 J. Schereschewsky, 'The health of garment workers', *Publ. Hlth Bull.*, no. 71, May 1915.

677

35

17. J. Schereschewsky and D. H. Tuck, 'The hygienic conditions of illumination in workshops of the women's garment industry', ibid.

18. *Second report of the New York State Factory Investigating Commission*, January 1913, vols. I and II, Albany, N.Y., J. B. Lyon, 1913.

19. *Transactions of the Fifteenth International Congress on Hygiene and Demography*, Washington, D.C., Government Printing Office, 1913. Especially: vol. III, part I, 'Hygiene of infancy and childhood: school hygiene'; vol. III, part II, 'Hygiene of occupations'; vol. IV. part I, 'Control of infectious diseases'; vol. IV; part II, 'State and municipal hygiene'.

20. *Twelfth annual report of the Factory Inspector of the State of New York (1897)*, New York, 1898.

21. B. S. Warren and Edgar Sydenstricker, 'Health of garment workers', *Publ. Hlth Rep.*, 26 May 1916, **31**, no. 21.

678

D. *Tuberculosis*

1. Emil Bogen, 'Tuberculosis among the Jews', *Medical Leaves*, 1940, **3**: 123–129.

2. Charity Organization Society (COS), *A handbook on the prevention of tuberculosis; the first annual report of the Committee on the Prevention of Tuberculosis of the COS*, New York, 1903; *Second annual report*, 1903–04; *Third annual report*, 1904–05.

3. COS, *Preventing tuberculosis in New York City*, Ninth annual report of the Committee, [n.d.].

4. Department of Health, City of New York, Clinic for the Treatment of Communicable Pulmonary Diseases, *First report*, 1906.

5. Department of Health of the City of New York and the Committee on the Prevention of Tuberculosis of the COS, *What you should know about tuberculosis*, New York City, 1910.

6. Maurice Fishberg, 'The relative infrequency of tuberculosis among the Jews', *Amer. Med.*, 1901, **2**: 695–698.

7. S. A. Knopf, *Tuberculosis as a disease of the masses and how to combat it*, New York, Fred P. Flori, 1907.

8. John H. Pryor, 'The tenement and tuberculosis', *Charities Rev.*, 1900–1901, **10**: 440–446.

9. *Sixth International Congress on Tuberculosis*, Philadelphia, William F. Fell, 1908; especially vol. III: *Hygienic, social, and industrial, and economic aspects of tuberculosis*.

10. 'Studies in immunity to tuberculosis', *J. med. Res.*, April 1910, **22**, no. 2.

11. 'Tuberculosis among Jews', *Br. med. J.*, 1908, **i**: 1000–1002.

12. Tostivint and Remlinger, 'Note sur la rareté de la tuberculose chez les Israélites Tunisiens', *Rev. Hyg. Police Sanitaire, Paris*, 1900, **22**: 984–986.

E. *Tenements*

1. Lawrence Veiller and Robert De Forest (editors), *The tenement house problem*, 2 vols., New York, Macmillan, 1903.

2. *Fifth Report of the Tenement House Department of the City of New York*, 1909,

*...conditions of immigrant Jews on the Lower East Side of New York: 1880–1914*

New York, J. J. Little & Ives.

1. Joseph Lee. 'Preventive work', *Charities Rev.*, 1900–1901, **10**: 469–485.
2. Sixth report of the Tenement House Department of the City of New York, New York City, Allied Printing, 1910–1911.
3. *Plumber and Sanitary Engineer*, March 1879, **2**, no. 4: 89–91; December 1878, pp. 1, 12.

F Social commentaries, tracts, pamphlets, and articles

1. Annie S. Daniel, 'The wreck of the home', *Charities*, 1905, **14**: 624–629.
2. Harold M. Finley, 'The congestion of Manhattan', *Federation*, May 1908, **5**, no. 1: 10–18, also, entire issue of *Federation*, April 1906, **4**, no. 3.
3. Burton J. Hendrick, 'The Jewish invasion of America', *McClure's Mag.*, March 1913, pp. 126–165.
4. Arthur Henry, 'Among the immigrants', *Scribner's Mag.*, 1901, **29**: 301–311.
5. Claude H. Miller, 'The menace of crowded cities', *World's Work*, 1908, **16**: 10268–10272.
6. George Price, 'The Russian Jews in the United States', *Amer. Jew. hist. Soc.*, September 1958, **48**, no. 1: 28–62; ibid., December 1958, **48**, no. 2: 78–133.
7. Jacob Riis, *How the other half lives*, New York, Hill & Wang, 1957.
8. Jacob Riis, *The children of the poor*, London, Sampson, Low, Marston, 1892.
9. Jacob Riis, *The peril and the preservation of the home*, Philadelphia, George W. Jacobs, 1903.
10. Jacob Riis, *A ten years' war*, Boston and New York, Houghton, Mifflin, 1900.
11. Mary Sherman, 'Manufacturing of foods in the tenements', *Charities and the Commons*, 1905–06, **15**: 669–672.
12. 'The moral side of the tenement problem', *Catholic Wld*, May 1885, **41**: 160–164.
13. Richard Wheatley, 'The Jews in New York', *Century Mag.*, January 1892, **43**, no. 3: 323–342.

G Fiction, fictionalized accounts

1. Sholem Aleichem, 'Off for the Golden Land', *Jewish Immigration Bull.*, February 1917, pp. 10–11.
2. Arthur Bullard, *Comrade Yetta*, New York, Macmillan, 1913.
3. Abraham Cahan, *The imported bridegroom and other stories*, Boston and New York, Houghton, Mifflin, 1898.
4. Abraham Cahan, *The rise of David Levinsky*, New York, Harper, 1917.
5. Michael Gold, *Jews without money*, New York, Horace Liverwright, 1930.
6. Hutchins Hapgood, *The spirit of the ghetto*, Cambridge, Mass., Belknap Press of Harvard University Press, 1967.
7. Theresa Server Malkiel, *The diary of a shirtwaist striker*, New York, Socialist Literature, Co-Operative Press, 1910.
8. I. L. Nascher, *The wretches of Povertyville*, Chicago, Joseph J. Lanzit, 1909.
9. James Oppenheim, *Doctor Rast*, New York, Sturgis & Walton, 1909.
10. S. B. Ornitz, *Haunch, paunch and jowl*, New York, Boni & Liverwright, 1923.
11. Ernest Poole, *His family*, New York, Macmillan, 1917.
12. Ernest Poole, *His second wife*, New York, Macmillan, 1918.

679

37

13. Ernest Poole, *The harbor*, New York, Macmillan, 1915.

14. Jacob Riis, *Children of the tenements*, New York, Macmillan, 1903.

15. Jacob Riis, *Neighbors*, New York, Macmillan, 1919.

16. Jacob Riis, *Out of Mulberry Street*, New York, Century, 1898; republished 1970 by Literature House.

17. Irvin Swerdlow, *All for one*, New York City, I.L.G.W.U. Education Department, [n.d.].

18. Anzia Yezierska, *Children of Loneliness*, New York and London, Funk & Wagnalls, 1923.

19. Anzia Yezierska, *Hungry hearts*, Boston and New York, Houghton, Mifflin, 1920.

20. Anzia Yezierska, *Salome of the tenements*, New York, Boni & Liverwright, 1923.

H. *Memoirs, autobiography*

1. Charles Bernheimer, *Half a century in community service*, New York, Association Press, 1948.

2. Miriam Blaustein, *Memoirs of David Blaustein*, New York, McBride, Nast, 1913.

3. Michael Charnofsky, *Jewish life in the Ukraine*, New York, Exposition Press, 1965.

4. Fannie Edelman, *The mirror of life*, New York, Exposition Press, 1961.

5. Emma Goldman, *Living my life*, Garden City, N.Y., Garden City Publishing Co., 1931.

6. Benjamin Lee Gordon, *The memoirs of a physician*, New York, Bookman Associates, 1962.

7. Mary Asia Iliff, *No time for tears*, New York, Thomas Yoseloff, 1964.

8. Oral histories, especially from the men and women of the Golden Age Club and the Happy Club of the Mosholu Montefiore Senior Center, DeKalb Avenue, Bronx, New York 10467.

9. Lillian Wald, *The house on Henry Street*, New York, Henry Holt, 1915.

10. Lillian Wald, *Windows on Henry Street*, Boston, Mass., Little, Brown, 1934.

11. Gregory Weinstein, *The ardent eighties*, New York, International Press, 1928.

12. Anzia Yezierska, *Red ribbon on a white horse*, New York, Charles Scribner's Sons, 1950.

I. *Miscellaneous*

1. Charles Bernheimer, *The Russian Jews in the United States*, Philadelphia, John C. Winston, 1905

2. Harry Chase Brearly, *The problem of Greater New York and its solution*, New York City, Search-Light Corporation, 1914.

II. SECONDARY SOURCES

A. *General*

1. Louis Finkelstein, *The Jews*, (vols. I and II), New York, Harper, 1960.

2. Irving Howe, *World of our fathers*, New York and London, Harcourt, Brace, Jovanovich, 1976.

680

38

3. Moses Rischin, *The promised city*, Cambridge, Mass., Harvard University Press, 1962.
4. Ronald Sanders, *The downtown Jews*, New York, Harper & Row, 1969.
5. *YIVO Annual of Social Science*, Yiddish Scientific Institute, New York. This is a necessary secondary source for any work in Jewish history. For the purposes of this work, volumes II/III, and IX are especially helpful.

B. *Population statistics*
1. Lloyd P. Gartner, 'The Jews of New York's East Side, 1890–1893', *Amer. Jew. hist. Quart.*, March 1964, pp. 266–281.
2. Samuel Joseph, *Jewish Immigration to the United States from 1881–1910*, Ph.D. Thesis, Columbia University, New York, 1914.
3. Walter Laidlow, *Population of the City of New York, 1890–1930*, New York, Cities Census Committee, 1932.
4. Jacob Lestschinsky, 'Jewish migration, 1840–1956', in Louis Finkelstein (editor), *The Jews*, vol. II, New York, Harper, 1960.

C. *Occupation distribution and labour unions*
1. John Commons, *History of labour in the United States*, New York, Macmillan, 1918 (especially vol. II).
2. Max Danish, *I.L.G.W.U. News–History 1900–1950*.
3. Nathan Goldberg, 'Occupational patterns of American Jews', *Jewish Rev.*, April 1945, **3**, no. 1: 3–24.
4. Simon Kuznets, 'Economic structure and life of the Jews', in Louis Finkelstein (editor), *The Jews*, vol. II, New York, Harper, 1960.
5. Harry Lang, *'62', Biography of a union*, printed by Undergarment and Negligee Workers' Union, Local 62, of the International Ladies' Garment Workers Union, [n.d.].
6. Louis Levine, *The women's garment workers*, New York, B. W. Huebsch, 1924.

D. *Public health and medical history*
1. John Duffy, *A history of public health in New York City, 1866–1966*, New York, Russell Sage Foundation, 1974.
2. Mazÿck Ravenal, *A half century of public health*, New York, American Public Health Association, 1921.
3. A. J. Rongy, 'Half a century of Jewish medical activities in New York City', *Medical Leaves*, Chicago, 1937, pp. 151–163.
4. George Rosen, *Preventive medicine in the United States*, New York, Science History, 1975.

E. *History of philanthropy*
1. Boris D. Bogen, *Jewish philanthropy*, New York, Macmillan, 1917.
2. Jewish Social Service Association, *Fifty years of social service*, New York City, 1926.
3. Roy Lubove, 'The New York Association for Improving the Condition of the Poor: the formative years', *N. Y. hist. Quart.*, 1959, **43**: 307–329.

681

F. *Biography*
1. R. L. Duffus, *Lillian Wald*, New York, Macmillan, 1939.
2. Roy Lubove, 'Annie Sturges Daniel', in Edward T. James (editor), *Notable American women, 1607–1950*, Boston, Mass., Harvard University Press, vol. I, 1971, pp. 429–431.
3. *Med. J. Rec.*, 16 November 1927, p. 632, (obituary notice for William Gilman Thompson).

G. *Newspaper articles (collections)*
1. Isaac Metzker, *A bintel brief*, Garden City, N.Y., Doubleday, 1971.
2. Allan Schoener, *Portal to America*, New York, Holt, Rhinehart & Winston, 1967.

H. *Miscellaneous*
1. Ezekiel Lifschutz, 'Yiddish autobiographies as a source of American Jewish history', *Amer. Jew. hist. Quart.* March 1964, pp. 253–263.
2. Roy Lubove, *The progressives and the slums*, Pittsburgh, University of Pittsburgh Press, 1962.

# THE JEWISH LABOR MOVEMENT
# IN THE UNITED STATES
## By WILL HERBERG

For an understanding of the history of the Jewish labor movement in the United States, the early 1930's may profitably be taken as constituting in some sense a watershed or turning point in the development of that movement. These years marked the end of one epoch and the beginning of another, not only for Jewish labor but for the nation as a whole.

The early 1930's proved so crucial for a number of interrelated reasons:

1. During these years the effects of the stoppage of foreign immigration, resulting from World War I and the passage of a series of restrictive laws in the 1920's, began to be felt in the profound changes of composition and structure which the American Jewish community was undergoing.

2. By the early 1930's the Communist bid for power which had shaken the Jewish labor movement to its foundations had been definitely defeated. But the decade of bitter civil war had left permanent marks which contributed to the making of the new period.

3. The economic, social, and labor world into which the Jewish unions emerged out of the 1920's was in many ways a new world. Franklin Delano Roosevelt was in the White House and the New Deal, with incredible speed, was remaking American social policy and transforming the lives and outlook of millions of Americans, particularly those composing the working classes of the nation.

4. The labor movement, after a decade of decline and crisis, was staging a spectacular come-back. It was a time of vast change, of far-reaching transformation in tradition, ideas, and purposes, for the Jewish labor movement as for American labor and the American people generally.

5. If the New Deal is taken as one pole of the new era, the upsurge of Nazism and anti-Semitism in Europe must be taken as the other. Both of these developments profoundly affected the character and outlook of Jewish labor in America.

Cumulatively, these factors contributed to remake the Jewish labor movement almost beyond recognition. It is the purpose of this study to look backward and forward from the vantage point of the early 1930's and to indicate what the Jewish labor movement once was, what

3

Originally published in *American Jewish Year Book* (1952). Reprinted by permission of the *American Jewish Year Book*.

it came to be under the new conditions, and what its prospects are for the future. In this way, we may hope to assess its significance in the general context of American life.

## The "Old" Jewish Labor Movement

### The Formative Period

The Jewish labor movement in the United States was a product of the "new" immigration that deposited millions of East European Jews on American shores within the space of a few decades after 1870. Jews had, of course, reached the New World long before, and in the early part of the nineteenth century they had begun to arrive in considerable numbers. This earlier immigration, except for a small Sephardic element, was largely Western, predominantly Central European. The early immigrants—some two or three hundred thousand in all—soon found their way into business or the professions; they left few traces on the labor movement and contributed almost nothing to the emergence of a Jewish proletariat in the United States. That was reserved for the East Europeans who came in vast numbers during the last three decades of the nineteenth and the first two or three decades of the twentieth century.

It has been noted that "the curve of Jewish immigration to the United States runs remarkably parallel to that of general immigration to America," a fact which tends to suggest that "the decisive forces were the general ones common to the whole movement." [1] The social composition of the Jewish immigrants was, however, markedly different. The non-Jewish immigrants from Eastern Europe were very largely peasants; the Jewish immigrants, on the other hand, were town dwellers, a large proportion being employed as artisans or laborers.

Hence, more than 64 per cent of the gainfully employed Jewish immigrants during 1900–25, government reports indicate, were "skilled workers," as compared with 8.5 per cent and 7.2 per cent of the non-Jewish immigrants from Russia and Poland, respectively. During the same period, domestic servants formed 13.7 per cent of the Jewish immigration, unskilled workers 11.2 per cent, merchants 6.2 per cent, and professionals 2.0 per cent. [2] Of course, very few of the "skilled workers" were factory workers in modern industry; almost all were artisans who frequently combined petty business with their crafts. Nevertheless, these figures are enough to indicate that the usual picture of the East European Jewish immigrant as a *luftmensh* without occupation is by no means true. There were many *luftmenshn* among them, no doubt, but the largest part of the East European immigrants of those days seem to have been artisans or artisan-merchants, a smaller part laborers, and still smaller parts professionals or intellectuals. In any case, once they had arrived in the United States, almost all the Jewish immigrants turned to manual labor.

## EARLY OCCUPATIONAL PATTERN

The occupational pattern that emerged among the Jewish immigrant workers in the last decades of the nineteenth century was the product of many factors, economic, social, and ethnic, which have not yet been sufficiently explored. Most of the Jewish newcomers landed at the port of New York and a very large part either remained there or moved on to other large urban centers near by. Before the last third of the century they apparently turned for work to a wide variety of trades, including even heavy industry. But this wide range soon began to narrow down. Some of the immigrants left industry altogether and went into petty trade; the great majority tended to gravitate toward occupations involved in the production of consumers' goods and services. The natural impulse to seek work in fields where friends and *lantslayt* (countrymen) were already employed contributed to this tendency. In any case, as the preponderant majority of Jews in America became wageworkers, a number of "Jewish trades" in which the great mass of workers and most of the employers were Jewish began to emerge.

685

These trades were of two types. The first type consisted of those which from their very nature were necessarily open only to Jews, such as Jewish slaughtering, baking, printing, acting, etc. Here the characteristic structure and way of life of the Jewish community conditioned the occupational pattern. But there were also some trades, particularly the needle and building trades, to which the immigrant Jews flocked perhaps partly by reason of their previous training and handicraft skills. It was the "Jewish trades" of the second type that became so significant in the emergence of a Jewish labor movement toward the end of the nineteenth century and in the development of this movement through later decades.

## EARLY ORGANIZATION

The Jewish immigrant worker did not take to trade unionism easily. Indeed, the "individualism" and "unorganizability" of the Jewish worker were familiar complaints until relatively recent times. In 1901, the distinguished labor economist, John R. Commons, in his report for the United States Industrial Commission, went to some length to explain why unionism was such a failure among Jewish workers. Whatever the validity of his arguments, he did point to an undeniable fact: the newly proletarianized Jewish worker was quick to strike, enthusiastic, and determined in struggle, but "when once the strike is settled, either in favor of or against the cause . . . that ends the union." [3] The Jewish worker apparently did not possess the tenacity or discipline necessary for enduring labor organization.

As a matter of fact, the first stirrings of what was to become the Jewish labor movement were rather in the political and ideological fields than in the field of trade unionism. In this as in other respects, the pattern and direction of the Jewish labor movement were originally the *reverse* of what was normative in American trade unionism; it followed far more closely the Continental than the native American model. The American labor movement, like the British, emerged and remained typically a *trade-union* movement; moreover, it developed *from the bottom up,* from the self-organization of groups of workers in their trades. Jewish trade unionism in the United States, on the other hand, was built *from the top down,* largely under the tutelage of ideological radicals who undertook the hard task of organizing Jewish workers as part of their revolutionary program. The increasing adaptation of the Jewish labor movement to the general American pattern in later decades should not blind us to this very great difference in its origins and beginnings. [4]

The early Jewish immigrants were, by and large, not radicals; there was among them, however, a tiny but very aggressive minority of intellectuals and intellectually minded workers who had received some radical indoctrination in the revolutionary movements of Eastern Europe. These radicals included Socialists of different degrees of extremism; anarchists, "philosophical" and violent; Comtean positivists; land reformers; ethical culturists; and doctrinaires of almost every other school. Though engaged in continuous and bitter conflict among themselves, with few exceptions all these radical groups agreed on the necessity of reaching the masses with the gospel of "education and organization."

Early in the "new" immigration, at the beginning of the 1880's, an attempt had been made by a Socialist-nationalist group, Am Olam (Eternal People), to found Jewish agricultural and industrial communes in the New World. The attempt soon failed, though the memory lingered on. Thereafter, the radicals were concerned primarily with revolutionizing the consciousness of the Jewish working masses and organizing them for the class struggle.

They succeeded in becoming the leaders of the Jewish masses, although the outcome of their work was not such as would have commended itself to them in their early days. Their quick success was due, in part at least, to the fact that they came with a new "faith" to fill the impossible spiritual void produced by the shattering impact of American life upon the traditional pattern of existence brought by the immigrant from the Old World. There, even through the nineteenth century, life had been ruled by religious law and had been organized around the synagogue. *Halakah* and synagogue afforded the Jew a strong measure of spiritual security amidst the miseries of the world; they provided him with an accepted system of standards and a context of meaning for life. In the United States, under drastically different social and economic conditions, the old ways were no longer tenable, not even for the most tradition-bound. The age-old continuities of life were disrupted; long-accepted standards and values were challenged by the demands of the new life as well as by the entire spiritual climate of the New World. There was little chance for slow organic transition. Spiritual confusion, insecurity, and normlessness were the result. It was the dreadful anomy of early immigrant life that gave the fervent young radicals the opportunity to establish a predominant influence among the Jewish workers in the formative period of the Jewish labor movement in the United States.

JEWISH WORKERS UNION

The first organizations of Jewish radicals in the United States were educational and propaganda societies, such as the Propaganda Union (1882), the Russian (i.e., Russian Jewish) Labor Union (1884), the Russian Labor Lyceum (1884), etc. (Most of the Russian Jewish radicals at this time, it should be noted, considered themselves primarily Russians and only turned to Yiddish in order to spread their propaganda.) At first the radicals rather looked down on the idea of organizing the Jewish workers into unions, although they passionately warned the inexperienced immigrants against scabbing and strike-breaking. But by 1885 a Yidisher Arbeter Farayn (Jewish Workers Union) was in existence which definitely set about the task of organizing the masses of Jewish workers. The older German Socialists played an important part in gathering together and orienting their Jewish comrades.

The Jewish Workers Union, though not itself a trade union, included in its ranks hundreds of workers—garment workers, capmakers, barbers, clerks. It was very active in New York City in the Henry George mayoralty campaign of 1886, which most Jewish radicals supported, but it did not survive the next year. The Jewish Workers Union was followed by what may properly be regarded as the parent institution of the Jewish labor movement in America—the United Hebrew Trades (Faraynikte Yidishe Geverkshaftn).

UNITED HEBREW TRADES

The United Hebrew Trades (UHT) came into being in October, 1888, under the leadership of Bernard Weinstein, Jacob Magidoff, Morris Hillquit, and Henry Miller, and with the direct assistance of Samuel Gompers. Its model was the United German Trades, one

of a number of "national," foreign-language labor federations that
had sprung up in the United States in the course of the second half
of the nineteenth century. The new Jewish group took as its main
purpose the organization of the Jewish workers into unions. The
UHT had only three affiliates at the time of its formation: the Jewish
compositors, the Jewish actors, and the Jewish choral singers. But it
grew rapidly and within four years had twenty-eight trade-union
affiliates, most of them organized through UHT efforts. The UHT
covered the Greater New York area, where the vast majority of working-class Jews were then and still are to be found. Similar federations
were set up in Chicago, Philadelphia, and Baltimore, and an attempt
was even made to launch a national Jewish labor federation; however,
these latter efforts proved short-lived, while the New York organization still exists, though its role has changed very considerably with the
passage of time.[5]

The establishment of the United Hebrew Trades brought to the
fore a problem that gave some concern to American labor leaders,
Jewish and non-Jewish alike—the problem of the propriety of organizing
"separate" Jewish unions. Samuel Gompers had his qualms about the
UHT because he did not believe in organizing workers along "religious" lines; but he wisely saw that "to organize Hebrew trade unions
was the first step in getting those immigrants into the American labor
movement." It was not, of course, a matter of religion, but of language, culture, community ties, and the characteristic structure of the
Jewish trades. In 1892, the Jewish Socialists discussed the question of
"Jewish" or "mixed" unions; principle was all on the side of the latter, the pressure of reality on the side of the former, and so they
decided to leave the choice to local option. History made its own
decision, considerably aided by the hostility that Jewish workers encountered when they tried to join some of the established unions.
Jewish unions were formed. In the long run, Gompers was right: the
Jewish unions were the first step in bringing the Jewish workers into
the American labor movement.

WORKING CONDITIONS

There would be little point in summarizing here the familiar facts
about the miserable conditions under which the garment workers
toiled in these early days. The industry was rapidly expanding and,
following the Irish and other earlier immigrants, Jews were being
absorbed into it in large numbers. Their entry was facilitated by the
fact that some Jews were already active in the clothing industry as
manufacturers. By 1890, over 13,000 Jews were employed in the garment trades on the East Side of New York alone, and their numbers
increased by leaps and bounds in the course of the next two decades.

Low wages, long hours, protracted slack seasons, home work, contracting and sub-contracting, absence of even the most elementary safeguards of health and decency made the garment trades notorious as a "sweated" industry. The workers were restless, shop strikes were frequent, and conflicts on a larger scale were not unusual. In 1885, the entire cloak trade in New York came to a stop, and a Cloak and Dressmakers Union constituted itself an assembly of the Knights of Labor. The year before, in the fall of 1884, the men's clothing workers in New York had successfully struck and set up the Progressive Tailors Union No. 1, also a part of the Knights. These unions split, disappeared, rose again, and merged with other groups; but in a very real sense they initiated the movement that culminated in the formation of the great garment unions of today. The connection with the Knights of Labor did not last very long.

Other strikes and other unions followed in rapid succession, not only in New York but in other cities as well. In the spring of 1886, a great cloakmakers' strike broke out in Chicago, out of which a union was born. During the next two or three years, cloakmakers' unions were launched in Philadelphia and Boston. But New York remained the main scene of the rising movement.

Capmakers' organizations go back to the 1870's. Some of the workers in those years were German Jews; Russian Jews and Italians began entering the trade a decade later. The Russian Jews found it especially difficult to secure entry into the existing unions, and so separate "Hebrew" unions were formed which were not absorbed into the larger organizations until the end of the 1890's. The UHT was largely instrumental in bringing about this unification.

The last two decades of the nineteenth century also witnessed the organization, mainly upon the initiative or with the help of the UHT, of Jewish bakery workers, tinsmiths, barbers, shoe workers, bookbinders, textile workers, theater employees, and the workers of the many other crafts and trades that year by year were added to the roster of the UHT. It was a difficult period, one of confusion and frequent defeat, yet a period in which the ground was broken and the foundations laid for what was to come.

INDUSTRIAL UNIONS

It is perhaps worth noting as a very fortunate circumstance in the early development of the Jewish labor movement that the fateful cleavage between the skilled and the unskilled, which so deeply affected American unionism generally, was hardly felt in the Jewish unions. This was primarily due to the structure of the industries in which these unions operated—some degree of skill was required of practically all workers in the garment and associated trades—but also

689

in part perhaps to the Socialist ideology of the builders of the movement. In any case, the Jewish unions, especially in the needle trades, developed from the very beginning as semi-industrial organizations, the special interests of the various crafts remaining subordinate. This proved an important source of strength to the unions, and also tended to define the direction of their influence in the American labor movement as a whole.

## NATIONAL ORGANIZATION

In many cases, the Jewish unions formed upon the initiative or with the help of the UHT were local or regional bodies that had to be affiliated with an existing national organization. This was sometimes quite difficult, for only too often the Jewish workers were not received into the older unions. Such was the case, for example, in the building trades. Jewish workers penetrated virtually every branch of these trades in New York, as did Jewish builders and contractors. However, the building trades unions not only would not admit Jewish workers into their ranks, but actually took measures to exclude them from the more desirable occupations and employments. Barred from the existing unions, the Jewish building trades workers formed their own organizations, under the guidance of the UHT; it required considerable effort, including the intervention of top leaders of the American Federation of Labor (AFL), to prevail upon the national unions in the building trades to admit them. Indeed, not until well into the twentieth century were the bars really let down.

But in many of the Jewish trades, typically in the needle trades, the task was even more difficult, for there were no national unions in the field and they had to be created in the process of union building. In the men's clothing trade, this step was taken in the last decade of the nineteenth century. In 1889, the UHT helped form the United Tailors Brotherhood, which led a successful strike the same year. In the full flush of victory, this union called a national conference for June 13, 1890, in New York City, to set up a nation-wide body in the industry. The International Tailors and Cutters Union was formed, but it died within the year. In 1891 another attempt was made, again at the initiative of the UHT. At a convention held in New York on April 12, attended by delegates from that city, Boston, Philadelphia, Chicago, Baltimore, and from a few smaller centers, the United Garment Workers was formed. It was at bottom a coalition of men's tailors, largely radical-minded immigrant Jews and Italians, on the one hand, and conservative American overall and work-clothes makers, on the other. The coalition could not last, and when the break-up came, the Amalgamated Clothing Workers emerged.

The women's garment workers had to wait another decade for a

690

national organization. This finally came in 1900. A call for a nation-wide conference was issued by the New York cloakmakers. Eleven delegates, representing seven local unions with about 2,000 members in New York and the vicinity, were present when the convention opened on June 3 in New York. The International Ladies Garment Workers Union (ILGWU) was formed and, like the United Garment Workers, it affiliated with the AFL.

The beginnings of the ILGWU were promising. By 1903, it already had nearly 10,000 members, about a third of whom were women. More than half its membership in that year was outside of New York. The onset of a business depression toward the end of 1903, however, brought an abrupt halt to this forward development, and the ILGWU entered a critical period from which it did not really emerge until the stormy days of 1909–10.

The formation of the UGW helped very little in improving the state or organization of the men's garment workers. The membership, as already indicated, consisted of two diverse elements, differing in ethnic origin, background, and outlook. The overall makers relied largely on the union label, which was of little use to the tailors. The tailors, for their part, complained of the lack of sympathy and under-standing shown by their leaders and of the dubious practices carried on under the protection of headquarters. They drifted away from the UGW. In the industry unrest was rife, and in 1901, 1902, and again in 1904, general strikes broke out in New York under the leader-ship of the United Brotherhood of Tailors, an affiliate of the UGW. These strikes had repercussions outside of New York, in St. Louis, Baltimore, and other cities. Very little was achieved, either by way of standards or organization. Then came the depression. Prospects in 1905 seemed no brighter for the men's tailors than for the women's garment workers.

The capmakers' union showed signs of greater stability. Conflict in the Socialist movement had split the capmakers' local in New York, but by 1900 some unity was restored and thoughts began to turn to a national organization. The New York local changed its name to United Cloth Hat and Capmakers Union of North America, and sent out a call for a convention. On December 27, 1901, the convention assembled in New York. There were 21 delegates, representing 1,200 workers in New York, Chicago, Boston, Detroit, and Baltimore. In order to avoid conflict in its own ranks, which included a number of strong DeLeonites, the national organization launched at the confer-ence did not affiliate with the AFL until the following year. The organization made steady progress until the recession of 1904. In that year the workers were forced into a costly general strike.

Jewish workers began to enter the fur industry in the 1890's. The

691

UHT formed a Jewish furriers' union in 1892, and a successful general strike for the eight-hour day was launched shortly thereafter. Both the union and the fruits of the strike disappeared next year. It required another decade for the UHT to re-establish a furriers' union in New York; this was done in 1904. In 1906, an attempt was made to set up a national organization, but this failed. A stable nation-wide organization was not established until 1913.

POLITICAL ACTIVITY

This laying of the foundations of the Jewish trade union movement can from our vantage point be seen to have been the most important work of those early decades.[6] But it hardly seemed so to the men of those days. To them, the Jewish labor movement meant primarily the *Socialist* movement, of which the trade unions were to be a kind of auxiliary or "arm." And indeed, political-ideological activity was at first much more exciting and immediately rewarding than the slow, ungrateful work of organizing "individualistic" and "unorganizable" workers. Until the second decade of the twentieth century, it was Socialist politics that absorbed the interest of the most gifted leaders of the Jewish workers.

Jewish radical clubs were already in existence in New York in the 1870's. Vigorous ideological battles were fought between the anarchists and the Socialists throughout the next two decades. Slowly, the Socialists established their predominance. Jewish Socialists took active part in the Henry George campaign for the mayoralty of New York on the United Labor Ticket in 1886. The next year, partly as a result of contacts established during the campaign, a group of Jewish Socialists asked the Socialist Labor party (SLP) to set them up as a Jewish branch, and Branch 8 was formed. Not all Jewish Socialists, however, wanted to belong to a Jewish organization, since they felt themselves to be really Russian. As a consequence, another SLP group, Russian Branch 17, was chartered, including among its members the celebrated American Socialist leader of later years, Morris Hillquit.

Hardly had the Jewish Socialists begun their party work when a split divided the party, one of the many that marked the few years of the SLP's significant life. It was over the atttude to be taken to unions. The New York Socialists favored working in the existing unions; the national leaders insisted on building separate radical unions. The New York position, which had the support of almost all Jewish Socialists, easily prevailed.

Within five years, however, the party was caught in an even worse crisis, in which the new Jewish unions were seriously involved. Daniel DeLeon, the new leader of the SLP, was determined to establish the hegemony of the party over the trade union movement. At first, he

692

tried to bore from within the AFL; but the results were not encouraging, so DeLeon set up a dual New York central body and launched an all-out attack on Gompers and his federation. Under orders from the party, the Jewish Socialists detached their unions from the AFL and affiliated them with the new SLP center. DeLeon now developed his strategy; he decided to make the declining Knights of Labor the base of his campaign to capture the labor movement. He easily took over District Assembly 49, a mixed group of intellectuals and radical workers of which he was a member, and then proceeded to take over the Knights. But in this he was balked; so in 1895 DeLeon finally left the Knights of Labor and set up a new dual trade union federation under strict party control, the Socialist Trades and Labor Alliance. Orders went out to all SLP members and Socialist-controlled unions to join the Alliance.

It is not difficult to imagine the confusion in the ranks of the Jewish Socialists and trade unionists. A good number of them, under the leadership of the *Jewish Daily Forward,* refused to go along with De-Leon, and together with other recalcitrant party members prepared for another split. The leaders of the UHT, however, proved loyal to DeLeon and took that organization into the Alliance, although many of the UHT affiliates remained in the AFL. The United German Trades refused to join, but permitted its affiliates to do so if they wished. District Assembly 49 of the K of L was shattered. To counteract the shift of the UHT, the Socialists of the *Forward* set up a Federated Hebrew Trades loyal to the AFL. All the while, the anarchists were following their own line.

It is impossible to describe in brief space the tortuous complications of the disastrous struggle in the SLP. Suffice it to say that in 1896 a series of splits began which culminated in 1900 in the defection of a large part of the membership of the SLP from the party, and the fusion of this dissident element with other Socialist forces to form the Socialist party of America in 1901.[7] Under the leadership of the *Forward,* which finally broke away from the SLP in 1899, the overwhelming majority of the Jewish Socialists went into the new organization. The unions that had followed DeLeon, including the UHT, reaffiliated with the AFL. The Socialist Trades and Labor Alliance, which never had more than 20,000 members, lingered on until it was merged by DeLeon into the Industrial Workers of the World (IWW) in 1905.

LABOR PRESS

One of the most important aspects of the political-ideological struggle in the Jewish radical movement was the development of a labor press. Two private journals of a labor cast had been established in

693

New York in 1886, but they did not last very long. The first Yiddish Socialist paper was the *Arbeter Tsaytung* ("Workers Paper"), a weekly established in 1890. It soon achieved a circulation of about 7,000. Two years later, the monthly *Zukunft* ("Future") appeared, and finally in 1892 the daily *Abendblat* ("Evening Paper"), with a circulation of perhaps 10,000. All were issued by a publishing association under SLP (DeLeonite) control. Against the Socialist press, the anarchists had the *Freie Arbeiter Stimme* ("Free Workers Voice"), a weekly set up in 1890 on an allegedly non-partisan basis.

As the crisis in the SLP sharpened, discontent with the DeLeonite control of the press grew by leaps and bounds. Abraham Cahan and Louis Miller made themselves the expression of this resentment. The conflict over the trade unions added fuel to the fire. A bewildering series of resolutions, negotiations, and conferences followed; the upshot was that on April 22, 1897, there appeared the first issue of the *Jewish Daily Forward (Forverts)*, destined to be the single most influential force in the making of the Jewish labor movement. Abraham Cahan was elected editor, a position he held, aside from the years 1898–1902, to the day of his death (August 31, 1951).

The role of the *Forward* in the Jewish labor movement, especially during the early days, emphasizes the very important fact that for the Jewish workers of four or five decades ago, Socialism was not so much a social ideology or political creed as a *moral cement* that joined them together into a cohesive force and made collective action possible. The Jewish trader or artisan came to the United States burdened with the divisive, individualistic habits born out of the desperate competition that had dominated his precarious life in the old country. He had little of the "social" spirit, of the solidarity so essential to unionism, and it is no wonder that he was given up as hopeless from the trade union standpoint. Yet within a decade or two, he was to become a stalwart and responsible trade unionist, accustomed to discipline and collective action. More than anything else it was Socialism, preached and propagated with all the fervor of a religious creed, that effected this moral revolution. Above and beyond the interminable factional conflict and ideological hairsplitting was a glowing ideal of brotherhood and solidarity; it was this "moral" Socialism that overcame the centrifugal forces of background and habituation and engendered the atmosphere of "decency" in which trade unionism could arise and sustain itself.[8]

WORKMEN'S CIRCLE

The third "wing" of the Jewish labor movement—alongside of trade unions and political Socialism—was the great Jewish fraternal society, Arbeter Ring (Workmen's Circle). The Workmen's Circle (WC) was established in 1892, upon the initiative of two cloakmakers. It was a genuine rank-and-file enterprise and proved able to maintain its autonomous character through the decades. The purposes of the WC, as formulated at the foundation meeting, were to provide "mutual assistance to members in time of need and trouble," to stimulate the "education of the members," and to promote the "organization of co-operative business enterprises." The last aim was soon dropped; the only co-operative enterprise that the WC was able to launch was a barber shop, and that lasted only two years. But the other two purposes—mutual aid and education—remained the foundation of the order and developed beyond the dreams of its founders.

The society was reorganized in 1900, and the journalist, B. Feigenbaum, became its general secretary. At its second convention in 1901, the membership stood at 650, and at the third in 1902, at more than 1,200. After some difficulty, involving the readjustment of its statutes and practices, it was awarded a charter under the New York State Insurance Department in 1905. In that year the WC already had 6,700 members. Despite difficulties, conflicts, and crises, its progress was solid and substantial. Other workers' fraternal societies appeared, but the Workmen's Circle remained the outstanding Jewish labor fraternal order.[9]

Thus Jewish labor emerged from its formative period, which may be held to have closed somewhere between 1905 to 1908, with a weak but definitely established trade union movement, a relatively strong political Socialist movement and press, and a promising fraternal order. A great period of upsurge, growth, and consolidation lay ahead.

*Growth and Consolidation*

The new period of consolidation and growth was ushered in by two events that set their mark on the Jewish labor movement: the economic recovery that followed the crisis of 1905, and the new wave of Jewish immigration that came in the wake of the Kishinev massacre (1903). The latter event was the more decisive factor. Not only was there a sudden and sustained rise in immigration—from 76,000 in 1903 to 106,000 in 1904 and 149,000 in 1906 [10]—but the Jewish immigrants entering at this time were notably different from the earlier immigrants. The new immigrants were younger, more radical, more modern, more involved in the progressive causes and movements of the day. They were also much more culturally Yiddishist than the intellectuals among the immigrants of earlier times, who only with difficulty came to realize the vitality and indispensability of Yiddish in the life of the immigrant Jews. For the new arrivals, Yiddish was not only the natural medium of communication but was also and above all an instrument of group solidarity and a vehicle of cultural expression. From this point on, the Jewish labor movement became Yiddishist in a very conscious way.

Every variety of radical came with the new wave of immigration. The most significant group among the immigrants was made up of members and adherents of the Bund (General Jewish Workers Union), an organization of Jewish Socialists that was winning a name for itself in the Jewish communities of Eastern Europe. The Bundists made an immediate impression on American Jewish Socialist circles. With the Socialists came the anarchists and the first substantial groups of Poale (Labor) Zionists. But beyond the groups and their sectarian programs was the undifferentiated radicalism that expressed itself in a general ferment of idealism, in a yearning for the "finer things of life." A new spirit began to infuse the Jewish labor community of the United States, a spirit of intellectual alertness, social activism, and cultural striving. The young men and women of the newer immigration were deeply concerned with many things beyond merely earning a living. They were concerned with "ideas," with "causes," with literature, society, and the welfare of humanity. Social radicalism and cultural self-improvement were the marks of the new consciousness.

This new spirit and the economic upturn co-operated to bring about a revival of the trade union movement in 1907. In the men's clothing industry the Brotherhood of Tailors, a UGW affiliate, led a number of significant local strikes. But this only exacerbated its relations with the parent organization, which frowned upon such militancy as a threat to its union label system. A peace was patched up, but it was clear that the situation in the UGW was heading for an explosion.

The same year, 1907, witnessed a bitter strike by the Boston cloakmakers for union recognition and the fifty-hour week. Here too the strike was called against the express orders of the national officers, especially the secretary, John Dyche, who was an exponent of cautious piecemeal progress. Of wider significance was the strike of the reefermakers in New York in the same year. On March 22, 1907, 12,000 workers came out, stopping the entire trade. The battle was bitterly fought, and to a successful conclusion. In April, all of the major demands—recognition, the fifty-five-hour week, abolition of inside subcontracting among pressers, and the free supply of all "materials, tools and appliances" (including sewing machines)—were granted.

In other trades too, there were signs of an upswing. But the optimism engendered by these advances was suddenly quenched by the onset of another sharp depression toward the end of 1907. Within a few months, all gains were wiped out. Widespread unemployment overwhelmed the weak trade unions. Despair mounted. At the 1908 convention of the ILGWU, a resolution was introduced to return the union's charter to the AFL and merge with the UGW. But a few hardy spirits refused to surrender. In one way or another the unions survived the hard days, and by 1909 signs of revival were in the air.

The economic recovery of 1909 set off the greatest upsurge of trade unionism that Jewish labor in America was to experience until the New Deal. The five years from 1909 to 1914 worked a tremendous transformation in the power and status of the Jewish labor movement in the United States.

UPRISING OF THE TWENTY THOUSAND

In the women's garment industry, which was now employing scores of thousands of Jewish workers and an increasing number of Italians and members of other ethnic groups, the first explosion came among the shirtwaist makers in New York. This branch of women's apparel was relatively new and was enjoying a boom. Perhaps as many as 30,-000 workers were employed in the trade in New York, about 65 per cent of whom were Jews, 25 per cent Italians. A very large part of the workers were young women, eager, energetic, idealistic. Conditions were miserable, the union was weak and ineffectual, tension and rebellion were in the air. Upon the initiative of the UHT, a conference was called to see what could be done to meet the situation. Preparations for a general strike were decided upon, but nothing definite was contemplated until the historic meeting in Cooper Union on November 22, 1909. There the girls took things into their own hands. Rising to the appeal made by one of them, Clara Lemlich, the workers voted an immediate general strike. The response was immense and incredible. Nearly 20,000 girls came out in answer to the call. What this meant can be gathered from the fact that at the time the total membership of the ILGWU was scarcely 2,000. The entire labor movement, the public generally, was deeply stirred. The girls took over the everyday conduct of the strike, on the picket line, in the strike halls, on the various strike committees. The strike became their life. Public opinion rallied to their support. Through the help of the Women's Trade Union League, a bond was forged between the "girls" and the "ladies" that was to become a significant force in the development of unionism in the women's trades. Nothing could daunt the girls, neither the threats of the employers, nor the brutality of the police, nor the heartless harangues of the magistrates. In December, 1909, negotiations began, and at about the same time the strike spread to Philadelphia. The Philadelphia strike ended in failure and was called off in February, 1910. The New York strike, however, had another and more fortunate outcome. On February 10, 1910, a settlement was agreed upon. The manufacturers' association itself refused

697

to recognize the union, but 339 of the 353 members of the association signed up with the ILGWU. The workers won a fifty-two hour week, four paid legal holidays, and improvements in working conditions and methods of settling wages. Local 25, the union of the shirtwaist and dress makers, emerged with a membership of over 10,000. All in all, the "Uprising of the Twenty Thousand" was an epoch-making event.

## THE GREAT REVOLT

Hard on the heels of the "uprising" of the waistmakers came the "Great Revolt" of the New York cloakmakers. This strike was a very different affair from the spontaneous rebellion of the girls. It was carefully prepared in advance. The industry was older; the workers were mostly men; the union tradition was much stronger and had far deeper roots. Jews predominated, but Italians already formed a growing proportion of the working force. Preparations for the strike began as far back as the middle of 1908. All branches of the labor movement, including the WC, united in a conference arranged by the New York Cloak Joint Board in support of the movement. The membership of the Joint Board at the time was about 2,000.

The union issued the strike call for July 7, 1910. The strike was an immediate success. The entire cloak, suit, skirt, and reefer industry was at a standstill. Together with the several thousand raincoat makers and ladies' tailors who also took part, close to 60,000 workers were on strike. The struggle was well led and hard-fought. The employers refused to negotiate, and it was only through the personal intervention of A. Lincoln Filene, the Boston merchant, who came to New York with his attorney, Louis D. Brandeis, that the stalemate was broken. Negotiations began in July, and it was soon clear that the main difficulty was the union shop, which the strikers felt to be essential to union security. No agreement could be reached on this crucial matter; conferences broke off, and the employers tried to crush the strike with an injunction. Again there was outside intervention, this time on the part of a group of wealthy New York Jews headed by Louis Marshall and Jacob H. Schiff, who felt that the good name of the Jewish community was being imperilled by the conflict, particularly since public opinion was overwhelmingly on the side of the workers. Negotiations were resumed, and finally Brandeis' "invention" —the preferential union shop—was accepted. It was the union shop in substance if not in name, or so at least it turned out.

## PROTOCOL OF PEACE

The settlement that followed granted most of the particular demands of the workers, including the fifty-hour week, minimum wage

rates, abolition of subcontracting, etc. It also laid down the main outlines of the system of industrial relations that was thenceforth to
govern the garment trades. The Protocol of Peace, despite its many
deficiencies and its short life in its original form, marked an immense
and pioneering achievement in the institutional history of union-management relations in American industry. It provided for a Board of
Grievances, consisting of representatives of both sides, to deal with
disputes arising between workers and employers. All differences that
could not be settled by the parties themselves through this Board of
Grievances were to be referred to a higher Board of Arbitration, in
which impartial representatives of the public were the deciding factor.
Unless abrogated by one or the other party, the Protocol was to run
indefinitely; it had no time limit such as the more orthodox collective
agreements had. Brandeis' expectation clearly was that the procedure
of *conciliation* in the two-party Board of Grievances would be sufficient to deal with most of the conflicts and controversies arising in the
industry; the Board of Arbitration was to be only a court of last resort.
Actually, it worked out the other way: conciliation very soon proved
inadequate and rapidly shrank in importance; *arbitration*, adjudica-
tion by an impartial representative of the public, became the chief
instrumentality in industrial relations. Thus was born the celebrated
institution of the "impartial chairman," which came to permeate all
branches of the needle trades and, in one form or another, much of
American unionized industry as well.

699

The settlement also provided for the setting up of a bi-party Joint
Board of Sanitary Control, charged with wiping out the sweatshop
and maintaining decent conditions of hygiene and safety in the shops.
Out of this grew the vast structure of health and medical care that now
prevails in the garment trades.

The jubilation of the cloakmakers and of the entire Jewish labor
movement over the victory was immense. Difficulties, conflicts, and
troubles soon appeared, and before long the Protocol itself was
scrapped. But it was an historical achievement of the first order.

This remarkable achievement in collective bargaining was to a
great extent facilitated by certain imponderable factors, chief among
which was the common social and cultural background of the opposing parties. Employers and employees were in large majority Jewish, and predominantly of East European origin. They had behind
them an age-old tradition of arbitration, of settling their often bitter
disputes within the Jewish community without appealing to "outside"
authorities. They shared too, as a heritage of centuries of self-enclosed
minority existence, a marked concern for the good reputation of the
Jewish community with the outside world. New World conditions undermined and confused these traditional standards, but did not

entirely destroy them. Workers and employers spoke a common language, and thought in more or less the same terms. Both were amenable to having outstanding community leaders called in to compose their differences. In reading the documents of the time, one cannot but be struck with the uneasiness displayed by many of the employers and their representatives at what the "Gentiles" would think of the deplorable conditions in their shops. The union leaders, for their part, were also careful not to bring their people and their movement into disrepute. These imponderables—the sensitivity to public opinion, the strong tradition of arbitration, and the common ethnic, cultural, and religious background—probably contributed very considerably to the achievement of the Protocol of Peace and to the development of industrial relations in the major Jewish unions for some time thereafter.

700     The impetus of the two great strikes in New York carried over into other trades and centers as well. Powerful organizing drives were launched among the cloakmakers in Cleveland and Chicago in 1911, but without success. Chicago had to wait until 1915 and Cleveland until 1918 before the efforts of the ILGWU proved effective. In the other women's garment trades in New York, however, among the white-goods workers, wrapper and kimono makers, and children's dressmakers, progress was more marked. These were mostly trades in which girls worked, and the "uprising" of 1909 was repeated on a smaller scale. Agreements modeled on the Protocol of Peace were signed. The same was true of the waist- and dressmakers of Boston. Early in January, 1913, 40,000 waist- and dressmakers in New York went out on a short, prearranged strike. Settlement followed in ten days, with full recognition.

Despite its extension, the Protocol was not destined to live long. Its clumsiness of operation was a great handicap, and widespread unemployment in the New York cloak trade in 1913–14 reduced the power of the union and made the employers eager for another trial of strength. In May, 1915, the cloak manufacturers abrogated the Protocol. A general strike was for the time being averted by conciliation, but the conflict broke out in April, 1916, when the employers' association locked out 25,000 workers. The union answered with a strike, which lasted for fourteen weeks. The settlement abandoned many of the features of the Protocol, but preserved the "impartial chairman" system. In the course of the year the Protocols in Boston and Philadelphia were also replaced, and in 1917 the same development occurred in the New York waist and dress industry. By the end of the decade, very little was left of the earlier Protocol movement, yet the face of unionism in the garment trades had been changed.

Next in order during these eventful years were the furriers. The small union set up in 1904, which had struggled along through the years, took heart from the example of the women's garment workers and in 1912, jointly with the UHT, issued a call for a general strike. Over 9,000 workers, 7,000 of whom were Jewish, answered the call. The strike ended in virtually complete victory for the workers. In 1913, a national organization, the International Fur Workers Union, was launched at a convention in Washington. The new union joined the AFL. The next year the agreement in New York was renewed and a system of arbitration along "impartial chairman" lines was set up.

In the millinery industry too, unionism was making headway. Earlier efforts of the capmakers to organize this branch of the headgear industry had proved abortive. In 1910, the first step was taken as the result of a spontaneous strike in Brooklyn. Local 24 was set up by the United Cloth Hat and Capmakers Union. Two years later, Local 42 was organized among the blockers, and at the end of 1915 the union signed its first collective agreement in the millinery field. The agreement included impartial arbitration machinery.

701

As epoch-making as the two great strikes of the women's garment workers in 1909–10 was the history of the men's clothing workers during the years that followed. Here things were complicated by the irrepressible conflict between the tailors on the one side, and the leaders of the United Garment Workers, to which they belonged, on the other. The differences between these groups were many and far-reaching, differences in background, outlook, ideology, policy, and trade orientation. The UGW leaders were conservative and extremely reluctant to get involved in a struggle. The tailors, on the other hand, resembled the apparel workers much more closely than they did the other elements of their own union; they were mostly immigrants (largely Jews, but increasingly Italians and Slavs as well), militant, with great confidence in the organized power of the strike. They regarded their national leaders in the UGW as utterly incapable of understanding their problems and concerned primarily with suppressing their militancy. As events showed, they were right in their suspicions.

## AMALGAMATED CLOTHING WORKERS

On September 22, 1910, just three weeks after the settlement of the great cloak strike in New York, seventeen girls employed in one of the pants shops of Hart, Schaffner, and Marx in Chicago were given another wage cut. This proved a spark in the heavily charged atmosphere. A spontaneous strike movement was set off. Within three weeks all workers in the industry, about 38,000, were out, without leadership or demands. Public opinion was aroused and was overwhelmingly on the side of the insurgent workers. The leadership of the

702

UGW, however, was hardly adequate to the demands of the situation. After some weeks, President Thomas Rickert of the UGW, who had frowned on the whole movement from the beginning, announced that he had signed an agreement with Hart, Schaffner, and Marx calling for the return to work of the strikers, but barring recognition of the union and perpetuating the open shop. The workers were infuriated; they repudiated the agreement and called upon the Chicago Federation of Labor to take over direction of the strike. Finally, on January 14, 1911, a new settlement was achieved, providing for the return to work of the strikers, no discrimination against union members, and an arbitration committee of three to adjust all other grievances. For the 6,000 employees of Hart, Schaffner, and Marx, this was a considerable victory, and although the rest of the strikers could show no comparable gain, the Chicago strike movement of 1910 had a generally invigorating effect. Especially significant was the arbitration committee, which soon developed into an "impartial chairman" system. Thus both major branches of the garment trades produced this basic innovation in industrial relations almost simultaneously and to a large extent independently, although of course the Protocol of Peace must be presumed to have had some influence on the thinking of the Chicago leaders.

Resentment against the UGW leadership was rife among the men's tailors throughout the country. Giving up hope of obtaining leadership or support from the UGW, the New York Brotherhood of Tailors called a conference in New York, which was attended by delegates from that city, Newark, Philadelphia, Boston, Baltimore, and Chicago. The conference set up a council and called for a general strike in New York in 1912. The UGW national leaders at first refused to have anything to do with the strike, but later were persuaded by the UHT to give their passive consent. Energetic preparations were initiated and thousands of members were enrolled in the union. On December 30, 1912, the general strike was launched. Over 60,000 workers responded. The entire Jewish labor movement, and many other labor and liberal organizations, rallied to their support. By the end of February, more than half of the strikers had returned to work in shops which had agreed to settlements. Behind the backs of the workers and even of many of the strike leaders, the UGW officials now tried to bring the strike to an end with an agreement that enraged the strikers because it ignored the question of recognition and other essential demands. Despite the partial approval given by the *Forward* and some of the spokesmen of the UHT, the Brotherhood of Tailors rejected this settlement, and the strike went on for another three weeks. The settlement, when it finally came, provided for the fifty-three hour week to become fifty-two hours after the first year, an increase in wages, improved conditions, and virtual though not official recognition. It was an important achievement. The workers felt victorious and the union grew.

This strike was important for still another reason. The tailors remembered with resentment the dubious settlement which the leaders of the UGW had tried to put over with the support of the *Forward* and some spokesmen of the United Hebrew Trades. This resentment helped encourage an incipient anti-*Forward* sentiment among certain sections of the men's clothing workers of New York. It is significant that immediately after the strike, the Brotherhood of Tailors invited Joseph Schlossberg to become its secretary-treasurer. Schlossberg was a man completely outside the *Forward* circle; in fact, at the time he was still a member of DeLeon's SLP. His affiliation made little difference, but the appointment was symbolic. The "independent" position of the men's tailors was to be strengthened by the circumstances under which the Amalgamated Clothing Workers was formed and, in part at least, by Sidney Hillman's deliberate policy.

In the UGW, conflict was now out in the open. The tailors represented a majority of the membership, but control of the national organization rested in the hands of conservative leaders, who had lost the confidence of the decisive section of their membership. When the convention met at Nashville, Tenn., in October, 1914, each party was prepared for a showdown. President Rickert's hand-picked committee refused to seat 105 delegates, representing locals with a majority of the membership. The campaign against the "Jewish anarchists" from New York dominated the convention. A split was inevitable. The few tailors' delegates, mostly from Chicago, who had been admitted, led a bolt from the union and, joining with the excluded delegates, declared themselves to be the legitimate United Garment Workers. They chose Sidney Hillman of Chicago and Joseph Schlossberg of New York as their president and general secretary respectively. But, of course, they could not make good their claim to being the "real" UGW before the AFL; so, in December, 1914, they met in special convention in New York and formed the Amalgamated Clothing Workers of America as an independent union. The AFL branded the Amalgamated a dual union, but the other Jewish unions, for all their loyalty to the AFL, recognized it as a *bona fide* organization. For a time at least, the UHT had to bow to an AFL edict and exclude Amalgamated locals, but this was a mere formality. In or out of the AFL, independent or in the CIO, the Amalgamated has always been an integral element of the Jewish labor movement.

The new organization was soon confronted with a series of strikes: in New York, Boston, and Baltimore in 1915; in St. Louis and Philadelphia in 1916. The AFL proved bitterly hostile and the Amalga-

703

mated suffered serious setbacks. But these reverses were only temporary. Before long, it had established itself as a significant force in
every large center where men's clothing was being produced in the
United States and Canada.

GROWTH OF UNIONS, 1909–16

The years from 1909 to 1916 were decisive ones in the history of the
Jewish labor movement. When the year 1909 opened, the needle
trades unions were weak, unstable, without an assured prospect or
much influence on the conditions of the workers in their industries.
In the course of less than a decade, these unions, especially the
ILGWU and the Amalgamated, had become significant and seasoned
organizations, with an impressive record of militancy and constructive
achievement to their credit. At the same time, they had already taken
the first steps towards launching the "extra-curricular" activities in
education, recreation, and membership welfare that were to gain them
such renown in coming years. They were, in fact, established institutions within the labor movement and within the American community generally. And what was true of these two great unions was true,
to some degree at least, of the smaller organizations as well. By 1917,
well over 150,000 workers were affiliated with the UHT in New York.

The entire character of the Jewish labor movement underwent a
significant change during the second decade of the twentieth century.
At the beginning of the decade, or just before, *circa* 1908, the Jewish
labor movement in the United States was a structure erected along
European lines, a politico-cultural Socialist movement with rather
weak trade union offshoots. Within ten years, the entire picture had
changed, although the full meaning of the transformation had not
yet become evident to contemporary observers. The Jewish labor
movement now consisted very largely, even primarily, of trade unions,
and it was the trade unions which now served as the foundation and
source of strength for the other branches—political, cultural, and fraternal—of the movement. In other words, the transformation of the
Jewish labor movement from the European to the American model
had already begun. Later developments were to extend and complete
the process, but the change itself was, in large part at least, essentially
the fruit of the great wave of strikes and organization drives that began with the Uprising of the Twenty Thousand in 1909.

INDUSTRIAL WORKERS OF THE WORLD

We cannot close our account of this period without a word about
an episode that loomed large in its time but which is now almost forgotten—the rise and decline of the Industrial Workers of the World
(IWW). The IWW emerged in 1905 out of a coalition of western semi-

proletarian radicals, the Socialist advocates of industrial unionism, and the remnants of DeLeon's Alliance. Its official program was to organize the unorganized along industrial lines, but it promptly set to work raiding the existing unions in order to establish "revolutionary" dual organizations. The Jewish labor movement suffered particularly from IWW incursions, and benefited not at all, as did some groups of textile workers, from its militancy. The IWW established dual unions in several branches of the women's garment trades in New York and elsewhere, among the capmakers, among the bakery workers, and in two or three other fields. Within a few years, however, the "invasion" was over. Some of the IWW militants remained within the main stream of the labor movement and played a significant role in after years; perhaps the best known among them was Morris Sigman.

705

POLITICAL PROGRESS

Quite as impressive as the upbuilding of the trade unions, at least in the eyes of most contemporaries, was the great progress Jewish labor was making on the political and cultural fronts. The advance of the Socialist movement was sensational. From a membership of less than 25,000 in 1905, the Socialist party (SP) grew rapidly to 41,000 in 1908, 58,000 in 1910, and 118,000 in 1912, the high point in its history. There was some falling off thereafter, but in 1917, the year of America's entry into World War I, membership was still above 80,000. Within the general movement, the Jewish Socialists made corresponding gains in membership and influence. The access of Bundist militants to the Jewish Socialist movement possessed a significance beyond their numbers. In 1912, through the exertion of the Bundists, a Jewish Socialist Federation uniting the Jewish branches throughout the country was set up within the SP. There had been a Central Jewish Agitation Bureau in existence since 1907, but it had been merely a translation and propaganda agency. The new Federation, on the other hand, was an autonomous body, virtually a Jewish Socialist party within the SP. It soon became a real force among the more radical Jewish workers in America.

Not all Jewish members of the party belonged to the Federation or approved of it. For one thing, it was politically more to the left than the *Forward* and the UHT or, for that matter, than the party as a whole. But it was in Jewish affairs that the greatest conflict was felt. The vigorous Yiddishism and cultural nationalism of the Bundist intellectuals were in large part foreign to the "old guard," which shared the traditional cosmopolitanism of Socialist ideology. In a sense, the Federation and the Forward Association became rival centers of leadership and influence in the Jewish labor movement. But they co-operated in the WC, in party work, and in the manifold activities of the movement.

Along with the orthodox Marxist Socialists of the Federation and the *Forward*, the Zionist Socialists of the Poale Zion movement began to make their voice heard. Scattered elements were to be found in America in earlier years, but it was not until 1904 that the first Poale Zion group was set up in New York. Two years later, *Der Yiddisher Kempfer* ("The Jewish Fighter") was launched in Chicago as a Poale Zion weekly. Within a decade (1912), a Labor-Zionist fraternal order, the Natsionaler Yidisher Arbeter Farband (Jewish National Workers' Alliance of America), was launched. Sharp differences relating rather to the Zionist than to the Socialist concerns of the movement agitated its ranks in the early years, but Labor Zionism succeeded in winning an assured place for itself in the American Jewish labor community.

706

CRISIS IN THE WORKMEN'S CIRCLE

The Workmen's Circle (WC), the "third arm" of the Jewish labor movement, underwent in this period a significant crisis of growth. Its numerical advance was spectacular. From 6,700 in 1905, the WC grew to 31,000 in 1909, 49,000 in 1913, and over 60,000 in 1918. By that time it had stabilized its functioning on a recognized system of actuarial rates, and was becoming one of the most important fraternal societies in the United States. It was, of course, entirely Socialist in character, and the same differences in orientation that were being felt among Jewish Socialists generally now broke out in accentuated form within the WC. A prolonged struggle set in between the "old" and the "young." These labels designated not so much age groups as philosophies and outlooks. The "young," prompted by the Bundists, demanded a "broadening" of WC activities, particularly in the direction of education and culture along Yiddishist lines. They urged the establishment of Yiddish schools for children, the large-scale publication of books and pamphlets, the initiation of workers' choruses, and similar cultural ventures. The "old" desired to hew to the line along which the society had been founded. The battle raged for eight years. When, in 1917, peace was re-established, the old guard was still in possession of the leadership, but the rebels had won the main points of their platform. Education and culture became central to WC activity, and the spirit of the new program was the Yiddishist cultural nationalism of the "young." It is interesting to note that this conflict cut across party lines. Socialists, anarchists, Poale Zionists, were to be found in both factions, and the Socialist party, which enjoyed ideological leadership, made no attempt to dictate policy or lay down a line.

CULTURAL RENAISSANCE

In a way almost without parallel, Jewish labor in America nourished and promoted a rich cultural renaissance that spread far beyond the narrow bounds of the labor movement. Closest to the unions was, of course, the press. Throughout this period the *Forward* grew in circulation and influence. Its circulation in 1905 was 52,000, somewhat less than the 55,000 of the conservative *Morgen Zhurnal* (*Jewish [Morning] Journal and Daily News*). But in 1911, its circulation had already risen to 123,000, while in 1916, the figure stood at just under 200,000, almost double that of its nearest competitor. The *Forward* became not merely the guide, mentor, and organizer of the Jewish trade unions, not only a Socialist educational agency of first importance, but also, and perhaps pre-eminently, a powerful cultural and spiritual force among all sections of the Jewish community in New York and near-by centers. And the *Forward* at this time, as throughout most of its long history, was Abraham Cahan.[11]

707

In addition to the *Forward* there were dozens of other periodicals: some—like *Naye Velt* ("New World"), the organ of the Jewish Socialist Federation, the *Freie Arbeiter Stimme,* the anarchist weekly, and the *Zukunft,* the Socialist monthly—serious general journals of politics and culture; others, like the growing number of trade union organs, devoted largely to their institutional affairs but never forgetting their responsibilities as instruments of education. Even the general Jewish press—and New York had as many as five Yiddish dailies in 1916 and Chicago three—was deeply affected by the ideas that emanated from the labor publications.

A remarkable upsurge of literary creativity in Yiddish was the most important aspect of the new cultural revival, and it expressed itself in poetry, novels, theatrical writing, and journalism of a high order. Most of these younger writers found their audience and vehicles in the radical and labor movement, and however far they strayed in later years their early sentiments and attitudes could never be entirely eradicated. It was the Jewish labor community that sustained them, inspired them, and indeed gave them their living context.[12] Particularly influential in developing mature and responsible literary standards was the *Freie Arbeiter Stimme* and its long-time editor, S. Yanofsky.

Institutionally, the most important aspect of the cultural revival was the establishment of secular Yiddish schools for the children of the immigrants. The movement was a reflection both of the new spirit of cultural nationalism, and of the consternation of the older generation of immigrant parents at the growing alienation of their American-born or bred children. Such schools were first established on a very small scale in 1912. The WC launched a school program in 1918, and the Poale Zionists somewhat earlier. (In later years, the Communists set up a Jewish school system of their own.) These schools differed considerably in ideology and orientation, but they were all secular and Yiddishist. It was this that constituted the foundation of the movement.

The cultural renaissance that began with the post–1904 immigration lasted well into the 1920's. It was an integral part, and, in a way, the most colorful aspect of the "old" Jewish labor movement.

BASIC TRENDS

The immense progress made by the Jewish labor movement in the decade and a half after 1905 helped obscure certain underlying trends that were already beginning to outline the shape of things to come. From the very beginning a tendency toward *de-proletarianization* was noted by perceptive observers. The Jewish factory workers, it was a common saying, were "neither the sons nor the fathers of workers." While the first part of this saying may not have been entirely true, the second part was becoming ever more true. Many of the Jewish workers themselves left the factory to go into business or even into the professions, despite the immense difficulties that had to be overcome. The "studying mania" among the intellectuals-turned-workers was noted in the columns of the labor press as early as the opening years of the twentieth century. Many of the most fervent Socialist agitators soon became doctors, lawyers, and teachers. But as a rule, they did not sever their connections with the radical or labor movement out of which they had come. On the contrary, these "men with diplomas" became the aristocracy within the movement, and their influence can be traced to the present day.

But it was quite otherwise with the children of the immigrants. Of these, only a relatively small proportion followed their parents into the shops. No sacrifice was too great for the immigrant parents to make in order to send their sons to college and their daughters through high school. Business, office work, or a profession was their goal for their children; above all, the children must be kept out of the shop. The de-proletarianization of the Jewish labor community was therefore quite rapid. It was more than a mere change of economic status. To the great majority of the American children of immigrant parents, if contemporary accounts are to be trusted, the Jewish labor movement was something alien, even offensive; it was part of the immigrant background that had to be sloughed off as fast as possible. A chasm, spiritual and cultural, developed between the generations, one that all the Yiddish-labor schools in the world could not hope to overcome.

This growing chasm between the immigrant parents and the first American generation affected all sections and classes of the Jewish community, and of course other immigrant groups. But among the Jewish workers, cultural alienation was reinforced by another factor. The American daughter would often work in the same shop with her Italian mother, just as the American son would frequently follow his Slav father into the mines; in this way, a certain community was maintained, despite all cultural differences. But it was not so among the Jews; there the rift was both cultural and social, both economic and ideological, and it was only the obscure, little-understood forces of Jewish family solidarity that staved off complete chaos. In any case, most of the remedies that the perturbed older generation tried to apply proved futile, for they were all predicated on somehow perpetuating the immigrant status. It was not until after World War I that the meaning of the changing situation was fully defined.

709

EXTERNAL RELATIONS

It might be well at this point to survey the Jewish labor movement, as it stood on the eve of the United States' entry into World War I, in its triple relation—to the American Jewish community, to the American labor movement, and to American national life generally.

The position of Jewish labor in the Amerian Jewish community was strange and hard to define. In New York particularly, it was a very important part of the community and yet was, in a way, alien to it; in the "provinces" (outside of New York), this alienation was even more marked. Jewish labor was an important part of the community because, in the larger centers, it constituted a major section of the Jewish population and set its mark on the emerging American Yiddish culture. But the radicalism of the Jewish labor movement, especially its secularist, antireligious bias, actually made it a schismatic element in American Jewish life, very much as it had been in earlier days in Eastern Europe. Speaking of the situation of the WC in the "middle-sized and smaller towns" of America, Epstein notes: "Relations between [the WC branch] and the rest of [the Jewish population of] the town were none too friendly. The former, not participating in the congregational life of the community, were looked upon as outsiders." [13] In practice, Jewish labor recognized and took for granted its schismatic position within the Jewish community, for it turned all its energies to building up a completely autonomous institutional structure that would make it possible for the Jewish worker to satisfy all his needs and meet all his problems within the framework of the labor movement. It was, in effect, a process of building up a self-enclosed Jewish labor community within, or rather side by side with, the general Jewish community. Not until the middle of the 1930's did the schismatic walls of the Jewish labor movement begin to crumble under the impact of new times and new forces.

The emergence of a self-enclosed Jewish labor community, reflecting though it did a schism in the traditional community organization, also in a way foreshadowed the transformation of Jewish life under American conditions. The Jewish Socialists and unionists were conscious that their institutions and institutional loyalties took them outside the Jewish community, as that had been understood in Europe; but they were also, in large part, conscious of themselves as Jews and of their institutions as Jewish institutions. In the United States, apparently, it was possible to build a Jewish community life that was not part of "the" Jewish community in the European sense. Jewish labor institutions thus marked a phase of the transition from the traditional Jewish community along East European lines to the American Jewish community of today, with its decentralized, pluralistic structure.

The historical process, however, was slow, and Jewish labor remained for a long time somewhat outside of general Jewish community life. But this was not the case in relation to the American labor movement. The Jewish unions very soon found their place in the AFL, and that place was never seriously questioned. Samuel Gompers well understood that the idiosyncracies of the Jewish unions, their quasi-separatist organization, their radical ideology and Socialist alliances, were merely temporary phenomena, phenomena of transition and acculturation. Basically, the Jewish unions, for all their "European" rhetoric, were *bona fide* trade union institutions of the American type, committed to the responsible conduct of industrial relations under capitalism. In this respect, for all their foreignness, they were more authentically American than such native-born movements as the IWW. The Jewish unions long constituted an element of Socialist, radical, or "progressive" dissidence within the family of American labor, but their full citizenship and legitimate status were never challenged.

AMERICANIZATION

The part played by the labor movement in the Americanization of the Jewish immigrant will be examined at greater length below. All that needs to be pointed out here is that almost from the very beginning, the orientation of the immigrant workers and especially of their leaders was toward the United States. The United States was the new home, and to win an assured place in American life was their goal. The eagerness of the immigrants to learn about America and American ways was proverbial. None of the Socialist gibes at "American democracy," none of the bitter immigrant disillusionment with the

710

unfulfilled promises of the "golden land," not even an intensely self-conscious Yiddishist cultural nationalism, could change or even blur this basic orientation. The Jewish worker was in the United States to stay, and American institutions and American values soon became the framework of his social existence. In time, he acquired citizenship and entered politics, usually under the Socialist banner. In 1906, he just barely failed to send Morris Hillquit to Congress, and in 1914 he succeeded in electing Meyer London Socialist Congressman from the 12th district in New York's East Side. If the Jewish worker did not become identical with the New England Yankee or the Midwestern Hoosier, he did develop into a recognized urban type, as authentically American as any other.

The Jewish immigrant worker accepted the United States and accepted it essentially without reservation. But did the United States accept him? In time it did, but it took a long time. It came hard for the older Americans to realize that the strange creature from Eastern Europe was to become—was in fact becoming—an integral part of the American national community. The great mass strikes that ushered in and marked the course of the second decade of the twentieth century contributed a great deal to this eventual recognition. The splendid spirit and idealism of the young men and women who were rebelling against economic degradation won the admiration of the best sections of American public opinion and made valuable friends in influential circles. But perhaps the most important factor was the unification of Jew and non-Jew, immigrant and native American, that, despite all hesitations and shortcomings, was affected through the American labor movement. Trade unionism helped very materially to obtain acceptance for the immigrant Jewish worker in the United States, for it was trade unionism, along with the public school, that constituted for the mass of immigrant Jews their first real initiation into American institutional life. As a trade unionist, the immigrant Jew began to speak a "language" that Americans could understand, whether they liked it or not; as a trade unionist, he was behaving in a familiar way, behaving like an American: it was the visible sign of his Americanization, as authentic as speaking English. Even the newspapers and public figures who denounced him for striking, made it the burden of their charge that he was too quick to learn the "bad ways" of the American trade unionist.

## World War I

World War I exerted a political effect on the Jewish labor movement in America second only in significance to that of the New Deal a decade and a half later. To the American labor movement as a whole, the United States' participation in the war brought not merely definite advances in organization and standards, but also a new role in national life and a new concern for the national interest, a new feeling of "belonging" to the national community. The War Labor Board, created early in 1918, gave organized labor a recognized though by no means clearly defined status in the institutional structure of the "American way of life." The membership of the AFL rose rapidly to a high point of over 4,000,000 in 1920, and labor leaders came closer to the centers of national power and prestige than ever before in American history, nearer in fact than they were again to come until 1933.[14]

For the Jewish labor movement, however, the situation seemed much more ambiguous. The Jewish unions benefited at least proportionately from the favorable conditions, but their position as radical and Socialist organizations was by no means an easy one. For the Jewish unions as well as for the other sections of the Jewish labor movement, this was a critical time; despite surface appearances, the outcome was a fundamental *de-radicalization* and a preparation for the thoroughgoing integration into the nation which was to take place under the New Deal.

The American Socialist movement was predominantly non-interventionist and antiwar, although some pro-Allied sentiment made itself felt. (The somewhat stronger pro-German sentiment did not express itself independently, but tended rather to strengthen the official non-interventionism.) Socialists had opposed Wilson's preparedness drive, and after the United States' entry into the war the Socialist party's special convention at St. Louis (April, 1917) officially reaffirmed its antiwar stand.[15] This vague, highly emotional sentiment pervaded the ranks of Jewish labor and was reinforced by a traditional detestation of Tsarist Russia, one of the Allies.

Samuel Gompers repudiated his earlier pacifism some time in 1915, and within a few months he was working vigorously for the Wilson program of military preparedness. In October, 1916, he was named a member of the Advisory Commission to the newly created Council of National Defense. Early in 1917, he took steps to call together in Washington a nation-wide conference of AFL affiliates in order to proclaim officially the patriotic, pro-preparedness stand of the American labor movement. This conference met on March 12, 1917. It was attended by the executive council of the AFL and by the officers of seventy-nine international unions, including the railway brotherhoods. Four important international unions were absent: the Western Federation of Miners, the Journeymen Barbers, the Typographical Union, and the biggest of the Jewish unions, the ILGWU.[16] The Amalgamated Clothing Workers, being outside the ranks of the AFL, was not expected to attend, but there can be little doubt that its attitude fell in with the abstentionism of the ILGWU. The United States' entry into the war did not materially change the situation. In fact, the Russian Revolution and the withdrawal from the war of the new Russian regime, with which in those early days so many of the Jewish workers sympathized, only intensified the antiwar feeling and deepened the cleavage.

It is hard today to appreciate how deep the cleavage really was. Gompers and the AFL leaders were greatly disturbed at the influence which the Socialist unions, primarily Jewish, were exerting in New York, and particularly disturbed at their attempt to "capture" the New York Central Federated Union for their "peace" program. The executive council of the AFL even decided to initiate a campaign to "Americanize" the labor movement in New York City and the metropolitan area; in this enterprise the Committee on Public Information, a government agency headed by George Creel, eagerly co-operated. To counteract the antiwar sentiment encouraged by the Socialists was also one of the purposes of the American Alliance for Labor and Democracy, formed at about this time by a number of prominent labor leaders and pro-war Socialists.

713

The suddenly emerging cleavage between the Jewish labor movement and the national community, including the great body of American labor, was serious while it lasted, but fortunately it was short-lived. It was, in fact, the last real spasm of radical non-conformism on the part of Jewish labor. Within the Socialist movement generally, a reversal of sentiment was beginning to make itself felt. Using the German attack on the new Soviet government as well as Wilson's Fourteen Points as arguments, a number of influential Socialists came out for at least partial support of the United States in the war. By the middle of 1918, decisive sections of the Socialist party were no longer opposed to the war, and the Socialist unions in the needle trades had begun quite openly, if not very enthusiastically, to favor it.[17] The General Executive Board of the ILGWU bought $100,000 in Liberty Bonds, and the Amalgamated also made heavy purchases. By and large, the reversal of sentiment was stronger in the Jewish unions than in the Socialist political movement. The difficult position in which the Jewish unions found themselves during the early preparedness and war years made many of the union leaders rather uneasy about Socialist political tutelage, and thus facilitated the formal breaking-away of their unions from the Socialist movement in later years.

ECONOMIC ADVANCES

On the economic front, the Jewish labor movement made notable advances during the war years, especially in the garment trades. After a brief flurry of unemployment, boom conditions set in. The federal agencies (Board of Control, Administrator of Labor Standards) in charge of government work used their influence, by and large, to protect the workers' right of self-organization and collective bargaining. Headway was made by the Amalgamated and ILGWU in almost every important center in the country. The unions gained significantly in numbers and power.

The shortening of hours was, next to organization, the primary objective of the needle trades unions in this period. The Amalgamated reduced the work week to forty-four hours in Toronto, New York, Chicago, Rochester, and Philadelphia during 1917–19. The ILGWU won the forty-four hour week in 1919; the capmakers and furriers, in the same year. These gains proved enduring.

The advance of the labor movement continued through 1919 and into 1920. Late in 1920, the situation suddenly changed. A depression set in and the employers launched a general offensive with the purpose of re-establishing open-shop conditions and destroying the gains of the war and immediate post-war period. In New York, Philadelphia, and Chicago, the cloak manufacturers moved against the union, but the attacks were beaten back. The ILGWU, however, suffered losses in the waist and dress industry and in some of the smaller cloak centers.

The most important development in the women's garment field during the early post-war years took place in Cleveland. This was one of the most difficult anti-union markets in the industry, but the war experience had made some influential manufacturers in the area, particularly Morris A. Black, ready to accept trade unionism under certain conditions. In December, 1919, an agreement was signed in the Cleveland cloak trade providing for the formulation of production standards on the basis of time studies. Two years later, a provision was included guaranteeing each regular worker under the plan forty-one weeks of work a year, with the payment of two-thirds of the minimum wage for each week of unemployment beyond eleven. Although the "Cleveland experiment" was eventually dropped, it represented a pioneering venture into an area that was later to become of real significance.

The Amalgamated during this period fought spirited contests in its various markets—Rochester, Philadelphia, New York, Boston, and Cincinnati—with results that were variable, but on the whole favorable. The events in Cincinnati were particularly important, for they

714

led to the lasting unionization of "Golden Rule" Nash's large concern, one of the leading non-union firms in the industry. It was at this
time that New York lost its old pre-eminence in the men's clothing
trade.

Both branches of the headgear industry were involved in struggles
in the immediate post-war years. The Hat and Capmakers suffered a
setback in 1919, and in the same year a general strike of the millinery
workers in New York City resulted in a partial victory. Internal administrative changes of importance also took place during these years.
The headgear workers' long-standing jurisdictional conflict with the
United Hatters of North America was finally settled in 1924, on the
basis of a division of the field. In recognition of the growing prominence of the millinery workers, the name of the organization was
changed to Cloth Hat, Cap, and Millinery Workers International
Union. The union now rejoined the AFL, in which it came to play a
role far out of proportion to its limited size.

715

The furriers' union also made advances during the war, but the
loss of a thirty-week strike in 1920 seriously weakened the organization. Internal conditions became increasingly bad as demoralization
and dissatisfaction spread among the ranks of the workers.

The needle trades unions had always felt themselves to be closely
akin industrially and ideologically. During and after the war, efforts
were made to establish some kind of organizational unity among
them. At the 1917 convention of the AFL, the ILGWU proposed that
a needle trades department be established within the AFL, but this
came to nothing. The following year, the headgear workers' union
called for the formation of a needle trades federation, and such a
body was actually launched in December, 1920, under the name of
Needle Trades Workers Alliance. The Alliance, however, remained
a paper organization, and it finally disintegrated.

On the whole, despite difficulties and setbacks, the war and the
immediate post-war years constituted a period of considerable advance
for the Jewish labor movement, both organizationally and ideologically. The "time of troubles," however, was just ahead.

## Inner Disruption and Economic Depression

The period immediately following World War I was one of continuing prosperity and the American labor movement kept growing
through 1920. A brief recession then set in, but before the middle
of the decade the "Coolidge boom" was well under way. Strangely
enough, however, the labor movement did not benefit from this economic advance. A sharp decline in labor organization set in during

1921–22, and this decline continued, with slight variations, until well into the next decade; it was not until 1933 that the trend was reversed. This anomalous development—for hitherto business prosperity had generally meant progress in labor organization—has puzzled students of the labor movement. Of the fact itself, however, there can be no doubt.

The Jewish labor movement, as part of the totality of organized labor in America, reflected this anomalous development. It, too, made little headway during the years of "New Era" prosperity. In fact, it was precisely during these years that it went through what may well be regarded as the most difficult period of its entire history. But in the case of the Jewish labor movement, the economic, social, and political influences that affected the course of organized labor as a whole were much aggravated by a factor that soon threw everything else into the background—the Communist drive for power.

### COMMUNIST DRIVE FOR POWER

Through the 1920's, the Jewish unions and such allied organizations as the WC were the scene of the best-planned and most nearly victorious drive for control that American labor history has to record. The Jewish labor organizations were, in the end, able to beat back the Communist offensive and save themselves from succumbing to Communist control, but only after a long and bitter struggle that left them shattered and at the brink of ruin. Had not the New Deal with all that it meant for the labor movement supervened, it is by no means certain what the status of unionism in the garment trades might have become.

The Communist drive for power in the Jewish unions—and for our purposes that means primarily in the needle trades, although other unions too were affected—was part of a more comprehensive program launched by the Communist International in 1921 to capture the "reactionary" unions in Western Europe and America. In the needle trades, the Communist campaign developed against the background of an earlier, essentially non-political, tradition of insurgency. As far back as 1917, a group of radical members of Waist and Dressmakers Local 25 of the ILGWU had formed a Current Events Committee, to bring, as they put it, "a bit of fresh air into the stagnant life of the union." Similar signs of restlessness could be detected in other unions as well. The Russian Revolution, when it came that year, had a terrific impact on the Jewish workers of the United States, an impact felt far beyond the confines of the incipient Communist movement. For a brief period, the Jewish masses in and out of the unions were indeed radicalized and thrown into a ferment of insurgency and expectation. Within the unions, leagues, clubs, and groups of all sorts

sprang up. A shop delegates' movement, modeled after the then celebrated British shop steward system, spread through the needle trades;
most characteristic of the time, perhaps, were such organizations as
the Workers' Council group and the Welfare and Propaganda League,
which managed to combine in the same program demands for the
democratization of the unions and slogans that recalled the mani-
festoes of the new Soviet state.

This strange combination was indeed characteristic of the insurgent
movement in its earliest stages. There was much in the unions—
ancient abuses, narrow-visioned, over-cautious policies, undemocratic
structures and practices—against which "idealistic" members might
revolt; it was not unnatural, considering the times, that this revolt
should have been linked with the upsurge of radical sentiment associated with the Russian Revolution. Yet until 1921, the explicit Communist aspect of this insurgency was largely peripheral.

717

### TRADE UNION EDUCATIONAL LEAGUE

The chief instrument of the Communist drive for power in the
Jewish unions, and indeed in the American labor movement as a
whole, was the Trade Union Educational League (TUEL). This organization had been formed in 1920 by William Z. Foster to promote
a policy of "boring from within" the American labor movement. In
1921, Foster joined the Communist party and the TUEL became a
key agency of the party. It was officially recognized as the American
affiliate of the newly formed Red International of Labor Unions
(RILU) in Moscow.

The TUEL almost literally took over the earlier radical insurgency
in the Jewish unions and used it as so much raw material to be ma-
nipulated and fashioned by the top Communist leaders. A "left wing"
movement arose in which Communists and non-Communist insurgents co-operated, obviously under the leadership of the former. On
the periphery of the "left wing" movement were the so-called "center"
or "non-partisan" elements, who for one reason or another pretended
to an independent position which, not unexpectedly, usually ended
up as support of the Communists. Before very long, a complicated
machinery was developed to implement the Communist drive for
control: At the center were the party leaders in charge of "trade
union work"; then came the party "fraction" (cell), made up of the
party members in the particular union; at a still further remove was
the TUEL group, including the Communists and their sympathizers
and followers; and finally, a "progressive" movement in which the
"center" elements were also included. The picture was rendered even
more complicated by the very important fact that the party leaders,
who of course had the last word, only too often did not see eye to

eye with the leading Communists in the unions; the "trade union comrades" were after all in daily contact with the life of their unions, while the party leaders always decided and issued orders in terms of the current "party line." Not infrequently during this decade, a decision concerning the fate of scores of thousands of workers was made by a factional vote in some party headquarters or secret hotel room and had to be carried out by Communist leaders in the unions who were bitterly hostile to the line handed down to them.

Opposed to the growing "left-wing" movement was the so-called "right-wing." The core of the "right-wing" was composed of the older leadership of the unions and of the masses of the more stable, more trade-union-minded workers. The leadership of the "right-wing" came from the old-line Socialists, grouped primarily around the *Forward,* and from the remnants of the once powerful anarchist tendency. The struggle in the Jewish unions thus took on, in part at least, the aspect of a phase of the struggle between Socialists and Communists that raged with such fury in the decade after the founding of the Communist International in 1919.

In the American Socialist movement generally, the Russian Revolution brought a wave of intense excitement and enthusiasm which few could resist and amidst which no critical voice could be heard. In the course of the years that followed (1918–21), the lines began to form and a violent conflict broke out in the Jewish Socialist Federation. The Federation was finally split when the Communists captured control of it in 1921; soon thereafter they converted it into the Jewish section of the Workers Party, which served as the "overground" of the Communist party formed in December of the same year. The Socialist elements, supported by what was almost certainly a majority of the membership, formed the Jewish Socialist Farband. The Farband retained control of the important federation institutions and press. Above all, it was closely associated with the *Forward,* which achieved a circulation of 205,000 in 1924–25 and which was by all odds the single most effective force in defeating the Communist drive for power in the Jewish labor movement.[18]

ILGWU AND THE COMMUNISTS

The main battleground in the conflict with the Communists was the ILGWU. Several factors made the ILGWU the chief theater in the civil war. Economic conditions, resulting from the decline of the cloak trade and the demoralizing effects of the jobber-contractor system, were particularly difficult during the first post-war decade, and naturally gave rise to serious grievances among the membership which the Communists were quick to exploit. Equally valuable from the Communist standpoint was the background of hostility between the

ILGWU international office and the larger locals in New York. Opposition movements, too, had a long tradition among the New York women's garment workers, a tradition which the Communists knew how to exploit. For these and other reasons, the ILGWU became the primary target in the Communist offensive.

By the end of 1921, the TUEL was already established in New York and other centers of the ILGWU, and soon the "left-wing" scored important election victories in New York, Philadelphia, and Chicago. By 1923 this conflict was raging throughout the union. In that year, Local 22 (a newly chartered offshoot of Local 25, consisting of dressmakers) was captured by the Communists; however, the "left-wing" members of the administration were removed from office by the General Executive Board (GEB). Similar action was taken against "left wingers" in Chicago and Philadelphia. In August, 1923, the GEB illegalized the TUEL and other intra-union groups. Despite the fact that all candidates were required to disavow membership in the outlawed groups, the chief cloakmakers' and dressmakers' locals in New York were captured by the "left-wing" in 1924–25. The Communist officers were removed and suspended. Thereupon they formed the Joint Action Committee, through which they functioned virtually as an independent union, issuing membership cards, collecting dues, and controlling shops by their own authority. Yet a final split was, for the moment, averted through a compromise that constituted a substantial victory for the "left-wing." The "left-wing" officers were reinstated, new elections were held, and the Communists and their allies returned to power.

719

The "peace" did not last long. The eighteen-day convention held in Philadelphia during November and December, 1925, was a continuous battle between the two factions. The "left wing" probably represented a majority of the membership; the ILGWU administration, however, controlled a majority of the convention votes. This convention, at which the "left wing" was defeated by a vote of approximately three to two, was the prelude to the most violent and, as it turned out, decisive battle in the long-drawn-out conflict. This was the Communist-conducted general strike in the New York cloak industry in 1926.

The strike broke out when the "left-wing" leaders, under direct instructions of the Communist party, rejected proposals of the Governor's Advisory Commission, despite the fact that the ILGWU leadership urged their acceptance. The "left wing" took over complete and exclusive control of the general strike machinery. The strike was bitterly fought from the beginning, but there were several moments when it might have been settled to some advantage. Indeed, there is good evidence that the leading Communist trade unionists, had they been left to themselves, would have settled much sooner and under better conditions; they were, however, forced to protract the strike by peremptory orders from party headquarters. Finally, after the situation had become utterly chaotic and it was disclosed that the "left-wing" leadership had misused $800,000 of employers' securities deposited with the union, the ILGWU's General Executive Board took over the strike and brought it to a quick conclusion. It had lasted twenty-six weeks and involved the expenditure of $3,500,-000, never fully accounted for; the workers, furthermore, had lost an entire season. Yet the terms upon which the union was forced to settle were less favorable than the original proposals of the Governor's Commission which the "left-wing" leaders had so violently rejected. The strike was a disastrous defeat and the very existence of the union was imperilled.

720

The ILGWU was done with compromises. The "left-wing" organizations were dissolved and a new registration of all workers was ordered; locals were reorganized with new charters. The Communist leaders refused to recognize the measure and called upon their sympathizers not to register, but the great mass of the workers went back to the ILGWU. In Chicago and other out-of-town centers, the struggle took a very similar course, though one by no means so acute. All in all, it may be said that by the end of 1926 the Communist bid for power had been defeated. But the union was shattered: the membership was depleted, the treasury empty, huge debts overwhelmed the organization, control over industrial conditions was virtually gone. There were many who despaired of the union.

COMMUNISTS AND THE FUR INDUSTRY

The conflict in the fur industry was almost as violent as in the women's garment trades; the opposing forces were largely the same, though the final outcome was very different. Organized opposition in the fur workers' union was already marked in 1919; for a time, it expressed itself through the same shop stewards' movement that was the vehicle of "left-wing" discontent in other branches of the needle trades. A disastrous strike in 1920 spurred on the insurgent movement, which made sufficient headway to win control of the New York Joint Board in 1921. Defeated in the elections the following year, the "left-wing" formally organized a section of the TUEL and prepared for a bitter-end struggle. The administration answered with suspensions. A crucial stage was reached in 1925. The Communists, operating through the TUEL, formed a "united front" with some "non-partisan" elements on a program of democracy and reform. In the elections of that year, the Communists again gained control of New York, and promptly used their office to aid the "left-wing" Joint Action Committee in the ILGWU. A special convention, meeting in November, settled nothing, because the "non-partisans," who held the balance of power, prevented any decisive action. The conflict flared up again with full fury the next year (1926), in the course of a general strike in New York conducted by the "left-wing" Joint Board. The strike lasted seventeen weeks and culminated in a partial victory. The furriers won the forty-hour week and a wage increase. Though (as the "right-wing" leaders charged) the same terms might have been obtained considerably earlier in the strike, the settlement was a victory and helped very considerably in raising the prestige of the Communist leadership.

Immediately after the strike, on the basis of a prior agreement, the AFL appointed a committee headed by Matthew Woll to investigate the entire internal situation of the fur workers' union. The report of the committee revealed a "shocking state of affairs," financial and organizational, in the conduct of the union by the "left wingers." The Communist-controlled Joint Board was dissolved and replaced by a "right-wing" Joint Council, with which the workers were called upon to register. But only a small minority apparently did so, and, unlike the situation in the ILGWU after the 1926 cloak strike, the "left wing" continued to enjoy the support of the bulk of the membership in New York. Enjoying such strength, the Communists were able to stimulate dissension in the Joint Council and heighten the demoralization in "right-wing" ranks.

721

## DUAL UNIONISM

In both the women's garment and the fur industries, the "left-wing" rapidly moved toward dual unionism. Early in 1928 the Communist authorities in Moscow ordered a change of line in the direction of extreme revolutionism; this new "third-period" turn seemed to offer the bankrupt Communist strategists a way out. For the United States, the Moscow directives meant the abandonment of "boring from within" in favor of a policy of setting up dual "Red" unions. The Trade Union Educational League was transformed into the Trade Union *Unity* League (TUUL), which began to operate as an independent trade union center. Wherever the Communists could muster any strength, they set up their own Communist-controlled unions affiliated with the TUUL. The "Red" union in the garment trades, the Needle Trade Workers Industrial Union, was formed toward the end of 1928. Its main sections consisted of a strong contingent of furriers and the remnants of the left wing of the ILGWU. It was De-Leon's Socialist Trades and Labor Alliance all over again; but this time the initiative had come from Moscow, whose policy of dual unionism was in fact bitterly, though unsuccessfully, opposed by the

American Communists. Indeed, it was primarily as a result of this resistance to the new Moscow line that a split developed in American Communist ranks which was to prove of considerable importance in the subsequent history of the Jewish labor movement.

## THE AMALGAMATED AND THE COMMUNISTS

In the Amalgamated Clothing Workers the course of events was rather different; the struggle in this organization never reached the acuteness of the civil war that was fought in the fur or the women's garment unions. For one thing, Communist strength did not have the same weight in the Amalgamated as in the other unions. For in the men's clothing industry out-of-town centers, such as Chicago and Rochester, played a very important role, while in the fur union and the ILGWU, New York embraced the bulk of the membership. Moreover, the national officers of the Amalgamated, particularly Sidney Hillman, were not identified with the *Forward* and right-wing Socialists, and so could for some time play at being non-partisans. For their part, the Communists refrained from attacking the national administration of the Amalgamated because of its pro-Soviet attitude. In 1922, the Amalgamated endorsed Hillman's plan for a joint Amalgamated-Soviet men's clothing enterprise in Russia (the Russian-American Industrial Corporation), and in 1924 Robert Minor, a national Communist leader, delivered a laudatory address at the Amalgamated convention held that year. Meanwhile, skirmishing had begun in New York and other centers. Late in 1924, the breach was widened because of a falling-out between the Communist party and the Amalgamated over the presidential campaign, the former putting up William Z. Foster and the latter supporting Robert La Follette. By the end of the year the Communist drive in the Amalgamated had assumed the same ferocity as it had in the other needle trades unions. A TUEL section was set up and Local 5, the coat operators' union in New York, was made the base of operations. The Communist fight was conducted under the direction of an Amalgamated Joint Action Committee, which was immediately branded a dual union by the national office. The prestige of the national leadership among the members was raised considerably by the successful outcome of some important strikes, and in 1926 the showdown came. The General Executive Board outlawed the TUEL and proceeded to reorganize the New York organization. "Left-wing" resistance proved futile. In Chicago, Rochester, and other centers, the defeat of the "left-wing," after a period of initial advance, was even more pronounced. By the time of the 1926 convention, it was obvious that the Communist drive had utterly failed. The "right-wing" victory came much more easily than in the ILGWU and did not leave the union in so ruinous a state.

### THE CAP AND MILLINERY WORKERS AND THE COMMUNISTS

Least affected among the important Jewish unions was the Cap and Millinery Workers Union. True to its tradition of "tolerating" various political factions, this union for some years tried to "get along" with the Communists. There were also, at the time, fewer issues dividing the cap and millinery workers than divided the workers in the other needle trades. The Communist-directed "left-wing" went ahead slowly building up its strength, making considerable headway in New York and other centers. The struggle became intense after the 1923 convention, and by 1925 it had reached a crucial point. Here, as elsewhere, the TUEL began to function as a dual union, sending out organizers, holding conferences, and imposing discipline. The 1927 convention was dominated entirely by a struggle in which the "left-wing" received a smashing defeat. In Chicago, St. Paul, and Boston, too, the "left-wing" was routed. To all intents and purposes, the war was over by the end of 1928. The remnants of the "left-wing," in both the Amalgamated and in the Cap and Millinery Union, soon joined the dual Needle Trades Workers Industrial Union.

723

### COMMUNIST DRIVE IN OTHER UNIONS

The needle trade unions were the main target of the Communists in their drive for control, but the other unions in the Jewish labor movement were not spared. Under various circumstances and on a scale reflecting the degree of "left-wing" strength, the same sort of internal disruption was precipitated in the bakery and food unions, in branches of the building trades (painters, carpenters), among the upholstery workers, the pocketbook workers, the suitcase and bag makers, and other unions associated with the Jewish labor movement. In virtually all cases, the Communists were ultimately beaten back, but in all cases the unions suffered seriously from the effects of the inner conflict.

### THE COMMUNISTS AND WORKMEN'S CIRCLE

Beginnings of the "left-right" struggle in the WC were already visible in 1920; within the next few years the conflict flared up with increasing violence. The big issue, sometimes relegated to the background, sometimes pushed to the fore, was Communism and the Soviet government. This issue found expression in 1921 in the refusal of the WC convention to endorse the "left-wing" (i.e., Communist) press, but perhaps it was most clearly reflected in the resolution adopted by the 1922 convention: to "join in the request of the Socialist movement of the world that the Soviet government grant full freedom to all Socialist political prisoners who, throughout their ideological opposition, did not make common cause with the counter-revolutionary elements against the Soviet government." The issue of Soviet political prisoners became central in the conflict.

The Communists, in the WC as elsewhere, soon established a left-wing machine for winning control of the organization. The Communist-directed left wing immediately came into conflict with the national leadership of the organization, closely associated with the *Forward* and the Jewish Socialist Farband. Years of internal warfare followed, involving severe disciplinary measures, reorganizations, and suspensions. Throughout, the national leadership had the support of the overwhelming majority of the WC. Thus, at the 1925 convention, a resolution to vest the National Executive Committee with adequate power to deal with Communist disruption was carried by a vote of 834 to 171.

Toward the end of the decade, the internal struggle in the WC approached its last phase. The Communists now turned to the Independent Workmen's Circle—a small group that had been formed in 1909 because of some legal difficulties which the WC encountered in Massachusetts—and decided to make it the base of their operations. They seized the Independent WC convention in 1929, only to be repudiated in a subsequent referendum. Meanwhile, the Communist-controlled National Conference of Left and Progressive Branches of the Workmen's Circle was mobilized to carry through a split in the WC, in line with the new "third-period" turn of Communist tactics. In October, 1929, a call for a split was issued. The response was disappointing, and the Communists broadened their line. A new fraternal order was formed in March, 1930, under the name of International Workers Order (IWO). Into this organization went not only the Jewish groups drawn from the WC and the Independent WC, but also whatever organizations or split-off sections the Communists could mobilize in other "foreign-language" fields. The Jewish section assumed the name of the Jewish People's Fraternal Order. The WC easily overcame the Communist split; later developments in the organization will be commented upon below.

### UHT, FORWARD, AND THE COMMUNISTS

Although the big unions had already thrown off its tutelage, the UHT played a large role in the struggle to beat back the Communist offensive. It was unwearying in its assistance to the smaller unions and in its efforts to co-ordinate the activities of the anti-Communist forces on the various fronts. But the most formidable power with which the Communists had to contend in the Jewish labor movement was the *Forward*. From the very beginning, they recognized the *Forward* as their main enemy and conducted the entire struggle as one against the *"Forward* clique." In this long and bitter conflict the *Forward* was organizer, mobilizer, co-ordinator, agitator, and morale-builder, all in one.

CONSEQUENCES OF THE COMMUNIST DRIVE

The events of this period had an important effect in bringing the Jewish unions closer to the AFL. AFL assistance was often desperately needed and usually freely given in these troubled years, and the Jewish workers, particularly the union leaders, came to lose most of their Socialist and immigrant prejudices against the "backward" American labor movement. The Americanization of the Jewish labor movement was thus considerably speeded up as a result of the close bonds of co-operation that developed in the common struggle against the Communists.

It is still hard to assess the over-all consequences of this period of civil war that raged through the 1920's. With the exception of the furriers' union, the Jewish labor organizations were saved from Communist control and hence from destruction as legitimate labor organizations. But they were left fearfully depleted in numbers, power, and industrial control; above all, they were left in a state of utter demoralization. As a consequence of the prolonged emergency situation, in which administrative actions such as suspensions, expulsions, and reorganizations were the order of the day, the traditional habits and concepts of trade union democracy were considerably weakened. The very legitimacy of opposition movements in the unions was called into question, since opposition came more and more to be identified with Communism. The effects of this change in the intra-union atmosphere are still to be felt. Still to be felt, too, are the effects of what may ultimately turn out to be the most important aspect of the entire conflict. This was the partial frustration of the natural process of development of a new generation of leadership in the unions. A sizeable number of younger leaders were cut off from positions of authority because of their identification with the Communist cause; although, as we shall see, many of the most active Communists later returned to, and were freely admitted by, the unions against which they had fought, the damage could not be fully repaired. Nor was the tense, suspicious atmosphere prevailing in the unions after the costly victory had been won, an atmosphere particularly conducive to the development of the independence, self-reliance, and mass appeal that effective leadership in the labor movement requires. The acute problem of developing new leaders, which confronts so many of the unions today, may be traced, at least in part, to the delayed effects of the civil war.

725

ECONOMIC DEPRESSION

Very little opportunity was given the unions to recover the ground they had lost as a result of the internal conflict precipitated by the Communist offensive. Hardly had the Communists been beaten off than the United States was plunged into the greatest economic depression in its history. The Amalgamated, first of the unions to emerge from the chaos of civil war, was able to launch an effective drive in 1928, which brought the open-shop Philadelphia market into the union camp. Early the next year, the ILGWU made an earnest effort at recovery, with some success. But by the end of the year, the "New Era" prosperity had collapsed and the country was gripped in an ever deepening crisis. Even the strongest unions were seriously affected; for the needle trades, weak, demoralized and impoverished as they were, the depression proved disastrous. The hard-won gains of decades were wiped out, union control was virtually eliminated, and the sweatshop conditions of an earlier generation were again widely prevalent. Bitter strikes, in desperate resistance to wage-cutting and union-smashing, could not halt the catastrophic downward trend. The ILGWU was reduced to a skeleton organization of 40,000, and the other unions in the Jewish labor movement were in little better state. To make matters worse, gangsterism and racketeering, which had arisen in these industries in the early 1920's, now managed to gain a hold that threatened to prevent responsible industrial relations. Despite their weakness, the unions fought back, but it was not until after 1933 that the tide of battle turned against the racketeers.

Thus, half a century after its hopeful beginnings, after decades of achievement and progress, the Jewish labor movement, concentrated largely in the needle trades, stood at the brink of ruin. Disorganized and enfeebled from within, beset from without, it faced a threatening future with no resources and with almost no hope. A few hardier spirits, a handful of leaders and rank-and-filers, kept the organizations going, waiting and working for the return of better times. It was their loyalty, their courage, and their vision that enabled the Jewish labor movement to take full advantage of the sudden turn initiated by the New Deal in 1933 and stage a spectacular comeback almost without precedent in our labor history. But when the Jewish labor movement re-emerged in the first hectic months of the New Deal, it was something very different from what it had been a decade and a half earlier, at the close of World War I.

726

## The "New" Jewish Labor Movement

### The "Rebirth" of Unionism

Efforts to regain the ground lost during the decade of civil war followed by depression did not wait until the New Deal. By 1932, the ILGWU, the Amalgamated, and the Hatters felt themselves in a position to hit back. Particularly impressive was the successful strike conducted by the ILGWU in the Philadelphia dress market in the spring of 1933, some months before the passage of the National Industrial Recovery Act (NIRA). This achievement had an invigorating effect on the entire union, and on the other needle trades organizations as well.

Much of the renewed vigor of the needle trades unions in this period can undoubtedly be traced to the return of a considerable number of former Communists. The American Communist party had passed through a profound crisis in 1929–30, in the course of which hundreds of members were expelled for refusing to go along fully with the new union-splitting line decreed by Moscow. These dissidents (known as "Lovestoneites" after their leader, Jay Lovestone) included many active trade unionists, particularly in the apparel industries. Perhaps the most outstanding among them was Charles S. Zimmerman, today a vice-president of the ILGWU. The "Lovestoneites" did not take long to effect a thorough reorientation in their trade union policy and basic political line. Inside the unions once more, they became loyal and indefatigable union builders and very soon regained positions of leadership. Other defections from Communist ranks followed in later years and today some of the most important and highly placed executives in the needle trade unions, as well as some of the most active workers at all levels, are former Communists who broke with the party and returned in good faith to their unions. They are, incidentally, among the most vigorous and effective opponents of Communism in the trade union movement.[19]

In a sense, therefore, the unions were prepared for the magnificent opportunity that the inauguration of the New Deal and the passage of the NIRA with its Section 7a (guaranteeing the right of self-organization and collective bargaining) presented to the entire labor movement. All unions in the country profited by this opportunity, but it is a matter of record that the Jewish unions, particularly the two large garment workers' organizations, made the most spectacular gains. Brilliant planning and vigorous action, manifested in a series of whirlwind strikes, raised the membership of the ILGWU from less than 50,000 in the spring of 1933 to 200,000 one year later, brought a substantial measure of organization to every field of the industry

727

and almost complete unionizaton to the cloak and silk dress trades, cut the working week to thirty-five hours, and made notable improvements in wages and working standards. Almost equal progress was made by the Amalgamated and the headgear union. Only the Fur Workers Union, still beset by dual unionism, lagged behind.

The phenomenal success of the unions in expanding organization and industrial control in the early days of the New Deal was reflected in the codes approved by the National Recovery Administration (NRA) for their fields. Coming to the code hearings as representatives of large masses of workers, these unions were able to have their gains enacted into the codes as provisions governing labor standards. Where unions had not managed to take advantage of the opportunity and establish themselves prior to code hearings, the results were obviously not so favorable. On the whole, however, it may be said that the labor provisions of the codes in the women's cloak and dress trades and the men's garment industry were among the best that the NRA had to show. The degree and effectiveness of enforcement also depended in great measure upon the power and alertness of the union operating in the field. Policing the codes became an important part of union activity.

Union progress, which began even before the enactment of the NIRA, continued uninterruptedly after this central New Deal measure was voided by the Supreme Court in May, 1935. The entire structure of code provisions and enforcement was wiped out at one stroke. The unions reacted promptly and succeeded in retaining in their collective agreements all the gains that had been guaranteed under the NRA codes. Here, again, there was a striking contrast between the strongly organized fields and those in which unionism was weak or non-existent; in the latter, conditions rapidly deteriorated to pre-NRA levels. No such retrogression was permitted by the ILGWU, the Amalgamated, and the headgear workers in the areas under their control. Indeed, not only were standards and membership maintained; it even proved possible to continue many of the functions of the old code authorities through new non-governmental bodies. In 1935, the employers and the union set up a National Coat and Suit Industrial Recovery Board to enforce fair labor standards and fair trade practices in all cloak markets of the country; a little over a year later, a very similar body, the Millinery Stabilization Commission, was set up jointly by the employers and the union in that field. The stability of the leading Jewish unions was proven by the very satisfactory way in which they weathered the crisis precipitated by the voiding of the NIRA.

728

UNIFICATION OF LABOR

The "rebirth"of the labor movement with the advent of the New Deal naturally tended to stimulate the unification of labor. Close relations between Sidney Hillman, president of the Amalgamated, and the leaders of the AFL in the top economic recovery bodies helped bring about a settlement of the long-standing jurisdictional conflict between the Amalgamated and the UGW. In the fall of 1933, the Amalgamated, which had been independent since its formation in 1914, affiliated with the AFL. A few months later, early in 1934, the Cloth Hat, Cap, and Millinery Workers International Union finally merged with the United Hatters, each of the unions becoming an autonomous department in the new organization. The departments were abolished and the merger completed two years later.

Less substantial and lasting was the unity achieved among the fur workers. With the dissolution of the Communist-controlled TUUL late in 1934, the "Red" fur workers' union was left free to try to return to the AFL. Negotiations with the AFL organization in the field, in the course of which the Communists were again able to make a deal with the "non-partisans," led to a merger which put the Communists in so advantageous a position that before three years were over, they were in control of the national organization, as well as of the New York Joint Council. A number of splits took place, as a result of which the AFL chartered federal locals of furriers in Toronto, Seattle, and New York.

729

INDUSTRIAL UNION MOVEMENT

Hardly had the Amalgamated rejoined the ranks of the AFL than it left again to become one of the founders of the Committee for Industrial Organization (CIO). All three of the major Jewish unions —the ILGWU, the Amalgamated, and the Hat, Cap, and Millinery Workers—participated in the launching of this new industrial union movement at the 1935 convention of the AFL. Dubinsky, Hillman, and Zaritsky were members of the original CIO, Zaritsky representing not his entire union but the cap and millinery department of the combined union. (The furriers, too, later joined the CIO.) But it would be wrong to think that the women's garment and the headgear unions abandoned their loyalty to the AFL. They were not intent on building a rival or dual movement; what they wanted was to break through the craft inhibitions of American unionism and to force it to go out and organize the mass production workers along industrial lines at the moment when such organization was both possible and mandatory. Because the leaders of the AFL refused to do so, action had to be taken against their will and outside the official bounds of the AFL. But the division was to be only temporary; ultimate re-unification was the goal envisaged from the very beginning. Such, at least, were the views of Dubinsky and Zaritsky when they went into the CIO; Hillman's attitude was not quite so unequivocal, since, after all, the Amalgamated could not be expected to be greatly attached to the AFL. In September, 1936, the ILGWU and the Amalgamated were suspended from the AFL because of their refusal to leave the CIO. No action was taken against Zaritsky's union because it was not affiliated as an international with the CIO, though the cap and mil-linery department was. Even this partial affiliation came to an end in October, 1936, when departments were abolished in the united organization.

From the very beginning, Zaritsky and Dubinsky were advocates of peace and re-unification. When it became clear, toward the end of 1938, that the CIO was determined to establish itself on a permanent basis as the Congress of Industrial Organizations, the ILGWU left that body and for the next year and a half remained independent. It returned to the AFL in 1940, after some of the conditions it had made were partially met. The Amalgamated, on the other hand, went along with the CIO, but had no easy time of it there: first, because of the break of John L. Lewis, president of the United Mine Workers, with President Franklin D. Roosevelt, whom Hillman ardently supported, and second, because of the increasingly obvious Communist influence in the newer CIO unions. In the end, it was Lewis and his miners, not Hillman and his men's clothing workers, who left the CIO.

Thus did the fortunes of trade union politics bring it about that of the two largest Jewish unions, one was an important affiliate of the AFL and the other of the CIO. Apart from the Communist-controlled fur workers' organization, all of the remaining unions associated with the Jewish labor movement were to be found in the AFL.

## EDUCATIONAL ACTIVITIES

The tremendous expansion of the early years of the New Deal brought into the ranks of the ILGWU, the Amalgamated, and other unions hundreds of thousands of new members with little background or experience in the labor movement. These "NRA babies" had to be trained and assimilated if the unions were to survive as great mass organizations in their fields. Much of this training was, of course, achieved through the everyday routine of work and struggle in the shops and on the picket line, but more planned and systematic educa-tion was early felt to be necessary. Hence, most of the unions quickly expanded to very considerable proportions the vestigial educational machinery that had survived the hard times. Both the ILGWU and the Amalgamated launched impressive programs of education, cul-

730

ture, and recreation for their members which easily placed them at the head of the American labor movement in these respects. Just what these educational activities contributed to the result cannot easily be determined; it is a fact, however, that scores and hundreds of thousands of "NRA babies" soon matured into loyal and seasoned unionists, a tower of strength for their organizations.

## JEWISH LABOR UNIONS IN NEW DEAL POLITICS

With the New Deal, the unions also went into politics in a way which, for the Jewish labor movement at least, represented a very considerable break with past traditions. In the spring of 1933, American labor, almost in a body, turned to Roosevelt and became part of the New Deal political machine. In 1936, the CIO leaders launched Labor's Non-Partisan League to mobilize labor's forces in the campaign to re-elect Roosevelt. In New York, an independent party, the American Labor Party (ALP), was set up as the state branch of Labor's Non-Partisan League. Most Jewish unions, AFL and CIO alike, affiliated with the ALP, which soon became a considerable force in local politics. Before long, however, the ALP was torn apart by an internal conflict with the Communists, who, with the help of some union leaders, had succeeded in getting a grip upon the organization. Ultimately (1944), a split took place, the ALP remaining in the hands of the Communists, and the *bona fide* trade unionists and liberals forming the Liberal party as its successor. In other parts of the country, too, the unions began to go into politics in support of the New Deal. On this front the Jewish labor leaders were everywhere most active, operating through the AFL's Labor's League for Political Action, the CIO's Political Action Committee (headed by Jack Kroll of the Amalgamated), as well as through such special organizations as the Liberal party of New York.

It is hard to appreciate what a rupture with tradition this new venture into politics represented for the Jewish workers under Socialist influence. For decades, it had been a cardinal principle of their faith that the two "old" parties were corrupt, "capitalistic outfits," with little difference between them, and that the only hope of the workers lay in building up an independent Socialist party. To vote for "old party" candidates was felt to be an act akin to treason to labor's cause. Now, Jewish unions with long Socialist records behind them were openly calling upon their members to vote for "capitalist" candidates in state and nation. The Jewish Socialist workers responded with enthusiasm. That this drastic turnabout could be accomplished so quickly without any serious protest or defection suggests that much of the Socialism of the Jewish Socialist unions had, by 1933, become largely formal, a mere sentimental vestige. By 1933, in fact, Socialism

731

had long since fulfilled its original function of creating a spirit of solidarity and co-operation among the Jewish workers, and it no longer bore any real relation to the actualities of the labor movement. It is noteworthy that not merely the Jewish unions but the Jewish Socialist organizations and press—in fact, all branches of the Jewish labor movement—were involved in this break with tradition. Here and there some of the old Socialist terminology was retained, but it was obviously merely vestigial, oddly out of place in the new situation. In this way, as in so many others, the New Deal "revolution" speeded the process of the Americanization of the Jewish labor movement.

## Reaction to Nazism

Another new departure of the Jewish labor movement in the early years of the New Deal came in reaction to the dreadful events that were beginning to unfold in Europe. The rise of Hitler to power induced in Jewish labor circles in the United States not merely a strong sentiment of solidarity with the imperilled Socialist and trade union movements in Germany, but also a growing concern for the fate of the Jews and Jewish life in Europe. As an expression of both of these concerns, the Jewish Labor Committee (JLC) was founded in 1933 by a group of Jewish unionists and Socialists headed by B. Charney Vladeck. The JLC's first tasks were naturally to mobilize all possible resources to support the developing anti-Nazi labor underground in Europe, and to relieve the sufferings of the victims of the Hitler terror. Rescue work, too, became a central activity. But before very long the JLC began to think of itself, however vaguely, as the representative of the specifically Jewish interests of the American Jewish workers in community and national affairs. About 1941 the JLC began to initiate activities in the domestic field. The most significant of these enterprises was a sustained and well-organized campaign against anti-Semitism and other forms of racial, religious, and ethnic intolerance in the United States.[20] This concern with things Jewish beyond the narrow bounds of class was one of the most significant aspects of the new orientation that was developing in the Jewish labor movement.

## Inner Transformation

The Jewish labor movement as it was "reborn" under the New Deal was something very different from what it had been a decade or two before; a profound inner transformation in composition, outlook, and interests had taken place which prompted observers to speak of it as the "new" Jewish labor movement. And yet this transformation, precisely because it was so profound and far-reaching, was not the work of a year or even of a decade; it was really the culmination of trends and tendencies that had been operating almost since the very inception of the movement. Sensational events of the new times—the Roosevelt "revolution" on the one side and the Hitler terror on the other— helped to bring out some of the hidden implications of these tendencies, but it would be a mistake to regard them as entirely the work of the 1930's.

What was the Jewish labor movement in its older form? Basically, it was a fairly compact and thriving group of unions of Jewish membership and leadership, using Yiddish as a means of communication. These unions were concentrated in New York and its environs, where they were federated into the UHT. They were strongly Socialist in outlook and were closely linked with the Jewish section of the SP and the WC. They commanded a large and influential Yiddish press and were a force to be reckoned with in the Jewish community. Their Jewish interests, however, were, by present standards, very narrow and peripheral.

Clearly, this is not the Jewish labor movement of 1951. Let us glance briefly at some of the aspects of the transformation.[21]

CHANGE IN COMPOSITION AND CONCERNS

Almost from the beginning, observers had noted that the Jewish worker in America was typically a man of one generation: he was "neither the son nor the father" of a proletarian. In the "old country," his father, or he himself, had most probably been a petty merchant or artisan; in this country, he had become a factory worker; his son and daughter, however, were not following him into the factory or trade, but were going into business, office work, or the professions.[22] This occupational "escalator" reflected the progress of many immigrant groups in the United States, but of none so clearly as of the Jews. Socialists had noted and bemoaned this tendency as far back as the first decade of the century; but until World War I the annual inflow of Jewish immigrants was so immense that it more than compensated for the relatively slight depletion through de-proletarianization. The number of Jewish workers grew quickly, but the growth was in large part due to replenishment from the outside. When Jewish immigration was brought to an abrupt halt by the outbreak of war in 1914, and later greatly reduced by the quota legislation of the early 1920's, the trend emerged quite clearly. The Jewish unions were becoming less and less Jewish in composition; the number of Jewish workers was beginning to decline absolutely as well as in proportion to the total Jewish population; and the average age of the Jewish segment in the once Jewish unions was constantly rising, since the Jewish worker was getting older and ever fewer younger workers were entering the factories or trades.

Before the second decade of the century was over, many of the big Jewish unions already had a considerable non-Jewish membership, primarily of Italians and Slavs. Before the end of the next decade, large numbers of Negroes and Latin Americans had begun to find their way into the unions. This movement has continued almost without interruption. Thus, in 1909 and 1910, the waistmakers and cloakmakers who went out in the great strikes of those years were very largely Jewish, most of them recent immigrants. Over 80 per cent of the men's clothing workers in 1913 were Jewish. But in 1950 less than 30 per cent of the members of the ILGWU and about 25 per cent of the members of the Amalgamated were Jewish.[23] Yiddish-speaking locals, once the rule, grew quite rare. There was still a Yiddish trade union press and "labor sections" in the New York Yiddish dailies, but their influence was limited to a declining number of "old-timers." Apart from a few small organizations, such as those of Jewish butchers, actors, writers, etc., there were no longer any Jewish unions in the older sense of the term.

Many factors contributed to this change. The geographical decentralization of the garment trades—i.e., the emergence of new production centers in sections of the United States where there are almost no Jews—was one important element. Another was the increasing division of labor ("section work") in the various branches of the needle trades, making possible the utilization of labor with little skill or training. But the main factor, combined with the virtual cessation of the stream of immigration in the 1920's, was unquestionably the deep-seated reluctance of Jewish workers to have their children follow them into manual occupations instead of rising in the social scale to professional or white-collar status. This naturally led to a continuous and accelerating shrinkage, both absolute and relative, of the Jewish sector in the most important of the formerly Jewish unions. Viewed simply in terms of composition, there was no longer a Jewish labor movement in this country.

And yet, in another sense, the Jewish labor movement became more Jewish than it had ever been. For although in earlier days the Jewish labor movement was Jewish in the obvious sense of composition and culture, its "Jewish" outlook was very ambiguous. Largely under radical "internationalist" influence, the Jewish labor leaders not only took a hostile attitude to Jewish religion, which they denounced as "reactionary benightedness and a prop of capitalism"; they virtually repudiated any Jewish interest that transcended class lines. Their Jewish concern was limited to Yiddish secular culture and to those areas into which labor solidarity or sentimental ties with the "old country" might bring them. They were, of course, bitterly anti-Zionist, nor, aside from one or two notable exceptions, would they admit of any real Jewish interests, political, social, or philanthropic, that went beyond proletarian bounds. Strong assimilatory trends also made themselves felt, though they never became dominant, perhaps because of the recency of the immigration. By and large, the "Jewishness" of the Jewish labor movement, or rather of the Jewish labor leaders who set the tone for the movement, was a matter of immigrant associations and the use of the Yiddish language as a cultural vehicle. Their attitude to anything Jewish that went beyond this was essentially negative, if not actually hostile.

Strangely enough, as the Jewish labor movement became less Jewish in composition, it grew more Jewish in breadth and intensity of concern. This paradox is to be accounted for on two closely related grounds. In the first place, however the membership might have changed, the leadership of the formerly Jewish unions still remained predominantly Jewish, and this was generally the more true the higher the rank of leadership. (This disproportion was perfectly natural and, in a sense, quite unavoidable, since the higher levels of leadership had necessarily to include a greater percentage of veteran union executives, who were so very largely Jewish.) But the high proportion of Jews in the leadership of the formerly Jewish unions might have proved of no particular importance had the old negative attitude to things Jewish continued among them or among the rank and file of Jewish workers. But precisely at the point in the early 1930's when the unions were ceasing to be Jewish in composition, their Jewish leaders began to acquire a new and far broader interest in Jewish affairs, and a much deeper concern for the fate and welfare of the Jewish people throughout the world. The collapse of the old dogmatic radical-"internationalist" outlook which forbade any all-Jewish concern transcending class or labor lines came just at the time when the demonic fury of anti-Semitism in Europe was bringing to even the most minimal Jew a consciousness of his Jewishness and a new sense of identification with the Jewish people of all classes and nations. The effects of this new consciousness among Jewish unionists were vast and sweeping. For one thing, the ancient, deeply rooted hostility to Zionism in Jewish labor circles was all but wiped out.

### RELATIONS WITH HISTADRUT

It was the Histadrut, the Labor Federation of Israel, which served as the bond between the predominantly anti-Zionist Jewish labor movement in the United States and the Yishuv ("Settlement") in Palestine, and greatly facilitated a rapprochement between the two. As a labor organization, the Histadrut could make its appeal and gain

735

support even among those who were hostile to the Zionist ideology and program. In 1923–24, under Poale Zionist auspices, the National Labor Committee for Palestine (Geverkshaftn Campaign) was launched, with the formal approval of all sections of Jewish labor opinion, as an agency for mobilizing aid for the Histadrut. The campaign did not really begin to take hold, however, until the 1930's, when in reaction to events in Europe, American Jewish sentiment began to undergo a notable shift. The historical events that led to the emergence of the state of Israel and the courageous struggle of the new state to maintain itself completed the process. A large part of the Jewish labor movement, both leaders and members, became explicitly Zionist, and even those who still remained non-Zionist were generally eager and enthusiastic in their support of the new state. Labor leaders entered prominently into all pro-Israel activities, initiating a number of enterprises of considerable economic importance in the development of Israel (*e.g.*, the Amun-Israeli Housing Corporation, launched by a group of American unionists and civic leaders headed by Charles S. Zimmerman).

736

The new Jewish concern of American Jewish labor was not limited to, though it tended to center around, the state of Israel. All aspects of Jewish existence in the United States, in Europe, and in Palestine were felt to be to some degree relevant. Even a more positive attitude to Jewish faith and religious tradition began to creep into the thinking and public expression of the notoriously secular-minded Jewish labor leaders. These factors tended to account for the persistence of the Jewish labor movement at a time when its "material" base—the "Jewish trades" with their unions of predominantly Jewish membership—had virtually disappeared. The truth is that, although the development was continuous, the term "Jewish labor movement" meant something very different in the 1930's from what it once had. Once it had meant a compact bloc of labor organizations—trade union, political, fraternal—making use of Yiddish as their vehicle of communication. Now, insofar as it was not merely a historical reminiscence, the term referred to a kind of semi-organized grouping of Jewish labor leaders combined for the purpose of promoting relevant Jewish interests in this country and throughout the world. To advance these interests, the Jewish labor leaders not only mobilized their own organizations, they also set up bodies (such as the JLC) to co-ordinate their efforts and to represent their organizations and their Jewish concerns in the general labor and national communities. Jewish labor participation in general Jewish communal and philanthropic efforts was also becoming increasingly common. It was primarily in this sense—in the sense of an interest group of which the Jewish labor leaders were the authorized representatives—that one could speak of a Jewish labor movement in the new period.

## NEW POLITICAL INTERESTS

Quite as striking as the transformation in the "Jewish" character of the Jewish labor movement was the change in its political orientation. The Jewish labor movement, as we have seen, was Socialist from its inception and remained so officially until the election of Roosevelt in 1932.[24] Then a startling shift took place. The Jewish labor movement in all its branches almost in a body joined the New Deal-Democratic coalition in support of the new administration. Many of the labor leaders had already dropped out of the Socialist Party during or immediately after the internal crisis of 1931, but even those who remained in the Social-Democratic Federation and the Jewish Socialist Farband entered the New Deal camp. Some, in their enthusiasm, insisted that Roosevelt had become a Socialist; others, somewhat more soberly, pointed to the new situation and called for a revision of the "rigid political purism" of old-line Socialist politics. But the result was the same: the Jewish labor movement, for all its "Socialist soul," was openly abandoning the cardinal principle of the Socialist faith.

But again, paradoxically, as the Jewish labor movement dropped its traditional Socialism it became more and more involved in the nation's political life. For, apart from a brief period just before and during the early years of World War I, Socialist politics in this country was largely peripheral, exhausting itself in radical propaganda and rarely touching the actualities of the political power conflict. When the Jewish labor movement joined the New Deal coalition, it found itself at the center of contemporary American politics. Jewish labor leaders, such as Sidney Hillman, David Dubinsky, and Alex Rose, emerged as political personalities of major importance with influence on policy and with considerable power to make or mar the political fortunes of aspirants for office on the major party tickets, especially in New York State. Other leaders of lesser prominence, trade unionists and former Socialists, obtained judicial or administrative positions of some significance. The great masses of members in the unions were periodically mobilized in election campaigns not, as in the past, simply to make Socialist propaganda, but to turn out the vote that would mean victory or defeat for some Democratic (or, less frequently, Republican) candidate. The Jewish labor movement, in the Roosevelt era, became centrally involved in politics because, with its new orientation, it soon emerged in New York and in one or two other places as a real force in the actual political struggle. Whether the Jewish labor movement utilized its power to best advantage has

737

been much discussed, but its new importance in politics can hardly be questioned.

## AMERICANIZATION

The various tendencies to which we have called attention amounted in fact to the total Americanization of the Jewish labor movement. Obviously, the turn away from traditional Socialism to New Deal politics brought Jewish labor much closer to the general body of American trade unionism, virtually obliterating any significant distinctions in practical political activity, which in this period began to figure very prominently in total labor strategy. No less obviously, the transformation in the composition and character of the Jewish labor movement contributed toward its Americanization. The "old" Jewish labor movement was essentially an immigrant enclave in American life; the "new" Jewish labor movement was spiritually and culturally very much a part of American labor. Even its growing "Jewish" concern, whether directed toward problems at home or abroad, fell in with the general tendency, for this concern was something that American labor, from its own past, could well understand. By becoming more Jewish in its concerns, Jewish labor in America paradoxically became more American.

## The Last Decade: 1941–50

Through the midcentury decade (1941–50), the advance of the unions included in the Jewish labor movement was steady and impressive. During the years of American involvement in war during the earlier part of this period, these organizations participated vigorously and effectively in the war effort as well as in all forms of war relief, in contrast to the suspicious, even hostile attitude displayed by the Jewish unions a quarter of a century earlier during the first world conflict. This wholehearted participation in a common national enterprise of such importance helped considerably to remove any barriers, traditional or ideological, still separating Jewish labor from American labor and the American nation as a whole. In this way the experience of the war completed the process that the New Deal had already carried so far.

The war economy, by shutting off the supply of "hard goods" for civilian consumption, as well as in other ways, greatly favored the garment industries and thus spurred the advance of the major Jewish unions in membership, industrial power, and the improvement of standards. Nor did the immediate post-war situation, for all its diffi-

738

culties, bring this progress to a halt. The forward movement that began so spectacularly in 1933 continued without much abatement.

## THE "BIG THREE"

By the end of the decade, half a century after its formation, the ILGWU (AFL) had a membership of over 400,000, of whom about 200,000 were to be found in New York. Almost 30 per cent of the national membership and perhaps 35 per cent of the New York membership were Jewish. David Dubinsky, who had become president in 1932, remained head of the organization. The Amalgamated Clothing Workers (CIO) stood second in size. It had about 375,000 members throughout the country (25 per cent Jewish), of whom 100,000 were in New York (30–40 per cent Jewish). Jacob Potofsky was president, having succeeded the founder and first president, Sidney Hillman, upon the latter's death in 1946. The membership of the United Cloth Hat, Cap and Millinery Workers Union (AFL) stood at 45,000, of whom nearly 45 per cent were Jewish. Most of the Jewish membership was to be found in New York, in the millinery division of the union. In 1950, Alex Rose became president, upon the retirement of Max Zaritsky. These were the "big three" in the Jewish labor movement. With them were associated many smaller organizations, some still retaining a predominantly Jewish membership.

These unions, especially the "big three," progressed not only in respect to membership, which in most cases reached an all-time high, but also in range and effectiveness of union activities. It was during this period that the big needle trades organizations either initiated or immensely developed their health, welfare, and security systems, their programs of industrial co-operation and stabilization, their research and publicity agencies, their educational, cultural, and co-operative enterprises. It was during this decade particularly that political activity assumed the scope and importance it possesses today in the life of these unions.

### SMALLER UNIONS

The progress registered by the bigger unions was not always equalled by the smaller groups forming part of the Jewish labor movement. With the passing of the older Yiddish-speaking immigrant Jewish community, many of the earlier "Jewish trades" had shrunk to very small proportions or had disappeared entirely. Other Jewish unions (*e.g.*, in the building trades) were adversely affected by the economic difficulties under which their industries labored. Yet on the whole, the last midcentury decade was a favorable one even for these smaller organizations.

## FUR WORKERS

We have still to mention the fur workers. This organization, as already indicated, early fell under Communist control and never succeeded in emancipating itself. In 1938, the fur union joined the CIO, and two years later it merged with the National Leather Workers Association to form the International Fur and Leather Workers' Union, with Ben Gold as president. Its position in the CIO was not an easy one; in 1950, along with other Communist-controlled groups, it was expelled from that federation. At that time the IFLW claimed a membership of 40,000 in the fur division. Owing in part to difficulties in the industry, but in part also to the exigencies of the Communist "party line," the fur union did not make progress comparable to that which the other needle trades unions were able to achieve in the period we are considering. Because of its Communist leadership, it was to all intents and purposes outside the American and Jewish labor movements and did not figure in any of their corporate enterprises.

## UNITED HEBREW TRADES

A summary view of the trade union basis of the Jewish labor movement, as it stood at the midcentury mark, may be gained by examining the roster of affiliates of the UHT in 1950. In addition to locals of the ILGWU, Amalgamated, and the Cap and Millinery Workers, the following were listed: food employees; shoe workers; musicians; theatrical managers, agents, and workers; bakery and pastry workers; confectionery workers; bartenders; teamsters and truck drivers; sales clerks; brushmakers; building service employees; butcher workers; cafeteria, restaurant, and delicatessen employees; funeral chauffeurs; motion picture operators; bath workers; seltzer and soft drink workers; sheet metal workers; suitcase, bag, and pocketbook makers; window trimmers; painters and decorators; button makers; kosher butchers and slaughterers; Jewish writers; printers; actors and radio performers. (This listing indicates the areas covered, not the individual unions; frequently several unions fall under a single designation.) The total membership of the affiliates of the UHT in 1950 was estimated at between 400,000 and 500,000.

## FRATERNAL GROUPS

The period was one of consolidation rather than growth for the WC, since that organization was necessarily almost entirely Jewish in composition and predominantly Yiddish in culture and language.

740

The WC emerged from the internal struggle against the Communists largely unimpaired. At the end of the decade, it had a total membership of about 70,000, some 10,000 of whom were in English-speaking branches. The order also possessed a youth movement (Young Circle League), which was entirely English-speaking. The Poale Zionist Jewish National Workers Alliance escaped much of the brunt of the Communist attack and gained considerably from the pro-Zionist sentiment in Jewish circles. In 1950, it had a membership of some 30,000.

In these fraternal organizations the structural change in the American Jewish labor community, to which reference has been made, manifested itself most clearly. Originally almost entirely proletarian in composition, they became with the years increasingly middle class, reflecting the de-proletarianization of the Jewish workers. The age level also rose steadily; from 28.7 in 1909, the average age of the WC membership rose to 36.5 in 1924 and 50.0 in 1946.[25] At the same time, the shift from Socialism to New Deal democracy and, in the case of the WC, from old-line "internationalism" to Jewish "nationalist" concern, drastically changed the ideological character of the fraternal wing of the Jewish labor movement.

As noted above, the Communists had their Jewish fraternal organization too. It was the Jewish People's Fraternal Order, a division of the International Workers Order (IWO). Accurate membership figures could not be ascertained, but something like 35,000 would probably be near the mark. In 1950, the IWO was being investigated by state insurance agencies in New York and other states as a Communist organization. Its dissoluton seemed probable.

As might be expected from an examination of the basic tendencies to which attention has been called, the Jewish Socialist political organizations were in decline during this decade. The turn away from Socialism in the Jewish labor movement, and the rapid linguistic assimilation which made Yiddish increasingly obsolescent, restricted the scope and influence of the Jewish Socialist Farband to a narrowing circle of "old-timers," still important in their organizations, but obviously the last of their kind. The same declining trend was to be noted in the Yiddish press, both trade union and general, and in the various Yiddish cultural and educational enterprises with which the Jewish labor movement had been so closely associated throughout the 1920's.

STATISTICAL SUMMARY

To conclude this brief sketch of the present (1951) standing of the Jewish labor movement, a statistical summary, based on the best available data supplemented by estimates, is offered:

741

TABLE 1

MEMBERSHIP IN JEWISH UNIONS, 1951[a]

| Union | Total Membership | Jewish Membership |
|---|---|---|
| ILGWU............... | 400,000 | 120,000 |
| Amalgamated.......... | 375,000 | 95,000 |
| Cap and millinery....... | 45,000 | 25,000 |
| Furriers................ | 40,000 | 25,000 |
| Other Jewish unions...... | 60,000 | 40,000 |
| Fraternal orders [b]........ | 70,000 | 70,000 |
| Miscellaneous [c]......... | 10,000 | 10,000 |
| TOTAL............ | 1,000,000 | 385,000 |

[a] This estimate is made on the basis of official statistics, critically examined and supplemented by data obtained through personal inquiry.

[b] The *total* membership of the fraternal societies is about 145,000. But a good part of the membership also belongs to the Jewish unions and is therefore already included in the compilation. The above estimate is of the *non-overlapping* membership, which consists of Jewish businessmen, professionals, and the like, as well as of Jewish workers not in Jewish unions.

[c] The "miscellaneous" category refers to cultural societies, Socialist political groups, etc., insofar as the membership is non-overlapping. No accuracy is claimed for this figure.

On the whole, it may therefore be said that the Jewish labor movement, in its newer sense, is a loose coalition of organizations with a membership of about a million, of whom less than 40 per cent are Jewish. The most all-inclusive organization is probably the Jewish Labor Committee, with an affiliated Jewish membership of 280,000; but even this group does not include the Communists at one end and the Poale Zionists at the other.

The approximately 385,000 Jews here estimated as belonging to the Jewish labor movement do not by any means constitute the total number of Jews in trade unions. The latter figure, though quite impossible to estimate, would naturally be considerably higher. Jews belonging to the teachers, newspaper, and public workers unions, for example, cannot be counted in the Jewish labor movement, since these unions never did and do not now constitute part of the entity so designated. They do not, by and large, through their organizations, play any specifically Jewish role or exert any specifically Jewish influence on labor or national affairs. And ultimately, it is in terms of such historical and functional categories that the Jewish labor movement must be defined.

ROLE IN GENERAL LABOR MOVEMENT

What role did the Jewish unions and the "new" Jewish labor movement which they constituted play, *as a Jewish entity,* in the general labor movement of this country during the past decade?

Of all Jewish labor groups, the ILGWU was probably the union most consistently concerned with Jewish affairs and most active in promoting them in the labor movement. The Cap and Millinery Workers, under its former president, Max Zaritsky, himself a Zionist, also became a significant factor, especially in AFL circles. The leaders of the New York organization of the Amalgamated, the only Jewish union in the CIO, and Joseph Schlossberg, retired general secretary-treasurer, a Labor Zionist, helped to make that union an important Jewish force in the labor movement. The smaller Jewish unions, all in the AFL, generally followed the "big three."

Insofar as there existed a Jewish labor movement within the larger body of American labor, it was as a loose coalition for the promotion of Jewish causes and interests. The existence of a Jewish labor grouping in this sense was recognized in responsible AFL and CIO circles and its legitimacy never questioned. The leaders of the general labor movement expected prominent Jewish labor leaders who identified themselves as such to represent Jewish interests within the labor movement, and to raise in labor councils questions and issues of vital importance to the Jewish people. They acknowledged the propriety of the Jewish labor leaders forming a kind of pressure group on these matters—within the framework, of course, of the general commitments of the labor movement. Since there was no problem of anti-Jewish discrimination within organized labor (as there was, for example, one of anti-Negro discrimination), the Jewish interests with which the Jewish labor leaders were expected to be concerned were primarily anti-Semitism at home and displaced persons and Palestine (later Israel) abroad. In these and related fields, joint action by Jewish labor leaders was sanctioned and approved by the public opinion of the labor movement.

743

What would not have been tolerated within the labor movement would have been the formation of a Jewish bloc along ethnic ("national," "racial") lines with the aim of corporate self-aggrandizement, i.e., with the aim of obtaining a greater share of positions and power "for the Jews." But there was never the slightest question of such a power bloc. Not only was there no basis for it in the labor movement, but it was an idea that every responsible Jewish labor leader would have rejected with repugnance had it ever been suggested.

The influence of Jewish labor was thus primarily the influence exerted by the Jewish unions and their leaders in the general labor movement, which was ready to give a sympathetic hearing to their appeals. It was not an influence created by special organizations and agencies; on the contrary, the influence that such agencies enjoyed in the labor movement was directly derived from the prestige and standing of the unions of which they were composed.

## JEWISH LABOR IN THE AMERICAN JEWISH COMMUNITY

In the American Jewish community, Jewish labor was almost from the beginning a factor of considerable weight, far more so, prior to the New Deal, than organized labor was in American life generally. The biggest and most important Jewish daily in the country, the *Forward*, was a labor paper; many of the most vital Jewish social and cultural institutions were in one way or another associated with the labor movement. Jewish labor was often at war with the spokesmen of Jewish community affairs and in many ways regarded itself as a kind of separate Jewish community, independent and self-sufficient, but its influence on American Jewish life could not be denied.

With the changing occupational-class structure of American Jewry and the passing of the older immigrant Yiddish culture, labor gradually lost its importance in Jewish community life. But as the "new" Jewish labor movement began to emerge through the transition period, it came to achieve a new though very different position in community affairs. The Jewish trade unions were now no longer impoverished radical groups battling against the established order. They were powerful, wealthy, and respected institutions, with fast-growing influence in public affairs. They could enter Jewish community life not as the representatives of a submerged group but as the dispensers of considerable funds and influence. Particularly striking was the new role of such unions as the ILGWU and the Amalgamated in the field of Jewish philanthropy. The ILGWU's contribution of $250,000 to the United Jewish Appeal in 1950–51 was said to have been the largest single donation to that cause then on record. The same union had two years earlier (June, 1948) lent $1,000,000 to the state of Israel, after having made outright donations totalling $220,000 to Jewish institutions in Palestine. Progressive unions had long been accustomed to give financial support to "outside causes," but hitherto these contributions had been largely limited to labor and radical purposes. Now, however, non-labor, non-radical causes of general community concern began to acquire an equal if not superior claim. This not only reflected a drastic change of attitude in Jewish labor circles but also forecast the increasing significance of labor unions in institutional philanthropy.

In view of the diverse ethnic composition of the Jewish unions, in which the Jewish segment was often a minority, it might perhaps be thought that such large donations to Jewish causes would have been likely to arouse considerable opposition. But such was not the case. The Jewish contributions were more than matched by those reflecting the concerns of other sections of the membership, or arising out of general American needs and interests (American Red Cross, United Services Organizations [USO], etc.). Organizations like the ILGWU or Amalgamated could no longer be regarded as merely Jewish unions; they were also in a very real sense "Italian" unions, playing an important part in Italian American community life and contribut-

744

THE JEWISH LABOR MOVEMENT IN THE UNITED STATES    65

ing heavily to Italian institutions in the United States and abroad.[26] As for the membership of the unions, they readily approved of these philanthropic expenditures. The intense concerns of the war and post-war years made them unusually accessible to humanitarian appeals, not only for their own particular causes, but also for those in which their fellow-workers might be interested. This "balance" system of philanthropy soon became institutionalized, and a number of leading unions established special funds for large-scale contributions. The likelihood was that the importance of labor unions in this field would continue to grow.

## SPECIAL ASPECTS OF THE JEWISH LABOR MOVEMENT

### Jewish Labor as a Factor in Americanization

The Jewish labor and Socialist movements played an enormous role in the acculturation of the Jewish immigrant worker to his new American environment. That the Jewish immigrants did not fall into a state of demoralization in face of the disappointments and difficulties of life in the sweatshop and tenement at the end of the century, that they indeed soon came to appreciate the fundamental values of American democracy, was very largely the work of the Jewish labor movement. It lifted the immigrants out of their material misery and slowly improved the conditions of their life and work. But even more important, the Jewish labor movement brought the immigrants a sense of status and belonging. Through the UHT, the immigrant workers were brought into contact with American laboring men whom —for all their strangeness—they felt they could trust and even understand. Through the Jewish labor movement they became part of the United States.

The Jewish Socialist movement, with which the unions were of course closely linked, also served another important function: it introduced the immigrant worker to American politics. The excited election campaigns in the big Jewish centers, the great political rallies addressed by Jewish and non-Jewish Socialist spellbinders, did more to integrate the Jewish worker into American political life than any number of civics classes or formal Americanization programs could possibly have done.

The unions, the WC, and the Socialist Party were also a laboratory and training ground in the practice of collective self-government through the democratic process. Union meetings, debates, conventions, and elections taught the politically inexperienced Jewish immigrants how public affairs could be run by free discussion, the ballot, and mutual tolerance.

The Yiddish press, too, particularly the *Forward,* which from the first occupied a commanding position in the field, was a primary agency of acculturation for the immigrant in his new environment.[27] Abraham Cahan and his colleagues understood the spiritual plight of the immigrant worker as few others did, and they addressed themselves with indefatigable energy to the task of interpreting the United States to him and of integrating him into American life. The earlier generations of Jewish workers learned most of what they knew about the United States, American history, and the American way of life from the columns of the *Forward.*

The Jewish unions showed an early and persistent interest in workers' education, under which head were included courses in the English language, as well as classes in and lectures on American social, economic, and political problems. Education began almost as soon as the union got under way; indeed, sometimes even before, since some of the unions had their beginning in "educational societies." The ILGWU and later the Amalgamated Clothing Workers were pioneers in workers' education, and other Jewish unions followed their lead. Unions that could not conduct programs of their own sent their members to such central institutions in New York City as Labor Temple, Cooper Union, and the Socialist Party's Rand School. Nor should one fail to mention the extensive educational activity carried on by the WC for its members and their families. All of these programs, which were followed to the best of their ability by Jewish unions and Socialist groups outside of New York, were consciously oriented toward bringing a knowledge and appreciation of the United States, however critical, to the immigrant Jewish workers.[28]

In retrospect, it may well be said that, next to the public school, the Jewish labor movement was the most sustained and effective institutional force making for the Americanization of the Jewish immigrant.

## *Jewish Labor as a Pioneer in Industrial Relations*

The extension of the processes of democratic control and self-government to economic life is perhaps the fundamental problem of contemporary democracy. To the solution of this problem under American conditions the Jewish labor movement made a contribution of basic significance. In the realization of industrial democracy, the Jewish labor movement was the pioneer for almost half a century.

Coming relatively late upon the American labor scene, the Jewish unions of course found a tradition of collective bargaining already in existence. But they did not merely follow in the wake of that tradition. They immediately began to make labor history and they have continued to do so to the present day.

Unionism in the women's garment industry, it will be remembered, was established by two great strikes conducted by the ILGWU—the strike of the waistmakers in 1909, and that of the cloakmakers in 1910, both in New York. The "Protocol of Peace," the collective agreement in which the latter culminated, was recognized at the time as a great "social invention" of profound significance for the future of industrial relations. This is still the verdict today.

"Protocolism" soon became dominant as a principle of industrial relations in the organized sector of both the women's and men's garment industries. Before long, a body of industrial usage and custom arose which "like English common law, grew into a codified system," a path of constitutionalism in the jungle of American industrial relations.[29] The "impartial chairman" idea sooner or later spread to other industries and trades and permanently affected the course of industrial relations in this country.

The ILGWU, the Amalgamated, and the Cap and Millinery Workers' Union continued to serve as trail blazers for the labor movement. The first important program of union-management co-operation for more efficient production was initiated by the ILGWU in Cleveland in 1919, and within five years it became the policy of the Amalgamated as well.[30] The first step in making the health and welfare of the workers a concern of the industry and a matter for collective bargaining, was taken by the ILGWU as far back as 1910 in the establishment of the Joint Board of Sanitary Control. Out of this grew the vast and complex system of union welfare funds, in the development of which the ILGWU and the Amalgamated again took the lead.[31]

Perhaps the best publicized and certainly one of the most interesting examples of pioneering in industrial relations was the program of industry planning and modernization advanced in 1941 by Julius Hochman for the New York Dressmakers Joint Board of the ILGWU. Here, for the first time, a militant union with an extremely "class-conscious" background came forward and demanded, for the sake of the workers, the public, and the industry alike, that the latter establish minimum standards of managerial efficiency and devise a program of concerted action in sales promotion and planning. The union itself presented such a program in outline form.[32] Under union pressure, provisions for plant efficiency and promotion were incorporated in the collective agreement. The reaction of the press throughout the country and abroad indicated that the full significance of this development was appreciated: a "new concept of unionism" had been brought into being, a concept that represented the farthest reach and highest level of collective bargaining yet achieved in this country. At about the same time, the ILGWU general office established a management engineering department to serve as information center for manufacturers, union officials, government agencies, and industrial engineers, and to provide practical assistance in solving technological and managerial problems that might arise in any branch of the industry.

Industrial stabilization was the concern of the Amalgamated from its very inception, and its famous "stabilization program" made history in its time. The National Coat and Suit Recovery Board of the ILGWU and the Millinery Stabilization Commission were set up in the wake of the NRA to adapt the same idea to their respective trades.

748

By and large, collective bargaining proved most stable and enduring and achieved the greatest measure of security in the unions that grew out of the old-line Jewish labor movement and that are still led and directed by Jewish labor leaders.[33] A wide variety of factors contributed to this stability. But there can be no doubt that what the Jewish unions did for the consolidation and extension of collective bargaining and union-management co-operation represents a great and enduring contribution to American democracy.

## Jewish Labor in the Struggle Against Communism

The attitude of the Jewish labor movement in America toward Communism in the days immediately after the Russian Revolution followed in many ways the attitude of the Jewish labor and Socialist organizations in the Russo-Polish areas from which so many of American Jews came. Contrary to the usual impression, Jewish labor and political groups in Russia and Poland were almost uniformly hostile to the Bolshevik adventure; indeed, the Bolsheviks never made any headway among the Jewish proletariat [34] until after they had taken power. In the American Socialist movement generally, the Russian Revolution at first called forth a wave of intense excitement and support. Among the first critical voices to be raised were those of the Jewish Socialists associated with the *Forward*. The "right-wing" Jewish Socialists, in fact, proved the most conscious and persistent opponents of Communism in the United States.

The story of the Communist offensive against the Jewish trade unions in the 1920's and of the successful stand of these unions has already been told. The Communists made the Jewish unions their special target, but except for the furriers, it was in these unions that they met their most disastrous defeat. In the ILGWU particularly, where once they were so near to taking power, their rout has been complete.

In the 1947 general elections, for example, the Communists were unable to get more than 14,711 votes out of a total of 126,960 cast in the city of New York; not one of their candidates for any policy-making or executive position was elected. In the rest of the country, their showing was even more insignificant. It is noteworthy that the elimination of Communist influence in the ILGWU and other garment unions was achieved not primarily by administrative measures, but by the effective mobilization of the masses of the membership operating through democratic channels.[35]

But Jewish labor was not content with eliminating Communist influence within its own ranks; it took the initiative in fighting Communism on many fronts at home and abroad. The JLC made the struggle against totalitarianism the central part of its original program, and that meant not only Nazi but also Communist totalitarianism. The ILGWU was the backbone of the resistance to Communist infiltration in the American Labor Party, and after the split became the mainstay of the Liberal Party. ILGWU leaders, especially David Dubinsky, proved most influential in helping to mold the international policy of the AFL in the direction of closer co-operation with the democratic elements of the Continental labor movements. The revival of democratic unionism in France and Italy after World War II and the decline of Communist influence in the labor movements of these countries, may in good part be traced to the help given by American labor under the stimulus of the ILGWU. The ILGWU, and David Dubinsky personally, also played a significant part in bringing about the formation of the International Confederation of Free Trade Unions in 1949, as the rallying center for democratic, anti-Communist unionism throughout the world.[36]

## Conclusion: Prospects

A survey of its development through seven decades leads to the conclusion that the Jewish labor movement in the United States has always been, in a sense, a transitory phenomenon in American social life. Even in its most flourishing period, it was never really a permanent institution, as the American labor movement is a permanent part of the social structure of the United States. For almost from its inception, the Jewish labor movement in this country has been in process of dissolution through de-proletarianization. It was essentially a one-generation phenomenon whose function was to bring the immigrant Jew-turned-proletarian into the stream of American labor and American life generally. When this function became obsolescent, it was replaced by another, that of representing Jewish interests in labor and national life. Some new agencies, such as the JLC, were added, but by and large the old institutional framework was preserved and turned to new purposes. The transition was made possible because large numbers of Jewish workers of immigrant background still remained in the unions and the other branches of the Jewish labor movement. But obviously even in its new form, the Jewish labor movement was essentially impermanent, representing perhaps a last stage of dissolution.

The ultimate disappearance of the Jewish labor movement in any form that we can think of it today seems to be conditioned upon the two factors above noted. These factors will presumably continue to operate in the foreseeable future, and as long as they continue to operate—as long as the children of Jewish workers do not follow their parents into the shops and as long as there is no large-scale immigration to make up their loss—the base of the Jewish labor movement in any form will continue to shrink.

The actual trend is fairly clear, despite the paucity of statistical data. In the once Jewish unions, which are necessarily all-proletarian in composition, the proportion of *Jews,* both immigrant and non-immigrant, is declining; in institutions such as the WC, which are all-Jewish in composition, it is the proportion of *workers* that is in decline. In both cases, the number and proportion of *Jewish workers* are becoming steadily smaller with the years. This trend is pretty certain to continue, though at varying rates, depending on location, trade, and type of institution. Hundreds of thousands of Jewish workers will, of course, be found in the trade unions in coming years, but rarely will they be such as to constitute a "Jewish element," and almost never will they be in sufficient concentration to make their organizations Jewish unions in the familiar sense. The day of the old-time Jewish labor movement, everything seems to indicate, is over.

For the immediate future, the Jewish labor movement in the newer sense—in the sense of a loosely organized grouping of Jewish labor leaders combined for the purpose of promoting appropriate Jewish concerns—seems likely to continue with considerable vigor. The two conditioning factors here involved are, first, the persistence of Jewish leadership at various levels in organizations that have long ceased to be predominantly Jewish in membership; and secondly, the maintenance of the Jewish self-consciousness that has emerged in recent years. The first factor will, of course, decline, since the "old-timers" are bound to be gradually replaced by newer leaders, increasingly non-Jewish. As to the intensity of Jewish self-consciousness, it is hard to be certain, but it seems safe to suggest that it is not likely to diminish measurably in the next decade at least. On the whole, therefore, we would appear justified in saying that in the sense in which we can speak of a Jewish labor movement today, it will continue to exist and function in the coming period. But almost as probably—barring wholly unexpected and unpredictable developments—the long-term prospect is one of decline and ultimate dissolution.

Yet when that day comes, and if it comes, the Jewish labor movement will not have disappeared without a trace. It will have left an enduring contribution to our national labor and Jewish life in the United States. It is a contribution which is still being made in the everyday activity of the hundreds of thousands of men and women, leaders and rank-and-filers, who constitute the Jewish labor movement in the United States.

## SELECTED BIBLIOGRAPHY                                    751

This list is primarily one of important and easily accessible secondary sources. In the preparation of this study, primary sources—reports of conventions and minutes of trade union meetings; reports, articles, letters, and official documents in trade union journals, the Yiddish and general press, etc.—were employed and supplemented by personal interviews and inquiries. However, it has not been felt possible to include specific references to this material in a limited bibliography such as this.

*Annual Report of the Commissioner General of Immigration,* 1901–26

BRAUN, KURT, *Union-Management Cooperation: Experience in the Clothing Industry* (1947)

BUDISH, J. M. and SOULE, GEORGE, *The New Unionism in the Clothing Industry* (1920)

CAHAN, AB., *Bleter fun mayn leben* (1912), 5 Vols.

COHEN, ELI E., "The American Jew: Economic Status and Occupational Structure," AMERICAN JEWISH YEAR BOOK, 1950, Vol. 51

COMMONS, JOHN R. and Associates, *History of Labor in the United States* (1918), 2 Vols.

DUBINSKY, DAVID, "A Warning Against Communists in Unions," *The New York Times Magazine,* May 11, 1947

DUBINSKY, DAVID, "Rift and Realignment in World Labor," *Foreign Affairs,* January, 1949

EPSTEIN, MELECH, *Jewish Labor in USA* (1950)

FINE, NATHAN, *Labor and Farmer Parties in the United States* (1928)

FONER, PHILIP, *History of the Fur and Leather Workers Union* (1950)

GOLDBERG, N., "Occupational Patterns of American Jews," *The Jewish Review,* Vol. III (1945)

GREEN, CHAS. H., *The Headwear Workers* (1944)

HANDLIN, OSCAR and MARY, "A Century of Jewish Immigration to the United States," AMERICAN JEWISH YEAR BOOK, Vol. 50 (1948–49)

HARDY, JACK, *The Clothing Workers* (1935)

HILLQUIT, MORRIS, *Loose Leaves from a Busy Life* (1934)

HOCHMAN, JULIUS, *Industry Planning Through Collective Bargaining* (1941)

HOWARD, E. D., "Cooperation in the Clothing Industry," *Proceedings of the American Academy of Political Science,* Vol. IX

HURWITZ, M., *The Workmen's Circle* (1936)

Jewish Labor Committee, *The Jewish Labor Committee in Action* (1948)
Jewish Labor Committee, *The Time Is Now: Report of Activities, Anti-Discrimination Department* (1951)
Jewish Socialist Farband, *Tsen Yor Sotsialistishe Arbet* (1931)
JOSEPH, SAMUEL, *Jewish Immigration to the United States from 1881 to 1910* (1914)
LANG, H. and FEINSTONE, M., eds., *Geverkshaftn: Zamelbukh tsu fuftsik vor leben fun di Farainikte Yidishe Geverkshaftn* (1943)
LEVINE, LOUIS, *The Women's Garment Workers* (1924)
LORWIN, LEWIS L., *The American Federation of Labor* (1933)
MINKOFF, N. M., *Union Health and Welfare Plans* (Bulletin No. 200, U.S. Bureau of Labor Statistics)
PAT, EMANUEL, "Mitn Ponim tsum Amerikaner Idntum," *Der Veker*, Feb. 15, 1951
PERLMAN, SELIG, *History of Trade Unionism in the United States* (1922)
PERLMAN, SELIG, *A Theory of the Labor Movement* (1928)
PERLMAN, SELIG and TAFT, PHILIP, *History of Labor in the United States* (1935), Vol. IV.
RICH, J. C., "The Role of the *Jewish Daily Forward* in the Trade Union Movement," *Forward*, May 25, 1947
RICH, J. C., "How the Garment Workers Licked the Communists," *Saturday Evening Post*, August 7, 1947
RICH, J. C., "The Jewish Labor Movement in the United States," *The Jewish People Past and Present* (1948), Vol. ii
ROBINSON, DONALD B., *Spotlight on a Union* (1948)
SEIDMAN, JOEL, *The Needle Trades* (1942)
SELIGMAN, BEN B., "The American Jew: Some Demographic Features," AMERICAN JEWISH YEAR BOOK, 1950, Vol. 51
SHERMAN, B., *Yidn un andere etnishe grupn in di Farainikte Shtatn* (1948)
SLICHTER, S. H., *Union Policies and Industrial Management* (1941)
SOLTES, MORDECAI, *The Yiddish Press: an Americanizing Agency* (1924)
STOLBERG, BENJ., *Tailor's Progress* (1944)
STRONG, EARL D., *The Amalgamated Clothing Workers of America* (1940)
TCHERIKOWER, E., ed., *Geshikhte fun der yidisher arbeter-bavegung in di Farainitke Shtatn* (1945), 2 vols.
United States Industrial Commission, *Report*, 1901, Vol. XV.
WEINRYB, BERNARD D., "The Adaptation of Jewish Groups to American Life," *Jewish Social Studies*, Vol. VIII (1946), no. 4
WEINSTEIN, B., *Di yidishe yunions in America* (1929)
WEINSTEIN, B., *Fertsik yor in der yidisher arbeter-bavegung* (1924)
ZARETZ, CHAS. E., *The Amalgamated Clothing Workers of America* (1934)

# FOOTNOTES

1. Oscar and Mary Handlin, "A Century of Jewish Immigration to the United States," AMERICAN JEWISH YEAR BOOK, Vol. 50 (1948–49), p. 10.
2. *Annual Report of the Commissioner General of Immigration . . .* , 1901–26; Bernard D. Weinryb, "The Adaptation of Jewish Groups to American Life," *Jewish Social Studies*, Vol. VIII (1946), No. 4, p. 223.
3. United States Industrial Commission, *Report*, 1901, Vol. XV, pp. 325-27.
4. Melech Epstein, *Jewish Labor in USA*, p. 168; J. C. Rich, "The Jewish Labor Movement in the United States," *The Jewish People Past and Present*, Vol. II, p. 401b.
5. E. Tcherikower, ed., *Geshikhte fun der yidisher arbeter-bavegung in di Farainikte Shtatn*, Vol. II, chap. X; B. Weinstein, *Di yidishe yunions in America*, pp. 143-49; H. Lang and M. Feinstone, eds., *Geverkshaftn: Zamelbukh tsu fuftsik yor leben fun di Farainikte Yidishe Geverkshaftn.*
6. Among the more important studies in English of Jewish unions in this and later periods are: [general] Epstein, *op. cit.*, and Joel Seidman, *The Needle Trades;* [women's garment workers] Louis Levine, *The Women's Garment Workers*, and

Benjamin Stolberg, *Tailor's Progress;* [men's clothing workers] Chas. E. Zaretz, *The Amalgamated Clothing Workers of America,* and Earl D. Strong, *The Amalgamated Clothing Workers of America;* [hat, cap, and millinery workers] D. B. Robinson, *Spotlight on a Union.* Two books written from the Communist standpoint are: Jack Hardy, *The Needle Trades,* and Philip Foner, *History of the Fur and Leather Workers.*

7. Nathan Fine, *Labor and Farmer Parties in the United States,* chaps. vi, vii.

8. I owe this insight as well as many others in this paper to the suggestions of Professor Selig Perlman.

9. M. Hurwitz, *The Workmen's Circle.*

10. Samuel Joseph, *Jewish Immigration to the United States from 1881 to 1910,* p. 93.

11. *See* the articles in the jubilee issue of the *Forward,* May 25, 1947, especially J. C. Rich, "The Role of the *Jewish Daily Forward* in the Trade Union Movement." *See also* Harry Lang, "Di geverkshaftn un Ab. Cahan," in *Geverkshaftn,* ed. by H. Lang and M. Feinstone.

12. Epstein, *op. cit.,* chap. 16.

13. *Ibid.,* p. 311.

14. Lewis L. Lorwin, *The American Federation of Labor,* chap. vii; Selig Perlman and Philip Taft, *History of Labor in the United States,* Vol. IV, pp. 403-11.

15. Fine, *op. cit.,* chap. x.

16. Lorwin, *op. cit.,* pp. 142-45.

17. Fine, *op. cit.,* p. 322.

18. For the early work of the Farband, *see Tsen Yor Sotsialistishe Arbet,* a publication of the Farband.

19. David Dubinsky has spoken of them as "the most effective fighters against Communist influence" (*The New York Times Magazine,* May 11, 1947).

20. For the work of the Jewish Labor Committee, see *The Jewish Labor Committee in Action; The Time is Now: Report of Activities, Anti-Discrimination Department,* and other publicatons of the JLC.

21. For a study of certain aspects of this transformation, see Weinryb, *op. cit.*

22. According to N. Goldberg ("Occupational Patterns of American Jews," *The Jewish Review,* Vol. III [1945], pp. 265, 274-75), the shift in the occupational structure of the Russian Jews in the United States during the past three and a half decades is reflected in the following figures:

| Occupation | 1900 | 1934 |
|---|---|---|
| Manufacturing | 59.6% | 13.7% |
| Trade | 20.6 | 51.1 |
| Professions | 2.6 | 13.1 |
| Other | 17.2 | 22.1 |

These figures are for the country as a whole; of course, the proportion of Jews in manufacturing is considerably higher in the big cities, but the trend is the same. Goldberg also points out another basic trend: "No less significant is the fact that the proportion of Jewish factory workers to manufacturers has decreased. 96.5 per cent of the Jews from Russia in manufacturing were in 1900 employees and approximately only 63 per cent in the 1930's" (pp. 275-76).

23. For data on the ethnic groups in the needle trades, *see* Seidman, *op. cit.,* pp. 30-39, 43-49. A closer view of the shift in membership composition of a large and important needle trades union is afforded by the following figures showing the composition of new members (applicants accepted) from 1934 to 1948:

| Year | Jewish | Non-Jewish |
|---|---|---|
| 1934 | 65.5% | 34.5% |
| 1940 | 61.9 | 38.1 |
| 1945 | 33.2 | 66.8 |
| 1946 | 24.5 | 75.5 |
| 1948 | 24.2 | 75.8 |

As a result, the composition of the *total membership* of this union has changed during the period 1934–48 as follows:

| Year | Jewish | Non-Jewish |
|------|--------|------------|
| 1934 | 70.5% | 29.5% |
| 1948 | 53.9 | 46.1 |

Accurate data are not obtainable for this organization before 1934, but it is known that a generation ago the membership was almost entirely Jewish and the language used in union affairs was Yiddish.

24. In 1912, there had been some sentiment among a limited group of Jewish Socialist intellectuals to support Woodrow Wilson on the platform of the "New Freedom." It found no response, however, in Socialist and Jewish labor ranks. That was the year of Eugene V. Debs' sensational campaign, in which he received over 900,000 votes.

25. Weinryb, *op. cit.*, p. 238.

26. Thus, corresponding to the Jewish Labor Committee, though with very different functions, there was the Italian-American Labor Council, headed by Luigi Antonini, first vice-president of the ILGWU, and composed of labor organizations with large Italian membership.

27. See Mordecai Soltes, *The Yiddish Press: an Americanizing Agency* (1924).

28. For the educational activities of the ILGWU, *see* Levine, *op. cit.*, chap. xxxvi; Stolberg, *op. cit.*, chap. xi, esp. pp. 281-84. For the Amalgamated Clothing Workers, *see* Strong, *op. cit.*, chap. ix; Seidman, *op. cit.*, pp. 285-86. For the WC, *see* Hurwitz, *op. cit.*, chap. xiv, xv.

29. E. D. Howard, "Cooperation in the Clothing Industry," *Proceedings of the American Academy of Political Science*, Vol. IX, pp. 607-10.

30. S. H. Slichter, *Union Policies and Industrial Management*, chaps. xiv, xvii; Levine, *op. cit.*, chap. xxxi; Strong, *op. cit.*, chap. v, also chaps. xi, xii, xiv. For similar developments among the Hat, Cap and Millinery Workers, *see* Robinson, *op. cit.*, chap. xiv.

31. N. M. Minkoff, *Union Health and Welfare Plans* (Bulletin No. 900, U. S. Bureau of Labor Statistics).

32. Julius Hochman, *Industry Planning Through Collective Bargaining* (1941).

33. "As in other parts of our economy, business depressions subjected the bridge between labor and management to serious trials of load. While cooperative systems in other industries collapsed, union-management cooperation in the clothing industry by and large withstood the pressure. . . . Collective bargaining in the clothing industry has become more and more peaceful. . . . Clothing manufacturers and unions cooperate with a strikingly sober and circumspect note." (Kurt Braun, *Union-Management Cooperation: Experience in the Clothing Industry*, pp. 52, 56, 57). The reference is primarily to the ILGWU and the Amalgamated Clothing Workers.

34. "In the first period of the October Revolution," a Russian Communist party memorandum of 1919 declared, "the Jewish workers were but little affected by it; they remained indifferent to the slogans of the revolution" (*Lenin über die Judenfrage*, p. 70). "The Jewish Socialist groups carried on a theoretical struggle against Bolshevism. . . . The Jewish workers resisted the Bolsheviks with armed force, particularly in the Ukraine" (*Communist International*, April, 1920). "Fully 90 per cent of all Jewish votes cast in the last free election in Russia in 1917 had gone to the nationalist, principally Zionist, candidates" (S. Baron, *Modern Nationalism and Religion*, p. 239).

35. *See* J. C. Rich, "How the Garment Workers Licked the Communists," *Saturday Evening Post*, August 7, 1947.

36. *See* David Dubinsky, "Rift and Realignment in World Labor," *Foreign Affairs*, January, 1949.

# The Russian Roots of the American Jewish Labor Movement

By Ezra Mendelsohn

(Hebrew University)

The massive emigration of Russian Jews to America, in the wake of the pogroms of 1881–1882, was chiefly a movement of poor artisans, traders, and "people who lived on nothing" (*luftmentshn*) who came to the New World in search of an opportunity to work, to grow prosperous, and to live without fear. The emigration, however, was not homogeneous. Along with the Jewish "masses" there appeared on American soil in the 1880s a very different type, the Russian Jewish intellectual, whose condition and motivation for the voyage often had little in common with the typical Jewish immigrant. The gulf separating the two immigrant types was keenly felt by the intellectuals, who were quick to call attention to their unique status. Thus Alexander Harkavy, who reached New York in 1882, remarks in his memoirs: "The members of our society [the *Am Olam* group, which is discussed below] felt themselves to be on a higher level than the masses. They are not like us, we thought. We are not journeying to America for ordinary reasons; are we not idealists, who will demonstrate to the nations of the world that the children of Israel are capable of being farmers?" A decade later Leon Kobrin observed that his shipmates on the way to America were divided into "we" (the intellectuals) and "they" (everyone else). The relatively tiny number of intellectuals were prepared "to struggle and to die for the happiness of mankind" and earnestly discussed the great question—what is to be done in America to further this noble goal? The masses, on the

150

Originally published in *YIVO Annual of Jewish Social Science* (1976). Reprinted by permission of YIVO Institute for Jewish Research.

other hand, "did not share our worries about what to do in America. They didn't think about such things. Each of them had already answered the question as follows: 'I have hands, I'll do allright.' "[1] In the end, the "we and they" dichotomy was resolved; the intellectuals, with their contempt for the materialistic Jewish immigrant masses, eventually came to involve themselves in the masses' struggle for a better life by organizing unions and preaching socialism to the Jewish proletariat. One of the aims of this essay is to investigate this process, which is of great significance in the history of organized Jewish labor in America.

What do we mean by the term "Russian Jewish intelligentsia?" At its most basic level, the word "intellectual" was employed to describe those Jews who, thanks to the Jewish "Enlightenment" (Haskalah) movement, to the russifying and relatively liberal policy of the Russian state during the reign of Alexander II, and to their own desire for education, had broken with the traditional Jewish way of life in the Pale of Settlement and had acquired a secular education. By the 1880s a considerable number of Jewish youths had attained the requisite secular education—by attending a Gymnasium, a Russian University, or a state-run Jewish institution of higher learning—to qualify formally as intellectuals.[2] The Jewish intellectual proudly wore his student uniform, striking evidence of his separation from the traditional Jewish world; above all, he spoke Russian rather than Yiddish. Indeed, when Abraham (Abe) Cahan, future editor of Forverts (Forward) and a graduate of the Vilna Jewish Teachers' Institute, sought out fellow-intellectuals in Brody on his way to America, he used a simple criterion: "I walked along the streets and listened to whether someone spoke Yiddish or Russian. If it was Russian that meant that he was an intellectual." [3]

The Russian Jewish intellectuals were therefore "russified"— a word which must be used cautiously, and should not be considered synonymous with "assimilated"—and one aspect of this russification was a disdain for the "jargon" (Yiddish) and traditional Jewish culture. The typical Jewish intellectual was alienated from the Jewish religion and from the world-outlook of the Jewish masses, who were regarded as still living in the "Middle Ages." Having discarded one identity the intellectual acquired a new one by identifying with the general Russian intelligentsia, which, as is

756

well known, was the bearer of revolutionary ideologies within the
Empire. Thus, along with our definition of the Russian Jewish intellectual as educated and russified, we should add that he was
likely to be radical; in fact, owing to the all-pervasive nature of
Czarist anti-Semitism he was even more likely to be radical than
his Russian counterpart. We shall have occasion to examine in
some detail the revolutionary baggage which the Jewish intelligentsia brought from Russia to America. Suffice it to say at this
point that many Jewish intellectuals were convinced that the only
life worth living was a life of service, and that the object of this
service was commonly conceived to be the long-suffering Russian
people. These views, of course, were transmitted to the Jewish students by Russian radicals who, despite the rising Marxist challenge, were largely of the Populist school.[4]

757

Given this dedication to serving the people, the true hallmark of the radical Russian intellectual, why did some Jewish intellectuals emigrate to America? The historian finds various motives.
Some, like Louis Miller, who was to become an important labor
leader in New York, and the famous anarchist Shoel Yanovsky, fled
because their revolutionary activities attracted the attention of the
police. And yet others left simply because in anti-Semitic Russia
there was not much future. Y. Kopelov, who became an anarchist in
America, recalls in his memoirs that ". . . to sit and wait for a
wedding match with a dowry and then to become middlemen, store-
keepers, or do nothing at all—for us, worldly, enlightened, socialist-
minded youths this was impossible."[5]

Miller, Yanovsky, and Kopelov left Russia as individuals.
There was, however, an organized emigration of Russian Jewish
intellectuals to America in the early 1880s known as the *Am Olam*
(*Eternal People*) movement. This movement, rather loosely organized but with a clear ideological position, developed as a result of the most important event in the history of Russian Jewry
in the last quarter of the nineteenth century—the pogroms of 1881–
1882. These pogroms had a devastating impact upon the Jewish
intelligentsia, who were spared the actual physical torment of the
victims only to suffer from acute psychological distress. For the
pogroms seemed to demonstrate that the hopes of the russified intelligentsia had been dashed, that the longed-for rapprochement
between the intelligentsia and the "people" was now an impossible

dream, at least for Jews. Nothing in their world-outlook had prepared them for this upsurge of irrational hatred, hatred deriving from the very "people" in whom the intelligentsia had placed its trust. A young *Am Olam* participant who was in Odessa on the eve of the pogroms found that the Jewish students believed that "only peasants are people and [are] entitled to the attention of the intelligentsia." [6] These populist views were hard pressed by the peasants' participation in the pogroms, and many Jewish students found themselves shaken to the core. In Warsaw Yankev Milkh, a "one-half" intellectual who was to become a labor leader in New York, felt that "All my thoughts were overturned" and that his love for life had disappeared; an Odessa student informs us that, as a result of the pogrom in that city "people abandoned their studies and began to search for ways to escape from their miserable condition."[7]

What was to be done? The problem was to translate the general feeling of "bitterness" [8] into action, and there were various proposals. It was in the wake of the pogroms that Leo Pinsker wrote his famous pamphlet *Auto-Emancipation,* an affirmation of Jewish nationalism which nurtured the first generation of Russian Zionists. But those who were attracted to the idea of national rebirth on the ancestral soil were outnumbered by those who looked to America as a source of new life and new hope. In the major centers of Jewish life in Southern Russia (where the pogroms were concentrated)—in Odessa, Kiev, Kremenchug, Elizavetgrad, and Balta—circles of like-minded intellectuals and "one-half" intellectuals formed in order to promote the idea of organized emigration to the New World. [9] These students had come to the sorrowful conclusion that "emigration is the only way out." "We are far from idealizing America," one of them wrote, "we know that much suffering awaits us at first; but we are prepared to endure a hundred times as much material suffering than we endure at the present time, if only we can be freed from the Damoclean sword . . ." [10] They resolved, in the words of M. Bokal, one of the leaders of the movement, to ". . . disperse among the *free* nations in a new world. We shall be compelled to become agriculturalists and we shall be like other people—we will live like other people." [11]

If the *Am Olam* despaired of the future in Russia, it by no

758

means abandoned the idealism of the intelligentsia. On the contrary, the movement fed on and lent new impetus to this idealism by presenting the migration to America as a migration of missionaries. The movement's ideologists advanced the notion that the Russian Jews, hitherto a race of unproductive middlemen, can redeem themselves only by adopting agriculture. This idea had long since been advocated by various would-be reformers of the Jewish condition, and was an integral part of the program of the Jewish "Enlightenment" movement in Russia. By adopting it the *Am Olam* signalled its acceptance of the accusation, usually associated with anti-Semitism, that the Jews were a parasitic people; like the Zionists, they felt that a return to the soil would guarantee a return to health. And, if the Jewish intelligentsia was barred from serving the Russian *muzhik,* it might nonetheless transform itself into a new class of Jewish peasants in a more favorable environment.

759

The idea of returning to the soil in the new world had great appeal to the intelligentsia. One member of *Am Olam* noted: ". . . it is a disgrace that a people should live off what others produce;" another wished ". . . to show the world that a Jew was able to become a productive worker if given the proper chance." [12] Shneyer Beyly was delighted with the opportunity ". . . to wipe away the stain that Jews were not agriculturists . . . ," and Moses Freeman, member of the Odessa *Am Olam,* defined the aims of his group as follows: "To settle on the land and to live from our own labor and to serve as an example to others. There in the colony, close to the tilled soil and in nature's bosom, the local storekeeper, middleman and 'luftmentsh' will be transformed into a useful member of society, for himself and for the world!" [13]

The *Am Olam* members, it should be noted, were interested not only in establishing colonies but in establishing these colonies on communal principles. They went off to America ". . . to demonstrate to the world that Jews are capable of being agriculturists; and as progressive, advanced and intelligent humans—live on communist principles." [14] The return to the soil would not take the form of private farming, but rather of sharing in the blessings of nature. It was in this sense, of course, that the colonists hoped to act as models; this would be their service to humanity.

The *Am Olam* groups began arriving in New York in 1882;

according to one source more than 1,000 intellectuals participated in the movement and set out to establish communal farms with such names as New Odessa and Bethlehem-Yehudah.[15] For various reasons—lack of funds, lack of experience, and the frailties of human nature—the colonies were largely unsuccessful. We need not go into the story of their collapse here; what is important is, first of all, that the movement brought to the new world a large contingent of Russian Jewish intellectuals and secondly, that these intellectuals had come to America embued with the general idealism of the Russian intelligentsia and the special mission of *Am Olam*. The failure of the colonies did not destroy this idealism, which was eventually channelled in new directions. The *Am Olam* pioneers became, in time, pioneers of the American Jewish labor movement.

Having accounted for the fact that the early 1880s witnessed the arrival in America of a rather sizeable number of Russian Jewish intellectuals (though they were, of course, vastly outnumbered by the "masses" of Russian Jewish immigrants) we must now consider more closely the political attitudes of these intellectuals. We have already noted their predeliction for radical views, but it is noteworthy that only a small minority were actually veterans of the Russian revolutionary movement. Among these veterans was Abraham Cahan, who had discovered an illegal revolutionary "circle" (*kruzhok*) while studying at the Jewish Teacher's Institute in Vilna. Cahan joined the group and, after his graduation, carried on socialist propaganda in Velich, a small town where he was employed as a teacher. In 1881, under police surveillance and agitated by the pogroms, he left for America.[16] Another Russian revolutionary activist who was to make a name for himself in the American Jewish labor movement was Isaac Hourwich, who participated in socialist circles in Minsk in the late 1870s and who came to America in 1890.[17] Phillip Krantz, editor of the famous London Yiddish socialist journal *Arbayter fraynd*, who in 1890 became editor of the New York socialist organ *Di arbayter tsaytung*, was active in the illegal circles of the Petersburg Polytechnical Institute in the late 1870s. And Michael Zametkin, a major figure in the Jewish labor movement in New York in the 1880s, had participated in revolutionary circles in Odessa in 1877–1878 and came to America to avoid incarceration.[18]

The historian is struck, however, by the fact that even the veterans were vague as to the ideological content of their radicalism. Thus Cahan admits that "I had no exact grasp" of socialist doctrine, and if this was true of a "circle" participant it was certainly true of the vast majority of other intellectuals. Khayim Spivakovsky (Spivak), a participant in the *Am Olam* movement, informs us that the Russian Jewish intelligentsia brought with it "no clearly defined political, social, and economic views;" and Morris Hillkowitz, who under the name Hillquit was to become one of the leaders of American socialism, remarks in his memoirs that ". . . my socialism was largely emotional and sentimental. My notions about the philosophy and practical program of the movement were quite vague." [19] In this Hillkowitz speaks for almost all his fellow intellectuals of the 1880s.

761

This ideological confusion is, of course, directly related to the state of Russian radical thought in the 1870s. While Marxist thought was beginning to make inroads among the radical intelligentsia it was still comparatively unknown, and only a few Jewish radicals who came to America in the 1880s were acquainted with the theories of scientific socialism. The prevailing theory was still populist, and here, surely, is the source of the vague radicalism of the Russian Jewish intelligentsia. For what the Jewish intellectuals acquired from their acquaintance with the Russian populist tradition—an acquaintance picked up, as we have seen, not so much through active participation in a circle as through reading and discussion—was a certain *mood* of revolutionary dedication and enthusiasm. The ideological content was, indeed, vague; what was clearly expressed was the revolutionary form, as manifest in the desire for rapid change, an end to oppression, a love for the "people," a hatred for authority. The typical Russian Jewish intellectual in America in the 1880s was more a revolutionary *type* than he was the bearer of a coherent ideology of revolution. William Frey, the Russian utopian socialist who was associated with those *Am Olam* members who established New Odessa in Oregon in 1883, has left us a most revealing portrait of the young intellectuals:

> All members were young Russians . . . thoroughly imbued with the individualism and revolutionism of our age. Like all Russian nihilists they stood for the extremes of individual liberty; they had aversion to everything pertaining to order and moral discipline. The

mere word "religion" was odious to them . . . The altruistic aim of my friends was in flat contradiction with their individualistic theory. Consciously they stood for anarchy, unconsciously they were led by a strong instinct towards a harmonious brotherly social life. This lack of unity, this combination of mean theory with a noble impulse was the cause of all troubles in the community.

Despite their dislike for order, which was, in Frey's view, an obstacle to the creation of a harmonious community, their enthusiasm was most engaging: "If you be present," wrote Frey to a friend, "at our meetings on New Year Day (a meeting specially appointed to celebrate the festival of humanity) if you would see their enthusiasm and the outburst of their best feelings, their wines mixed with the tears of pure brotherly love—you would say you are present at another descension of Holy Spirit." [20]

The process by which the Russian Jewish intellectuals assimilated the attitudes of the populist movement was not always identical, but certain recurrent patterns are clear. Most of them had read certain classics of populist literature—the most commonly read was perhaps Chernyshevsky's celebrated novel *What is to be Done?* All knew of, and revered, the terrorists who had taken the lives of many Russian officials and who were, in 1881, to assassinate Alexander II. And all had participated in fervent discussions with their fellow students on ". . . dimly understood high themes with the oft-recurring refrain of 'Bazarov, Hegel, liberty, Chernyshevsky, *v narod*' . . ." [21] The impression made by these conversations and readings was deep and lasting. Emma Goldman, the famous anarchist who came to America from Russia in 1885 was, at that time, "ignorant of the real meaning of socialism" but nonetheless sought to pattern her life after that of Vera, the heroine of Chernyshevsky's novel, who established a dressmaking shop to aid the poor working girls of St. Petersburg.[22] Goldman's close friend Alexander Berkman also found a suitable model in *What is to be Done?*—that of Rakhmetov, the dedicated revolutionary. "I am simply a revolutionist," Berkman writes in his memoirs, "an instrument for furthering the cause of humanity; in short, a Rakhmetov." [23] Dovid Edelshtat, the Yiddish poet and anarchist, relates in an autobiographical story how, at the age of fifteen, he encountered a populist named Vera who urged him to read the populist literature and added: "May Rakhmetov serve as a model for

762

your life." The revolutionary, who was eventually arrested, made a striking impression on the young boy:

> She not only preached that we must sacrifice all for the oppressed and the down-trodden, but her whole heart, her soul, her every thought, her whole life was devoted to those who had been the victims, to those who had borne on their shoulders the yoke of tyranny and despotism.[24]

It was, indeed, precisely this heroic quality of populism which attracted the Jewish intellectuals, and which they sought, with all their heart, to emulate. In the words of Moissaye Olgin, himself a Russian Jewish intellectual who became a Communist in America, "They [the Russian radical intellectuals] stand out like so many pillars of fire in the desert. Their voices sound like beautiful music in a prison-house. Their eyes saw the dawn when dark reigned all around. And their call stirred the depths of young souls when all was apathy and gloom." And the Russian Jewish intellectuals who arrived in America in the 1880s saw themselves as the inheritors of this glorious tradition, which represented everything good and noble in the world.[25]

763

Having arrived in the New World, the young idealists were faced with a severe problem—how to implement their ideals in a totally new environment. The problem was made especially acute by the general failure of the colonies, which were to serve as a sign of the redemption of a parasitic people. As one would-be pioneer commented, "If we can't be agriculturalists, why go to America?" Rather than engage in "unproductive" labor (as Mandelkorn termed his job as a clerk) some of the youths returned, disillusioned, to Russia.[26]

Most, however, stayed, and sought to find themselves in a world which seemed quite inhospitable to their ideals. The memoirs of a good number of these intellectuals testify to the extremely difficult early years. In the words of Khayim Spivakovsky (Spivak),

> After the stormy revolutionary life in Russia and the collapse of our ideals, we, the first Russian immigrants, spent our first years in America in a state of suspended animation. Without a goal in life, without ideals—in a word, we all felt like the *melamed* (traditional Jewish teacher) without pupils.[27]

Kobrin's friend, Boris, found America to be "A land without a and without a spirit," while Shmuel Garson, a graduate of the Vilna Jewish Teacher's Institute and one of the few intellectuals to have actually participated in the Russian revolutionary movement, was dismayed by the contrast between the "American spirit of materialism" and the "Russian spirit." The latter was ". . . what I had acquired from the Russian literature of my time —the spirit of compassion, the desire to build a society where there would be no oppressed or suffering." The belief in "going to the people," which Garson had received from his populist mentors, was not easily acted on in Boston, where he found himself in 1884.[28] And Phillip Krantz, too, the editor of *Di arbayter tsaytung,* confessed to the same feeling of alienation. The Russian revolutionary, he wrote in a letter to the Russian socialist journal *Znamia,* is hard pressed to maintain his revolutionary passion once he has left sacred Russia behind. "In a word, there is nothing sadder that the lot of the Russian intellectual abroad." [29] Emma Goldman and Alexander Berkman thought occasionally of returning to Russia, for "What could we hope to achieve in barren America? . . . In Russia we could engage in conspiratorial work. We belonged to Russia." [30] And Dovid Edelshtat wrote romantic poetry glorifying the Russia of his dreams, when

> Old Moscow is no longer seen,
> in the place of the ancient Kremlin—
> a great monument to Perovskaia
> erected by the Russian land! [31]

Alienation from American life and a romantic desire to return to an idealized Russia was the common lot of the Russian Jewish intellectuals in the 1880s. We now must consider the ways in which this alienation was eventually resolved.

In 1889 Michael Zametkin, one of the most notable of the Russian Jewish radicals in New York, wrote a letter expressing the dilemma of the radical intelligentsia in its new home:

> Some persecuted defenders of their country's [Russia's] rights found refuge in foreign countries. But the manly heart that beats in full accord with the interests of the unfortunate victims of universal plunder, tells its brave owner that here, too, there is work for him to do. And consciously and conscientiously he undertakes to fulfill his duty towards his brethren in his new country. But how changed the situation! How changed the environments. Free assemblage, free speech, self-government and many other things that stood as a leading-star and shone upon him who bravely fought

with the tyranny of a barbarian tzardom, these beautiful things, they are already here.[32]

In other words, how does one retain that glorious revolutionary purity, that legacy of Russian populism which the Jewish radical intellectuals had adopted as their own, in a country where basic freedoms are assured and the police is not particularly interested in making martyrs out of radicals? The first reaction to this serious dilemma was to cast doubts on the existence of American freedoms, to reject the "reformism" of American radicalism, and to create, on American soil, societies and, indeed, a social life which aimed at perpetuating the heroic and enthusiastic student life in Russia. Even Zametkin, whose admission of the completely changed American environment is an admission of the dilemma confronting the intelligentsia, asked: "Will the American hangman ever force upon *Znamia*'s mind the deplorable fact that the difference between tzardom and full-fledged plutocracy is but nominal after all? That remains to be seen." [33] A poet in the anarchist journal *Fraye arbayter shtime* noted that the old country was one of prisons and blood but America is no better than "a free land of slaves;" another correspondent, writing in 1890, made this comparison: "The Russian regime suffocates its freedom fighters, the American —well, I hope you have not yet forgotten the 11th of November, when five freedom fighters were legally murdered in the Russian manner." [34]

765

The general tendency to consider America no more free than Czarist Russia—despite certain obvious but superficial liberties enjoyed in the New World—was accompanied by an attempt, in the early years, to withdraw from American reality and establish a self-contained Russian radical community. As Spivak recalls in his memoirs, "Poor and lost we were here in the '80s, and friendship and love were the only sources of refreshment and strength." [35] And so the streets and cafes of the lower East Side in New York were converted into islands of Russian student life; the mood is well described by Morris Hillquit:

> They [the intellectuals] felt unhappy and forlorn in their workshops, but at night on the roofs they again lived in a congenial atmosphere. Once more they were students among students, forgetting the miseries of their hard and toilsome lives and enjoying the pleasures of freedom and companionship with the abandon and enthusiasm of youth . . . It was a slice of old Russian life that was

thus transported to Cherry Street by the uprooted young immigrants . . . Most of their evenings were spent in discussion. And what discussion! There was not a mooted question in science, philosophy, or politics that was not aired on the roofs in ardent, impassioned, and tumultuous debate . . . Communist anarchism, as it was then termed, was a simple creed and a romantic movement filled with thrilling conspiracies and acts of heroism and self-sacrifice. It had an irresistible attraction for the young and found many advocates on the Cherry Street roofs . . . It was amusing to hear these mild-mannered and soft-spoken boys and girls talk glibly about blowing up buildings and killing tyrants.

766 And Hillquit goes on to observe, "The fraternity on the roofs for a time was the main link between the idealism of my youth and the sordid realities of my new daily occupations." [36] It was, in a word, a method of resolving the deep feeling of alienation which seized the intellectuals in a country oblivious to their mission and their gifts.[37]

Along with informally structured efforts to recreate radical Russia in America went formal attempts to establish revolutionary organizations. A large number of these were founded in the 1880s —the "Propaganda Union," the "Russian Workers' Union," the "Russian Labor Lyceum," the "Russian Jewish Workers' Union," the "Jewish Workers' Union," the "Knights of Liberty," the "Pioneers of Liberty," the "Russian Progressive Union," and so forth.[38] Their names notwithstanding, these groups were, by and large, debating societies. In a clubbish atmosphere the Jewish radicals would meet to listen to lectures and to discuss various problems. Not surprisingly, a good deal of attention was paid to Russian problems (the language of these societies remained Russian though, as we shall see, attacks on this practice were soon forthcoming) and to the question of the Russian revolutionary's dilemma in America. Thus Abe Cahan, in a speech delivered at the Propaganda Union in 1882, had the following to say:

> We find ourselves in a country which is relatively free. We are looking here for a new home. But we dare not forget that great struggle for freedom which we experienced in our former home. At a time when we are concerned only with ourselves, our comrades, our heroes, our martyrs struggle over there, or suffer in Russian prisons.
>
> We dare not forget the struggle for freedom in our former home. We cannot do much from afar, but we can collect money.

> We must support that holy movement. The struggle of the Russian revolutionaries must remain deep in our hearts. We must not forget the martyrs who martyr themselves in Siberia, at hard labor.[39]

This interesting speech, which demonstrates the urgent desire on the part of Cahan and his colleagues to maintain their revolutionary credentials despite their having abandoned Russia (Cahan's guilty feelings are readily apparent) set the tone for the activities of this and the other societies. They established Russian libraries, celebrated such great events as the anniversary of Alexander II's assassination and, as Cahan had suggested, raised money for the Russian revolutionary movement.[40] The "stars" of the Russian Jewish colony in New York appeared before these societies and lectured, not only on socialist theory, but on such topics as "the family" and "the evolution of plants and animals." The organizations stood apart from the masses, catered to the intellectual elite, and, in the words of a contemporary, served as a "refuge" (*miklat*) for the alienated intelligentsia.[41] Thus Shoel Yanovsky attended a meeting of the "Russian Progressive Union" despite the fact that ". . . the actual aim of the meeting interested me very little; but the fact that the meetings were held in Russian, that people were coming to hear what others were saying in Russian, interested me very much." The meetings, Yanovsky continues, ". . . took me back, in my fantasies, to the old times, when I was still in Russia, when I had such beautiful and wonderful dreams."[42] For Alexander Berkman, too, ". . . the Fridays in the little dingy hall in the Ghetto, where bold imprecations are thundered against the tyranny and injustice of the existing, and winged words prophesy the near approach of a glorious dawn" served as a link between past and present, and made the present more bearable.[43] Far more important than the actual organizing achievements of these societies (we shall see that this amounted to very little) was their social function, which was to shield the little band of Russian Jewish intellectuals from the harshness of the American experience.

Along with this voluntary segregation from American life, quite naturally, went a rejection of American radical politics, which the young populist-minded youths regarded with no little scorn and condescension. Dovid Edelshtat, for example, made the point (a point often repeated by his colleagues) that the American radicals were far inferior to their Russian counterparts:

767

> When we consider the holy images of the Russian revolutionaries, full of self-sacrifice and immortal courage, and then we consider those who, in America, bear the name revolutionaries, what a sad comparison it is. At a time when the Russian revolutionaries amaze the world with their iron energy and holy spirit, our American revolutionaries offer empty phrases, with disgusting metaphysics, which they pass off as philosophy . . .[44]

Isaac Hourwich held similar opinions. Having personally known many Russian revolutionaries, and having participated in the movement in Petersburg and Minsk, he was contemptuous of American radicalism: "I have spent half my life in America," he writes in his memoirs, "where there never was and still is no revolutionary movement. Revolutionary declarations, which can be easily combined with daily business, I do not consider to constitute a revolutionary movement."[45] This attitude helps to explain why so many of the Russian Jewish intellectuals in the New World were attracted to the anarchist movement, which, at least in the early years of the Russian Jewish socialist movement, was its strongest faction. In this connection it is particularly instructive to quote the words of Leon Moiseyev (M. Leontiev) who came to America in 1891 and became active in the anarchist movement. When he arrived in New York, Moiseyev recalls,

768

> My ideological orientation was Marxist: science, capitalist development, concentration of capital, proletarianization and revolution. My revolutionary education, my feelings, my tradition was incompatible with the variety of socialism as taught in Germany and America. I would go to listen to a social democratic speaker and everything would please me until the last ten or five minutes when he would . . . claim that only through politics and votes might the workers take power. I couldn't swallow that. When I went to hear an anarchist speaker and he would say the same thing with a bit more heart, but without mentioning voting, my heart would beat faster, though I knew scarcely anything about anarchism.[46]

As Alexander Berkman noted, describing the Jewish intellectuals, ". . . the fire of Russia still smolders in their hearts;" it is remarkable to what extent, throughout the 1880s, even those intellectuals who rejected anarchism continued to regard the Russian terrorists as, in Hillquit's words, "the best and noblest people in the world." [47]

The political sentiments of the intellectual immigrants, while shielding them from the "mainstream," if such a term can be used, of American radical thought, predisposed them towards making alliances in America with people who reminded them of their Russian heroes. A case in point was William Frey, whose remarks on the New Odessa pioneers have been quoted above. Frey, whose real name was Vladimir Geins, was born into the Russian gentry class in 1839; a typical "repentent noble" type, he became a populist and came to the United States in 1868 where he established several utopian societies. In 1881 he came to New York to lecture, and found a ready audience among the Jewish intellectuals of *Am Olam*. Mandelkorn, whose Odessa *Am Olam* group persuaded Frey to join them in New Odessa in 1883, found him to be ". . . an extraordinary character of his kind, a man of beauty and refinement of the old Russian military aristocracy," while Abe Cahan, despite his skepticism concerning utopian ventures, describes Frey as "one of the most remarkable people whom I have ever met. Such personalities appear on the earth only seldom . . . a few of us fell under his influence like disciples of a hassidic 'Rebbe.' " [48] Gregory Weinstein, an *Am Olam* member from Vilna, found Frey to be a "unique personality" while Hillquit remarks that his ". . . nobility of character and purity of life made a profound impression on the youthful members of the Russian colony . . ." [49] While the love-affair between Frey and the intellectuals did not last long—he managed to alienate even his most devoted supporters with his increasingly eccentric ways in New Odessa—the episode is a revealing one. For Frey possessed precisely what the intellectuals found lacking in American radicalism—that total devotion and dedication, that "holiness" (Mandelkorn actually describes Frey's family as the "holy family") which had characterized the fanatics of the populist movement.

Another political figure who excited the imagination of the intellectuals—and for the same reasons—was the German anarchist Johann Most. Emma Goldman, who was to become Most's lover, quickly fell under his spell and found herself "almost hypnotized." [50] Y. Benekvit converted to anarchism after hearing him speak, and Y. Kopelov, revealingly enough, found that Most resembled the "Rebbe" Leybele Kapitser, whose sermons he had heard in Bobruisk. He possessed "The same enthusiasm, the same devotion to his ideal and to his truth, and the same readiness to

769

sacrifice himself for the ideal. Khayim Vaynberg, who also became a "Mostian," recalls that Most knew how "to hypnotize his audience so that they would follow him whenever he might call them to struggle on the barricades." [51]

The very refusal of men like Frey and Most to consider compromise and, indeed, to make the slightest effort to surrender to the American way of life, made them venerated figures on the lower East Side of New York. Their attractiveness to the intellectual immigrants had its roots in the same psychological need as did the attraction of the "society of the roofs" and the various organized "Unions" of the 1880s. And yet, this need to be sheltered from the new environment, this rejection of the environment, could not endure forever. The history of the radicals in the 1880s is, to a great extent, the history of their coming to terms with American life. Despite their occasional longing for the excitement and danger of Russia, the intellectuals came to realize that they had come to stay, and by 1891 Cahan had gone so far as to announce that "Yes, America is the new home, the only home of the Jewish people . . . America is the only place where Jews can find a little peace." [52] This process of "americanization" was, of course, a reflection of the simple passage of time—it is difficult to remain an "internal emigré" forever. But the process was a paradoxical one, for it was intricately involved with the intellectuals' discovery of the Jewish proletariat and their creation of a new movement which spoke, not Russian, and not English, but Yiddish. The creation of this Yiddish-speaking movement served as a final resolution of that alienation which was the hallmark of the intellectuals' condition in America.

We have seen that the Russian Jewish intellectuals who came to America were basically "populist," and initially rejected the practical socialism which they encountered in the New World. They were certainly not oriented towards the creation of a labor movement concerned with dollars and cents issues—Cahan tells us, for example, that the leader of the "Jewish Propaganda Union" considered labor organization "not dangerous enough" to interest a real revolutionary.[53] But as the years passed their attitude towards such activities changed. Central to this change was their "discovery" of the Jewish proletariat in New York and its desperate situation. Such a discovery was by no means inevitable and is to be

770

associated, first of all, with the important fact that the Jewish working class as it evolved in New York (as in London) struck the radicals as being quite different from that which they had known in the old country. They had never regarded the traditional Jewish *bal-melokhe* (artisan) in the Pale of Settlement as a worthy subject for their energies, a view which their colleagues who remained in Russia continued to hold until the early 1890s.[54] But, as Hillquit remarks in his memoirs, they found that, in New York, the Jewish artisans ". . . evolved for the first time a solid proletarian block." The same point was made by the Jewish socialist pioneer Morris Vintshevsky, who discovered in London (he did not arrive in America until 1894) that the Jewish artisans from Russia had been transformed into "a modern proletariat. . . . What our little circle of propagandists had previously encountered almost only in the literature now stood before our eyes." [55] Perhaps this modern proletariat, created by the great needle industries, might take the place of the Russian peasantry as a class upon which the radical intelligentsia would lavish its attentions.

771

This all-important discovery of the Jewish proletariat was made inevitable by an important change in the social situation of the Jewish intelligentsia. In Russia they had, by and large, supported themselves by teaching. Isaac Hourwich had given lessons to Jewish students seeking secular knowledge; Israel Mandelkorn served in Odessa as a tutor to Jewish students hoping to enter Gymnasium; Abe Cahan was a teacher at an elementary school in Velich before coming to America. But in America there was no need for this type of teacher, and since the radical immigrants had to earn a living, they had no choice but to follow the "masses" into the shops of the garment industry. They were obliged to remove their gymnasium uniforms and don the clothes of an American working man.[56] They therefore became, in America, not the peasants which they hoped to become, but simple workers laboring for low wages in sweatshops.

The favorite trade of the intelligentsia was shirt-making, because it could be learned easily and was not particularly demanding. As Hillquit informs us, it was ". . . the favorite occupation of the circle of young Russian intellectuals in which I moved . . . the work was not exacting, and the surroundings were not uncongenial. The operators in the stuffy little workshop spent at least as much time in discussing social and literary topics as in turning out shirts, and the whir of the sewing machines was often accompanied by the loud and hearty sound of revolutionary songs." [57] Among the more celebrated shirt-makers were Louis Miller and Michael Zametkin; Leon Kobrin, who remarks in his memoirs that he and his fellow intellectuals were "mama's boys" in Russia, became a shirt-maker because "one didn't need any special skills" and only took two weeks to learn.[58] Abe Cahan went to work in a cigar factory, where he converted the Jewish labor organizer Bernard Vaynshteyn to socialism; Shoel Yanovsky became a hat-maker, Emma Goldman made waists, and the radical poet Yoysef Bovshover became a furrier. Khayim Vaynberg became a cigar-maker, and Hillel Solotarov worked as a tailor. In this manner the Russian Jewish intelligentsia was "proletarianized" in the New World.

This "proletarianization" was of relatively short duration—many of the intellectuals—among them Spivak, Alenikov, and Solotarov—took advantage of American opportunities and became professionals. Abe Cahan and Louis Miller left the shops to become English teachers at immigrant schools. But we may assume that their exposure to working conditions made them more sensitive to the needs of the Jewish working class and presented to them the possibility of organizing this class into unions. Unlike the radicals who had remained in Russia, and who by their own admission were quite isolated from the Jewish masses, conditions in America brought the "people" and the intelligentsia together. And this led to extremely important results. We know, for example, from the account of Bernard Vaynshteyn, that the "intellectual proletariat" in the shirt-making trade established a union to improve working conditions in 1884—in 1888, when the United Hebrew Trades was established, this union was re-founded and became the "pride" of the Jewish labor movement because "The entire Jewish-Russian intelligentsia belonged to it." [59] Indeed, the United Hebrew Trades itself, which was organized in order to encourage the organization of Jewish labor, was conceived by Y. Magidov, an intellectual from Odessa who came to America in 1886 and worked as a shirt-maker. The first secretary was Bernard Vaynshteyn, who had come to America with the *Am Olam* and who had also worked in various factories.[60] We know that Michael Zametkin, who became a shirt-maker in New York, also became

772

one of the leading union organizers in that city; and Shoel Yanovsky, despite his typical Russian radical background, became conscious of the extremes of proletarian exploitation only after his
experiences in an American sweatshop.[61] We may assume that Hillquit's realization that the situation of the Jewish proletariat
"fairly cried out for sympathy" was a result of his actual experience in the shop.[62]

To be sure, the proletarianization of the Jewish intelligentsia
was not the only reason for its decision to "go to the people,"
the people now being the Jewish workers. There was, too, the
very important influence of the German social democrats in New
York. For Cahan, as for many of his colleagues, the *Volks-Zeitung*
(the German social democratic organ) was a particularly important influence: "In each number we found Marxist explanations
for daily events—food for new thought." Some of the leading German socialists became familiar figures at Jewish radical meetings—
especially Sergei Shevich, whose Baltic German origins and knowledge of Russian made him a particularly acceptable figure.[63] But
the German influence—which was also most instrumental in the
founding of the United Hebrew Trades itself—was not as important as the discovery of the masses via proletarianization.

By the second half of the decade of the 1880s we detect a
striking change in the ideas of the radical intelligentsia. In 1887
Nikolai Alenikov, the former leader of the Kievan *Am Olam*,
made a speech urging Jewish Russian radicals to enter the Jewish labor movement; speaking at a meeting of the "Russian Progressive Union," held in 1887, another *Am Olam* alumnus, Rayevsky, made the point that the place of the Jewish intelligentsia
was in the Jewish labor movement, and that the use of Russian
should give way to the use of Yiddish.[64] In 1890 an unnamed socialist remarked in the pages of *Znamia* that the ". . . Jewish
workers, who were looked upon up until this time as a hindrance
to the workers' movement, can be extraordinarily useful in the
ranks of the organized proletariat." [65] By 1890, Cahan informs us,
"As speakers, agitators, and organizers we were closely connected
with every important event in the life of the Jewish unions. We
took part in every strike and in almost every settlement. We were
in the center of all union activity." [66] From messianic politics and
the worship of Russian terrorists, the intelligentsia had proceeded

to trade union activities which nothing in their radical background had truly prepared them for.

The transformation of the intelligentsia into labor leaders also implied its transformation into a Yiddish-speaking group. Abe Cahan pioneered in the use of the people's language, and was the first to address (in 1882) a workers meeting in that language.[67] Yiddish was resisted by the intelligentsia at first, as was the notion of a specifically *Jewish* labor movement. The populist background of the intellectual radicals had definitely not included any recognition of the need for a Jewish movement—on the contrary, the russified intelligentsia was far from being interested in Jewish survival. And while the *Am Olam* was a movement dedicated to renewal through agriculture, it had, in fact, little Jewish content. This, at least, was the opinion of Israel Mandelkorn, who reports that the New Odessa group decided against the adoption of any specific Jewish characteristics. "The majority were far from Jewish life," he tells us, and the members regarded themselves as "a community of *workingmen*." [68] William Frey, while reporting that the Jews in New Odessa "are proud of their nationality" added that they had all abandoned their religion and did not even perform circumcision.[69] But if the intellectuals, having discovered the Jewish proletariat, were to have any success in organizing it, they must speak its language. Thus A. Ortman, who came to America in 1888, joined the Russian language branch of the American Socialist Labor Party, and participated in the journal *Znamia,* observed: "We became quickly convinced that in order to influence the masses we had to speak to them in their own language."[70] And Phillip Krantz, in a letter to the editors of *Znamia,* urged his fellow intellectuals to learn Yiddish; "Nothing is easier than to learn to write in Yiddish," he informs his colleagues, adding that he himself didn't know a word of the language five years ago but quickly learned.[71]

The Russian Jewish intelligentsia was therefore "yiddishized;" Dovid Edelshtat, a Russian poet in Russia, became a Yiddish poet in America so that his poetry might reach the Jewish working class; Leon Kobrin assiduously read the Yiddish press so that he could write short stories in the "jargon," as the language was affectionately (and also scornfully) called.[72] And the intelligentsia soon became not only users of Yiddish but its champion; as was the case, later on, within the ranks of the Russian Bundists, Yiddish came to be glorified as the language of the Jewish masses.[73] And, as is well known, the American Jewish labor movement gave enormous impetus to the flourishing of Yiddish culture in America.

Let us attempt a summary of the points made in this essay. The Russian Jewish intellectuals who came to America in the 1880s—whether on their own or as members of the *Am Olam* movement, were radicals whose political ideology was vague but populist-inspired. In America they sought to shield themselves against the strange environment of the New World by creating their own societies—formal and informal—which sought to perpetuate the Russian radical tradition as they understood it. For this reason many became anarchists, and many became followers of political leaders who reminded them of the martyr-heroes of the People's Will and the other populist factions. Gradually, however, this intelligentsia became "americanized," a process which was the result of their discovery of the Jewish proletariat and their acceptance of a new mission—to organize this proletariat and to uplift it economically and spiritually. This new orientation—the result of the passage of time, the influence of the German social democrats, and, above all, the proletarianization of the intelligentsia in the New World—was accompanied by a shift to Yiddish on the part of the intellectuals. They therefore gave up their essentially Russian orientation, though they certainly retained a sentimental attachment to the old country and to the politics of the Russian revolutionary movement.[74]

775

One final point must be made. While it is true that the intelligentsia was americanized, and largely abandoned its absolute devotion to messianic politics, it also retained the radical zeal of the Russian movement. This radical background, which was reinforced through the arrival of new intellectuals from the old country in the 1890s and, especially, following the revolution of 1905, imparted to the Jewish labor movement a radical orientation largely lacking in other labor movements in the United States. In other words, we have here a two-way process, whereby the Russian intelligentsia was americanized and therefore became concerned with trade unionism, while the Jewish labor movement was to a certain extent russified via the leadership of the Russian radical intelligentsia. This radical orientation has certainly been a distinguishing feature of the Jewish labor movement throughout its history.

## NOTES

1 Aleksander Harkavy, *Perakim mi-khayai* (New York, 1935), p. 39; Leon Kobrin, *Mayne fuftsik yor in Amerike* (Buenos Aires, 1955), p. 20. Another intellectual immigrant of the period describes how he and his friends voyaged to America in a special cabin, apart from the other travelers; see Yisroel Iser Katsovitsh, *Zekhtsik yor lebn* (New York, 1919), p. 214.

2 In 1881 Jews constituted 12.3% of all Russian Gymnasium (High School) students—in 1863 the figure was 3.2%. See P. Marek, *Ocherki po istorii prosveshcheniia evreev v Rossii* (Moscow, 1909), pp. 166–167. Those Jews who attained a certain level of secular knowledge through self-education but were unable to finish Russian schools, were often called "one-half intellectuals."

3 Kahan, *Bleter fun mayn lebn*, II (New York, 1926), 34; see also pp. 82–83. Another intellectual immigrant describes his dress upon arriving in America; he had ". . . long hair, a pince-nez, a peaked cap and the uniform of the 'real school' (technical High School) . . ." Before applying for work he acquired "American working clothes," thus symbolizing his transformation from student-intellectual to proletarian; see "Iz vospominanii emigranta" in G. M. Prais, *Russkie evrei v Amerike* (St. Petersburg, 1893), p. 10.

4 There is an extensive literature on the Russian intelligentsia. A useful source is Richard Pipes, ed., *The Russian Intelligentsia* (New York, 1961).

5 Y. Kopelov, *Amol in Amerike* (Warsaw, 1928), p. 7.

6 Israel Mandelkorn, *My Recollections* (n.d., typescript located in the Frey Papers in the New York Public Library), p. 12.

7 Yankev Milkh, *Oytobiografishe skitsn* (New York, 1946), pp. 183–184; Shneyer Beyly, *Zikhroynes* (New York, American Jewish autobiographies, typescript, YIVO Institute, archives), p. 17.

8 Beyly, *op. cit.*, p. 17.

9 A group was also formed in Vilna, although the wave of pogroms did not reach Lithuania. The best general study of the movement is A. Menes, "Di 'Am Olam'—bavegung," in E. Tsherikover, ed., *Geshikhte fun der yidisher arbeter-bavegung in di Fareynikte shtatn*, II (New York, 1945), 203–238. It should be pointed out that the reaction on the part of Russian radicals to the pogroms was mixed; some went so far as to praise the anti-Semitic excesses as "revolutionary" acts by the oppressed peasants. Some Jewish radicals shared this view, as is demonstrated by the following remarks of Isaac Hourwich, a pioneer of the Russian Jewish socialist movement and later an activist in New York: ". . . we in our revolutionary circle remained indifferent to the affair [the pogroms]. We were also under the influence of the theory that it was an uprising of the folk, and all such uprisings are good since they revolutionize the masses. As for the fact that Jews suffered—did not the Russian revolutionaries of gentry origin call upon the peasants to stage an uprising against their own fathers and brothers?" See

Yitskhok-Ayzik Ben Arye Tsvi Ha-Leyvi (Isaac Hourwich), "Zikhroynes fun an apikoyres," *Fraye arbayter shtime*, June 23, 1922. Yankev Gordin, the celebrated Jewish playwright, published an article in 1881 blaming the Jewish moneylenders ("protsentniks") for the pogroms; see Kalmen Marmor, *Yankev Gordin* (New York, 1953), pp. 36 ff. For a study of the reaction of Pavel Axelrod, the Menshevik leader, see Abraham Asher, "Pavel Axelrod: A Conflict between Jewish Loyalty and Revolutionary Dedication," *Russian Review*, XXIV, No. 3 (July, 1965), 249–265.

[10] "Iz vospominanii emigranta," *op. cit.*, p. 5.

[11] As quoted by Mandelkorn, *op. cit.*, p. 37.

[12] Katsovitsh, *op. cit.*, p. 211; Katherine Sabsovich, *Adventures in Idealism. A Personal Record of the Life of Professor Sabsovich* (New York, 1922), p. 13. Sabsovich was one of the leaders of the Odessa *Am Olam* and later the founder of the Woodbine colony in New Jersey.

[13] Beyly, *op. cit.*, p. 20; Moses Freeman, *Fuftsik yor geshikhte fun yidishn lebn in Filadelfye* (Philadelphia, n.d.), p. 199. In the words of a Russian Jewish colonist who reported back to Russia in 1886, "The only salvation for oppressed Israel lies in agricultural labor." See M. Zayfert, "Russkie evrei i zemledelenie v Amerike," *Nedel'naia khronika voskhoda*, No. 34, Aug. 24, 1886, p. 925.

[14] Mandelkorn, *op. cit.*, p. 65. For Bokal's views on the problem of establishing communistic colonies see Ben-Ami's report, originally published in 1882 and republished in *Tsherikover, op. cit.*, 471–474.

[15] The estimate is from Prais, *op. cit.*, 46. In 1886 Zayfert, *op. cit.*, p. 925, estimated that 344 Russian Jewish families, or 1,720 people in all, were settled in colonies.

[16] *Bleter, op. cit.*, I (New York, 1926), 386 ff.

[17] "Zikhroynes," *op. cit.*; for his description of the Minsk circle see *Fraye arbayter shtime*, March 16, 1923.

[18] On Krantz's revolutionary past see his remarks in *Di arbayter tsaytung*, I, No. 19, July 11, 1890 ("Mayne erinerungen vegn Grinevetsky"). For Zametkin's biography see the obituary in *Forverts*, March 7, 1935 and the *Leksikon fun der nayer yidisher literatur* (New York, 1960), III, 543 ff. Louis Miller, who together with his brother L. S. Bandes participated in revolutionary circles in Vilna, is another example. Miller came to America in 1886 and became one of the leaders of the Jewish socialist and trade union movement; he also worked on the Russian socialist paper *Znamia*, which appeared in 1889–1890.

[19] Kahan, II, *op. cit.*, 44; Kh. Spivak, "Erinerungen fun Kahan's grine tsaytn," *Yubileyum-shrift tsu Ab. Kahan's 50stn geburtstog* (New York, 1910), p. 33; Morris Hillquit, *Loose Leaves from a Busy Life* (New York, 1934), p. 8. Kopelov, *op. cit.*, p. 138, comments that "The majority of them [the intellectuals] knew very little about socialism and especially about various socialist factions."

[20] The first quotation is from an undated letter from Frey to an unnamed correspondent, presumably written in 1884 (Frey papers, New York Public Library). The second is from a letter by Frey to Edward King, dated Jan. 4, 1884. Frey is of the opinion, in this letter, that ". . . the Semitic race, which gave to the world the three grate (sic) religions of the past will be a leading race in the next religious revival." Frey, of whom more will be said below, was by this time an apostle of Compte's "religion of humanity."

777

21 The quotation is from Alexander Berkman, *Prison Memoirs of an Anarchist* (New York, 1912), p. 5. Berkman, who was from Kovno in Russia, came to America in 1887. Bazarov was the controversial hero of Turgenev's *Fathers and Sons*, while *v narod* ("to the people") was the slogan of the populist movement in the 1870s.

22 Emma Goldman, *Living My Life* (New York, 1934), pp. 9, 26. While still in Russia, she tells us, the populist terrorists ". . . became to me heroes and martyrs, henceforth my guiding stars." (28).

23 Berkman, *op. cit.*, pp. 9–10. In fact, he assumed the name Rakhmetov upon arriving in Pittsburgh to carry out his "deed," that is to assassinate the steel magnate Frick.

24 Dovid Edelshtat, "Vera," in *Dovid Edelshtat gedenk-bukh* (New York, etc., 1953), pp. 294, 293.

25 Moissaye Olgin, *The Soul of the Russian Revolution* (New York, 1917), p. 44. There is abundant material in the literature concerning the populist attitudes of the Jewish intelligentsia in America. The intellectuals whom Mandelkorn encountered in Odessa ". . . only offered me talk and disputes about the heroes of the novel *What is to be Done?* or Turgeneff's Bazaroff" (Mandelkorn, *op. cit.*, p. 12); Cahan's introduction to socialism was via the literature of the populist parties "Land and Freedom" and the "People's Will," as well as the inevitable *What is to be Done?* (*Bleter*, I, *op. cit.*, 386 ff.); Sh. Yanovsky was influenced by his reading of Dobroliubov, Belinsky, Pisarev, and the radical poet Nekrasov, who was also Edelshtat's hero (Shoel Yanovsky, *Ershte yorn fun yidishn frayhaytlekhn sotsyalizm* (New York, 1948), pp. 23–24; Kh. Rayevsky, who together with Cahan edited a Yiddish socialist paper in 1886, refers in a memoir to his "nihilist" past (*Yubileyum-shrift, op. cit.*, p. 15); M. Kats, a leading Jewish anarchist in America, is described by his biographer as having arrived in America in 1888 as a full-fledged *narodovoletz* (populist), (M. Melamed, "Kinder-yorn, ertsiung un der ershter aroystrit in der velt" in *M. Kats zamlbukh*, Philadelphia, 1925, pp. 5 ff.); Shneyer Beyly, *op. cit.*, recalls in his memoirs that he read the works of Mikhailovsky, Belinsky, Dobroliubov, and Pisarev; Leon Kobrin, who became a well known Yiddish writer, writes that he and his friends had no definite ideology but hated Russian despotism and believed simply in "revolution, whatever kind it might be." (*Mayne fuftsik yor, op. cit.*, p. 28.) In America among the favorite books of the intelligentsia was Stepniak's celebration of populist virtues, *The Career of a Nihilist*, which was serialized in *Di arbayter tsaytung* and, naturally enough, Chernyshevsky's *What is to be Done?* which was also published in the Yiddish socialist press (it appeared in *Der morgenshtern*, apparently in a translation by M. Zametkin).

26 The quotations are from Katsovitsh, *op. cit.*, p. 223, and Mandelkorn, *op. cit.*, p. 55. For information concerning the return of disappointed *Am Olam* members to Russia see Beyly, *op. cit.*, p. 20.

27 "Erinerungen," *op. cit.*, p. 31. For another description of the sad lot of the Russian Jewish intellectual in America see *Russkie evrei*, IV, No. 24, June 18, 1882, 926; the correspondent notes that the intellectual's ". . . Russian education doesn't do him any good, and no aid awaits him, for he is immediately seen to

the door with the words: 'be proud, you are an educated man, you must help yourself!' "

28 Kobrin, *op. cit.*, p. 122; memoirs of Shmuel Garson (typescript available at the YIVO Institute, American Jewish autobiographies collection), p. 34. On a somewhat different level, another educated immigrant was annoyed by the fact that Americans had no interest in his cultural achievements: "In the old home," he says, "I was able to speak with the Jews in Yiddish, with the local Germans in German (the author came from Courland) and in Russian with the intelligentsia, and now I find myself in a country where no one is interested in my knowledge and education in Hebrew, Yiddish, German, and Russian, so long as I don't know any English." (Memoirs of Philip Bernhardt, 1942, typescript available at the YIVO Institute, American Jewish autobiographies collection.)

29 *Znamia*, No. 3, Feb. 15, 1890.

30 *Living My Life, op. cit.*, p. 70.

31 *Fraye arbayter shtime*, No. 31, Jan. 30, 1891. Sofia Perovskaia was executed in 1881 for her role in the assassination of Alexander II.

32 The letter was published in the *Workmen's Advocate*, V, No. 8, Feb. 23, 1889, on the occasion of the publication of *Znamia*, a Russian-language socialist journal which appeared in New York.

33 *Ibid.*

34 R. Rozenblum, "Kenst du dos land?," *Fraye arbayter shtime*, No. 110, May 26, 1893; Yoysef Maytes, *ibid.*, No. 11, Sept. 12, 1890. The latter reference is to the execution of the anarchists involved in the Chicago Haymarket Affair of 1886, an event which made a great impression on the Jewish radicals. In *Di Nyu yorker yudishe folkstsaytung*, hereafter referred to as *Folkstsaytung*, a Yiddish socialist paper which began to appear in 1886, M. Zayfert published a list of thirteen "credos" (modelled after Maimonides' credo of Jewish faith) one of which reads as follows: "I believe that America is a free country, but only for the capitalist; he is free to suck the blood of the workers." (No. 4, July 16, 1886.) Abe Cahan's reaction to America was particularly interesting: "I felt America's liberty every minute. It seemed to me I could breathe more freely and more deeply than ever before. At the same time however I said to myself: 'But this is all a prison of capital.'" (*Bleter, op. cit.*, II, 90.)

35 Spivak, *op. cit.*, p. 31.

36 Hillquit, *op. cit.*, pp. 2 ff.

37 For an interesting description of another meeting place for the Jewish radicals—the home of Abraham Netter—see Michael Kan, "In Neters keler," *Dovid Edelshtat gedenk-bukh, op. cit.*, pp. 183–184. A description of a cafe on the lower East Side, to which Emma Goldman was taken in 1889 upon her arrival in New York, is found in her memoirs *Living My Life, op. cit.*, p. 5: "Everybody talked, gesticulated, and argued, in Yiddish and Russian, each competing with the other." This hot-house atmosphere was regarded by some observers as unhealthy; thus Anna Strunsky wrote to a young Jewish intellectual in 1897 urging him not to come to New York: ". . . there is even danger of your getting into bad society—for our Jewish socialist comrades who are ignorant and ill-mannered and who sit all day and night talking sophistry in the coffee-saloons or Labor Lyceum, make a very bad society indeed." (Edlin Papers, YIVO Institute.)

38 The general history of these societies is to be found in *Tsherikover*, II, *op. cit.*, 239 ff.

39 *Bleter*, II, *op. cit.*, 105. In 1887 N. Alenikov, the former leader of the Kiev *Am Olam*, spoke at the "Russian Progressive Union" on the "Duties of the Russian-Jewish youth in the United States." Alenikov urged the Russian Jewish intellectuals not to forget the Russian struggle; see *Folkstsaytung*, No. 30, Jan. 14, 1887. But Alenikov had another message as well; see note 64.

40 The best source for the activities of these various societies is the Yiddish socialist press of the 1880s, which clearly demonstrates their continued Russian orientation. Thus as late as 1889 the "Russian Progressive Union" announced the founding of a new Russian library "so that every worker, who understands Russian, will be able to read about and study social questions, for a small fee" (*Folkstsaytung*, No. 137, Jan. 4, 1889).

41 Kopelov, *op. cit.*, p. 174. See also, on the character of the early societies, Kahan, *Bleter*, *op. cit.*, II, 139. B. Vaynshteyn describes the "Russian Labor Union" as "aristocratic" in nature (*Fertsik yor in der yidisher arbeter bavegung*, New York, 1924, p. 45) but also notes that the "Russian Jewish Workers' Union" catered to the less educated because Yiddish was spoken there. Y. A. Benekvit, *Durkhgelebt un durkhgetrakht* (New York, 1934) attended, in 1887, meetings of the "Russian National League," which had been established by the intellectuals in order to protest the signing of a Russian-American trade agreement; he found that it had no connection with the masses (p. 55).

42 Yanovsky, *op. cit.*, p. 59.

43 Berkman, *op. cit.*, p. 207.

44 Dovid Edelshtat, "Eyn vort tsu di yidishe revolutsyonern," *Fraye arbayter shtime*, No. 5, Aug. 1, 1890.

45 "Zikhroynes fun an apikoyres," *Fraye arbayter shtime*, Nov. 11, 1921.

46 Leon Moiseyev, "M. Kats—der fareynignder element in der bavegung," *M. Kats zamlbukh*, *op. cit.*, p. 39.

47 Berkman, *op. cit.*, p. 84; *Di arbayter tsaytung*, No. 7, April 18, 1890. Hillquit also includes under this heading the Chicago martyrs of the Haymarket affair and the Paris communards. A. Mirovich, one of the founders of the "Jewish Propaganda Union," went so far as to name his son after one of the terrorists who had assassinated Alexander II; see Kahan, *op. cit.*, II, 139.

48 Mandelkorn, *op. cit.*, p. 62; Kahan, *op. cit.*, II, 123.

49 Gregory Weinstein, *The Ardent Eighties and After* (New York, 1947), p. 84; Hillquit, *op. cit.*, pp. 5–6. For information on Frey see Avrahm Yarmolinsky, *A Russian's American Dream. A Memoir on William Frey* (Lawrence, 1965).

50 Goldman, *op. cit.*, p. 38.

51 Benekvit, *op. cit.*, pp. 48 ff.; Kopelov, *op. cit.*, p. 114; Khayim Leyb Vaynberg, *Fertsik yor in kamf far sotsyaler bafrayung* (Los Angeles & Philadelphia, 1952), p. 26.

52 *Di arbayter tsaytung*, II, No. 21, May 22, 1891.

53 *Bleter*, *op. cit.*, II, 139.

54 Throughout the so-called "circle period" or the period of "propaganda," which lasted until the early 1890s, the Russian Jewish socialists active in the north-west provinces of the Empire did not consider the Jewish artisans of such

cities as Vilna and Minsk as a real proletariat; they changed their minds only with the transition from "propaganda" to "agitation." The "discovery" of the Jewish proletariat by the Jewish intelligentsia was made first in London, and then in New York.

55 Hillquit, *op. cit.*, p. 16; M. Vintshevsky, *Erinerungen* (Moscow, 1926), p. 170. Vintshevsky goes on to compare the Jewish proletarians in London, whom he regarded as true "wage slaves," with the journeymen of Russia who might be workers today, and owners of a shop tomorrow.

56 There is a description of this external transformation in "Iz vospominanii emigranta," *op. cit.*, pp. 10–11.

57 Hillquit, *op. cit.*, p. 32; see also Yanovsky, *op. cit.*, p. 53; Vaynshteyn, *op. cit.*, pp. 65 ff.

58 Kobrin, *op. cit.*, p. 28.

59 Vaynshteyn, *op. cit.*, p. 68.

60 On Magidov see *Leksikon, op. cit.*, V, 389–390. Vaynshteyn, *op. cit.*, pp. 75 ff.; see also Vaynshteyn, *Yidishe yunyons in Amerike* (New York, 1929), pp. 143 ff.

61 Yanovsky, *op. cit.*, pp. 54 ff. Yanovsky writes that the exploitation of Jewish workers in New York was far worse than anything he had known in his native city, Pinsk, where "The air in the workroom was fine and clear."

62 Hillquit, *op. cit.*, p. 17.

63 Kahan, *op. cit.*, II, 87–88. German, moreover, was an easier language for the intellectual immigrants than English; a good many had some acquaintance with it. See, for example, G. Weinstein, *op. cit.*, p. 23, and Benekvit, *op. cit.*, pp. 48 ff.

64 *Folkstsaytung*, No. 30, Jan. 14, 1887; *ibid.*, No. 40, March 25, 1887.

65 *Znamia*, No. 3, Feb. 15, 1890.

66 Kahan, *op. cit.*, III, 49.

67 *Ibid.*, II, 107 ff., and the description in Vaynshteyn, *op. cit.*, pp. 43 ff.

68 Mandelkorn, *op. cit.*, pp. 67, 68.

69 Frey, "Lecture to American Neighbors on Life at New Odessa" (1884?), Frey Papers, New York Public Library.

70 A. Ortman, "A bletl geshikhte (erinerungen, vi azoy di 'Tsukunft' iz gegrindet gevorn)," *Di tsukunft*, XVII, No. 1, Jan. 1912, 58.

71 *Znamia*, No. 3.

72 Another example was the case of Yankev Gordin, a russified intellectual from Poltava who, in America, became a celebrated Yiddish dramatist. Gordin was not involved directly in the labor movement but his first Yiddish writing appeared in the *Arbayter tsaytung*. See Marmor, *op. cit.*, pp. 47 ff.

73 See the interesting exchange between J. Finn, a Jewish radical from Boston, and Rabbi Solomon Schindler on the question of Yiddish in the pages of the *Workmen's Advocate*, No. 14, April 6, 1889. Schindler claims that Yiddish is a jargon "which only the *unintelligent* speak" while Finn says that ". . . I must say that the jargon is as much worthy of being called a language as the Roumanian or Bulgarian, so long as 6 millions of people speak it." In the next issue M. Kohn, a leading anarchist, writes: ". . . how do you [Schindler] know

whether our jargon is spoken by the unintelligent only, since you do not understand that tongue at all?" (No. 15, April 15, 1889).

[74] Most of the radicals were, in later years, only too happy to lend their financial support to Russian radicals. Y. Kopelov, *op. cit.*, p. 454, writing on the occasion of a trip to the United States by a Russian social revolutionary emissary, confesses that "Every party which struggled against Czarism was dear and beloved to me." M. Kats aided G. Gershuni when the famous Russian populist came to America in 1907 (Kopelov, "M. Kats's tetikayt in der anarkhistisher un sots. revolutsyonerer bavegung," *M. Kats zamlbukh, op. cit.*, p. 28).

# THE JEWISH LABOR MOVEMENT IN AMERICA:
## A Social Interpretation

by MOSES RISCHIN

Over half a century ago, William M. Leiserson prepared the first scholarly study of the origins of the Jewish labor movement in America.[1] Ever since, historians of American labor have incorporated the story of this development into their texts. Yet until recently, little appreciating the movement's dynamics, scholars have failed to probe for its larger significance. It is the intent of this study to place the Jewish labor saga of the early twentieth century in the wider perspective of American social history. In so doing, an interpretation will emerge which, hopefully, will lend depth to our understanding of the American labor movement.

783

Labor historians have alluded to English and German no less than to Jewish and other group influences upon the American labor scene. But they have regarded these influences as at best tangential. Consequently, they have taken little account of the ethnic context of American life. Nowhere did they recognize or attempt to relate the differently paced, often contrasting, ethnic styles to one another. The crucial turning points in immigrant histories, the play of trans-Atlantic forces, and the sea-changes in the group lives of America's immigrants —these were peripheral to their chief concerns. As a result, the American labor story was left devoid of its significant and exciting ethnic dimension.

In part, the parochialism of labor historians has been due to a failure in discernment as well as in sensibility. Trained as labor economists, they were confined by the narrowness of both their dis-

---

[1] William M. Leiserson, *History of the Jewish Labor Movement in New York City* (B.A. thesis, 1908, University of Wisconsin, on deposit at YIVO Institute of Jewish Research).

MOSES RISCHIN, *author of* The Promised City: New York's Jews, 1870-1914 *(Harvard University Press, 1962), is currently visiting lecturer in American history at the University of California at Los Angeles.*

Originally published in *Labor History* (Fall 1963). Reprinted by permission of *Labor History*.

cipline and their interests. More fundamentally, their preconceptions were molded by a climate of opinion in the first four decades of the twentieth century that shunned sympathetic investigations of the nation's ethnic patterns. The progressive spirit shaped the writing of American labor history, and it was committed to the gospel of social uniformity. The fear that the country would be Europeanized, indeed Balkanized, before the latest immigrants could be assimilated intimidated even those humanitarian reformers most deeply involved in the fight for social justice for immigrants. Inordinately sensitive to racial differences, these scholars rejected all ethnic ties—except, of course, the Anglo-Saxon—as inimical to American nationality and to the American labor scene. In an era given to validating the Americanness of the American past, John R. Commons inevitably espoused racism and ultra-nationalism. The author of *Races and Immigrants* (1907), convinced of the superiority of American democratic ideas and institutions no less than his midwestern colleague, Frederick Jackson Turner, avidly sought to demonstrate an indigenous point of view. By so doing, however, he deliberately bypassed the omnipresence of a Europe-in-flux in America.

784

As a matter of course, Commons and his team of assistants patterned the classic *History of Labor in the United States* on an economic-environmentalist formula that all but ignored the immigrant texture of American life. Indeed, individual no less than group personalities were merged beneath a colorless, if meticulous, scholarship that only occasionally veered away from strict trade union history. Labor historians, Americanists, and Progessives echoed the chauvinistic slogans of the American Federation of Labor. In muted tones they proclaimed the impeccable Americanism of the craft unions. Seeking to win over a public persuaded that labor was deserving of its lot, they distinguished between the worthy "old" immigrants and the unworthy "new," the superior western immigrants and the inferior eastern immigrants. In effect, a strenuously American rationale for the beleaguered craft unions became the synthesizing principle for the writing of American labor history. Whatever its tactical merits, this apologetic posture obscured the complex human-relations problems that society was reluctant to confront, and lulled the imagination and the historical sense of a whole generation of historians. American labor history had become trade union bound.

Much has happened, however, to open the way to a more sensitive appreciation of group differences since World War II. First, labor's place has been legitimized beyond repeal. Second, an immigration restriction policy of forty years' standing has contributed to increased social homogeneity. Third, the racist assumptions of an earlier era have happily fallen into disuse. And finally, the American acceptance of a large role in world affairs has fostered cultural maturity. For the first time, the creative interaction of the ethnically different in the American past has excited a confident, if as yet unstructured, curiosity. The memory of group differences has come to arouse feelings of nostalgia rather than strain.

Thus the spirit of the times is especially conducive to an appreciative study of the challenge presented to American labor by an ethnically diverse people. It is perhaps no exaggeration to say that American labor's single most creative achievement has been the social and spiritual integration of the nation's immigrant peoples through democratic organization.[2] It is the contention of this paper that the Jewish labor movement, by force of historical circumstances, was propelled into a position which enabled its leaders to play an important role in this process.

785

In the last decade or so, a new spirit of inquiry has influenced the work of scholars studying the Jewish labor movement.[3] At conferences and in scholarly papers they have voiced their discontent with labor history conceived solely as trade union history. In their studies, without exception, the folk distinctiveness of the Jewish labor movement has emerged as the critical shaping factor. In fact, the industrial and business features of the needle trades that an earlier generation of historians saw as critical to the accomplishment of the Jewish labor movement have now been overshadowed by this new awareness.

---

[2] Rowland T. Berthoff, "The American Social Order: A Conservative Hypothesis," *American Historical Review* (April, 1960), LXV, 508.

[3] The major points in the reinterpretation of the Jewish labor movement are to be found in the following articles and books: Selig Perlman, "Jewish American Unionism, Its Birth Pangs and Contributions to the General American Labor Movement," *Publications of the American Jewish Historical Society* (June, 1952), XLI; Will Herberg, "Jewish Labor Movement in the United States: Early Years to World War I," *Industrial and Labor Relations Review* (July, 1952), V; Will Herberg, "Jewish Movement in the United States: World War I to the Present," *"Industrial and Labor Relations Review* (October, 1952). VI; Jack Barbash, "Ethnic Factors in the American Labor Movement," in Industrial Relations Research Association, *"Interpreting the Labor Movement* (New York, 1952); J. B. S. Hardman, "Jewish Workers in the American Labor Movement," *YIVO Annual of Jewish Social Science* (1953), VIII; Melech Epstein, *Jewish Labor in USA* (New York, 1950-1953), 2 vols; Moses Rischin, "From Gompers to Hillman: Labor Goes Middle Class," *Antioch Review* (Summer, 1953); "Summary of the Proceedings of the First Session of the Editorial Advisory

As has been suggested, the Jewish labor movement's most significant achievement is intimately related to the central social fact of the ethnic heterogeneity of the American labor force. Labor unions did not compile ethnic statistics; the dissemination of such data, in an era when ethnic prejudices ran strong, seemed contrary to the spirit and interests of the labor movement. Ethnic diversity seemed in fact to be its nemesis. Unions continually faced the exhausting task of organizing workmen differing not only in kind and grade of skill but in language, religion, national origin, customs, political experience, and habits of mind. In the late nineteenth century the rise of big business only helped to polarize the labor force into craft and industrial unionists, skilled and unskilled, natives and immigrants, Catholics and Protestants. Consequently, a divided laboring population confronted a relatively homogeneous big business community of men committed to a belief in their moral and racial superiority. The racist assumptions of the age were rendered even more plausible by the geographically and socially selective process of immigration.[4] The whole social order seemed to vindicate a hierarchic ethnic pattern.

786

The ethnic strains of this society were vividly reflected in the trade unions. While native Americans regarded the unions as "un-American," "old" immigrant trade unionists viewed themselves as the true Americans. Despite a professed internationalism, the "old" scorned and feared the "new" who appeared to threaten their jobs and their status. In the 1880s, the long lists of unpronounceable names being added to their membership lists alarmed union officials, them-

---

Council of the YIVO History of the Jewish Labor Movement in the United States, September 13, 1953," *YIVO Bleter: Studies in American Jewish History and Culture* (1954), XXXVIII; Abraham Menes, "The East Side—Matrix of the Jewish Labor Movement," *Judaism* (Fall, 1954), III; Selig Perlman, "America and the Jewish Labor Movement: A Case of Mutual Illumination;" Henry David, "Jewish Labor History: A Problem Paper;" Daniel Bell, "Jewish Labor History"; Moses Rischin, The Human Element and Jewish Labor;" all in *The Writing of American Jewish History Proceedings of the Conference of Historians* edited by Moshe Davis and Isidore S. Meyer (New York, 1957); Clifton K. Yearley, Jr., "Samuel Gompers: Symbol of Labor," *South Atlantic Quarterly* (Summer, 1957), LVI; J. B. S. Hardman, "The Needle-Trades Unions: A Labor Movement at Fifty," *Social Research* (Autumn, 1960), XXVII; Moses Rischin, "European Influences upon the Jewish Labor Movement," unpublished paper read at a session of the Mississippi Valley Historical Association devoted to "Immigrant Influences in the American Labor Movement;" Moses Rischin, "The Jews and the Liberal Tradition in America," *American Jewish Historical Quarterly* (September, 1961), LI; Melvin Dubofsky, "Organized Labor and the Immigrant in New York City, 1900-1918," *Labor History* (Spring, 1961), II; Moses Rischin, *The Promised City: New York's Jews 1870-1914* (Cambridge, 1962).
4 William Miller, "American Historians and the Business Elite," *Journal of Economic History* (November, 1949), IX, 208.

selves relative newcomers from the British Isles. In the following two decades, the craft unions consolidated the "old" immigrants and closed out the "new." By drawing the line in this manner, the unions thus resolved a social, cultural, and economic dilemma with which they were unprepared to cope. To limit competition, trade unions resorted to defensive measures. Exorbitant initiation fees, the approval and consent of the officers of the international unions, the insistence on a foreign union card, and the requirement of naturalization or the declaration of intention to become a citizen—all these comprised labor's equivalent of industry's high protective tariff. These measures virtually barred all but a handful of the "new" immigrants from union membership. By 1910, the United States Immigration Commission could report that the trade unions, a few years earlier regarded as a dangerous element, were bulwarks of Americanism and that they themselves were now menaced by the "new" immigrants. Not until the labor upheaval of the 1930s was the guild unity of the American Federation of Labor to be breached. In the interim, a craft-proud federation successfully integrated a predominantly British, German, and Irish constituency into a privileged labor class. But the understandable anxieties of its members, and their desire to dissociate themselves in every way from the newcomers, robbed the AFL of much of its earlier effectiveness as a social movement.[5]

787

Yet it was no mean achievement to weld the disparate elements of the "old" immigration into a coherent labor organization at a time when British-America, German-America, and Irish-America stood at the high tide of hyphen-consciousness.[6] In the still untold story of the social integration of the "old" immigrants, Samuel Gompers, more so than any other man, anticipated the role that leaders of the Jewish labor movement were destined to play in integrating the "new" immigrants. By the 1880s, before the great Jewish migration hit the labor market, this English-born Jew had lived through the full cycle of labor growth, upheaval, decline, and revival. Gompers learned the lessons of failure more thoroughly than any other labor leader,

---

[5] Rena M. Atchison, *Un-American Immigration* (Chicago, 1894), 105; William M. Leiserson, *Adjusting Immigrant and Industry* (New York, 1924), 170ff.; Frank J. Carlton, *The History and Problems of Organized Labor* (Boston, 1911), 63; Herman Feldman, *Racial Factors in American Industry* (New York, 1931), 145, 221; David J. Saposs, *Left-Wing Unionism* (New York, 1926), 11, 163.

[6] Michael Williams, *The Shadow of the Pope* (New York, 1932), 97ff.; Coleman J. Barry, *The Catholic Church and German-Americans* (Washington, 1953), 105; John Higham, *Strangers in the Land* (New Brunswick, N. J., 1955), 84ff.

and thereafter proceeded to mold the American Federation of Labor
with the tactile skill of the expert cigar maker that he was. Gompers
was fitted for his labor role in the cigar trade, a metropolitan New
York-centered consumer industry, similar in these years to the subsequent clothing-trade milieu of the Jews of the great migration.
Jews were among diverse laboring men employed at the cigarmaker's
bench, and, being active unionists, they partly provided the lively
labor environment that schooled Gompers in human relations and
that also supplied a base from which he rose to become American
labor's first secretary-general.[7] Gompers, of course, also educated himself and applied the fruits of this self-education to his union activities.
For example, learning German in order to read Karl Marx, as he
says in his autobiography, he inadvertently fortified himself as a labor
virtuoso and coordinator among English and German-speaking unionists. His gift for rising above the divisions of language, religion, and
nationality were essential to his role as leader and arbiter.

788

But if Gompers symbolized the solidarity of the "old" immigrant
craft unionists, his cosmopolitanism did not stop there. He repeatedly
fought to bring the "new" immigrants into the Federation. Federation
strategy, however, limited these efforts to extend the benefits of organization to the unorganized, and, unfortunately, his words obscured
and belied his actions. As a result, Gompers and his Jewish antagonists,
in their assertion of labor's rights, were locked in a dialogue that
for intensity and articulate concern stood second to none. For nearly
forty years, the spokesman for the "old" immigrants of the AFL
served as the chief whipping boy for the leaders of the "new" immigrants of the Jewish labor movement.

The leaders of the Jewish labor movement, rather than the officers
of the AFL, were destined to extend the bounds of Americanness to
include the "new" immigrants. Hovering strategically between the
"old" and the "new" immigrants, they were the natural promoters
of inclusive as opposed to exclusive unions. But for a generation
after 1880 one of the "new" blocs—East European Jewish workmen—

---

[7] T. W. Glocker, "The Structure of the Cigar Makers' Union," in J. H. Hollander and
G. E. Barnett (eds.), *Studies in American Trade Unionism* (New York, 1907), 51-52;
Bernard Mandell, "The Great Uprising of 1877," *Cigar Makers' Official Journal*
(December, 1953); Isaac Markens, *The Hebrews in America* (New York, 1888),
155-156; Arthur Mann, *Yankee Reformers in the Urban Age* (Cambridge, 1954),
187ff.; George H. Evans, Jr., "Geographical Differences in the Use of the Corporation
in American Manufacturing in 1899," *Journal of Economic History* (Spring, 1954),
XIV, 117.

remained on the edge of organized labor. Unreliable as unionists, they were at once attracted by opportunities for independence in the fluid and fast-growing apparel trades and repelled by a business jungle that victimized employer and employee alike. Yet by the close of the first decade of this century, "new" Jewish immigrants entered upon a Jewish labor mission that was to culminate in the great labor gains of the 1930s.

The progressive years of the early twentieth century set the stage for labor action in the great urban centers. Mounting protest by the victims of industrialism, the public's grudging recognition of the AFL craft unions, and widespread alarm at big business' threat to democracy and individual liberty reopened the labor question. A decade of reform,     789
vitalized by a concern for the alien other half, paved the way for a new climate of opinion. Health, housing and factory conditions, the welfare of child and female factory labor, education, the arts, and recreation—all became as central to the promise of a new urban democracy as political reform. Inspired by European example, the nationwide liberal revival, and the discontent of urban Americans, middle-class reformers labored to arouse a sense of community and social responsibility among hosts of strangers.

The first of the "new" immigrant strangers to be imbued en masse with the revived democratic impulse were East European Jews. An array of circumstances compelled these tenement dwellers and sweatshop workmen to focus their classic group consciousness upon the labor movement with an intensity that could not be ignored. New York and Chicago, unlike the factory and mill towns of Homestead and Lawrence, were metropolitan nerve centers of innovation and urban reform. By 1910, East European Jews, one-quarter of New York's inhabitants, made up nearly one-half of its industrial labor force. There and in the other great clothing centers, this cohesive group impressed a social and cultural homogeneity upon a major industry unique to the nation's economic life. By then, the high tide of progressivism had prepared the way for public acceptance of the claims of the most assertive and visible of these "'new" immigrants. Their leaders, inspired by Russian revolutionary developments, were ready to press home the program of the Jewish labor movement.

Significantly, this movement crystallized into solid unionism just as the momentum of revolution in Eastern Europe slackened (after 1905). Immigrant leaders then turned energies, formerly directed outward toward the creation of a free Russia, inward toward the democratization of American industry. By the eve of World War I, successive strikes in New York and Chicago placed the semi-industrial needle-trade unions, led by Russian-Jewish immigrants, in the forefront of organized labor.

In the next few decades, the garment unions were to gain national attention. They were to become known as exemplars and sounding boards of the new. In their ranks, labor leader and labor philosopher were joined. The seeming paradox of unions committed to socialism pioneering in union-management cooperation reflected a common-sense acceptance of the realities of American industrial life that transcended the artificial categories of capitalism and socialism. Initial experiments in industrial democracy in an industry divided into many small segments, where the unions alone were in a position to serve as agents of social cohesion, were to develop a unique style of union-management cooperation. Patterns of industry-wide collective bargaining were accepted. Impartial chairmen adjudicated major disputes as well as minor grievances, which led to the establishment of an industrial common law that moved the class struggle from the picket line to the bargaining table. A Joint Board of Sanitary Control administered health and safety standards that were to become models of their kind. By the mid-twentieth century, joint union-management activities were to encompass virtually all problems in the garment trades. Competition, trade practices, technological progress, security of employment, improved marketing, labor and management education, labor and commercial legislation, wage cost and production stabilization—all were marked by a degree of unparalleled mutuality. These practices, growing out of the unusual pattern of organization in the garment industries, nevertheless served as measuring rods of industrial progress for the nation. The unions themselves functioned as schools of industrial and labor relations that were to have a widespread influence.

Their successes would lift the leaders of the Jewish labor movement into the position of spokesmen for less articulate and experienced fellow "new" immigrants. Many of these newcomers were in the semi-industrial needle-trade unions, which were half way between the craft unions and the unorganized workers in the mass production industries, and which were committed to an all-inclusive industrial unionism. In the great depression, the apostles of this new unionism were to make themselves heard among the leading voices of the loyal opposition in and out of the American Federation of Labor. The Jewish labor unions, it should be pointed out, were far more than labor unions. In many respects, the Jewish labor movement represented no less than the aspirations of a Jewish world in turmoil. The early years of this movement paralleled the years of struggle for the emancipation of Russia's five million Jews. And the fight for liberation placed its mark on succeeding generations. In the briefest time, Eastern European Jews were driven to modify or to discard religious habits that were positively physical in the intensity with which they were practiced. Tradition gave way to a voracious urge for the most cosmopolitan modes of thought, trimmed of course to the measure of the Jewish folk past. Yiddish newspapers, theaters,         791 and public forums raised a village vernacular into a language of great cities; framed universal issues in terms of a morally intense Judaic heritage; and furnished the binding terms of discourse that kept immigrants, on the way to becoming contemporary Americans, precariously balanced between an ancient past come to life and a nearer past falling to pieces. Out of the debris, Jewish immigrants forged a religiously-informed socialism and cultural modernism. All their strivings bore witness to their aspiration toward high civilization, to their acceptance of the enlightenment's faith in science, liberalism, and limitless human progress. With the conviction of a folk committed to the belief that knowledge made men free, they looked to an era of unrelieved social justice. With the emotional urgency of a long-persecuted people, they envisaged a promised land where differences of race, religion and nationality would no longer divide mankind, where worldly goods would be apportioned equitably and all energies would be devoted to the cultivation of the arts of peace.

From its founding, the Jewish labor movement's sense of mission and vocation was fired by this social and cultural awakening. Messianic fervor sustained a sense of high moral purpose that was to serve as proof of a great Jewish ethic. The Jewish labor movement, like the Jews, was on trial. A community of immigrants, forming a new group personality, yearned to assimilate the best that was being said and thought and done in the modern world. "The East Side, like Boston, is a state of mind, but unlike the Hub, it is a state of mind which is always in flux. No new idea is unwelcome here," wrote Henry Moskowitz, Ethical Culture Society leader, Progressive candidate for

Congress, and East Side settlement leader in 1912.[8]

The Jewish labor movement hummed with this larger social consciousness, spiritual restlessness, and sense of world and folk rebirth.
The labor spirit that stirred the market place was both cause and
effect of the movement's precipitous awakening. In revolt against
traditional Judaism, Jewish labor spokesmen were not at all secular
by the standards of their time; indeed, their religious *élan* was all-
pervasive. Jewish labor apologists, in an effort to prove themselves
modern men devoid of superstition and the tribal mind, proved too
much. Labor leaders and rank-and-filers, nurtured in a tradition that
did not admit apostasy, were imbued with a religious ethos that
informed their lives and their organizations, even as they declared
themselves free thinkers. Industrial exploitation and a Marxist dialectic
combined to crystallize a folk religious ethic. Scriptural calls to a
courageous new era betrayed continuity with the past. Ineluctably,
the Jewish labor movement assumed a tone and coloration rooted in
Jewish habits of mind and communal modes of justice, and these
were emboldened and transformed by an industrial society. In this
respect, the leaders of the Jewish labor movement were closest in
spirit to the British labor movement of Kier Hardie. They were
righteously angry, intolerant of injustice, and eager for social service.
The dual awakening to prophetic injunctions and to the promise of
a true modern community sustained their conviction in the triumph
of a new social ethic and their sense of their own worthiness as Jews.[9]

Many non-Jewish reformers envisioned a magnificent mission for
the Jews. Indeed, in the early years of the twentieth century they
indiscriminately assigned all Jews, as many Jews assigned themselves,
to the forefront of the reform crusade. David Graham Phillips planned
an epic of Jewish progress through the ages. Thomas Davidson saw
his young Jewish disciples on the Lower East Side as the heirs of
Isaiah, destined vessels of a revolutionized social order, if they would
but will it. Ray Stannard Baker extolled the Jewish gift for prophecy,
exemplified by Frederick Lasalle, Karl Marx, and Felix Adler:

> The Jewish people [he wrote] have always possessed the genius for

792

---

[8] Henry Moscowitz, "The East Side in Oil and Crayon," *Survey* (May 11, 1912), XXVIII,
272.

[9] Curiously, Selig Perlman, who was quite sensitive to the religious dimension of the
British labor movement, failed to perceive the extent to which religious influences
were operative in the Jewish labor movement. Cf. H. Richard Niebuhr, *The Social
Sources of Denominationalism* (New York, 1929), 74ff.

declaring revolutionary truths, for prophecy. We sometimes forget that modern civilization rests largely upon Jewish prophecy and Jewish law-giving. Moses and David and Isaiah, Jesus and Paul—all Jews.

The great garment strikes, as a matter of course, inspired an exalted proletarian theme. "Marx was a Hebrew—wasn't he?" exclaimed the labor heroine of Phillips' novel, *The Conflict:* "Yes, he was a Jew. Both were Jews . . ., Marx and Jesus. . . . And they were both labor leaders . . ., labor agitators." In 1913, John E. Williams, who was to play a major role in striking new paths in labor-industrial relations, predicted that Russian Jews would make their most creative contribution to American life in labor relations. The editor of the Streator, Illinois *Independent Times* insisted further that their wide grasp of human relations problems, their alert minds, and their susceptibility to ethical ideals equipped them uniquely for the task of humanizing economic society.[10] After 1914, however, the tragic complexity of world events curbed the enthusiasm of reformers and cut short their rhapsodizing while the Jewish labor movement was convulsed by the reality of nascent world revolution.

793

Ever since the opening years of this century, Jewish immigrants shared the exhilaration and horror that were part of the upheaval that shook the foundations of East European Jewish life. During World War I, the immigrant community reached the heights of spiritual turmoil. The quick succession of events in 1917—the emancipation of Russia's Jews, the revolutionary overturn of Tsarist autocracy, and the proclamation of the Balfour Declaration—rekindled Messianic expectations. Immigrant Jewry looked to this-worldly salvation both for their kinsmen overseas and for all humanity. But salvation did not come, at least not in the form that was anticipated. Between 1915 and 1924, 300,000 Jews entered the United States from an Eastern Europe in chaos. Like their pre-war predecessors, the newcomers dangled between a world fallen to pieces and one that was struggling to be born. Bringing with them the prestige of the Russian revolution, they helped revive—indeed pervert—an earlier Russian revolutionary tradition committed to social democracy. Their readiness to believe

[10] Louis Filler, *Crusaders of American Liberalism* (New York, 1939), 118; Morris R. Cohen, *A Dreamer's Journey* (Boston, 1949), 95-96; R. S. Baker, *The Spiritual Unrest* (New York, 1909), 111; David Graham Phillips, *The Conflict* (New York, 1911), 62; Walter B. Rideout, *The Radical Novel in the United States 1900-1954* (Cambridge, 1956), 61-62; Matthew Josephson, *Sidney Hillman* (New York, 1952), 81-82. Cf. Mabel Dodge Luhan, *Intimate Memories* (New York, 1936), III, 96ff.

in Utopia kept the Russian-Jewish immigrant community astir for years to come. The Jewish labor movement, pledged to the highest form of democracy, inevitably became the focus for all the revolutionary will-o'-the-wisps that momentarily dazzled the idealistic and impressionable.

In the 1920s, the Jewish unions provided the first American forum for the pro and anti-Soviet debate. Nostalgic Russian immigrants, intimidated by the world around them, participated vicariously in the march of events that promised to turn "the home that had never been a home" into a paradise. Ideological conflict weakened the Jewish unions. The disordered state of the needle trades, the tensions between immigrant parents and their American children, fear and hope for families divided between Eastern Europe and the United States by immigration laws, and harsh anti-immigrant sentiments helped keep these unions vulnerable throughout the decade.

794

> The great majority of them come from Russian; a large number of them have been engaged at home in fighting autocracy, in fighting ukases of the Czar, and to a great many of them even obeying an order, even though the order comes from the union, is repugnant . . . .
>
> Of course, if a situation arises where the honesty and good faith of the leaders is attacked, naturally the opportunity of getting discipline at all is almost impossible . . . .

This characterization of the state of mind of Jewish unionists in 1912 by an officer of the ILGWU (at a session of the United States Industrial Commission) was equally valid for succeeding decades; and in the '20s it proved nearly catastrophic. Everyday labor politics became clothed in the rhetoric of the Russian revolution. The needle-trade unions became the key target in the Communist Party's bid for power in the American labor movement. William Z. Foster's Trade Union Educational League aimed to amalgamate the four major garment unions, so heavily populated with Russian immigrants. It proceeded to found needle-trade and furriers' sections and a Yiddish daily newspaper. In 1926, the Communists nearly overwhelmed the ILGWU, while the International Union of Fur and Leather Workers succumbed completely to Communist control. But the Jewish labor movement as a whole emerged still vital, even if somewhat chastened.[11]

---

[11] Irving Bernstein, *The Lean Years: A History of the American Worker 1920-1933*, (Boston, 1960), 136ff.; Melech Epstein, *Jewish Labor in USA 1914-1952*, 124ff.; Melech Epstein, *The Jew and Communism 1919-1941* (New York, 1959), 274ff.

The propensity of many East European Jews and their sons to be attracted to Communism has been variously explained.[12] Fundamentally, though, the fact that they were in the throes of Russian emancipation, with all that it implied, must account in large part for their political judgment. Indeed, these newcomers, eager to embrace a democratic tradition that they might call their own, found themselves out of joint with the times. Disoriented and often brutalized, they lost all sense of proportion. In the 1920s, they confronted an exclusive Americanism, not merely indifferent, but hostile to egalitarian ideals and intolerant of cultural differences. No better account of the jagged sensibilities of second generation American Jews of Russian parentage is likely to be found than in Joseph Freeman's *An American Testament: A Narrative of Rebels and Romantics* (New York, 1936) and in the opening chapters of Eugene Lyon's autobiographical memoir, *Assignment in Utopia* (New York, 1937). But Max Beer, the erudite Austrian-born historian of British socialism, best summed up the hurt, real or imagined, of the heirs of an antique moral culture who yearned to enter a world which appeared to reject them:

795

> It is not . . . political inequality which set his feelings on edge; it is the social inequality and human indignity to which he is subjected that causes him to leave the open road, and move from the center to the farthest extreme. It is a terrible state of mind to feel oneself the legitimate heir of three thousand years of spiritual wrestling and unique historical experience, and at the same time to be socially outlawed . . . .[13]

If easily ensnared by calls to Utopia, once disillusioned by Soviet realities, Jews in the labor movement became the keenest adversaries of all forms of totalitarianism while persisting as champions of advanced democratic ideals. Despite a great range of differences among themselves, Jews in the 1930s were politically the most openly disturbed and concerned of Americans. They were among the first to sound the alert on the domestic as well as on the international scene. As early as 1931, Socialist intellectuals forecast the coming of German totalitarianism. Always part of a larger world consciousness, the Jewish

---

[12] Werner Cohn, "Sources of American Jewish Liberalism" (Unpublished doctoral dissertation, New School for Social Research, 1956), 134ff.; Nathan Glazer, *The Social Basis of American Communism* (New York, 1961), 130ff, 223ff.; Maldwyn A. Jones, *American Immigration* (Chicago, 1960), 229-230; Philip Rieff, "The Mirage of College Politics," *Harper's Magazine* (October, 1961), CCXXIII, 159.

[13] Max Beer, *Fifty Years of International Socialism* (New York, 1935), 105. Cf. Daniel Aaron, *Writers on the Left* (New York, 1961), 130ff.; Lewis S. Feuer, "Travelers to the Soviet Union 1917-1932: The Formation of a Component of New Deal Ideology," *American Quarterly* (Summer, 1962), XIV.

working-class leaders sensed the perils to democracy and to civilization.[14]

For many reasons, labor's lean years were not at all lean for the Jewish labor movement. For these unions, the great strides in labor organization and toward social democracy in the New Deal era were rooted almost as solidly in the 1920s as in the progressive years. In a decade when the value of order overshadowed the value of freedom, a heady sensitivity to the promise of American life was no less salutary for being unfashionable. Jewish immigrants had never subscribed to the laissez-faire tenets of the business creed which was accepted as axiomatic by the AFL. They viewed the ideals of social democracy that had gained recognition in Western Europe, and especially in England, as common sense statesmanship that in modern form approximated Jewish communal and humanitarian ideals. It is well to remember that in the '20s New York City, the base of the Jewish labor movement, was the most liberal metropolis in the nation. Racism, still very much present in America, hardened class and ethnic lines, and isolationism—all of which undermined the earlier optimistic process of gradual and casual assimilation of all immigrants—was here most forcefully and constructively contested. Historians may differ as to the relative merits of the claims of Congressman Fiorello H. LaGuardia, Governor Alfred E. Smith, and Governor Franklin D. Roosevelt to be regarded as the progenitors of the New Deal. But there is no doubt that they were all products of the New York milieu and its energetic social consciousness. In these years, the city's East European Jews played a significant role by articulating and defining social issues that in the succeeding decade were to become national in scope.[15]

The centrality of the labor milieu to the Jewish immigrant experience in the 1920s also makes the role of the Jewish labor movement in the 1930s more intelligible. In 1925, it was estimated that Jews made up

---

[14] Henry F. May, *The End of American Innocence* (New York, 1959), 394; Louis Adamic, *My America 1928-1938* (New York, 1938), 253; Henry Cohen, "Crisis and Reaction," *American Jewish Archives* (June, 1953), V, 104.

[15] John Higham, "American Immigration Policy in Historical Perspective," *Law and Contemporary Problems* (Spring, 1956), XXI, 219; Sidney Fine, *Laissez-Faire and the General Welfare State* (Ann Arbor, 1956), 3ff.; Arthur Mann, *La Guardia: A Fighter Against His Times 1882-1933* (Philadelphia, 1959), 223; Oscar Handlin, *Alfred E. Smith and His America* (Boston, 1958), 75ff.; Bernard Bellush, *Franklin D. Roosevelt as Governor of New York* (New York, 1955), 282-283; Daniel R. Fusfeld, *The Economic Thought of Franklin D. Roosevelt and the Origins of the New Deal* (New York, 1956), 154ff.

over one-third of New York City's organized labor force; and over half of them were in the garment trades, the metropolis' first industry. But Jews were also dispersed throughout the unionized labor force. In the transportation and communication industry alone—second only to the needle trades in union members—were their numbers few. In these industries, Jews accounted for only eight per cent of the membership. But they comprised over one-sixth of the printers, nearly one-quarter of the building-trades workmen, over one-third of those employed in the jewelry, amusement, and ornament trades, over half of the workmen in food preparation and distribution, two-thirds of the labor force in the leather trades, and virtually all the members of the retail salesmen's unions. This variegated yet compact labor force with its special labor culture helped nurture a core of young men eager to further the good society through the labor movement. The crisis brought on by the depression crisis was to give them their opportunity.[16]

797

Furthermore, in the '20s the labor movement rather than politics provided the chief avenue to leadership for the foreign-born and their sons. In this golden decade, evangelical fervor and intense democratic sentiment were hardly to be found outside the labor movement; only there was the immigrant's background an asset rather than a liability. According to a statistical study prepared by Professor Sorokin and based on the *American Labor's Who's Who* (New York, 1926), one-third of the nation's labor leaders in 1925 were immigrants. Of these, 22.2 per cent were of Russian birth—twice the proportion of Russian-born immigrants in the country—and most of them were Jews.[17] If the American-born of East European parentage also had been accounted for, the proportion of Jews among labor spokesmen would most likely have been even higher.

Despite a veneer of rhetoric, one of the great garment unions made a solid and unequalled institutional record in the 1920s. In a decade when the AFL suffered severe setbacks, the independent Amalgamated Clothing Workers' Union served as a laboratory of the new

---

[16] H. S. Linfield, "Jews in Trade Unions in the City of New York," *The Communal Organizations of the Jews in the United States* (New York, 1927), 129. Cf. C. Wright Mills, *The New Men of Power: American Labor Leaders* (New York, 1948), 2ff.

[17] Pitrim A. Sorokin, "Leaders of Labor and Radical Movements in the United States and Foreign Countries," *American Journal of Sociology* (November, 1927), XXII, 391; Sumner H. Slichter, "The Worker in Modern Economic Society," *Journal of Political Economy* (February, 1926), XXXIV, 120.

unionism. The Amalgamated provided comprehensive unemployment benefits, ventured into low-cost cooperative housing, established the only successful labor bank, inaugurated a research department that encouraged scientific management, and invited the interest of all men of good will in the labor movement.

The humanistic ends of the Jewish labor movement also attained full expression in these years. Even those of modest intellectual capacity were encouraged to share the movement's militant belief in culture. Workers' education in the social sciences and the humanities was given special attention. The Rand School and the Workers' University, no less than the earlier Breadwinners' College and the People's Institute at Cooper Union, gave larger institutional form to the scores of educational self-help, literary, and musical societies that had flourished in Yiddish colonies in urban centers, particularly in New York, ever since the 1880s. The philosophical issues that went to the roots of industrial society—social problems, sociology, the social interpretation of literature, and labor legislation—were the staples of a people with a tradition of intellectual and moral inquiry. The studious Lowell mill girls of the 1840s had worthy successors in the classes of the Workers' Education Department of the ILGWU led by Fannia Cohn. Indeed, the ILGWU spent more on labor education and recreation than did any other union. It coined its own songs, slogans, and literature. In 1937 its labor theater was to gain national recognition with the production of "Pins and Needles." The ILGWU example spurred the AFL to inaugurate its own educational program.[18]

The great garment unions were also acutely sensitive in the 1920s to the challenge of an ethnically heterogeneous membership. Their multilingual house periodicals aimed to Americanize union members. The ILGWU's *Justice* (published in Yiddish, English, Italian, French, and later in Spanish editions) and the Amalgamated's *Advance* (issued in Yiddish, English, Italian, French, Bohemian, Polish, Lithuanian, and Russian editions) reflected a vision of the labor movement as a cosmopolitan community of equals bound together by their common citizenship in the job.

Throughout the heyday years of the Jewish labor movement, newspapers, fraternal orders, and a wider Yiddish world of small shop-

---

18 J. M. Budish & George Soule, *The New Unionism*, New York, 1920), 205ff.; Margaret T. Hodgen, *Workers' Education in England and the United States* (London, 1925), 196ff., 214ff.

keepers and professionals helped provide the middle-class support that gave the Jewish labor movement its communal flavor and *éclat*. Unlike the other "new" immigrants, the newcomers of the great Jewish migration almost from the start had the makings of a variegated middle class. Over the years their range of talents and skills mounted steadily. Yet despite a remarkable rate of economic and social mobility, the successful in great numbers continued to respect, if not always to identify themselves with, the world of Jewish labor.

Intellectuals, too, played an important role in the Jewish labor movement, and their talents and esprit were communicated to the American labor movement as a whole. Russian-educated intellectuals had played the key role in 1888 in the founding of the United Hebrew Trades. For over two decades, the UHT served as the central organizing committee of the Jewish labor movement. After 1910, these intellectuals played a less direct role in the now soundly established Jewish labor unions. But they continued to serve as advocates, as gadflies, as advisors, and as emissaries of Jewish labor culture to the world at large. These heralds of the coming new world served as newspaper editors, intellectual leaders, political candidates, officers of fraternal orders, and popular lecturers. They included such men as Isaac Hourwich, economist and immigration expert and the first Russian immigrant to receive a doctorate at Columbia; Paul Abelson, pioneer in adult education and labor arbitration; Dr. George M. Price, leader in industrial health; Morris Hillquit and Meyer London, early labor lawyers and Socialist Party stalwarts; and, above all, Abraham Cahan, the editor of the *Jewish Daily Forward* for nearly half a century and the elder statesman of Yiddish America.

The little known career of Isaac M. Rubinow (1875-1936) provides the most cogent example of the independent Russian intellectual quietly dedicated to the ideals of social democracy. Rubinow helped bridge the gap between Europe and America, between the progressive era and the era of the New Deal, between the university and the factory. As physician, economist, statistician, actuary, social worker, and Jewish leader, he combined many careers into a lifetime directed to the single goal of human betterment. Rubinow's broad social interests, magnificent technical equipment, panoramic view of the ills of society, and wide human contacts uniquely fitted him for the pioneer intellectual role in the American social security movement. In 1910, Rubinow and his associates submitted a two-volume report to the

799

Department of Commerce and Labor, commissioned two years earlier, for which he received his doctorate from Columbia. Rubinow's *Studies in Workmen's Insurance: Italy, Russia, Spain,* was followed in 1913 by his pioneering book, *Social Insurance.* In the next six years, state after state passed workmen's compensation laws based on Rubinow's findings. In 1916, he advocated the adoption of an insurance plan that would guard against wage losses due to sickness and invalidism and that would cover the cost of medical care. Rubinow was even chosen executive secretary of a social insurance committee created by the American Medical Association. But because of strong opposition to compulsory health insurance, nothing came of it. In 1927, he became vice-president of the American Association for Social Security, founded by Abraham Epstein, a fellow Russian Jew and a leading unemployment insurance expert. Together scholar and publicist popularized the social security idea. Although Rubinow was not appointed to Franklin Roosevelt's Committee on Economic Security (headed by Edwin E. Witte of the University of Wisconsin), he served as a consultant when the Social Security law was drawn up.[19]

800

Renewing the national attack upon social problems, the New Deal opened a new era for labor. In a climate molded by a renewed democratic spirit, men and women of many backgrounds, drawing upon over half a century of European and American social experience, converged upon the nation's capital. They brought with them the cosmopolitanism and zeal that had marked an earlier generation of reformers.

Both the first and the second New Deal drew upon the know-how and the enthusiasm of the new unionism, but it derived from the World War I government-business-labor partnership experience which instituted standards in wages, hours, bargaining, etc. This experience provided the only precedent for large-scale government intervention in the economy to insure fair dealing between management and labor. Young Sidney Hillman, a member of the Board of Control and Labor Standards for Army Clothing, never forgot this model and precedent for a welfare state. The War Labor Board's recognition of collective bargaining and union wage standards seemed to Hillman merely an extension of the Hart, Schaffner and Marx plan. In 1931, Hillman and

---

[19] Joseph Dorfman, *The Economic Mind in American Civilization* (New York, 1959), IV, 116-123; Wilbur J. Cohen, "Edwin E. Witte (1887-1960): Father of Social Security," *Industrial and Labor Relations Review* (October, 1960), XIV, 7ff.; A. M. Schlesinger, Jr., *The Coming of the New Deal* (Boston, 1958), 302, 306.

his union could anticipate the benefits to be derived from government intervention. In 1933, Hillman and Dr. Leo Wolman of the Amalgamated were appointed to the five-member Labor Advisory Board of the NRA, and played a major role in formulating the labor code which they had sketched two years earlier.[20]

With their dedication to industrial unionism, their will to organize, and their evangelical fervor, the needle-trade unions were to relive Jewish labor's heroic age in the upheaval of the 1930s. The great strikes in the first and second decades of the century had established the needle-trade unions as potential spearheads for the extension of labor organization and industiral unionism. But before the New Deal era, the great steel strike of 1919 provided the only major occasion for the needle-trade unions to demonstrate their solidarity with labor and their will to expand the labor movement to the unorganized workers in basic industries. In that year the garment unions alone contributed $200,000 to the steel workers' relief fund, more than was raised by the twenty-four AFL unions combined with twenty-five times the membership. Indeed, the Amalgamated's $100,000 contribution was the largest ever made in the United States up to that time. But in 1935 the opportunity for wholesale industrial unionism had arrived. The needle-trade unions, helped by the Committee for Industrial Organization, organized, financed, and staffed the Textile Workers' Organizing Committee. They loaned their talents to organizing the auto and steel workers. And together with the mine workers, they supplied the backbone and were the chief advocates of industrial unionism.[21]

The most impressive achievements of the garment unions since World War II have been in the realm of charitable aid. Now that the great years of basic organizing had passed, an era of labor trusteeship had arrived. The emphasis on giving was not superimposed as a philanthropic gloss, but arose from a traditional religious mandate. During World War I, the ILGWU membership had contributed over $250,000 to East European war relief, inaugurating a manner of domestic and overseas aid that was to become habitual. The Jewish Labor Committee, founded in 1934 to fight fascism at home and

801

[20] William Leuchtenburg, *The Perils of Prosperity 1914-1932* (Chicago, 1958), 41-42; Matthew Josephson, *Sidney Hillman, Statesman of American Labor* (New York, 1952), 166ff.
[21] Josephson, *Sidney Hillman,* 200, 373, 417-418.

abroad, also undertook certain philanthropic functions. But it was in the wake of World War II that the garment unions blossomed forth into massive aid societies. Between 1947 and 1950, the ILGWU membership, through voluntary donations, responded to requests for aid from other labor unions, community causes, and worthy institutions both at home and abroad by contributing some $4,600,000. This pattern of civic and overseas responsibility was soon emulated by other unions.

The garment unions also took the initiative after World War II in helping to revive the labor movement abroad. The ILGWU, in an effort to build democratic unions overseas as a bulwark against communism, probably expended more than all other unions combined in this effort. If Sidney Hillman proved overly sanguine in supporting the World Federation of Trade Unions, organized in 1945, and soon to be dominated by the Soviet Union, the leaders of the Amalgamated Clothing Workers' Union quickly saw his mistake and joined fellow unionists in backing the new International Confederation of Free Trade Unions.[22]

The political tradition of the Jewish labor movement, which in the early decades of the twentieth century expressed itself directly through the Socialist Party, still survived, though in attenuated form. In the years since World War II, the habit of dissent has been reflected in the persistence in New York State of the only third parties in the nation. Both the American Labor Party and the Liberal Party, organized by leaders of the needle-trade unions and supported largely by Jewish ballots, are lineally descended from the Socialist Party of Eugene V. Debs and Morris Hillquit. The alliance between Morningside Heights professors and theologians and Jewish trade-union leaders, renewing the ties of the early decades of the century between Christian and Jewish socialists, continues to serve a largely educational purpose, although at times its leaders also have demonstrated considerable political acumen.[23]

---

22 Herman D. Stein, "Jewish Social Work in the United States (1654-1954)," *American Jewish Yearbook* (1956), v.57, 97; Max Danish, *The World of David Dubinsky* (New York, 1957), 41, 184ff.; Lewis Lorwin, *The International Labor Movement* (New York, 1953), 180; A. H. Raskin, "The Dubinsky Concept of Unionism," *New York Times Magazine* (June 9, 1957), 29ff.; John P. Windmuller, *American Labor and the International Labor Movement 1940-1953* (Ithaca, N. Y., 1954), 74-75, 77-78.

23 William Spinrad, "New York's Third Party Voters," *Public Opinion Quarterly* (Winter, 1957-1958), XXI, 548ff.

The Jewish labor movement was shaped by the tensions of a Jewish religio-communal tradition, by a messianic bent, by the historical circumstances of the great Jewish migration that favored Jews with a trau-matic preview of events to come, and by a direct as well as vicarious share in the travail of the two great world powers of the mid-twentieth century. In the liberating climate of the late nineteenth and early twentieth centuries, Jewish ethnic solidarity was attuned to the highest ethical ideals. Mankind was to be united by the ties of brotherhood that through the ages had bound Jews together. The moral unity of the *shtetl*, the Jewish small town of Eastern Europe, was to be scaled to fit the needs of a world community; and the Jewish labor movement served as a temple of spiritual fraternity. Despite excesses, the informing vision and the utopian hopes of "social unionism" remain part of a creative phase in the American labor experience that is worth remembering.[24]

803

If the faith in the labor movement as ethical preceptor for the larger society has dimmed over the years, labor's responsibility to elect and to seek the better life remains a lasting conviction. The appointment in 1960 of two sons of Russian-Jewish immigrants to the posts of Secretary of Labor and Secretary of Health, Welfare and Education, the first of the newer ethnic groups to be elevated to Cabinet rank, is in a sense a tribute to the continued viability of the Jewish labor tradition.[25] At first primarily by virtue of its existence, and eventually by its influence throughout the industrial world, the Jewish labor movement has played a significant role. As an agent of social change and cosmopolitan democracy, its spirit persists into the present.

---

[24] J. B. S. Hardman, *American Labor Yearbook* (New York, 1916), 33; Herbert Harris, *American Labor* (New Haven, 1938), 193ff.

[25] Cf. Solomon Barkin, *The Decline of the Labor Movement and what can be done about it* (Center for the Study of Democratic Institutions, 1960); Robert Shaplen, "Peace-maker," *New Yorker* (April 7, 1962), 49ff., (April 14, 1962), 49ff.

# American Jewish Labor: Historiographical Problems and Prospects

## By IRWIN YELLOWITZ

The history of American Jewish labor has been a subject of inquiry and discussion for over a half century. Yet one must conclude that major problems in concept and method have not been resolved, and that a definitive and comprehensive history of American Jewish labor remains to be written.

Perhaps the most basic problem faced by historians of American Jewish labor has been the precise nature of the subject.[1] Most historians have limited their interest to the American Jewish labor movement, often without discussion of the implications of such a step. As in other areas of historical inquiry, leadership and institutions have received extensive attention. However, the unorganized aspects of the subject have been largely ignored. In part, this flows from the availability of materials, which are generated and preserved mainly by institutions and their leaders. Yet the movement is not synonymous with American Jewish labor, and thus significant areas of study remain.

The scope of American Jewish labor is also important even when one studies the institutional component. Traditionally, historians have studied the Jewish leaders of trade unions and socialist movements as representatives of Jewish labor. However, the membership of the International Ladies' Garment Workers' Union was no longer predominantly Jewish by the 1920's, while the workers in the men's clothing industry were never predominantly Jewish. Is there not an assumption of identity that goes beyond number, and which links these leaders to a fundamental Jewish consciousness?

The boundaries of American Jewish labor should be defined by the influence of Jewish identity and concerns upon leaders and institutions, and, in turn, the impact of these major figures and their organizations upon the Jewish community in general and Jewish workers in particular. Clearly the trade unions in the needle

[1] Nathan Reich, "The Organization of the YIVO History of the Jewish Labor Movement in the United States," *YIVO Annual of Jewish Social Science,* IX (1954), 389; Hyman Berman, "A Cursory View of the Jewish Labor Movement: An Historiographical Survey," *American Jewish Historical Quarterly, [=AJHQ],* LII (December, 1962), 79-82.

Originally published in *American Jewish Historical Quarterly* (March 1976). Reprinted by permission of the American Jewish Historical Society.

trades have served significant numbers of Jewish workers, and these organizations were in constant touch with the major issues that faced the Jewish community in general. Moreover, the attempt of the Jewish labor movement to create a distinct sub-culture within American Jewry significantly affected workers and the entire Jewish community.[2] Yet one must not forget that this same leadership had a strong commitment to socialism, which led them to build bridges out of the ethnic community. Trade union leaders, such as Benjamin Schlesinger, Morris Sigman and David Dubinsky of the International Ladies' Garment Workers' Union, Sidney Hillman and Jacob Potofsky of the Amalgamated Clothing Workers and Max Zaritsky of the United Cloth Hat and Capmakers' Union, desired to integrate Jewish workers more fully into the larger American labor movement—which they hoped would ultimately become socialist. The socialists Morris Hillquit and Meyer London believed in a universal working class, and they opposed tendencies and movements within Jewish labor that might elevate ethnic or national concerns above class identification. However, this position was modified by their involvement in the activities of political groups and trade unions that were closely related to Jewish workers.

The boundaries of American Jewish labor are also defined by who is excluded. Samuel Gompers was of Jewish origin, but clearly should not be placed within the confines of American Jewish labor.[3] Gompers' activities generally had little direct effect upon Jewish workers or the American Jewish community. He operated within the broader American labor movement. Although Robert Asher's article in this volume indicates that Gompers' Jewish origin was not forgotten by other labor leaders, it was of little importance in the decisions that he made. In this connection, Sheila Polishook's comments on Gompers' attitude toward Zionism are quite instructive.[4]

Similarly, the United Federation of Teachers (New York City), which has a large number of Jews in its leadership, plus a membership that is heavily Jewish, has not identified itself with American Jewry, nor has the union had an appreciable influence upon the Jewish community. In this respect, the United Federation of

---

[2] Arthur Goren, *New York Jews and the Quest for Community: The Kehillah Experiment* (New York: 1970), pp. 19-20 and ch. 9.

[3] On Gompers, see Bernard Mandel, *Samuel Gompers: A Biography* (Yellow Springs: 1963); William Dick, *Labor and Socialism in America: The Gompers Era* (Port Washington: 1971); Stuart B. Kaufman, *Samuel Gompers and the Origins of the American Federation of Labor, 1848-1896* (Westport: 1973).

[4] See the article by Sheila Polishook, below pp. 228-244.

Teachers differs from the unions in the needle trades during an earlier generation. In both cases, the leadership represented their members, as workers, but the unions in the needle trades also had a significant effect upon the Jewish community. With the exception of the school strike of 1968, and its continuing consequences in some local school districts, the United Federation of Teachers has not had such an impact upon its members as Jews or upon the Jewish community.[5] The differences between unions that represented first and second generation Jews and unions, often of a professional or white collar type, that contain Jewish leaders and members today, reveal much about the changes that have taken place in American Jewry in the last half century.

The complex interaction of Jewish, American, trade union and socialist concerns deserves further study. We need a clearer statement of the impact of labor leaders, such as Sidney Hillman and David Dubinsky, upon workers as Jews, and upon the Jewish community as a whole.[6] The same holds true for Morris Hillquit and Meyer London. The existing studies stress broader concerns, in the case of Hillquit, or the work in print is inadequate, as is true for London. Both men desired an American socialism, yet both had their political base within the Jewish community. In addition, we have no biography of Abraham Cahan, one of the most significant of the Jewish socialist leaders. He played a central role in harmonizing the universalism and the ethnic concerns and identity of the first generation Jewish community in America.[7]

807

[5] The strike of 1968 produced severe stress between Jews and Blacks in New York City, which intensified the already existing ethnic tensions in the political life of the City. For a discussion of religious identification as a variable affecting militancy within the United Federation of Teachers, see Stephen Cole, *The Unionization of Teachers: A Case Study of the UFT* (New York: 1969), pp. 79-84.

[6] On Sidney Hillman, see Matthew Josephson, *Sidney Hillman: Statesman of American Labor* (Garden City: 1952). On David Dubinsky, see Max Danish, *The World of David Dubinsky* (Cleveland: 1957). In chapter 22, Danish gives some attention to Dubinsky's attitudes toward, and involvement with, Jewish issues; also *Labor History*, IX, Special Supplement (Spring, 1968) which was devoted entirely to Dubinsky.

[7] On London, the only complete account is Harry Rogoff, *An East Side Epic: The Life and Work of Meyer London* (New York: 1930); a shorter sketch appears in Melech Epstein, *Profiles of Eleven* (New York: 1965), pp. 159-187; Gordon J. Goldberg is at work on London's career, and hopefully a full-length scholarly book will result; see his "Meyer London and the National Social Insurance Movement, 1914-1922" in *AJHQ* LXV (Sept., 1974), 59-73. On Hillquit, see Ira Kipnis, *The American Socialist Movement, 1897-1912* (New York: 1952); David Shannon, *The Socialist Party of America* (New York: 1955); James Weinstein, *The Decline of Socialism in America, 1912-1925* (New York: 1967); Epstein, *Profiles of Eleven*, pp. 189-231; Robert Iversen, "Morris Hillquit: American Social Democrat," Ph.D. dissertation, University of Iowa, 1951; Norma Pratt of U.C.L.A. is at work on Hillquit, including his relationship to Jewish issues. On Cahan, see Epstein, *Profiles of Eleven*, pp. 49-109 and Ronald Sanders, *The*

In an article in this volume, L. Glenn Seretan presents a perceptive analysis of the effect of Jewish identity upon Daniel DeLeon.[8]
Seretan's use of the theme of the Wandering Jew as an interpretive
tool in analyzing DeLeon's career is innovative methodologically,
and it provides new insights on the relationship between ethnic
factors and DeLeon's activities and policies. Specific attention to
the impact of ethnic factors upon other socialists of Jewish origin
should produce valuable material on the complex relationship between Jewish and non-Jewish factors within the American context.

The literature on American Jewish labor has also traditionally
included the studies of unionism in the needle trades. However,
most of this work focusses on the growth of unions and labor-
management relations in these trades, with only sparse reference
to the impact of ethnic factors.[9] The work on trade unionism in
the needle trades by persons who were themselves involved as
participants offers little more on this score.[10] There is still need
for an examination of how the trade unions in the needle trades
were affected by their large Jewish membership.

One barrier to such studies has been the relative paucity of material on the Jewish worker as distinguished from trade unions that
contained such workers.[11] This has been true for labor history

808

---

*Downtown Jews* (New York: 1969); Leon Stein presented a paper on Cahan at the
meeting of the American Historical Association in December, 1975. Zosa Szajkowski,
*Jews, Wars and Communism* (New York: 1972) is a rich source on Jewish socialists
generally.

[8] On DeLeon, see Howard Quint, *The Forging of American Socialism* (Indianapolis:
1953); Don McKee, "Daniel DeLeon: A Reappraisal," *Labor History,* I (Fall, 1960),
264-297; L. Glenn Seretan, "The Personal Style and Political Methods of Daniel DeLeon:
A Reconsideration," *Labor History,* XIV (Spring, 1973), 163-201.

[9] J.M. Budish and George Soule, *The New Unionism in the Clothing Industry* (New
York: 1920); Louis Levine, *The Women's Garment Workers: A History of the International Ladies' Garment Workers' Union* (New York: 1924); Charles Zaretz, *The Amalgamated Clothing Workers of America: A Study in Progressive Trades-Unionism* (New
York: 1934); Earl Strong. *The Amalgamated Clothing Workers of America* (Grinnell:
1940); Wilfred Carsel, *A History of the Chicago Ladies' Garment Workers' Union* (Chicago:
1940); Joel Seidman, *The Needle Trades* (New York: 1942). Seidman devotes some
attention to ethnic factors; see chapter 2 and pp. 49-50. Other works on the needle
trades are Charles Green, *The Headwear Workers.* (New York: 1944); Donald Robinson,
*Spotlight on a Union: The Story of the United Hatters, Cap and Millinery Workers
International Union* (New York: 1948); Philip Foner, *The Fur and Leather Workers
Union* (Newark: 1950); and Jesse T. Carpenter, *Competition and Collective Bargaining
in the Needle Trades, 1910-1967* (Ithaca: 1972). A good review of this literature is contained in Berman, "A Cursory View of the Jewish Labor Movement."

[10] James Oneal, *A History of the Amalgamated Ladies' Garment Cutters' Union,
Local 10* (New York: 1927); Benjamin Stolberg, *Tailor's Progress* (Garden City: 1944);
Harry Haskell, *A Leader of the Garment Workers: The Biography of Isidore Nagler*
(New York: 1950); Marx Lewis, *A Half Century of Achievement: The History of Millin-
ery Workers' Union Local 24* (New York: 1960).

[11] On this point see Henry David, "Jewish Labor History: A Problem Paper," in Moshe

generally. However, in recent years, historians such as Herbert Gutman have stressed the need for studies of the context in which organized labor operated.[12] The culture, economic situation and broad attitudinal structure of American workers have received increasing attention. A similar need exists for American Jewish labor. Lloyd Gartner provided a model for such studies in 1960.[13] His book on Jewish immigrants in England covers the totality of life. There are discussions of trade unionism and radical political activity, but most of the volume discusses the slighted areas of occupation, housing, health, welfare institutions, domestic life, crime, education and religious affairs. Thus Jewish labor is examined within the context of the total community.

Moses Rischin has done a similar work on the Jews of New York City.[14] When compared to Gartner's work, Rischin's book gives more attention to the labor and radical movements and to political developments in general. There is less emphasis on subjects such as education, religious affairs and Zionism. Yet Rischin's volume is most valuable in developing the life of Jewish immigrants in their major American center. His chapters on the economic situation, housing, crime, sanitation, cultural developments, and the conflict between German and Russian Jews provide the background against which trade unionism and socialist politics must be viewed.

809

In an article in this volume, Selma Berrol adds to this work on the life of the Jewish immigrant community by examining the much discussed relationship between mobility and education. She concludes that education may have been less important than previously thought for the first and second generation of Jewish immigrants. Her study points to other avenues of mobility. It is the kind of work that is needed on the basic life experience of the Jewish community.

Beyond the confines of New York City, even the institutional side of American Jewish labor history has been barely touched. In general, American Jewish labor has been studied as though it were equivalent to New York Jewish labor. Developments in Chicago are perhaps the single exception to this fascination with the largest Jewish community in America. Yet as Jews from beyond the Hudson River never tire of repeating, the experience of Jews in New

---

Davis and Isidore Meyer, *The Writing of American Jewish History* (New York: 1957), pp. 83-88 and Berman, "A Cursory View of the Jewish Labor Movement," pp. 82, 94.

[12] Herbert Gutman, "Work, Culture and Society in Industrializing America, 1815-1919," *American Historical Review*, LXXVIII (June, 1973), 535-537.

[13] Lloyd Gartner, *The Jewish Immigrant in England, 1870-1914* (London: 1960).

[14] Moses Rischin, *The Promised City: New York's Jews, 1870-1914* (Cambridge: 1962).

York City does not necessarily reflect the situation elsewhere in the nation. We will not know if Jewish workers in smaller cities followed a similar path to those in New York City until Jewish labor is studied around the country. Once again sources are a major reason for this particular lacuna in the study of American Jewish labor. Unlike New York City, Jewish workers in smaller cities were less able to create institutions which they led, or in which they were a major constituent, and thus the history of Jewish workers tends to become part of the general labor history of the area.[15] Within the Jewish community of these cities, the institutional record is left largely by communal organizations or leaders, not by the labor movement.

810

Progress in this area is possible, however, through the use of census materials and oral history. In recent years, historians have used computers to help analyze large bodies of quantitative data. In addition, the possibilities of the manuscript census records have become clearer as a resource for studying the living conditions of workers.[16] At the opposite pole from quantitative data, oral history adds to the traditional historical record. A recent oral history of Jewish workers in Pittsburgh indicates that such material can become a valuable resource.[17]

Ida Cohen Selavan's contribution to this volume is a rare effort to discuss Jewish labor in a medium-sized American city. She combines oral history material with more traditional sources in exploring the almost unknown world of Jewish workers outside New York City. It should serve to stimulate further work of this type.

Students of American Jewish labor have stressed the uniqueness of the trade union policies and political activities carried through by the Jewish labor movement. Although the unions in the needle trades did not follow identical policies, as a group they pioneered in the use of impartial umpire systems for settling grievances; they had concern for the economic health of their industries, including use of the unions to control competition among employers; they used the contract process to build up job control for the unions; they developed a wide range of welfare programs that included banks, health institutions, leisure facilities and social insurance;

[15] This is clearly seen in Sara Cogan, comp. *The Jews of San Francisco and the Greater Bay Area, 1849-1919: An Annotated Bibliography* (Berkeley: 1973).
[16] For the use of census materials in an earlier period, see Sophia M. Robison, *Jewish Population Studies* (New York: 1943).
[17] National Council of Jewish Women, Pittsburgh Section, *By Myself I'm a Book: An Oral History of the Immigrant Jewish Experience in Pittsburgh* (Waltham: 1972).

and they took an active role in politics, with the International Ladies' Garment Workers' Union particularly active in this respect.[18] While none of these features were unique to the unions in the needle trades, the complete range produced a distinctive brand of unionism within the American labor movement. How does one account for this distinctive type of unionism?

An explanation must be fashioned from three interconnected themes. First, the socialist background and commitment among the leadership of the unions in the needle trades; second, characteristics of the Jewish community which significantly affected trade unionism and the Jewish labor movement generally; and third, the economic structure of the needle trades.

The socialist leadership hoped that the Jewish labor movement would become a distinct sub-community within American Jewry. Such a sub-community would have a socialist and secular ideology, its own communal institutions, and a distinctive culture. Vigorous trade unionism in the industries that employed a large portion of the Jewish work force was part of this labor movement, as was solidarity with other American workers and an emphasis on political action. Yet socialism did not operate independently within the Jewish community: it constantly was modified and influenced by traditional cultural, religious and social attitudes. Ultimately these restraints, the impact of the Americanization of the immigrant, and changes in the political attitude of the leadership—produced by the weaknesses of socialism as a political movement and the appearance of a revitalized reform impulse in the New Deal—ended the attempt to build a socialist community within the larger Jewish population.

A number of scholars have investigated the relationship between the socialists and the larger Jewish community. Moses Rischin has pointed out that the secular Jewish socialists really did not escape the religious past of the Jewish people. Instead they developed a "folk religious ethic" that combined socialist ideology, and an emphasis on industrial exploitation, with scriptural references.[19] C. Bezalel Sherman has suggested that there is a connection between

811

[18] Selig Perlman, "Jewish-American Unionism, Its Birth Pangs and Contributions to the General American Labor Movement," *Publications of the American Jewish Historical Society*, XLI (June, 1952), 297-337; J.B.S. Hardman, "The Jewish Labor Movement in the United States: Jewish and Non-Jewish Influences," *ibid.* (December, 1952), 98-132; Moses Rischin, "The Jewish Labor Movement in America: A Social Interpretation," *Labor History*, IV (Fall, 1963), 234.

[19] *Ibid.* p. 236.

the messianic image in Judaism and the attraction of the messianic aspects of socialism for Jews.[20] On a more concrete level, Abraham Cahan opposed the efforts of some Jewish socialists to attack traditional religious practices. He feared such attacks would hinder the ability of socialists to reach Jewish workers.[21] Several scholars have stressed that most Jewish immigrants remained loyal to the religious practices that they had brought from Europe, and Sherman has claimed that such identification interferred with the efforts of the International Ladies' Garment Workers' Union to organize the Jewish workers in the trade.[22] Yet he also notes that socialism attracted many Jews, who were seeking the status denied to them within the traditional Jewish community. Socialism gave these persons the opportunity to gain self-esteem through their identification with the course of history and their role in the creation of a Jewish labor movement that would further the ultimate transformation of society. Thus the American Jewish labor movement not only protected the concrete interests of workers, but it also provided purpose and meaning through identification with the ultimate victory of socialism.[23]

Even at a less millennial level, Abraham Menes has suggested that strikes were affected by intangible psychological factors that flowed from the position of the worker within the larger Jewish community. Strikers often walked out to win recognition as individuals of worth, who had some influence in the economic world, even if they lacked such impact within the larger Jewish community.[24]

One must also consider the competing loyalties of class, as demanded by the socialists, and of place, as found in the landsmanschaften. So strong was this sense of geographical identity that the socialist Workmen's Circle had to make a place for landsmanschaften within its ranks. In addition, the Jewish labor movement faced the constant threat of the individual's desire for material success, which weakened his commitment to socialism and unionism.

The complexity of these issues only enhances their interest and importance. Although valuable work has been done, it has been in

---

[20] C. Bezalel Sherman, "Labor in the Totality of Jewish Life," *YIVO Annual of Jewish Social Science,* IX (1954), 384.

[21] C. Bezalel Sherman, "Nationalism, Secularism and Religion in the Jewish Labor Movement," *Judaism,* III (Fall, 1954), 356-357.

[22] Abraham Menes, "The East Side-Matrix of the Jewish Labor Movement," *Ibid.,* p. 369; Goren, *New York Jews and the Quest for Community,* ch. 9; Sherman, "Nationalism, Secularism and Religion," p. 356.

[23] Sherman, "Labor in the Totality of Jewish Life;" Menes, "The East Side".

[24] *Ibid.,* p. 377.

shorter, basically interpretive pieces, or as part of studies that are devoted primarily to other subjects. If work proceeds on the nature of the workers' lives within the immigrant Jewish community, the raw material will emerge for a full-scale assessment of the relationship between major characteristics of that community and the Jewish labor movement.

The economic structure of the needle trades themselves is also a vital factor in explaining the activities of the unions in these industries. Some of the policies adopted by the garment unions relate directly to the need of both employers and workers to control non-union shops; to the relatively small size of enterprises in the needle trades when compared to companies in major American industries; to the seasonality of production, which made job control even more crucial an issue; to the lack of welfare capitalism on the part of the small employers, which left the field open for unions; and to the relatively mild impact of strikes in the needle trades upon the general public.[25] This last factor, combined with the poor labor conditions in the industries, roused considerable support from reformers, and even led to some positive response from conservative sources. When such considerations are combined with the ideology of the leadership, and the characteristics of the Jewish work force, the total picture is before us. The best synthesis of these factors to date is by Melvyn Dubofsky for the period 1910-1918 in New York City.[26] Work of this type for other periods and places needs to be done.

813

Jewish labor must be studied not only within the broader Jewish community, but within the larger American scene as well.[27] The Jewish labor movement may have influenced the practices of American labor unions, but influences from beyond the Jewish community were also important in the activities of the unions that contained the bulk of the organized Jewish work force. Jewish labor leaders always planned to integrate their unions fully into the larger American labor movement; but their socialist ideology, and in the case of the Amalgamated Clothing Workers, the problem of dual unionism, slowed this development.[28] Such an inte-

[25] Carpenter, *Competition and Collective Bargaining;* Melvyn Dubofsky, *When Workers Organize: New York City in the Progressive Era* (Amherst: 1968); Selig Perlman, "America and the Jewish Labor Movement: A Case of Mutual Illumination," in Davis and Meyer, *The Writing of American Jewish History,* p. 95.

[26] Dubofsky, *When Workers Organize.*

[27] On this point, see Hardman, "The Jewish Labor Movement in the United States," especially pp. 122-130; Perlman, "America and the Jewish Labor Movement," p. 100; Berman, "A Cursory View of the Jewish Labor Movement," p. 94.

[28] C. Bezalel Sherman, *The Jew Within American Society: A Study in Ethnic Individu-*

gration ultimately did take place as the radicalism of Jewish labor leaders cooled by the 1930's while the climactic events of the Great Depression led the American labor movement to a greater acceptance of industrial unionism, political action and other features of unionism in the needle trades. Today Jewish labor is American labor—one can make no real distinction.[29] However, examination of the relationship between Jewish labor and the broader American labor movement, in the years when there was a separate identity, can be most useful.

Jewish workers created a defineable labor movement, but so did the Germans. A study of differences and similarities would be rewarding. The Finns shared many of the characteristics of Jewish labor, but they did not dominate an industry. As a result, the Finns failed to achieve control over a national labor organization. How many of the differences between Jewish labor leaders and the heads of the craft unions—who were often of English or Irish origin—flowed from differences in the experiences of the ethnic groups? What portion of the differences is related to conditions in specific industries or to changes in the American economy as a whole? Is the continued leadership of the unions in the needle trades by Jews, even after the work force has become largely non-Jewish, as significiant a development when it is viewed against the broader situation? Irish and German labor leaders also continued to maintain leadership despite changes in the ethnic make-up of their unions. Clearly, a study of Jewish labor, within the broader American situation, is a valuable conceptual tool.

To date relatively little has been done in this area. Melvyn Dubofsky's fine study of New York City in the Progressive era is based upon a comparison of the Jewish trade unions and other labor organizations.[30] John Laslett has provided us with a valuable comparative study of socialism in a number of American unions including the International Ladies' Garment Workers' Union.[31] The comparative approach once again provides insights that would

814

---

*ality* (Detroit: 1961), pp. 166-167. Will Herberg has pointed out that the rank and file of Jewish workers sought acceptance within the larger American community. However, America often failed to reciprocate. See Will Herberg, "Jewish Labor Movement in the United States: Early Years to World War I," *Industrial and Labor Relations Review*, V (July, 1952), 523.

[29] This point was strongly made in the 1950's. See the remarks by David Saposs (pp. 371-372) and by Philip Taft (p. 387) in "Proceedings of the First Session of the Editorial Advisory Council of the YIVO History of the Jewish Labor Movement in the United States (Sept. 13, 1953)," *YIVO Annual of Jewish Social Science*, IX (1954).

[30] Dubofsky, *When Workers Organize.*

[31] John Laslett, *Labor and the Left: A Study of Socialist and Radical Influences in the American Labor Movement, 1881-1924* (New York: 1970).

not appear in studies that focussed only on one or another of these unions.

Two articles in this volume seek to continue work on the relationship between Jewish labor and the broader American labor movement. Robert Asher discusses the role played by the needle trades unions within the American Federation of Labor. He believes that their influence within the organizational structure of the A.F.L. was minor even though, by virtue of size, the International Ladies' Garment Workers' Union should have had a greater role. Asher clearly indicates the reasons for this lack of influence, and he surveys the complex relationship between the American Federation of Labor and the International Ladies' Garment Workers' Union. The article reveals once again the usefulness of viewing the Jewish labor movement within a larger framework.

Sheila Polishook's contribution to this volume explores another aspect of the relationship between the American Federation of Labor and Jewish labor. She discusses the little known support of Zionism by the A.F.L. in 1917, and the reasons for such a step when the socialist Jewish labor leaders opposed Zionism on ideological grounds. The analysis of Samuel Gompers' motivation, and the relationship between the activities of organized labor and the policies of the Wilson Administration, is most valuable. The importance of the connection between Jewish and American concerns becomes quite apparent. Thus one can only renew the calls made over the last two decades that more serious attention be devoted to the relationship between Jewish labor and the general American labor movement.

In the literature on the American Jewish labor movement, only two books have attempted to provide a comprehensive account. The history of the early Jewish labor movement, edited originally by Elias Tcherikower, and later translated from Yiddish and abridged in the English version by Aaron Antonovsky, is a fine scholarly effort that connects the institutions of the Jewish labor movement to the conditions of Jewish workers, both in Europe before the passage and after their arrival in the United States.[32] Unfortunately, it ends in 1890, and efforts to continue this history have thus far failed to produce the remaining volume.[33]

815

[32] Aaron Antonovsky, *The Early Jewish Labor Movement in the United States* (New York: 1961). On the European background, also see Ezra Mendelsohn, *Class Struggle in the Pale: The Formative Years of the Jewish Workers' Movement in Tsarist Russia* (Cambridge, England: 1970).

[33] See footnote 29. In the late 1960's, Ezra Mendelsohn tried to bring together a number of scholars, under the auspices of YIVO, to prepare a companion volume to the original one edited by Tcherikower. To date, this volume has not appeared.

In the absence of a comprehensive scholarly account, Melech Epstein's two volumes remain as the only work that presents the total history of the American Jewish labor movement.[34] The volumes have the virtues of completeness in time coverage, and attention to the full breadth of the Jewish labor movement. This includes not only trade unions and radical parties, but fraternal organizations and the press. However, the weaknesses are also quite clear. The books are overly descriptive and so poorly footnoted that they provide little basis for further scholarly investigation. In addition, the focus is squarely on the Jewish labor movement—not Jewish labor—with only minimal connections to the broader characteristics of the Jewish community or the American labor movement. Thus after more than a half century of work on American Jewish labor, we still await a comprehensive, scholarly and definitive treatment. Hopefully we will not have to wait much longer for such a volume to appear.

816

[34] Melech Epstein, *Jewish Labor in U.S.A.* (New York: 1969). This revised edition contains the two volumes originally published in 1950 and 1953 plus a new Preface that updates the work.

# Jewish Immigrants and the American Labor Movement, 1900-1920

Irwin Yellowitz

America was the land of opportunity for immigrants so long as they did not make any demands upon, nor challenge the interests of, those people already in the country. Fortunately, the economic growth of the United States in the years 1880-1920 was so enormous that newcomers often could find their way without directly opposing more established groups and without requiring their support. However, immigrants found that the more desirable skilled jobs in many of the major cities were within the jurisdiction of labor organizations. In addition, Jews who sought to unionize in the garment industry faced difficulties with existing groups of organized workers. Jewish immigrants had to enter these unions as a means to better jobs and improved working conditions. Their efforts to do so, and the responses by the trade unions, are the subject of this article.

The reaction of the American labor movement to the Jewish immigrant is clear: in a word – cool. Why this is so is less obvious. Jews who attempted to enter trade unions often ascribed their difficulties to prejudice and disinterest.[1] Comments by some labor leaders lend apparent credence to such charges.[2] In addition, there were sharp political differences. Jewish workers were usually led by radicals whose concept of unionism was profoundly different from the non-Marxist orientation of most American trade unions.[3] However, as

---

1  In 1918 and 1919, David Saposs conducted a series of interviews with officials of trade unions, including Jewish labor leaders. The major subject discussed was the organization of immigrants. Jewish newcomers received considerable attention. I am indebted to Professor Robert Asher of the University of Connecticut for suggesting the significance of this source. On the issue of prejudice and disinterest, see the interviews with Hyman Schneid, M. Feinstone, United Hebrew Trades; David Wolff, Joseph Schlossberg, Amalgamated Clothing Workers; Philip Zausner, J. C. Skemp et al, Painters, Decorators and Paper Hangers; Sol Broad, Structural Iron Workers; David T. Davies, Bookbinders, David B. Saposs Papers, State Historical Society of Wisconsin.

2  See the interviews with J. E. Roach, New York office, American Federation of Labor; Benjamin Schweitzer and Ephraim Kaufman, United Garment Workers; Louis Sylvester, Wood, Wire and Metal Lathers; Carl Andelin, Boot and Shoe Workers; Thomas McMahon et al, United Textile Workers, Saposs Papers.

3  See interviews with Max Zuckerman, Cloth Hat and Cap Makers; Michael Newman, Bookbinders; L. Siskind, Tinsmiths and Metal Workers of New York State; Marsden G. Scott, Typographical; Frank Hoschang, Barbers; George W. Perkins, R. Youkelson, Cigar Makers; Joseph Schlossberg; David Wolff; Benjamin Schweitzer and Ephraim Kaufman; Carl Andelin; J. C. Skemp et al; Sol Broad, Saposs Papers.

Originally published in *American Jewish History* (December 1981). Reprinted by permission of the American Jewish Historical Society.

one examines the American labor movement of the early twentieth century closely, it becomes clear that the resistance to organizing Jewish workers was only part of a similar attitude toward immigrants generally. This, in turn, was a manifestation of a basic policy that excluded all those who were not considered essential to the trade interests of the existing union membership.[4]

American craft unions stressed control over the supply of labor. However, the forces liberated by the industrial revolution reduced the role of skill as a limitation upon the labor supply, and this led unions to renewed efforts to find other devices for this purpose.[5] Exclusion of new workers of all types – including of course immigrants – accordingly became common. The anomaly of trade unions that sought *not* to organize workers led many to cite prejudice as the cause, but in fact such a policy operated in many cases in which ethnic or religious differences were not a factor.

Such behavior was based on perceived self-interest, and it could operate even in unexpected situations. Thus the politically progressive Tapestry Workers' Union ignored those outside its stronghold of Philadelphia until the threat from cheaper non-union labor made organization of such workers necessary. The effort failed and the union ultimately collapsed.[6] After much conflict, the Hebrew Hatters' Union won admission to the United Hatters of North America, but the formerly Jewish union then proceeded to use restrictive devices to control new entrants into its ranks. The United Cloth Hat and Cap Makers' Union had a heavily Jewish membership, strong socialist sympathies and an industrial union structure, yet this did not prevent consideration of means to restrict entry into the more skilled jobs during the slow season of 1904.[7] Thus the immigrants, including Jewish newcomers, faced a trade union movement that had little interest in organizing them unless they constituted a threat or a clear addition to a specific organization's strength. Such a determination varied with conditions in different trades, and thus the sub-

---

4   On the activities and policies of American trade unions, see Sumner Slichter, *Union Policies and Industrial Management* (Washington: 1941); William Haber, *Industrial Relations in the Building Industry* (Cambridge: 1930); Lloyd Ulman, *The Rise of the National Trade Union* (Cambridge: 1955); Philip Taft, *The A.F.L. in the Time of Gompers* (New York: 1957); and George Barnett, *Chapters on Machinery and Labor* (Cambridge: 1926).

5   Irwin Yellowitz, *Industrialization and the American Labor Movement, 1850-1900* (Port Washington: 1977).

6   Gladys Palmer, *Union Tactics and Economic Change* (Philadelphia: 1932), pp. 36-37, 46-47.

7   Moses Rischin, *The Promised City: New York's Jews, 1870-1914* (Cambridge: 1962), p. 189.

ject requires careful study of those industries that employed significant numbers of Jews.

Exclusion was most important in craft unions composed mainly of the more skilled workers. The few industrial unions in the American labor movement took a quite different attitude toward immigrants, but one that again flowed from their understanding of the basic interests of the membership and the organizations themselves. Industrial unions generally represented less skilled workers even though some members might be skilled. As a result, entry into the industry was relatively easy, and attempts at exclusion nearly impossible. The influence of an industrial union rested not on control over a group of key skilled workers, but in its inclusion of a significant portion of the total work force. Accordingly, the United Mine Workers of America had a long-standing policy of organizing all the workers in the industry.[8] As we shall see, the Amalgamated Meat Cutters and Butcher Workmen of North America became increasingly interested in recruiting immigrants as it changed from a craft to an industrial union. Ethnic and religious factors were less important than trade considerations in these cases just as they were in the instances of exclusion.

Union officials naturally were aware of the widespread hostility toward immigrants that existed among their members, yet reactions differed according to the union's situation. In many craft unions, the national officers were prepared more quickly than the members to accept newcomers. However, their efforts to carry out such a policy were incomplete and slow. Only when trade interests were directly imperilled did they act decisively and quickly. On the other hand, Frank Kasten, president of the United Brick and Clay Workers, an industrial union of unskilled workers, claimed that immigrants were better unionists than the natives because the newcomers were less individualistic and had fewer opportunities for better jobs. Kasten believed "All that is necessary is sympathetic understanding" in order to organize the immigrants. He was determined to do

819

---

8 John Laslett, *Labor and the Left: A Study of Socialist and Radical Influences in the American Labor Movement, 1881-1924* (New York: 1970), pp. 192-193, 197; Herbert Gutman, "The Negro and the United Mine Workers of America: The Career and Letters of Richard L. Davis and Something of Their Meaning: 1890-1900" in Julius Jacobson, ed., *The Negro and the American Labor Movement* (Garden City: 1968); Victor Greene, in his *Slavic Miners on Strike: Immigrant Labor in Pennsylvania Anthracite* (Notre Dame: 1968), argues that immigrants were eager to support the union. He believes labor leaders did not do enough to recruit them. Metal miners in the West freely admitted European immigrants. See Mark Wyman, *Hard Rock Epic: Western Miners and the Industrial Revolution, 1860-1910* (Berkeley: 1979), ch. 2.

so, and his plan was to expel any members who attacked the immigrants as such. As a result, Kasten concluded that his "national organization has had no trouble with race prejudice."[9] Clearly the union could not be effective without the immigrants, and thus Kasten acted in a way quite different from officers in other unions.

The activities of American labor have been labelled "business unionism" – a seemingly contradictory term that actually describes the situation well. American unions often shared a fundamental outlook with the firms against which they contended. Basic to both was the survival and expansion of the organization. Its interests determined the answer to almost every question. Within the labor movement, this led to jurisdictional disputes, and, even inside a union, locals or particular groups of workers quarrelled with their fellow unionists since even the craft was often too broad a vessel to prevent conflicts based on still smaller units of self-interest.

It is important to realize that this type of unionism arose to meet the difficulties of organizing workers in the United States. Although not confined to America, here it was not significantly affected by socialism and industrial unionism – two forces that mitigated its impact elsewhere. In an environment in which employers used a wide variety of tactics – both legal and illegal – to weaken unions; in which basic American traditions of individualism, competition, equal opportunity and mobility were offered as a powerful alternative to the collective advance demanded by the unions; in which the courts and other agencies of government often openly allied themselves with employers against the labor movement; in which constant and increasing immigration, plus migration from rural America, provided a pool of workers whose poverty and need for work made them ready to seize opportunities at the expense of those already on the job, or those on strike – in such an environment one can understand why the labor movement would turn to the type of organization and tactics that seemed to allow for survival and some degree of effectiveness.

American unions generally chose to concentrate on the most organizable workers, usually those most skilled, to group these workers around a common bond – similar job interests – and to reject

820

---

9    Interview with Frank Kasten, Saposs Papers. See also the interview with Charles Dold, Piano and Organ Workers, *Ibid*. Dennis Lane, Secretary-Treasurer of the Amalgamated Meat Cutters and Butcher Workmen, which also was committed to industrial unionism by World War I, echoed these sentiments: "As to educating the foreigner into the trade union and its principles, I find that the immigrant worker is educated and grasps the fundamental principles quicker than the white or Negro Americans." Lane to Saposs, March 12, 1919, *Ibid*.

those persons or policies that diluted this common bond. Attempts to establish alternative types of unions usually failed. Business unionism thus meant that the trade interests of a union were paramount, and this was no less true in terms of Jewish immigrants than in other areas.

This does not discount ethnic and religious prejudice. Examples abound of hostility among ethnic groups within the American work force, and these often were exploited or encouraged by employers.[10] Moreover, ethnic and religious tensions could add emotional force to policies of exclusion directed against Jewish workers and other immigrants. Yet they were not the basic factor, but an additional force that intensified and supplemented the fundamental trade interests.[11] In this article, I propose to test this judgment by examining a number of different industries in which Jewish workers were found.

The men's clothing industry had large numbers of Jewish workers. The disputes between the leadership of the established union, the United Garment Workers, and representatives of the semi-skilled and unskilled workers who produced the great bulk of the clothing, ultimately led to a split that created the Amalgamated Clothing Workers in 1914 as the organization for the great majority of those in the industry.[12] The conflict between the national leaders of the United Garment Workers, who were of older immigrant stock, and the newcomers in the major garment centers led to charges on both sides in 1914 that ethnic and religious prejudices were at work. President Thomas Rickert of the United Garment Workers charged that

821

---

10 For examples of hostility between Jews and other workers, see Melech Epstein, *Jewish Labor in U.S.A.* (New York: 1950), vol I, pp. 77–79, 101, 116, 187, 253, 372; Joel Seidman, *The Needle Trades* (New York: 1942), pp. 90–91. John Dyche, Secretary-Treasurer of the International Ladies' Garment Workers' Union, reported in 1906 that the Philadelphia local of waistmakers consisted almost entirely of Jews because the non-Jewish girls, who constituted one-half the labor force, refused to join. See *Proceedings*, 1906, p. 13. For a similar situation in the men's clothing industry of Rochester, New York, see the United Garment Workers, *Proceedings*, 1897, p. 7. Ethnic and religious problems persisted in the Amalgamated Clothing Workers Union after its formation in 1914. See the interviews with David Wolff and Sam Levin in the Saposs Papers. There was also trouble between German and East European Jews. See Epstein, *Jewish Labor*, vol. I, pp. 101, 109, 111, 126.
11 Rischin, *Promised City*, p. 189.
12 J. M. Budish and George Soule, *The New Unionism in the Clothing Industry* (New York: 1920), pp. 73–76, 85–95, 118–124; Matthew Josephson, *Sidney Hillman: Statesman of American Labor* (Garden City: 1952), chs. 4–6; Seidman, *Needle Trades*, ch. 6; Epstein, *Jewish Labor*, vol. I, pp. 367–369, 381–382, 414–419; vol. II (New York: 1952), ch. 4.

plans to take over the union were discussed widely in the Jewish press prior to the 1914 convention, and that "the Jewish workers were urged to 'come into their own' and select for their leaders 'people of their own flesh and blood' and put out of business the 'Irish and Catholics' who from their point of view were running the organization."[13] Rickert's opponents in turn contended that the leaders of the union had stirred up anti-Semitism among the delegates to the 1914 convention. The insurgents claimed the union's officers regarded their opponents as "greenhorn tramps." In addition, one member of the General Executive Board, Margaret Daley, supposedly told a meeting of female delegates that the challengers "were Jews, [who] sought to put Jewish officers in the places of the non-Jews, and as decent American women they must stand solidly against [them]."[14] As late as 1919, two Jewish organizers for the United Garment Workers still claimed that "the Jews have been poisoned against the United Garment Workers. Their leaders and newspapers feature the issue as a struggle between Jews and Gentiles."[15]

Despite the heat generated by this issue, it was not at the root of the difficulties. Instead, ethnic and religious prejudice were used by both sides at the climactic moment to organize their forces and to build emotional resentment against the other side. The opponents of the United Garment Workers' leadership concentrated on Thomas Rickert and B. A. Larger – both Catholics – but generally ignored the Jews who dominated the General Executive Board.[16] While some of these were German Jews of an earlier generation, one would have to stretch the well-known tensions between these segments of America's Jewish community to conclude that the issue was basically a question of prejudice. The fundamental reasons lay in the conditions of the trade and the composition of the union.

The United Garment Workers had been founded in 1891 to orga-

---

13 United Garment Workers, *Proceedings*, 1918, p. 40. For similar charges made by officers of the union at the 1914 convention, see *Proceedings*, 1914, pp. 103, 116, 231.

14 Report of the New York delegation to the 1914 convention of the United Garment Workers in Amalgamated Clothing Workers, *Documentary History of the Amalgamated Clothing Workers, 1914–1916* (New York: 1920), p. 24. See also pp. 21, 31–32.

15 Interview with Benjamin Schweitzer and Ephraim Kaufman, Saposs Papers.

16 For exceptions see the interviews by Hyman Schneid and A. D. Marimpietri of the Amalgamated Clothing Workers, Saposs Papers. There was a significant group of Jews on the General Executive Board throughout the decade prior to the split in 1914. The boards elected in 1910 and 1912 had as many as six Jews out of the eleven members. See United Garment Workers, *Proceedings*, 1910, pp. 192–199; 1912, pp. 245–249.

nize all aspects of the men's clothing industry within an industrial union framework. However, organizing proceeded best among the most skilled workers in the industry – the cutters – and in the work clothes segment. This situation led to a heavy reliance on the union label. Manufacturers of work clothes recognized that their clientele was likely to be influenced by the union label, and this led to contracts with the United Garment Workers. The result of these developments was that the union contained only a small portion of the work force in the industry even though it claimed jurisdiction over the whole.

The leaders of the immigrant workers opposed this traditional policy.[17] The union label could not be used successfully in the men's coat and suit trade since the general body of customers ignored it. Thus manufacturers had no incentive to accept the union. Occasional efforts to organize by means other than the label also proved to be ineffective. Organizing trips to Chicago by the presidents of the union in 1899 and 1900 produced little, which led the two men to suggest a more modest approach with attention to a single firm or the more skilled workers.[18] In addition, the union's officers were unsympathetic to poorly organized strikes by locals. These might weaken the national organization and were bound to fail.[19] The situation also was complicated by the existence of a few organized shops, or a small group of organized cutters, in the midst of a mass of unorganized workers. The union insisted that its agreements with employers be maintained, yet efforts by locals to organize the majority of the workers dragged those already under union contracts into the fray. In 1907, this problem led the leaders of the United Garment Workers to expel its affiliate in New York City.[20]

823

In the years between 1891 and 1910, the union of the garment workers had become the union of some of the garment workers. Once this occurred, the interests of those inside the organization rapidly diverged from those outside. Although there were ethnic and religious differences between the two groups, the conflict between them resulted from their fundamentally different trade interests. This emerged clearly in the strikes of 1910 and 1913 in Chicago and New York City.

The Chicago strike of 1910 was the most significant effort to that

---

17 Interviews with Hyman Schneid, A. D. Marimpietri, David Wolff and Sam Levin, Saposs Papers.
18 President Edward Sabine, United Garment Workers, *Proceedings*, 1900, p. 2; President B. A. Larger, *Proceedings*, 1901, p. 10.
19 United Garment Workers, *Proceedings*, 1901, p. 25.
20 Epstein, *Jewish Labor*, vol I, pp. 381–382.

date to organize the mass of immigrants in the men's clothing industry. All agreed this was a difficult task. It was a highly competitive industry that ground down wages. As those most sympathetic to a major effort at immediate organization later pointed out, the workers "were almost without exception recently arrived immigrants unable to speak English and ignorant of the customs and conditions of other American workers. The racial and linguistic differences among the workers themselves made common understanding and action extremely difficult."[21] After the split of 1914, the Amalgamated Clothing Workers made a strenuous effort to organize the industry in Chicago. Not until 1919 did a breakthrough occur.[22] Thus the task was a formidable one. Equally important, the trade interests of the United Garment Workers prevented it from making a major effort to organize these immigrants.

The strike began among the workers themselves in September 1910, and the United Garment Workers subsequently authorized it. However, the strikers demanded that all shops and workers, even those under union agreements, join the strike. President Rickert assented only reluctantly.[23] He feared that these contracts might be imperilled if workers violated them to support the unorganized strikers. The organized were being asked to make a sacrifice for the unorganized. In this case, as in so many others, the union that represented the organized workers refused to take more than token steps in this direction.

President Rickert then made every effort to settle the strike as soon as possible. A very poor agreement in early November was quite properly rejected by the strikers. Rickert was castigated for this proposed agreement, which the strikers regarded as a sell-out.[24] On December 1, Rickert proposed a second agreement, which this time had the support of the Joint Strike Board that included representatives of progressive organizations and the Chicago Federation of Labor. Although again turned down by the strikers, Rickert had gained about all that he could, and the agreement of January 11, 1911, that ended the strike at Hart, Shaffner and Marx, the largest manufacturer, and that had the support of Sidney Hillman and A. D. Marimpietri, two of Rickert's critics within the union, essentially restated the terms of December 1. The agreement of January 11 still left the

21 Amalgamated Clothing Workers of America, Chicago Joint Board, *The Clothing Workers of Chicago, 1910–1922* (Chicago: 1922), pp. 18–19.

22 *Ibid.*, p. 2.

23 *Ibid.*, p. 27.

24 United Garment Workers, *Proceedings*, 1912, p. 26; interview with Sam Levin, Saposs Papers.

strikers at other shops out.[25] On February 3, 1911, Rickert called off the strike for these workers, as hopeless, without further consultation with them.[26] This led to renewed charges of sell-out against the leaders of the United Garment Workers.

Rickert's objectives seem clear. He did not favor the strike, did not believe it could succeed, and did not propose to risk the gains made by the union to date in pursuit of a vain objective. In this regard, he followed the earlier policy of the union. Once the strike was underway, Rickert did not sell out the immigrant workers so much as refuse to take major risks on their behalf. His first concern was to preserve his organization and its gains. In contrast, the leaders of the immigrants demanded that unionization of the great mass of garment workers receive first priority.

825

Such a demand raised the issue of whether the addition of the immigrant workers to the union might not produce more problems than gains for the existing membership and its leaders. The United Garment Workers followed the common policy among American trade unions of prohibiting partisan politics by the organization. This was to avoid disturbing the frail harmony within the union. The leaders of the immigrants were socialists who made it clear they wanted the United Garment Workers to take a strong political stance.[27] The leadership of the union also followed the great majority of labor organizations in demanding restriction of immigration to reduce competition in the work force. The leaders of the newly arrived immigrants naturally wanted the doors to remain open.[28] As we have noted, the reliance on the union label received scant support from the leaders of the immigrant workers. Ultimately, the leadership of the United Garment Workers did not want the newcomers, who were so numerous they might soon take over the union.[29] Yet the union would not give them up for fear that a new labor organization would be a potential competitor, and that jurisdictional disputes would develop. Thus the immigrants received minimal attention and support from the United Garment Workers; yet they were not permitted to organize separately.

---

25 *Clothing Workers of Chicago*, pp. 43–46.
26 United Garment Workers, *Proceedings*, 1912, p. 31.
27 United Garment Workers, *Proceedings*, 1899, p. 2; 1901, pp. 18–19; 1903, pp. 161–162, 190; *Amalgamated Clothing Workers Documentary History*, pp. 53, 72, 94–95.
28 United Garment Workers, *Proceedings*, 1900, p. 15; 1914, pp. 94–95; *Amalgamated Clothing Workers Documentary History*, pp. 92–93.
29 The workers on strike in 1910 ultimately numbered 18,000, more than the entire membership of the United Garment Workers. See Josephson, *Sidney Hillman*, p. 49.

The events in Chicago led to renewed efforts to organize immigrants elsewhere in the men's clothing industry. In 1911, locals of the United Garment Workers in New York City and Baltimore challenged the leadership for its failure to stress organization, and its over-emphasis upon the interests of the label shops. The group in New York City began to plan for an organizing strike, and in an attempt to maintain influence over events, the leaders of the United Garment Workers joined the effort. Ultimately, a general strike in the men's clothing industry of New York City was called on December 30, 1912.[30] Events followed the pattern of Chicago. Again Rickert did his utmost to end a strike he really did not want. He did not sell out the interests of the workers since the agreements proposed were reasonable, the privation of the strikers was great, and the employers seemed unlikely to give in.[31] In fact, Rickert tried to establish the type of labor-management-public system of labor relations introduced into the ladies' garment industry by the Protocol of 1910. This would benefit the workers by establishing machinery for conciliation and adjustment of grievances, and for improvement of working conditions, while meeting the union's desire to avoid major strikes, especially the bitter ones over formal recognition. However, the leaders of the immigrant workers in New York City insisted on the acceptance of the union by employers. In addition, they made demands, such as a forty-eight hour week, that Rickert considered unattainable at the time.[32] The strike ended in March, 1913 without major gains for those who had braved a winter without work.

By 1914, the leaders of the immigrants had the choice of trying to seize control of the union or of bolting to form their own organization. They first made the effort to take power, a difficult task because the constitution of the union provided representation to the convention so as to favor small locals over bigger ones.[33] The leadership was able to charter new small locals whose delegates supported them. Amendment of the constitution required convention action or a two-thirds vote of the membership, both of which were beyond the power of the insurgents. Rickert and the other officers also strictly

---

30 Epstein, *Jewish Labor*, vol. I, pp. 414–416.
31 Once the Amalgamated Clothing Workers was formed, Sidney Hillman acted much as Rickert had, when, as President of the new union, he tried to resolve a bitter strike in Baltimore in 1915. See *Amalgamated Clothing Workers Documentary History*, pp. 56–59.
32 United Garment Workers, *Proceedings*, 1914, pp. 44–52.
33 This provision was part of the original constitution of 1891, and it remained unchanged. For an effort to alter it, see United Garment Workers, *Proceedings*, 1903, p. 222.

enforced long-standing rules about dues in arrears to exclude their opponents in New York City from the 1914 convention.[34] It was during this struggle for power in the union that the ethnic and religious charges became part of the campaign. The leaders of the immigrant workers finally decided that the struggle to seize control of the union would be a protracted one. Secession was the only alternative and they chose it in 1914.

In the ladies' garment industry, which had even more Jewish workers than the men's trade, internal conflict also developed. The issue of organizing new Jewish immigrants reappeared, as did the commitment of the more skilled to the less skilled newcomers. Moreover, the conflict developed between skilled cutters, who were mostly native born, or of old-time Irish and German origins,[35] and the newly arrived immigrants from Eastern Europe. However, in this case, the International Ladies' Garment Workers' Union (ILGWU), founded in 1900, ultimately supported the newcomers, and the skilled workers were the ones to leave the union, although the breach eventually was healed. Thus there was once more an obvious ethnic and religious division, but the importance of these differences again requires careful attention to conditions in the industry.

There were two distinct problems that involved the cutters. The first concerned the acceptance of new cutters into the union. In the early years of the ILGWU, the major local of cutters (No. 6) consistently opposed the existence of other locals in their craft. The major problem was with new Jewish immigrants who entered the trade with cutting experience. As the delegate of Local 6 explained in 1903, the local "could not afford to lower the standard of high grade work and reasonable wages in order to accept every cutter at work in the trade into the Union."[36] Thus the immigrant Jewish cutters were to be left unorganized because their entrance would adversely affect the interests of Local 6. The new immigrants worked for about half the scale of Local 6, and, if admitted, under the conditions of relative weakness that existed, the employers would pressure the local to lower its scale closer to the wages of the newcomers.

In addition, a skilled union, such as Local 6, tried to limit the supply of union workers to the number of jobs available. In the ladies' garment trade, there were relatively few of the best paid cutter's

827

---

34 In a similar situation earlier, the rules were applied less harshly. United Garment Workers, *Proceedings*, 1904, p. 33.
35 Louis Levine, *The Women's Garment Workers: A History of the International Ladies' Garment Workers' Union* (New York: 1924), p. 135.
36 International Ladies' Garment Workers' Union, *Proceedings*, 1903, p. 16.

posts. If the local increased its membership, it also intensified competition for these desirable jobs. Thus Local 6 had refused admission even to cutters who could earn the scale in an effort to monopolize the best positions for the existing membership. It amalgamated with a smaller local of cutters only reluctantly in 1905 since refusal to do so could lead to a destructive competition between the two to the advantage of the employer.[37] This type of thinking affected locals of the less skilled as well once they grew in power. Thus President Abraham Rosenberg of the ILGWU reported in 1912 that jurisdictional disputes among locals within the union had been unknown before 1910. However, after that date, "when these unions grew into thousands of members, the problem of finding employment for all of them made its appearance."[38] The result was conflict among the locals.

828

A local of cutters on the East Side of New York City did exist within the ILGWU, and Local 6 repeatedly demanded its abolition. In response, the cutters from the East Side pointed out that such action would leave the great mass of newly arrived cutters unorganized in favor of the few highly paid cutters of Local 6.[39] The ILGWU wrestled with the problem over several years, and in 1904 President Benjamin Schlesinger proposed a compromise that would make the Jewish immigrant cutters members of a sub-local under the control of Local 6.[40] Thus he hoped to meet the trade interests of the cutters in Local 6, but not stop the organizing of Jewish immigrant cutters.

Both groups resisted this compromise. The local of cutters from the East Side bolted the union. The two older locals of cutters seriously considered secession and the creation of a national union of their craft. However, opposition from President Samuel Gompers of the American Federation of Labor blocked such action.[41] Gompers opposed the separation of the cutters for fear this would destroy the fledgling ILGWU and the chances for organization of the industry.

In 1907, the conflict reappeared when a new independent union of Jewish immigrant cutters approached the predominantly Jewish ILGWU just as Jewish independent unions asked for admission to non-Jewish labor organizations. The spokesman for the new union stressed that his organization reached out to "quite a different class

37 *Ibid.*, 1904, pp. 10, 18; 1906, p. 20.
38 *Ibid.*, 1912, p. 18.
39 *Ibid.*, 1903, p. 22.
40 *Ibid.*, 1904, p. 18.
41 James O'Neal, *A History of the Amalgamated Ladies' Garment Cutters' Union, Local 10* (New York: 1927), pp. 71-73.

of people working under different conditions for a different class of employers." Since they could not achieve the wage scale of the cutters within the ILGWU (now renumbered Local 10), a separate charter was necessary if these workers were to be organized at all. The delegates from Local 10 did not oppose the idea of a charter for "Hebrew speaking cutters," but only if they had the union scale of wages. Clearly this new organization once again represented lesser paid cutters.[42] To resolve the impasse, the convention of the ILGWU returned to the sub-local scheme of 1904, but this time Local 10 refused to admit the newcomers under any arrangement. The General Executive Board of the ILGWU responded by organizing a new local to contain the immigrant cutters.[43] This threat to its trade interests was one major factor that led Local 10 to leave the ILGWU in 1908 – a break that lasted until 1910.

829

In his study of the cutters' local, the socialist James O'Neal recognized that the issue was not ethnic but economic. As he observed with disapproval: "The upper layer of skilled workers in all industries where trade unions have appeared have always passed through a period of exclusiveness and many skilled workers have never advanced beyond this stage."[44] This basic policy clearly dictated the specific reactions of the cutters in response to the new body of immigrant Jewish workers in their craft.

The second issue involved the relationship between the cutters and the general body of less skilled workers in the union, most of whom were recent Jewish immigrants. One reason the cutters joined the ILGWU originally was to enlist the aid of other garment workers in support of their strikes. Yet it quickly became apparent that the less skilled expected help from the cutters in return. This posed a problem for the cutters in the ILGWU similar to that faced by the officers of the United Garment Workers. The response was the same: the skilled workers refused to subordinate their interests to the organizing needs of the poorly unionized, less skilled immigrants. A District Council of cutters and tailors, established by the convention of 1906, failed to overcome "years of ill-will and mutual distrust." In 1907, Local 10 refused to withdraw its members from shops struck by order of the New York Joint Board and the General Executive Board of the union. This led to a temporary revocation of Local 10's charter. The dispute came at a weak point for the young union, and it nearly destroyed the organization.[45]

42 International Ladies' Garment Workers' Union, *Proceedings*, 1907, pp. 28-29.
43 *Ibid.*, p. 38; 1908, p. 30.
44 O'Neal, *History of Local 10*, p. 88.
45 International Ladies' Garment Workers' Union, *Proceedings*, 1905, p. 16; 1906,

The intra-union strife ended in 1910 for several reasons. The ILGWU had begun its growth into a major union with the Shirtwaist Strike of 1909. The cutters recognized that their interests were better served by being part of a growing union. Also it was clear that a stronger ILGWU would challenge Local 10's control over cutters in the better paid shops by introducing the lower paid immigrant cutters. Thus Local 10 opened its ranks to the newcomers. This process was to be repeated in many other trades. Once faced with a serious threat from the immigrant workers, the union admitted them. Otherwise trade interests often dictated exclusion.

Clearly there were ethnic and religious differences between the cutters in Local 10 and the other members of the union. As the reporter from the *Forward* put it in describing the departure of Local 10 from the convention of 1908: "The Christian delegates have left the hall. . . ."[46] Yet one must agree with the conclusion of John Dyche, Secretary-Treasurer of the ILGWU. In 1905, he pointed out the distrust and suspicion that existed among workers in the various branches of the industry. He then added that "the ill-will between the cutters and the tailors in our own trade is accentuated by the differences of language, race and religion. . . ."[47] Dyche correctly understood that the basic issue was the conflicting trade interests, and that these were enhanced by ethnic and religious differences.

Admission of the newcomers did not end the conflict among the cutters. The old-timers in Local 10 continued to monopolize the best jobs. In addition, during the long periods of lay-off or short time, the old-timers controlled the limited amount of work available. Finally, the newcomers were led by socialists in contrast to the traditional politics of the existing leadership. Thus the newcomers sought control of the local. Since they soon outnumbered the old-timers, it was not long until this occurred.

By 1918, the newcomers had won all the leadership posts, but even before that the impact of socialist politics could be seen as the local opposed the American Federation of Labor's support for American participation in World War I. Most important, the equal distribution of work during slow times was established as policy in March, 1914. The better jobs also began to flow to the newcomers on a more regular basis. In 1919, a small group of old-timers tried to use the job issue, and the supposed radicalism of the local's leaders, to

830

---

p. 16–17; 1907, pp. 23, 31; 1908, pp. 10–12; Levine, *Women's Garment Workers*, pp. 135–142; O'Neal, *History of Local 10*, chs. 6–7.

46 Levine, *Women's Garment Workers*, p. 139n.

47 International Ladies' Garment Workers' Union, *Proceedings*, 1905, Secretary-Treasurer's Report, p. 8.

regain control. In this effort, help came from James P. Holland, President of the New York State Federation of Labor, who opposed all radicals within the labor movement. Considering the numerical superiority of the newcomers in Local 10, it is no surprise that this challenge failed.[48] Other groups of immigrant Jewish workers also found that entrance into a union did not guarantee acceptance or equal treatment.

When one leaves the garment industry, Jewish workers were a small minority in trades dominated by non-Jewish workers. Yet trade interests continued as the basic motive for the unions' response to Jews and other immigrants. This is well illustrated in the bookbinding industry.

831

Most Jewish bookbinders brought the trade with them from Europe, but since methods were different in the United States, they had to relearn much of the work. This, together with the fact that they had recently arrived and were deficient in their knowledge of English, resulted in Jewish bookbinders working in small shops, owned by Jews, mostly on the Lower East Side of New York City, and at much lower wages than in the larger shops. The Irish workers who dominated Local 1 of the International Brotherhood of Bookbinders in New York City, and the union generally, ignored the Jews in the trade. However, they soon realized the newcomers had to be "organized as a matter of self-defense . . . as the workers learned American ways they threatened the bookbinders in the rest of the city."[49] On the other hand, Jewish workers sought affiliation with the International Brotherhood "because of the prestige and desire to be part of the American labor movement," but also because unemployed members of Local 1 often replaced Jewish strikers.[50] This would be prevented by membership in the American union.

The willingness of Local 1 to accept Jewish workers also was influenced by the fact that the newcomers already had organized their own independent union in 1910 with the help of the United Hebrew

---

48 On the conflict within Local 10, see O'Neal, *History of Local 10*, chs. 9–12. According to David Dubinsky, President of the ILGWU from 1932 to 1966, Samuel Gompers told Holland that the socialist leaders of Local 10 were not a front for the Bolsheviks. This action continued Gompers' efforts to build the strength and unity of the ILGWU. On this incident, see David Dubinsky and A. H. Raskin, *David Dubinsky: A Life with Labor* (New York: 1977), p. 51. For a similar struggle between old-timers and new Jewish members in the painters' union, see Philip Zausner, *Unvarnished: The Autobiography of a Union Leader* (New York: 1941), pp. 56 ff. and the discussion below.
49 Interviews with H. Kaplan and Michael Newman, Bookbinders, Saposs Papers.
50 Interview with Sigmund Skolnik, Bookbinders, Saposs Papers.

Trades.[51] Thus the Jewish bookbinders could be even more effective competitors. Shortly thereafter, the Jewish union joined Local 1 as an auxiliary. As we observed in the case of the ladies' garment cutters, this device was used to allow the admission of those regarded as less desirable members under the control of the existing local. The relationship between the Jewish auxiliary and Local 1 remained uneasy because Jewish workers continued to work for lower wages, which endangered the wage scale of the parent local. Ultimately, the Jewish workers were placed into their own local in 1918, apparently because they might otherwise leave the International Brotherhood. Clearly the union organized these Jewish workers reluctantly and only when its own interests seemed threatened.

832

In evaluating the role of ethnic and religious prejudice among the bookbinders, one must study the history of the union as a whole. Such an examination indicates that the more powerful locals also maintained a policy of exclusion on issues that did not have ethnic or religious ramifications. In the late 1890's, the locals in New York City opposed both the inclusion of other skilled bookbinders in their locals, and a universal travelling card. As one spokesman for these locals remarked, many of the workers involved "would be only too glad to come into our shops and deprive our people of work."[52] Local 1 also hesitated to organize new shops, apparently content with the relationship between its membership and the number of jobs it controlled. Pressure from employers who recognized the union, and who thus faced competition from non-union firms with lower labor costs, led the International's officers in 1902 to try to increase the pace of unionization. Despite this effort, the convention of 1910 heard the old complaint that "many locals are making little or no effort to increase their membership."[53]

If the skilled bookbinders were reluctant to organize workers of a similar level of skill, it should not be surprising that they had little interest in the less skilled. President Robert Glackling acknowledged in 1910 "that the attitude of our male members in the matter of organizing women in the bindery has been one of apathy and non interest generally." As early as 1906, Glackling had urged that women be organized precisely because they were cheaper labor. If left out of the union, they might ultimately be used to replace the skilled workers, particularly as machinery reduced the level of skill.[54] Yet locals con-

---

51 It was at this time that Local 1 called for the organization of the Jewish bookbinders. International Brotherhood of Bookbinders, *Proceedings*, 1910, pp. 227, 239.
52 *Ibid.*, 1898, pp. 27–29, 53, 72; 1900, pp. 27–28, 51–52.
53 *Ibid.*, 1902, p. 109; 1910, pp. 202, 224, 229, 239.
54 *Ibid.*, 1910, pp. 262, 224, 242, 243, 260; 1906, pp. 168–169.

tinued to resist, especially if the women were to be organized within the existing local. As one female delegate commented in 1914: "The men are afraid of the women. They are afraid the women will out-vote them."[55] In general, the national officers, often backed by the convention, urged the organization of all workers in the trade, but powerful locals refused to carry out the policy. The job interests of these locals led them to policies of exclusion and non-cooperation. As one participant in the struggles in New York City noted: "For years past everything but harmony has existed . . . It has always been a case of each local for itself and the devil take the hindmost."[56] The attitude toward the Jewish bookbinders fits within this broader pattern.

The reaction of the International Cigar Makers' Union to Jewish immigrants also reflects the interests of the existing membership. George W. Perkins, the President of the union, and Samuel Gompers, who remained an officer of the Cigar Makers during his many years as President of the American Federation of Labor, tried to have the union accept the production of cigars by division of labor and the use of machinery. However, many locals still represented workers who made more expensive cigars by hand, and they resisted opening the union to the less skilled for fear it would accelerate technological change in their segment of the industry.[57] Despite the efforts of the leadership, it was not until the 1920's that the union removed the major restrictions on the entry of the unskilled. However, by that time "the manufacture of cigars had largely passed into the hands of non-union workers, and the restrictive policies of the union had made these workers either indifferent or positively hostile to it."[58]

Jewish workers had been in the skilled work force, and they were members and leaders of the union.[59] As with the United Garment Workers, trade issues divided these Jews from the new Jewish workers as fully as they separated Jewish immigrants from non-Jews. Newer immigrants, including Jews, entered the industry as unskilled workers and the existing locals of skilled workers generally ignored them. However, in Chicago, the new Jewish cigar makers organized under the aegis of the United Hebrew Trades.[60] Perkins regarded this

---

55 *Ibid.*, 1914, p. 324.
56 *Ibid.*, 1912, p. 313.
57 For the history of the issue, see Yellowitz, *Industrialization and the American Labor Movement*, pp. 63-71.
58 Slichter, *Union Policies*, pp. 216-222. The quotation is from p. 221.
59 Jews were prominent among delegates to the union's convention. See Cigar Makers' International Union, *Proceedings*, 1912, pp. 47-49.
60 Interview with Hyman Schneid, Saposs Papers.

new organization as a distinct threat because it could become the basis for a dual union of the unskilled cigar makers, not only in Chicago, but elsewhere. This was even more likely since the new union was headed by Jewish socialists who were committed to militant organizing. To head off this possibility, Perkins favored the admission of the new organization into the Cigar Makers' Union even though he regarded the Jewish workers as radicals and troublemakers.[61]

The new local (527) was 65 percent Jewish, and it had a largely Jewish and socialist leadership that was hostile to traditional trade agreements and emphasis on the union label, and that criticized the union for not organizing the unskilled.[62] Local 527's delegate to the convention of 1920 demanded increased rank and file participation in the affairs of the national union, and he called for a variety of political steps in line with radical opinion at the time.[63] In addition, the leaders of Local 527 supported a variety of specific policies to advance the interests of the unskilled workers within the union.[64] Clearly the entry of the unskilled immigrants – in the case of Local 527, largely Jewish – introduced not so much new ethnic groups into the union as new trade interests. Such interests had determined the policies of the union up to the entry of Local 527, and they were to continue to do so.

The complex relationship between ethnic and trade issues is perhaps most clearly revealed in the entrance of the skilled Jewish hatters into the United Hatters of North America in 1899. Skilled Jewish workers had begun to enter the trade in the 1880's. After efforts to join the existing craft unions generally failed, the newcomers began to organize their own local organizations. In 1892, 1895 and once again in 1899, efforts were made to merge with the national unions in the trade. However, these efforts failed.[65] The ostensible reason for this rejection was the familiar one that the immigrants were poorer workers, and that they accepted wages below the union scale. If admitted, they supposedly would lower standards in the union shops. After the admission of the Jewish workers into the United Hatters, Martin Lawlor, one of the union's officers, indi-

834

---

61 Interview with George W. Perkins, Saposs Papers.
62 Interview with R. Youkelson, Saposs Papers.
63 Cigar Makers' International Union, *Proceedings*, 1920, pp. 14, 16, 17, 32, 35, 38, 60, 64, 71, 79, 80.
64 *Ibid.*, pp. 44, 45, 63, 72-73, 80, 83-84.
65 Donald B. Robinson, *Spotlight on a Union: The Story of the United Hatters, Cap and Millinery Workers International Union* (New York: 1948), p. 75; Charles Green, *The Headwear Workers: United Hatters, Cap and Millinery Workers International Union* (New York: 1944), p. 55.

cated how flimsy such an argument was. He claimed that the quality of work done by the Jewish skilled hatters was comparable to that among union hatters. However, if the immigrants demanded prices equivalent to the union scale, employers saw no reason not to recognize the union and thus secure the advantage of its national label. Accordingly, the Jewish workers had no inducement to raise their wages and thereby forfeit jobs to the United Hatters.[66]

Beyond this problem lay the more fundamental one that the United Hatters followed an exclusionary policy. As Lawlor, now Secretary-Treasurer, pointed out twenty years later, the union still did not seek out immigrants. The union stressed the union label, and there was only a limited market for label goods. Too many union shops meant that this market might be exceeded, which weakened the appeal of union recognition to employers.[67] As we have observed, much the same policy existed in the United Garment Workers.

The membership figures for the United Hatters in this period demonstrate the effects of such an approach. In 1896, the union's membership stood at approximately 5800. It was much the same until the entrance of the Jewish hatters in 1899. Between 1896 and 1898, only eight locals gained members while thirteen declined and one remained even. The number of apprentices was tightly controlled, and a $25 initiation fee further limited new members.[68]

The national officers of trade unions often realized the negative effects of an exclusionary policy before the membership. The same situation developed in the United Hatters. President Edward Barrett opposed the limitations on new members. He believed that the union had to grow to retain its bargaining power, but he ruefully pointed out in 1897 that "in most every instance where a shop could be gained we have met with more or less opposition to taking even a few men into the Union, and sometimes we have lost good shops in consequence of such opposition from our own members."[69] Thus the rank and file of hatters shared the belief of the cigar makers and many other skilled workers that a small union limited to areas of strength could protect their interests best.

In addition to this barrier, the Jewish hatters faced prejudice as well. The lengthy verbatim record of the United Hatters' proceedings in 1900 – when the issue of admitting the Jewish workers was exhaustively debated – reveals this clearly. Several delegates indicated

835

66 United Hatters of North America, *Proceedings*, 1900, pp. 31–32.
67 Interview with Martin Lawlor, Saposs Papers.
68 United Hatters of North America, *Semi-annual Reports*, December 1896–1898.
69 *Ibid.*, December 1897, President's Address, p. 3.

their negative attitude and sense of superiority toward Jews. Thus one officer, who had been charged with accepting an illegal payment from a Jewish hatter to secure him a union card, denied the allegation and then added: "Mr. Moffat [President of the United Hatters] I have no doubt believes it to-day, and would prefer to take that Jew's word to mine." A delegate from Boston charged that the six or seven "Hebrews" in his local were responsible for the internal discord over the admission of the Jewish hatters. When union cards had to be distributed to the new Jewish members, one officer reported that several of the small number of Jews already in the union had to be called upon since "you will understand that the names of these Jews are very hard to pronounce, and these gentlemen were employed to write them out in English. . . ."[70] It is significant that all three of these delegates voted to admit the Jewish hatters.

Secretary George Phillips of the United Hatters strongly supported the admission of the Jewish workers. At one point, he remarked

> I hate this prejudice against people on account of their race or faith. I dislike it very much. It is very prevalent in our trade. I know men who have been refused admission into the association just because they were Jews. It is prevalent in the district where I come from [Brooklyn]. I have seen it, and is it not a mean, contemptible principle to say, 'because you are a Jew you cannot associate with us? Because you cannot speak the English language, you cannot associate with us.'[71]

Considering the barriers of trade union policy and prejudice among the workers, how did the Jewish hatters win entry into the union?

To begin with, as we have noted, there was sentiment among many of the national officers to open membership more widely. Their pressure in this direction did allow small groups of specialized workers to enter the union.[72] However, the addition of the 1462 Jewish hatters in 1899 would have increased the union's membership by about 25 percent. The national officers were not prepared to upset the exclusionary principle in so major a way unless forced to do so. This compulsion arose as a result of the union's decision to strike against the firm of F. Berg and Company in September, 1899.

The strike was an outgrowth of the union's attempt to offset surplus labor in the hat manufacturing center of Orange, New Jersey by reducing hours to fifty-five per week. Manufacturers who had agreements with the union protested that this rule placed them at a severe

---

70 United Hatters of North America, *Proceedings*, 1900. The statements by the delegates are from pp. 99, 82 and 95 respectively.
71 *Ibid.*, p. 172.
72 Green, *Headwear Workers*, pp. 72–73.

836

competitive disadvantage since non-union shops continued to work longer hours. The major problem was F. Berg and Company, the second largest soft hat factory in the nation. Although the local union had only 110 members there out of a total work force of 500, it called a strike to enforce shorter hours.[73] The strike started auspiciously as all but 29 of the workers left their jobs. However, Berg and Company quickly turned to the Jewish hatters' union – still outside the United Hatters – and offered them the jobs of the strikers.

Before the strike began, the Jewish hatters had been negotiating to enter the United Hatters. They now seized the opportunity and told the leaders of the national union that unless they were admitted immediately, Jewish hatters would fill all the jobs in the struck factory. The officers of the United Hatters still tried to avoid admitting the Jewish workers, but the options finally became clear: admit the new members or lose the strike. The leaders of the United Hatters then decided to admit the Jewish workers in toto.[74] A decade of exclusion, job competition and strikebreaking ended in a week.

The admission of the Jewish hatters provoked strong opposition from a small group within the union led by Edward Moore of Philadelphia. Since the inclusion of so many new workers altered the basic membership policy of the union, Moore claimed it was unconstitutional unless approved by two-thirds of the members in a referendum. He argued that the Berg strike could have been won without the admission of the Jewish hatters and defended the traditional policies based on exclusion and the union label. The officers responded by stressing the need to remove the significant threat to the union posed by a large and well-organized body of hatters who were excluded from membership. The delegates agreed as they voted 44 to 3 to support the admission of the Jewish hatters.[75]

The trade interests of the United Hatters ultimately dictated inclusion of the Jewish workers just as for years such interests had encouraged exclusion. The ability of the Jewish hatters to maintain an independent union increased the pressure on the United Hatters to absorb the newcomers. Obviously the personal prejudice against Jews had not changed overnight. However, since it had not been the major reason for exclusion prior to 1899 – although it certainly reinforced such a policy – when the choice between trade interests and prejudice had to be made, that choice was clear.

837

---

73 United Hatters of North America, *Proceedings*, 1900, pp. 288–290.
74 *Ibid.*, pp. 86–89, 290–295. On a similar situation in Newark, New Jersey in 1894, see pp. 95–96. In a further effort to win the strike against Berg, the United Hatters also organized immigrant workers in Reading, Pennsylvania. See pp. 73–74, 76–77.
75 For Moore's arguments, see *Ibid.*, passim. The vote is on pp. 284–285.

838

Exclusion as a device to protect existing interests reached its peak in the building trades. Yet it was more a matter of degree than kind. The situation of Jewish workers in the structural iron industry is a fine example.

The bulk of the membership in the International Association of Bridge and Structural Iron Workers was from the native born or older immigrant groups. It was concerned with the construction of buildings, bridges and piers. Jewish workers, known as shop men, entered the trade by working "at the fabrication of bridge, structural, ornamental and grill work." These jobs were judged by many in the union to be peripheral to the trade interests of the majority. Moreover, although relatively skilled, the shop men earned considerably less than the so-called "outside" workers.[76] The International President admitted that the slow progress in organizing shop workers was not only because "there are a large percentage of the foreign element . . . who cannot speak or read English," and who often indulged in ill-prepared strikes, but also as a result of lack of cooperation by outside locals.[77] Once again, the international officers stressed the need to organize the newcomers since to control the outside work "it is necessary that we control the men that fabricate as well as erect the material."[78] In addition, the shop men constituted a pool of new members that could offset any losses from the many jurisdictional conflicts which affected the union. However, locals often disagreed with this policy.

In New York City, many shop workers were Jewish, and originally they had been organized within an existing local of outside workers. As Sol Broad, one of the leaders of the shop men later reported, this arrangement did not work well. He complained that the Jews had been only "reluctantly admitted" and that they were not "recognized and were looked down upon as foreigners who were unworthy of consideration. A Jew was seldom given the floor to discuss matters or to bring up new matters. If a Jew did get a chance to speak, he was disregarded."[79] This lack of acceptance by the Irish and German members of the local reflected not only personal differences, based on ethnicity and religion, but basic trade conflicts as well. This becomes clear if we follow the subsequent history of the Jewish shop workers.

The local of outside workers and shop men collapsed, following

---

76 International Association of Bridge and Structural Iron Workers, *Proceedings*, 1914, p. 656; 1916, p. 687; 1918, p. 609.
77 *Ibid.*, 1914, p. 656; 1915, p. 768; 1916, p. 596; 1920, p. 547.
78 *Ibid.*, 1918, p. 609.
79 Interview with Sol Broad, Saposs Papers.

an unsuccessful strike, and the shop workers organized their own independent union with the help of the United Hebrew Trades. Subsequently, this union, which had almost as many members as the largest of the locals inside the International Association, was admitted to the national union in 1913. As in most situations where organizing was in an early stage, frequent strikes took place among the shop men. The Jewish leaders of the shop workers' local in New York City claimed that the outside men – their fellow unionists who were not on strike – continued to use material made by scabs in the struck shops. They demanded that the outside workers boycott all products from struck shops and that the union prohibit agreements with employers that prevented sympathy strikes.[80] The outside workers did not oppose sympathetic action when their own interests were involved, but they felt no real connection to the problems of the shop workers. Although the issue in New York City could be framed in ethnic and religious terms, this was not the case elsewhere. Thus in Kansas City, shop workers, whose ethnicity differed little from the outside local in the city, also complained that their calls for a boycott of products produced by scab labor in struck shops were ignored by fellow unionists who used this material in their outside work.[81]

839

Even among the international officers, there were definite limits on their positive attitude toward the shop men. While anxious to organize shop workers, the international officers were not prepared to allow the power of the large, socialist led and Jewish dominated local in New York City to grow. Thus in 1918, the local was divided into three over the bitter objections of its Jewish leadership. A Jewish issue might seem involved, but when one compares the strong business unionism of the international officers with the quite different principles held by the leaders of the shop men in New York City, the ethnic and religious differences assume less significance.

Reluctant acceptance of immigrants, including Jews, when trade interests required, also marked the policies of other unions in the building trades. The case of the Jewish house painters in New York City is significant in this regard.

The national union of painters was established in 1887, but during the 1890's it split into two hostile factions. The local unions of painters in New York City stayed aloof from this struggle. However, when the split was healed, and the Brotherhood of Painters reestablished in 1901, the painters' unions in New York City and Philadelphia still refused to join the national organization. They did so a few

---

80 International Association of Bridge and Structural Iron Workers, *Proceedings*, 1916, pp. 759, 779; 1918, pp. 707, 744; 1920, pp. 563, 573-574, 733-737.
81 *Ibid.*, 1920, pp. 703-704.

years later only under the strongest pressure, which included threats by the Brotherhood to charter dual unions.[82]

As we noted with the bookbinders, the intense localism of locals in New York City largely resulted from fears that members of the national union from other parts of the country would move to the metropolis to take advantage of the higher wages generally found there.[83] In addition, the high rate of unemployment in the trade intensified the fear of outsiders.[84] Finally, the trade was becoming less skilled as ready mixed paints allowed employers to stress quantity over quality of work.[85] Older union painters had organized around the value of their skill to employers, and they viewed the immigrants as generally inferior workers who would accelerate the decline in the level of skill. In fact, the immigrants merely took advantage of developments already well underway.

Beyond these trade factors lay ethnic and religious prejudice. J. C. Skemp, the General Secretary-Treasurer of the Brotherhood of Painters, Decorators and Paperhangers, was sympathetic to the organization of immigrants for trade reasons. Skemp viewed Jewish workers in the trade positively: they were hard workers, courageous strikers and good unionists. He also pointed out that immigrants often were more open to unionism than the native born from small cities. Despite this, he acknowledged that there was ethnic prejudice within the union that led to separate foreign language locals. Moreover, he expressed several stereotypical views of his own concerning Jews. Thus Skemp characterized the Jews as clannish because of their desire for officers from their own group. He cited their supposed radicalism, yet also claimed that the Jew quickly gave up Yiddish as a result of "his business instinct and his desire to exercise the rights of citizenship. . . ."[86] Among those less inclined to accept Jewish workers for trade reasons, such stereotypes contributed to prejudice.

The painters' locals in New York City accepted some Jews.[87]

---

82 Brotherhood of Painters, Decorators and Paperhangers of America, Proceedings, 1903 in *Official Journal*, XVII (September, 1903), 617–623.

83 Report of J. C. Skemp, General Secretary-Treasurer, *The Painter and Decorator*, XXVII (September, 1913), 563–564. For a similar situation in other unions, see the United Brotherhood of Carpenters and Joiners of America, *Proceedings*, 1900, p. 15; the Amalgamated Meat Cutters and Butcher Workmen of North America, *Proceedings*, 1902, p. 18; and the discussion of the bookbinders above.

84 Zausner, *Unvarnished*, pp. 106–109, 112.

85 *Ibid.*, p. 87.

86 Interview with J. C. Skemp et al, Saposs Papers.

87 Zausner, *Unvarnished*, p. 91. Local 123 of the Brotherhood (Cleveland) was a Jewish local. Lloyd Gartner, *History of the Jews of Cleveland* (Cleveland: 1978), p. 119.

However, they resisted admission of any large number of Jews or other immigrants. These locals controlled the better paid work on new buildings and they shared the widespread desire of skilled workers to maintain a balance between jobs and members.[88] This policy was so widespread in the Brotherhood that J. C. Skemp pointedly attacked it in 1913 as a threat to the union. He believed that new members lagged behind new jobs, and this encouraged non-union conditions.[89] A challenge to the policy of exclusion arose from the large and growing force of Jewish painters who entered the trade in the years after 1900. Barred from the better work by the locals of the Brotherhood, these men became "cockroach chasers" who did the so-called alteration jobs repainting older buildings. Wages were lower for such work, and the speed-up and unemployment even greater than elsewhere in the trade. It is no wonder immigrant Jews sought entrance into the Brotherhood to gain access to better jobs.

When refused admission, the Jewish painters formed their own Alteration Painters' Union in New York City in 1909. As with the Jewish hatters, the immigrants' ability to organize separately made them a threat to the national union, especially since the membership of the Jewish union soon exceeded that of the Brotherhood's locals in New York City.[90] Once again the national officers recognized the need to organize the newcomers, but the locals resisted.[91] Outnumbered by the immigrants, the old-timers stood to lose control over any merged organization. Such sentiments ultimately yielded to the reality of the situation, and in 1914 the Jewish painters' union joined the Brotherhood.

The newcomers quickly repeated the developments that took place in Local 10 of the ILGWU as they organized and gained control of the New York City District Council of Painters in 1915. This effort required the help of the national officers who set up a special electoral procedure to prevent fraud.[92] Control was necesary to prevent discrimination in job arrangements for the newcomers. The Jewish painters in the Brotherhood before 1914 originally had been in regular locals, but they had switched to a separate Jewish local to

841

---

88 Zausner, *Unvarnished*, p. 40.
89 *The Painter and Decorator*, XXVII (September, 1913), 563.
90 The Jewish bricklayers' union of Cleveland also had to prove it could survive as an independent organization before Local 5 of the International Bricklayers and Stonemasons Union would agree to a merger. See Gartner, *Jews of Cleveland*, pp. 134, 351n, 131.
91 Interview with Philip Zausner, Saposs Papers.
92 Zausner, *Unvarnished*, pp. 71–72.

try to get a larger share of the better jobs.[93] The new members expected no better treatment, but they had the votes to take charge.

The conflict between newcomers and old-timers assumed some strange forms. In the Wood, Wire and Metal Lathers International Union, the old-timers contended that new Jewish and Italian members in New York City were undercutting existing union rates. Supposedly to prevent this, a minimum 50 percent of all the lathers on a job had to be "Americans" so that they "could see that the Jewish and Italian members received the scale which the locals were maintaining."[94] Yet this policy also had another result – unstated by union officials. Since immigrants often predominated on certain jobs done by Jewish or Italian contractors, the 50 percent rule would open places for "American" workers. Yet there was no corresponding 50 percent rule on jobs where old-timers predominated. This policy could lead to bitter competition for jobs within the union. Thus one local of the Lathers struck against some of its own members, who were working for a Jewish contractor and supposedly were rate cutting. The Jewish and Italian union members refused to leave their jobs, which led to a sympathy strike by other unions in support of the Lathers' leadership. Ultimately, only the intervention of the police forced the immigrants out.[95]

Immigrants had no sentimental attachment to American trade unions, especially in the face of prejudice from the old-timers. Although some Jewish radicals viewed entrance into the national unions as a base for increased political activity, for most Jews the attraction was practical and material. Access to better jobs was clearly paramount, but there were other advantages as well. David Brodsky, President of a largely Jewish local in the Amalgamated Sheet Metal Workers' International Alliance, made these quite clear. As the interviewer's summary put it:

> A worker affiliated with international will find his card recognized all over the country. This local also benefited in one case where the teamsters refused to haul work of a non-union shop. This forced the employer to recognize the union. In another shop only Hungarian Jews were employed. They considered themselves superior to the Russian Jews and would not join the union. Brodsky appealed to the building trades council which called a sympathetic strike where material was used upon which the Hungarian Jews worked. They joined in short order.[96]

---

93 *Ibid.*, p. 91.
94 Ralph Brandt, General Secretary-Treasurer, Wood, Wire and Metal Lathers International Union to Saposs, November 14, 1918, Saposs Papers.
95 Interview with Louis Sylvester, Wood, Wire and Metal Lathers Union of Hudson County, New Jersey, Saposs Papers.
96 Interview with David Brodsky, Local 137, Saposs Papers.

On occasion, Jewish immigrants did not find it to their advantage to join the national union. One group of tinsmiths and metal workers had been in the Sheet Metal Workers' union in 1908, but despite some help from the national organization, they lost a hastily called strike and subsequently disbanded. When the local union reappeared in 1916, it chose not to join the national despite pressure from Brodsky's local to do so. The advantages to be gained seemed too few to justify the high initiation fee and per capita tax. In addition, the officers of the independent union were believers in industrial unionism and "revolutionary ideals," and they found the Sheet Metal Workers' union inhospitable to their views.[97] This type of situation, however, clearly was the exception.

Where the trade interests of a craft union called for militant organizing rather than exclusion, immigrants found entry much easier. The activities of the Brotherhood of Carpenters illustrate this point.

The carpenter's trade had undergone rapid technological change in the last quarter of the nineteenth century with the result that the work was greatly simplified.[98] This eased entry into the trade, which made a policy of exclusion even less likely to succeed than elsewhere. Thus the United Brotherhood of Carpenters and Joiners of America, founded in 1881, adopted a policy of aggressive organization. Unlike the painters' union, the national leaders of the carpenters could establish new locals in an area without the approval of the existing ones.[99] In addition, the Brotherhood of Carpenters recognized that there were many new immigrants in the trade, and the union not only enrolled them into the existing locals (where a two-thirds vote of the members was necessary to admit), but also created new foreign language locals to encourage their admission. These foreign language locals were an important part of the organizing strategy of the Brotherlood almost from its inception.[100] Up to 1900, the major foreign language locals were composed of German, French-Canadian and Scandinavian workers. At a later point, Italian and Mexican immigrants also were organized into separate locals. Throughout the period, separate locals of Black workers existed in the South.[101]

Jewish workers were members of regular locals, but as early as

843

---

97 Interview with L. Siskind, Saposs Papers.

98 Robert A. Christie, *Empire in Wood: A History of the Carpenters' Union* (Ithaca: 1956), pp. 25–28.

99 United Brotherhood of Carpenters and Joiners of America, *Constitution*, 1891, p. 7.

100 Between 1888 and 1900, 9.3 percent of the new locals were organized on a foreign language basis. United Brotherhood of Carpenters and Joiners of America, *Proceedings*, 1888–1900.

101 *Ibid.*, 1908, pp. 20, 208–209, 308, 345; 1912, pp. 29, 403, 763.

1892, separate Jewish locals appeared. The number of these locals increased as more Jews entered the trade. Once again, the attitude toward organizing Jews was a reflection of the more general admission policy of the national union or its locals. In the case of the Carpenters, this allowed Jewish workers to enter the national union steadily throughout the period. By 1908, a perhaps overenthusiastic estimate placed their number at 20,000 out of a total membership of 178,000.[102] Our own survey shows that sixteen Jewish locals were organized between 1892 and 1912 in addition to the Jewish carpenters who were members of regular locals.[103]

Unlike independent Jewish unions in other trades, the Jewish locals in the Brotherhood of Carpenters either gained the standard union conditions for their locality soon after their formation or moved steadily toward such standards. The Jewish locals in Boston, Chelsea, New York City, Philadelphia, Baltimore and Newark achieved parity with existing locals almost immediately. Those in Montreal and New Haven lagged behind for five or six years, but then gained equal conditions. Only in Cleveland did the Jewish local fail to reach the standard of other locals.[104] This equality of conditions allowed for consolidation with non-Jewish locals, or led members of Jewish locals that lapsed to move easily to other locals. Jews were not invisible in these regular locals. Although only one separate Jewish local had existed in New York City and it had been suspended in 1912, seven other locals there in 1916 had at least one Jewish officer.[105]

Jewish locals of the carpenters' union took little part in the national affairs of the organization. They rarely sent delegates to conventions, and they voted rather spottily in the elections for officers. There is no evidence that Jewish locals saw their interests as different from those of other members. Jewish locals did not differ markedly from other locals in their localities in voting patterns. Lloyd Gartner contends that the Jewish carpenters' local in Cleveland was not marked by the secularist and socialist views of the garment unions.[106] The behavior of other Jewish locals in the Brotherhood suggests this point may have wider validity.

The openness of the Carpenters to new immigrants waned after 1910. Although separate ethnic locals still were organized, the

---

102 *Ibid.*, 1908, p. 269.
103 Based on the proceedings of the union for the period 1894–1920.
104 See United Brotherhood of Carpenters and Joiners of America, *Proceedings*, 1906–1914, Secretary's Report; *The Carpenter* (August, 1916), 8–32.
105 *The Carpenter* (December, 1916), 25ff.
106 Gartner, *Jews of Cleveland*, p. 133.

Brotherhood deemphasized them. In addition, the union retreated from the use of foreign languages in its affairs. The subject always had provoked lively debate within the organization. German and French were used in the union's magazine and some other publications, but the efforts of other groups to gain similar concessions failed. In 1916 and 1917, the union insisted on the sole use of English in its major publications, and it then added a constitutional provision that after January 1, 1919 all business in locals of the union "shall be transacted in English." Any local that did not comply would have its charter revoked.[107]

The separate ethnic local always had been regarded as a necessary evil. The Brotherhood had been a leader within organized labor in calling for major restrictions on immigration. In the absence of such legislation, the union was prepared to organize the newcomers in order to protect the interests of its members. The increased strength of the Brotherhood and the heightened sense of hostility toward immigrants that marked the period of World War I led the Carpenters to reduce significantly the role of separate locals as an organizing device.

845

As we noted earlier, labor organizations that followed the principle of industrial unionism were much more open to immigrants. The Amalgamated Meat Cutters and Butcher Workmen of North America had started as a craft union, but technological change in the meatpacking industry led increasingly to an industrial organizing strategy. By World War I, the leadership recognized that newly arrived immigrants, Black migrants from the South and women had to be recruited if a strong union was to be built.[108] Before the switch in tactics, the attitude toward Jewish meat cutters had been ambivalent. By 1904, a "Hebrew Meat Cutters" local in New York City existed within the national union. However, the local soon folded and it was followed by other Jewish locals in New York City, both outside and inside the Amalgamated Meat Cutters.[109] With the decision to organize all workers in the industry, Jewish locals appeared in

---

107 United Brotherhood of Carpenters and Joiners of America, *Constitution*, 1917, p. 26. In 1921, the provision was softened a bit to "must be recorded" in English. This wording remained until 1975.

108 See David Brody, *The Butcher Workmen: A Study in Unionization* (Cambridge: 1964).

109 In 1895, before the national union was established, the United Hebrew Trades had sponsored a union of workers in the kosher butcher shops of New York City. *Ibid.*, p. 20. On the union that existed in 1904, see *Ibid.*, p. 118; Amalgamated Meat Cutters and Butcher Workmen of North America, *Proceedings*, 1904, p. 41. For later years, *Ibid.*, 1914, p. 77; 1917, pp. 76-77; *The Butcher Workman*, I

Chicago, Detroit and other cities during and after World War I.[110] Jewish workers also were members of regular locals, and, on occasion, they held local union offices.[111]

846

Organizing workers in the kosher meat and chicken trades did raise several problems for the national union. Conflict arose concerning the Sunday closing law in New York State. Workers in kosher butcher shops opposed this law because it provided no alternative Sabbath closing, and thus they lost two days' work per week. Although leaders of the Amalgamated were sympathetic to the position of the kosher butchers, the great majority of the union's members opposed any alternative Sabbath, claiming it would set back efforts to win a Sunday closing law elsewhere.[112] In addition, there was a religious complication in organizing the kosher chicken slaughterers. If a rabbi opposed the union, the workers were almost powerless because the chickens might be called unkosher. Union leaders tried to separate the labor and religious questions, but they were not always successful.[113] Despite these problems, the union recruited workers in the kosher meat and chicken trades as part of its broader effort to organize the entire industry.

In sum, the attitude of trade unions to the immigrants, including Jews, was motivated in the main by trade interests and the principles of business unionism. These permitted the organization of Jewish immigrants in many cases, but the ultimate determinant was always the effect on the interests of the existing union. Accordingly, recruitment efforts among immigrants differed from union to union, and they were often incomplete within a union. One must study the situation in each trade. As we have seen, the results of such a survey include basic similarities, but they also indicate differences which are equally part of the immigrants' relationship to the labor movement. Neither element should be lost in the continuing effort to understand the Jewish experience in America.

(June, 1915), 7; (November, 1915), 2 and Joseph Belsky, *I, The Union: Being the Personalized Trade Union Story of the Hebrew Butcher Workers of America* (New York: 1952).

110 Amalgamated Meat Cutters and Butcher Workmen of North America, *Proceedings*, 1917, p. 118; 1920, p. 227; *The Butcher Workman*, III (May, 1917), 4; (July, 1917), 2; Belsky, *I, The Union*, pp. 130-132.

111 Amalgamated Meat Cutters and Butcher Workmen of North America, *Proceedings*, 1920, p. 134; *The Butcher Workman*, IV (September, 1918), 5; V (August, 1919), 5; VI (July, 1920), 6.

112 *The Butcher Workman*, II (February, 1916), 3; (April, 1916), 1.

113 Amalgamated Meat Cutters and Butcher Workmen of North America, *Proceedings*, 1920, p. 81; Brody, *Butcher Workmen*, pp. 118-119.

# Reflections on the Anglo-American Jewish Experience: Immigrants, Workers, and Entrepreneurs in New York and London, 1870-1914

By ANDREW S. REUTLINGER

Between 1870 and 1915 more than 120,000 East European Jews came to Great Britain, some two million to the United States. The settlement pattern of these two immigrant streams was quite similar. In each case more than half made their homes in the great entrepôts of London and New York. And of these, few moved far from their point of disembarkation, settling by the water's edge in the East End and the East Side. In both cities petty commerce and light manufacture were the newcomers' primary sources of income. And in both England and America, established Jewry—sympathetically aware of the conditions that drove the immigrants to their shores, but unsure of their impact on the status of Jews in the larger society—gave them an ambiguous reception.

Yet for all these similarities, the evolution of the east European Jewish settlements in London and New York was marked by sharp differences. One example of this was the experience of Jewish labor unionism in the two countries. The successful unionization of the American immigrants is a familiar story. But Jewish immigrant workers in England were wracked by ideological dissension, and failed to create a form of unionization adapted to the conditions of twentieth century urban-industrial life. Instead, more traditional forms of communal organization, the *chevra* and the *landsmanschaft*, were adapted to the English environment, creating a social and economic network of minor synagogues and friendly societies.

The task before us is to describe those factors that contributed significantly to the divergent patterns of communal development among the East European Jewish immigrants to London and New York. Many of these factors lay outside the ghettos of the East End and the East Side, residing in the process of migration itself or in the differences between British and American values and

Originally published in *American Jewish Historical Quarterly* (June 1977). Reprinted by permission of the American Jewish Historical Society.

institutions during the late nineteenth and early twentieth centuries.

While much is known about the general patterns of westward movement of East European Jewry around the turn of the century, only conjecture has been offered as to who went where, when, and why.[1] While the United States received over 70% of the Russian Jewish immigrants of the period, many others found their way to Canada, South Africa, South America, and even a few to Palestine. About five percent settled permanently in Great Britain. One of these offered the most common explanation of this choice:

848

> In England, chiefly in London, the emigrants were composed chiefly of those who had to leave their countries because of social conditions and had not enough fare [to reach the United States] and had to leave their homes, suddenly, in haste, like refugees, and so on. About ninety percent of the immigrants in London had in mind to go on to America by saving up enough fare. The remaining ten percent remained in London, because their parents or children, family or fellow-townsmen made them comfortable, and they settled with the intention of remaining there permanently.[2]

The British Board of Trade gathered data on the preferences of East European immigrants which suggested that a large proportion intended to stay in England. But the Board of Deputies of British Jews, wishing to fend off the rising demand for restrictive legislation, contended that it was impossible to ascertain the ultimate purpose of the immigrants: "Jewish immigrants who wish to avail themselves of the cheap passages offered by English Shipping Companies are, in almost every case, obliged to conceal the fact that they are coming to England *en route* only, and accordingly they appear on the alien list as 'not stated to be en route'."[3]

Paucity of means and the prospect of another ten days to three weeks of steerage travel across the North Atlantic may well have induced immigrants to settle in England. Nevertheless, many remained there only briefly before travelling on. They carefully saved pennies from their starvation wages, or waited for family or friends to send the tickets that would enable them to complete

[1] See, however, Simon Kuznets, "Immigration of Russian Jews to the United States: Background and Structure," *Perspectives in American History*, IX (1975), 35-124.

[2] T. Eyges, *Zikhroynes fun die Yiddishe Arbeter Bavegung in London, England [Memoirs of the Jewish Labour Movement in London, England]*, quoted in Lloyd P. Gartner, *The Jewish Immigrant in England, 1870-1914* (London: 1960), p. 44.

[3] The London Committee of Deputies of the British Jews, *Annual Report* (1900), p. 28. See also Bernard Gainer, "The Alien Invasion: The Origins of the Alien Act," (unpublished Ph.D. thesis, Trinity College, Cambridge University, 1969), p. 11.

their voyage. Others turned to institutions such as the Jewish Board of Guardians, who gladly transported immigrants to the New World or back to Eastern Europe. When the "Atlantic Rate Wars" dropped the fare from England to America from £6 10s to £2, even an unskilled immigrant working in the English garment trade could save enough in a few months to make the journey.[4]

Several selective factors determined the destinations of those who emigrated from Eastern Europe. The traditional religious orthodoxy of many East European Jews had been shaken by the *Haskala* and the internal migration brought about by economic change, which uprooted many a *shtetl* family. Those most tradition-bound rightly believed that to emigrate was to endanger their devotion to their faith. But for religious leaders who took a more moderate view of emigration, England as compared to America was the lesser of two evils:

849

> The native Jews of England had long been praised for their faithful observance of traditional Judaism, and their well-organized community was elevated as a model. . . . there can have been little doubt of the religious acceptability of England as a land for Jewish settlement in comparison with the much laxer situation in America as it was reported back to Eastern Europe.[5]

Thus (all other things being equal) the traditionalist East European Jew was more likely to set sail for London than New York. It would be reasonable to assume that this distinction extended beyond the realm of piety. It took a more adventurous, hardy— and uprooted—spirit to make so great a break with the Old World.

Aside from those who made the choice in Eastern Europe, many more experienced England and found it wanting before moving on to America. They often did so on economic grounds, encouraged by less than charitable Anglo-Jewish institutions and glowing reports of America's opportunities. For others, the social cost of London life may have been too heavy a burden to bear. One student of Anglo-Jewish social structure stresses the importance of the breakdown of the family unit in promoting transmigration to the New World. There could be other pressures too: a Russian Jewish immigrant, arrested and brought to trial for begging in London in the summer of 1903, was given a suspended

[4] Frank C. Bowen, *A Century of Atlantic Travel 1830-1930* (Boston: 1930), pp. 191-192, 211; Moses Rischin, *The Promised City* (Cambridge: 1962), p. 33.
[5] Gartner, *op. cit.*, p. 30. Maurice Orbach, a Jewish Member of Parliament, discounted the economic factor as a goad to Jewish migration from England to the United States: "if New York's streets were paved with gold, London's were paved with platinum and diamonds." Interview with the author, June 23, 1972.

sentence after he told the bench of his desire to go on to the United States.[6]

Whether England pushed the migrant Jew more than America pulled him is difficult to assess. But there can be no doubt that the prevailing winds of migration were westward. Indeed, the United Kingdom itself sent nearly as many emigrants to the United States in a typical year during the late nineteenth and early twentieth centuries as it received from East European Jewry during the entire forty-five years of Jewish mass migration.[7] England to the overwhelming majority of East European Jews was little more than a way station.

850

But the importance of that role ought not to be minimized. Great Britain long had been a launching pad for East European Jews aiming to settle in the United States. A German-Jewish correspondent writing from New York in 1846 observed that many of the so-called English Jews in the United States were born east of the Oder, and came to the United States only "after having spent a lengthy time in England and [after having] adopted the English way of life." The American Jewish historian Ronald Sanders recalled that his East European immigrant mother "had lived in England long enough to finish her elementary schooling there and develop an unwarranted cultural pride that made her look upon the Brownsville Jewish environment with a touch of disdain." Professor Lloyd Gartner has concluded that between four and five hundred thousand Jewish migrants to America spent some time in Great Britian before crossing the Atlantic. Because of this, they "knew a bit of English and had experience of the urban life in which their lives would be spent. Their children were attending school and had quickly made the linguistic transition. In short, Great Britain served as a staging area for trans-Atlantic migration."[8]

Two other aspects of the "experience of urban life" gained in London and other English cities would be important for the social and economic evolution of New York Jewry. These were the

---

[6] Howard M. Brotz, "The Outlines of Jewish Society in London," in Maurice Freedman, ed., *A Minority in Britain* (London: 1955), p. 139n; *The East London Observer*, July 11, 1903.

[7] See Lloyd P. Gartner, "Notes on the Statistics of Jewish Immigration to England, 1871-1914," *Jewish Social Studies*, XXII, 2 (April, 1960), 97-102.

[8] A. R. Rollin, "Russo-Jewish Immigrants in England before 1881," *Transactions of the Jewish Historical Society of England*, XXI (1968), 206; Ronald Sanders, *Reflections on a Teapot* (New York: 1972), p. 21; Lloyd P. Gartner, "North Atlantic Jewry," *Migration and Settlement* (London: 1971), p. 121. Mayor Abraham Beame of New York City, who was in England, is a very good example.

transmission of an industrial process, and a group of men whose raison d'être was to humanize the consequences of that productive system. The factory method of garment manufacture (as for other modes of large-scale production) entailed "a minute subdivision of processes and the employment of each worker on a single task." Brought to the United States in the mid-1890's, it was amalgamated with the more traditional artisan team and task system employed by early Russian Jewish immigrant tailors. It has long been held that those who introduced this system to the United States were "English Jews." But as we have seen, most of these were themselves not more than one generation (and more likely just a few months or years) removed from Eastern Europe.[9]

While these English garment makers introduced a mode of production that was to have a long-term impact on the conduct of the American garment trade, other "English" Jews sailed westward with social and economic ideas that in part were a response to this mode of production. They had common East European roots with the entrepreneurs, and had been wrenched from their places of origin by the same socioeconomic upheaval of the late nineteenth century. But theirs was a different perspective, one gained in the sweatshops of London's Whitechapel or Leeds's Leylands ghetto.

One of these was the Yiddish poet Morris Rosenfeld. Of him, Ronald Sanders has written: "though this poetic formulation [of social protest] flowered in New York under Rosenfeld's pen, the seeds of it were first planted in London, during the brief season of Yiddish proletarian culture that had begun in the East End in the early eighties and was moribund a decade later. . . . Rosenfeld's vision is largely attributable to the influence of one man: the poet and feuilletonist Morris Winchevsky, who was the chief mentor of that East End Jewish culture when it was at its height." Like Winchevsky, Rosenfeld drifted across western Europe until he found a temporary resting place in London's East End. Both poets spent their days on the benches of the clothing contractors' sweatshops; by night they nurtured a Dickensian sense of social injustice while they learned the English language. Their growing indignation over social and economic exploitation spilled out in the Yiddish sweatshop poetry of their New York years. Rosenfeld told a correspondent of the London *Jewish Chronicle* during a return visit in 1904 that he had worked in London "as a tailor, but hearing of the victories won by the tailors of New York, he proceeded to

851

---

[9] Edna Bryner, *The Garment Trades* (Cleveland: 1916), pp. 13-14; Jesse E. Pope, *The Clothing Industry in New York* (New York: 1905), p. 70.

America, where he worked in the sweatshops till about three years ago." Rosenfeld and Winchevsky (who followed him to the United States in 1894) were committed to arousing the Jewish immigrant worker to his economic plight. They saw in trade union socialism the solution to the abuses of the sweated garment trades.[10]

Theirs was not a unique experience. Many Jewish youths in the eastern Europe of the 1870's and 1880's had been exposed to socialist ideas. Cast ashore in Great Britain by the turn-of-the-century westward migration and forced into the sweatshops to survive, their religious beliefs and social ideas were put to the test. Some turned to anarchism in the 1880's, and marched with black banners unfurled, carrying ham sandwiches to demonstrate their defiance of traditional Judaism as well as the prevailing social system. But while this ideological liberation from the *shtetl* may have met the needs of educated revolutionaries, most of their fellow immigrant workers remained tied to the traditional forms of Judaism, and would not march behind their banners.

Jewish immigrant labor in London remained sweated and un-unionized. Like Rosenfeld and Winchevsky the secular radicals who might have organized them made their way to New York. There they continued their association with the Jewish labor movement. While most abandoned their anarchism, leaders such as Joseph Barondess, John Dyche, Benjamin Feigenbaum, Joseph Jaffe, Philip Krantz, Morris Sigman, and others applied their Whitechapel experience of the 1880's to the lower East Side labor movement at the turn of the century. Moses Rischin has said of the ethical imperative that spurred them on: "the leaders of the Jewish labor movement were closest in spirit to the British labor leader Keir Hardie. They were righteously angry, intolerant of injustice, and eager for social service."[11]

It is evident that in terms of goals, methods of operation, organizational structure, ideology, and ethics, the years of English acculturation were of great importance to the leadership of the American Jewish garment trade unions. But if the strategy and tactics of the docks of Merseyside and the collieries of Northumberland were adaptable to the sidewalks of New York, why were they not equally applicable to the sweatshops of Whitechapel? It has been argued that the East End garment industry of small

[10] Ronald Sanders, *The Downtown Jews* (New York: 1969), pp. 137, 143; *The Jewish Chronicle*, June 1, 1900; "Vinchevsky, Morris," *Encyclopaedia Judaica*, XVI, 154.
[11] Moses Rischin, "The Jewish Labor Movement in America," *Labor History*, IV (1963), 236. John H. M. Laslett, *Labor and the Left* (New York: 1970), p. 101, notes John Dyche's English experience.

852

shops, little capital, scant overhead, and high rates of business mortality militated against unionization.[12] Yet similar conditions in New York gave rise to the powerful International Ladies Garment Workers Union (ILGWU).

Part of the answer lies in the fact that failure in London did not mean the end of the line (or a return to Eastern Europe) either for the petty entrepreneur or for the labor organizer. The *goldener land* beckoned to sweater and sweated alike. What is more, two political events in 1905, one occurring in Russia and one in Great Britain, had a lasting impact on the immigrant labor movement in New York and London. In Russia the Czarist repression that followed the 1905 revolution struck hard at the Jewish masses and their revolutionary elite. Masses of Jews fled Russia: in 1906 more than 152,000 entered the United States, the crest of the early twentieth century Jewish immigrant wave. Among the new arrivals were experienced *Bund* leaders, some of whom had undergone forced labor and exile in Siberia. The post-1905 immigrants had a substantial impact on the American labor movement:

> Whereas the earlier arrivals—of the eighties—had been composed largely of dreamy visionaries, men who had emerged from the *class-room* or the secret circle of theoretical world redeemers, these latter men and women had been baptized in the fire of revolution, had faced bullet and knout, and were thoroughly conversant with *action* in all its implications. It was their spirit that was responsible for the great series of strikes that followed their incursion into the ranks of labor in America.[13]

If earlier migration patterns had persisted, London's Whitechapel and Leeds' Leyland ghettos would have shared in this infusion of experienced, committed Jewish labor organizers. But in 1905 the demand for legislation restricting the entry of "aliens"— a code word for East European Jews—peaked in Great Britain. A racist demagoguery that played on the fears of East End London Gentiles; the disarray of the parliamentary parties, in a state of realignment and highly responsive to organized interest group demands; and the belief on the part of the Anglo-Jewish elite that restrictive legislation was inevitable, assured the passage of the Conservatives' Alien Restriction Bill of August 1905.

The Liberal ministry that swept into office in January 1906

853

---

[12] John W. Carrier, "Working Class Jews in Present-Day London: A Sociological Study," (unpublished M. Phil. thesis, London University, 1969), p. 51.

[13] Harold Berman, "The Decline of Jewish Labor," *The Reflex*, I (October, 1927), 34; Judah J. Shapiro, *The Friendly Society* (New York: 1970), p. 45.

quickly weakened the force of the act: the Home Office made it clear that it would not be used to block those seeking sanctuary from religious or political persecution. But word of the bill had spread rapidly through Eastern Europe, and the image of England as a land of refuge was seriously tarnished. In 1905 nearly 15,000 Jews—many of them recent arrivals who now felt less welcome—left Great Britian for the United States. It was clear that twentieth century America, not Great Britain, was to be the land of opportunity for entrepreneur, worker, and labor leader alike.[14]

854

The contrast between the British Isles as a land of emigration and the United States as a nation of immigrants was but one manifestation of profound cultural differences. An examination of the economic organization and social structure of the two nations' garment industries makes it clear that the transmigration of labor leadership was more a symptom than a cause of the successful unionization of the New York industry and the relative failure in London.

In London the labor pool on which small garment contractors could draw was composed not only of immigrant Jews but also of the wives of Irish immigrant dockers, recent arrivals from rural England, and Cockneys of long residence in East London. That this labor force should fail to unite is not surprising, considering its diverse ethnic strains and the antagonism that typified their relations in the hemmed-in slum quarters of the East End. The Cockneys whom Jack London found "on the doss" ascribed "their homelessness to foreign immigration, especially of Polish and Russian Jews, who take their places at lower wages and establish the sweating system."[15]

While ethnic diversity and intergroup antagonisms also posed a threat to collective action in New York, common experiences of emigration and exploitation proved to be more decisive. The number of new immigrants was so overwhelming, and other opportunities for retail and clerical employment drew so many old stock female workers out of the labor force, that the only exploitable ethnic distinctions lay among immigrant workers themselves. More than ninety percent of these were East European Jews and

---

[14] Charles F. Fraser, *Control of Aliens in the British Commonwealth of Nations* (London: 194- ), pp. 59-60; Gartner, *Jewish Immigrant*, p. 49.

[15] Jack London, *The People of the Abyss* (New York: 1903), p. 106. See also C. Russell and H. S. Lewis, *The Jew in London* (London: 1900), p. 8; G. Stedman-Jones, "Some Social Consequences of the Casual Labour Problem in London, 1860-90, with Particular Reference to the East End," (unpublished D. Phil. Thesis, Oxford University, 1968).

southern Italians. Rudolf Glanz's conclusion that the association of Jewish and Italian immigrants has been perhaps *the most* harmonious historical relationship ever to exist among ethnic groups in America may be overstated; but it is clear that the two groups largely managed to subordinate ethnic differences as they engaged in industry-wide strikes to organize hundreds of shops. The ILGWU successfully responded to the pressing economic needs of the workers and to their demand for recognition of their social identities. While union locals were organized on a linguistic base— Italian or Yiddish—the interethnic shop committee was the source of union action. True, the Italian minority at times resented the dominance of the Jewish majority, and insisted on guarantees that proportional representation rather than majority control would prevail in ILGWU governance. And many a union meeting was marked by demands from Italian members that Jewish spokesmen refrain from addressing the gathering in Yiddish. But the prevailing experience was one of amity and cooperation.[16]

855

How was this Italian-Jewish alliance forged and maintained? It would seem that their common experience of emigration from the Old World, their shared status as members (and second-class members at that) of minority religious groups in the United States, and the prevalence of a moderate, widely acceptable socialist ideology among leaders in both ghettos, contributed to worker unity and made unionization feasible.

Yet the union leadership and the most enthusiastic and committed organizers and activists were Jews, not Italians. Melvyn Dubofsky argues that while the East European Jews brought with them a "tradition of working-class, political-economic action," Italian immigrants placed greater stress on the importance of maintaining Old World family or provincial ties, and on returning home once a financial surplus was secured—tendencies which lessened their need to come to terms with the economic realities of their American experience.[17]

But it may be questioned whether the cultural baggage of the Jewish immigrants really was so different. Undoubtedly the Bundist (and the English) experience of many union leaders prepared them for the struggle of organizing the New York garment indus-

[16] Rudolf Glanz, *Jew and Italian* (New York: 1971); cf. Edwin Fenton, "Immigrants and Unions, A Case Study: Italians and American Labor, 1870-1920," (unpublished Ph.D. thesis, Harvard University, 1957).
[17] Melvyn Dubofsky, *When Workers Organize* (Amherst: 1968), pp. 17-18. Cf. also William J. Fishman, *Jewish Radicals: From Czarist Stetl to London Ghetto* (New York: 1975).

try. But much older traditions, not unlike the provincial and village ties of Italian immigrants, had perhaps even greater weight among the Jews. The *landsmanschaft*—the home town benefit society—often was the creation of garment trade entrepreneurs, who hired (and exploited) their workers on the basis of a shared Old World experience. This paternalistic institution had its roots in the old East European *chevra*, and often was deliberately designed to prevent unionization of the garment trade shop.[18]

Yet by 1910 these benefit societies, the rough equivalent of company unions, failed in the face of the challenge posed by the ILGWU. What in the American Jewish immigrants' experience led them to place their faith in a democratic, class-oriented trade union rather than traditional paternalistic, provincial benefit societies?

Once again the comparative perspective offers a possible explanation. During these years there were numerous attempts to organize the English garment trades, but none was as lasting or as successful as the ILGWU. The English unions were splintered by ethnic, ideological, and regional disputes. In the sphere of Jewish communal life, however, the reverse was true: it was American Jewry that was deeply divided internally, while English Jews, native as well as immigrant, created lasting and cohesive institutions. The highly structured character of Anglo-Jewish associational life, and the absence of equivalent institutions in the United States, went far to determine how the new immigrants in each country adjusted to the conditions that confronted them.

The structural models for Anglo-Jewish religious institutions were the English churches—established and dissenting—of the nineteenth century. This might be seen in bodies such as the office of the Chief Rabbi, the Board of Deputies of London (and later British) Jews, the United Synagogue, and the Board of Jewish Guardians. The paternalism exercised by the Anglo-Jewish "Cousinhood" of the Rothschilds, Montefiores, Goldschmidts, Salomons, Waleys, Cohens, Sebags, Franklins, Samuels, and others resembled nothing so much as the style as the British elites. No less than their English upper class counterparts, they stood aloof from the Anglo-Jewish middle and working classes. These bankers, bullion merchants, and City investment brokers shared only a religious heritage with the mass of English Jews, native or immigrant. The only contact between the "Cousinhood" and the rest of English Jewry was a philanthropic one. At the same time—and this too was

[18] Rischin, *Promised City*, pp. 104-105, 182-183.

typically English—because their status in the larger society was so high they could act as the spokesmen of English Jewry in secular as well as religious matters. Thus Samuel Montagu, a Member of Parliament and City of London banker, sought to create a communal base to rival the Rothschild-led United Synagogue. He was able to organize the immigrant East London store-front synagogues into a Federation of Minor Synagogues which maintained standards of housing, finances, and decorum and helped them to function as benefit societies. At the same time he served as a mediator in disputes between Jewish master tailors and the garment workers, who were the congregants of these synagogues. The garment workers, who rejected the radical labor leaders' disdain for religious traditions, made these minor synagogues their most important form of extra-familial association; and in this they were joined by their employers the master tailors. Together, contractor and worker showed a high degree of deference to the white-bearded, devout Montagu. For all the exploitation of worker by employer that characterized the English garment trade, the vastness of the gulf that separated both sweater and sweated from the "Cousinhood" made their differences subject to mediation by those who stood above them.

857

The social situation in the United States precluded the establishment of all-inclusive communal institutions or the secular and religious deference to the Jewish elite that prevailed in England. The earlier Jewish migrants to the United States were widely dispersed; "national" institutions were unfeasible. No American Jewish families commanded the wealth or the deference of the Rothschild. Neither the "Sephardic Elite" nor "Our Crowd" could match the "Cousinhood" in social status or communal leadership.

When the Jewish mass of migrants from Eastern Europe struck New York, there were no institutions or individuals with the social standing to organize, lead, or mediate among them. Those who sought to play these roles were unacceptable to the new immigrants not only because of their class and religious differences, but also because the more settled American Jews had a major economic stake in the garment trades that most of the new arrivals entered. The East European immigrants supplied the labor and the earlier German Jewish immigrants supplied the capital for the rapidly growing mass market in ready-made clothing.

The slower growth of consumer purchasing power in Great Britain engendered a conflict between the native artisan clothing trade and the Jewish ready-to-wear industry that did not exist in the United States. This conflict demanded Jewish group solidarity, and the mitigation of economic conflict within the group such as was sought by Samuel Montagu in his Federation of Minor Synagogues. But in the United States, the very fact that there was no external challenge to the Jewish garment industry increased the opportunity for employer-employee conflict within it.

A final consequence of the peculiar conditions prevailing in the United States was the appearance in the early twentieth century of a distinctive new social type. Large numbers of East European immigrant Jews emerged as entrepreneurs, supplanting old German-Jewish manufacturers. They moved beyond the management of small sweatshops to employ hundreds of workers in modern factory lofts. East European *yichus* meant nothing in the volatile garment trade; a sense of timing and responsiveness to public taste enabled many an immigrant with little capital and limited tailoring skill to rise by the sweat of his and other brows.[19]

As this development took place, Old World bonds which at one time may have checked the impulse to worker unionization became increasingly attenuated. The appearance of the garment trade entrepreneur, no less than the Jewish workers' militant leadership, helped to foster the emergence of the ILGWU.

What appeared to the sweated workers, the trade union leaders, social reformers, and the older German Jewish immigrants as the rise of a dangerous and unethical class of entrepreneurs was to the participants in that rise an American dream fulfilled. The garment trade entrepreneur was both a Babbitt and a *Balebos*, a master of middling rank, and his accommodation to his social and economic roles calls for further study.

858

[19] *Ibid.*, p. 245; Abraham Cahan's famous novel *The Rise of David Levinsky* ably illustrates this point.